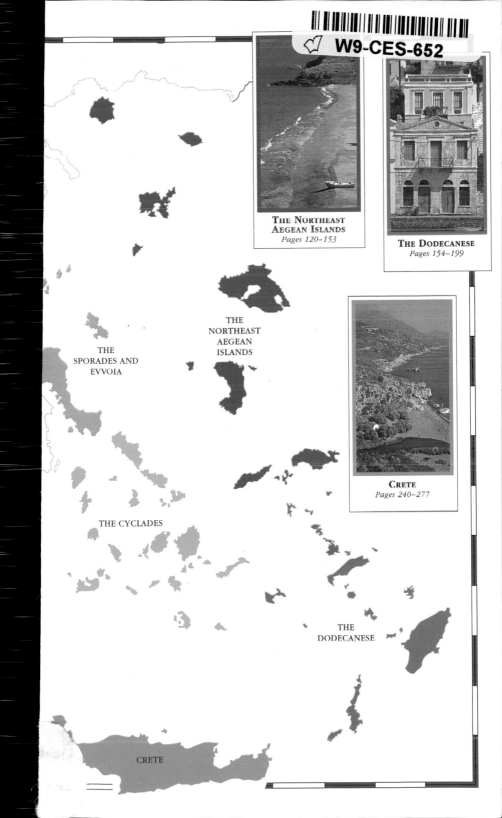

W9-CES-652

THE NORTHEAST AEGEAN ISLANDS
Pages 120–153

THE DODECANESE
Pages 154–199

CRETE
Pages 240–277

THE
NORTHEAST
AEGEAN
ISLANDS

THE
SPORADES AND
EVVOIA

THE CYCLADES

THE
DODECANESE

CRETE

THE
GREEK
ISLANDS

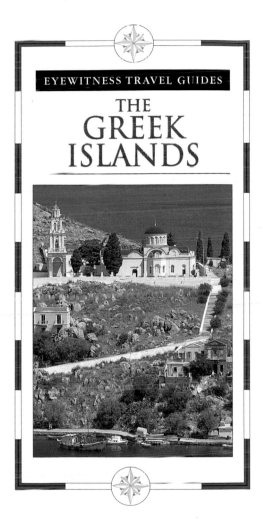

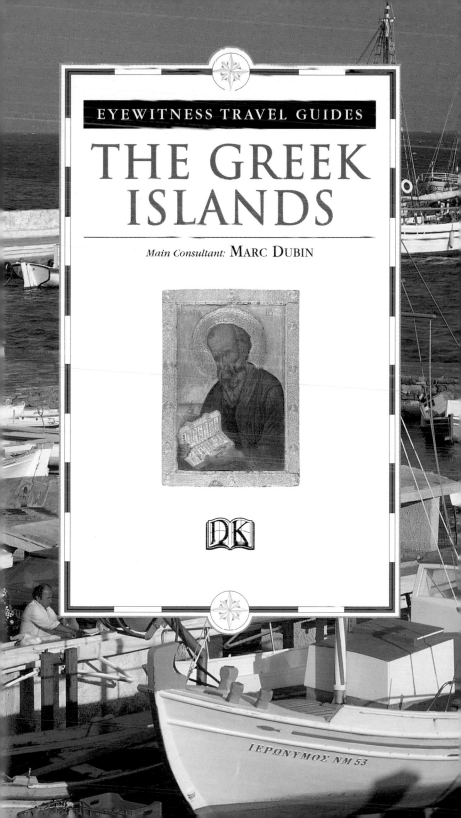

EYEWITNESS TRAVEL GUIDES

THE GREEK ISLANDS

Main Consultant: MARC DUBIN

LONDON, NEW YORK,
MELBOURNE, MUNICH AND DELHI
www.dk.com

PROJECT EDITOR Jane Simmonds
ART EDITOR Stephen Bere
EDITORS Isabel Carlisle, Michael Ellis, Simon Farbrother,
Claire Folkard, Marianne Petrou, Andrew Szudek
US EDITORS Michael Wise, Mary Sutherland
DESIGNERS Jo Doran, Paul Jackson, Elly King, Marisa Renzullo
MAP CO-ORDINATORS Emily Green, David Pugh
VISUALIZER Joy Fitzsimmons
LANGUAGE CONSULTANT Georgia Gotsi

CONTRIBUTORS AND CONSULTANTS
Rosemary Barron, Marc Dubin, Stephanie Ferguson, Mike Gerrard,
Andy Harris, Lynette Mitchell, Colin Nicholson, Robin Osborne,
Barnaby Rogerson, Paul Sterry, Tanya Tsikas

MAPS
Gary Bowes, Fiona Casey, Christine Purcell (ERA-Maptec Ltd)

PHOTOGRAPHERS
Max Alexander, Joe Cornish, Paul Harris, Rupert Horrox,
Rob Reichenfeld, Linda Whitwam, Francesca Yorke

ILLUSTRATORS
Stephen Conlin, Steve Gyapay, Maltings Partnership, Chris Orr &
Associates, Mel Pickering, Paul Weston, John Woodcock

Reproduced by Colourscan (Singapore)
Printed and bound by L. Rex Printing Company Limited, China

First American Edition, 1997
04 05 10 9 8 7

Published in the United States by
DK Publishing, Inc., 375 Hudson Street,
New York, New York 10014

**Reprinted with revisions 1998, 1999, 2000,
2001, 2002, 2003, 2004**

Copyright © 1997, 2004 Dorling Kindersley Limited, London

ISSN 1542-1554
ISBN 0-7894-9425-6

FLOORS ARE REFERRED TO THROUGHOUT IN ACCORDANCE WITH EUROPEAN USAGE;
IE THE "FIRST FLOOR" IS THE FLOOR ABOVE GROUND LEVEL.

**The information in this
DK Eyewitness Guide is checked regularly**.
Every effort has been made to ensure that this book is as up-to-date as
possible at the time of going to press. Some details, however, such as
telephone numbers, opening hours, prices, gallery hanging
arrangements and travel information are liable to change. The publishers
cannot accept responsibility for any consequences arising from the use
of this book, nor for any material on third party websites, and cannot
guarantee that any website address in this book will be a suitable source
of travel information. We value the views and suggestions of our readers
very highly. Please write to: Publisher, DK Eyewitness Travel Guides,
Dorling Kindersley, 80 Strand, London WC2R 0RL, Great Britain.

The harbor at Réthymno, Crete

CONTENTS

HOW TO USE THIS GUIDE 6

The Turkish Prince Cem arriving
in Rhodes (15th century)

INTRODUCING THE GREEK ISLANDS

PUTTING GREECE ON
THE MAP 10

A PORTRAIT OF
THE GREEK ISLANDS 12

THE HISTORY
OF GREECE 22

THE GREEK ISLANDS
THROUGH THE YEAR 42

◁ Fishermen unloading their catch at Mýkonos harbor in the Cyclades

Gorgon's head from Evvoia

ANCIENT GREECE

GODS, GODDESSES, AND HEROES 50

THE TROJAN WAR 52

GREEK WRITERS AND PHILOSOPHERS 54

TEMPLE ARCHITECTURE 56

VASES AND VASE PAINTING 58

Family on a scooter

THE GREEK ISLANDS AREA BY AREA

THE GREEK ISLANDS AT A GLANCE 62

THE IONIAN ISLANDS 64

THE ARGO-SARONIC ISLANDS 88

THE SPORADES AND EVVOIA 100

THE NORTHEAST AEGEAN ISLANDS 120

THE DODECANESE 154

THE CYCLADES 200

CRETE 240

A SHORT STAY IN ATHENS 278

Garídes saganáki, shrimp with feta in a tomato sauce

TRAVELERS' NEEDS

WHERE TO STAY 294

WHERE TO EAT 312

SURVIVAL GUIDE

PRACTICAL INFORMATION 336

Kámpos beach on Ikaría in the Northeast Aegean Islands

TRAVEL INFORMATION 352

GENERAL INDEX 362

PHRASE BOOK 396

MAP OF FERRY ROUTES
Inside back cover

Néa Moní on Chíos, Northeast Aegean Islands

HOW TO USE THIS GUIDE

THIS GUIDE helps you to get the most from your visit to the Greek Islands. It provides both expert recommendations and detailed practical information. *Introducing the Greek Islands* maps the country in its historical and cultural context. *Ancient Greece* gives a background to the many remains and artifacts to be seen. The seven regional chapters, plus *A Short Stay in Athens,* describe important sights, with maps and illustrations. Restaurant and hotel recommendations can be found in *Travellers' Needs.* The *Survival Guide* has tips on everything from the Greek telephone system to transport networks.

THE GREEK ISLANDS AREA BY AREA

The islands have been divided into six groups, each of which has a separate chapter. Crete has a chapter on its own. A map of these groups can be found inside the front cover of the book. Each island group is colour coded for easy reference.

1 Introduction
The landscape, history and character of each island group is described here, showing how they have developed over the centuries and what they offer to the visitor today.

Each island group can be quickly identified by its colour coding.

A locator map shows you where you are in relation to other island groups.

2 Pictorial Map
This shows all the islands covered in the chapter. Main ferry routes are marked and there are useful tips on getting around the islands.

Islands at a Glance lists the islands alphabetically. Each island has a cross reference to its entry.

The main ferry routes, roads and transport points are marked on each map.

A locator map shows you where you are in relation to other islands in the group.

3 Detailed information
Most of the islands are described individually. Within each island entry there is detailed information on all the sights. Major islands have an island map showing all the main towns, villages, sights and beaches.

Story boxes highlight special or unique aspects of a particular sight.

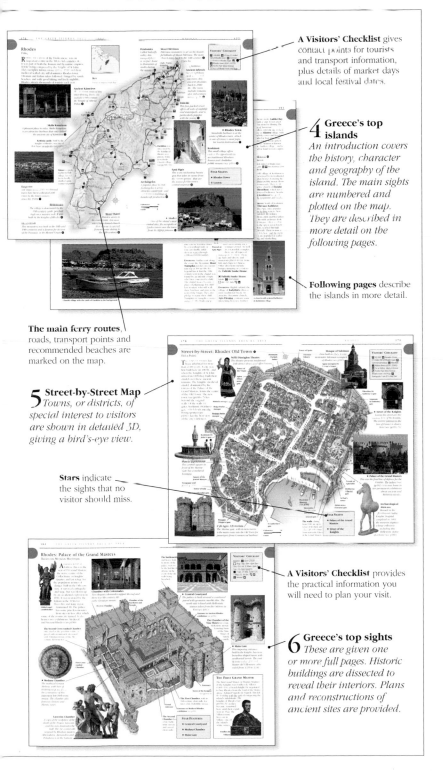

A Visitors' Checklist gives contact points for tourists and transport information, plus details of market days and local festival dates.

4 Greece's top islands
An introduction covers the history, character and geography of the island. The main sights are numbered and plotted on the map. They are described in more detail on the following pages.

Following pages describe the islands in more detail.

The main ferry routes, roads, transport points and recommended beaches are marked on the map.

5 Street-by-Street Map
Towns, or districts, of special interest to visitors are shown in detailed 3D, giving a bird's-eye view.

Stars indicate the sights that no visitor should miss.

A Visitors' Checklist provides the practical information you will need to plan your visit.

6 Greece's top sights
These are given one or more full pages. Historic buildings are dissected to reveal their interiors. Plans and reconstructions of ancient sites are provided.

Introducing the Greek Islands

PUTTING GREECE ON THE MAP 10-11
A PORTRAIT OF THE GREEK ISLANDS 12-21
THE HISTORY OF GREECE 22-41
THE GREEK ISLANDS THROUGH THE YEAR 42-47

Putting Greece on the Map

Occupying the southernmost tip of the Balkan peninsula, Greece divides into over 2,000 islands stretching from the Ionian Sea in the west to the Aegean Sea in the east. The mainland has borders with Albania, Bulgaria, Turkey and the FYR of Macedonia. Of Greece's 10.2 million people, over 10 per cent live on the islands, while a third live in Athens.

KEY

⛴ Main international ferry service

✈ International airport

═══ Motorway, dual-carriageway

━━━ Major road

──── Railway line

– ∙ – National boundary

A PORTRAIT OF THE GREEK ISLANDS

G REECE IS ONE OF THE MOST VISITED *European countries, but also one of the least known. At a geographical crossroads, the modern Greek state dates only from 1830, and combines elements of the Balkans, Middle East and Mediterranean.*

Of the thousands of Greek islands, large and small, only about a hundred are today permanently inhabited. Barely 10 per cent of the country's population of just over ten million lives on the islands, and for centuries a large number of Greek islanders have lived abroad: currently there are over half as many Greeks outside the country as in. The proportion of their income sent back to relatives significantly bolsters island economies. Recently there has been a trend for reverse immigration, with expatriate Greeks returning home to influence the architecture and cuisine on many islands.

Islands lying within sight of each other can have vastly different

Greek priest

histories. Most of the archipelagos along sea lanes to the Levant played a crucial role between the decline of Byzantium and the rise of modern Greece. Crete, the Ionian group and the Cyclades were occupied by the Venetians and exposed to the influence of Italian culture. The Northeast Aegean and Dodecanese islands were ruled by Genoese and Crusader overlords in medieval times, while the Argo-Saronic isles were completely resettled by Albanian Christians.

Island and urban life in contemporary Greece were transformed in the 20th century despite years of occupation and war, including a civil war, which only ended after

Fishermen mending their nets on Páros in the Cyclades

◁ **A backstreet in Anógeia on Crete**

A village café on Crete's Lasíthi Plateau

the 1967–74 colonels' Junta. Recently, based on the revenues from tourism and the EU, there has been a rapid transformation of many of the islands from backwater status to prosperity. Until the 1960s most of the Aegean Islands lacked paved roads and basic utilities. Even larger islands boasted just a single bus and only a few taxis as transport and emigration, either to Athens or overseas, increased.

RELIGION, LANGUAGE AND CULTURE
During the centuries of domination by Venetians and Ottomans (see pp36–7) the Greek Orthodox church preserved the Greek language, and

Frescoed saint from monastery of St John, Pátmos

with it Greek identity, through its liturgy and schools. The query *Eísai Orthódoxos* (Are you Orthodox?) is virtually synonymous with *Ellinas eísai* (Are you Greek?). Today, the Orthodox Church is still a powerful force, despite the secularizing reforms of the first democratically elected PASOK government of 1981–5. While no self-respecting couple would dispense with church baptisms for their children, civil marriages are now as valid in law as the religious service. Sunday Mass is popular, particularly with women, who often socialize there as men do at *kafeneía* (cafés).

Many parish priests, recognizable by their tall stovepipe hats and long beards, marry and have a second trade (a custom that helps keep up the numbers of entrants to the church). However, there has also been a recent renaissance in celibate monastic life, perhaps as a reaction to postwar materialism.

The beautiful and subtle Greek language, that other hallmark of national identity, was for a long time

Traditional houses by the sea on Kefalloniá, the Ionian Islands

Stepped streets and pastel colours at Oía on Santoríni in the Cyclades

DEVELOPMENT AND DIPLOMACY

While compared to most of its Balkan neighbours Greece is a wealthy and stable country, by Western economic indicators Greece languishes at the bottom of the EU league table and will be a net EU beneficiary for several years to come. The country's persistent negative trade deficit is aggravated by the large number of luxury goods imported on the basis of *xenomanía* – the belief that goods from abroad are of a superior quality to those made at home. Cars are the most conspicuous of these imports, since Greece is one of the very few European

A family in Kós on their scooter

countries not to manufacture any of its own.

a field of conflict between the written *katharévousa*, an artificial form hastily devised around the time of Independence, and the slowly evolved everyday speech, or *dimotikí* (demotic Greek).

Today's prevalence of the more supple *dimotikí* was perhaps a foregone conclusion in an oral culture. Storytelling is still as prized in Greece as in Homer's time, with conversation pursued for its own sake in *kafeneía*. The bardic tradition is alive with poet lyricists such as Mános Eleftheríou, Níkos Gátsos and Apóstolos Kaldáras. Collaborations such as theirs have produced accessible works which have played an important role keeping *dimotikí* alive from the 19th century until today.

During recent times of censorship under dictatorship or foreign rule, writers and singers have been a vital source of news and information.

Greece still bears the hallmarks of a developing economy, with profits from the service sector and agriculture accounting for two-thirds of its GNP. With EU membership since 1981, and an economy that is more capitalist than not, Greece has lost its economic similarity to Eastern Europe before the fall of the Iron Curtain. Recent years have seen many improvements: loss-making enterprises

A beach at Plakiás on Crete

Windmills at Olympos on the island of Kárpathos, in the Dodecanese

have been sold off by the state, inflation has dipped to single figures for the first time since 1973, interest rates are falling and Greece was accepted as a member of the EU monetary union. The euro has been its sole currency since March 2002.

Tourism ranks as the largest hard currency earner, compensating for the depression in world shipping and the fact that Mediterranean agricultural products are duplicated within the EU. Now the lifeblood of many islands,

Children dressed for a festival in Koskinoú village, Rhodes

tourism has only been crucial since the late 1960s. The unprepossessing appearance of many island tourist facilities owes much to a megadevelopment ethos and permit-granting policy formulated under the Junta. More recent developments have an appearance that is more in harmony with their natural surroundings. Planners hope that traditional high-volume and low-spending package tourism will defer to the new rich of central Europe, pan-Orthodox pilgrimages and special-interest tourism. To attract higher spenders the infrastructure of the islands is being upgraded, with plans for spas, yacht marinas, new airports and telecommunication links.

The fact that the Greek state is less than 200 years old and in the years since 1922 has been politically unstable means that Greeks have very little faith in government institutions. Everyday life operates on networks

Threshing with donkeys in the Cyclades

Festival bread from Chaniá's covered market on Crete

of personal friendships and official contacts. The classic political designations of Right and Left have only acquired their conventional meanings in Greece since the 1930s. Among politicians, the dominant figure of the early 20th century was the anti-royalist Liberal Eleuthérios Venizélos, who came from Crete. The years since World War II have been over-shadowed by two politicians: the late Andréas Papandréou, three times premier as head of the Panhellenic Socialist Movement (PASOK), and the late conservative premier Konstantínos Karamanlís, who died in 1998.

Thriving Pythagóreio harbour on the island of Sámos

With the Cold War over, Greece looks more than likely to assert its underlying Balkan identity. Relations with its nearest neighbours, and particularly with Albania, have improved considerably since the fall of the Communist regime there in 1990. Greece is already the number-one investor in neighbouring Bulgaria, and after a recent rapprochement with Skopje, (formerly Yugoslavian Macedonia) it seems as if Greece is now poised to become a significant regional power.

HOME LIFE

The family is still the basic Greek social unit. Under traditional island land distribution and agricultural practices, one family could sow, plough and reap its own fields, without the help of cooperative work parties. Today's family-run businesses are still the norm in the many port towns. Arranged marriages and granting of dowries, though not very common, persist; most single young people live with their parents or another relative until marriage; and outside the largest university towns, such as Rhodes town, Irákleio or Mytilíni, few couples dare to cohabit "in sin". Children from the smaller islets board with a relative while attending secondary school on the larger islands. Despite the renowned Greek love of children, Greece has a very low birth rate – in Europe, only Italy's is lower. Currently, the Greek birth rate is less than half of pre-World War II levels.

Fish at Crete's Réthymno market

Macho attitudes persist on the islands and women often forgo any hope of a career in order to look after the house and children. Urban Greek women are seeing a rise in status as new imported attitudes have started to creep in. However, no amount of outside influence is likely to jeopardize the essentially Greek way of life, which remains vehemently traditional.

A man with his donkey in Mýkonos town in the Cyclades

Vernacular Architecture on the Greek Islands

Greek island architecture varies greatly, even between neighbouring islands. Yet despite the fact that the generic island house does not exist, there are shared characteristics within and between island groups. The Venetians in Crete, the Cyclades, Ionian Islands and Dodecanese, and the Ottomans in the Northeast Aegean strongly influenced the indigenous building styles developed by vernacular builders.

View of the town of Chóra on Astypálaia in the Dodecanese, with the kástro above

Venetian-style external chimney

Carved stone ornamentation

Sachnísia, or overhangs, were built of lath and plaster and supported by wooden cantilevers.

Venetian-style town houses on Crete date from Venice's 15th- to 17th-century occupation. Often built around a courtyard, the ground floor was used for storage.

Sash windows with shutters

The top floor was for receiving guests and sleeping.

The kitchen was on the middle storey.

The stone ground floor housed animals and tools.

Lesvian pýrgoi are fortified tower-dwellings at the centre of a farming estate. First built in the 18th century, most surviving examples are 19th century and found near Mytilíni town.

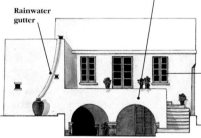

Rainwater gutter

Arcade on ground floor supporting veranda

Double "French" windows of the parlour

Sífnos archontiká or town houses are found typically in Kástro, Artemónas and Katavatí. They are two storeyed, as opposed to the one-storey rural cottage.

Kastro Architecture

The kástro or fortress dwelling of Antíparos dates from the 15th century. It is the purest form of a Venetian pirate-safe town plan in the Cyclades.

Chimneypot from broken urn

Stairway to central court

Plaster and whitewash surface

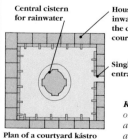

Central cistern for rainwater

Houses facing inwards on to the central court

Single entrance

Plan of a courtyard kástro

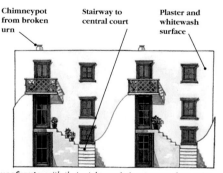

Kástro housefronts, with their right-angled staircases, face either on to a central courtyard or a grid of narrow lanes with limited access from outside. The seaward walls have tiny windows. Kástra are found on Síkinos, Kímolos, Sífnos, Antíparos and Folégandros.

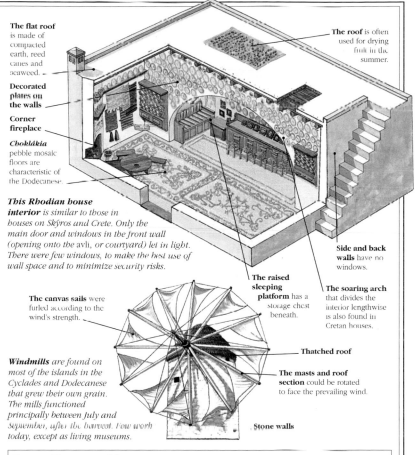

The flat roof is made of compacted earth, reed canes and seaweed.

Decorated plates on the walls

Corner fireplace

Choklákia pebble mosaic floors are characteristic of the Dodecanese.

The roof is often used for drying fruit in the summer.

This Rhodian house interior is similar to those in houses on Skýros and Crete. Only the main door and windows in the front wall (opening onto the avlí, or courtyard) let in light. There were few windows, to make the best use of wall space and to minimize security risks.

Side and back walls have no windows.

The raised sleeping platform has a storage chest beneath.

The soaring arch that divides the interior lengthwise is also found in Cretan houses.

The canvas sails were furled according to the wind's strength.

Windmills are found on most of the islands in the Cyclades and Dodecanese that grew their own grain. The mills functioned principally between July and September, after the harvest. Few work today, except as living museums.

Thatched roof

The masts and roof section could be rotated to face the prevailing wind.

Stone walls

LOCAL BUILDING METHODS AND MATERIALS

Lava masonry is found on the volcanic islands of Lésvos, Límnos, Nísyros and Milos. The versatile and easily split schist is used in the Cyclades, while lightweight lath and plaster indicates Ottoman influence and is prevalent on Sámos, Lésvos, the Sporades and other northern islands. Mud-and-rubble construction is common on all the islands for modest dwellings, as is the *dóma* or flat roof of tree trunks supporting packed reed canes overlaid with seaweed and earth.

Unmortared wall of schist slabs

Masoned volcanic boulders

Slate (or "fish-scale") roof

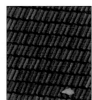

Pantiled roof, found in the Dodecanese

Flat earthen roof or *dóma*

Arched buttresses for earthquake protection

Marine Life

B Y OCEANIC STANDARDS, the Mediterranean and Aegean are small, virtually land-locked seas with a narrow tidal range. This means that relatively little marine life is exposed at low tide, although coastal plants and shoreline birds are often abundant. However, if you snorkel close to the shore or dive below the surface of the azure coastal waters, a wealth of plant and animal life can be found. The creatures range in size from myriad shoals of tiny fish and dainty sea slugs to giant marine turtles, huge fish and imposing spider crabs.

Triton shell

The great pipefish's elongated body is easily mistaken for a piece of drifting seaweed. It lives among rocks, pebbles and weed, often in rather shallow water, and can be spotted when snorkelling.

Sea spurge

Mediterranean gull

Masked crab

Tamarisk

Yellow-horned poppy

The spiny spider crab is ungainly when removed from water but agile and surprisingly fast-moving in its element. The long legs allow it to negotiate broken, stony ground easily.

Neptune grass (Posidonia)

Fan mussels

Red mullet

Codium bursa

Sea slug

Murex

TOP SNORKELLING AREAS

Snorkelling can be enjoyed almost anywhere around the Greek coast, although remoter areas are generally more rewarding.
• Kefalloniá and Zákynthos: you may find a rare loggerhead turtle *(see p87)* off the east coast.
• Rhodes: wide variety of fish near Líndos on the sheltered east coast.
• Evvoia: the sheltered waters of the west coast harbour sponges.
• Santoríni: the volcanic rock of the caldera has sharp drop-offs to explore.

The octopus catches its prey of crabs and small fish with the rows of powerful suckers along each of its eight legs. It can also change its colour and squeeze through the tiniest of crevices.

The sea turtle, or loggerhead, needs sandy beaches to lay its eggs and has been badly affected by the intrusion of tourists. The few remaining nesting beaches are now given a degree of protection from disturbance.

This jellyfish, called a "by-the-wind-sailor", uses a buoyant float to catch the wind and skim across the sea. Storms will often wash them up on to the beach. Swimmers beware: even the detached thread-like tentacles of some species can inflict painful stings.

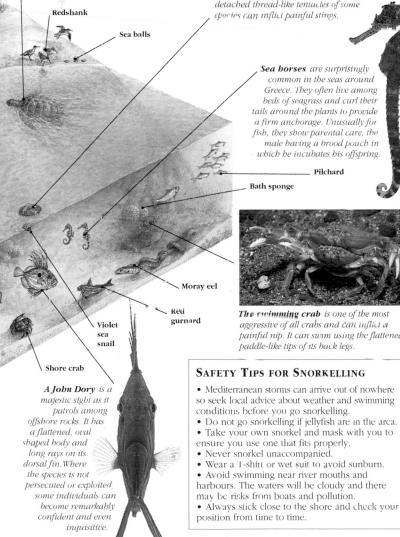

Redshank

Sea balls

Sea horses are surprisingly common in the seas around Greece. They often live among beds of seagrass and curl their tails around the plants to provide a firm anchorage. Unusually for fish, they show parental care, the male having a brood pouch in which he incubates his offspring.

Pilchard

Bath sponge

Moray eel

Red gurnard

Violet sea snail

Shore crab

A John Dory is a majestic sight as it patrols among offshore rocks. It has a flattened, oval shaped body and long rays on its dorsal fin. Where the species is not persecuted or exploited, some individuals can become remarkably confident and even inquisitive.

The swimming crab is one of the most aggressive of all crabs and can inflict a painful nip. It can swim using the flattened, paddle-like tips of its back legs.

SAFETY TIPS FOR SNORKELLING

• Mediterranean storms can arrive out of nowhere so seek local advice about weather and swimming conditions before you go snorkelling.
• Do not go snorkelling if jellyfish are in the area.
• Take your own snorkel and mask with you to ensure you use one that fits properly.
• Never snorkel unaccompanied.
• Wear a T-shirt or wet suit to avoid sunburn.
• Avoid swimming near river mouths and harbours. The waters will be cloudy and there may be risks from boats and pollution.
• Always stick close to the shore and check your position from time to time.

THE HISTORY
OF GREECE

THE HISTORY of Greece is that of a nation, not of a land: the Greek idea of nationality is governed by language, religion, descent and customs, not so much by location. Early Greek history is the story of internal struggles, from the Mycenaean and Minoan cultures of the Bronze Age to the competing city-states that emerged in the 1st millennium BC.

Alexander the Great, by the folk artist Theófilos

After the defeat of the Greek army by Philip II of Macedon at Chaironeia in 338 BC, Greece became absorbed into Alexander the Great's empire. With the defeat of the Macedonians by the Romans in 168 BC, Greece became a province of Rome. As part of the Eastern Empire she was ruled from Constantinople and became a powerful element within the new Byzantine world.

In 1453, when Constantinople fell to the Ottomans, Greece disappeared as a political entity. The Venetian republic quickly established fortresses on the coast and islands in order to compete with the Ottomans for control of the important trade routes in the Ionian and Aegean seas. Eventually the realization that it was the democracy of Classical Athens that had inspired so many revolutions abroad gave the Greeks themselves the courage to rebel and, in 1821, to fight the Greek War of Independence. In 1830 the Great Powers that dominated Europe established a protectorate over Greece, marking the end of Ottoman rule.

After almost a century of border disputes, Turkey defeated Greece in 1922. This was followed by the dictatorship of Metaxás, and then by the war years of 1940–4, during which half a million people were killed. The present boundaries of the Greek state have only existed since 1948, when Italy returned the Dodecanese. Now an established democracy and member of the European Union, Greece's fortunes seem to have come full circle after 2,000 years of foreign rule.

A map of Greece from the 1595 Atlas of Abraham Ortelius called *Theatrum Orbis Terrarum*

◁ The Knights of the Order of St John from a 15th-century history of the siege of Rhodes

Prehistoric Greece

DURING THE BRONZE AGE three separate civilizations flourished in Greece: the Cycladic, during the 3rd millennium; the Minoan, based on Crete but with an influence that spread throughout the Aegean Islands; and the Mycenaean, which was based on the mainland but spread to Crete in about 1450 BC when the Minoans went into decline. Both the Minoan and Mycenaean cultures found their peak in the Palace periods of the 2nd millennium when they were dominated by a centralized religion and bureaucracy.

Mycenaean gold brooch

PREHISTORIC GREECE

☐ *Areas settled in the Bronze Age*

Neolithic Head *(3000 BC)*
This figure was found on Alónnisos in the Sporades. It probably represents a fertility goddess who was worshipped by farmers to ensure a good harvest. These figures indicate a certain stability in early communities.

The town is unwalled, showing that inhabitants did not fear attack.

Cycladic Figurine
Marble statues such as this, produced in the Bronze Age from about 2800 to 2300 BC, have been found in a number of tombs in the Cyclades.

Multistorey houses

Minoan Bathtub Sarcophagus
This type of coffin, dating to 1400 BC, is found only in Minoan art. It was probably used for a high-status burial.

TIMELINE

	200,000 BC	5000 BC	4000 BC	3000 BC	2000 B

7000 Neolithic farmers in northern Greece

3200 Beginnings of Bronze-Age cultures in Cyclades and Crete

2000 Arrival of first Greek-speakers on mainland Greece

200,000 Evidence of Palaeolithic civilization in northern Greece and Thessaly

"Frying Pan" vessel from Sýros (2500–2000 BC)

2800–2300 Kéros-Sýros culture flourishes in Cyclades

2000 Building of palaces begins in Crete, initiating First Palace period

Mycenaean Death Mask
Large amounts of worked gold were discovered in the Peloponnese at Mycenae, the ancient city of Agamemnon. Masks like this were laid over the faces of the dead.

Forested hills

WHERE TO SEE PREHISTORIC GREECE

The Museum of Cycladic Art in Athens *(see p287)* has the leading collection of Cycladic figurines in Greece. In the National Archaeological Museum *(p282)* Mycenaean gold and other prehistoric artifacts are on display. Akrotíri *(p237)* on Santoríni in the Cyclades has Minoan buildings surviving up to the third storey. The city of Phyla-kopi on Mílos *(p233)* also has Mycenaean walls dating to 1500 BC. Crete, the centre of Minoan civilization, has the palaces of Knosós *(pp268–71)*, Phaestos *(pp262–3)* and Agía Triáda *(p259)*.

The inhabitants are on friendly terms with the visitors.

Cyclopean Walls
Mycenaean citadels, such as this one at Tiryns in the Peloponnese, were encircled by walls of stone so large that later civilizations believed they had been built by giants. It is unclear whether the walls were used for defence or just to impress.

Oared sailing ships

MINOAN SEA SCENE
The wall paintings on Santoríni *(see pp234–7)* were preserved by the volcanic eruption at the end of the 16th century BC. This section shows ships departing from a coastal town. In contrast to the warlike Mycenaeans, Minoan art reflects a more stable community which dominated the Aegean through trade, not conquest.

Mycenaean Octopus Jar
This 14th century BC vase's decoration follows the shape of the pot. Restrained and symmetrical, it contrasts with relaxed Minoan prototypes.

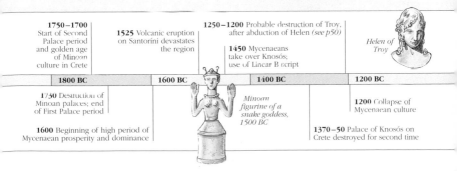

1750–1700 Start of Second Palace period and golden age of Minoan culture in Crete	**1525** Volcanic eruption on Santoríni devastates the region	**1250–1200** Probable destruction of Troy, after abduction of Helen *(see p50)* **1450** Mycenaeans take over Knosós; use of Linear B script	*Helen of Troy*
1800 BC	**1600 BC**	**1400 BC**	**1200 BC**
1750 Destruction of Minoan palaces; end of First Palace period		*Minoan figurine of a snake goddess, 1500 BC*	**1200** Collapse of Mycenaean culture
1600 Beginning of high period of Mycenaean prosperity and dominance			**1370–50** Palace of Knosós on Crete destroyed for second time

The Dark Ages and Archaic Period

I N ABOUT 1200 BC, Greece entered a period of darkness. There was widespread poverty, the population decreased and many skills were lost. A cultural revival in about 800 BC accompanied the emergence of the city-states across Greece and inspired new styles of warfare, art and politics. Greek colonies were established as far away as the Black Sea, present-day Syria, North Africa and the western Mediterranean. Greece was defined by where Greeks lived.

Silver coin from Athens

Kouros *(530 BC)*
Koúroi *were early monumental male nude statues. Idealized representations rather than portraits, they were inspired by Egyptian statues, from which they take their frontal, forward-stepping pose.*

Bronze breastplate

MEDITERRANEAN AREA, 479 BC

▨ *Areas of Greek influence*

The double flute player kept the men marching in time.

Bronze greaves protected the legs.

Solon *(640–558 BC)*
Solon was appointed to the highest magisterial position in Athens. His legal, economic and political reforms heralded democracy.

HOPLITE WARRIORS

The "Chigi" vase from Corinth, dating to about 750 BC, is one of the earliest clear depictions of the new style of warfare that evolved at that period. This required rigorously trained and heavily armed infantrymen called hoplites to fight in a massed formation or phalanx. The rise of the city-state may be linked to the spirit of equality felt by citizen hoplites fighting for their own community.

TIMELINE

Vase fragment showing bands of distinctive geometric line patterns

900 Appearance of first Geometric pottery

1100 BC	1000 BC	900 BC
1100 Migrations of different peoples throughout the Greek world	**1000–850** Formation of the Homeric kingdoms	

6th-Century Vase
This bowl (krater) *for mixing wine and water at elegant feasts is an early example of the art of vase painting. It depicts mythological and heroic scenes.*

Spears were used for thrusting.

Bronze helmets for protection

The phalanxes shoved and pushed, aiming to maintain an unbroken shield wall, a successful new technique.

Gorgon's head decoration

Characteristic round shields

WHERE TO SEE ARCHAIC GREECE

Examples of *koúroi* can be found in the National Archaeological Museum (*see p282*) and in the Acropolis Museum (*p286*), both in Athens. The National Archaeological Museum also houses the national collection of Greek Geometric, red-figure and black-figure vases. Old *koúroi* lie in the old marble quarry on Náxos (*pp226–9*). Sámos boasts the impressive Efpalíneio tunnel (*p151*) and a collection of *koúroi* (*p150*). Delos has a terrace of Archaic lions (*pp214–15*) and the Doric temple of Aphaia on Aígina is well preserved (*pp94–5*). Palaiókastro on Nísyros has huge fortifications (*p171*).

Hunter Returning Home (*500 BC*)
Hunting for hares, deer, or wild boar was an aristocratic sport pursued by Greek nobles on foot with dogs, as depicted on this cup.

Darius I (*ruled 521–486 BC*)
This relief from Persepolis shows the Persian king who tried to conquer the Greek mainland, but was defeated at the Battle of Marathon in 490.

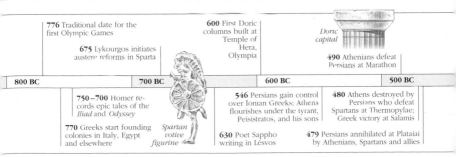

800 BC

776 Traditional date for the first Olympic Games

675 Lykourgos initiates austere reforms in Sparta

700 BC

750–700 Homer records epic tales of the *Iliad* and *Odyssey*

770 Greeks start founding colonies in Italy, Egypt and elsewhere

Spartan votive figurine

600 First Doric columns built at Temple of Hera, Olympia

600 BC

546 Persians gain control over Ionian Greeks; Athens flourishes under the tyrant, Peisistratos, and his sons

630 Poet Sappho writing in Lésvos

Doric capital

490 Athenians defeat Persians at Marathon

500 BC

480 Athens destroyed by Persians who defeat Spartans at Thermopylae; Greek victory at Salamis

479 Persians annihilated at Plataiai by Athenians, Spartans and allies

Classical Greece

Trading amphora

THE CLASSICAL PERIOD has always been considered the high point of Greek civilization. Around 150 years of exceptional creativity in thinking, writing, theatre and the arts produced the great tragedians Aeschylus, Sophocles and Euripides as well as the great philosophical thinkers Socrates, Plato and Aristotle. This was also a time of warfare and bloodshed, however. The Peloponnesian War, which pitted the city-state of Athens and her allies against the city-state of Sparta and her allies, dominated the 5th century BC. In the 4th century Sparta, Athens and Thebes struggled for power only to be ultimately defeated by Philip II of Macedon in 338 BC.

CLASSICAL GREECE, 440 BC

■ *Athens and her allies*

■ *Sparta and her allies*

Fish Shop
This 4th-century BC Greek painted vase comes from Cefalù in Sicily. Large parts of the island were inhabited by Greeks who were bound by a common culture, religion and language.

Theatre used in Pythian Games

Temple of Apollo

Siphnian Treasury

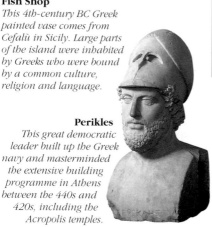

Perikles
This great democratic leader built up the Greek navy and masterminded the extensive building programme in Athens between the 440s and 420s, including the Acropolis temples.

THE SANCTUARY OF DELPHI

The sanctuary in central Greece, shown in this 1894 reconstruction, reached the peak of its political influence in the 5th and 4th centuries BC. Of central importance was the Oracle of Apollo, whose utterances influenced the decisions of city-states such as Athens and Sparta. Rich gifts dedicated to the god were placed by the states in treasuries that lined the Sacred Way.

TIMELINE

Detail of the Parthenon frieze

462 Ephialtes's reforms pave the way for radical democracy in Athens

431–404 Peloponnesian War, ending with the fall of Athens and start of 33-year period of Spartan dominance

c.424 Death of Herodotus, historian of the Persian Wars

475 BC	450 BC	425 BC

478 With the formation of the Delian League, Athens takes over leadership of Greek cities

451–429 Perikles rises to prominence in Athens and launches a lavish building programme

447 Construction of the Parthenon begins

Bust of Herodotus, probably of Hellenistic origin

Gold Oak Wreath from Vergína
By the mid-4th century BC, Philip II of Macedon dominated the Greek world through diplomacy and warfare. This wreath comes from his tomb

WHERE TO SEE CLASSICAL GREECE

Athens is dominated by the Acropolis and its religious buildings, including the Parthenon, erected as part of Perikles's mid-5th-century BC building programme (*see pp284–6*). The island of Delos, the mythological birthplace of Artemis and Apollo, was the centre for the Delian League, the first Athenian naval league. The site contains examples of 5th-century BC sculpture (*pp214–5*). On Rhodes, the 4th-century Temple of Athena at Líndos (*pp192–3*) is well preserved.

Votive of the Rhodians

Stoa of the Athenians

Sacred Way

Athenian Treasury

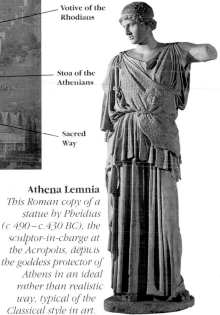

Slave Boy (*400 BC*)
Slaves were funda-mental to the Greek economy and used for all types of work. Many slaves were foreign; this boot boy came from as far as Africa.

Athena Lemnia
This Roman copy of a statue by Pheidias (c.490–c.430 BC), the sculptor-in-charge at the Acropolis, depicts the goddess protector of Athens in an ideal rather than realistic way, typical of the Classical style in art.

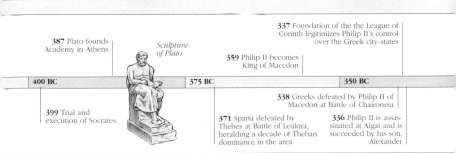

387 Plato founds Academy in Athens

Sculpture of Plato

337 Foundation of the the League of Corinth legitimizes Philip II's control over the Greek city-states

359 Philip II becomes King of Macedon

400 BC

375 BC

350 BC

399 Trial and execution of Socrates

338 Greeks defeated by Philip II of Macedon at Battle of Chaironeia

371 Sparta defeated by Thebes at Battle of Leuktra, heralding a decade of Theban dominance in the area

336 Philip II is assas-sinated at Aigai and is succeeded by his son, Alexander

Hellenistic Greece

Alexander the Great

ALEXANDER THE GREAT of Macedon fulfilled his father Philip's plans for the conquest of the Persians. He went on to create a vast empire that extended to India in the east and Egypt in the south. The Hellenistic period was extraordinary for the dispersal of Greek language, religion and culture throughout the territories conquered by Alexander. It lasted from after Alexander's death in 323 BC until the Romans began to dismantle his empire in the mid-2nd century BC. For Greece, Macedonian domination was replaced by that of Rome in AD 168.

Relief of Hero-Worship *(c.200 BC)*
Hero-worship was part of Greek religion. Alexander, however, was worshipped as a god in his lifetime.

Péla was the birthplace of Alexander and capital of Macedon.

The Mausoleum of Halicarnassus was one of the Seven Wonders of the Ancient World.

Issus, in modern Turkey, was the site of Alexander's victory over the Persian army in 333 BC.

BLACK SEA

• Péla

• Athens

Mausoleum of Halicarnassus

ASIA MINOR

• Issus

MEDITERRANEAN SEA

Ammon •

Lighthouse at Alexandria

Ishtar Gate i Babylon

Alexander died in Babylon in 323 BC.

Alexander Defeats Darius III
This Pompeiian mosaic shows the Persian leader overwhelmed at Issus in 333 BC. Macedonian troops are shown carrying their highly effective long pikes.

EGYPT

RED SEA

ARABIA

The Ammon oracle declared Alexander to be divine.

Alexandria, founded by Alexander, replaced Athens as the centre of Greek culture.

Terracotta Statue
This 2nd-century BC statue of two women gossiping is typical of a Hellenistic interest in private rather than public individuals.

KEY

- - - Alexander's route

▢ Alexander's empire

▢ Dependent regions

TIMELINE

333 Alexander the Great defeats the Persian king, Darius III, and declares himself king of Asia

323 Death of Alexander, and of Diogenes

301 Battle of Ipsus, between Alexander's rival successors, leads to the break-up of his empire into three kingdoms

268–261 Chremonidean War, ending with the capitulation of Athens to Macedon

325 BC	300 BC	275 BC	250 BC

322 Death of Aristotle

331 Alexander founds Alexandria after conquering Egypt

287–275 "Pyrrhic victory" of King Pyrros of Epirus who defeated the Romans in Italy but suffered heavy losses

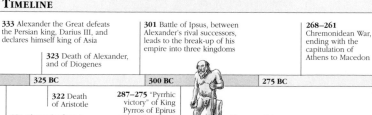

Diogenes, the Hellenistic philosopher

Fusing Eastern and Western Religion

This plaque from Afghanistan shows the Greek goddess Nike, and the Asian goddess Cybele, in a chariot pulled by lions.

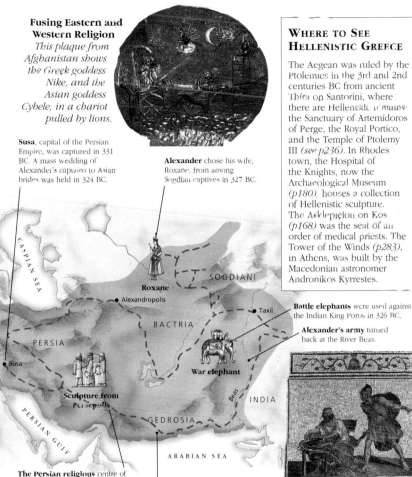

Susa, capital of the Persian Empire, was captured in 331 BC. A mass wedding of Alexander's captains to Asian brides was held in 324 BC.

Alexander chose his wife, Roxane, from among Sogdian captives in 327 BC.

Battle elephants were used against the Indian King Poros in 326 BC.

Alexander's army turned back at the River Beas.

The Persian religious centre of Persepolis, in modern Iran, fell to Alexander in 330 BC.

Alexander's army suffered heavy losses in the Gedrosia desert.

Roxane

Alexandropolis

SOGDIANI

CASPIAN SEA

BACTRIA

Taxil

PERSIA

War elephant

INDIA

Susa

Beas

Sculpture from Persepolis

GEDROSIA

PERSIAN GULF

ARABIAN SEA

ALEXANDER THE GREAT'S EMPIRE

In forming his empire Alexander covered huge distances. After defeating the Persians in Asia he moved to Egypt, then returned to Asia to pursue Darius, and then his murderers, into Bactria. In 326 his troops revolted in India and refused to go on. Alexander died in 323 in Babylon.

The Death of Archimedes

Archimedes was the leading Hellenistic scientist and mathematician. This mosaic from Renaissance Italy shows his murder in 212 BC by a Roman.

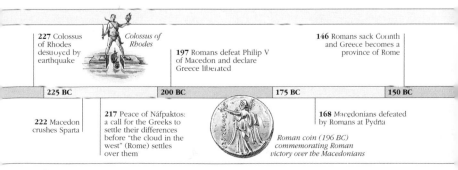

227 Colossus of Rhodes destroyed by earthquake

Colossus of Rhodes

197 Romans defeat Philip V of Macedon and declare Greece liberated

146 Romans sack Corinth and Greece becomes a province of Rome

225 BC

200 BC

175 BC

150 BC

222 Macedon crushes Sparta

217 Peace of Náfpaktos: a call for the Greeks to settle their differences before "the cloud in the west" (Rome) settles over them

168 Macedonians defeated by Romans at Pydna

Roman coin (196 BC) commemorating Roman victory over the Macedonians

Roman Greece

Mark Antony

AFTER THE ROMANS GAINED CONTROL of Greece with the sack of Corinth in 146 BC, Greece became the cultural centre of the Roman Empire. The Roman nobility sent their sons to be educated in the schools of philosophy in Athens. The end of the Roman civil wars between leading Roman statesmen was played out on Greek soil, finishing in the Battle of Actium in Thessaly in 31 BC. In AD 323 the Emperor Constantine founded the new eastern capital of Constantinople; the empire was later divided into the Greek-speaking East and the Latin-speaking West.

ROMAN PROVINCES, AD 211

Mithridates
In a bid to extend his territory, this ruler of Pontus, on the Black Sea, led the resistance to Roman rule in 88 BC. He was forced to make peace three years later.

Bema, or raised platform, where St Paul spoke

Roman basilica

Bouleuterion

Notitia Dignitatum *(AD 395) As part of the Roman Empire, Greece was split into several provinces. The proconsul of the province of Achaia used this insignia.*

Springs of Peirene, the source of water

RECONSTRUCTION OF ROMAN CORINTH

Corinth, in the Peloponnese, was refounded and largely rebuilt by Julius Caesar in 46 BC, becoming capital of the Roman province of Achaia. The Romans built the forum, covered theatre and basilicas. St Paul visited the city in AD 50–51, working as a tent maker.

Baths of Eurycles

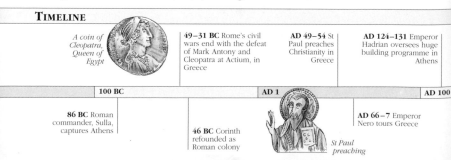

TIMELINE

A coin of Cleopatra, Queen of Egypt

86 BC Roman commander, Sulla, captures Athens

100 BC

49–31 BC Rome's civil wars end with the defeat of Mark Antony and Cleopatra at Actium, in Greece

46 BC Corinth refounded as Roman colony

AD 1

St Paul preaching

AD 49–54 St Paul preaches Christianity in Greece

AD 66–7 Emperor Nero tours Greece

AD 124–131 Emperor Hadrian oversees huge building programme in Athens

AD 100

Mosaic *(AD 180)*
*This highly
sophisticated
Roman mosaic of
Dionysos riding
on a leopard comes
from the House of
Masks, on Delos.*

Temple of
Octavia

Odeion or Roman
covered theatre

Greek open-air
theatre

Archaic
Greek
Temple of
Apollo

WHERE TO SEE ROMAN GREECE

In Athens the Theatre of
Herodes Atticus *(see p284)*
at the foot of the Acropolis
is an example of Roman
architecture. To the southwest
of the Acropolis, Hadrian's
Arch, which leads from the
Roman into the old Greek
city, is still standing next to
the Temple of Olympian Zeus
(p281). On Sámos *(p151)*
and Santorini *(p256)* there are
remains of Roman baths. On
Delos, Roman houses with
mosaics survive *(pp214–15)*.
Among them, the House of
the Dolphins and the House
of the Masks are particularly
well-preserved examples.

**Arch of
Galerius**
*This arch at
Thessaloníki
commemorates the
Emperor Galerius's
victory over the
Persians. The carved
panel shows Galerius
in his chariot.*

Apollo Belevedere
*Much Greek sculpture
is known to us only
through Roman copies
of Greek originals, like
this statue of Apollo.*

170 Pausanias completes
Guide to Greece for
Roman travellers

267 Goths
pillage Athens

324 Constantine becomes sole
emperor of Roman Empire
and establishes his capital in
Constantinople

395 Goths devastate Athens
and Peloponnese

381 Emperor
Theodosius I makes
Christianity state religion

AD 200   AD 300

*Coin of the
Roman Emperor
Galerius*

293 Under Emperor
Galerius, Thessaloniki
becomes second city to
Constantinople

393 Olympic games banned

395 Death of Theodosius I; formal
division of Roman Empire into
Latin West and Byzantine East

Byzantine and Crusader Greece

Byzantine court dress arm band

UNDER THE BYZANTINE EMPIRE, which at the end of the 4th century succeeded the old Eastern Roman Empire, Greece became Orthodox in religion and was split into administrative *themes*. When the capital, Constantinople, fell to the Crusaders in 1204 Greece was again divided, mostly between the Venetians and the Franks. Constantinople and Mystrás were recovered by the Byzantine Greeks in 1261, but the Turks' capture of Constantinople in 1453 marked the final demise of the Byzantine Empire. It left a legacy of hundreds of churches and a wealth of religious art.

BYZANTINE GREECE IN THE 10TH CENTURY

Watch-tower of Tsimiskís

Chapel

Refectory

Two-Headed Eagle
In the Byzantine world, the emperor was also patriarch of the church, a dual role represented in this pendant of a two-headed eagle.

GREAT LAVRA

This monastery is the earliest (AD 963) and largest of the religious complexes on Mount Athos in northern Greece. Many parts have been rebuilt, but its appearance remains essentially Byzantine. The monasteries became important centres of learning and religious art.

Defence of Thessaloníki
The fall of Thessaloníki to the Saracens in AD 904 was a blow to the Byzantine Empire. Many towns in Greece were heavily fortified against attack from this time.

TIMELINE

578–86 Avars and Slavs invade Greece

Gold solidus of the Byzantine Empress Irene, who ruled AD 797–802

400	600	800
529 Aristotle's and Plato's schools of philosophy close as Christian culture supplants Classical thought	**680** Bulgars cross Danube and establish empire in northern Greece	**726** Iconoclasm introduced by Pope Leo III (abandoned in 843) **841** Parthenon becomes a cathedral

Constantine the Great
The first eastern emperor to recognize Christianity, Constantine founded the city of Constantinople in AD 324. Here he is shown with his mother, Helen.

Cypress tree of Agios Athanásios

Christ Pantokrátor
This 14th century fresco of Christ as ruler of the world is in the Byzantine city and monastic centre of Mystrás.

WHERE TO SEE BYZANTINE AND CRUSADER GREECE

In Athens, the Benáki Museum *(see p287)* contains icons, metalwork, sculpture and textiles. On Pátmos, the treasury of the Monastery of St John, founded in 1088 *(pp160–61)*, is the richest outside Mount Athos. The 11th-century convent of Néa Moní on Chios *(pp146–7)* has magnificent gold-ground mosaics. The medieval architecture of the Palace of the Grand Masters and the Street of the Knights on Rhodes *(pp182–5)* is particularly fine. Buildings by the Knights on Kos *(pp166–9)* are also worth seeing. The Venetian castle on Páros *(p223)* dates from 1260.

Chapel of Agios Athanásios, founder of Great Lávra

Combined library and treasury

Fortified walls

The katholikón, the main church in Great Lávra, has the most magnificent Byzantine murals on Mount Athos.

1054 Patriarch of Constantinople and Pope Leo IX excommunicate each other

Frankish Chlemoútsi Castle

1081–1149 Normans invade Greek islands and mainland

1354 Ottoman Turks enter Europe, via southern Italy and Greece

1390–1450 Turks gain power over much of mainland Greece

1000

1200

1400

Basil the Bulgar Slayer, Byzantine emperor (lived 956–1025)

1204 Crusaders sack Constantinople. Break-up of Byzantine Empire as result of occupation by Franks and Venetians

1210 Venetians win control over Crete

1261 Start of intellectual and artistic flowering of Mystrás

1389 Venetians in control of much of Greece and the islands

Venetian and Ottoman Greece

**Venetian lion
of St Mark**

FOLLOWING THE OTTOMANS' momentous capture of Constantinople in 1453, and their conquest of almost all the remaining Greek territory by 1460, the Greek state effectively ceased to exist for the next 350 years. Although the city became the capital of the vast Ottoman Empire, it remained the principal centre of Greek population and the focus of Greek dreams of resurgence. The small Greek population of what today is modern Greece languished in an impoverished and underpopulated backwater, but even there rebellious bands of brigands and private militias were formed. The Ionian Islands, Crete and a few coastal enclaves were seized for long periods by the Venetians – an experience more intrusive than the inefficient tolerance of the Ottomans, but one which left a rich cultural and architectural legacy.

GREECE IN 1493

Areas occupied by Venetians

Areas occupied by Ottomans

Cretan Painting
This 15th-century icon is typical of the style developed by Greek artists in the School of Crete, active until the Ottomans took Crete in 1669.

Battle of Lepanto *(1571)*
The Christian fleet, under Don John of Austria, decisively defeated the Ottomans off Náfpaktos, halting their advance westwards.

ARRIVAL OF TURKISH PRINCE CEM ON RHODES

Prince Cem, Ottoman rebel and son of Mehmet II, fled to Rhodes in 1481 and was welcomed by the Christian Knights of St John *(see pp184–5)*. In 1522, however, Rhodes fell to the Ottomans after a siege.

TIMELINE

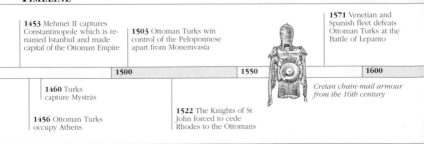

1453 Mehmet II captures Constantinople which is re-named Istanbul and made capital of the Ottoman Empire

1503 Ottoman Turks win control of the Peloponnese apart from Monemvasía

1571 Venetian and Spanish fleet defeats Ottoman Turks at the Battle of Lepanto

1500　　**1550**　　**1600**

1460 Turks capture Mystrás

1456 Ottoman Turks occupy Athens

1522 The Knights of St John forced to cede Rhodes to the Ottomans

Cretan chain-mail armour from the 16th century

Shipping

Greek merchants traded throughout the Ottoman Empire. By 1800 there were merchant colonies in Constantinople and as far afield as London and Odessa. This 19th-century embroidery shows the Turkish influence on Greek decorative arts.

The Knights of St John defied the Turks until 1522.

The massive fortifications eventually succumbed to Turkish artillery.

The Knights supported Turkish rebel, Prince Cem.

WHERE TO SEE VENETIAN AND OTTOMAN ARCHITECTURE

The Ionian Islands are particularly rich in buildings dating from the Venetian occupation. The old town of Corfu *(see pp70–73)* is dominated by its two Venetian fortresses. The citadel in Zákynthos *(p86)* is also Venetian. Crete has a number of Venetian buildings: the old port of Irákleio *(pp264–5)* and some of the back streets of Chaniá *(pp248–9)* convey an overwhelming feeling of Venice. Irákleio's fort withstood the Great Siege of 1648–69. Some Ottoman-era houses survive on Thásos *(p127)*. Several mosques and other Ottoman buildings, including a library and *hammam* (baths), can be seen in Rhodes old town *(pp178–87)*.

Dinner at a Greek House in 1801

Nearly four centuries of Ottoman rule profoundly affected Greek culture, ethnic composition and patterns of everyday life. Greek cuisine incorporates Turkish dishes still found throughout the old Ottoman Empire.

1650	1700	1750	1800

1687 Parthenon seriously damaged during Venetian artillery attack on Turkish magazine

1715 Turks reconquer the Peloponnese

Ali Pasha (1741–1822), a governor of the Ottoman Empire

1814 Britain gains possession of Ionian Islands

1684 Venetians reconquer the Peloponnese

Parthenon blown up

1778 Ali Pasha becomes Vizier of Ioánnina and establishes powerful state in Albania and northern Greece

1801 Frieze on Parthenon removed by Lord Elgin

1814 Foundation of *Filikí Etaireía*, Greek liberation movement

The Making of Modern Greece

THE GREEK WAR of Independence marked the overthrow of the Ottomans and the start of the "Great Idea", an ambitious project to bring all Greek people under one flag *(Enosis)*. The plans for expansion were initially successful, and during the 19th century the Greeks succeeded in doubling their national territory and reasserting Greek sovereignty over many of the islands. However, an attempt to take the city of Constantinople by force after World War I ended in disaster: in 1922 millions of Greeks were expelled from Smyrna in Turkish Anatolia, ending thousands of years of Greek presence in Asia Minor.

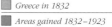

THE EMERGING GREEK STATE

▢ *Greece in 1832*

▨ *Areas gained 1832–1923*

Klephts (mountain brigands) were the basis of the Independence movement.

Massacre at Chíos
This detail of Delacroix's shocking painting Scènes de Massacres de Scio *shows the events of 1822, when Turks took savage revenge for an earlier killing of Muslims.*

Weapons were family heirlooms or donated by philhellenes.

Declaration of the Constitution in Athens
Greece's Neo-Classical parliament building in Athens was the site of the Declaration of the Constitution in 1843. It was built as the Royal Palace for Greece's first monarch, King Otto, in the 1830s.

TIMELINE

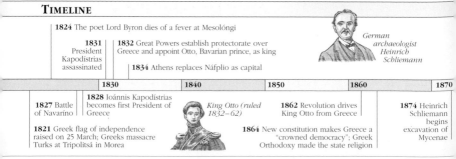

1824 The poet Lord Byron dies of a fever at Mesolóngi

1831 President Kapodístrias assassinated

1832 Great Powers establish protectorate over Greece and appoint Otto, Bavarian prince, as king

1834 Athens replaces Náfplio as capital

German archaeologist Heinrich Schliemann

1830	1840	1850	1860	1870

1827 Battle of Navaríno

1828 Ioánnis Kapodístrias becomes first President of Greece

King Otto (ruled 1832–62)

1862 Revolution drives King Otto from Greece

1874 Heinrich Schliemann begins excavation of Mycenae

1821 Greek flag of independence raised on 25 March; Greeks massacre Turks at Tripolitsá in Morea

1864 New constitution makes Greece a "crowned democracy"; Greek Orthodoxy made the state religion

Life in Athens
By 1836 urban Greeks still wore a mixture of Greek traditional and Western dress. The Ottoman legacy had not totally disappeared and is visible in the fez worn by men.

FLAG RAISING OF 1821 REVOLUTION
In 1821, the Greek secret society *Filikí Etaireía* was behind a revolt by Greek officers which led to anti-Turk uprisings throughout the Peloponnese. Tradition credits Archbishop Germanós of Pátra with raising the rebel flag near Kalávryta in the Peloponnese on 25 March. The struggle for independence had begun.

WHERE TO SEE 19TH-CENTURY GREECE
In Crete, Moní Arkadíou *(see p256)* is the site of mass suicide by freedom fighters in 1866; the tomb of Venizélos is at Akrotíri *(p247)*. The harbour and surrounding buildings at Sýros *(p216)* are evidence of the importance of Greek seapower in the 19th century.

Corinth Canal
This spectacular link between the Aegean and Ionian seas opened in 1893.

Elefthérios Venizélos
This great Cretan politician and advocate of liberal democracy doubled Greek territory during the Balkan Wars (1912–13) and joined the Allies in World War I.

1893 Opening of Corinth Canal

1896 First Olympics of modern era, held in Athens

1908 Crete united with Greece

1921 Greece launches offensive in Asia Minor

1917 King Constantine is deposed; Greece joins World War I

1922 Turkish burning of Smyrna signals end of the "Great Idea"

1880	1890	1900	1910	1920

Spyridon Louis, Marathon winner at the first modern Olympics

1899 Arthur Evans begins excavations at Knosós

1912–13 Greece extends its borders during the Balkan Wars

1920 Treaty of Sèvres gives Greece huge gains in territory

1923 Population exchange agreed between Greece and Turkey at Treaty of Lausanne. Greece loses previous gains

Twentieth-Century Greece

THE YEARS after the 1922 defeat by Turkey were terrible ones for Greek people. The influx of refugees contributed to the political instability of the interwar years. The dictatorship of Metaxás was followed by invasion in 1940, then Italian, German and Bulgarian occupation and, finally, the Civil War between 1946 and 1949, with its legacy of division. After experiencing the Cyprus problem of the 1950s and the military dictatorship of 1967 to 1974, Greece is now an established democracy and became a member of the European Economic and Monetary Union in 2000.

1947 Internationally acclaimed Greek artist, Giánnis Tsaroúchis, holds his first exhibition of set designs, in the Romvos Gallery, Athens

1938 Death of sculptor Giannoúlis Chalepás, best known for his *Sleeping Girl* funerary statue

1946 Government institutes "White Terror" against Communists

1958 USSR threatens Greece with economic sanctions if NATO missiles installed

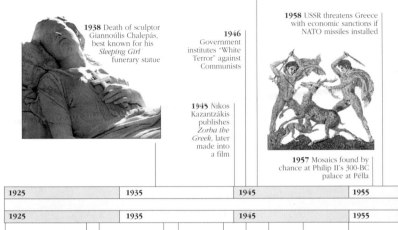

1945 Níkos Kazantzákis publishes *Zorba the Greek*, later made into a film

1957 Mosaics found by chance at Philip II's 300-BC palace at Pélla

1925	1935	1945	1955

1925	1935	1945	1955

1933 Death of Greek poet, Constantine (C P) Cavafy

1951 Greece enters NATO

1955 Greek Cypriots start campaign of violence in Cyprus against British rule

1932 Aristotle Onassis purchases six freight ships, the start of his shipping empire

1939 Greece declares neutrality at start of World War II

1948 Dodecanese becomes part of Greece

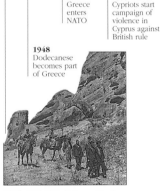

1925 Mános Chatzidákis, who wrote music for the film *Never on Sunday*, is born

1946–9 Civil War between Greek government and the Communists who take to the mountains

1944 Churchill visits Athens to show his support for Greek government against Communist Resistance

1960 Cyprus declared independent

1940 Italy invades Greece. Greek soldiers defend northern Greece. Greece enters World War II

1963 Geórgios Papandréou's centre-left government voted into power

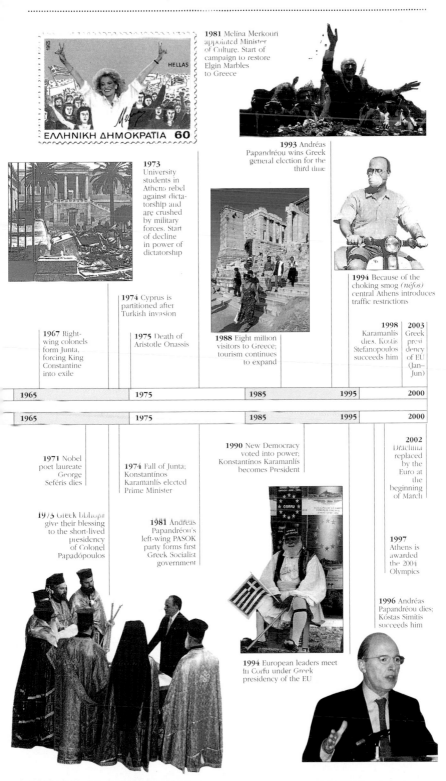

1981 Melína Merkoúri appointed Minister of Culture. Start of campaign to restore Elgin Marbles to Greece

1993 Andréas Papandréou wins Greek general election for the third time

1973 University students in Athens rebel against dictatorship and are crushed by military forces. Start of decline in power of dictatorship

1974 Cyprus is partitioned after Turkish invasion

1967 Right-wing colonels form Junta, forcing King Constantine into exile

1975 Death of Aristotle Onassis

1988 Eight million visitors to Greece; tourism continues to expand

1994 Because of the choking smog (néfos) central Athens introduces traffic restrictions

1998 Karamanlís dies. Kostas Stefanopoulos succeeds him

2003 Greek presidency of EU (Jan–Jun)

1965   1975   1985   1995   2000

1965   1975   1985   1995   2000

1971 Nobel poet laureate George Seféris dies

1974 Fall of Junta; Konstantínos Karamanlís elected Prime Minister

1990 New Democracy voted into power; Konstantínos Karamanlís becomes President

2002 Drachma replaced by the Euro at the beginning of March

1973 Greek bishops give their blessing to the short-lived presidency of Colonel Papadópoulos

1981 Andréas Papandréou's left-wing PASOK party forms first Greek Socialist government

1997 Athens is awarded the 2004 Olympics

1996 Andréas Papandréou dies; Kóstas Simítis succeeds him

1994 European leaders meet in Corfu under Greek presidency of the EU

THE GREEK ISLANDS
THROUGH THE YEAR

May Day wreath

REEK ISLAND LIFE revolves around the seasons, and is punctuated by saints' days and colourful religious festivals, or *panigýria*. Easter is the most important Orthodox festival of the year, but there are lively pre-Lenten carnivals on some islands as well. The Greeks mix piety and pleasure, with a great enthusiasm for their celebrations, from the most important to the smallest village fair. There are also festivals that have ancient roots in pagan revels. Other festivals celebrate harvests of local produce, such as grapes, olives and corn, or re-enact various victories for Greece in its struggle for Independence.

SPRING

THE GREEK WORD for spring is *ánoixi* (the opening), and it heralds the beginning of the tourist season on the islands. After wintering in Athens or Rhodes, hoteliers

Children in national dress, 25 March

and shopkeepers head for the smaller islands to open up. The islands in spring are at their most beautiful, carpeted with red poppies, camomile and wild cyclamen. Fruit trees are in blossom, fishing boats and houses are freshly painted and people are at their most welcoming. Orthodox Easter is the main spring event, preceded in late February or March with pre-Lenten carnivals. While northern island groups can be showery, by late April, Crete, the Dodecanese and east Aegean islands are usually warm and sunny.

MARCH

Apókries, or Carnival Sunday *(first Sun before Lent)*. There are carnivals on many islands for three weeks leading up to this date, the culmination of pre-Lenten festivities. Celebrations are exuberant at Agiásos on Lésvos and on Kárpathos, while a goat dance is performed on Skýros.
Katharí Deftéra, or Clean Monday *(seven Sundays before Easter)*. This marks the start of Lent. Houses are spring-cleaned and the un-leavened bread *lagána* is baked. Also, a huge kite-flying contest takes place in Chalkída on Evvoia.

CELEBRATING EASTER IN GREECE

Greek Orthodox Easter can fall up to three weeks either side of Western Easter. It is the most important religious festival in Greece, and Holy Week is a time for Greek families to reunite. It is also a good time to visit Greece, to see the processions and church services and to sample the Easter food. The ceremony and symbolism is a direct link with Greece's Byzantine past, as well as with earlier more primitive beliefs. The festivities reach a climax at midnight on Easter Saturday when, as priests intone "Christ is risen", fireworks explode to usher in a Sunday of feasting, music and dancing. The Sunday feasting on roast meat marks the end of the Lenten fast, and a belief in the renewal of life in spring. Particularly worthwhile visiting for the Holy Week processions and the Friday and Saturday night services are Olympos on Kárpathos, Ýdra, Pátmos and just about any village on Crete.

Priests in robes at the Easter parade of icons

***Christ's bier**, decorated with flowers and containing His effigy, is carried in solemn procession through the streets at dusk on Good Friday.*

***Candle lighting** takes place at the end of the Easter Saturday Mass. In pitch darkness, a single flame is used to light the candles held by worshippers.*

A workers' rally in Athens on Labour Day, 1 May

Independence Day and **Evangelismós** *(25 Mar)*. A national holiday, with parades and dances nationwide to celebrate the 1821 revolt against the Ottoman Empire. The religious festival, one of the Orthodox church's most important, marks the Archangel Gabriel's announcement to the Virgin Mary that she was to become the Holy Mother. Name day for Evángelos and Evangelía.

APRIL

Megáli Evdomáda, Holy Week *(Apr or May)*, including *Kyriakí tōn Vaïōn* (Palm Sunday), *Megáli Pémpti* (Maundy Thursday), *Megáli Paraskeví* (Good Friday),

Megálo Sávvato (Easter Saturday) and the most important date in the Orthodox calendar, *Páscha* (Easter Sunday).

Agios Geórgios, St George's Day *(23 Apr)*. A day for celebrating the patron saint of shepherds. This date traditionally marks the beginning of the grazing season in Greece

Kite-flying competition in Chalkída, Evvoia

MAY

Protomagiá, May Day or Labour Day *(1 May)*. Traditionally, wreaths made with wild flowers and garlic are hung up to ward off evil. In major towns and cities, the day is marked by workers' demonstrations and rallies.

Agios Konstantínos kai Agía Eléni *(21 May)*. A nationwide celebration for the saint and his mother, the first Orthodox Byzantine rulers.

Análipsi, Ascension *(40 days after Easter, usually in May)*. An important Orthodox feast day, celebrated across the nation.

Easter biscuits celebrate the end of Lent. Another Easter dish, mayerítsa soup, is made of lamb's innards and is eaten in the early hours of Easter Sunday.

Easter dancing, for young and old alike, continues the outdoor festivities after the midday meal on Sunday.

Egg loaves, made of sweet plaited dough, contain eggs with shells dyed red to symbolize the blood of Christ. Red eggs are also traditionally given as presents on Easter Sunday.

Lamb roasting is traditionally done in the open air on giant spits over charcoal, for lunch on Easter Sunday. The first retsina wine from last year's harvest is opened and for dessert there are sweet cinnamon-flavoured pastries.

Harvesting barley in July, on the island of Folégandros

SUMMER

WITH ISLANDS parched and sizzling, the tourist season is now in full swing. Villagers with rooms to let meet backpackers from the ferries, and prices go up. The islands are sometimes cooled by the strong, blustery *meltemi*, a northerly wind from the Aegean, which can blow up at any time to disrupt ferry schedules and delight windsurfers.

In June, the corn is harvested and cherries, apricots and peaches are at their best. In July herbs are gathered and dried, and figs begin to ripen. August sees the mass exodus from Athens to the islands, especially for the festival of the Assumption on 15 August. By late summer the first of the grapes have ripened, while temperatures soar.

JUNE

Pentikostí, Pentecost, or Whit Sunday *(seven weeks after Orthodox Easter)*. An important Orthodox feast day, celebrated throughout Greece.
Agíou Pnévmatos, Feast of the Holy Spirit, or Whit Monday *(the following day)*. A national holiday.
Athens Festival *(mid-Jun to mid-Sep)*, Athens. A cultural festival with modern and ancient theatre and music.
Klídonas *(24 Jun)* Chaniá, Crete *(see pp248–9)*. A festival celebrating the custom of water-divining for a husband. An amusing song is sung while locals dance.
Agios Ioánnis, St John's Day *(24 Jun)*. On some islands bonfires are lit on the evening before. May wreaths are consigned to the flames and youngsters jump over the fires.
Agioi Apóstoloi Pétros kai Pávlos, Apostles Peter and Paul *(29 Jun)*. There are festivals at dedicated churches, such as St Paul's Bay, Líndos, Rhodes *(see p193)*.
Agioi Apóstoloi, Holy Apostles *(30 Jun)*. This time the celebrations are for anyone named after one of the 12 apostles.

Consecrated bread for religious festivals

JULY

Agios Nikódimos *(14 Jul)*, Náxos town. A small folk festival and procession for the town's patron saint.

Festivities on Tínos for Koímisis tis Theotókou, 15 August

Agía Marína *(17 Jul)*. This day is widely celebrated in rural areas, with feasts to honour this saint. She is revered as an important protector of crops and healer of snakebites. There are festivals throughout Crete and at the town of Agía Marína, Léros.
Profítis Ilías, the Prophet Elijah *(18–20 Jul)*. There are high-altitude celebrations in the Cyclades, Rhodes and on Evvoia at the mountain-top chapels dedicated to him. The chapels were built on former sites of Apollo temples.
Agíou Panteleïmonos Festival *(25–28 Jul)*, Tílos *(see p173)*. Three days of song and dance at Moní Agíou Panteleïmonos, culminating in "Dance of the Koupa", or Cup, at Taxiárchis, Megálo Chorió. There are also celebrations at Moní Panachrántou, Andros *(see p205)*.
Simonídeia Festival *(1–19 Aug)*, Kea. A celebration of the work of the island's famous lyric poet, Simonides (556–468 BC), with drama, exhibitions and dance.
Réthymno Festival *(Jul and Aug)*, Réthymno, Crete. The event includes a wine festival and Renaissance fair.

AUGUST

Ippokráteia, Hippocrates Cultural Festival *(throughout Aug)*, Kos *(see p166)*. Art exhibitions are combined with concerts and films, plus the ceremony of the Hippocratic Oath at the Asklepieion.

One of the many local church celebrations during summer, Pátmos

Dionysía Festival *(first week of Aug)*, Náxos town. A festival of folk dancing in traditional costume, with free food and plenty of wine.
Metamórfosi, Transfiguration of Christ *(6 Aug)*. An important day in the Orthodox calendar, celebrated throughout Greece. It is a fun day in the Dodecanese, and particularly on the island of Chálki, where you may get pelted with eggs, flour, yoghurt and squid ink.
Koímisis tis Theotókou, Assumption of the Virgin Mary *(15 Aug)*. A national holiday, and the most important festival in the Orthodox calendar after Easter. Following the long liturgy on the night of the 14th, the icon of the Madonna is paraded and kissed. Then the celebrations proceed, and continue for days, providing an excellent opportunity to experience traditional music and spontaneous dance. There are spectacular celebrations at Olympos on Kárpathos *(see p199)*, with women wearing dazzling costumes, and at Panagía Evangelístria on Tínos *(see pp208–9)*.

Women in ceremonial costume, Kárpathos

Autumn

THE WINE-MAKING months of September and October are still very warm in the Dodecanese, Crete and the Cyclades, although they can be showery further north, and the sea can be rough. October sees the "little summer of St Dimitrios", a pleasant heatwave when the first wine is ready to drink. The shooting season begins and hunters take to the hills in search of pigeon, partridge and other game. The main fishing season begins, with fish such as bream and red mullet appearing on restaurant menus. By the end of October many islanders are heading for Athens, packing the ferries and wishing each other *Kaló Chimóna*

The year's first wine

(good winter). But traditional island life goes on: olives are harvested and strings of garlic, onions and tomatoes are hung up to dry for the winter; flocks of sheep are brought down from the mountains; and fishing nets are mended.

September

Génnisis tis Theotókou, birth of the Virgin Mary *(8 Sep)*. An important feast day in the Orthodox church calendar. Also on this day, there is a re-enactment of the Battle of Spétses (1822) in the town's harbour *(see p97)*, followed by a fireworks display and feast.
Ypsosis tou Timíou Stavroú, Exaltation of the True Cross *(14 Sep)*. Though in autumn, this is regarded as the last of Greece's summer festivals. The festivities are celebrated with fervour on Chálki.

Strings of tomatoes hanging out to dry in the autumn sunshine

October

Agios Dimítrios *(26 Oct)*. A popular and widely celebrated name day. It is also traditionally the day when the first wine of the year is ready to drink.
Ochi Day *(28 Oct)*. A national holiday, with patriotic parades in the cities, and plenty of dancing. The day commemorates the famous reply by Greece's prime minister of the time, Metaxás, to Mussolini's 1940 call for Greek surrender: an emphatic no *(Ochi)*.

Greek veterans on Ochi Day

November

Ton Taxiarchón Michaíl kai Gavriíl, *(8 Nov)*. Ceremonies at many monasteries named after Archangels Gabriel and Michael, such as at Panormítis, on Sými *(see p175)*. This is an important name day throughout Greece.
Eisódia tis Theotókou, Presentation of the Virgin in the Temple *(21 Nov)*. A religious feast day, and one of the most important for the Orthodox church. Name day for María, Mary.

Diving for the cross at Epiphany, 6 Jan

WINTER

LASHED BY wild winds and
high seas, the islands can
be bleak in winter. *Kafeneía*
are steamed up and full of
men playing cards or back-
gammon. Women
often embroider or
crochet, and cook
warming stews
and soups. Fisher-
men celebrate
Agios Nikólaos,
their patron
saint, and then
preparations get underway
for Christmas. The 12-day
holiday begins on Christmas
Eve, when the wicked gob-
lins, *kallikántzaroí*, are about
causing mischief, until the
Epiphany in the new year,
when they are banished. Pigs
are slaughtered for Christmas
pork, and cakes representing
the swaddling clothes of the
infant Christ are made. The
Greek Father Christmas
comes on New Year's Day
and special cakes, called
vasilópita, are baked with
coins inside to bring good
luck to the finder.

DECEMBER

Agios Nikólaos *(6 Dec).*
This is a celebration for the
patron saint of sailors. *Panigýria* (religious ceremonies)

are held at harbourside
churches, and decorat-
ed boats and icons are
paraded on beaches.
Agios Spyrídon
(12 Dec), Corfu *(see
pp70–75).* A celebra-
tion for the patron saint
of the island, with a
parade of his relics.
Christoúgenna,
Christmas *(25 Dec).*
A national holiday.
Though less significant
than Easter in Greece,
Christmas is still an
important feast day.
**Sýnaxis tis Theotó-
kou**, meeting of the
Virgin's entourage *(26
Dec).* A religious cele-
bration nationwide, and
a national holiday. The
next day *(27 Dec)* is a popular
name day for Stéfanos and
Stefanía, commemorating the
saint Agios Stéfanos.

JANUARY

**Almond biscuits eaten at
Christmas and Easter**

Agios Vasíleios, also
known as *Proto-
chroniá (1 Jan).*
A national holiday
to celebrate this
saint. The day
combines with
festivities for
the arrival of
the new year. Gifts are ex-
changed and the new year
greeting is *Kalí Chroniá*.
Theofánia, or Epiphany
(6 Jan). A national holiday
and an important feast day.
There are special ceremonies

**MAIN PUBLIC
HOLIDAYS**

These are the dates when
museums and public sites
are closed nationwide.

Agios Vasíleios (1 Jan).
Evangelismós (25 Mar).
Protomagiá (1 May).
Megáli Paraskeví
(Good Friday).
Páscha (Easter Sunday).
Christoúgenna (25 Dec).
Sýnaxis tis Theotókou
(26 Dec).

to bless the waters at coastal
locations throughout many
of the islands. A priest at the
harbourside throws a crucifix
into the water. Young men
then dive into the sea for the
honour of retrieving the cross.

FEBRUARY

Ypapantí, Candlemas *(2
Feb).* An important Orthodox
feast day throughout Greece.
This festival celebrates the
presentation of the infant
Christ at the temple.

**Priests in ceremonial robes at
Ypapantí, 2 February**

NAME DAYS

In the past, most Greeks did not celebrate their birthdays
past the age of about 12. Instead they celebrated their
name days, or *giortí*, the day of the saint after whom they
were named at their baptism. Choice of names is very
important in Greece, and children are usually named after
their grandparents – though in recent years it has become
fashionable to give children names from Greece's history
and mythology. On St George's day or St Helen's day (21
May) the whole nation seems to celebrate, with visitors
dropping in, bearing small gifts, and being given cakes
and liqueurs in return. On a friend's name day you may
be told *Giortázo símera* (I'm celebrating today) – the
traditional reply is *Chrónia pollá* (many years). Today, most
people also celebrate their birthdays, regardless of their age.

The Climate of the Greek Islands

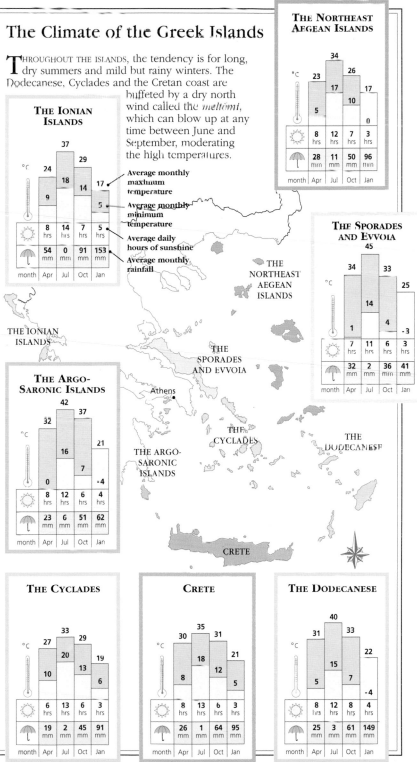

THROUGHOUT THE ISLANDS, the tendency is for long, dry summers and mild but rainy winters. The Dodecanese, Cyclades and the Cretan coast are buffeted by a dry north wind called the *meltémi*, which can blow up at any time between June and September, moderating the high temperatures.

THE NORTHEAST AEGEAN ISLANDS

°C			
23	34	26	
5	17	17	10
			0

☀	8 hrs	12 hrs	7 hrs	3 hrs
☂	28 mm	11 mm	50 mm	96 mm
month	Apr	Jul	Oct	Jan

THE IONIAN ISLANDS

°C			
24	37	29	
9	18	14	17
			5

☀	8 hrs	14 hrs	7 hrs	5 hrs
☂	54 mm	0 mm	91 mm	153 mm
month	Apr	Jul	Oct	Jan

Average monthly maximum temperature

Average monthly minimum temperature

Average daily hours of sunshine

Average monthly rainfall

THE NORTHEAST AEGEAN ISLANDS

THE SPORADES AND EVVOIA

°C			
34	45	33	
1	14	4	25
			-3

☀	7 hrs	11 hrs	6 hrs	3 hrs
☂	32 mm	2 mm	36 mm	41 mm
month	Apr	Jul	Oct	Jan

THE IONIAN ISLANDS

THE ARGO-SARONIC ISLANDS

°C			
32	42	37	
0	16	7	21
			-4

☀	8 hrs	12 hrs	6 hrs	4 hrs
☂	23 mm	6 mm	51 mm	62 mm
month	Apr	Jul	Oct	Jan

THE SPORADES AND EVVOIA

Athens

THE CYCLADES

THE DODECANESE

THE ARGO-SARONIC ISLANDS

CRETE

THE CYCLADES

°C			
27	33	29	
10	20	13	19
			6

☀	6 hrs	13 hrs	6 hrs	3 hrs
☂	19 mm	2 mm	45 mm	91 mm
month	Apr	Jul	Oct	Jan

CRETE

°C			
30	35	31	
8	18	12	21
			5

☀	8 hrs	13 hrs	6 hrs	3 hrs
☂	26 mm	1 mm	64 mm	95 mm
month	Apr	Jul	Oct	Jan

THE DODECANESE

°C			
31	40	33	
5	15	7	22
			-4

☀	8 hrs	12 hrs	8 hrs	4 hrs
☂	25 mm	3 mm	61 mm	149 mm
month	Apr	Jul	Oct	Jan

ANCIENT GREECE

GODS, GODDESSES AND HEROES 50-51
THE TROJAN WAR 52-53
GREEK WRITERS AND PHILOSOPHERS 54-55
TEMPLE ARCHITECTURE 56-57
VASES AND VASE PAINTING 58-59

Gods, Goddesses and Heroes

THE GREEK MYTHS that tell the stories of the gods, goddesses and heroes date back to the Bronze Age when they were told aloud by poets. They were first written down in the early 6th century BC and have lived on in Western literature. Myths were closely bound up with Greek religion and gave meaning to the unpredictable workings of the natural world. They tell the story of the creation and the "golden age" of gods and mortals, as well as the age of semimythical heroes, such as Theseus and Herakles, whose exploits were an inspiration to ordinary men. The gods and goddesses were affected by human desires and failings and were part of a divine family presided over by Zeus. He had many offspring, both legitimate and illegitimate, each with a mythical role.

Hades and Persephone *were king and queen of the Underworld (land of the dead). Persephone was abducted from her mother Demeter, goddess of the harvest, by Hades. She was then only permitted to return to her mother for three months each year.*

Zeus was the father of the gods and ruled over them and all mortals from Mount Olympos.

Eris was the goddess of strife.

Clymene, a nymph and daughter of Helios, was mother of Prometheus, creator of mankind.

Poseidon, *one of Zeus's brothers, was given control of the seas. The trident is his symbol of power, and he married the sea-goddess Amphitrite, to whom he was not entirely faithful. This statue is from the National Archaeological Museum in Athens (see p282).*

Hera, sister and wife of Zeus, was famous for her jealousy.

Athena was born from Zeus's head in full armour.

Paris was asked to award the golden apple to the most beautiful goddess.

Paris's dog helped him herd cattle on Mount Ida where the prince grew up.

Dionysos, *god of revelry and wine, was born from Zeus's thigh. In this 6th-century BC cup, painted by Exekias, he reclines in a ship whose mast has become a vine.*

A DIVINE DISPUTE

This vase painting shows the gods on Mount Ida, near Troy. Hera, Athena and Aphrodite, quarrelling over who was the most beautiful, were brought by Hermes to hear the judgment of a young herdsman, the Trojan prince, Paris. In choosing Aphrodite, he was rewarded with the love of Helen, the most beautiful woman in the world. Paris abducted her from her husband Menelaos, King of Sparta, and thus the Trojan War began (*see pp52–3*).

Artemis, the chaste goddess of the hunt, was the daughter of Zeus and sister of Apollo. She can be identified by her bow and arrows, hounds and group of nymphs with whom she lived in the forests. Artemis was also the goddess of childbirth.

Happiness, here personified by two goddesses, waits with gold laurel leaves to garland the winner. Wreaths were the prizes in Greek athletic and musical contests.

Helios, the sun god, drove his four-horse chariot (the sun) daily across the sky.

Hermes was the gods' messenger.

Aphrodite, the goddess of love, was born from the sea. Here she has her son Eros (Cupid) with her.

Apollo, son of Zeus and brother of Artemis, was god of healing, plague and also music. Here he is depicted holding a lyre. He was also famous for his dazzling beauty.

THE LABOURS OF HERAKLES

Herakles (Hercules to the Romans) was the greatest of the Greek heroes, and the son of Zeus and Alkmene, a mortal woman. With superhuman strength he achieved success, and immortality, against seemingly impossible odds in the "Twelve Labours" set by Eurystheus, King of Mycenae. For his first task he killed the Nemean lion, and wore its hide ever after.

Killing the Lernaean hydra was the second labour of Herakles. The many heads of this venomous monster, raised by Hera, grew back as soon as they were chopped off. As in all his tasks, Herakles was helped by Athena.

The huge boar that ravaged Mount Erymanthus was captured next. Herakles brought it back alive to King Eurystheus who was so terrified that he hid in a storage jar.

Destroying the Stymfalian birds was the sixth labour. Herakles rid Lake Stymfalia of these man-eating birds, which had brass beaks, by stoning them with a sling, having first frightened them off with a pair of bronze castanets.

The Trojan War

Ajax carrying the body of the dead Achilles

THE STORY of the Trojan War, first narrated in the *Iliad*, Homer's 8th-century BC epic poem, tells how the Greeks sought to avenge the capture of Helen, wife of Menelaos, King of Sparta, by the Trojan prince, Paris. The Roman writer Virgil takes up the story in the *Aeneid*, where he tells of the sack of Troy and the founding of Rome. Recent archaeological evidence of the remains of a city identified with ancient Troy in modern Turkey suggests that the myth may have a basis in fact. Many of the ancient sites in the Peloponnese, such as Mycenae and Pylos, are thought to be the cities of some of the heroes of the Trojan War.

Achilles binding up the battle wounds of his friend Patroklos

GATHERING OF THE HEROES

WHEN PARIS *(see p50)* carries Helen back to Troy, her husband King Menelaos summons an army of Greek kings and heroes to avenge this crime. His brother, King Agamemnon of Mycenae, leads the force; its ranks include young Achilles, destined to die at Troy.

At Aulis their departure is delayed by a contrary wind. Only the sacrifice to Artemis of Iphigeneia, the youngest of Agamemnon's daughters, allows the fleet to depart.

FIGHTING AT TROY

THE ILIAD OPENS with the Greek army outside Troy, maintaining a siege that has already been in progress for nine years. Tired of fighting, yet still hoping for a decisive victory, the Greek camp is torn apart by the fury of Achilles over Agamemnon's removal of his slave girl Briseis. The hero takes to his tent and refuses adamantly to fight.

Deprived of their greatest warrior, the Greeks are driven back by the Trojans. In desperation, Patroklos persuades his friend Achilles to let him borrow his armour. Achilles agrees and Patroklos leads the Myrmidons, Achilles' troops, into battle. The tide is turned, but Patroklos is killed in the fighting by Hector, son of King Priam of Troy, who mistakes him for Achilles. Filled with remorse at the news of his friend's death, Achilles returns to battle, finds Hector, and kills him in revenge.

King Priam begging Achilles for the body of his son

PATROKLOS AVENGED

REFUSING HECTOR'S dying wish to allow his body to be ransomed, Achilles instead hitches it up to his chariot by the ankles and drags it round the walls of Troy, then takes it back to the Greek camp. In contrast, Patroklos is given the most elaborate funeral possible with a huge pyre, sacrifices of animals and Trojan prisoners and funeral games. Still unsatisfied, for 12 days Achilles drags the corpse of Hector around Patroklos's funeral mound until the gods are forced to intervene over his callous behaviour.

PRIAM VISITS ACHILLES

ON THE INSTRUCTIONS of Zeus, Priam sets off for the Greek camp holding a ransom for the body of his dead son. With the help of the god Hermes he reaches Achilles' tent undetected. Entering, he pleads with Achilles to think of his own father and to show mercy. Achilles relents and allows Hector to be taken back to Troy for a funeral and burial.

Although the Greek heroes were greater than mortals, they were portrayed as fallible beings with human emotions who had to face universal moral dilemmas.

Greeks and Trojans, in bronze armour, locked in combat

ACHILLES KILLS THE AMAZON QUEEN

Penthesileia was the Queen of the Amazons, a tribe of warlike women reputed to cut off their right breasts to make it easier to wield their weapons. They come to the support of the Trojans. In the battle, Achilles finds himself face to face with Penthesileia and deals her a fatal blow. One version of the story has it that as their eyes meet at the moment of her death, they fall in love. The Greek idea of love and death would be explored 2,000 years later by the psychologists Jung and Freud.

Achilles killing the Amazon Queen Penthesileia in battle

THE WOODEN HORSE OF TROY

As was foretold, Achilles (see p79) is killed at Troy by an arrow in his heel from Paris's bow. With this weakening of their military strength, the Greeks resort to guile.

Before sailing away they build a great wooden horse, in which they conceal some of their best fighters. The rumour is put out that this is a gift to the goddess Athena and that if the horse enters Troy, the city can never be taken. After some doubts, but swayed by supernatural omens, the Trojans drag the horse inside the walls. That night, the Greeks sail back, the soldiers creep out of the horse and Troy is put to the torch. Priam, with many others, is murdered. Among

An early image of the Horse of Troy, from a 7th-century BC clay vase

the Trojan survivors is Aeneas who escapes to Italy and founds the race of Romans: a second Troy. The next part of the story (the *Odyssey*) tells of the heroes' adventures on their way home (see p83).

DEATH OF AGAMEMNON

Klytemnestra, the wife of Agamemnon, had ruled Mycenae in the ten years that he had been away fighting in Troy. She was accompanied by Aigisthos, her lover. Intent on vengeance for the death of her daughter Iphigeneia, Klytemnestra receives her husband with a triumphal welcome and then brutally murders him, with the help of Aigisthos. Agamemnon's fate was a result of a curse laid on his father, Atreus, which was finally expiated by the murder of both Klytemnestra and Aigisthos by her son Orestes and daughter Elektra. In these myths, the will of the gods both shapes and overrides that of heroes and mortals.

GREEK MYTHS IN WESTERN ART

From the Renaissance onwards, the Greek myths have been a powerful inspiration for artists and sculptors. Kings and queens have had themselves portrayed as gods and goddesses with their symbolic attributes of love or war. Myths have also been an inspiration for artists to paint the nude or Classically draped figure. This was true of the 19th-century artist Lord Leighton, whose depiction of the human body reflects the Classical ideals of beauty. His tragic figure of Elektra is shown here.

Elektra mourning the death of her father Agamemnon at his tomb

Greek Writers and Philosophers

Playwrights Aristophanes and Sophocles

THE LITERATURE OF GREECE began with long epic poems, accounts of war and adventure, which established the relationship of the ancient Greeks to their gods. The tragedy and comedy, history and philosophical dialogues of the 5th and 4th centuries BC became the basis of Western literary culture. Much of our knowledge of the Greek world is derived from Greek literature. Pausanias's *Guide to Greece*, written in the Roman period and used by Roman tourists, is a key to the physical remains.

Hesiod with the nine Muses who inspired his poetry

EPIC POETRY

AS FAR BACK as the 2nd millennium BC, before even the building of the Mycenaean palaces, poets were reciting the stories of the Greek heroes and gods. Passed on from generation to generation, these poems, called *rhapsodes*, were never written down but were changed and embellished by successive poets. The oral tradition culminated in the *Iliad* and *Odyssey* (see p83), composed around 700 BC. Both works are traditionally ascribed to the same poet, Homer, of whose life

nothing reliable is known. Hesiod, whose most famous poems include the *Theogony*, a history of the gods, and the *Works and Days,* on how to live an honest life, also lived around 700 BC. Unlike Homer, Hesiod is thought to have written down his poems, although there is no firm evidence available to support this theory.

PASSIONATE POETRY

FOR PRIVATE OCCASIONS, and particularly to entertain guests at the cultivated drinking parties known as *symposia*, shorter poetic forms were developed. These poems were often full of passion, whether love or hatred, and could be personal or, often, highly political. Much of this poetry, by writers such as Archilochus, Alcaeus, Alcman, Hipponax and Sappho, survives only in quotations by later writers or on scraps of papyrus that have been preserved by chance from private libraries in Hellenistic and Roman Egypt. Through these fragments we can gain glimpses

of the life of a very competitive elite. Since *symposia* were an almost exclusively male domain, there is a strong element of misogyny in much of this poetry. In contrast, the fragments of poems discovered by the poet Sappho, who lived on the island of Lésvos, are exceptional for showing a woman competing in a literary area in the male-dominated society of ancient Greece, and for describing with great intensity her passions for other women.

HISTORY

UNTIL THE 5th century BC little Greek literature was composed in prose – even early philosophy was in verse. In the latter part of the 5th century, a new tradition of lengthy prose histories, looking at recent or current events, was established with Herodotus's account of the great war between Greece and Persia (490–479 BC). Herodotus put the clash between Greeks and Persians into a context, and included an ethnographic account of the vast Persian Empire. He attempted to record objectively what people said about the past. Thucydides took a narrower view in his account of the long years

Herodotus, the historian of the Persian Wars

of the Peloponnesian war between Athens and Sparta (431–404 BC). He concentrated on the political history, and his aim was to work out the "truth" that lay behind the events of the war. The methods of Thucydides were adopted by later writers of Greek history, though few could match his acute insight into human nature.

An unusual vase painting of a *symposion* for women only

The orator Demosthenes in a
Staffordshire figurine of 1790

ORATORY

PUBLIC ARGUMENT was basic
to Greek political life
even in the Archaic period.
In the later part of the 5th
century BC, the techniques
of persuasive speech began
to be studied in their own
right. From that time on
some orators began to
publish their speeches. In
particular, this included those
wishing to advertise their
skills in composing speeches
for the law courts, such as
Lysias and Demosthenes.
The texts that survive give
insights into both Athenian
politics and the seamier side
of Athenian private life. The
verbal attacks on Philip of
Macedon by Demosthenes,
the 4th-century BC Athenian
politician, became models
for Roman politicians seeking to defeat their oppo-
nents. With the 18th-century
European revival of interest
in Classical times, Demosthenes again became a
political role model.

DRAMA

ALMOST ALL the surviving
tragedies come from the
hands of the three great 5th-
century BC Athenians:
Aeschylus, Sophocles and
Euripides. The latter two
playwrights developed an
interest in individual psy-
chology (as in Euripides'
Medea). While 5th century
comedy is full of direct
references to contemporary
life and dirty jokes, the
"new" comedy developed
in the 4th century BC is
essentially situation comedy
employing character types.

Vase painting of two costumed
actors from around 370 BC

GREEK PHILOSOPHERS

The Athenian Socrates was recognized in
the late 5th century BC as a moral arbiter.
He wrote nothing himself but we know of
his views through the "Socratic dialogues",
written by his pupil, Plato, examining the
concepts of justice, virtue and courage.
Plato set up his academy in
the suburbs of Athens.

His pupil, Aristotle, founded the Lyceum,
to teach subjects from biology to ethics, and
helped to turn Athens into one of the first
university cities. In 1508–11 Raphael painted
this vision of Athens in the Vatican.

Aristotle, author of the Ethics, had
a genius for scientific observation.

Euclid laid
the rules of
geometry
in around
300 BC

Plato saw "the
seat of ideas"
in heaven.

Epicurus
advocated
the pursuit
of pleasure.

Socrates taught by debating his ideas.

Diogenes, the Cynic, lived like a beggar.

Temple Architecture

TEMPLES WERE THE most important public buildings in ancient Greece, largely because religion was a central part of everyday life. Often placed in prominent positions, temples were also statements about political and divine power. The earliest temples, in the 8th century BC, were built of wood and sun-dried bricks. Many of their features were copied in marble buildings from the 6th century BC onwards.

Pheidias, sculptor of the Parthenon, at work

TEMPLE CONSTRUCTION
This drawing is of an idealized Doric temple, showing how it was built and used.

The cella, or inner sanctum, housed the cult statue.

The cult statue was of the god or goddess to whom the temple was dedicated.

The pediment, triangular in shape, often held sculpture.

Fluting on the columns was carved *in situ*, guided by that on the top and bottom drums.

A ramp led up to the temple entrance.

The stepped platform was built on a stone foundation.

The column drums were initially carved with bosses for lifting them into place.

TIMELINE OF TEMPLE CONSTRUCTION

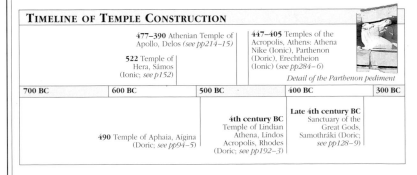

477–390 Athenian Temple of Apollo, Delos *(see pp214–15)*

522 Temple of Hera, Sámos (Ionic; *see p152*)

447–405 Temples of the Acropolis, Athens: Athena Nike (Ionic), Parthenon (Doric), Erechtheion (Ionic) *(see pp284–6)*

Detail of the Parthenon pediment

700 BC	600 BC	500 BC	400 BC	300 BC

4th century BC Temple of Lindian Athena, Líndos Acropolis, Rhodes (Doric; *see pp192–3)*

Late 4th century BC Sanctuary of the Great Gods, Samothráki (Doric; *see pp128–9)*

490 Temple of Aphaia, Aígina (Doric; *see pp94–5)*

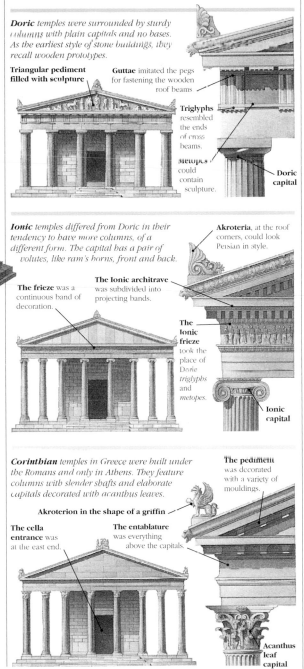

The gable ends of the roof were surmounted by statues, known as *akroteria*, in this case of a Nike or "Winged Victory". Almost no upper portions of Greek temples survive.

The roof was supported on wooden beams and covered in rows of terracotta tiles, each ending in an upright antefix.

Stone blocks were smoothly fitted together and held by metal clamps and dowels: no mortar was used in the temple's construction.

The ground plan was derived from the megaron of the Mycenaean house: a rectangular hall with a front porch supported by columns

THE DEVELOPMENT OF TEMPLE ARCHITECTURE

Greek temple architecture is divided into three styles, which evolved chronologically, and are most easily distinguished by the column capitals.

Doric temples were surrounded by sturdy columns with plain capitals and no bases. As the earliest style of stone buildings, they recall wooden prototypes.

Triangular pediment filled with sculpture

Guttae imitated the pegs for fastening the wooden roof beams

Triglyphs resembled the ends of cross beams.

Metopes could contain sculpture.

Doric capital

Ionic temples differed from Doric in their tendency to have more columns, of a different form. The capital has a pair of volutes, like ram's horns, front and back.

Akroteria, at the roof corners, could look Persian in style.

The frieze was a continuous band of decoration.

The Ionic architrave was subdivided into projecting bands.

The Ionic frieze took the place of Doric triglyphs and metopes.

Ionic capital

Corinthian temples in Greece were built under the Romans and only in Athens. They feature columns with slender shafts and elaborate capitals decorated with acanthus leaves.

The pediment was decorated with a variety of mouldings.

Akroterion in the shape of a griffin

The cella entrance was at the east end.

The entablature was everything above the capitals.

Acanthus leaf capital

Caryatids, or figures of women, were used instead of columns in the Erechtheion at Athens' Acropolis. In Athens' Agora (see p283), tritons (half-fish, half-human creatures) were used.

Vases and Vase Painting

THE HISTORY OF GREEK vase painting continued without a break from 1000 BC to Hellenistic times. The main centre of production was Athens, which was so successful that by the early 6th century BC it was sending its high-quality black- and red-figure wares to every part of the Greek world. The Athenian potters'

Donkey cup

quarter of Kerameikós, in the west of the city, can still be visited today. Beautiful works of art in their own right, the painted vases are the closest we can get to the vanished wall paintings with which ancient Greeks decorated their houses. Although vases could break during everyday use (for which they were intended), a huge number still survive intact or in reassembled pieces.

This 6th-century BC black-figure vase shows pots being used in an everyday situation. The vases depicted are hydriai. *It was the women's task to fill them with water from springs or public fountains.*

The naked woman holding a *kylix* is probably a flute girl or prostitute.

The white-ground lekythos was developed in the 5th century BC as an oil flask for grave offerings. They were usually decorated with funeral scenes, and this one, by the Achilles Painter, shows a woman placing flowers at a grave.

THE SYMPOSION

These episodes of mostly male feasting and drinking were also occasions for playing the game of *kottabos*. On the exterior of this 5th-century BC *kylix* are depictions of men holding cups, ready to flick out the dregs at a target.

THE DEVELOPMENT OF PAINTING STYLES

Vase painting reached its peak in 6th- and 5th-century BC Athens. In the potter's workshop, a fired vase would be passed to a painter to be decorated. Archaeologists have been able to identify the varying styles of many individual painters of both black-figure and red-figure ware.

The body of the dead man is carried on a bier by mourners.

The geometric design is a prototype of the later "Greek key" pattern.

Chariots and warriors form the funeral procession.

Geometric style characterizes the earliest Greek vases, from around 1000 to 700 BC, in which the decoration is in bands of figures and geometric patterns. This 8th-century BC vase, placed on a grave as a marker, is over 1 m (3 ft) high and depicts the bier and funeral rites of a dead man.

Eye cups *were given an almost magical power by the painted eyes. The pointed base suggests that they were passed around during feasting.*

The rhyton, *such as this one in the shape of a ram's head, was a drinking vessel for watered down wine. The scene of the symposion around the rim indicates when it would have been used.*

This kylix is being held by one handle by another woman feaster, ready to flick out the dregs at a *kottabos* target.

This drinker holds aloft a branch of a vine, symbolic of Dionysos's presence at the party.

Striped cushions made reclining more comfortable.

The drinking horn shape was copied in the pottery *rhyton*.

Black-figure style *was first used in Athens around 630 BC. The figures were painted in black liquid clay on to the iron-rich clay of the vase which turned orange when fired. This vase is signed by the potter and painter Exekias.*

Red-figure style *was introduced in c.530 BC. The figures were left in the colour of the clay, silhouetted against a black glaze. Here a woman pours from an oinochoe (wine-jug).*

VASE SHAPES

Almost all Greek vases were made to be used; their shapes are closely related to their intended uses. Athenian potters had about 20 different forms to choose from. Below are some of the most commonly made shapes and their uses.

The amphora *was a two-handled vessel used to store wine, olive oil and foods preserved in liquid such as olives. It also held dried foods.*

This krater *with curled handles or "volutes" is a wide-mouthed vase in which the Greeks mixed water with their wine before drinking it.*

The hydria *was used to carry water from the fountain. Of the three handles, one was vertical for holding and pouring, two horizontal for lifting.*

The lekythos *could vary in height from 3 cm (1 in) to nearly 1 m (3 ft). It was used to hold oil both in the home and as a funerary gift to the dead.*

The oinochoe, *the standard wine jug, had a round or trefoil mouth for pouring, and just one handle.*

The kylix, *a two-handled drinking cup, was one shape that could take interior decoration.*

THE GREEK ISLANDS AREA BY AREA

THE GREEK ISLANDS AT A GLANCE 62-63
THE IONIAN ISLANDS 64-87
THE ARGO-SARONIC ISLANDS 88-99
THE SPORADES AND EVVOIA 100-119
THE NORTHEAST AEGEAN ISLANDS 120-153
THE DODECANESE 154-199
THE CYCLADES 200-239
CRETE 240-277
A SHORT STAY IN ATHENS 278-291

The Greek Islands at a Glance

THE GREEK ISLANDS range in size from tiny uninhabited rocks to the substantial islands of Crete
and Evvoia. Over the centuries, the sea has brought
settlers and invaders and provided the inhabitants
with their way of life; it now attracts millions of
visitors. Each island has developed its own character
through a mix of landscape, climate and cultural
heritage. As well as the scattered historical sites, there
is enough remote, rugged terrain to satisfy the most
discerning walker and,
of course, the variety of
beaches is extraordinary.

Skópelos
*The capital of this rugged island (see
pp108–9), Skópelos town, spills down
from the hilltop kástro to the sea.*

Corfu
*The most visited of the Ionians,
Corfu (see pp68–79) is a green,
fertile island. Corfu town, its
capital, contains a maze of
narrow streets overlooked by two
Venetian fortresses.*

KEY

☐	The Ionian Islands *pp64–87*
☐	The Argo-Saronic Islands *pp88–99*
☐	The Sporades and Evvoia *pp100–19*
☐	The Northeast Aegean Islands *pp120–53*
☐	The Dodecanese *pp154–99*
☐	The Cyclades *pp200–39*
☐	Crete *pp240–77*

Athens

Aígina
*Home to the spectacular and well-preserved
ancient Temple of Aphaia, Aígina (see pp92–5)
has a rich history due to its proximity to Athens.*

Crete
*The largest Greek island, Crete (see pp240–77)
encompasses historic cities, ancient Minoan
palaces, such as Knosós, and dramatic
landscapes, including the Samaria Gorge (right).*

◁ **Windmills in the village of Olympos, Kárpathos**

Delos
This tiny island (see pp214–15) is scattered with the ruins of an important ancient city. From its beginnings as a centre for the worship of Apollo in 1000 BC until its sacking in the 1st century AD, Delos was a thriving cultural and religious centre.

Chíos
The Byzantine monastery of Néa Moní in the centre of the island (see pp142–9) contains beautiful mosaics, which survived a severe earthquake in 1881. The mastic villages in the south of the island prospered from the wealth generated by the medieval trade in mastic gum.

Pátmos
The "holy island" of Pátmos (see pp158–61) is where St John the Divine wrote the book of Revelation. Pilgrims still visit the Monastery of St John, a fortified complex of churches and courtyards.

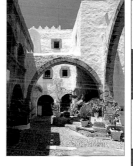

0 kilometres 100

0 miles 50

Rhodes
Rhodes town is dominated by its walled medieval citadel founded by the crusading Knights of St John. The island has many fine beaches and, inland, some unspoilt villages and remote monasteries (see pp176–93).

THE IONIAN ISLANDS

CORFU · PAXOS · LEFKADA · ITHACA · KEFALLONIA · ZAKYNTHOS

THE IONIAN ISLANDS *are the greenest and most fertile of all the island groups, characterized by olive groves and cypresses. Lying off the west coast of mainland Greece, these islands have been greatly influenced by Western Europe, in part because the Turks never managed to gain control here, except on the island of Lefkáda.*

Famous as the homeland of Homer's Odysseus, these islands were colonized by the Corinthians in the 8th century BC and flourished as a wealthy trading post. In the 5th century BC Corfu defeated Corinth and joined the Athenians, instigating the Peloponnesian War. The Ionians first became a holiday destination during the Roman era.

Gorgon pediment in Corfu town's Archaeological Museum

The islands were not politically grouped together until Byzantine times. They were later occupied by the Venetians whose rule began in 1363 and lasted until 1797. After a brief period of French rule the British took over in 1814. The islands were finally ceded to the Greek state in 1864.

Evidence of the various periods of occupation can be seen throughout the islands, especially in Corfu town which contains a mixture of Italian, French and British architecture.

Each island has its own distinct character, from tiny Paxós covered in olive groves, to rocky Ithaca, the rugged beauty of Kefalloniá and mountainous Corfu. The group historically includes Kýthira, but in this guide it is included under the Argo-Saronic Islands due to easier transport connections.

The islands lie on a fault line, which runs south down Greece's west coast, and have been subjected to much earthquake damage. Kefalloniá and Zákynthos in particular suffered massive destruction in the summer of 1953.

Summers are hot and dry but for the rest of the year the islands have a mild climate; the above-average rainfall supports the lush greenery. There is a huge variety of beaches throughout the Ionians, from resorts providing lively nightlife to quieter stretches, virtually untouched by tourism.

Watching from the shade as a ship comes into Sámi town, Kefalloniá

◁ **The islet of Vlachérna with its small convent, reached by a short causeway from Corfu island**

Exploring the Ionian Islands

THE WIDELY SCATTERED Ionian Islands are not particularly well connected with each other, though most are easily reached from the mainland. Corfu is the best base for the northern islands and Kefaloniá for the southern islands. There are few archaeological remains, and museums tend to concentrate on folklore, culture and historical European links. Today's Europeans come mostly for beach holidays. The main islands are large enough to cater for those who like bars and discos, as well as those who prefer a quieter stay, in a family resort or simply in a small fishing village. Traditional Greek life does exist here, inland on the larger islands and on islands such as Meganísi off Lefkáda, or Mathráki, Othonoí and Erikoúsa off northern Corfu.

ISLANDS AT A GLANCE

Corfu pp68–79
Ithaca pp82–3
Kefaloniá pp84–5
Lefkáda p81
Paxós p80
Zákynthos pp86–7

SEE ALSO

• *Where to Stay pp298–9*

• *Where to Eat pp322–3*

• *Travel Information pp356–9*

Looking down on Plateía Dimarcheíou in Corfu town with the Town Hall on the left

A typical house by the roadside in Stavrós village on Ithaca

KEY

▬▬	Major road
▬▬	Asphalt road
▬▬	Non-asphalt road
▬▬	Scenic route
– – –	High-season, direct ferry route
⁑	Viewpoint

0 kilometres   25

0 miles   25

The mountain landscape of Lefkáda

LOCATOR MAP

GETTING AROUND

Aside from Ithaca and Paxós, all the main Ionians can be reached by air, Préveza airport serving Lefkáda which is also connected to the mainland by a road bridge. Larger ferries often travel via the mainland but smaller boats offer direct connections between the islands. Islands often have several ports so check specific destinations. Buses in the capitals provide services radiating out round the islands, with taxis filling the gaps. Car and bike hire is widespread but road standards vary considerably, as do local road maps.

Párga

Pátra

Lefkáda Town

LEFKADA

Vasiliki Nydrí Vathý
Spartochóri

MEGANISI KALAMOS
ARKOUDI KASTOS

Fiskárdo ATOKOS Astakós

Fríkes

Pólis Bay ITHACA

KEFALLONIA Vathý

Piso Aetós

Agía Efthymía

Sámi

rgostóli

Póros Pátra

Pesáda

Agios Nikólaos

Kyllíni

Zákynthos Town

ZAKYNTHOS

An islander working on his boat in Gáïos harbour on Paxós

Holiday apartments at Fiskárdo on Kefalloniá

Corfu
Κέρκυρα

CORFU IS A GREEN ISLAND offering the diverse attractions of secluded coves, stretches of wild coast, bands of coast given over totally to resorts and traditional hill-villages. In 229 BC it became a colony of the Roman Empire, remaining so until AD 337. Byzantine rule then began, intermittently broken by the Goths, the Normans and Angevin rule. Situated between Italy and the Greek mainland, its strategic importance continued under Venetian rule (1386–1797). French rule (1807–14) saw the Greek language restored and the founding of the Ionian Academy, set up for the development of the arts. A period of British rule (1814–64) was followed by unification with Greece.

Detail from Corfu Town Hall

Sidári
Unusual rock formations, produced by the effect of sea on sandstone, give the resort of Sidári its appeal. Legend has it that any couple swimming through the Canal d'Amour will stay together forever ➎

Angelókastro
is a ruined 13th-century fortress, which stands across the bay from Palaiokastrítsa (*see p77*).

Myrtiótissa is one of Corfu's finest beaches (*see p78*).

Vátos
This traditional Greek hill-village is set above the fertile Ropa plain ➐

Korisíon Lagoon
This lake is a haven for wildlife and is separated from the Ionian Sea only by some beautiful beaches ➑

KEY

For key to map see back flap

0 kilometres   5

0 miles   3

Palaiokastrítsa
Three main coves cluster around a thickly wooded headland at Palaiokastrítsa. It is now one of the most popular spots on the island and is an ideal base for families, with watersports available and a friendly atmosphere ➏

STAR SIGHTS

★ **Corfu Town**

Kassiópi
The unspoilt bay at Kassiópi is overlooked by an attractive quayside lined with tavernas, shops and bars ❹

VISITORS' CHECKLIST

🏠 100,000. ✈ 3 km
(2 miles) S of Corfu town.
⛴ Xenofontos Stratigoú, Corfu
town. 🚌 ℹ Corfu town (26610·
42070). 🎭 Cultural festival at
Ano Korakiána: 1–15 Aug;
festival at Benítses: 17 July

ℹ 🚌
Kassiópi
❹

Avláki ✈

Perítheia   Koulóura
etália ❸

Mount   Kalámi
Pantokrátor   🚌 ✈

artýlas   Nisáki
yrgí

sos

asiá

ouviá

Mount Pantokrátor
This is the highest point on Corfu and offers excellent views over the island and, on a clear day, as far as Italy ❸

PTICHIA

CORFU TOWN
❶ 🚌 ℹ ⛴
Potamós
✈
Kanóni   Igoumenítsa,
Vlachérna   Paxos, Pátra

Pontikonísi

❿ Achílleion Palace 🚌

❾ Benítses
🚌 ✈

Strongylí

Agios
Mattháios
Moraïtika
✈
Mesongí

Chlomós
🚌   Alykés   Igoumenítsa
Korision
❽ Lagoon   Argyrádes

Perivóli   Léfkímmi ⛴

✈
Kávos

Dragótina

Kalámi
Made famous by the author Lawrence Durrell, this remains an attractive coastal village ❷

★ Corfu Town
Corfu town is a delightful blend of European influences. The Liston, focus of café life, was built during the brief French rule. It overlooks the Esplanade that dates to Venetian rule in the town ❶

Achílleion Palace
The Empress Elizabeth of Austria built this palace (1890–91) ❿

Benítses
An archetypal package holiday resort, Benítses appeals to a young crowd. There is plenty of nightlife and the beach offers every conceivable watersport ❾

Gardíki Castle was built in the 13th century on the site of Paleolithic remains *(see p78).*

Street-by-Street: Corfu Old Town ●

Πόλη της Κέρκυρας

THE 20TH CENTURY has not spoiled Corfu town, and it continues to be a delightful blend of European influences. The Venetians ruled here for over four centuries, and elegant Italianate buildings, with balconies and shutters, can be seen above French-style colonnades. British rule left a wealth of monuments, public buildings, and also the cricket pitch, which is part of the Esplanade, or Spianáda *(see pp72–3)*. This large park, still a venue for cricket matches, is a focus for both locals and tourists, with park games and good walks. On its eastern side is the Old Fortress *(see p74)* standing guard over the town, a reminder that Corfu was never conquered by the Turks.

View of the Old Fortress from Corfu old town

New Fortress *(see p74)*

The Mitrópoli was built in 1577, and became Corfu's Orthodox cathedral in 1841. It is dedicated to St Theodora, whose remains are housed here along with some impressive gold icons.

FILELLINON

THERMISTOKLEOUS

AGIOU

SPYRIDONOS

N THEOTOKI

N THEOTOKI

KAPODISTRIOU

ELEFTHERI

STAR SIGHTS

* ★ **Palace of St Michael and St George**

* ★ **The Liston**

* ★ **Agios Spyrídon**

Town Hall *(see p74)*

The Paper Money Museum has a collection of Greek notes and tells Corfu's history through its changes of currency. There is also a display on modern bank-note production *(see p73)*.

Archaeological Museum *(see pp74–5)*

★ **Agios Spyrídon**

The red-domed belfry of this church is the tallest on Corfu. It was built in 1589 and dedicated to the island's patron saint, whose sarcophagus is just to the right of the altar (see p72).

The Corfu Reading Society
is housed in this building. The
society was founded in 1836
and was modelled on the
Reading Society of Geneva. It
is the oldest cultural institution
in modern Greece.

Byzantine
museum
(see p73)

ARSENIOU
KAPODISTRIOU
APOLLODOROU
ONTOS

KEY

– – – Suggested route

0 metres 250
0 yards 250

★ **Palace of St Michael
and St George**
*Built by the British between
1819 and 1824, the palace
later became the residence of
the Greek royal family. Today
it houses the Museum of
Asiatic Art (see p73).*

**The Cricket
Ground** was once a
Venetian firing range.
It was developed by
the British, and
local teams play
here regularly.

Old
Fortress
(see p74)

★ **The Liston**
*This elegant parade of cafés
was built as a copy of the Rue de
Rivoli in Paris. It is the place to sit
and relax while sipping Corfu's
most expensive coffee (see p72).*

Exploring Corfu Town

IN MIDSUMMER THE narrow streets of Corfu's old town may be packed with visitors, but there are always quiet places to be found down alleyways and shady cobbled squares. The Corfiot housewives string washing across the streets from their balconies and, below, silversmiths and woodcarvers' shops are hidden away in the maze of alleys. On Nikifórou Theotóki, the southern boundary of the old town, there are several elegant arcaded sections. Built by the French, they are now home to souvenir shops, chapels and churches. Parts of the surrounding new town are quite modern but many of the buildings date back to French and British rule.

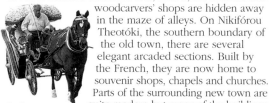

Corfu town by horse and trap

🔒 Agios Spyrídon

Agíou Spyrídonos. 📞 *26610 33059*. ☀ *daily.*

The distinctive red-domed tower of Agios Spyrídon guides the visitor to this church, the holiest place on the island. Inside, in a silver casket, is the mummified body of the revered saint, after whom many Corfiot men are named.

Spyrídon himself was not from Corfu but from Cyprus, where he was raised as a shepherd. Later he entered the church and rose to the rank of bishop. He is believed to have performed many miracles before his death in AD 350, and others since – not least in

1716 when he is said to have helped drive the Turks from the island after a six-week siege. His body was smuggled from Constantinople just before the Turkish occupation of 1453. It was only by chance that it came to Corfu, where the present church was built in 1589 to house his coffin.

The church is also worth seeing for the immense amount of silverware brought by the constant stream of pilgrims. On four occasions each year (Palm Sunday, Easter Saturday, 11 August and the first Sunday in November) the saint's remains are carried aloft through the streets.

✿ Esplanade

This mixture of park and town square is one of the reasons Corfu town remains such an attractive place. Known as the Esplanade, or Spianáda, it offers relief from the packed streets in summer, either on a park bench or in one of the elegant cafés lining the square on **The Liston**, overlooking the cricket pitch.

The Liston was designed by a Frenchman, Mathieu de Lesseps, who built it in 1807. The name Liston comes from the Venetian practice of having a "List" of noble families in the *Libro d'Oro* or Golden Book – only those on this list were allowed to promenade here.

There are a number of monuments in and around the Esplanade. Near the fountain is the **Enosis Monument**: the word *énosis* means unification, and this celebrates the 1864 union of the Ionian Islands with the rest of Greece, when British rule came to an end. The marble monument has carvings of the symbols of each of the Ionian Islands.

A statue of **Ioánnis Kapodístrias**, modern Greece's first president in 1827 and a native of Corfu, stands at the end of the street that flanks the Esplanade and bears

Agios Spyrídon, seen down one of the many small shopping alleyways

A game of cricket on the pitch by the Esplanade

his name. He was assassinated in Náfplio in the Peloponnese in 1831 by two Cretans whose uncle he had imprisoned.

Facing this is the **Maitland Rotunda** (1816), a memorial to Sir Thomas Maitland, who became Britain's first Lord High Commissioner to Corfu after the island became a British Protectorate in 1814, though neither he nor his policies were much liked.

🏛 Palace of St Michael and St George

Plateía Spianáda. ☎ 26610 30443. ◯ Tue–Sun. ● main public hols.

The Palace of St Michael and St George was built by the British between 1819 and 1824 from Maltese limestone. It served as the residence of Sir Thomas Maitland, the High Commissioner, and as such is the oldest official building in Greece. When the British left Corfu in 1864 the palace was used for a short time by the Greek royal family but it was later abandoned and left to fall into disrepair.

The palace was carefully renovated in the 1950s by Sir Charles Peake, British Ambassador to Greece, and now houses the traffic police, a library and some government offices. Conferences and exhibitions are also held in the palace from time to time.

The Palace of St Michael and St George also houses the **Museum of Asiatic Art**. The core of the museum's collection is the 10,000 items that were collected by a Corfiot diplomat, Grigórios Mános (1850–1929), during his travels overseas. He

offered his vast collection to the state on condition that he could retire and become curator of the museum. Unfortunately he died before he could realize his ambition. The exhibits include statues, screens, armour, silk and ceramics from China, Japan, India and other Asiatic countries.

In front of the building is a statue of **Sir Frederick Adam**, the British High Commissioner to Corfu from 1824–31. He built the Mon Repos Villa (see p75), to the south of town and was also responsible for popularizing the west coast resort of Palaiokastrítsa (see p77), one of his favourite spots on the island.

Statue of Sir Frederick Adam

🔲 Byzantine Museum

Prosfórou 30 & Arseníou. ☎ 26610 38313. ◯ 8:30am–3pm Tue–Sun. ● main public hols. 🌐

The Byzantine Museum opened in 1984 and is housed in the renovated church of Panagía Antivouniótissa, which provided some of the exhibits. The museum contains about 90 icons dating back to the 15th century. It also has work by artists from the Cretan School. Many of these artists worked and lived on Corfu, as it was a convenient stopping-off point on the journey between Crete and Venice from the 13th to the 17th centuries during the period of Venetian rule.

🔲 Paper Money Museum

Ioniki Trápeza, Plateía Iróon Kypriakoú Agóna. ☎ 26610 41552. ◯ Tue, Thu. ● main public hols.

This complete collection of Greek bank notes traces the way in which the island's currency has altered as Corfu's society and rulers changed. The first bank note on the island was issued in British pounds, while later notes show the German and Italian currency of the war years. Another intriguing display shows the process of producing a note from the artistic design to engraving and printing.

Maitland Rotunda situated in the Esplanade

The Old Fortress towering above the sea on the eastern side of Corfu town

⚓ Old Fortress

📞 26610 48310. ⏱ Apr–Oct: 8am–7pm daily. ● main public hols. 🎟 except Sun. ♿ limited.

The ruined Old Fortress, or Palaió Froúrio, stands on a promontory believed to have been fortified since at least the 7th or 8th century AD; archaeological digs are still underway. The Old Fortress itself was constructed by the Venetians between 1550 and 1559. The very top of the fortress gives magnificent views of the town and along the island's east coast. Lower down is the church of St George, a British garrison church built in 1840. The fortress is also a venue for summer sound and light shows, preceded by a truly Terpsichorean delight of Ionian folk dancing displays.

⚓ New Fortress

Plateía Solomoú. 📞 26610 27370. ⏱ Apr–Oct: daily. 🎟

The Venetians began building the New Fortress, or Néo Froúrio, in 1576 to further strengthen the town's defences. It was not completed until 1589, 30 years after the Old Fortress, hence their respective names. The fortress is used by the Greek navy as a training base, while the surrounding moat is the setting for the town's market.

⛪ Mitrópoli

Mitropóleos. 📞 26610 39409. ⏱ daily.

The Greek Orthodox church of the Panagía Spiliótissa, or Virgin Mary of the Cave, was built in 1577. It became Corfu's cathedral in 1841, when the nave was extended. It is

The 17th-century Catholic cathedral Agios Iákovos in Plateía Dimarcheíou

dedicated to St Theodora, a former Byzantine empress whose remains were brought to Corfu at the same time as those of St Spyrídon. Her body is in a silver coffin near the altar.

🏛 Plateía Dimarcheíou

Town Hall 📞 26610 10102. ⏱ daily. ● main public hols. 🎟 ♿
Agios Iákovos ⏱ daily.

Within this elegant square stands the **Town Hall**. It is a grand Venetian building, which began life in 1663 as a single-storey *loggia* or meeting place for the nobility. It was then converted into the San Giacomo Theatre in 1720, which made it the first modern theatre in Greece. The British added the second floor in 1903 when it became the Town Hall.

Adjacent to it is the Catholic cathedral **Agios Iákovos**, also known by its Italian name of San Giacomo. Built in 1588 and consecrated in 1633, it was badly damaged by bombing in 1943 with only the bell tower surviving intact. Services are held every day, with three Masses on Sundays.

🏛 Archaeological Museum

Vraïla 1. 📞 26610 30680. ⏱ Tue–Sun. ● main public hols. 🎟 ♿

The Archaeological Museum is situated a pleasant stroll south from the centre of town, along the seafront. The museum's collection is not large but a visit is worthwhile to see the centrepiece, the stunning Gorgon frieze.

The frieze, dating from the 6th century BC, originally formed part of the west pediment of the Temple of Artemis near Mon Repos Villa. The layout ensures that

CORFU TOWN CENTRE

Agios Spyrídon ⑤
Byzantine Museum ⑧
Esplanade ⑥
Mitrópoli ②
New Fortress ①
Palace of St Michael
   and St George ⑦
Paper Money Museum ④
Plateía Dimarcheíou ③

0 metres   250
0 yards   250

KEY

- Street-by-Street map (see pp70–71)
- Ferry port
- P Parking
- Church
- Old Town walls

The Gorgon frieze in Corfu town's Archaeological Museum

the frieze, a massive 17 m (56 ft) long, is not seen until the final room. The museum also displays other finds from the Temple of Artemis and the excavations at Mon Repos Villa.

ENVIRONS: Garítsa Bay sweeps south of Corfu town, with the suburb of Anemómilos visible on the promontory. Here, in the street named after it, is the 11th-century church of **Agion Iásonos kai Sosipátrou** (saints Jason and Sossipater). These disciples of St Paul brought Christianity to Corfu in the 1st century AD. Inside are faded wall paintings, including an 11th-century fresco.

South of Anemómilos is **Mon Repos Villa.** It was built in 1824 by Sir Frederick Adam, the second High Commissioner of the Ionian state, as a present for his wife, and was

later passed to the Greek royal family. The remains of the **Temple of Artemis** lie nearby. Opposite the villa are the 5th-century ruins of **Agia Kerkýra**, the church of the old city.

An hour's walk or a short bus ride south of Corfu town is **Kanóni,** with the islands of **Vlachérna** and **Pontikonísi** just off the coast. Vlachérna, with its tiny white convent, is a famous landmark and can be reached by a causeway. In summer boats go to Pontikonísi, or Mouse Island, said to be Odysseus's ship turned to stone by Poseidon. This caused Odysseus to be shipwrecked on Phaeacia, the island often identified with Corfu in Homer's Odyssey.

🏛 Mon Repos Villa
📞 26610 20980. **○** April–Oct: Tue–Sun (gardens open daily).

The church of Agion Iásonos kai Sosipátrou

Around Northern Corfu

NORTHERN CORFU, in particular the northeast coast, is emphatically holiday Corfu, with a string of resorts along the main coastal road. These include popular spots such as Kassiópi and Sidári, though there are also quieter villages like Kalámi. In the northwest is one of Corfu's prettiest areas, Palaiokastrítsa, a jigsaw of bays and beaches. Inland stands Mount Pantokrátor, a reminder that there is also a rugged interior to explore.

View looking southwards over the beach at Kalámi Bay

Kalámi ②

Καλάμι

26 km (16 miles) NE of Corfu town. 🏨 18. 🚌 to Kassiópi.

Kalámi village has retained its charm despite its popularity with visitors. A handful of tavernas line its sand and shingle beach, while behind them cypress trees and olive groves climb up to the lower slopes of Mount Pantokrátor. The hills of Albania are a little over 2 km (1 mile) across Kalámi Bay.

Kalámi's obvious appeal attracted the author Lawrence Durrell to the village in 1939.

Only during the day in high season, when visitors from holiday resorts throng his "peaceful fishing village", might Durrell fail to recognize the place. In the evenings and outside the months of July and August, normality returns.

Mount Pantokrátor ③

Όρος Παντοκράτωρ

29 km (18 miles) N of Corfu town. 🚌 to Petáleia.

Mount Pantokrátor, whose name means "the Almighty", dominates the northeast bulge of Corfu. It rises so steeply that its peak, at 906 m (2,972 ft), is less than 3 km (2 miles) from the beach resorts of Nisáki and Mparmpáti. The easiest approach is from the north, where a rough road goes all the way to the small monastery at the top. The mountain has great appeal to naturalists as well as walkers, but exploring its slopes is not something to be undertaken lightly as Corfu's weather can change suddenly. However, the reward is a view to Albania and Epirus in the east, of Corfu town to the south, and even west to Italy when weather conditions are clear.

Kassiópi ④

Κασσιόπη

37 km (23 miles) N of Corfu town. 🏨 600. 🚌 🚕 Avláki 2 km (1 mile) S.

Kassiópi has developed into one of Corfu's busiest holiday centres without losing either its charm or character. It is set around a harbour that lies between two wooded head-lands. Although there is plenty of nightlife to attract younger holiday-makers, there are no high-rise hotels to spoil the setting. The heart of the town is at its harbour, with tavernas and souvenir shops overlooking fishing boats moored alongside motor boats from the many watersports schools.

In the 1st century AD the Emperor Nero is said to have visited a Temple of Jupiter, which was situated on the western side of the harbour, where the church of **Kassio-pítissa** now stands. The ruins of a 13th-century castle are a short walk further west.

Fishing boats moored in Kassiópi harbour, east of the castle ruins

Caretaker monk at Moní Theotókou, Palaiokastrítsa

British High Commissioner, Sir Frederick Adam (see p73), loved to picnic here but did not like the awkward journey from Corfu town, so he had a road built between the two.

On the main headland stands **Moní Theotókou**, which dates from the 17th century, although the first monastery stood here in 1228. The church's ceiling features a fine carving of the *Tree of Life*.

Views from the monastery include **Angelókastro**, the ruined 13th-century fortress of Michaíl Angelos Komninós II, the Byzantine despot of Epirus. Situated above the cliffs west of Palaiokastrítsa, the fortress was never taken and in 1571 it sheltered locals from another failed Turkish attempt to conquer Corfu. The remains include a hilltop chapel and some hermit cells and caves.

OUTLYING ISLANDS

Corfu has three offshore islands. **Mathráki** offers the simplest Greek island life, with two villages and only a few rooms to rent. **Ereikoússa** is the most popular island, largely because of its glorious sandy beaches. **Othonoí** is the largest island and has the best facilities but lacks the finer beaches.

Sidári ❺
Σιδάρι

31 km (20 miles) NW of Corfu town.
🏠 *300.* 🚌 🚏 *Róda 6 km (4 miles) E.*

One of Corfu's first settlements, the village of Sidári has pre-Neolithic remains dating back to about 7000 BC. Today it is a bustling holiday centre with the twin attractions of sandy beaches and unusual rock formations. Erosion of the sandstone has created a number of caves and tunnels, the most famous being a channel between two rocks known as the Canal d'Amour (see p68).

Palaiokastrítsa ❻
Παλαιοκαστρίτσα

26 km (16 miles) NW of Corfu town.
🏠 *600.* 🚌

Palaiokastrítsa is one of Corfu's most popular spots. Three main coves cluster around a wooded headland, dividing into numerous other beaches which are popular with families because swimming is safe. Watersports are available as

well as boat trips out to see the nearby grottoes. Until the early 19th century the place was noted for its beauty but access was difficult. The

---

WRITERS AND ARTISTS IN CORFU

The poet Dionýsios Solomós lived on Corfu from 1828 until his death in 1857. He is best known for his poem Hymn to Freedom, part of which was adopted as the national anthem after Independence. Other writers have also found inspiration on Corfu, including the British poet and artist Edward Lear, who visited the island in the 19th century, and the Durrell brothers, who both wrote about Corfu. Gerald described his idyllic 1930s childhood in *My Family and Other Animals*, while Lawrence produced *Prospero's Cell* in 1945. He wrote this while staying in Kalámi, where he was visited by Henry Miller, whose 1941 book *The Colossus of Maroussi* is one of the most accurate and endearing books about Greece.

A view from the Benítses road near Gastoúri, by Edward Lear

Around Southern Corfu

Less MOUNTAINOUS but more varied than the north, southern Corfu encompasses Benítses' wild nightlife and the shy wildlife of the Korisíon Lagoon. Much of Corfu's produce grows in the fertile Rópa Plain north of Vátos. To the south lies Myrtiótissa, once described as the world's most beautiful beach. Bus services are good but to explore off the beaten track you will need your own car.

View inland over the freshwater Korisíon Lagoon

Vátos **7**
Βάτος

24 km (15 miles) W of Corfu town.
👥 480. 🚌 🚃 Myrtiótissa 2 km
(1 mile) S, Ermones 2 km (1 mile) W.

In the hillside village of Vátos, the whitewashed houses with flower-bedecked balconies offer a traditional image of Greece. Vátos has only two tavernas and a handful of shops and has mostly remained untainted by the impact of tourism. From the village, a steep climb leads up the mountainside to the top of Agios Geórgios (392 m; 1,286 ft), while below lies the fertile Rópa Plain and the beach at busy Ermones.

ENVIRONS: The glorious beach at **Myrtiótissa**, 2 km (1 mile) south of Vátos, is named after the 14th-century monastery behind it dedicated to Panagía Myrtiótissa (Our Lady of the Myrtles). The beach is a long golden sweep of sand backed with cypress and olive trees. Lawrence Durrell was fond of the area and, in his book *Prospero's Cell*, referred to Myrtiótissa as "perhaps the loveliest beach in the world".
    South of Vátos lies **Pélekas**, another picturesque and unspoilt hillside village. Its traditional houses tumble down wooded slopes to the small and secluded beach below. Above this is the **Kaiser's Throne**, the hilltop

from which Kaiser Wilhelm II of Germany loved to watch the sunset while staying at the Achílleion Palace.

Korisíon Lagoon **8**
Λίμνη Κορισσίων

42 km (26 miles) S of Corfu town.
🚃 Gardíki 1 km (0.5 mile) N.

The Korisíon Lagoon is a 5-km (3-mile) stretch of water, separated from the sea by some of the most beautiful dunes and beaches on Corfu. The lake

remains a haven for wildlife, despite the Greek love of hunting. At the water's edge are a variety of waders such as sandpipers and avocets, egrets and ibis. Flowers include sea daffodils and Jersey orchids.
    Almost 2 km (1 mile) north lies **Gardíki Castle**, built in the 13th century by Michaíl Angelos Komninós II *(see p77)*, with the ruined towers and outer castle walls still standing. The site is also known for a find of Paleolithic remains, now removed.

Benítses **9**
Μπενίτσες

14 km (9 miles) S of Corfu town.
👥 1,400. 🚌 🚃 Benítses.

Benítses has become the archetypal package holiday resort. Its appeal is to young people, and not to those seeking peace and quiet or a real flavour of Greece.
    The beaches offer every conceivable watersport, and at the height of the season are extremely busy. The nightlife is also very lively: the bars and discos close about the same time as the local fishermen return from their night at sea.
    There are few sights of interest in Benítses other than the remains of a Roman bathhouse near the harbour square.

A whitewashed house in the attractive village of Vátos

Achílleion Palace ⑩

Αχίλλειον

19 km (12 miles) SW of Corfu town.
📧 📞 26610 56210. **Palace &
gardens** ☐ daily.

A popular day trip from any of Corfu's resorts is to the Achílleion Palace. It was built in 1890–91 by the Italian architect Raphael Carita for the Empress Elizabeth of Austria (1837–98), formerly Elizabeth of Bavaria. She used it as a personal retreat from the problems she was enduring at the Hapsburg court. Her health was poor and her husband, Emperor Franz Josef, notoriously unfaithful. After the assassination of the Empress Elizabeth by an Italian anarchist in 1898, the palace lay empty for nearly a decade until it was bought by Kaiser Wilhelm II in 1907. The Achílleion is famous as the set used for the casino in the James Bond film *For Your Eyes Only*.

The outer entrance to the Achílleion's gardens

The Gardens

The lush green gardens below the palace are terraced on a slope which drops 150 m (490 ft) to the coast road. The views along the rugged coast both north and south are spectacular. In the grounds

A 19th-century painting of Elizabeth of Bavaria by Franz Xavier

the walls are draped with colourful bougainvillea and a profusion of palm trees. The gardens are also dotted with numerous statues, especially of Achilles, who was the empress's hero, after whom the palace is named. One moving bronze of the *Dying Achilles* is by the German sculptor, Ernst Herter. The statue is thought to have appealed to the unhappy empress following her tragic suicide of her second son, the Archduke Rudolph, at Mayerling. Another impressive statue of the hero Achilles is

the massive 15-m (49-ft) high, cast-iron figure, which was commissioned by Kaiser Wilhelm II.

The Palace

There have been numerous attempts to describe the Achílleion's architectural style, ranging from Neo-Classical to Teutonic, although Lawrence Durrell was more forthright, and declared it "a monstrous building". The empress was not particularly pleased with the finished building, but her fondness for Corfu made her decide to stay.

The palace does however contain a number of interesting artifacts. Inside, some original furniture is on display and on the walls there are some fine paintings of Achilles, echoing the bronze and stone statues seen in the gardens. Another exhibit is the strange saddle-seat that was used by Kaiser Wilhelm II whenever he was writing at his desk.

Visitors requiring a pick-me-up after touring the palace can try the Vasilákis Tastery, opposite the entrance, and sample this local distiller's many products, which include a number of Corfiot wines, ouzo and the speciality kumquat liqueur.

THE LEGEND OF ACHILLES

Shortly after his birth, Achilles was immersed in the River Styx by his mother Thetis. This left him invulnerable apart from the heel where she had held him. Achilles' destiny lay at Troy *(see pp52–3)*; Helen, the wife of King Menelaos of Sparta, was held by Paris at Troy where Menelaos and his allies laid siege. As the Greeks' mightiest warrior, it was Achilles who killed the Trojan hero Hector. However, he did not live to see Troy fall, since he was struck in the heel by a fatal arrow from Paris's bow.

Achilles victoriously dragging the body of Hector around the walls of Troy

Local fishing boats moored at the eastern end of the harbour at Gáïos

Paxós
Παξοί

🏠 2,700. 🚢 Gáïos, Lákka. 🚌 Gáïos.
ℹ️ Gáïos (26620 32222). 🚤
Mogonisi 3 km (2 miles) SE of Gáïos.

PAXÓS IS GREEN and wooded, with a few farming and fishing villages. The thick groves of olive trees are still a major part of the island's economy. In mythology, Poseidon created Paxós for his mistress, and its small size has saved it from the turbulent history of its larger neighbours. Paxós became part of the Greek state along with the other Ionians in 1864.

GAIOS
Gáïos is a lively, if small-scale, holiday town with two harbours: the main port where ferries dock and, a short walk away, the small harbour, lined with 19th-century houses with Venetian-style shutters and balconies. At the waterfront stands Pyropolitís, a statue of Constantínos Kanáris, hero in the Greek Revolution *(see pp38–9)*. The grandest house was once residence of the British High Commissioner of Corfu. Behind it are narrow old streets, bars and tavernas.

AROUND THE ISLAND
One main road goes from the south to the north of the island. There are few cars and the best way to get about is by bicycle or moped. Many pleasant tracks lead through woods to high cliffs or secluded coves. At the end of a deep, almost circular inlet on Paxós's northern coast lies the town of **Lákka**. This pretty

Statue of Pyropolitís on the waterfront in Gáïos

coastal town is backed by olive groves and pine-covered hills. Lákka is popular with day-trippers from Corfu, but at night it returns to being a quiet fishing village, with a few rooms to rent and only a scattering of restaurants and cafés.

To the east is the small village of **Pórto Longós**, which is the most attractive of the island's settlements. It has a pebble beach, a handful of houses, a few shops, and tavernas whose tables stand at the water's edge. Pórto Longós is a peaceful place where the arrival of the boat bringing fruit and vegetables every few days is a major event. Paths from the village lead through olive groves to several quiet coves, good for swimming.

OUTLYING ISLANDS
Around 100 people live on **Antípaxos**, south of Paxós, and mostly in Agrapidiá, although there are a few hamlets inland. The island is unusual in that olive trees are easily outnumbered by vines, which produce Antípaxos's potent and good-quality wine. There is little tourism and no accommodation available, although the sandy beaches do fill up in summer with visitors from Paxós. Offshore from Gáïos lie the two islets of Panagiá and Agios Nikólaos.

View overlooking Lákka to the south

Houses on a hillside near Kalamítsi

Lefkáda
Λευκάδα

🏛 25,000. 🚤 Nydrí, Vasilikí
🚌 Dimitroú Golémi, Lefkáda town.
ℹ Lefkáda town (26450 29379).
🗓 Lefkáda town: daily.

LEFKADA OFFERS variety, from mountain villages to beach resorts. It has had a turbulent history, typical of the Ionian Islands, since the Corinthians took control of the island from the Akarnanians in 640 BC, right up until the British left the island in 1864.

KEY

For key to map see back flap

0 kilometres 5

0 miles 3

LEFKADA TOWN
The town has suffered repeated earthquakes, but there are interesting back streets and views of the beautiful ruins of the 14th-century **Sánta Mávra fortress.** Situated on the mainland opposite, the fortress is connected to Lefkáda by a causeway. The main square, Plateía Agíou Spyrídona is named after the 17th-century church with its rare metal bell towers. Nearby, the **Phonograph Museum** houses a private collection of records and old

A bell at Moní Faneroménis

phonographs. The small **Folk Museum** has local costumes and old photographs of island life. Above the town, **Moní Faneroménis** was founded in the 17th century, though the present buildings date from the 19th century. Its icon of the Panagía is also 19th century.

📷 **Phonograph Museum**
Konstantínou Kalkáni 10.
☐ daily. ● main public hols. ♿

📷 **Folk Museum**
Stefanítsi 2. ☎ 26450 22473.
☐ call for opening times.
● main public hols

AROUND THE ISLAND
The best way to see the island is to hire a moped or bike, although bus services operate from Lefkáda town. **Agios Nikítas** is a traditional small resort with a harbour and beach. To the south, **Kalamítsi** is a typical Lefkáda mountain village. In the south, the main hill-village is **Agios Pétros,** still a rural community despite the nearby resort of **Vasilikí,** a windsurfer's paradise. **Nydrí** is the main resort on the east coast, with splendid views of the offshore islands.

OUTLYING ISLANDS
Meganísi has retained its rural lifestyle. Most boats from Nydrí stop at Vathý, the main port, whose harbour has chapels on each side and several tavernas. Uphill, the small village of Katoméri has the island's only hotel.

LEFKADA TOWN
🏛 📷 Moní Faneroménis
Agios Nikítas
Kalamítsi
Eláti Stavrotá
1,157m
3,795ft
Nydrí
SPARTI
SKORPIOS
Agios Pétros
Vathý
Vasilikí
Spartochóri
MEGANISI
Ithaca,
Kefalloniá
Kefalloniá

Sailing boats off the white-sand beach at Vasilikí

The pebble beach of Pólis Bay on the northwest coast of Ithaca

Ithaca
Ιθάκη

🏠 4,000. 🚢 Vathý. 🚌 ℹ️ Vathý
(26740 32110). 🚢 Pólis Bay 20 km
(12 miles) NW of Vathý.

SMALL AND RUGGED, Ithaca is famous, according to Homer's epic

KEY

For key to map see back flap

the *Odyssey*, as the home of Odysseus. Finds on Ithaca date back as far as 4000–3000 BC, and by Mycenaean times it had developed into the capital of a kingdom that included its larger neighbour, Kefalloniá.

VATHY
The capital, also known as Ithaca town, is an attractive port, its brown-roofed houses huddled around an indented bay. The surrounding hills were the site for the first settlement, but the harbour itself was settled in the medieval period,

0 kilometres   5

0 miles   2

and Vathý became the capital in the 17th century. Destroyed by an earthquake in 1953, it was reconstructed from the rubble and declared a traditional settlement, which requires all new buildings to match existing styles.

The **Archaeological Museum** contains a collection mainly of vases and votives from the Mycenaean period. In the church of **Taxiárchis** is a 17th-century icon of Christ, believed to have been painted by El Greco *(see p264)*.

🏛️ **Archaeological Museum**
Behind EOT office. 📞 26740 32200. ⬤
Tue–Sun. ⬤ main public hols. ♿ 📷

AROUND THE ISLAND
With just one main town, high hills, a few pebble beaches and little development, Ithaca is a pleasant island to explore. A twice-daily bus (four in season) links Vathý to villages in the north and there are some taxis.

Stavrós, the largest village in northern Ithaca, has only 300 inhabitants but is a thriving hill community and market centre. Nearby **Pólis Bay** is thought to have been the old port of ancient Ithaca, and site of an important cave sanctuary to the Nymphs. **Odysseus' Palace** may have stood above Stavrós on the hill known as Pilikáta. To find it ask for directions at the one-room **Archaeological Museum**, whose curator gives guided tours in several languages. Among the varied local finds is a piece of a terracotta mask from Pólis cave bearing the inscription "Dedicated to Odysseus".

🏛️ **Archaeological Museum**
Stavrós. 📞 26740 31305. ⬤ variable.
⬤ Mon, main public hols. ♿

The red-domed roof of a church in Stavrós

The Legend of Odysseus' Return to Ithaca

ODYSSEUS, THE KING OF ITHACA, had been unwilling to leave his wife Penelope and infant son Telemachos and join Agamemnon's expedition against Troy *(see pp52–3)*. But once there his skills as warrior and speaker, and his cunning, ensured he played a vital role. However, his journey home was fraught with such perils as the monstrous one-eyed Cyclops, the witch Circe, and the seductive Calypso. His blinding of the Cyclops angered the god Poseidon who ensured that, despite the goddess Athena's support, Odysseus lost all his companions, before the kindly Phaeacians brought him home, ten years after he left Troy. On Ithaca, Odysseus found Penelope besieged by suitors. Disguising himself as a beggar, and aided by his loyal swineherd Eumaios and his son, he killed them all and returned to his marriage bed and to power.

Odysseus' homecoming is depicted in this 15th-century painting attributed to Coracelli. Odysseus had been washed ashore on Phaeacia (Corfu), where King Alkinoös took pity and ferried him back to Ithaca.

Penelope wove a shroud for Odysseus' father Laertes, shown in this 1920 illustration by A F Gorguet. She refused to remarry until the shroud was finished; each night she would unpick the day's weaving.

Eumaios, Odysseus' faithful swineherd, gave his disguised master food and shelter for the night on his arrival in Ithaca. Eumaios then demonstrated his loyalty by praising his absent king while describing the situation on Ithaca to Odysseus. Their meeting is shown on this 5th-century BC Athenian vase.

Argus, Odysseus' aged dog, recognized his master without prompting, a feat matched only by Odysseus' old nurse, Eurykleia. Immediately after their meeting Argus died.

Telemachos had challenged Penelope's suitors to string Odysseus' bow and thereby to win his mother's hand in marriage. The suitors all failed the test. Odysseus locked them in the palace hall, strung the bow, and revealed his identity before slaughtering them.

Kefalloniá
Κεφαλλονιά

ARCHAEOLOGICAL FINDS date Kefalloniá's first inhabitants to about 50,000 BC. In Mycenaean times the island flourished and remained Greek until the 2nd century BC when it was captured by the Romans. It was squabbled over by many powers but from 1500 to 1700 it shared the Ionians' history of Venetian occupation. Kefalloniá's attractions range from busy beach resorts to Mount Aínos National Park, which surrounds the Ionians' highest peak.

A church tower in the countryside between Argostóli and Kástro

ARGOSTOLI

A big, busy town with lush surrounding countryside, Kefalloniá's capital is situated by a bay with narrow streets rising up the headland on which it stands. Its traditional appearance is deceptive as Argostóli was destroyed in the 1953 earthquake and rebuilt with donations from emigrants. The destruction and re-building is shown in a photographic collection at the **Historical and Folk Museum**. Other exhibits range from rustic farming implements to traditional folk costumes.

The nearby **Archaeological Museum** includes finds from the Sanctuary of Pan, based at the Melissáni Cave-Lake and an impressive 3rd-century AD bronze head of a man found at Sámi. From the waterfront you can see the **Drápanos Bridge**, built during British rule in 1813.

🏛 Historical and Folk Museum
Ilia Zervoú 12. ☎ 26710 28835.
🕘 9am–2pm Mon–Sat. ⬛ Dec or Jan for cleaning, main public hols.
🏛 Archaeological Museum
Rókkou Vergotí. ☎ 26710 28300.
🕘 8:30am–3pm Tue–Sun.
⬛ main public hols.

AROUND THE ISLAND

It takes time to travel around Kefalloniá, the largest of the Ionian Islands. Despite this, driving is rewarding, with some beautiful spots to discover. The island's liveliest places are **Lássi** and the south-coast resorts; elsewhere there are quiet villages and the scenery is stunning. A bus service links Argostóli with most parts of the island.

Capital of Kefalloniá until 1757, the whitewashed village of **Kástro** still flourishes outside the Byzantine fortress of Agios Geórgios. The Venetians renovated the fortress in 1504 but it was damaged by earthquakes in 1636 and 1637, and the 1953 earthquake finally ruined it. The large and overgrown interior is a haven for swallowtail butterflies.

In 1264 there was a convent on the site of **Moní Agíou Andréa**. The original church was

Visitors to the blue waters of the subterranean Melissáni Cave-Lake

damaged in 1953, but has been restored as a museum to house icons and frescoes made homeless by the earthquake. The new church houses the monastery's holiest relic, supposedly the foot of the apostle Andrew.

There was once a sanctuary to Aenios Zeus at the summit of **Mount Aínos**, which is 1,630 m (5,350 ft) high. Wild horses live in the Mount Aínos National Park, and the slopes of the mountain are covered with the native fir tree, *Abies cephalonica*. A road leads up towards the mountain's summit, but soon becomes a very rough track.

On the east coast, **Sámi** has ferry services to the Peloponnése and Ithaca. Nearby are two caves, Drogkaráti Cave, 3.5 km (2 miles) southwest and the Melissáni Cave-Lake, 2 km (1 mile) to the north. **Drogkaráti** drips with stalactites. It is the size of a large concert hall and is sometimes used as such due to its fine acoustics. The subterranean **Melissáni Cave-Lake** was a sanctuary of Pan in Mycenaean times. Part of its limestone ceiling has collapsed creating a haunting place with deep, blue water. A channel leads to the enclosed section, where legend says that the nymph Melissáni drowned herself when she was spurned by Pan.

Fiskárdo is Kefalloniá's prettiest village, undamaged by the 1953 earthquake. Its

Apostle Andrew from the Moní Agíou Andréa

pastel-painted 18th-century Venetian houses cluster by the harbour, which is a popular berth for yachts. It is also busy in the summer with daily ferry services and day trips from elsewhere on Kefalloniá. Despite the crowds and gift shops Fiskárdo retains its charm.

Asos is an unspoilt village on Kefalloniá's west coast. The surrounding hilly terrain is noted for its stone terracing, which once covered the island. On the peninsula across the isthmus from Asos is a ruined Venetian fortress, built in 1595, which has seen occupation by the Venetians, and stays by the French and Russians in the 19th century. Now Asos sees mostly day-trippers, as there is little accommodation in the village. South of Asos is **Mýrtou Bay**, a lovely cove with the most beautiful beach on the island.

🛕 Moni Agíou Andréa
Peratáta village. 🕿 26710 69700. 🕎 daily. 🎨 museum only.

A view overlooking Asos in the northwest of the island

Zákynthos
Ζάκυνθος

ZAKYNTHOS WAS INHABITED by Achaians until Athens took control in the 5th century BC. They were followed by a succession of rulers, including the Spartans, Macedonians, Romans and Byzantines. The Venetians ruled from 1484 until 1797 and Zákynthos finally joined the rest of Greece in 1864. An attractive and green island, there are mountain villages, monasteries, fertile plains and beautiful views to reward exploration.

Statue of the poet Solomós in the main square, Zákynthos town

ZAKYNTHOS TOWN
Completely destroyed in the 1953 earthquake that hit the Ionian Islands, Zákynthos town has now been rebuilt with efforts to recapture its former grace. The traditional arcaded streets run parallel to the waterfront, where fishing boats arrive each morning to sell their catch. Further down the waterfront the ferry boats dock alongside grand Mediterranean cruise ships.

At the southern end of the harbour is the impressive church of **Agios Dionýsios**, the island's patron saint (1547–1622). The church, which houses the body of St Dionýsios in a silver coffin, was built in 1925 and survived the earthquake. The **Byzantine Museum** has a scale model of the pre-earthquake

town, an elegant city built by the Venetians. It also houses a breathtaking collection of icons and frescoes rescued from the island's destroyed churches and monasteries.

North of here is the **Solomós Museum**, which contains the tomb of the poet Dionýsios Solomós (1798–1857), author of the Greek national anthem. The collection details lives of prominent Zákynthiot citizens.

A short walk north from the town centre, **Stráni hill** offers good views, while the Venetian kástro, above the town, has even more impressive views of the mainland. The ruined walls contain remnants of several churches and an abundance of plants and wildlife.

Byzantine Museum
26950 42714. ☐ Tue–Sun.
● main public hols. 🎫 ♿
Solomós Museum
26950 48982. ☐ daily.
● main public hols. 🎫

AROUND THE ISLAND
Outside the main resorts there is little tourist development on Zákynthos. It is possible to drive around the island in a day as most of the roads are in good condition. Hiring a

0 miles   5

0 kilometres   5

LOGGERHEAD TURTLES

The Mediterranean green loggerhead turtle *(Caretta caretta)* has been migrating from Africa to Laganás Bay, its principal nesting site, for many thousands of years. These giant sea creatures can weigh up to 180 kg (400 lb). They lay their eggs in the sand, said to be the softest in Greece, at night. However, disco and hotel lights disorientate the turtles' navigation and few now nest successfully. Of the eggs that are eventually laid, many are destroyed by vehicles or by

the poles of beach umbrellas. The work of environmentalists has led to some protection for the turtles, with stretches of beach now off-limits, in an attempt to give the turtles a chance to at least stabilize their numbers.

car or a powerful motorbike is the best idea, though buses from Zákynthos town are frequent to resorts such as Alykés, Tsiliví and Laganás.

The growth of tourism on Zákynthos has been heavily concentrated in **Laganás** and its 14-km (9-mile) sweep of soft sand. This unrestricted development has decimated the population of loggerhead turtles that nests here – only an estimated 800 remain. Efforts are now being made to protect the turtles and to ensure their future survival. Visitors may take trips out into the bay in glass-bottomed boats to see the turtles, and all sorts of turtle souvenirs fill the large number of trinket shops. An equally large

number of bars and discos ensure the nightlife here continues till dawn.

Head to the north coast for the busy beach resorts of **Tsiliví** and **Alykés**, the latter being especially good for windsurfing.

The 16th-century **Moní tis Panagías tis Anafonítrias** in the northwest has special appeal for locals as it was here the island's patron saint, Dionýsios, spent the last years of his life as an abbot. During his time here, it is said that Dionýsios heard a murderer's confession; the murderer received the saint's

Coat of arms at **Moní tis Panagías tis Anafonítrias**

forgiveness, never knowing that his victim was the abbot's brother. When questioned by the authorities, Dionýsios denied seeing the man, which was the only lie he ever told. Dionýsios lived in a cell here which still stands and contains many of the saint's revered possessions. The three-aisled church and the tiny chapel alongside are rare in that they survived the 1953 earthquake.

At the northernmost tip of the island are the unusual **Blue Caves**, formed by the relentless action of the sea on the coastline. The principal cave, the Blue Grotto, lies directly underneath the lighthouse on Cape Skinári. It was discovered in 1897 and has become well known for its stunningly blue and clear water. The caves can be visited by boat from the resort of Agios Nikólaos and the round-the-island boat trips from the main resorts also stop here

The Blue Caves of Zákynthos on the northern tip of the island

THE ARGO-SARONIC ISLANDS

SALAMINA · AIGINA · PÓROS · YDRA · SPETSES · KYTHIRA

ALTHOUGH STILL SUPPORTING *fishing and farming communities, the Argo-Saronic Islands have succumbed to a degree of tourism. Many Athenians visit the islands at weekends, when the beaches can become very busy. Kýthira, off the tip of the Peloponnese, shares its history of Venetian and British rule with the Ionians, but is today administered with the Argo-Saronics.*

The islands' location close to Athens has given them a rich history. Aígina was very prosperous in the 7th century BC as a maritime state that minted its own coins and built the magnificent temple of Aphaia. Salamína is famed as the site of the Battle of Salamis (480 BC), when the Greek fleet defeated the Persians. Wealth gained from maritime trading also assured the Argo-Saronics' cultural and social development, seen today in the architectural beauty of Ydra and in the grand houses and public buildings of Aígina. Ydra and Spétses were important in the War of Independence *(see p38–9)*, both islands producing brave fighters, including the notorious Laskarína Bouboulína and Admiral Andréas Miaoúlis.

Terracotta ornament

Salamína and Aígina are so easy to reach from the capital that they are often thought of as island suburbs of Athens. Póros hardly seems like an island at all, divided from the Peloponnese by a narrow channel. However, despite modern colonization peaceful spots can still be found. Póros and Spétses are lush and green, covered with pine forests and olive groves, in contrast to the other more barren and mountainous islands. Scenically, Kýthira's rugged coastline has more in common with the Ionians than the Argo-Saronics. The island's position on ancient shipping routes has led to some major finds, such as the bronze *Youth of Antikýthira*, now in the National Archaeological Museum *(see p282)*.

The chapel of Agios Nikólaos on Aígina

◁ **Póros town with the mountains of the Peloponnese in the background**

Exploring the Argo-Saronic Islands

CLOSE PROXIMITY TO ATHENS makes the Argo-Saronic Islands suitable for short visits as well as longer stays. The islands have a lush landscape, with pine forests and crystal-clear waters in secluded bays. Aígina is an ideal base and, like the other islands, has picturesque ports with cobbled streets and Neo-Classical buildings. Packed with smart bars and shops, the cosmopolitan atmosphere of the Argo-Saronics is tempered by harbourside caïques selling vegetables and horse-drawn carriages driving along the seafront. Horse power is particularly evident in Póros, Ydra and Spétses where no cars are allowed. Kýthira remains a well-kept secret. This large island has beautiful villages and deserted beaches to explore.

The harbour in Aígina town

ISLANDS AT A GLANCE

Aígina *pp92–5*
Kýthira *pp98–9*
Póros *p96*
Salamína *p92*
Spétses *p97*
Ydra *pp96–7*

SEE ALSO

- **Where to Stay** p299
- **Where to Eat** p323
- **Travel Information** pp356–9

The rugged scenery of Palaióchora on Kýthira

KEY

▨ Asphalt road

⠿ Non-asphalt road

▨ Scenic route

-- High season, direct ferry route

⚘ Viewpoint

KOLPOS EPIDAVROU

Ermióni

DOKOS

SPETSES
Spétses Town

SPETSOPOULA TRIKERI ALEXANDROS

0 kilometres   20

0 miles   10

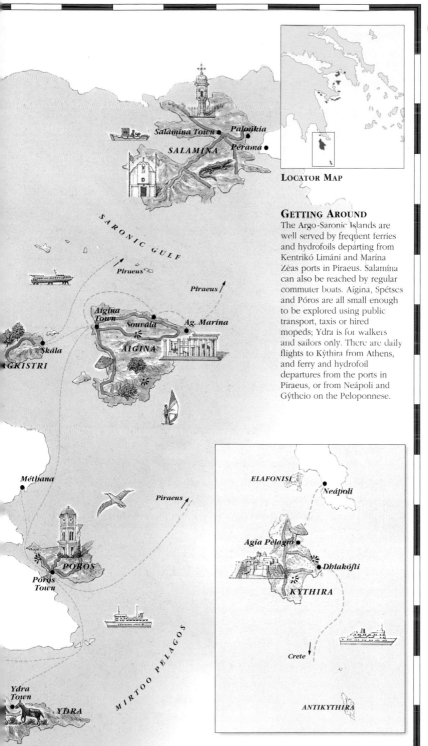

LOCATOR MAP

GETTING AROUND

The Argo-Saronic Islands are
well served by frequent ferries
and hydrofoils departing from
Kentrikó Limáni and Marína
Zéas ports in Piraeus. Salamína
can also be reached by regular
commuter boats. Aígina, Spétses
and Póros are all small enough
to be explored using public
transport, taxis or hired
mopeds; Ydra is for walkers
and sailors only. There are daily
flights to Kýthira from Athens,
and ferry and hydrofoil
departures from the ports in
Piraeus, or from Neápoli and
Gýtheio on the Peloponnese.

Salamína
Σαλαμίνα

23,000. 🚢 Paloúkia & Selínia.
🚌 Salamína town. 🚢 Thu at
Salamína town, Sat at Aiánteio.

SALAMINA IS THE LARGEST of the Saronic Gulf islands, and so close to Athens that most Greeks consider it part of the mainland. The island is famed as the site of the decisive Battle of Salamis in 480 BC, when the Greeks defeated the Persians. The king of Persia, Xerxes, watched the humiliating sight of his cumbersome ships being destroyed in Salamis Bay, trapped by the faster triremes of a smaller Greek fleet under Themistokles. The island today is a cheerful medley of holiday homes, immaculately whitewashed churches and cheap tavernas, although its east coast is lined with a string of marine scrapyards and naval bases.

The west coast capital of **Salamína town** is a charmless place, straddling an isthmus of flat land filled with vineyards. Both the town and the island are known as Koúlouri, nick-named after a biscuit that resembles the island's shape.

East of Salamína town **Agios Nikólaos** has far more character, with 19th-century mansions lining the quayside and small caïques off-loading their catch of fish. A road from Paloúkia meanders across the south of the island to the villages of Selínia, Aiánteio and Peristéria.

In the northwest of the Salamína, the 17th-century **Moní Faneroménis** looks across a narrow gulf to Ancient Eleusis on the Attic coast. The monastery was used during the War of Indepen-dence *(see pp38–9)* as a hiding place for Greek freedom fighters. Its Byzantine church was restored by the Venetians, and has fine 18th-century frescoes vividly depicting the *Last Judgment*. Today nuns welcome visitors, and tend the gardens, home to a number of peacocks.

Shrine opposite Moní Faneroménis

Fishing boats sailing into Aígina harbour

Aígina
Αίγινα

12,400. 🚢 🚌 Aígina town.
ℹ️ Leonárdou Ladá, Aígina town
(22970 27777).

ONLY 20 km (12 miles) southwest of the port of Piraeus, Aígina has been in-habited for over 4,000 years, and has remained an impor-tant settlement throughout that time. According to Greek mythology, the island's name was changed from Oinóni to Aígina, who was the daughter of the river god Asopós, after Zeus installed her on the island as his mistress.

By the 7th century BC the second-largest Saronic island was the first place in Europe to mint its own silver coins, which became accepted currency throughout the Greek-speaking world. Plying the Mediterranean and the Black Sea, the people of Aígina controlled most foreign trade in Greece. However, their legendary nautical skills and vast wealth finally incurred the wrath of neigh-bouring Athens, who settled the long-term rivalry by conquering the island in 456 BC. Aígina's most famous site is the well-preserved **Temple of Aphaia** *(see pp94–5)*, built in about 490 BC, prior to Athenian control. Later, the island de-clined during the centuries of alternating Turkish and Venetian rule and the constant plague of piracy. However, Aígina enjoyed fame again for a brief period in 1828 when Ioánnis Kapodístrias (1776–1857) declared it the first capital of modern Greece.

The ruinous Venetian Pýrgos Markéllou in Aígina town

AIGINA TOWN
This picturesque island town is home to many churches, including the pretty 19th-century **Agía Triáda**, next to the fish market overlooking the harbour. At the quayside, horse-drawn carriages take visitors through narrow streets of Neo-Classical mansions to the Venetian tower **Pýrgos Markéllou** near the cathedral. **Agios Nektários** cathedral, inaugurated in 1994, is said to be the second-biggest Greek Orthodox church after Agía Sofía in Istanbul. Octopuses are hung out to dry at taver-nas in the street leading to the fish market. To the north-

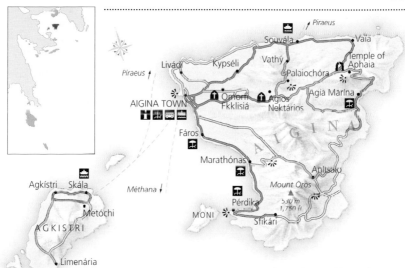

**Agios Nektários cathedral
in Aígina town**

west, past shops selling pistachio nuts and earthenware
jugs, are the remains of the
6th-century BC **Temple of
Apollo**. The 6th-century
Sphinx of Aígina, now in
the **Aígina Museum**, was
discovered here.

 **Aígina Museum**
Kolóna 8. [22970 22637.
◯ Tue–Sun. ◉ main public
hols. ◢ ⛾

ENVIRONS: North of Aígina
town, in Livádi, a plaque
marks the house where
Níkos Kazantzákis wrote
Zorba the Greek (see p272).

AROUND THE ISLAND
Aígina, at only 8 km (5
miles) across, is easy to
explore by bicycle. Just
off the main road east
from Aígina town is the

KEY

For key to map see back flap

13th-century Byzantine church,
Omorfi Ekklisiá, which has
some fine frescoes. Pilgrims
take this road to pay homage
at **Agios Nektários**. Archbishop Nektários (1846–1920)
was the first man to be canon-
ized in modern times (1961)
by the Orthodox Church.
Visitors can see his quarters
and the chapel where he rests.
On the opposite hillside are
the remains of the deserted
town of **Palaiochóra**. Populated since Byzantine times, it

**The scattered ruins of Byzantine chapels
around the deserted town of Palaiochóra**

was destroyed by Barbarossa,
the general of Sultan Suleiman
I, in 1537. The area around the
town was abandoned in 1826.
South from Aígina town, the
road hugs the shore, beneath
the shadow of **Mount Oros** at
530 m (1,750 ft). Passing the
pistachio orchards and the
fishing harbour of Fáros, this
scenic route ends at **Pérdika**
at the southwestern tip of the
island. Overlooking the harbour, this small, picturesque
fishing village has some excellent fish tavernas that are
packed at weekends with
Athenians over for a day trip.

OUTLYING ISLANDS
Just 15 minutes by caïque
from Pérdika is the island of
Moní, popular for its emerald-
green waters, secluded
coves and hidden caves.
Agkístri is easily accessible by caïque from
Aígina town or by ferry
from Piraeus. Originally
settled by Albanians, to-
day this island is colonized
by Germans who have
bought most of the houses
in the village of Metóchi,
just above Skála port.
Although many hotels,
apartments and bars have
been built in Skála and
Mílos, its other main port,
the rest of this hilly, pine-
clad island remains largely
unspoilt. Limenária, in the
south of the island, is a
more traditional, peaceful
community of farmers
and fishermen.

Aígina:Temple of Aphaia
Ναός της Αφαίας

SURROUNDED BY PINE TREES, on a hilltop above the busy resort of Agía Marína, the Temple of Aphaia is one of the best-preserved Doric temples in Greece *(see pp56–7)*. The present temple dates from around 490 BC, but the site is known to have been a place of worship from the 13th century BC. In 1901 the German archaeologist Adolf Furtwängler found an inscription to the goddess Aphaia, disproving theories that the temple was dedicated to Athena. Although smaller, the building is similar to the temple of Zeus at Olympia, built 30 years later.

Inner Walls
The inner wall was built with a thickened base and a minimal capital to correspond with the capitals of the colonnade.

The east pediment sculptures, with Athena at the centre, were replacements for an earlier set. The west pediment sculptures are Archaic in style.

Aerial view of the site from the south

Triglyph

Metope

Architrave

Corner Columns
These columns were made thicker for emphasis and to counteract the appearance of thinness in a column that was seen against the sky.

Ramp from altar to temple

Corner Architraves
Still in good condition, the stonework above the capitals consists of a plain architrave surmounted by a narrow band of plain metopes alternating with ornate triglyphs.

Inner Columns
The cella *is enclosed by two storeys of Doric columns, one on top of the other. The taper of the upper columns is continuous with that of the lower.*

VISITORS' CHECKLIST

12 km (7 miles) E of Aígina town.
📞 22970 32398. **Site** 🕐 Apr–
Oct: 8:15am–7pm daily;
Nov–Mar: 8:15am–5pm daily.
Museum 🕐 9am–1pm daily
(entry at 9am, 11am, noon, 1pm
only). ● 1 Jan, 25 Mar, Good
Fri am, Easter Sun, 1 May, 25, 26
Dec. 🖼 🦽 📷 🚮

The roof was made of terracotta tiles with Parian marble tiles at the edges.

Opisthodomos, or rear porch

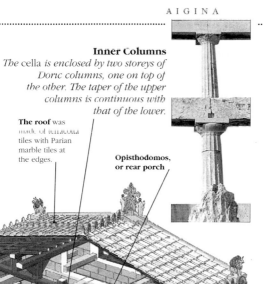

View of the Cella
The cella *was the inner room of the temple, and the home of the cult statue. Some temples had more than one, the back* cella *being reserved for the priestess alone.*

Cult statue of the goddess Aphaia

RECONSTRUCTION OF THE TEMPLE OF APHAIA
Viewed from the northwest, this reconstruction shows the temple as it would have been in c.490 BC. Built of local limestone covered in stucco and painted, it was highly colourful.

The pool of olive oil was a collection of the many libations (offerings) made to the goddess.

TEMPLE PEDIMENTS
The famous sculptures from the pediments of the temple of Aphaia were discovered by a group of British and German architects and artists, including John Foster, C R Cockerell, and Baron Haller von Hallerstein, in April 1811. They were later sold to the Crown Prince of Bavaria at auction and are now housed in the Glyptothek in Munich. They portray the struggles of various mythological heroes. The sculptures from the west pediment date from around 490 BC and are in the late Archaic style. Those from the east, with their more fluid movements and serious expressions, date from approximately 480 BC and foreshadow the Classical style.

Reconstruction of the *Warriors* sculpture from the west pediment

Póros
Πόρος

 *4,000.* 🚗 🚢 *Póros town.*
ℹ️ *Póros town (22980 22462).*
🎡 *Fri (am) at Paidikí Chará.*

POROS TAKES its name from the 400-m (1,300-ft) passage *(póros)* separating it from the mainland at Galatás. Póros is in fact two islands, joined by a causeway: pine-swathed Kalávria to the north, and the smaller volcanic islet of Sfairía in the south over which **Póros town** is built. In spite of much tourist development, the town is an appealing place, extending along the narrow straits, busy with shipping. Its 19th-century houses climb in tiers to its apex at a clock tower.

The **National Naval Academy**, northwest of the causeway and Póros town, was set up in 1849. An old battleship is usually at anchor there for training naval cadets.

The attractive 18th-century **Moní Zoödóchou Pigís** can be found on Kalávria, built around the island's only spring. There are the ruins of a 6th-century hilltop **Temple of Poseidon** near the centre of Kalávria, next to which the orator Demosthenes poisoned himself in 323 BC rather than surrender to the Macedonians. In antiquity the site was linked to ancient Troezen in the Peloponnese. The temple has unlimited access.

The busy waterfront on Ydra

Ydra
Ύδρα

🚶 *3,000.* 🚗 *Ydra town.*
ℹ️ *Ydra town (22980 52205).*
🚤 *Mandráki 1.5 km (1 mile) NE of Ydra town; Vlychós 2 km (1 mile) SW of Ydra town.*

ALONG, NARROW mass of barren rock, Ydra had little history before the 16th century when it was settled by Orthodox Albanians, who then turned to the sea for a living. Ydra town was built in a brief period of prosperity in the late 18th and early 19th centuries, boosted by blockade-running during the Napoleonic wars. After Independence, Ydra lapsed into obscurity again, until foreigners

Bell tower of Ydra's Panagía church

rediscovered it after World War II. By the 1960s, the trickle had become a flood of outsiders who set about restoring the old houses, transforming Ydra into one of the most exclusive resorts in Greece. Yet the island has retained its charm, thanks to an architectural preservation order which has kept the town's appearance as it was in the 1820s, along with a ban on motor vehicles. Donkey caravans perform all haulage on steep stair streets.

YDRA TOWN
More than a dozen three- or four-storeyed mansions *(archontiká)* survive around the port, though none are regularly open to the public. Made from local stone, they were

Póros town, its houses clustered on the hillside of Sfairía

built by itinerant craftsmen between 1780 and 1820. On the east side of the harbour the **Toamadoú mansion** is now the National Merchant Marine Academy. On the west, the **Tompázi mansion** is a School of Fine Arts. Just behind the centre of the marble-paved quay is the monastic church of the **Panagía**, built between 1760 and 1770 using masonry from Póros's Temple of Poseidon. The marble belfry is thought to have been erected by a master stonemason from Tinos.

AROUND THE ISLAND

Visitors must walk virtually everywhere on Ydra, or hire water taxis to go along the coast. **Kamíni**, 15 minutes' walk southwest along the shore track, has been Ydra's main fishing port since the 16th century. The farm hamlet of **Episkopí**, in the far southwest of the island, used to be a summer refuge and a hunting resort for the upper classes. An hour's steep hike above the town is the convent of **Agía Efpraxía**, which still houses nuns who are keen to sell you handicrafts. The adjacent 19th-century **Profítis Ilías** functions as a monastery. In the island's eastern half, visible from Profitis Ilías, are three uninhabited monasteries, dating from the 18th and 19th centuries. They mark the arduous 3-hour-long route to **Moní Panagía**, situated out near Cape Zoúrvas to the northeast of the island.

Spétses
Σπέτσες

The old harbour of Báltiza on Spétses

in 1460, and then by Albanians during the 16th century, the island developed as a naval power, and supplied a fleet for the Greek revolutionary effort. Possibly the most famous Spetsiot was Laskarína Boubou:lína, the admiral who menaced the Turks from her flagship *Agamemnon* and reputedly seduced men at gunpoint. She was shot in 1825 by the father of a girl her son had eloped with. During the 1920s and 30s, Spétses was a fashionable resort for British expatriates and anglophile Greeks. The ban on vehicles is not total: mopeds and horsecabs can be hired in town, and there are buses to the beaches.

Statue of Boubouilína in Spétses town

SPETSES TOWN

Spétses town runs along the coast for 2 km (1 mile). Its centre lies at Ntápia quay, fringed by cafés. The *archontiká* of Chatzi-Giánnis Méxis, dating from 1795, is now the **Chatzi-Giánnis Méxis Museum**. Bouboulína's coffin is on display as well as figureheads from her ship. Her former home is now the privately run **Boubouilína Museum**. Southeast from here lies the old harbour at **Báltiza** inlet, where wooden boats are still built using the traditional

methods. Above the harbour is the attractive 17th-century church of **Agios Nikólaos**, which has some fine pebble mosaics and a belfry made by craftsmen from Tínos.

Chatzi Giánnis Méxis Museum
300 m (985 ft) from the port.
📞 22980 72994. ⏰ Tue–Sun.
● main public hols. 🈂

Boubouilína Museum
Behind Plateía Ntápia. 📞 22980 72416. ⏰ 25 Mar–28 Oct: 9:45am–8:30pm daily. 🈂 📷 📹

AROUND THE ISLAND

A track, only partly concreted, runs all the way round the island, and the best way to get around is by bicycle or moped. East of the town stands the Anargýreios and Korgialéneios College, which is now closed. British novelist John Fowles taught there briefly in the early 1950s. He later used Spétses as the setting for *The Magus*. The pebble beaches on Spétses are the best in the Argo-Saronic group, including **Ligonéri**, **Vréllas**, and **Agía Paraskeví**. **Agioi Anárgyroi** is the only sandy one.

Pebble mosaic from the church of Agios Nikólaos, Spétses town

🏠 3,700. 🚢 🚌 Spétses town.
🛈 Spétses town (22980 73100).
🎪 Wed at Kokinária.

SPETSES IS A CORRUPTION of Pityoússa, or "Piney", the ancient name for this round, green island. Occupied by the Venetians in 1220, by the Turks

Kýthira
Κύθηρα

CALLED TSERIGO by the Venetians, Kýthira is one of the legendary birthplaces of Aphrodite. Historically, the island shared Venetian and British rule with the Ionian islands; today it is governed from Piraeus with the other Argo-Saronics. Clumps of eucalyptus seem emblematic of the Island's modern alias of "Kangaroo Island"; return visits from 60,000 Australian Kythirans are central to Kythiran life. The island is also popular with Athenians seeking unspoilt beaches and holiday homes, many of which are the typical mix of Aegean and Venetian architecture.

Kapsáli harbour seen from Chóra

Platiá Ammos
Karavás
Neápoli
Agía Pelagía
Potamós
Palaióchora
Gýtheio
Douriánika
Moní Agíou Theodórou
Diakófti
Crete
Agía Sofía Cave
Friligkiánika
Mylopótamos
Mitáta
Agios Geórgios
Avlémonas
Káto Chóra
Fónissa
Palaiópoli
Kastrí
Limniónas
Frátsia
Kaladí
Limnária
Kalokairínes
Komponáda
Livádi
Kálamos
Moní
Agios Ioánnis
sto Gkremó
Fyrí Ammos
Melidóni
CHORA
Kapsáli
Chalkós

KYTHERA

0 kilometres   5
0 miles   3

CHORA

Chóra has been Kýthira's capital only since the destruction of Palaióchora in 1537. Its magnificent **kástro** was built in two phases during the 13th and 15th centuries. A multidomed cistern lies intact near the bottom of the castle; at the summit, old cannons surround the church of **Panagía Myrtidiótissa**. The steepness of the drop to the sea below and Avgó islet, thought to be the birthplace of Aphrodite, is unrivalled throughout the Greek islands. A magnet for wealthy Athenians, the appealing lower town with its solidly built, flat-roofed mansions dates from the 17th to 19th centuries. The **Archaeological Museum** just outside Chóra has finds from Mycenaean and Minoan sites, plus gravestones dating from the British occupation of 1809–64.

🔲 Archaeological Museum
📞 27360 31739. **🕐** 8:45am–2pm Tue–Sat, 9:30am–1pm Sun. **⚫** main public hols. 💶

ENVIRONS: Yachts, hydrofoils and, occasionally, large ferries drop anchor at the harbour of **Kapsáli**, just east of Chóra. The beach is mediocre, but most foreigners stay here. In the cliff above the pine wood is the 16th-century **Moní Agios Ioánnis sto Gkremó**, built on to the cliff edge. The nearest good beaches are pebbly **Fyrí Ammos**, 8 km (5 miles) northeast via Kálamos, with sea caves at its south end; and sandy **Chalkós**, 7 km (4 miles) south of Kálamos.

The houses of Chóra clustered on the hillside at dusk

Whitewashed house in Mylopotamos

AROUND THE ISLAND

Like many Greek islands, the best way to get around Kýthira is by car, particularly as it is quite mountainous. A bus runs to the main towns once a day during the summer from Agía Pelagía to Kapsáli. **Avlémonas**, with its vaulted warehouses and double harbour, forms an attractive fishing port at the east end of a stretch of rocky coast. Just offshore the *Mentor*, carrying many of the Elgin Marbles, sank in 1802. Excellent beaches extend to either side of Kastrí point. The 6th-century hilltop church of **Agios Geórgios**, which has a mosaic floor, sits high above Avlémonas.

Roadside shrine on Kýthira

On the other side of the island is **Mylopótamos**. From here a track leads west to the small Fónissa waterfall, downstream from which is a millhouse, and a tiny stone bridge.

In its blufftop situation with steep drops to the north and west, and a clutch of locked chapels, the Venetian kástro at **Káto Chóra** superficially resembles Palaióchora. It was not a military stronghold but a refuge prepared in 1565 for the peasantry in unsettled times. The Lion of St Mark presides over the entrance; nearby an English-built school of 1825 is being restored.

Agía Sofía Cave, 2.5 km (1.5 miles) from Káto Chóra and 150 m (490 ft) above the sea, has formed in black lime stone strata. At the entrance, a frescoed shrine, painted by a 13th-century hermit, depicts Holy Wisdom and three attendant virtues. **Palaiochóra**, the Byzantine "capital" of Kýthira after 1248, was sited so as to be nearly invisible from the sea, but the pirate Barbarossa detected and destroyed it in 1537. The ruins of the town perch on top of a sheer 200-m (655-ft) bluff. Among six churches in Palaióchora, the most striking and best preserved is the 14th-century **Agía Varvára**.

To the south, **Moní Agíou Theodórou** is the seat of Kýthira's bishop. The church, originally 12th century, has

been much altered, and the Baroque relief plaque over the door is a rarity in Greece.

To the north, the main port, **Agía Pelagía**, has a handful of hotels. **Karavás**, 5 km (3 miles) northwest is, in contrast, an attractive oasis village, with clusters of houses overhanging the steep banks of a stream valley.

Agía Sofía Cave

Mylopótamos. 27360 33754. Tue–Sun. Nov–Mar. Jul & Aug.

OUTLYING ISLANDS

Directly north of Kýthira, the barren islet of **Elafonísi** is visited mostly by Greeks for the sake of the best desert-island beaches in the country. The better of the two is Símos on the east side of a peninsula 5 km (3 miles) southeast of the port town. The remote island of **Antikýthira**, southeast of Kýthira, has a tiny population and no beaches.

View to the east across a gorge from Palaióchora

THE SPORADES AND EVVOIA

SKIATHOS · SKOPELOS · ALONNISOS
SKYROS · EVVOIA

THE LUSH LANDSCAPE *of Evvoia and the Sporades comes as a surprise after barren and arid islands such as the Cyclades. Since ancient times, settlers and pirates alike have been lured by the pine-clad mountains, abundant springs and rivers, endless beaches and hidden coves that are found throughout these islands.*

Being close to the mainland, the Sporades and Evvoia have been easily conquered throughout history. They were colonized in the prehistoric era by nearby Iolkos (Vólos), and also by the Minoans, who introduced vine and olive cultivation. More than any other island, Evvoia reveals its diverse history in the large number of buildings remaining from the long periods of Venetian and Turkish occupation. Susceptible to pirate raids, the inhabitants of the Sporades lived in the safety of fortified towns until as late as the 19th century. Even in Evvoia, when life proved too difficult in coastal villages such as Límni, the residents simply migrated to Skiáthos for a few generations. The islanders

Mariner statue in Kárystos, Evvoia

have a rich heritage of maritime trading around the Aegean and are still noted today as sailors. The islands' patchworked interiors of fertile fields and orchards, watered by ample springs and rivers, also encouraged agricultural self-sufficiency and wealth. Particularly on remote and rugged Skýros, such insularity has nurtured some unique folk art and colourful traditions. Its inaccessible coastline enables it to remain relatively unaffected by the numerous tourist hotel complexes that have sprung up on Skiáthos and Skópelos.

The size of Evvoia also means it is one of the few places in the Greek islands where life carries on during the summer, undeterred by the annual invasion of holiday-makers.

Castel Rosso near Kárystos on Evvoia

◁ **The harbour of Agnóntas on Skópelos in the evening sun**

Exploring the Sporades and Evvoia

Tʜᴇ ʀɪᴄʜ ᴀɴᴅ ꜰᴀᴍᴏᴜꜱ first flocked in their yachts to the deserted beaches of Skiáthos, Skópelos and Alónnisos in the 1960s and 1970s. Although no longer so exclusive, the beautiful coastlines of these islands still lure Greek and foreign holiday-makers alike. There are facilities for windsurfing and boats for hire on most beaches. Skópelos and Skiáthos have a sophisticated array of nightclubs and bars. Quieter Skýros and Evvoia, offering a varied culture and landscape, are perfect for rambling holidays, punctuated by visits to local folk art museums and lingering days on the fine beaches.

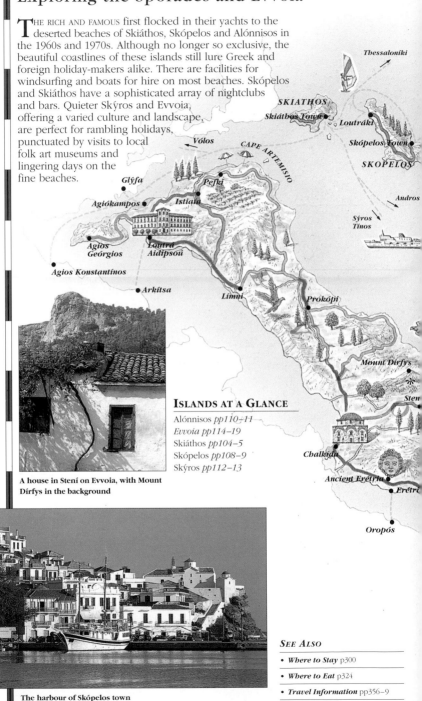

Thessaloníki

SKIATHOS
Skiáthos Town • Loutráki
Vólos
CAPE ARTEMISIO
Skópelos Town •
SKOPELOS

Andros

Sýros
Tínos

Glýfa
Pefki
Agiókampos • Istiaía
Agios Geórgios
Loutrá Aidipsoú
Agios Konstantínos
• Arkítsa
Limni
Prokópi

Mount Dírfys

Sten

Islands at a Glance

Alónnisos *pp110–11*
Evvoia *pp114–19*
Skiáthos *pp104–5*
Skópelos *pp108–9*
Skýros *pp112–13*

Chalkída

Ancient Erétria
• Erétri

Oropós

A house in Steni on Evvoia, with Mount Dírfys in the background

The harbour of Skópelos town

See Also

• *Where to Stay* p300

• *Where to Eat* p324

• *Travel Information* pp356–9

GIOURA

KIRA
PANAGIA

PIPERI

ALONNISOS

Palaia
Alonnisos

PERISTERA

Patitiri

LOCATOR MAP

SKANTZOURA

GETTING AROUND

Skýros and Skiáthos are both connected
with Athens by internal flights. Skiáthos's
international airport also caters for charter
flights. Island-hopping is easy in the
summer season, with frequent ferries
and Flying Dolphin hydrofoils plying
between the Sporades, Evvoia and
the mainland. It is also possible to
connect by ferry with the Cyclades
and Thessaloníki. Kárystos is the
best base for touring the south of
Evvoia; stay at Kými for the east
coast, and Límni or Loutrá
Aidipsoú for a tour of the
north. There are good
roads around Evvoia and a
frequent, reliable bus service.

Skýros
Town

Linariá

SKYROS

Kými

Paralía Kýmis

Ochthoniá

View of Skýros town from the kástro

Agía
Marína

Néa Stýra

KEY

▬	Major road
▬	Asphalt road
▬	Scenic route
▬	River
--	High-season, direct ferry route
✺	Viewpoint

Mount Ochi

Rafína

Marmári

Kárystos

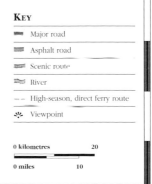

0 kilometres   20

0 miles   10

Skiáthos
Σκιάθος

Sκιάτηος has always been an unashamedly hedonistic island from its early tourist development in the 1960s, when it attracted the rich and famous with its legendary beaches, to its current role as bucket-and-spade paradise for family package tours. Although the introduction of direct package flights has diminished Skiáthos's exclusive status, the luxury yachts are still in evidence off Koukounariés beach. In spite of the tourism, the island retains its scenic beauty and a scattering of atmospheric churches and monasteries.

The sweeping bay of Koukounariés

KEY

For key to map see back flap

0 kilometres   2

0 miles   1

SKIÁTHOS TOWN

Still picturesque, the island town is a charming place with its red-tiled roofs and maze of cobbled back streets. It is built on two small hills, dominated by the large 19th-century churches of **Trión Ierarchón** and **Panagía Limniá**, which offer excellent views of the bustling harbour below. The main street winds up between the two hills to the old quarter of Limniá, a quiet neighbourhood of restored sea captains' houses, covered with trailing bougainvillea and trellised vines. The town is excellent

for shopping, full of aromatic bakeries, smart boutiques and antique shops, some of which specialize in genuine folk artifacts, including ceramics, icons, jewellery and embroidery.

The town has twin harbours, separated by **Bourtzi** islet, which is reached by a narrow

causeway. The pine-covered islet, once a fortress, is now a cultural centre and hosts the annual Aegean festival of dance, theatre and concert performances each summer.

Bourtzi is dominated by a handsome Neo-Classical building, with a statue of the famous Greek novelist Aléxandros Papadiamántis standing guard. Life in Skiáthos town centres on the long, sweeping quaysides lined with numerous *kafeneía*, specializing in *loukoumádes* (small honeyed fritters). In the evenings the waterside attracts many people for a stroll in the cool night air. During the day there is the spectacle of arriving and departing flotilla yachts, ferries and hydrofoils. The western end of the quay has a good fish market, and an *ouzerí* frequented by locals. It is also where small boats and caïques depart for day trips to some of the island's famous beaches,

View of Skiáthos town from the church of Profítis Ilías

An ornate fresco in the Christós sto Kástro church

VISITORS' CHECKLIST

5,000. ✈ 2 km (1 mile) NE of Skiáthos town. 🚢 Harbour-front, Skiáthos town. ℹ 24270 23172. 🎭 Aegean Festival of Dance, Skiáthos town: Jul.

such as Koukounariés and Laláría, or to the nearby islands of Tsougkriá and Argos.

Behind the harbour is the **Papadiamántis Museum**, former home of the locally born novelist, whose name it takes. Although tiny, the museum shows the simplicity of local island life prior to the invasion of tourism.

📷 **Papadiamántis Museum**
📞 24270 23843. ⏰ May–Oct. 🏛

Moní Agíou Charalámpou, set in the hills above Skiáthos town

AROUND THE ISLAND

The interior of the northern side of the island, with its verdant landscape of pine and olive trees, reveals deserted monasteries and churches, springs and plenty of birdlife. This is in contrast to the overdeveloped southern coast. It is still possible to find deserted beaches and coves scattered along the northern coast. Many of these, such as **Kechriá** and **Mandráki**, can only be visited when the excursions stop for a few hours on their day trips around the island.

The main road south from Skiáthos town passes Fteliá and branches to the west just before Troúllos for **Asélinos** beach and **Moní Panagías Kounístras**. The monk who founded this 17th-century monastery, originally called Panagía Eikonístria, discovered a miraculous icon in a nearby tree. The icon is kept in Trión Ierarchón in Skiáthos town.

The path north from here leads to **Agios Ioánnis**, where it is customary to stop and ring the church bell after completing the steep walk through pine trees.

Further north still is the tiny 19th-century chapel of **Panagía Kechriás**, with its blue ceiling covered in stars, which perches high above **Kástro**. Abandoned in 1829, remains of the 300 houses are still visible in this deserted town and three churches have been restored. The 17th-century **Christós** church has a fine iconostasis.

On the road heading northwest out of Skiáthos town lies the barrel-vaulted 20th-century church of **Profítis Ilías**, which has a good taverna nearby with stunning views over the town. Continuing north, past rich farms and the 20th-century **Agios Apóstolos** church, the track descends through sage and bracken to **Moní Agíou Charalámpou**, built in 1809. Aléxandros Moraítidis, the writer, spent his last days here as a monk in the early 1920s. Just south of here is **Moní Evangelismoú**. Founded in 1775 by monks from Mount Athos, it played a crucial role in the War of Independence (see pp38–9), hiding many freedom fighters.

To the south of Moní Agíou Charalámpou, on the way back to Skiáthos town, is the beautiful church of **Taxiárchis**. It is covered in plates in the shape of a cross, and the best mineral spring water on the island flows out of a tap that is by the church.

ALEXANDROS PAPADIAMANTIS

The island's most famous native is one of Greece's outstanding literary figures. Aléxandros Papadiamántis spent his early childhood on the island, with five brothers and sisters, before leaving to study in Athens where he began his career in journalism. He wrote more than 100 novellas and short stories, all set against the backdrop of island life. Among his best-known works are *The Gypsy, The Murderess*, a compulsive psychological drama, and *The Man Who Went to Another Country*. In 1908 he returned to Skiáthos where he died a few years later in 1911 at the age of 60.

Skópelos
Σκόπελος

Surprisingly, given its close proximity to Skiáthos, Skópelos has not totally succumbed to tourism. It is known to have been colonized by the Minoans as far back as 1600 BC and was used as a place of exile by the Byzantines. The Venetians held power for about 300 years after 1204. Famed for its wine in ancient times, Skópelos is still renowned for its fruit today. It offers many good beaches, and has a beautiful pine-covered interior.

The way up to Panagía tou Pýrgou above Skópelos town

KEY

For key to map see back flap

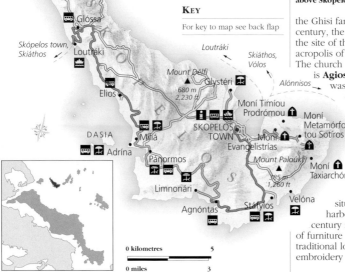

Glóssa

Skópelos town, Skiáthos

Loutráki

Skiáthos, Vólos

Mount Délfi
680 m
2,230 ft

Glystéri

Alónnisos

Elios

Moní Timíou Prodrómou

Moní Metamórfosis tou Sotíros

DASIA

Miliá

SKOPELOS TOWN

Adrína

Moní Evangelistrías

Pánormos

Mount Paloúki
385 m
1,260 ft

Moní Taxiarchón

Limnonári

Velóna

Agnóntas

Stáfylos

0 kilometres   5

0 miles   3

the Ghisi family in the 13th century, the castle stands on the site of the 5th-century BC acropolis of ancient Skópelos. The church nearest the castle is **Agios Athanásios**. It was built in the 11th century, but the foundations date from the 9th century. There are some fine 16th-century frescoes inside. The **Folk Art Museum** is situated behind the harbourfront in a 19th-century mansion. Pieces of furniture and examples of traditional local costumes and embroidery are on display.

⊙ Folk Art Museum
Chatzistamáti. ☎ 24240 23494.
◯ Nov–May: 8:30am–2:30pm daily; Jun–Oct: 10:30am–2:30 pm & 6–10:30pm daily. ⌂

Environs: In the hills above Skópelos town there are numerous impressive monasteries. Reached by the road going east out of the town, they all have immaculate

Skopelos Town

This charming town proudly reveals its rich pedigree with 123 churches, many fine mansion houses and myriad shops selling local delicacies such as honey, prunes and various delicious sweets. The cobbled streets wind up from the waterfront, and are covered with intricate designs made from sea pebbles and shells. There are numerous classic examples of the old Sporadhan town house, with its wooden balcony and fish-scale, slate-tiled roof.

In the upper town the cruciform church of **Panagía Papameletíou** is particularly splendid. Built in 1662, it is also known as Koímisis tis Theotókou. It has a well-kept interior, with an interesting display case of ecclesiastical *objets d'art* and a carved iconostasis by the Cretan

craftsman Antónios Agorastós. Perched on a clifftop above the town, the landmark church of **Panagía tou Pýrgou**, with its shining fish-scale roof, overlooks the harbour.

The old quarter of Skópelos town, the Kástro, sits above the modern town and is topped by the remains of the Venetian **castle**. Built by

The attractive bay of Skópelos town, viewed from the Kástro

Fish tavernas around the bay at Agnontas in the late afternoon

VISITORS' CHECKLIST

🏠 5,000. ⛴ 🚌 Skópelos town.
🛈 Harbourfront (24240 23220).
🎉 Panaqía: 15 Aug.

churches with carved iconostases and icons. **Moní Evangelistrías** (also known as Evangelismós) was built in 1712 and is one of the largest on the island. The nuns sell their handicrafts, including weavings, embroidery and food. Further up the road is **Metamórfosis tou Sotíros**, one of the oldest monasteries on Skópelos. It was built in the 16th century and is now inhabited by a solitary monk.

Moní Timíou Prodrómou, north of Moní Metamórfosis tou Sotíros, was restored in 1721. It has been inhabited by nuns, who also sell crafts, since the 1920s, and has a commanding view of Skópelos. From here a rough track leads up to **Mount Paloúki**. The deserted **Moní Taxiarchón** is reached by a track from Mount Paloúki that hugs the *sares*, the local name for the steep cliffs facing Alónissos.

AROUND THE ISLAND
The island is easy to explore, with its main road traversing the developed southern coast, and continuing as far as Glóssa to the northwest. It has a beautiful interior, full of plum orchards, pine forests and *kalývia* (farmhouses), but beware of the lack of signposts when travelling inland.

A steep road leads down to the popular beaches south of Skópelos town, Stáfylos and Velóna. **Agnóntas**, which serves as a port for ferries in rough weather, is quieter than Skópelos town. It is popular with locals who come for the

fish tavernas beside its pebble beach. Nearby **Limnonári**, with its stunning pebble beach and azure-coloured water, is reached by boat or along the narrow clifftop road.

Whitewashed houses in Glóssa with colourful doors and shutters

Before reaching the modern village of Elios, there are two thriving resorts at Miliá and Pánormos. For a quieter location, the tiny beach of **Adrína** nearby is often deserted. Sitting oposite the beach is wooded Dasiá island, named after a female pirate who drowned there long ago.

Glóssa is the other major settlement on the island, and sits directly opposite Skiáthos. Reminders of the Venetian occupation of Skópelos are evident in the picturesque remains of Venetian towers and houses. The small port of **Loutráki** below Glóssa is a sleepy place with little charm, but most ferries stop here as well as at Skópelos town

On the north coast, caïques shuttle every half-hour between the pebbled **Glystéri** beach and Skópelos town. From Glystéri a winding road leads inland to the wooded region just east of the island's highest peak, **Mount Délfi**. A short walk through the enchanting pine forest leads to four mysterious niches, signposted as *sentoúkia*, literally "crates", that are carved in the rocks. Believed to be Neolithic sarcophagal tombs, their position offers fine views over the island.

KALYVIA

Skópelos's interior is covered with an unusual array of beautiful *kalývia* (farmhouses). Some of these traditional stone buildings are still occupied all year round, others are only used during important seasonal harvests or for celebratory feasts on local saints' days. They all have distinctive outdoor prune ovens – a legacy from the days when Skópelos was renowned for its prunes. They provide a rare insight into the rural life that has virtually disappeared on neighbouring islands.

A traditional *kalívi* among olive and cypress trees

Two of the old houses in Palaiá Alónnisos in the process of restoration

Alónnisos
Αλόννησος

3,000. *Patitíri.*
*Kokkinókastro 6 km (4 miles)
N of Patitíri.*

SHARING a history of attacks by the pirate Barbarossa with the other Sporades and having endured earthquake damage in 1965, Alónnisos has suffered much over the years. However, the island is relatively unspoilt by tourism, and most of the development is centred in the main towns of Patitíri and Palaiá Alónnisos.

PATITÍRI
The port of Patitíri is a centre of bustling activity. Boats are available for day trips to the neighbouring islands, and there is excellent swimming off the rocks, northeast of the port. The picturesque back-streets display typical Greek pride in the home, evident in the immaculate whitewashed courtyards and pots of flowers.

Fishing vessels and cargo boats moored in Patitíri harbour

Rousoúm Gialós and Vótsi, 3–4 km (1–2 miles) north of Patitíri, are quieter alternatives with their natural cliff-faced harbours and tavernas.

AROUND THE ISLAND
This quiet island has a surfeit of beaches and coves and the interior is crisscrossed by dirt tracks accessible only to intrepid shepherds and motorbikes. The old capital of **Palaiá Alónnisos**, west of Patitíri, perches precariously on a clifftop. There are ruins of a 15th-century Venetian castle and a beautiful small chapel, Tou Christoú, that has a fish-scale roof. The town was seriously damaged by the earthquake in 1965, and the inhabitants were forced to leave their homes. They were rehoused initially in makeshift concrete homes at Patitíri. Today, the houses of Palaiá Alónnisos have been bought and restored by German and British families, and the town retains all the architectural beauty of a traditional Sporadhan village.
  The road across the island, northeast from Patitíri, reveals a surprisingly fertile land of pine, olive and arbutus trees. At **Kokkinókastro**, a popular pebble

beach edged by red cliffs and pines, there are scant remains of the site of ancient Ikos – the old name of the island.
  Further north lies the seaside village of **Steni Vála**. From here, a road snakes towards **Gérakas**, at the wild northern tip of the island. This lovely deserted beach is now home to the main research centre for the **HSSPMS** (Hellenic Society for the Study and Protection of the Monk Seal), with information displays and a video show.

Hellenic Society for the Study and Protection of the Monk Seal (HSSPMS)
Gérakas. *210 522 2888.* *Apr–Oct: daily; Nov–Mar: on request.*

Taverna at Steni Vála

Two endangered Mediterranean monk seals

Sporades Marine Park
Θαλάσσιο Πάρκο

🚢 from Skiáthos, Skópelos, Alónnisos.

FOUNDED IN 1992, the National Marine Park of Alónnisos and the Northern Sporades, to give it its full name, is an area of great environmental importance. It is the only such park in the Aegean, and includes not just Alónnisos but also its uninhabited outlying islands of Peristéra, Skantzoúra and Gioúra. Day trips by boat are possible but access is limited.

The park was created to protect an important breeding colony of the endangered Mediterranean monk seal and a fragile marine ecosystem of other rare wildlife, flora and fauna. Thanks to the pioneering efforts of marine biologists from the University of Athens, who first formed the Hellenic Society for the Study and Protection of the Monk Seal in 1988, Greece's largest population of the elusive Mediterranean monk seal is now scientifically monitored. Fewer than 500 of these seals exist worldwide, making it one of the world's most endangered species. There is an estimated population of 300 seals around the Aegean, with about 50 in the marine park. A recent campaign to promote awareness of the endangered status of the seals and restrictions on fishing in the area seems to be paying off.

Sightings of seals are not always guaranteed and there is no longer access for the public to view the wild goats on Gioúra, Audouin's gull or Eleonora's falcons on the islet of Skantzoúra: only scientists are now permitted.

The marine park is also an important route and staging post for many migrant birds during the spring and autumn. Land birds, ranging in size from tiny warblers through to elegant pallid harriers, pass through the region in large numbers to and from their breeding grounds in northeast Europe.

MARINE WILDLIFE IN THE SPORADES

Visitors can observe a wide range of other wildlife in the Sporades while watching out for monk seals. Grey herons and kingfishers are both birds of the coast here, a surprise for many birdwatchers from northern Europe who usually associate them with freshwater habitats. Spring and autumn in particular are good times for seeing several species of gulls and terns and, when venturing close to sea cliffs, keep an eye out for the Eleonora's falcons which nest on the inaccessible ledges; in the air, they are breathtakingly acrobatic birds.

Further out to sea, look for jellyfish in the water and the occasional group of common dolphins which may accompany the boat for a while. Cory's shearwaters fly with rigid wings close to the waves and head towards the shore in high winds and as dusk approaches. If you are at sea after dark, you are likely to see a glowing bioluminescence on the surface of the waves, caused by microscopic marine animals.

Cory's shearwaters glide low over the water. They are a common sight around Alónnisos.

Jellyfish flourish in the seas off the Sporadic islands. This is a *Pelagia noctiluca*.

Mediterranean gulls are easily recognized by the pure white wings and black hood that characterize their summer plumage.

Common dolphins can sometimes be seen in small groups diving in and out of the waves around the boat's wake or swimming alongside.

Skýros
Σκύρος

RENOWNED IN MYTH as the hiding place of Achilles *(see p79)* and the home-in-exile of the hero Theseus, Skýros has always played an important role in Greek history. A rich Athenian colony from 476 BC, it later became a place of exile for the wealthy from Byzantine Constantinople. Currently one of the homes of the Greek Navy and Air Force, its unique heritage, landscape and architecture bear more resemblance to the Dodecanese than the Sporades.

Skýrian pony

An example of traditional Skýrian embroidery in the Faltáits Museum

SKYROS TOWN

The main town is architecturally unusual in the Aegean; it has a fascinating mixture of cube-shaped houses, Byzantine churches and spacious squares. Although its main street has been spoilt by loud tavernas and bars, many backstreets give glimpses into Skýrian homes. Traditional ceramics, wood carving, copper and embroidery are always proudly on display.

Topping the kástro of the old town with its impressive mansion houses are the remains of the **Castle of Lykomedes**, site of both an ancient acropolis and later a Venetian fortress. It is reached through a tunnel underneath the whitewashed **Moní Agíou Georgíou**, which contains a fine painting of St George killing the dragon. The views from the kástro of the bay below are quite breathtaking. Nearby are the remains of two Byzantine churches, and three tiny chapels, with colourful pastel

Immortal Poetry in Plateía Rupert Brooke

pink and blue interiors. The town has two good museums. The **Archaeological Museum** displays some bracelets and pottery that were discovered during excavations of minor Neolithic and Mycenaean sites around the island. The museum also presents a traditional Skýrian town house that has been accurately recreated with local furnishings.

Housed in an old mansion owned by the Faltáits family, the excellent **Faltáits Museum** was opened in 1964 by one of their descendants, Manos Faltáits. It has a diverse collection of folk art including rare books and manuscripts, photographs and paintings, which reveal much about Skýrian history and culture. It not only shows how craftsmen absorbed influences from the Byzantine, Venetian and Ottoman occupations, but also

how the development of a wealthy aristocracy actively helped transform the island's woodcarving, embroidery, ceramics and copperware into highly sophisticated artforms.

One place to learn some of these crafts is the **Skýros Centre**, a unique holiday centre which also has courses in such wide-ranging subjects as yoga, reflexology, creative writing and windsurfing. The main branch is in Skýros town, with another branch at Atsítsa, on the west coast of the island.

Plateía Rupert Brooke, above the town, is famous for its controversial statue of a naked man by M Tómpros. Erected in 1930 in memory of the British poet Rupert Brooke who died on the island, the statue is known as *Immortal Poetry*.

Archaeological Museum
Plateía Brooke. **(** 22220 91327.
(Tue–Sun. **●** main public hols.

Faltáits Museum
Palaiópyrgos. **(** 22220 91232.
(daily. **●** Nov–Mar.

Skýros Centre
(020-7267 4424 *(contact London office for bookings).* **(** Apr–Oct.

ENVIRONS: Beneath Skýros town are the resorts of **Mólos** and **Magaziá**. Around these two resorts there are plenty of decent hotels, tavernas and rooms to rent. Further along the coast from Magaziá, there is another sandy stretch of beach at **Pouriá**, which offers excellent spear-fishing and snorkelling. At **Cape Pouriá** itself, the chapel of Agios Nikólaos is built into a cave. Just off the coast are the islets of Vrikolakonísia where the incurably ill were sent during the 17th century.

The Castle of Lykomedes towering above Skýros town

KEY

For key to map see back flap

VISITORS' CHECKLIST

3,000. ✈ 18 km (11 miles)
NW of Skýros town. 🚢 Linariá.
🚌 Skýros town. ℹ 22220 91600.
📅 Carnival around island: end
Feb–early Mar.

Access to Vounó, the mountainous southern part of the island, is through a narrow fertile valley south of **Ormos Achíli** between the island's two halves. The road continues south to **Kalamítsa** bay, and beyond to **Treis Mpoúkes**, a natural deep-water harbour used by pirates in the past and the Greek Navy today. Reached by dirt-track road, this is also the site of poet Rupert Brooke's simple marble grave, set in an olive grove. Brooke (1887–1915) died on a hospital ship that was about to set sail to fight at Gallipoli.

AROUND THE ISLAND

The island divides into two distinct halves, bisected by the road from Skýros town to the port of Linariá. Meroí, the northern part of the island, is where most people live and farm on the fertile plains of Kámpos and Trachý.

Skýros is famous for its indigenous ponies, thought by some to be the same breed as the horses that appear on the Parthenon frieze (see p286). It is certainly known that the animals have been bred exclusively on Skýros since ancient times and can still be seen in the wild on the island today, particularly in the south, near the grave of Rupert Brooke.

The road running north from Skýros town leads first to the airport and then west around the island through pine forests to **Kalogriá** and **Kyrá Panagiá**,

two leeward beaches sheltered from the *meltémi* (north wind). From here, the road leads to the small village and pine-fringed beach of **Atsítsa**, where there are rooms to rent and a good taverna. As noted above, Atsítsa is also home to the other branch of the Skýros Centre, the island retreat offering alternative holidays. A little way south are the two beaches of **Agios Fokás** and **Péfkos**. The road loops back from Péfkos to the port of Linariá. Caïques depart from here to the inaccessible sea caves at Pentekáli and Diatrýpti on the east coast.

The azure waters and tree-lined sand of Péfkos beach

THE SKYROS GOAT DANCE

This famous goat dance is one of Greece's few rites that have their roots in pagan festivals. It forms the centrepiece of the pre-Lenten festivities in Skýros, celebrated with dancing and feasting. Groups of masquerading men parade noisily around the narrow streets of Skýros town. Each group is led by three central characters, the *géros* (old man), wearing a traditional shepherd's outfit and a goatskin mask and weighed down with noisy bells, the *koréla*, a young man in Skýrian women's clothing, and the *frángos*, or foreigner, a comic figure wearing dishevelled clothes.

The géros in full costume

Evvoia
Εύβοια

AFTER CRETE, EVVOIA IS GREECE'S largest island. It is generally unspoilt by tourism, and its diverse landscape and history make it a microcosm of the whole country. From Macedonian rule in 338 BC, to Turkish government until 1833, the island has suffered many occupations. Traces of Evvoia's mixed history are widely evident, from the range of religious cultures in Chalkída to the descendants of 15th-century Albanian immigrants who still speak their own dialect of Arvanitika.

Cape Artemísio
This is the site of the Battle of Artemisium which took place in 480 BC ❽

Istiaía is the main town in the northern part of the island. It is a pretty market town with sleepy squares *(see p119)*.

Límni
This picturesque fishing town is full of narrow streets lined with white houses, and colourful flowers that pour out on to the pavement ❿

★ **Loutrá Aidipsoú**
Old-fashioned, this charming resort has attracted visitors for centuries with its warm spa waters. Local fishermen still continue their trade in the wide bay ❾

Prokópi
The large Kandíli estate, belonging to the English Noel-Baker family, sits just outside the quiet village of Prokópi ❼

STAR SIGHTS
───────────────
★ **Loutrá Aidipsoú**
───────────────
★ **Kárystos**

Chalkída
A modern town, Chalkída is the capital of the island, and has a mixed populace of Muslims, Jews and Orthodox Greeks. By the waterfront is a flourishing market ❶

Steni
Nestling in the green hills of Mount Dírfys, Stení's cool climate makes it a pleasant escape from the summer heat and a popular place for a day trip **6**

VISITORS' CHECKLIST

🏠 208,000. 🚢 Agiókampos, Erétria, Karystos, Loutrá Aidipsoú, Marmári, Néa Stýra, Paralía Kýmis. 🚌 🚕 Chalkída.
ℹ️ Chalkída (22210 77777).
🎭 Summer Drama Festival in Chalkída: May–Sep.

Kými
A wealthy port in the 1880s, Kými is quieter today, with a fine Folk Museum displaying traditional crafts such as this embroidered picture frame **5**

Ochthoniá
The wild and exposed beaches surrounding Ochthoniá are quiet and often deserted, offering a relaxing break from the busy village **4**

Mount Dírfys, the highest point on Evvoia, is a trekker's paradise *(see p118)*.

★ Kárystos
The traditional seaside and port town of Kárystos is overlooked by the dramatic slopes of Mount Ochi **3**

Lake Dýstos is a large swampy area on the road to Néa Stýra *(see p117)*.

Mount Ochi provides a scenic day's trek with excellent views *(see p117)*.

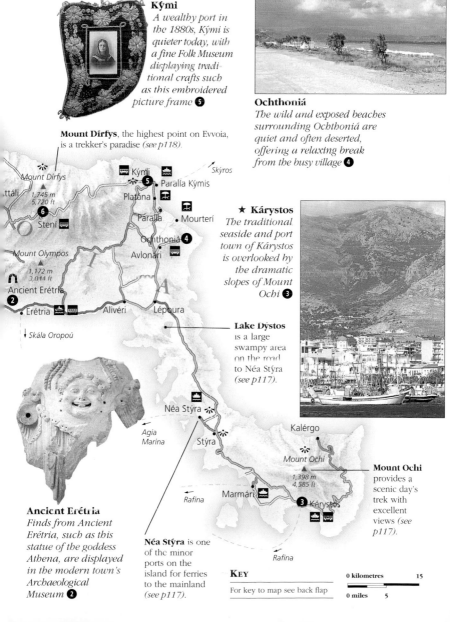

Mount Dírfys
1,745 m
5,720 ft

Kými
Paralía Kýmis
Platána
Paralía
Mourterí
Ochthoniá
Avlonári
Mount Olympos
1,172 m
3,844 ft
Ancient Erétria
Erétria
Alivéri
Lépoura
Skýros

Skála Oropoú

Néa Stýra
Agía Marína
Stýra
Kalérgo
Mount Ochi
1,398 m
4,585 ft
Marmári
Kárystos
Rafína
Rafína

Ancient Erétria
Finds from Ancient Erétria, such as this statue of the goddess Athena, are displayed in the modern town's Archaeological Museum **2**

Néa Stýra is one of the minor ports on the island for ferries to the mainland *(see p117)*.

KEY

For key to map see back flap

0 kilometres   15
0 miles   5

Chalkída ❶
Χαλκίδα

ANCIENT CHALKIS WAS ONE of the major independent
city-states until it was taken by Athens in 506 BC,
and it remained an Athenian ally until 411 BC. Briefly
Macedonian, the town was under Roman rule by 200
BC. There followed the same history of Byzantine,
Frankish and Venetian rule that exists in the Sporades.
A bridge has spanned the fast-flowing Evripos channel
since the 6th century BC. According to legend, Aristotle
was so frustrated at his inability to understand the ever-
changing currents that he threw himself into the water.

VISITORS' CHECKLIST

🏙 75,000. ✈ 🚌 Athinón.
corner of Athanasíou Diákou
& Frízi. 🆘 22210 77777.
🚢 Mon–Sat. 🎭 Agía Paraskeví
celebrations: 26 Jul–1 Aug.

Chalkída's waterfront market

Exploring Chalkída
Although much of modern
Chalkída is dominated by
commercial activity, there are
two areas of the town that are
worth a visit: the waterfront
which overlooks the Evripos
channel, and the old Kástro
quarter, on the slopes
overlooking the seafront.

The Waterfront
Lined with old-fashioned
hotels, cafés and restaurants,
Chalkída's waterfront also
has a bustling enclosed
market where farmers from
the neighbouring villages sell
their produce. This often
leads to chaotic traffic jams
in the surrounding narrow
streets, an area still known by
its Turkish name of Pazári,
where there are interesting
shops devoted to beekeeping
(No. 6 Neofýtou) and other
rural activities.

Kástro
In the old Kástro quarter,
southeast of the Evripos
bridge, the deserted streets
reveal a fascinating architectural history. Many houses
still bear the traces of their
Venetian and Turkish
ancestry, with timbered
façades or marble heraldic

carving. Now inhabited by
Thracian Muslims who settled
here in the 1980s, and the
surviving members of the
oldest Jewish community
in Greece, the Kástro also
has an imposing variety of
religious buildings. Three
examples of these include
the 19th-century **synagogue**
on Kótsou, the beautiful 15th-
century mosque, **Emir Zade**,
in the square marking the
entrance to the Kástro, and
the church of **Agía Paraskeví**.
The mosque is usually
closed, but outside is
an interesting marble
fountain with an
Arabic inscription.
  Agía Paraskeví,
situated near the
Folk Museum,
reveals the diverse
history of Evvoia more
than any other building
in Chalkída. This huge
13th-century basilica is built
on the site of a much earlier
Byzantine church. Its exterior

resembles a Gothic cathedral
but the interior is a patchwork of different styles, a
result of years of modification
by invading peoples, including
the Franks and the Turks. It
has a marble iconostasis, a
carved wooden pulpit, brown
stone walls and a lofty wooden
ceiling. Opposite the church
on a house lintel is a carving
of St Mark's winged lion, the
symbol of Venice.
  Housed in the vaults of the
old Venetian fortress at the
top of the Kástro quarter, the
Folk Museum presents a
jumble of local costumes,
engravings and a bizarre set
of uniforms from a brass band,
suspended with their instruments from the ceiling. The
Archaeological Museum is a
more organized collection
of finds from ancient
Evvoian sites such as
Kárystos. Exhibits
include some 5th-
century BC grave-
stones and vases.

**Roman horse
head in Archaeo-
logical Museum**

🏛 **Folk Museum**
Skalkóta 4. 🆘 22210
21817. ⭕ Wed–Sun. 🚫
🏛 **Archaeological Museum**
Venizélou 13. 🆘 22210 76131.
⭕ Tue–Sun. ⬤ main public hols. 🌀

The 15th-century mosque in the Kástro, home to some Byzantine relics

Around Evvoia

THE FORESTS OF PINE and chestnut trees, rivers and deserted beaches in the fertile north contrast dramatically with the dry and scrubby south. Separated by the central mountains, the south becomes rough and dusty with sheep grazing in flinty fields, snaking roads along cliff tops and the scree slopes of Mount Ochi.

Picturesque Kárystos harbour, with Mount Ochi in the background

Ancient Erétria ❷
Αρχαία Ερέτρια

22 km (14 miles) SE of Chalkída. 🚌

Excavations begun in the 1890s in the town of Néa Psará have revealed the sophistication of the ancient city-state of Erétria, which was destroyed by the Persians in 490 BC and the Romans in AD 198. At the height of its power it had colonies in both Italy and Asia Minor. Although the ancient harbour is silted up, evidence of its maritime wealth can be seen in the ruined agora, temples, gymnasium, theatre and sanctuary, which still remain around the modern town.

Artifacts from the ancient city are housed in the **Archaeological Museum**. The tomb finds include some bronze cauldrons and funerary urns. There are votive offerings from the Temple of Apollo, gold jewellery and a terracotta gorgon's head, which was found in a 4th-century BC Macedonian villa.

Archaeologists have also restored the **House with Mosaics** (ask for the key at the museum). Its floor mosaics are of lions attacking horses, sphinxes and panthers.

🏛 Archaeological Museum
On the road from Chalkída to Alivéri.
📞 22290 62206. ◯ Tue–Sun. 🎦 ♿

ENVIRONS: Past **Alivéri**, with its medieval castle and ugly power station, the road divides at the village of **Lépoura**. Venetian towers can be seen on the hillside here, and also around the Dýstos plain northwards to Kými and south to Kárystos. A road twists through tiny villages such as **Stýra**, with their surrounding wheat fields and olive trees. Below lie the seaside resorts of Néa Stýra and Marmári, both of which provide ferry services to the mainland port of Rafína.

Gorgon's head, Archaeological Museum, Erétria

Kárystos ❸
Κάρυστος

130 km (80 miles) SE of Chalkída.
🏘 4,600. 🚢 🚌

Kárystos, overlooked by the imposing Castel Rosso and the village of Mýloi where plane trees surround the *kafeneía*, is a picturesque town. The modern part of the town dates from the 19th century, and was built during the reign of King Otto. Kárystos has five Neo-Classical municipal buildings, excellent waterfront fish tavernas close to its Venetian Bourtzi fortress and a **Folk Museum**. Set up as a typical Karystian house, the museum contains examples of rural life – copper pots and pans, oil amphorae and ornate 19th-century furniture and embroidery. Kárystos is also famed for its green and white marble and green slate roof and floor tiles.

🏛 Folk Museum
50 m (165 ft) from the town square.
📞 22240 22452.
◯ Apr–Oct: Tue–Sun; Nov–Mar: Wed.
🈂 main public hols.

ENVIRONS: Southeast of Kárystos, remote villages, such as Platonistós and Amigdaliá, hug the slopes of Mount Ochi. Caïques from these villages take passengers on boat trips to visit nearby coves where there are prehistoric archaeological sites.

DRAGON HOUSES

Off the main road at Stýra, a signpost points the way to the enigmatic dragon houses, known locally as *drakóspita*. Red arrows mark the trail that leads to these low structures. Constructed with huge slabs of stone, they take their name from the only creatures thought capable of carrying the heavy slabs. There are many theories about the *drakóspita*, but the most plausible links them to two other similar sites, on the summits of Mount Ochi and Mount Ymittós in

Attica. All three are near marble quarries, and it is believed that Carian slaves from Asia Minor (where there are similiar structures) built them as temples in around the 6th century BC.

Scenic road running through olive groves between Ochthoniá and Avlonári

Ochthoniá ❹
Οχθωνιά

90 km (56 miles) E of Chalkída.
🏃 1,140. 🚌

Both Ochthoniá and its neighbouring village of Avlonári, with their Neo-Classical houses clustered around ruined Venetian towers, are reminiscent of protected Umbrian hill-towns.

A Frankish castle overlooks the village of Ochthoniá, and just west of Avlonári is the distinctive 14th-century basilica of Agios Dimítrios, which is the largest Byzantine church in Evvoia. Beyond the fertile fields that surround these villages, wild beaches, such as those at Agios Merkoúris and Mourterí, stretch out towards the forbidding cliffs of Cape Ochthoniá.

Kými ❺
Κύμη

90 km (56 miles) NE of Chalkída.
🏃 4,000. 🚤 🚌 ⛴ Sat. 🚉
Platána 7 km (4.5 miles) S.

Four km (2 miles) above Paralía Kýmis, lies the thriving town of Kými. With a commanding view of the sea, this remote settlement had surprisingly rich resources, derived from silk production and maritime trading, in the 19th century. In the 1880s,

45 ships from Kými plied the Aegean sea routes. The narrow streets of elegant Neo-Classical houses testify to its past wealth. It is known today mainly for the medicinal spring water from nearby Choneftikó, and a statue in the main square of Dr Geórgios Papanikoláou, Kými's most famous son and inventor of the cervical smear "Pap test". An extensive and well-organized **Folk Museum** contains many exhibits from Kymian life, such as a fine collection of unique cocoon embroideries and costumes. On the road north of Kými, the 17th-century **Moní Metamórfosis tou Sotíra**, now inhabited by nuns, perches on the cliff edge.

Dr Papanikoláou
(1883–1962)

📷 **Folk Museum**
📞 22220 22011. ⏱ by appointment only. ⬤ main public hols.

Steni ❻
Στενή

31 km (20 miles) NE of Chalkída.
🏃 1,250. 🚌

This mountain resort is much loved by Greeks who come for the cool climate and fine scenery. Steni is also popular with hikers setting their sights on Mount Dírfys, the island's highest peak at 1,745 m (5,720 ft), with spectacular views from the summit. A brisk walk followed by a lazy lunch of classic mountain cuisine – grilled meats and oven-baked beans – make for a pleasant day. The main square is also good for shops selling local specialities, such as wild herbs and mountain tea.

The road from Steni to the northern coast snakes up the mountain. It passes through spectacular scenery of narrow gorges filled with waterfalls and pine trees, and cornfields that stretch down to the sea.

Moní Sotíra in the mountains near Kými overlooking the sea

Prokópi **❼**
Προκόπι

52 km (32 miles) NW of Chalkída.
🏃 1,200. 🚌 🚍 Sun. 🚂 Krýa Vrýsi
15 km (9 miles) N

Sleepy at most hours, Prokópi
only wakes when the tourist
buses arrive with pilgrims
coming to worship the remains
of St John the Russian (Agios
Ioánnis o Rósos), housed in
the modern church of Agíou
Ioánnou tou Rósou. Souvenir
shops and hotels around the
village square cater fully for
the visiting pilgrims. In reality
a Ukranian, John was captured
in the 18th century by the
Turks and taken to Prokópi
(present-day Ürgüp) in central
Turkey. After his death, his
miracle-working remains were
brought over to Evvoia by the
Greeks during the exodus from
Asia Minor in 1923.

Prokópi is also famous for
the English Noel-Baker family,
who own the nearby Kandíli
estate and most of the local
land. Although the family have
done much for the region,
local feeling is mixed about
the once-feudal status of this
estate. Many locals, however,
now accept the important role
Kandíli plays in its latest
incarnation as a specialist
holiday centre, by bringing
money into the local economy.

ENVIRONS: The road between
Prokópi and Mantoúdi runs
by the river Kiréa, and a path
leads to one of the oldest trees
in Greece, said to be over
2,000 years old. This huge
plane tree has a circumference
of over 4.5 m (15 ft). Sadly, it
is sinking into the sludge
created by a nearby mine.

Façade of the mansion on the Noel-Baker Kandíli estate, Prokópi

View across the beach at Cape Artemísio

Cape Artemísio **❽**
Ακρωτήριο Αρτεμίσιο

105 km (65 miles) NW of Chalkída.
🚌 to Agriovótano. ℹ️ Agriovótano
(22260 41720). 🚂 Psaropoúli 15 km
(9 miles) SE.

Below the picturesque village
of Agriovótano sits Cape
Artemísio, site of the Battle
of Artemisium. Here
the Persians, led by
King Xerxes, defeat-
ed the Greeks in 480
BC. In 1928, local
fishermen hauled a
famous bronze
statue of Poseidon
out of the sea at the
cape. It is now on
show in the National
Archaeological
Museum in Athens *(see p282).*

Old Mercedes truck delivering produce

ENVIRONS: About 20 km (12
miles) east lies **Istiaía**, a
pleasant market town with
sleepy squares, white chapels
and ochre-coloured houses.

Loutrá Aidipsoú **❾**
Λουτρά Αιδηψού

90 km (56 miles) NW of Chalkída.
🏃 5,000. 🚌 ℹ️ 22260 22456.
🚍 Mon–Sat. 🚂 Giáltra 20 km
(12 miles) SW.

Loutrá Aidipsoú is Greece's
largest spa town, popular
since antiquity for its cure-all
sulphurous waters. These
waters bubble up all over the
town and many hotels are
built directly over hot springs
to provide a supply to their
treatment rooms. In the rock
pools of the public baths by
the sea, the steam rises in
winter scalding the red rocks.

The old hotel Thérmai Sýlla
has a rickety lift and a marble
staircase down to its splendid
basement treatment rooms.
These luxuries are reminders
of the days when the rich and
famous came to take the cure.
Other faded Neo-Classical
hotels along the seafront also
recall the town's days of glory
in the late 19th century.
The town has a relaxed
atmosphere and in
summer the beach
is popular with
Greek families.

ENVIRONS: In the
summer a ferry
service goes across
the bay to **Loutrá
Giáltron** where
warm spring water mixes
with the shallows of a quiet
beach edged by tavernas.

Límni **❿**
Λίμνη

87 km (54 miles) NW of Chalkída.
🏃 2,100. 🚌 ℹ️ 22270 32111.

Once a wealthy 19th-century
seafaring power, the pleasant
town of Límni has elegant
houses, cobbled streets and a
charming seafront. Just south
of the town is the magnificent
Byzantine **Moní Galatáki**, the
oldest monastery on Evvoia,
etched into the cliffs of Mount
Kandíli. Inhabited by nuns
since the 1940s, its church is
covered with beautiful frescoes.
The *Last Judgment* is shown
in particularly gory detail, with
some souls frantically climbing
the ladder to heaven, while
others are dragged mercilessly
into the leviathan's jaws.

THE NORTHEAST AEGEAN ISLANDS

THASOS · SAMOTHRAKI · LIMNOS · LESVOS
CHIOS · IKARIA · SAMOS

*M*ORE THAN ANY OTHER ARCHIPELAGO IN GREECE, *the seven major islands of the Northeast Aegean defy easy categorization. Though they are neighbours, sharing a common history of rule by the Genoese and lively fishing industries, the islands are culturally distinct, encompassing a range of landscapes and lifestyles.*

Although Sámos and Chíos were prominent in ancient times, few traces of that former glory remain. Chíos offers the region's most compelling medieval monuments, including the Byzantine monastery of Néa Moní and the mastic villages, while Sámos has a fascinating museum of artifacts from the long-venerated Heraion shrine. In Límnos's capital, Mýrina, you encounter evidence of the Genoese and Ottoman occupations, in the form of its castle and domestic architecture.

Lésvos shares the fortifications and volcanic origin of Límnos, though the former's monuments are grander and its topography more dramatic. To the south, the islands of Sámos, Chíos and Ikaría have mountainous profiles and are forested with

Assumption of the Virgin by Theófilos (1873–1934), Mytilíni's Byzantine Museum, Lesvos

pine, olive and cypress trees. Most of the pines of Thásos were devastated by forest fires in the 1980s, though Samothráki remains unspoilt; its numerous hot springs and waterfalls, as well as the brooding summit of Mount Fengári, are a counterpoint to the long-hallowed Sanctuary of the Great Gods.

Beaches come in all sizes and consistencies, from the finest sand to melon-sized volcanic shingle. Apart from Thásos, Sámos and Lésvos, package tourism is scarce in the north where summers are shorter. Wild Ikaría, historically a backwater, will appeal mostly to spa-plungers and beachcombers, while its tiny dependency, Foúrnoi, is an ideal do-nothing retreat owing to its convenient beaches and abundant seafood.

Mólyvos harbour, Lésvos, overlooked by the town's 14th-century Genoese castle

◁ The broad, sandy beach near the village of Kámpos, Ikaría

Exploring the Northeast Aegean Islands

FOR ITS BEACHES AND ANCIENT RUINS, both composed of white marble, Thásos is hard to fault, while Samothráki has long been a destination for hardy nature lovers. Less energetic visitors will find Límnos ideal, with picturesque villages and beaches close to the main town. Olive-rich Lésvos offers the greatest variety of scenery but requires time and effort to tour. For first-time visitors to the eastern isles, Sámos is the best touring base, though the cooler climate of Chíos is more attractive, and its main town offers good shopping. Connoisseurs of relatively unspoiled islands will want to sample a slower pace of life on Ikaría, Psará or Foúrnoi.

Kaválta
Thásos Town
THÁSOS
Kamariótissa
SAMOTHRAKI
THRACIAN SEA
Kavála
LÍMNOS
Mýrina
Thessaloníki
Rafína
AGIOS EFSTRATIOS
Vólos
AEGEAN SEA
Rafína
Piraeus, Rafína
PSAR.
Piraeus
Piraeus, Sýros

0 kilometres 20
0 miles 10

Fishing boat in Mólyvos harbour, Lésvos

ISLANDS AT A GLANCE

Chíos *see pp142–8*
Ikaría *see p149*
Lésvos *see pp132–41*
Límnos *see pp130–31*
Sámos *see pp150–53*
Samothráki *see pp128–9*
Thásos *see pp124–7*

Byzantine monastery of Néa Moní, Chíos, seen from the southwest

KEY

━━ Minor road
┈┈ Non-asphalt road
━━ Scenic route
-- High-season, direct ferry route
☀ Viewpoint

Alexandroúpoli

Volcanic landscape near Kontiás, Límnos

SEE ALSO

- *Where to Stay* pp300–301
- *Where to Eat* pp325–6
- *Travel Information* pp356–9

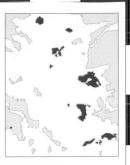

LOCATOR MAP

GETTING AROUND

Thásos and Samothráki have no airports, but are served by ferries from Alexandroúpoli and Kavála on the mainland, while Límnos and Lésvos have air and ferry links with Athens and Thessaloníki. Bus services vary from virtually non-existent on Límnos and Samothráki, or Lesvos's functional schedules, to Thásos's frequent coaches. Chíos, Ikaría and Sámos are served by flights from Athens, and are connected by ferry. Chíos has an adequate bus service but is best explored by car; Sámos has more frequent buses, and is small enough to be toured by motorbike; Ikaría has skeletal public transport and steep roads requiring sturdy vehicles.

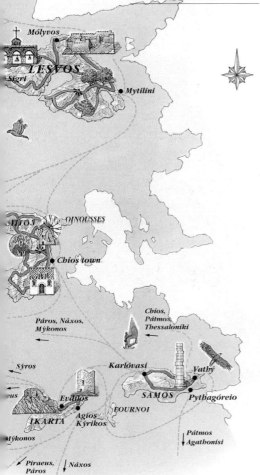

Sandy Messaktí beach, Ikaría

Thásos
Θάσος

T HASOS HAS BEEN INHABITED since the Stone Age, with
settlers from Páros colonizing the east coast during
the 7th century BC. Spurred by revenues from gold deposits near modern Thásos town, Ancient Thásos became
the seat of a seafaring empire, though its autonomy
was lost to the Athenians in 462 BC. The town thrived
in Roman times, but lapsed into medieval obscurity.
Today, the island's last source of mineral wealth is delicate white marble, cut from quarries whose scars are
prominent on the hillsides south of Thásos town.

**Exterior of the Archaeological
Museum, Thásos**

Thásos town harbour, viewed from the agora

Thásos Town ❶
Λιμένας

🏃 3,000. ⛴ 🚌 ℹ️ 25930 23111.
🚪 daily. 🚉 Pachýs 9 km (6 miles) W.

Modern Liménas, also known
as Thásos town, is an undis-
tinguished resort on the coastal
plain which has been settled
for nearly three millennia.
Interest lies in the vestiges

SIGHTS AT A GLANCE

Alykí ❸
Kástro ❻
Megálo Kazavíti ❽
Moní Archangélou Michaïl ❹
Potamiá ❷
Sotíras ❼
Thásos Town ❶
Theológos ❺

of the ancient city and the manner in which they blend into
the modern town. Foundations
of a Byzantine basilica take
up part of the central square,
while the road to Panagiá
cuts across a vast shrine of
Herakles before passing a
monumental gateway.

⋒ Ancient Thásos
Site & Museum 【 25930 22180.
🔾 daily. 🌑 main public hols.
Museum closed to public.
Founded in the 7th century BC,
Ancient Thásos is a complex
series of buildings, only the
remains of which can be seen
today. French archaeologists
have conducted excavations
here since 1911; digs were
recently resumed at a number
of locations in Thásos town.
The **Archaeological Museum**,
next to the agora, houses
treasures from the site.
  Well defined by the ruins
of four stoas, the Hellenistic
and Roman **agora** covers a
vast area behind the ancient
military harbour, today the
picturesque Limanáki, or
fishing port. Though only
a few columns have

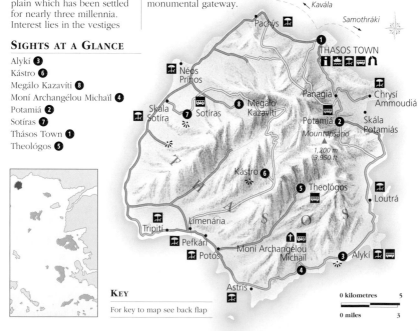

0 kilometres   5

0 miles   3

PLAN OF ANCIENT THASOS

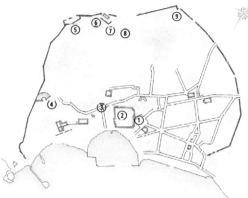

KEY TO PLAN

① Archaeological Museum
② Agora
③ Temple of Dionysos
④ Theatre
⑤ Citadel
⑥ Walls
⑦ Temple to Athena Poliouchos
⑧ Shrine to Pan
⑨ Gate of Parmenon

0 kilometres 5

0 miles 3

The Gate of Parmenon in the
south wall of Ancient Thásos

been re-erected, it is easy to trace the essentials of ancient civic life, including several temples to gods and deified Roman emperors, foundations of heroes' monuments and the extensive drainage system.

Foundations of a **Temple of Dionysos**, where a 3rd-century BC marble head of the god was found, mark the start of the path up to the acropolis. Partly overgrown by oaks, the Hellenistic **theatre** has spectacular views out to sea. The Romans adapted the stage area for their bloody spectacles; it is now being excavated with the intent of complete restoration.

The ancient **citadel**, once the location of an Apollo temple, was rebuilt during the 13th century by the Venetians and Byzantines. It was then ceded by Emperor Manuel II Palaiológos to the Genoese Gatelluzi clan in 1414, who enlarged and occupied it until 1455. Recycled ancient masonry is conspicuous at the south gateway. By the late 5th century BC, substantial walls of more than 4 km (2 miles) surrounded the city, the sections

by the sea having been mostly wrecked on the orders of victorious besiegers in 492 and 462 BC.

Foundations of a **Temple to Athena Poliouchos** (Patroness of the City), dated to the early 5th century BC, are just below the acropolis summit; massive retaining walls support the site terrace. A cavity hewn in the rocky outcrop beyond served

as a **shrine to Pan** in the 3rd century BC; he is depicted in faint relief playing his pipes.

Behind the summit point, a steep 6th-century BC stairway descends to the **Gate of Parmenon** in the city wall. The gate retains its lintel and takes its name from an inscription "Parmenon Made Me" (denoting its mason), on a nearby wall slab.

Columns of the agora, with the town church in the background

Around Thásos Island

THÁSOS IS JUST SMALL ENOUGH to explore by motorbike, though the bus service along the coastal ring road is good and daily hydrofoils link Thásos town with the western resorts. The best beaches are in the south and east, though the coastal settlements are mostly modern annexes of inland villages, built after the suppression of piracy in the 19th century.

Sculpture at the Vágis Museum

Boats in the peaceful harbour of Skála Potamiás

Potamiá **2**

Ποταμιά

9 km (6 miles) S of Thásos town.
🏠 1,000. 🚌 🛳 daily. 🚗 Loutrá 12 km (7 miles) S; Chrysi Ammoudiá 5 km (3 miles) E.

Named after the perennial river in the valley behind, Potamiá is a small village with one of the most popular paths leading to the 1,200-m (3,950-ft) summit of Mount Ipsário. Following bulldozer tracks upstream brings you to the trailhead for the ascent, which is a 7-hour excursion; although the path is waymarked by the Greek Alpine Club, it is in poor condition.

The sculptor and painter Polýgnotos Vágis (1894–1965) was a native of the town, although he emigrated to America at an early age.

Blue-washed house in Panagiá

Before his death, the artist bequeathed most of his works to the Greek state and they are now on display at the small **Vágis Museum**, situated in the village centre. His work has a mythic, dreamlike quality; the most compelling sculptures are representations of birds, fish, turtles and ghostly faces which he carved on to boulders or smaller stones.

🏛 **Vágis Museum**
📞 25930 61400. ⭕ Tue–Sun.

ENVIRONS: Many visitors stay and enjoy the traditional Greek food at **Skála Potamiás,** 3 km (2 miles) east of Potamiá, though **Panagiá,** 2 km (1 mile) north, is the most visited of the inland villages. It is superbly situated above a sandy bay, has

a lively square and many of its 19th-century houses have been preserved or restored.

Alykí **3**

Αλυκή

29 km (18 miles) S of Thásos town.
🚌 🚗 Astris 12 km (7 miles) W.

Perhaps the most scenic spot on the Thasian shore, the headland at Alykí is tethered to the body of the island by a slender spit, with beaches to either side. The westerly cove is fringed by the hamlet of Alykí, which has well-preserved 19th-century vernacular architecture due to its official classification as an archaeological zone. A Doric temple stands over the eastern bay, while behind it, on the headland, are two fine Christian basilicas, dating from the 5th century, with a few of their columns re-erected.

Local marble was highly prized in ancient times; now all that is left of Alykí's quarries are overgrown depressions on the headland. At sea level, "bathtubs" (trenches scooped out of the rock strata) were once used as evaporators for salt-harvesting.

Moní Archangélou Michaïl, perched on its clifftop

Moní Archangélou Michaïl **4**

Μονή Αρχαγγέλου Μιχαήλ

34 km (21 miles) S of Thásos town.
📞 25930 31500. 🚌 ⭕ daily.

Overhanging the sea 3 km (2 miles) west of Alykí, Moní Archangélou Michaïl was founded early in the 12th century by a hermit called Luke, on the spot where a spring had appeared at the behest of the Archangel. Now a dependency of Móni Filothéou on Mount Athos in northern Greece, its most treasured relic is a Holy Nail from the Cross. Nuns have occupied the grounds since 1974.

Slate-roofed house with characteristically large chimney pots, Theológos

Theológos **9**
Θεολόγος

50 km (31 miles) S of Thásos town.
👥 900. 🚌 🚲 daily. 🚕 Potós 10 km (6 miles) SW.

Well inland, secure from attack by pirates, Theológos was the Ottoman era capital of Thásos. Tiered houses still exhibit their typically large chimneys and slate roofs. Generous gardens and courtyards give the village a green and open aspect. A ruined tower and low walls on the hillside opposite are evidence of Theológos's original 16th-century foundation by Greek refugees from Constantinople.

Kástro **6**
Κάστρο

45 km (28 miles) SW of Thásos town.
👥 6. 🚕 Tripití 13 km (8 miles) W of Limenária.

At the centre of Thásos, 500 m (1,640 ft) up in the mountains, the village of Kástro was even more secure than Theológos. Founded in 1403 by Byzantine Emperor Manuel II Palaiológos, it became a stronghold of the Genoese, who fortified the local hill which is now the cemetery. Kástro was slowly abandoned after 1850, when a German mining concession created jobs at Limenária, on the coast below.

This inland hamlet has now been reinhabited on a seasonal basis by sheep farmers. The *kafeneío*, on the ground floor of the former school, beside the church, shelters the single telephone; there is no mains electricity.

Sotíras **7**
Σωτήρας

23 km (14 miles) SW of Thásos town.
👥 12 🚌 🚕 Skála Sotíra 3 km (2 miles) E.

Facing the sunset, Sotíras has the most alluring site of all the inland villages – a fact not lost on the dozens of foreigners who have made their homes here. Under gigantic plane trees watered by a triple fountain, the tables of a small taverna fill the relaxed balcony-like square. The ruin above the church was a lodge for German miners, whose exploratory shafts still yawn on the ridge opposite.

Traditional stone houses with timber balconies, Megálo Kazavíti

Megálo Kazavíti **8**
Μεγάλο Καζαβίτι

22 km (14 miles) SW of Thásos town.
👥 1,650. 🚌 🚲 daily. 🚕 Néos Prínos 6 km (4 miles) NE.

Greenery-shrouded Megálo Kazavíti (officially Áno Prínos) surrounds a central square, which is a rarity on Thásos. There is no better place to find examples of traditional domestic Thasian architecture with its characteristic mainland Macedonian influence: original house features include narrow-arched doorways, balconies and overhanging upper storeys, with traces of the indigo, magenta and ochre plaster pigment that was once commonly used across the Balkans.

Taverna overhung by plane trees in Sotíras village

Samothráki
Σαμοθράκη

🏛 2,700. ⛴ 🚌 Kamariótissa.
🚌 Pachiá Ammos 15 km (9 miles)
SW of Kamariótissa.

WITH VIRTUALLY NO level terrain, except for the western cape, Samothráki is synonymous with the bulk of Mount Fengári. In the Bronze Age the island was occupied by settlers from Thrace. Their religion of the Great Gods was incorporated into the culture of the Greek colonists in 700 BC, and survived under Roman patronage until the 4th century AD. The rawness of the weather seems to go hand in hand with the brooding landscape, making it easy to see how belief in the Great Gods endured.

CHORA

Lying 5 km (3 miles) east of Kamariótissa, the main port of the island, Chóra is the capital of Samothráki. The town almost fills a pine-flecked hollow which renders it invisible from the sea.

With its labyrinthine bazaar, and cobbled streets threading past sturdy, tile-roofed houses, Chóra is the most handsome village on the island. A broad central square with two tavernas provides an elegant vantage point, looking out to sea beyond the Genoese **castle**. Adapted from an earlier Byzantine fort, little other than the castle's gateway remains,

The town of Chóra with the remains of its Genoese castle in the background

though more substantial fortifications can be found downhill at Chóra's predecessor, **Palaiópoli**; here

---

Sanctuary of the Great Gods
Ερείπια του Ιερού των Μεγάλων Θεών

THE SANCTUARY of the Great Gods on Samothráki was, for almost a millennium, the major religious centre of ancient Aeolia, Thrace and Macedonia. There were similar shrines on Límnos and Ténedos, but neither commanded the following or observed the same rites as the one here. Its position in a canyon at the base of savage, plunging crags on the northeast slope of Mount Fengári was perhaps calculated to inspire awe; today, though thickly overgrown, it is scarcely less impressive. The sanctuary was expanded and improved in Hellenistic times by Alexander's descendants, and most of the ruins visible today date from that period.

Nike Fountain
A marble centrepiece, the Winged Victory of Samothráki, once decorated the fountain. It was discovered by the French in 1863 and is now on display in the Louvre, Paris.

The stoa is 90 m (295 ft) long and dates to the early 3rd century BC.

Hall for votive offerings

The theatre held performances of sacred dramas in July, during the annual festival.

Hieron
The second stage of initiation, epopteia, *took place here. In a foreshadowing of Christianity, this involved confession and absolution followed by baptism in the blood of a sacrificed bull or ram. Rites took place in an old Thracian dialect until 200 BC.*

three Gatelluzi *(see p134)* towers of 1431 protrude above the extensive walls of the ancient town.

AROUND THE ISLAND

Easy to get around by bike or on foot, Samothráki has several villages worth visiting on its southwest flank, lost in olive groves or poplars. The north coast is moister, with plane, chestnut and oak trees lining the banks of several rivers. Springs are abundant, and waterfalls meet the sea at Kremastá Nerá to the south. Stormy conditions compound the lack of adequate harbours.

Thérma has been the island's premier resort since the Roman era, due to its hot springs and lush greenery. You

Three Gatelluzi towers at ancient Palaiópoli

can choose among two rustic outdoor pools of about 34° C (93° F), under wooden shelters; an extremely hot tub of 48° C (118° F) in a cottage, only for groups; and the rather sterile modern bathhouse at 39° C (102° C). Cold-plunge fans will find rock pools and low waterfalls 1.5 km (1 mile) east at **Krýa Váthra**. These

are not as impressive or cold as the ones only 45 minutes' walk up the Foniás canyon, 5 km (3 miles) east of Thérma.

The highest summit in the Aegean, at 1,600 m (5,250 ft), is the granite mass of **Mount Fengári**. Although often covered with cloud, it serves year round as a seafaring landmark and the views from the top are superb. In legend, the god Poseidon watched the Trojan War from this mountain. The peak is usually climbed from Thérma as a 6-hour round trip, though there is a longer and easier route up from Profítis Ilías village on its southwest flank.

Arsinoeion

At over 20 m (66 ft) across, this rotunda is the largest circular building known to have been built by the Greeks. It was dedicated to the Great Gods in the 3rd century BC.

VISITORS' CHECKLIST

6 km (4 miles) NE of Kamariótissa. ☐ to Palaiópoli. **Site & Museum** ☎ 25510 41474. ☐ 8:30am–3pm (site till 8:30pm May–Sep) Tue–Sun. ● main public hols. ◉

Sanctuary of Anaktoron

This building was where myesis, *the first stage of initiation into the cult, took place. This involved contact with the* kabiri *mediated by prior initiates.*

The Temenos is a rectangular space where feasts were probably held.

Small theatre

DEITIES AND MYSTERIES OF SAMOTHRAKI

When Samothráki was colonized by Greeks in 700 BC, the settlers combined later Olympian deities with those they found here. The principal deity of Thrace was Axieros, the Great Mother, an earth goddess whom the Greeks identified with Demeter, Aphrodite and Hekate. Her consort was the fertility god Kadmilos and their twin offspring were the *kabiri* – a Semitic word meaning "Great Ones" which soon came to mean the entire divine family. These two deities were later recognized as the *dioskouri* Castor and Pollux, whose emblems were snakes and a star. The cult was open to all comers of any age or gender, free or slave, Greek or barbarian. Details of the mysteries are unknown as adherents honoured a vow of silence.

The twin *kabiri*, Castor and Pollux

The Propylon (monumental gate) was dedicated by Ptolemy II of Egypt in 288 BC.

Museum

Límnos
Λήμνος

THE MYTHOLOGICAL LANDING PLACE OF HEPHAISTOS, the god of metalworking cast out of Olympos by Zeus, Límnos is appropriately volcanic; the lava soil crumbles into broad beaches and grows excellent wine and herbal honey. Controlling the approaches to the Dardanelles, the island was an important outpost to both the Byzantines and the Turks, under whom it prospered as a trading station. The Greek military still controls much of the island, but otherwise it is hard to imagine a more peaceful place.

VISITORS' CHECKLIST

12,000. 22 km (14 miles) NE of Mýrina. Mýrina. Plateía Kída, Mýrina. Town Hall, on the waterfront Mýrina (22540 22200). 15 Aug.

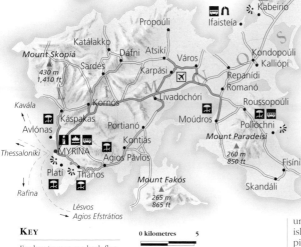

KEY

For key to map see back flap

0 kilometres   5
0 miles   3

been sent to Athens, however, leaving a collection dominated by pottery shards which may only interest a specialist. The most compelling ceramic exhibits are a pair of votive lamps in the form of sirens from the temple at Ifaisteía, while metalwork from Polióchni is represented by bronze tools and a number of decorative articles.

Spread across the headland, and overshadowing Mýrina, the **kástro** boasts the most dramatic position of any North Aegean stronghold. Like others in the region, it was in turn an ancient acropolis and a Byzantine fort, fought over and refurbished by Venetians and Genoese until the Ottomans took the island in 1478. Though dilapidated, the kástro makes a rewarding evening climb for views over western Límnos.

Archaeological Museum
Romeíkos Gialós. 22540 22990. Tue–Sun. main public hols.

Mýrina harbour, overlooked by the kástro in the background

MYRINA
Successor to ancient Mýrina, Límnos's second town in antiquity, modern Mýrina sprawls between two sandy bays at the foot of a rocky promontory. Not especially touristed, it is one of the more pleasant island capitals in the North Aegean, with cobbled streets, an unpretentious bazaar and

imposing, late-Ottoman houses. The most ornate of these cluster behind the northerly beach, Romeíkos Gialós, which is also the centre of the town's nightlife. The south beach, Toúrkikos Gialós, extends beyond the compact fishing port with its half-dozen quayside tavernas. The only explicitly Turkish relic is a fountain on Kída, inscribed with Turkish calligraphy, from which delicious potable water can still be drawn.

Housed in an imposing 19th-century mansion behind Romeíkos Gialós, the recently redesigned **Archaeological Museum** is exemplary in its display of artifacts belonging to the four main ancient cities of Límnos. The most prestigious items have

The volcanic landscape of Límnos, viewed from the village of Kontiás

AROUND THE ISLAND

Though buses run from Mýrina to most villages in summer, the best way to travel around Límnos is by car or motorbike; both can be hired at Mýrina. Southeast from Mýrina, the road leads to **Kontiás**, the third-largest settlement on Límnos, sited between two volcanic outcrops supporting the only pine woods on the island. Sturdily constructed, red-tiled houses, including some fine *belle époque* mansions, combine with the landscape to make this the island's most appealing inland village.

The bay of **Moúdros** was Commonwealth headquarters during the ill-fated 1915 Gallipoli campaign. Many casualties were evacuated to hospital here; the unlucky ones were laid to rest a short walk east of Moúdros town on the road to Roussopoúli. With 887 graves, this ranks as the largest Commonwealth cemetery from either world war in the Greek islands; 348 more English-speaking servicemen lie in another graveyard across the bay at **Portianoú**.

Founded just before 3000 BC, occupying a clifftop site near the village of Kamínia, the fortified town of **Polióchni** predates Troy on the coast of Asia Minor just across the water. Like Troy, which may have been a colony, it was levelled in 2100 BC by an earthquake. It was never resettled. The suddenness of the catastrophe gave many people no time to escape – skeletons were unearthed among the ruins. Polióchni was noted for its metalsmiths, who refined and worked raw ore from Black Sea deposits, and shipped the finished objects to the Cyclades and Crete. A hoard of gold jewellery, now displayed in Athens, was found in one of the houses. Italian archaeologists continue the excavations every summer, and have penetrated four distinct layers since 1930.

The patron deity of Límnos was honoured at **Ifaisteía**, situated on the shores of Tigáni Bay. This was the largest city on the island until the Byzantine era. Most of the site has yet to be completely revealed. Currently, all that is visible are outlines of the Roman theatre, parts of a necropolis and foundations of Hephaistos's temple.

Looking down on the remains of a Roman theatre, Ifaisteía

Rich grave offerings and pottery found on the site can be seen in the Mýrina Archaeological Museum.

The ancient site of the **Kabeirio** (Kavírio in modern Greek) lies across Tigáni Bay from Ifaisteía and has been more thoroughly excavated. The Kabeirioi, or Great Gods, were worshipped on Límnos in the same manner as on Samothráki *(see pp128–9)*, though at this sanctuary little remains of the former shrine and its adjacent stoa other than a number of column stumps and bases.

Below the sanctuary ruins, steps lead down to a sea grotto known as the Cave of Philoctetes. It takes its name from the wounded Homeric warrior who supposedly abandoned here by his comrades on their way to Troy until his infected leg injuries had healed.

OUTLYING ISLANDS

Certainly the loneliest outpost of the North Aegean, tiny, oak-covered **Agios Efstrátios** (named after the saint who was exiled and died here) has scarcely a handful of tourists in any summer. The single port town was damaged by an earthquake in 1967, with dozens of islanders killed; some pre-quake buildings survive above the ferry jetty. Deserted beaches can be found an hour's walk to either side of the port.

Lésvos
Λέσβος

O NCE A FAVOURED SETTING for Roman holidays, Lésvos, with its thick southern forests and idyllic orchards, was known as the "Garden of the Aegean" to the Ottomans. Following conquest by them, in 1462, much of the Greek population was enslaved or deported to Constantinople, and most physical traces of Genoese or Byzantine rule were obliterated by both the Turks and the earthquakes the island is prone to. Lésvos has been the birthplace of a number of artists, its most famous child being the great 7th-century BC lyric poet Sappho.

Ouzo from Plomári

★ Mólyvos
The tourist capital of the island, Mólyvos has a harbour overlooked by a Genoese castle with fine views of Turkey 6

Pétra
This popular resort takes its name from the huge perpendicular rock at its heart. Steps in the rock lead to an 18th-century church on the summit 7

Kalloní
Known mainly for the sardines caught off the coast of nearby Skála Kallonís, this is a crossroads for most of the island's bus routes 8

Antissa
Situated just below a pine grove, this is the largest village in the area. It has several excellent kafeneía in its central square, overshadowed by huge plane trees 9

Moní Ypsiloú
Straddling the summit of an extinct volcano on the edge of a fossilized forest, 12th-century Ypsiloú has a museum of ecclesiastical treasures 10

Sígri
Near the westernmost point of the island, this small chapel stands at the waterfront on the edge of the remote village of Sígri 11

Skála Eresoú
One of the largest resorts on the island, the beach at Eresós lies only a short walk from the birthplace of the poet Sappho 12

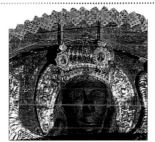

Skála Sykaminiás
Sykaminiá
Kagiá

Lepétymnos
968 m
3,176 ft

Mantamádos
This attractive village
is famous for both
its pottery and the
"black" icon at the
enormous Moní ton
Taxiarchón ❹

Tsónia

Mantamádos ❹

Sykaminiá
The harbour below the hill-town of Sykaminiá,
birthplace of modern novelist Strátis Myrivílis,
is one of the most picturesque in Greece ❺

Agía Paraskeví

Pigí
Thermi

↑ *Límnos*

★ Mytilíni
Just outside Mytilíni is a museum
devoted to the work of the painter
Theófilos Chatzimichaïl ❶

0 kilometres   10

0 miles   5

❸ Agiásos

Kólpos Géras

MYTILÍNI ❶

Olympos
968 m
3,176 ft

Vareiá

Melínta

Agios
Ermogénis

❷ Plomári

Charamída

Agios Isídoros

Oinoússes
& Chios

Plomári
This large coastal resort, with
its Varvagiánnis distillery, is
the ouzo capital of Lésvos ❷

Agiásos
Widely regarded as
the most beautiful
hill-town of the island,
Agiásos's main church
has an icon supposedly
painted by St Luke ❸

STAR SIGHTS

★ **Mólyvos**

★ **Mytilíni**

KEY

For key to map see back flap

Mytilíni ❶
Μυτιλήνη

Ottoman inscription above the castle gate

Modern mytilini has assumed both the name and site of the ancient town. It stands on a slope descending to an isthmus bracketed by a pair of harbours. An examination of Ermoú reveals the heart of a lively bazaar. Its south end is home to a fish market selling species rarely seen elsewhere, while at the north end the roofless shell of the Gení Tzamí marks the edge of the former Turkish quarter. The Turks ruled from 1462 to 1912 and Ottoman houses still line the narrow lanes between Ermoú and the castle rise. The silhouettes of such *belle époque* churches as Agioi Theódoroi and Agios Therápon pierce the tile-roofed skyline.

VISITORS' CHECKLIST

🏛 30,000. ✈ 8 km (5 miles) S.
⛴ 🚌 Pávlou Kountourióti.
ℹ Aristárchou 6 (22510 42511).
🚆 Agios Ermogénis 12 km
(7 miles) S; Charamída 14 km
(9 miles) S. 📅 15 Jul–15 Aug.

The dome of Agios Therápon

⚓ Kástro
📞 22510 27970. ◯ Tue–Sun.
● main public hols.

Surrounded by pine groves, this Byzantine foundation of Emperor Justinian (527–65) still impresses with its huge curtain walls, but it was even larger during the Genoese era. Many ramparts and towers were destroyed during the Ottoman siege of 1462 – an Ottoman Turkish inscription can be seen at the south gate. Over the inner gate the initials of María Palaiologína and her husband Francesco Gatelluzi – a Genoan who helped John Palaiológos regain the Byzantine throne – complete the resumé of the castle's various occupants. The ruins include those of the Gatelluzi palace, a Turkish *medresse* (theological school) and a dervish cell; a Byzantine cistern stands by the north gate.

🏛 Archaeological Museum
Argýris Eftaliótis. **New wing:** Corner of 8 Noemvríou & Melínas Merkoúri.
📞 22510 28032. ◯ Tue–Sun.
● main public hols.

Lésvos's archaeological collection occupies a *belle époque* mansion and a small annexe in its back garden. The most famous exhibits are Roman villa mosaics. Neolithic finds from the 1929–33 British excavations at Thermí, just north of town, can also be seen, while the garden contains grave stelae. A new building nearby displays additional finds.

🏛 Byzantine Museum
Agios Therápon. 📞 22510 28916.
◯ mid-May–mid-Oct: Mon–Sat.

This ecclesiastical museum is devoted almost entirely to exhibiting icons. The collection ranges from the 13th to the 18th century and also includes a more recent, folk-style icon by Theófilos Chatzimichaïl.

ENVIRONS: The **Theófilos Museum**, 3 km (2 miles) south, in Vareiá village, offers four rooms of canvases by Theófilos Chatzimichaïl (1873–1934), the Mytilíni-born artist. All were commissioned by his patron Tériade in 1927 and created over the last seven years of the painter's life. Theófilos detailed the fishermen, bakers and harvesters of rural Lésvos and executed creditable portraits of personalities he met on his travels. For his depictions of historical episodes or landscapes beyond his experience, Theófilos relied on his imagination. The only traces of our age are occasional aeroplanes or steamboats in the background of his landscapes.

Just along the road is the **Tériade Museum**, housing the collection of Stratís Eleftheriádis – a local who emigrated to Paris in the early 20th century, adopting the name Tériade. He became a publisher of avant-garde art and literature. Miró, Chagall, Picasso, Léger and Villon were some of the artists who took part in his projects.

🏛 Theófilos Museum
Mikrás Asías, Vareiá. 📞 22510 41644.
◯ Tue–Sun. ● main public hols.
🏛 Tériade Museum
Vareiá. 📞 22510 23372. ◯ Tue–Sun.
● main public hols.

***Daphnis and Chloe*, by Marc Chagall (1887–1984), in the Tériade Museum**

Olive growing in Greece

THE CRETAN MINOANS are thought to have been the first people to have cultivated the olive tree, around 3800 BC. The magnificent olive groves of modern Greece date back to 700 BC, when olive oil became a valuable export commodity. According to Greek legend, Athena, goddess of peace as well as war, planted the first olive tree in the Athenian Acropolis – the olive has thus become a Greek

Branch of ripening olives

symbol for peace. The 11 million or so olive trees on Lésvos are reputed to be the most productive oil-bearing trees in the Greek islands, Crete produces more and better-quality oil, but no other island is so dominated by olive monoculture. The fruits can be cured for eating throughout the year, or pressed to provide a nutritious and versatile oil; further crushing yields oil for soap and lanterns, and the pulp is a good fertilizer.

In myth, the olive is a virgin tree, sacred to Athena, tended only by virgin males. Its abundant harvest has been celebrated in verse, song and art since antiquity. This vase shows three men shaking olives from a tree, while a fourth gathers the harvest into a basket.

Olive groves *on Lésvos largely date from after a killing frost in 1851. The best olives come from the hillside plantations between Plomári and Agiásos, founded in the 18th century by local farmers desiring land relatively inaccessible to Turkish tax collectors.*

Greek olive oil, *greenish-yellow after pressing, is believed by the Greeks to be of a higher quality than its Spanish and Italian counterparts, owing to hotter, drier summers which promote low acid levels in olive fruit.*

The olive harvest *on Lésvos takes place from late November to late December. Each batch is brought to the local elaiotriveío (olive mill), ideally within 24 hours of being picked, pressed separately and tested for quality.*

TYPES OF OLIVE

From the mild fruits of the Ionians to the small, rich olives of Crete, the Greek islands are a paradise for olive lovers.

Kalamáta, the most famous Greek olive, is glossy-black, almond-shaped and cured in red-wine vinegar.

Elítses are small, sweetly flavoured olives from the island of Crete.

Tsakistés are picked young and lightly cracked before curing in brine.

Throúmpes are a true taste of the countryside, very good as a simple mezés with olive-oil bread.

Thásos olives are salt-cured and have a strong flavour that goes well with cheese.

Ionian greens are mild, mellow-flavoured olives, lightly brine-cured.

Around Eastern Lésvos

Miraculous icon of Agiásos

EASTERN LESVOS is dominated by the two peaks of Lepétymnos in the north and Olympos in the south, both reaching the same height of 968 m (3,176 ft). Most of the island's pine forests and olive groves are found here, as well as the two major resort areas and the most populous villages after the port and capital. There are also several thermal spas, the most enjoyable being at Loutrá Eftaloús, near Mólyvos.

With an early start from Mytilíni, which provides bus connections to all main towns and villages, the east of the island can be toured in a single day.

Plomári **②**
Πλωμάρι

42 km (26 miles) SW of Mytilíni.
🚶 3,600. 🚌 ⛴ Mon–Sat.
🚉 Agios Isidoros, 3 km (2 miles) NE; Melinta, 6 km (4 miles) NW.

Plomári's attractive houses spill off the slope above its harbour and stretch to the banks of the usually dry Sedoúntas river which runs through the central commercial district. The houses date mostly from the 19th century, when Plomári became wealthy through its role as a major shipbuilding centre. Today, Plomári is known as the island's "ouzo capital", with five distilleries in operation, the most famous being Varvagiánnis.

Agiásos **③**
Αγιάσος

28 km (17 miles) W of Mytilíni.
🚶 3,500. 🚌 ⛴ Mon–Sat.
🚉 Vaterá, 31 km (19 miles) S.

Hidden in a forested ravine beneath Mount Olympos, Agiásos is possibly the most beautiful hill-town on Lésvos. It began life in the 12th century as a dependency of the central monastic church of the **Panagía Vrefokratoússa** which was constructed to enshrine a miraculous icon reputed to have been painted by St Luke.

After exemption from taxes by the Sultan during the 18th century, Agiásos swelled rapidly with Greeks fleeing hardship elsewhere on the island. The town's tiled houses and narrow, cobbled lanes have changed little in recent years, except for stalls of locally crafted souvenirs which line the way to the church with its belfry and surrounding bazaar. The presence of shops built into the church's foundations, with rents going towards its upkeep, is an ancient arrangement. It echoes the country-fair element of the traditional religious *panigýria* (festivals), where pilgrims once came to buy and sell as well as perform devotions. Agiásos

Ouzo

Ouzo is the Greek version of a spirit found throughout the Mediterranean. The residue of grape skins left over from wine-pressing is boiled in a copper still to make a distillate originally called raki. The term ouzo may derive from the Italian *uso Massalia*, used to label early shipments leaving the Ottoman Empire for Marseille. Today it means a base of raki flavoured with star anise or fennel. Ouzo's alcohol content varies from 38–48 per cent, with 44 per cent considered the minimum for a quality product. When water is added, ouzo turns milky white – this results from the binding of anethole, an aromatic compound found in fennel and anise.

musicians are hailed as the best on Lésvos – they are out in force during the 15 August festival of the Assumption of the Virgin, considered one of the liveliest in Greece. The pre-Lenten carnival is also celebrated with verve at Agiásos; there is a special club devoted to organizing it.

Mantamádos **④**
Μανταμάδος

36 km (22 miles) NW of Mytilíni.
🚶 1,500. 🚌 ⛴ Mon–Sat.
🚉 Tsónia, 12 km (7 miles) N.

The attractive village of Mantamádos is famous for its pottery industry and the adjacent **Moní Taxiarchón**. The existing monastery dates from the 17th century and houses a black icon of the Archangel Michael, reputedly made from mud and the blood of monks slaughtered in an Ottoman raid. A bull is publicly sacrificed here on the third Sunday after Easter and its meat eaten in a communal stew, the first of several such rites on the island's summer festival calendar. Mantamádos ceramics come in a wide

Plomári, viewed from the extended jetty

Fishing boats at Mólyvos harbour with the castle in the background

range of sizes and colours, from giant *pythária* (olive oil containers) to smaller *koumária* (ceramic water jugs).

Sykaminiá ❺
Συκαμινιά

46 km (29 miles) NW of Mytilíni. 👥 300. 🚌 🚤 Mon–Sat. 🚢 *Kágia 4 km (2 miles) E; Skála Sykaminiás, 2 km (1 mile) N.*

Flanked by a deep valley and overlooking the straits to the Asia Minor coast, Sykaminiá has the most spectacular position of any village on Mount Lepétymnos, which stands at a height of 968 m (3,176 ft). Novelist Efstrátios Stamatópoulos (1892–1969), known as Strátis Myrivílis, was born close to the atmospheric central square. The jetty church, which featured in his novel *The Mermaid Madonna*, can be seen down in Skála Sykaminiás. One of Skála's tavernas is named after the *mouriá* or mulberry tree in which Myrivílis slept on hot summer nights.

Mólyvos (Míthymna) ❻
Μόλυβος (Μήθυμνα)

61 km (38 miles) NW of Mytilíni. 👥 1,500. 🚌 ℹ️ 22530 71347. 🚤 Mon–Sat.

Situated in a region celebrated in antiquity for its vineyards, Mólyvos is the most popular and picturesque town on Lésvos. It was the birthplace of Arion, the 7th-century BC

poet, and the site of the grave of Palamedes, the Achaian warrior buried by Achilles. According to legend, Achilles besieged the city until the king's daughter fell in love with him and opened the gates – though he killed her for her treachery. There is little left of the ancient town apart from the tombs excavated near the tourist office, but its ancient name, Míthymna, has been revived and is used as an alternative to Mólyvos (a Hellenization of the Turkish "Molova").

Before 1923 over a third of the population was Muslim, forming a landed gentry who built many sumptuous three-storey town houses and graced Mólyvos with a dozen street fountains, some of which retain original ornate inscriptions. The mansions, or *archontiká*, are clearly influenced by eastern architecture *(see p18)*; the living spaces are arranged on the top floor around a central stairwell, or *chagiáti* – a design which had symbolic, cosmological meaning in the original Turkish mansions from which it was taken. The picturesque harbour and cobbled lanes of tiered stone houses are all protected by law; any new development must conform architecturally with the rest of the town.

Overlooking the town, and affording splendid views of the Turkish coast, stands a sizeable Byzantine **kástro**.

The castle was modified by the Genoese adventurer Francesco Gatelluzi *(see p134)* in 1373, though it fell into Turkish hands during the campaign of Mohammed the Conqueror in 1462. Restored in 1995, the castle still retains its wood and iron medieval door and a Turkish inscription over the lintel. During summer, the interior often serves as a venue for concerts and plays.

As you head down to the port, the **Archaeological Museum** is worth visiting for its artifacts from Ancient Míthymna. A boatyard operates at the fishing harbour, a reminder of the days when Mólyvos was one of the island's major commercial ports.

🏛 **Kástro**
📞 22530 71803. ⬜ May–Oct: 8:30am–3pm Tue–Sun; Jun–Sep: 8am–7pm Tue–Sun 🟥 main public hols. 🈲
🏛 **Archaeological Museum**
⬜ Phone tourist office for details.

Colourfully restored Ottoman-style houses in Mólyvos

Tiered stone houses rising above the picturesque harbour of Mólyvos ▷

Around Western Lésvos

THOUGH MOSTLY TREELESS AND CRAGGY, western Lésvos has a severe natural beauty, broken by inland villages, beach resorts and three of Lésvos's most important monasteries. Many of the island's famous horses are bred in this region, and where the streams draining the valleys meet the sea, reedy oases form behind the sand providing a haven for bird-watchers during spring. Bus schedules are too infrequent for touring the area, but cars can be hired at Mólyvos.

Tiered houses of the village of Skalochóri

Pétra **❼**
Πέτρα

55 km (34 miles) NW of Mytilíni.
🏠 1,000. ▦ 🚤 Anaxos 3 km (2 miles) W.

The village of Pétra takes its name (meaning "rock") from the volcanic monolith at its centre. By its base is the 16th-century basilica of **Agios Nikólaos**, still with its original frescoes, while a flight of 103 steps climbs to the 18th-century church of **Panagía Glykofiloúsa** church. The **Archontikó Vareltzídainas**, one of the last of the Ottoman dwellings once widespread on Lésvos (see p137), is also 18th century.

▦ Archontikó Vareltzídainas
Sapphous. 【 22530 41510.
◯ Tue–Sun. ⬤ main public hols.

Kalloní **❽**
Καλλονή

40 km (25 miles) NW of Mytilíni.
🏠 1,600. ▦ 🚌 Mon–Sat.
🚤 Skála Kallonis 2 km (1 mile) S.

An important crossroads and market town, Kalloní lies 2 km (1 mile) inland from its namesake gulf. Sardines are netted at the beach of **Skála Kallonís**.

ENVIRONS: In 1527, the abbot Ignatios founded the rambling complex of **Moní Leimónos**, the second most important monastery on Lésvos. You can still view his cell, maintained as a shrine. A carved wood ceiling, interior arcades and a holy spring distinguish the central church. Moní Leimónos also has various homes for the infirm, a mini-zoo and two museums: one ecclesiastical and one of folkloric miscellany.

🏠 Moní Leimónos
5 km (3 miles) NW of Kalloní.
【 22530 22289. **Ecclesiastical Museum** ◯ daily. **Folk Museum** ◯ on request.

Antissa **❾**
Άντισσα

76 km (47 miles) NW of Mytilíni.
🏠 1,410. ▦ ◯ daily.
🚤 Kámpos 4 km (2.5 miles) S.

The largest village of this part of Lésvos, Antissa merits a halt for its fine central square alone, in which a number of cafés and tavernas stand overshadowed by three huge plane trees. The ruins of the eponymous ancient city, destroyed by the Romans in 168 BC, lie 8 km (5 miles) below by road, near the remains of the Genoese **Ovriókastro**. This castle stands on the shore, east of the tiny fishing port of Gavathás and the long sandy beach of Kámpos.

ENVIRONS: Although, unlike Antissa, there is no view of the sea, **Vatoússa**, 10 km (6 miles) east, is the area's most attractive village. Tiered **Skalochóri**, another 3 km (2 miles) north, does overlook the north coast and – like most local villages – has a ruined mosque dating to the days before the 1923 Treaty of Lausanne (see p39).
Hidden in a lush river valley, 3 km (2 miles) east of Antissa, stands the 16th-century **Moní Perivolís**, situated in the middle of a riverside orchard. The narthex features three 16th-century frescoes, restored in the 1960s: the apocalyptic the *Earth and Sea Yield Up Their Dead*, the *Penitent Thief of Calvary* and the *Virgin* (flanked by Abraham). The interior is lit by daylight only, so it is advisable to visit the monastery well before dusk.

Frescoes adorning the narthex of Moní Perivolís

Moní Ypsiloú
Μονή Υψηλού

62 km (39 miles) NW of Mytilíni
📞 22530 56259. ○ daily.

Spread across the 511-m
(1,676-ft) summit of Mount
Ordymnos, an extinct volcano,
Moní Ypsiloú was founded in
the 12th century and is now
home to just four monks. It has
a handsome double gate, and
a fine wood-lattice ceiling in its
katholikón (main church) beside which a rich exhibition of
ecclesiastical treasures can be
found. In the courtyard outside
stand a number of fragments of
petrified trees. The patron saint
of the monastery is John the
Divine (author of the book of
Revelation), a typical dedica-
tion for religious communities
located in such wild, forbidding scenery.

Triple bell tower of Moní Ypsiloú

ENVIRONS: The main entry to
Lésvos's **petrified forest** is just
west of Ypsiloú. Some 15 to
20 million years ago, Mount
Ordymnos erupted, beginning
the process whereby huge
stands of sequoias, buried in
the volcanic ash, were transformed into stone.

Sígri ⑪
Σίγρι

93 km (58 miles) NW of Mytilíni.
👤 400. ➥

An 18th-century Ottoman
castle and the church of **Agía
Triáda** dominate this sleepy
port, protected from severe
weather by long, narrow Nisópi
island. Sígri's continuing
status as a naval base has
discouraged tourist development, though it has a couple
of small beaches; emptier ones
are only a short drive away.

The peaceful harbour of Sígri

Skála Eresoú ⑫
Σκάλα Ερεσού

89 km (55 miles) W of Mytilíni town.
👤 1,500. ➥

Extended beneath the acropolis of ancient Eresós, the
wonderful, long beach at Skála
Eresoú supports the island's
third-largest resort. By climbing
the acropolis hill, you can spot
the ancient jetty submerged in
the modern fishing anchorage.
Little remains at the summit, but
the Byzantine era is represented
in the ancient centre by the
foundations of the basilica of
Agios Andreás; its 5th-century
mosaics await restoration.

ENVIRONS: The village of
Eresós, 11 km (7 miles)
inland, grew up as a refuge
from medieval pirate raids;
a vast, fertile plain extends
between the two settlements.
Two of Eresós's most famous
natives were the philosopher
Theophrastos, a pupil of
Aristotle *(see p55)*, and
Sappho, one of the greatest
poets of the ancient world.

SAPPHO, THE POET OF LESVOS

One of the finest lyric poets of any era, Sappho (c.615–562 BC)
was born, probably at Eresós, into an aristocratic family and
a society that gave women substantial freedom. In her own
day, Sappho's poems were known across the Mediterranean,
though Sappho's poetry was to be suppressed by the
church in late antiquity and now survives only in short
quotations and on papyrus scraps. Many of her poems
were also addressed to women, which has prompted
speculation about Sappho's sexual orientation. Much of her
work was inspired by female companions: discreet
homosexuality was unremarkable in her time. Even less

certain is the manner of her
death; legend asserts that she
fell in love with a younger
man whom she pursued as
far as the isle of Lefkáda.
Assured that unrequited
love could be cured by
leaping from a cliff, she did
so and drowned in the sea:
an unlikely, and unfortunate,
end for a poet reputed to be
the first literary lesbian.

Chíos
Χíος

Aℓℓℓℓℓℓℓℓℓ Cℕℐℴℴ has been prosperous since antiquity, today's island is largely a product of the Middle Ages. Under the Genoese, who controlled the highly profitable trade in gum mastic *(see pp144–5)*, the island became one of the richest in the Mediterranean. It continued to flourish under the Ottomans until March 1822, when the Chians became the victims of one the worst massacres *(see p147)* of the Independence uprising. Chíos had only partly recovered when an earthquake in 1881 caused severe damage, particularly in the south.

Shopfront in Chíos town bazaar

Chíos Town ❶
Χíος

🏠 25,000. ⛴ 🚌 *Polytechníou (around island), Dimokratías (environs).* ℹ️ *Kanári 18 (22710 44389).* 🏪 *Mon– Sat.* 🚕 *Karfás 7 km (4 miles) S.*

Chíos town, like the island, was settled in the Bronze Age and was colonized by the Ionians from Asia Minor by the 9th century BC. The site was chosen for its convenient position for travelling to the Turkish mainland opposite, rather than good anchorage: a series of rulers have been obliged to construct long breakwaters as a consequence. Though it is a modernized island capital (few buildings predate the earthquake of 1881), there are a number of museums and other scattered relics from the town's eventful past. Besides the kástro,

the most interesting sights are the lively bazaar at the top of Roïdou, and an ornate Ottoman fountain dating to 1768 at the junction of Martýron and Dimarchías.

♣ Kástro
Maggiora. ☎ *22710 22819.* ⬜ *daily.* ♿
The most prominent medieval feature of the town is the kástro, a Byzantine foundation improved by the Genoese after they acquired Chíos in 1346. Today the kástro lacks the southeasterly sea rampart, which fell prey to developers after the devastating earthquake in 1881. Its most impressive gate is the southwesterly Porta Maggiora; a deep dry moat runs from here around to the northwest side of the walls. Behind the walls, Ottoman-era houses line narrow lanes of what were once the Muslim and Jewish quarters of the town; after the Ottoman conquest, in 1566, Orthodox and Catholics were required to live out-side the walls. Also inside, a disused mosque, ruined Turkish baths and a small

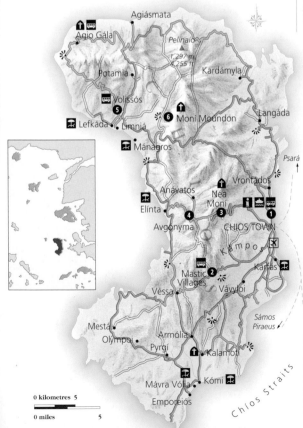

KEY
For key to map see back flap

↓ *Sámos*

SIGHTS AT A GLANCE

Avgónyma ❹
Chíos Town ❶
Mastic Villages ❷
Moní Moúndon ❻
Néa Moní ❸
Volissós ❺

0 kilometres 5

0 miles 5

Chíos town waterfront with the dome and minaret of the Mecidiye Mosque

VISITORS' CHECKLIST

🏠 45,000. ✈ 4 km
(2 miles) S of Chíos town.
🚌 Chíos town.
ℹ Chíos town (22710 44389).

Ottoman cemetery can be found. The latter contains the grave and headstone of Admiral Kara Ali who commanded the massacre of 1822. He was killed aboard his flagship when it was destroyed by the Greek captain Kanáris.

Porta Maggiora, the southwesterly entrance to the kástro

🏛 Justiniani Museum

Kástro. 📞 22710 22819. ◯ Tue–Sun. ⬤ main public hols. 🎟

This collection is devoted to religious art and includes a 5th-century AD floor mosaic rescued from a neglected Chian chapel. The saints featured on the icons and frescoes include Isídoros, who is said to have taught the islanders how to make liqueur from mastic (see pp144–5), and Matrona, a martyr of Roman Ankara whose veneration here was introduced by refugees from Asia Minor after 1923.

🏛 Byzantine Museum

Plateia Vounakíou. 📞 22710 26866. ◯ Tue–Sun. ⬤ main public hols. 🎟

Though called the Byzantine Museum, this is little more than an archaeological warehouse and restoration workshop. It is housed within the only mosque to have survived intact in the East Aegean, the former Mecidiye Cami, which still retains its minaret. A number of Jewish, Turkish and Armenian gravestones stand propped up in the courtyard, attesting to the multiethnic population of the island during the medieval period.

🏛 Philip Argéntis Museum

Koraïs 3. 📞 22710 44246. ◯ 8am–2pm Mon–Fri, 5–7:30pm Fri, 8am–noon Sat. 🎟

Endowed in 1932 by a member of a leading Chian family and occupying the floor above the Koraïs library, this collection features rural wooden implements, plus examples of traditional embroidery and costumes. Also on view, alongside a number of portraits of the Argéntis family, are rare engravings of islanders and numerous copies of the Massacre at Chíos by Delacroix (1798–1863). This painting, as much as any journalistic dispatch, aroused the sympathy of Western Europe for the Greek revolutionary cause (see pp38–9). The main core of the Koraïs library, situated on the ground floor, consists of a number of books and manuscripts bequeathed by the cultural revolutionary and intellectual Adamántios Koraïs (1748–1833); these include works given by Napoleon.

ENVIRONS: The fertile plain known as the **Kampos** extends 6 km (4 miles) south of Chíos town. The land is crisscrossed by a network of unmarked lanes which stretch between high stone walls that betray nothing of what lies behind. However, through an ornately arched gateway left open, you may catch a glimpse of what were once the summer estates of the medieval Chian aristocracy.

Several of the mansions were devastated by the 1881 earthquake, but some have been restored with their blocks of multicoloured sandstone arranged so that the different shades alternate. Many of them still have their own waterwheels, which were once donkey-powered and drew water up from 30-m (98-ft) deep wells into open cisterns shaded by a pergola and stocked with fish. These freshwater pools, which are today filled by electric pumps, still irrigate the vast orange, lemon and tangerine orchards for which the region is widely known.

Detail of Delacroix's Massacres de Chíos (1824) in the Philip Argéntis Museum

Mastic Villages ❷
Μαστιχοχώρια

T HE 20 SETTLEMENTS in southern Chíos known as the *mastichochória*, or "mastic villages", received their name from their most lucrative medieval product. Genoese overlords founded the villages well inland as an anti-pirate measure during the 14th and 15th centuries. Constructed to a design unique in Greece, they share common defensive features made all the more necessary by the island's proximity to the Turks. Though they were the only villages to be spared in the 1822 massacres *(see p147)*, most have had their architecture compromised by both earthquake damage and ill-advised modernization.

Armólian pottery

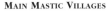

MAIN MASTIC VILLAGES

Fortification towers guarded each corner of the village.

Houses reached three storeys, with vaulted ceilings except on the top floor.

Véssa
This is the one village whose regular street plan can easily be seen from above while descending from Agios Geórgios Sykoúsis or Eláta.

Narrow passages were overarched by flying buttresses, to limit earthquake damage.

Streets followed an intricate grid plan designed to confuse strangers.

Pyrgí
Pyrgí is renowned for its bright houses, many patterned with xystá *("grating") decoration. Outer walls are plastered using black sand and coated with whitewash. This is then carefully scraped off in repetitive geometric patterns, revealing the black undercoat. An example of this is the church of Agioi Apóstoloi which also has medieval frescoes.*

Armólia
One of the smallest and simplest of the mastichochória, *Armólia is renowned for its pottery industry.*

Flat roofs of adjacent buildings were ideally of the same height to facilitate escape.

Olýmpoi

Olýmpoi is almost square in layout. Its central tower has survived to nearly its original height, and today two cafés occupy its ground floor. Here local men and women can be seen winnowing mastic.

VISITORS' CHECKLIST

28 km (17 miles) SW of Chíos town. 🚌 Pyrgí: 1,200; Mestá: 400; Olýmpoi: 350. 🚌 Mestá. 🌊 Mávra Vólia & Kómi 5 km (3 miles) SE of Pyrgí.

Vávyloi
The 13th-century Byzantine church of Panagía tis Krínis, on the edge of the village, is famed for its frescoes and its alternating courses of stone- and brickwork.

A square tower in the centre of the village was the last refuge in troubled times.

MASTIC PRODUCTION

The mastic bush of southern Chíos secretes a resin or gum that, before the advent of petroleum-based products, formed the basis of paints, cosmetics and medicines. Today it is made into chewing gum, liqueur and even toothpaste. About 300 tonnes of gum are harvested each summer through incisions in the bark, which weep resin "tears"; once solidified a day later, the resin is scraped off and spread to air-cure on large trays.

Mastic bush bark and crystals

Crystals separated from the bark

The outer circuit of houses doubled as a perimeter wall.

MESTA

Viewed here from the southwest, Mestá is considered the best preserved of the mastic villages. It has the most even roof heights and still retains its perimeter corner towers.

Taxiárchis Church
Mestá's 19th-century church, the largest on Chíos, dominates the central square. The atmospheric interior has a fine carved altar screen.

Néa Moní ●

Νέα Μονή

St Anne mosaic, inner narthex

H IDDEN IN A WOODED VALLEY 11 km (7 miles) west of Chíos town, the monastery of Néa Moní and its mosaics – some of Greece's finest – both date from the 11th century. It was established by Byzantine Emperor Constantine IX Monomáchos in 1042 on the site where three hermits found an icon of the Virgin. It reached the height of its power after the fall of the Byzantine Empire, and remained influential until the Ottoman reprisals of 1822. Néa Moní has now been a convent for decades, but when the last nun dies it is to be taken over again by monks.

Néa Moní, viewed from the west

St Joachim mosaic

The belfry is a modern structure, added after the 1881 earthquake.

Narthex

Seen here with the main church dome in the background, the narthex contains the most complex mosaics. Twenty-eight saints are depicted, including St Anne, the only woman. The Virgin with Child adorns the central dome.

Ornate marble inlays were highly prized in the Byzantine Empire.

STAR FEATURES

★ **Anástasis**

★ **Christ Washing the Disciples' Feet**

★ **Christ Washing the Disciples' Feet**

Here Christ washes the feet of Peter, who indicates he wishes his head and hands also to be bathed.

★ **Anástasis**
After the Resurrection, Christ rescues Adam and Eve from Hell before entering Heaven

St Mark the Evangelist mosaic

The dome was repaired after the 1881 earthquake, though its magnificent Pantokrátor was lost.

Descent from the Cross mosaic

The main apse has a mosaic of the Virgin. It is positioned above the walls and represents earthly subjects, while the dome depicts Christ.

Altar screen

Byzantine Clock
Standing beneath the Crucifixion mosaic, this Armenian-made clock came from Smyrna after its destruction in 1922.

THE MASSACRE AT CHÍOS

After 250 years of Ottoman rule, the Chians joined the Independence uprising in March 1822, incited by Samian agitators. Enraged, the Sultan sent an expedition that massacred 30,000 Chians, enslaved almost twice that number and brutally sacked most of the monasteries and houses. Many Chians fled to Néa Moní for safety, but they and most of the 600 monks were also killed. Just inside the main gate of the monastery stands a chapel containing the bones of those who died here. The savagery of the Turks is amply illustrated by the axe-wounds visible on many skulls, including those of children.

The floor is covered with marble segments which echo the disciplined architecture of the nave.

Betrayal in the Garden
A detail of this mosaic shows Peter lopping off the ear of Malchus, the High Priest's servant, following the betrayal of Jesus in Gethsemane. Unfortunately, the Kiss of Judas has been damaged.

Cabinet containing the skulls of the Chian martyrs of 1822

Around Chíos Island

Ceiling detail at Moní Moúndon

WITH ITS VERDANT, semi-mountainous terrain, edged by rocky cliffs in the south and sandy beaches to the north-west, Chíos is one of the Aegean's most beautiful isles. Roads and public transport radiate in all directions from Chíos town and the best bus service is to be found on the densely populated southeast coast; to explore anywhere else you need to hire a taxi, car or powerful motorbike.

Avgónyma **4**
Αυγώνυμα

20 km (12 miles) W of Chíos town.
🚶 15. 🚏 Elinta 7 km (4 miles) W.

This is the closest settlement to Néa Moní *(see pp146–7)* and the most beautiful of the central Chian villages, built in a distinct style: less labyrinthine and claustrophobic than the mastic villages, and more elegant than the houses of northern Chíos. The town's name means "clutch of eggs", perhaps after its clustered appearance when viewed from the ridge above. Virtually every house has been tastefully restored in recent years by Greek-Americans with roots here. The medieval *pýrgos* (tower) on the main square, with its interior arcades, is home to the excellent central taverna.

ENVIRONS: Few Chian villages are as striking glimpsed from a distance as **Anávatos**, 4 km (2 miles) north of Avgónyma. Unlike Avgónyma, Anávatos has scarcely changed in recent

decades; shells of houses blend into the palisade on which they perch, overlooking occasionally tended pistachio orchards. The village was the scene of a particularly traumatic incident during the atrocities of 1822 *(see p147)*. Some 400 Greeks threw themselves into a ravine from the 300-m (985-ft) bluff above the village, choosing suicide rather than death at the hands of the Turks.

Volissós **5**
Βολισσός

40 km (25 miles) NW of Chíos town.
🚶 500. 🚌 🚏 Mánagros 2 km (1 mile) SW.

Volissós was once the primary market town for the 20 smaller villages of northwestern Chíos, but today the only vestige of its former commercial standing is a single saddlery on the western edge of town. The strategic importance of medieval Volissós is borne out by the crumbled hilltop castle, erected by the Byzantines in the 11th century and repaired

One of the many restored stone houses of Avgónyma

by the Genoese in the 14th. The town's stone houses stretch along the south and east flanks of the fortified hill; many have been bought and restored by Volissós's growing expatriate population.

ENVIRONS: Close to the village of **Agio Gála**, 26 km (16 miles) northwest of Volissós, two 15th-century chapels can be found lodged in a deep cavern near the top of a cliff. The smaller, hindmost chapel is the more interesting of the two; it is built entirely within the grotto and features a sophisticated and mysterious fresco of the *Virgin and Child* in its apse. The larger chapel, which stands at the entrance to the cave, boasts an intricate carved *témblon* or altar screen. Agio Gála can be reached by bus from Volissós and admission to the churches should be made via the resident warden who holds the keys.

The largely deserted town of Anávatos with the few inhabited dwellings in the foreground

Moní Moúndon **6**
Μονή Μούνδων

35 km (22 miles) NW of Chios town
☎ 22740 21230. ▓ to Volissós.
◯ daily (ask for key at first house in
Diefha village).

Founded late in the 16th
century, this picturesque
monastery was once second
in importance to Néa Moní
(see pp146–7). The katholikón
(or central church) has a
number of interesting late-
medieval murals, the most
famous being the *Salvation of
Souls on the Ladder to Heaven*.
Although the church is only
open to the public during the
monastery's festival (29
August), the romantic setting
makes the stop worthwhile.

Moúndon's *Salvation of Souls
on the Ladder to Heaven* mural

OUTLYING ISLANDS

Domestic architecture on the
peaceful islet of **Oinoússes**, a
few miles east of Chíos town,
is deceptively humble, for it
is the wealthiest territory in
Greece. Good beaches can
be found to either side of the
port, and in the northwest of
the island is the Evangelismoú
convent, endowed by the
Pateras family.

Much of **Psará**, 71 km
(44 miles) to the west, was
ruined in the Greek War of
Independence (see pp38–9);
as a result, the single town,
built in a pastiche of island
architectural styles, is a product of the last 100 years. The
landscape is still desolate and
infertile, though there are
good beaches to visit east of
the harbour, and Moní Koímisis
tis Theotókou in the far north.

The remains of a Hellenistic tower near Fanári, Ikaría

Ikaría
Ικαρία

🏛 9,000. ✈ 🛥 🚌 Agios Kýrikos.
🛈 22750 22202. 🚆 Fanári 16 km
(10 miles) NE of Agios Kírykos.

LYING 245 km (150 miles)
south of Chíos, Ikaría is
named after the Ikaros of legend who flew too near the sun
on artificial wings and plunged
to his death in the sea when
his wax bindings melted.

Agios Kírykos, the capital
and main port, is a pleasant
town flanked by two spas,
one of them dating to Roman
times and still popular with
an older Greek clientele. A
number of hot baths can be
visited at **Thérma**, a short
walk to the northeast, while
at **Thérma Lefkádas**, to the
southwest, the springs still
well up among the boulders
in the shallows of the sea.

About 2 km (1.5 miles) west
of Evdilos, a village port on
the north coast, lies the
village of **Kámpos**. It
boasts a broad, sandy
beach and, beside the
ruins of a 12th-century
church, the remains of a
Byzantine manor house
can be seen. The building
recalls a time when the
island was considered a
humane place of exile
for disgraced noblemen;
there was a large settle-
ment of such officials in
Kámpos. A small museum
contains artifacts from the
town of Oinoe, Kámpos's
ancient predecessor.

Standing above Kosoíki
village, 5 km (3 miles) inland, the Byzantine castle
of **Nikariás** was built

during the 10th century to
guard a pass on the road to
Oinoe. The only other well-
preserved fortification is a
3rd-century BC **Hellenistic
tower (Drakánou)**, once an
ancient lighthouse, near Fanári.

Tiny **Armenistís**, with its
surrounding forests and fine
beaches, such as Livádi and
Messaktí to the east, is Ikaría's
main resort. The foundations
of a temple to the goddess
Artemis Tavropólos (Artemis
incarnated as the patroness of
bulls) lie 4 km (2 miles) west.

Home to the most active fishing fleet in the East Aegean, the
island of **Foúrnoi**, due east of
Ikaría, is far more populous
and lively than its small size
suggests. The main street of the
port town, lined with mulberry
trees, links the quay with a
square well inland, where an
ancient sarcophagus sits between the two cafés. Within
walking distance lie Kampí
and Psilí Ammos beaches.

Coastal town of Agios Kírykos,
the capital of Ikaría

Sámos
Σάμος

SETTLED EARLY, owing to its natural richness and ease of access from Asia, Sámos was a major maritime power by the 7th century BC and enjoyed a golden age under the rule of Polykrates (538–522 BC). After the collapse of the Byzantine Empire, most of the islanders fled from pirates and Sámos lay deserted until 1562, when Ottoman Admiral Kiliç Ali repopulated it with returned Samians and other Orthodox settlers. The 19th century saw an upsurge in fortunes made in tobacco trading and shipping. Union with Greece occurred in 1912.

Assyrian bronze horse figurine, Vathý Archaeological Museum

Fishermen at Vathý harbour

SIGHTS AT A GLANCE

Efpalíneio Orygma ➋
Heraion ➎
Karlóvasi ➐
Kokkári ➏
Moní Megális Panagías ➍
Mount Kerketéfs ➑
Pythagóreio ➌
Vathý ➊

Vathý ➊
Βαθύ

🏙 5,700. ⛴ 🚌 Ioánnou Lekáti.
ℹ 25 Martíou (22730 28530).
🛒 daily. 🚌 Psilí Ammos 8 km (5 miles) SE; Mykáli 6 km (4 miles) S.

Though the old village of Ano Vathý existed in the 1600s, today's town is recent; the harbour quarter grew up only after 1832, when the town became the capital of the island. Just large enough to provide all amenities in its bazaar, lower Vathý caters to tourists while cobble-laned Ano Vathý carries on oblivious to the commerce in the streets below.

The Sámos **Archaeological Museum** contains artifacts from the excavations at the Heraion sanctuary (see p152). Because of the far-flung origins of the pilgrims who visited the shrine, the collection of small votive offerings is one of the richest in Greece – among them are a bronze statuette of an Urartian god, Assyrian figurines and an ivory miniature of

Perseus and Medusa. The largest free-standing sculpture to have survived from ancient Greece is the star exhibit: a 5-m (16-ft) tall marble *koûros* dating from 580 BC and dedicated to the god Apollo.

🏛 **Archaeological Museum**
Kapetán Gymnasiárchou Kateváni.
📞 22730 27469. ◐ Tue–Sun.
● main public hols.

KEY

For key to map see back flap

Around Sámos Island

SAMOS HAS A PAVED ROAD around the island, but buses are frequent only between Pythagóreio and Karlóvasi, via Vathý. Vehicle-hire is easy, though many points can be reached only by jeep or foot. In the south and west there are many rough dirt roads where caution is necessary.

Efpalíneio Orygma ❷
Ευπαλίνειο Όρυγμα

15 km (9 miles) SW of Vathý.
22730 61400. Tue–Sun.
main public hols.

Efpalíneio Orygma (Eupalinos's tunnel) is a 1,040-m (3,410-ft) aqueduct, ranking as one of the premier engineering feats of the ancient world. Designed by the engineer Eupalinos and built by hundreds of slaves between 529 and 524 BC, the tunnel guaranteed ancient Sámos a water supply in times of siege, and remained in use until this century. Eupalinos's surveying was so accurate that, when the work crews met, having begun from opposite sides of the mountain, their vertical error was nil.

Visitors may walk along the ledge used to remove rubble from the channel far below. Half the total length is open to the public, with grilles to protect you from the worst drops.

Pythagóreio ❸
Πυθαγόρειο

13 km (8 miles) SW of Vathý.
1,500. Lykoúrgou Logothéti (22730 61389).
Potokáki 3 km (2 miles) W.

Cobble-paved Pythagóreio, named after the philosopher Pythagoras who was born here in 580 BC, has long been the lodestone of Samian tourism. The extensive foundations and walls of ancient Sámos act as a brake on tower-block construction; the only genuine tower is the 19th-century manor of **Lykoúrgos Logothétis**, the local chieftain who organized a decisive naval victory over the Turks on 6 August 1824, the date of the Feast of the Transfiguration. Next to this stronghold is the church of the **Metamórfosis**, built to celebrate the victory. At the far western edge of town are the extensive remains of

Pythagoras statue (1989) by Nikoláos Ikaris, Pythagóreio

Roman Baths, still with a few doorways intact. Further west, the Doryssa Bay luxury complex stands above the silted-in area of the Archaic harbour; all that remains is Glyfáda lake, crossed by a causeway.

Roman Baths
W of Pythagóreio. 22730 61400.
variable.

ENVIRONS: Polykrates protected Pythagóreio by constructing a circuit of walls enclosing Kastrí hill, to a circumference of more than 6 km (4 miles), with 12 gates. The walls were damaged by an Athenian siege of 439 BC, and today are most intact just above Glyfáda, where a fortification tower still stands. Enclosed by the walls, just above the ancient theatre, sits **Moní Panagías Spilianís** with its 100-m (330-ft) cave containing a shrine to the Virgin.

Moní Megális Panagías ❹
Μονή Μεγάλης Παναγίας

27 km (17 miles) W of Vathý.
May–Oct: daily.

Founded in 1586 by Nílos and Dionýsios, two hermits from Asia Minor, the monastery of Megális Panagías is the second oldest on Sámos and contains the island's best surviving frescoes from that period. The central church is orientated diagonally within the square compound of cells, now restored, probably built directly above a temple of Artemis which it replaced. Sadly, the area was ravaged by fire in 1990, shortly after the last monk died. Visiting hours depend on the whim of the caretaker.

Fresco of Jesus washing the apostles' feet, Moní Megális Panagías

The single remaining column of Polykrates' temple, Heraion

Heraion ❺
Ηραίον

21 km (13 miles) SW of Vathý.
📞 22730 95277. 🚌 Iraío.
🕐 Tue–Sun. ⬤ main public hols. 📷

A fertility goddess was worshipped here from Neolithic times, though the cult only became identified with Hera after the arrival of Mycenaean colonists (see pp24–5), who brought their worship of the Olympian deities with them. The sanctuary's site on flood-prone ground honoured the legend that Hera was born under a sacred osier (willow tree) on the banks of the Imvrasos and celebrated her nuptials with Zeus among the osiers here, in the dangerous pre-Olympian days when Kronos still ruled.

A 30-m (98-ft) long temple built in the 8th century BC was replaced in the 6th century BC by a stone one of the Ionic order, planned by Rhoikos, a local architect. Owing to earthquakes, or a design fault, this collapsed during the reign of Polykrates, who ordered a grand replacement designed by Rhoikos's son, Theodoros. He began the new temple in 525 BC, 40 m (130 ft) west of his father's, recycling building materials from its predecessor. Building continued off and on for many centuries, but the vast structure was never completed. The interior, full of votive offerings, was described by visitors in its heyday as a veritable art gallery.

Most of the finds on display at the Archaeological Museum in Vathý (see p150) date from the 8th to the 6th centuries BC, when the sanctuary was at the height of its prestige. The precinct was walled and contained several temples to other deities, though only Hera herself had a sacrificial altar. Pilgrims could approach from the ancient capital along a 4,800-m (15,750-ft) Sacred Way.

Despite diligent 20th-century German excavations, much of the sanctuary is confusing. Byzantine and medieval masons removed ready-cut stone for reuse in their buildings, leaving only one column untouched. Early in the 5th century, Christian masons built a basilica dedicated to a new mother figure: the Virgin Mary. Its foundations lie east of the Great Temple.

Kokkári ❻
Κοκκάρι

10 km (6 miles) W of Vathý. 🏠 1,000.
🚌 🛈 Agíou Nikoláou (22730 92333). 🏖 Tsamadoú & Lemonákia 2 km (1 mile) W.

Built on and behind twin headlands, this charming little port takes its name from the shallot-like onions once cultivated just inland. Today it is the island's third resort after Pythagóreio and Vathý, with its wind-blown location turned to advantage by a multitude of windsurfers. The town's two beaches are stony and often

Plinth from Polykrates' temple, Heraion

THE CULT OF HERA

Hera was worshipped as the main cult of a number of Greek cities, including Argos on the mainland, and always at out-of-town sanctuaries. Before the 1st millennium BC, she was venerated in the form of a simple wooden board which was later augmented with a copper statue. One annual rite, the Tonaia, commemorated a foiled kidnapping of the wooden statue by Argive and Etruscan pirates. During the Tonaia, the idol would be paraded to the river mouth, bound on a litter of osiers (sacred to Hera), bathed in the sea and draped with gifts. The other annual festival, the Heraia, when the copper statue was dressed in wedding finery, celebrated Hera's union with Zeus, and was accompanied by concerts and athletic contests. Housed in a special shrine after the 8th century, the statue of Hera was flanked by a number of live peacocks and sprigs from an osier tree. Both are shown on Samian coins of the Roman era stamped with the image of the richly dressed goddess.

Hera, led by peacocks, and depicted on Samian coins

The beach and harbour of Kokkári, flanked by its twin headlands

surf-battered, but the paved quay and its waterside cafés and tavernas are the busy focus of nightlife.

ENVIRONS: Though many of Sámos's hill-villages are becoming deserted, **Vourliótes** is an exception, thriving thanks to its orchards and vineyards. The picturesque central square is one of the most beautiful on the island, with outdoor seating at its four tavernas. Vourliótes is situated at a major junction in the area's network of hiking trails; paths come up from Kokkári, descend to Agios Konstantínos, and climb to Manolátes, which is the trailhead for the ascent of Mount Ampelos, a five-hour round trip.

Karlóvasi **⑦**
Καρλόβασι

33 km (20 miles) NW of Vathý. ⑦ 5,000. ⛴ 🚌 🚖 Potámi 2 km (1 mile) W.

Sprawling, domestic Karlóvasi, gateway to western Sámos and the island's second town, divides into four separate districts. Néo Karlóvasi served as a major leather production centre between the world wars, and abandoned tanneries and ornate mansions built on shoe-wealth can still be seen down by the sea. Meséo Karlóvasi, on a hill across the river, is more attractive, but most visitors stay at the harbour of Limín, with its tavernas and lively boatyard. Immediately

above the port, Ano, or Palaió Karlóvasi is tucked into a wooded ravine, overlooked by the landmark hilltop church of **Agía Triáda**, the only structure in Ano visible from the sea.

ENVIRONS: An hour's walk from Ano Karlóvasi, inland from Potámi beach, is the site of a medieval settlement. Its most substantial traces include the 11th-century church of **Metamórfosis**, the oldest on the island, and a Byzantine castle immediately above.

Mount Kerketéfs **⑧**
Όρος Κερκετεύς

50 km (31 miles) W of Vathý. 🚌 to Marathókampos. 🚖 Votsalákia, 2 km (1 mile) S of Marathókampos; Limniónas, 5 km (3 miles) SW of Marathókampos

Dominating the western tip of Sámos, 1,437-m (4,715-ft) Mount Kerketéfs is the second highest peak in the Aegean

after Sáos on Samothráki. On an island otherwise composed of smooth sedimentary rock, the partly volcanic mountain is an anomaly, with jagged rocks and bottomless chasms.

Kerketéfs was first recorded in Byzantine times, when religious hermits occupied some of its caves. Nocturnal glowings at the cave-mouths were interpreted by sailors as the spirits of departed saints, or the aura of some holy icon awaiting discovery. Today, two monasteries remain on Kerketéfs: the 16th century **Moní Evangelistrías**, perched on the south slope, and **Moní Theotókou**, built in 1887, tucked into a valley on the northeast side.

Despite recent forest fires, and the paving of a road to remote villages west of the summit, Mount Kerketéfs still boasts magnificent scenery, with ample opportunities for hiking. At Seïtáni Bay on the north coast, a marine reserve protects the Mediterranean monk seal *(see p111)*.

Mount Kerketéfs, seen from the island of Ikaría

THE DODECANESE

PATMOS · LIPSI · LEROS · KALYMNOS · KOS · ASTYPALAIA · NISYROS
TILOS · SYMI · RHODES · CHALKI · KASTELLORIZO · KARPATHOS

*SCATTERED ALONG THE COAST OF TURKEY, the Dodecanese are the most
southerly group of Greek islands, their hot climate and fine
beaches attracting many visitors. They are the most cosmopolitan
archipelago, with an eastern influence present in their architecture.
They were the last territories to be incorporated into modern Greece.*

Due to their distance from Athens and mainland Greece, these islands have been subject to a number of invasions, with traces of occupation left behind on every island. The Classical temples built by the Dorians can be seen on Rhodes. The Knights of St John were the most famous invaders, arriving in 1309 and staying until they were defeated by Suleiman the Magnificent in 1522.

A statue at Mandráki harbour in Rhodes

Ottoman architecture is most prominent on larger, wealthier islands, such as Kos and Rhodes. After centuries of Turkish rule, the Italians arrived in 1912 and began a regime of persecution. Mussolini built many imposing public buildings, notably in the town of Lakkí on Léros. After years of occupation, the islands were finally united with the Greek state in 1948.

Geographically, the Dodecanese vary dramatically in character: some are dry, stark and barren, such as Chálki and Kásos, while Tílos and volcanic Nísyros are fertile and green. Astypálaia and Pátmos, with their whitewashed houses, closely resemble Cycladic islands; the pale houses of Chóra, on Pátmos, are spectacularly overshadowed by the dark monastery of St John. Rhodes is the the capital of the island group, and is one of the most popular holiday destinations due to its endless sandy beaches and many sights.

The climate of these islands stays hot well into the autumn, providing a long season in which to enjoy the beaches. These vary from black pebbles to silver sands, and deserted bays to shingle strips packed with sunbathers.

One monk's method of travelling around on the holy island of Pátmos

◁ A façade on the waterfront of Sými town's harbour

Exploring the Dodecanese

THE DODECANESE offer an unparalleled range of landscapes and activities. There are beautiful beaches with all kinds of watersports, safe yachting harbours, lush valleys and barren mountains, caves and fjords, and even the semi-active volcano on Nísyros. Historical sights in the group are just as diverse, including the 11th-century Monastery of St John on Pátmos, the Hellenistic Asklepieíon of Kos, the medieval walled city of the Knights of Rhodes and the unique traditional village of Olympos on Kárpathos. This island group divides neatly into north and south. Kos in the north and Rhodes, the group's capital, in the south make good bases for air and ferry travel.

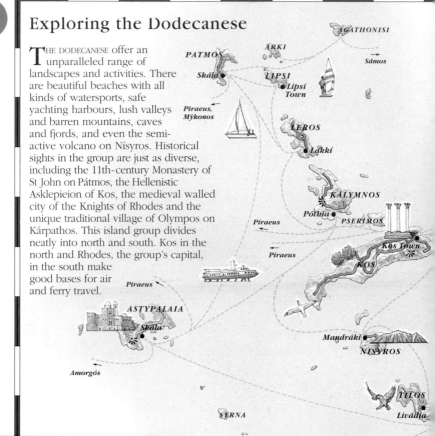

The domed entrance to the New Market in Rhodes town

ISLANDS AT A GLANCE

Astypálaia *p170*
Chálki *pp194–5*
Kálymnos *pp164–5*
Kárpathos *pp198–9*
Kastellórizo *p195*
Kos *pp166–9*
Pátmos *pp158–61*
Léros *pp162–3*
Lipsí *p162*
Nísyros *pp170–72*
Rhodes *pp176–93*
Sými *pp174–5*
Tílos *p173*

GETTING AROUND

Kos, Rhodes and Kárpathos have international airports; those at Léros, Astypálaia and Kásos are domestic. Travelling by sea, it is wise to plan where you want to go, as some islands do not share direct connections even when quite close. Also journeys can be long – it takes nine hours from Rhodes to Pátmos. If possible allow time for changes in the weather. The cooling *meltémi* wind is welcome in the high summer but, if strong, can mean ferries will not operate and even leave you stranded. Bus services are good, especially on the larger islands, and there are always cars and bikes for hire or taxis available, though the standard of roads can vary.

LOCATOR MAP

An aerial view of Sými town with its Neo-Classical houses

KEY

▬	Major road
▬	Asphalt road
▭	Non-asphalt road
▬	Scenic route
≈	River
– –	High season, direct ferry route
↯	Viewpoint

0 kilometres   25

0 miles   15

SEE ALSO

- *Where to Stay* pp302–4
- *Where to Eat* pp326–8
- *Travel Information* pp356–9

Pátmos

Πάτμος

KNOWN AS THE JERUSALEM of the Aegean, Pátmos's religous significance dates from St John's arrival in AD 95 and the founding of the Monastery of St John *(see pp160–61)* in 1088. Monastic control declined as the islanders grew rich through ship-building and trade, and in 1720 the laymen and monks divided the land. Today Pátmos tries to maintain itself as a centre for both pilgrims and tourists.

SKALA

Ferries, yachts and cruise ships dock at Skála, the island's port and main town, which stretches around a wide sheltered bay. As there are many exclusive gift shops and boutiques, Skála has a smart, up-market feel. There are several travel and shipping agencies along the harbourfront.

Skála's social life centres on the café-bar *Aríon*, a Neo-Classical building that doubles as a meeting place and waiting point for ferries. From the harbourfront caïques and small cruise boats leave daily for the island's main beaches.

ENVIRONS: The sandy town beach can get very crowded. To the north, around the bay, lies the shingly, shaded beach at **Melói**. There is an excellent campsite and taverna, and taxi boats also run back to Skála. Above Skála lie the ruins of the ancient acropolis at **Kastélli**. The remains include

KEY

For key to map see back flap

0 kilometres   2

0 miles   1

a Hellenistic wall. The little chapel of **Agios Konstantínos** is perched on the summit where the wonderful views at sunset make the hike up from Mérichas Bay well worthwhile.

CHORA

From Skála an old cobbled pathway leads up to the Monastery of St John *(see pp160–61)*, which crowns Chóra. The panoramic views

to Sámos and Ikaría are ample reward for the long trek. A maze of dazzling white narrow lanes with over 40 monasteries and chapels, Chóra is a gem of Byzantine architecture. Many of the buildings have distinctive window mouldings, or *mantómata*, decorated with a Byzantine cross. Along the twisting alleys, some doorways lead into vast sea captains' mansions, or *archontiká*, that were built to keep marauding pirates at bay.

View of Skála from the Monastery of St John

Stall owners selling souvenirs on the pathway to the Monastery of St John

Down the path to Skála is the church of **Agía Anna**. Steps decked with flowers lead down from the path to the church (1090) which is dedicated to the mother of the Virgin Mary. Inside the church is the **Holy Cave of the Apocalypse**, where St John saw the vision of fire and brimstone and dictated the book of *Revelation* to his disciple, Próchoros. The visitor can see the rock where the book of *Revelation* was written, and the indentation where the saint is said to have rested his head. There are 12th-century wall paintings and icons from 1596 of St John and the Blessed Christodoulos (*see p160*) by the Cretan painter Thomás Vathás. St John is said to have heard the voice of God coming from the cleft in the rock, still visible today. The rock is divided into three, symbolizing the Trinity.

Near Plateía Xánthou is an *archontikó*, **Simantíris House**, preserved as a Folk Museum. Built in 1625 by Aglaïnós Mousodákis, a wealthy merchant, it still has the original furnishings and contains objects from Mousodákis's travels, such as Russian samovars and four-poster beds.

Nearby, the tranquil convent of **Zoödóchou Pigís**, built in 1607, has some fine frescoes and icons and is set in peaceful gardens.

🏠 Holy Cave of the Apocalypse
Between Skála and Chóra.
📞 22470 31234. 🕐 daily.

🏛 Simantíris House
Chóra. 🕐 daily. 📷

Votive offerings from pilgrims to Pátmos

AROUND THE ISLAND
Pátmos has some unspoiled beaches and a rugged interior with fertile valleys. Excursion boats run to most beaches and buses from Skála serve Kámpos, Gríkos and Chóra.

The island's main resort is **Gríkos**, set in a magnificent bay east of Chóra. It has a shingly beach with fishing boats, watersports facilities and a handful of tavernas. From here the bay curves past the uninhabited Tragonísi islet south to the bizarre Kallikatsoús rock, perched on a sand spit, which looks like the cormorant it is named after. The rock has

been hollowed out to make rooms, possibly by 4th-century monks, or it could have been the 11th-century hermitage mentioned in the writings of Christodoulos

On the southwestern coast is the island's best beach, **Psilí Ammos**, with its stretch of fine sand and sweeping dunes. It is the unofficial nudist beach and is also popular with campers. Across the bay, the Rock of Genoúpas is marked by a red buoy. This is where, according to legend, the evil magician Genoúpas challenged St John to a duel of miracles. Genoúpas plunged into the sea to bring back effigies of the dead, but God then turned him to stone. Cape Genoúpas has a grotto that is said to be where the wizard lived.

Situated in the more fertile farming region in the north of the island, **Kámpos** beach, reached via the little hill-village of Kámpos, is another popular beach with watersports and a few tavernas. From Kámpos a track leads eastwards to the good pebble beaches at **Vagiá**, **Geranoú** and **Livádi**.

Windy **Lámpi** on the north coast is famous for its coloured and multipatterned pebbles. There are two garden tavernas and a little chapel set back from the reed-beds. You can walk here from the hamlet of Christós above Kámpos.

Holy Cave of the Apocalypse where St John lived and worked

Pátmos: Monastery of St John
Μονή του Αγίου Ιωάννου του Θεολόγου

THE 11TH-CENTURY Monastery of St John is one of the most important places of worship among Orthodox and Western Christian faithful alike. It was founded in 1088 by a monk, the Blessed Christodoulos, in honour of St John the Divine, author of the book of *Revelation*. One of the richest and most influential monasteries in Greece, its towers and buttresses make it look like a fairy-tale castle, but were built to protect its religious treasures, which are now the star attraction for the thousands of pilgrims and tourists.

Monastery of St John above Chóra

Chapel of John
the Baptist

Kitchens

Inner
courtyard

The Hospitality of Abraham
This is one of the most important of the 12th-century frescoes that were found in the chapel of the Panagía. They had been painted over but were revealed after an earthquake in 1956.

The monks' refectory has two tables made of marble taken from the Temple of Artemis, which originally occupied the site.

★ Icon of St John
This 12th-century icon is the most revered in the monastery and is housed in the katholikón, *the monastery's main church.*

The Chapel of Christodoulos contains the tomb and silver reliquary of the Blessed Christodoulos.

STAR FEATURES

★ **Main Courtyard**

★ **Icon of St John**

Chapel of the Holy Cross
This is one of the monastery's ten chapels built because church law forbade Mass being heard more than once a day in the same chapel.

Chrysobull
This scroll of 1088 in the treasury is the monastery's foundation deed, sealed in gold by the Byzantine Emperor Alexios I Comnenos.

The treasury houses over 200 icons, 300 pieces of silverware and a dazzling collection of jewels.

★ Main Courtyard
Frescoes of St John from the 18th century adorn the outer narthex of the katholikón, whose arcades form an integral part of the courtyard.

The Chapel of the Holy Apostles lies just outside the gate of the monastery.

The main entrance has slits for pouring boiling oil over marauders. This 17th-century gateway leads up to the cobbled main courtyard.

NIPTIR CEREMONY

The Orthodox Easter celebrations on Pátmos are some of the most important in Greece. Hundreds of people pack Chóra to watch the *Niptír* (washing) ceremony on Maundy Thursday. The abbot of the Monastery of St John publicly washes the feet of 12 monks, re-enacting Christ's washing of His disciples' feet before the Last Supper. The rite was once performed by the Byzantine emperors as an act of humility.

Embroidery of Christ washing the disciples' feet

Agios Ioánnis church in Lipsí village

Lipsí
Λειψοί

650. Lipsí town. Town hall, Lipsí (22470 41185). Platýs Gialós 4 km (2.5 miles) N of Lipsí town.

LITTLE LIPSI is a magical island characterized by green hills dotted with blue and white chapels, and village houses painted in a riot of colours. It is one of many islands claiming to be the enchanted place where Calypso beguiled Odysseus. Officially owned by the monastery at Pátmos since Byzantine times, Lipsí has excellent beaches, and is popular for day excursions from Pátmos and Kálymnos.

The island is only 10 sq km (4 sq miles) and remains a haven for traditional Greek island life, producing some good local wines and cheeses.

The main settlement, **Lipsí town** is based around the harbour. Here the blue-domed church of **Agios Ioánnis** holds a famous icon of the Panagía. Ancient lilies within the frame miraculously spring into bloom on 23 August, the feast of the Yielding of the Annunciation. In the town hall the **Nikofóreion Ecclesiastical Museum** features an odd collection of finds, from neatly labelled bottles of holy water to traditional costumes.

These sights are all signposted from the harbour, and there are informal taxi services to the more distant bays and beaches of **Platýs Gialós**, **Monodéntri** and the string of sandy coves at **Katsadiás**.

Nikofóreion Ecclesiastical Museum
May–Sep: daily.

Léros
Λέρος

8,000. Parthéni. Lakkí, Agía Marína (hydrofoils). Plateía Plátanos, Plátanos. Harbourfront, Lakkí (22470 23711).

ONCE FAMOUS AS the island of Artemis, Léros's more recent history, as the home of Greece's prison camps and later mental hospitals, has kept tourism low-key. The hospitals still provide the main source of employment for the locals. However, life here is traditional, and the people are very welcoming and friendly.

Neo-Classical façade of Maliamate villa, Agía Marína

The island was occupied by the Knights of St John in 1309, by the Turks from 1522 to 1831, and by the Italians in 1912 when they built naval bases in Lakkí bay. Under German rule from 1943 until the Allied liberation, Léros was eventually united with Greece in 1948. When the military Junta took power in 1967 they exiled political dissidents to Léros's prison camps.

Today, Léros is keen to emphasise its strong cultural and educational heritage. Famous for its musicians and poets, the island has preserved traditional folk dance and music through Artemis, the youth cultural society.

Lakki

Lakkí, the main port and former capital, has one of the best natural harbours in the Aegean, and served as an anchorage point in turn for the Italian, German and then the British fleets. Today it resembles a disused film set full of derelict Art Deco buildings, the remains of Mussolini's vision of a Fascist dream town. Lakkí is a ghost town during the day, but the seafront cafés come to life in the evening. Around the bay at Lépida, the former Italian naval base now houses the State Therapeutical Hospital and within the complex is a mansion once used as Mussolini's summer

The Art Deco Architecture of Lakki

Mussolini's vision of a new Roman Empire took shape here in 1923 when Italian architects and town planners turned their energies to building the new town. A quite remarkable example of Art Deco architecture, Lakkí was built around wide boulevards by the engineers Sardeli and Caesar Lois, an Austrian. The model town was all curves and featured a saucer-shaped market building with a clocktower, completed in 1936; a cylindrical Town Hall and Fascist centre, dating to 1933–34; and the vast Albergo Romana, later the Léros Palace Hotel. The Albergo, with the cinema and theatre complex, was completed in 1937 for visiting Italian performers. These days the majority of the buildings are crumbling and neglected.

Lakkí's Art Deco cinema building

0 kilometres 4
0 miles 2

KEY

For key to map see back flap

residence. Also in Lépida is the 11th-century church of **Agios Ioánnis Theológos** (St John the Divine), built over the remains of a Byzantine church by the monk Christodoulos (see p160).

AROUND THE ISLAND

Léros is a pretty, green island with an indented coastline sweeping into vast gulfs, the "four seas" of Léros. With craggy hills and fertile valleys, it is good walking country.

To defy the Italians, the Lerians abandoned Lakkí and made the village of **Plátanos** the capital. Straddling a hilltop, its houses spill down to the little port of Pantéli and to the fishing village of Agía Marína.

Perched above Plátanos, the Byzantine kástro offers fine views. Renovated by the Venetians and the Knights of St John, it houses the church of **Megalóchari or Kyrá tou Kástrou** (the Madonna of the Castle) famous for its miraculous icon. Nearby Pantéli is a fishing village with a tree-fringed beach and harbour.

The road north leads to Agía Marína, and is lined with impressive Neo-Classical mansions built between 1880 and 1920. **Agía Marína** is the principal port for hydrofoils. Following the coastal road north to Krithóni, the **British War Cemetery** is a site of pilgrimage for those who lost relatives in the 1943 Battle of Léros.

Beaches line the road leading further north to **Alínda**, the island's main resort, which has a long beach with watersports and seafront cafés. Alínta's **Historic and Folk Museum** is housed in the twin-towered Belénis Castle, built by an expatriate benefactor, Paríssis Belénis. Little remains of the once-powerful Temple of

Artemis, now overlooking the airport at Parthéni in the north. There are a few carved blocks of stone and fragments of pillars. The goddess still has some influence in Léros, however, as property passes down the female family line.

Early Christian basilicas have been found in the area, and south of the airport the 11th-century church of **Agios Geórgios**, built by the monk Christodoulos (see p160) using temple columns, has a fresco of the saint.

Agios Isídoros, on the west coast above sandy Goúrnas Bay, has a white chapel on an islet that can be reached by means of a narrow causeway.

At Drymónas, with its coves and oleander gorge, is the church of the **Panagía Gourlomáta**, which translates as the "goggle-eyed Virgin". Reconstructed in 1327 from an 11th-century chapel, the church takes its name from the wide-eyed expression of the Madonna seen in one of its frescoes.

The resort of **Xirókampos**, lying in a bay to the south of the island, is overlooked by ancient Palaiókastro, the former site of the 3rd-century castle of Lépida. The huge Cyclopean walls remain, and within them is the church of Panagía, that is home to some fine mosaics.

⌖ Historic and Folk Museum
Belénis Castle, Alínda
◯ May–Sep: daily.

Plátanos village with the kástro in the background

Kálymnos
Κάλυμνος

Famous today as the sponge-fishing island, Kálymnos's history can be traced back to a Neolithic settlement in Vothýnoi, near Póthia; it was colonized after the 1450 BC devastation of Crete. The people have been known for their resilience since the 11th-century massacre by the Seljuk Turks, which a few survived in fortified Kastélli.

POTHIA
The capital and main port of the island is a busy working harbour. Wedged between two mountains, the town's brightly painted houses curve around the bay.

Póthia is home to Greece's last sponge fleet and there is a sponge-diving school on the eastern side of the harbour. The waterfront is lined with cafés and the main landmarks are the pink, domed Italianate buildings, including the **Governor's Palace,** which now houses the market, and the silver-domed cathedral of **Agios Christós** (Holy Christ).

This 19th-century cathedral has a reredos (screen) behind the altar by Giannoúlis Chalepás *(see p40).* The *Mermaid* at the harbour is one of 43 works that were donated to the island by local sculptors Irene and Michális Kókkinos.

The **Archaeological Museum,** housed in a Neo-Classical mansion, has been lavishly reconstructed and there is a collection of Neolithic and Bronze-Age finds from the island plus local memorabilia. The **Sponge Factory**, just off Plateía Eleftherías, has a complete history of sponges.

The Mermaid at Póthia harbour

🏛 Archaeological Museum
Near Plateía Kýprou. ☎ *22430 23113.*
🕐 *Tue–Sun.* ⬤ *main public hols.*
🏛 Sponge Factory
Plateía Eleftherías. ☎ *22430 28501.*
🕐 *daily.* ⬤ *main public hols.*

AROUND THE ISLAND
Kálymnos is easy to get around with a good bus service to the villages and numerous taxis. This rocky island has three mountain ranges, the peaks offset by deep fjord-like inlets.

Northwest of Póthia the suburb of Mýloi, with its three derelict windmills, blends into **Chorió**, the pretty white town and former capital. On the way, standing to the left, is the ruined **Castle of the Knights**, and above, via steps from Chorió, is the citadel of **Péra Kástro**. Following a Turkish attack, this fortified village was inhabited from the 11th to the 18th century. It has good views and nine white chapels stand on the crags.

The **Cave of Seven Virgins** (Eptá Parthénon) shows traces of nymph worship. Legend has it that the seven virgins hid here from pirates, but disappeared in the bottomless channel below.

The main resorts on the island are strung out along the

View of Póthia and harbour

The deep Vathý inlet with the settlement of Rína at its head

west coast. The sunset over the islet of Télendos from **Myrtiés** is one of Kálymnos's most famous sights. Although Myrtiés and neighbouring Masoúri have now grown into noisy tourist centres, the Armeós end of Masoúri is less frenetic. To the north is the fortified **Kastélli**, the refuge of survivors from the 11th-century Turkish massacre. The coast road from here is spectacular, passing fish farms, inlets and the fjord-like beach at **Arginónta**. A visit to the northernmost fishing hamlet, **Emporeiós** makes a good day out and is in craggy walking

country. You can walk to **Kolonóstilo** (the Cyclops Cave), which is named after its massive stalactites.

In the southeast is the most beautiful area of Kálymnos: the lush Vathý valley which has three small villages at the head of a stunning blue inlet. Backed by citrus groves, **Rína**, named after St Irene, is a pretty hamlet with a working boatyard. **Plátanos**, the next village, has a huge plane tree and the remains of Cyclopean walls. There is a 3 hour trail from here via **Metóchi**, the third Vathý village, across the island to Arginónta.

Caïques from Rína visit the **Daskalió Cave** in the side of the sheer inlet, and Armiés, Drasónia and Palaiónissos beaches on the east coast.

OUTLYING ISLANDS
Excursion boats leave Póthia daily for **Psérimos** and the islet of **Nerá** with its Moní Stavroú. Psérimos has an often busy, sandy beach and a popular festival of the Assumption on 15 August.

Télendos, reached from Myrtiés, is perfect for a hideaway holiday, with a few rooms to rent and a handful of tavernas, plus shingly beaches. There are Roman ruins, a derelict fort and the ruined Moní Agíou Vasileíou, dating from the Middle Ages. The Byzantine castle of Agios Konstantínou also stands here,

SPONGE FISHING AROUND KALYMNOS

Kálymnos has been a sponge-fishing centre from ancient times, although fishing restrictions and sponge blight have hit the trade in recent years. Once in great demand, sponges were used for the Sultan's harem, for padding in armour and later for cosmetic and industrial purposes. Divers were **Sea sponge** weighed down with rocks or used crude air apparatus, and many men were drowned or died of the bends. The week before Kálymnos's fleet sets out to fish is the *Ipogros* or Sponge Week Festival. Divers are given a celebratory send off with food, drink and dancing in traditional costume.

A stone was used to weigh divers to keep them near to the seabed.

Diving equipment *varied greatly over the years. Early diving suits were made from rubber and canvas with huge helmets. You can see some on display in the sponge factory at Póthia and on stalls where divers sell their wares.*

This black-figure *Greek vase depicts an early sponge-diving scene. The diver, pictured standing at the front of the boat, is preparing to enter the sea to search for sponges. The vase dates back to around 500 BC.*

Kos
Κως

T HE SECOND LARGEST of the Dodecanese, Kos has a pleasant climate and fertile land, famous for producing the kos lettuce. Kos has attracted settlers since 3000 BC, and Hippocrates' teachings *(see p168)* increased the island's renown. By the 4th century BC Kos was a strong trading power, though it declined after the Romans arrived in 130 BC. The Knights of St John ruled from 1315, and the Turks governed from 1522–1912. Italian and German occupation followed until unification with Greece in 1948.

Yachts moored in the harbour at Kos town

Kos Town ❶
Κως

🏘 15,000. ✈ 🚢 *Akti Koudouriotou.* 🛈 *Vasiléos Georgíou 1 (22420 28724).* 🚌 *daily.* 🚕 *Kos town.*

Dominated by its Castle of the Knights, old Kos town was destroyed in the 1933 earthquake. This revealed many ancient ruins which the Italians excavated and restored.

The harbour bristles with yachts and excursion boats, and pavement cafés line the street. At night in high season you can almost get swept along by the crowds. There are palm trees, pines and gardens full of jasmine. Ancient and modern sit oddly side by side: Nafklírou, the "street of bars", runs beside the ancient agora,

at night lit up by strobes and lasers. Hippocrates' ancient plane tree, in Plateía Platánou, is said to have been planted by him 2,400 years ago. Despite its 14-m (46-ft) diameter the present tree is only about 560 years old and is

The water fountain near Hippocrates' plane tree

probably a descendent of the original. The nearby fountain was built in 1792 by the Turkish governor Hadji Hassan, to serve the Mosque of the Loggia. The water gushed into an ancient marble sarcophagus.

♦ Castle of Knights
Plateía Platánou. ☎ 22420 28326. 🕐 *Tue–Sun.* ⬤ *main public hols.* 🎫
The 16th-century castle gateway is carved with gargoyles and an earlier coat of arms of Fernández de Heredia, the Grand Master from 1376 to 1396. The outer keep and battlements were built between 1450 and 1478 from stone and marble, including blocks from the Asklepieíon *(see p168).* The fortress was an important defence for the Knights of Rhodes against Ottoman attack and the ramparts still offer great views.

⋔ Ancient Agora
South of Plateía Platánou.
This site is made up of a series of ruins; from the original Hellenistic city to Byzantine buildings. Built over by the Knights, the ancient remains were revealed in the 1933 earthquake. Highlights include

VISITORS' CHECKLIST

🏙 27,000. ✈ 27 km (16 miles)
W of Kos town. 🚢 Aktí Koud
ouriótou, Kos town. 🚌 Kos town.
🛈 Kos town (22420 28724).
🎭 Hippocrates Cultural Festival:
Jul–Sep; Panagia at Kardámaina:
8 Sep; Agios Geórgios Festival at
Palaió Pylí: 23 Apr.

Sights at a Glance

Antimácheia ❼
Asfendíou Villages ❸
Asklepicíon ❷
Kamári ❽
Kardámaina ❻
Kos Town ❶
Palaió Pylí ❺
Tigkáki ❹

the 3rd-century BC stoa Kamára tou Fórou (Arcade of the Forum), the 3rd-century BC Temple of Herakles, mosaic floors depicting Orpheus and Herakles, and ruins of the Temple of Pándemos Aphrodite. A 5th-century Christian basilica was also discovered, along with the Roman Agora.

🏛 Archaeological Museum
Plateía Eleftherías. 📞 22420 28326.
⭘ Tue–Sun. ⬤ main public hols.
The museum has an excellent collection of the island's Hellenistic and Roman finds, including a 4th-century BC marble statue of Hippocrates. The main hall displays a 3rd-century AD mosaic of Asklepios surrounded by 2nd-century statues of Dionysos with Pan and a satyr. The east wing exhibits Roman statues and the north Hellenistic finds, while the west room has later gigantic statuary.

🏛 Roman Remains
Grigoríou E. ⭘ Tue–Sun.
The most impressive of these ruins is the Casa Romana, built in the Pompeiian style. It had 26 rooms and three pools surrounded by shady courtyards lined with Ionian and Corinthian columns. There are mosaics of dolphins, pouncing lions and leopards. The dining room has decorated marble walls and several rooms are painted. In the grounds are the excavated thermal baths and part of the main Roman road, covered with ancient capitals and Hellenistic fragments. Set back off the road down an avenue of cypresses is the

Kos lettuce on a market stall in Plateía Eleftherías

ancient odeion or theatre. It has rows of marble benches – the first class seats – and limestone blocks for the plebeians.

The western excavations opposite reveal a mix of historical periods. There are Mycenaean remains, a tomb dating from the Geometric period and Roman houses with some fine mosaics. One of the most impressive sights is the gym or xystó with its 17 restored Doric pillars.

Rows of marble benches for the Roman audiences that came to the ancient odeion

Around Kos Island

MAINLY FLAT AND FERTILE, Kos is known as the "Floating Garden". It has a wealth of archaeological sites and antiquities, Hellenistic and Roman ruins, and Byzantine and Venetian castles. Most visitors, however, come for Kos's sandy beaches. Those on the southwest shore are some of the finest in the Dodecanese, while the northwest bays are ideal for watersports. Much of the coast has been developed, but inland you can still see remnants of Kos's traditional lifestyle.

Carving at the Asklepieíon

The seven restored columns of the Temple of Apollo at the Asklepieíon

Asklepieíon ②
Ασκληπιείο

4 km (2.5 miles) NW of Kos town. 🚌
📞 22420 28763. ⏱ Jul–Oct
8am–6:30pm Tue–Sun; Nov–Jun:
8:30am–3pm Tue–Sun. 🎟

With its white marble terraces cut into a pine-clad hill, the Asklepieíon site was chosen in the 4th century BC for rest and recuperation and still exudes an air of tranquillity. The views from the sanctuary are breathtaking and it is one of Greece's most important Classical sites.

Temple, school and medical centre combined, it was built after the death of Hippocrates and was the most famous of ancient Greece's 300 asklepieia dedicated to Asklepios, god of healing. The doctors, priests of Asklepiados, became practitioners of Hippocrates' methods. The cult's symbol was the snake, once used to seek healing herbs, and is the emblem of modern western medicine. There are three levels: the lowest has a 3rd-century BC porch and 1st-century AD Roman baths; the second has a 4th-century BC Altar of Apollo and a 2nd to 3rd-century AD Temple of Apollo; on the third level is the Doric Temple of Asklepios from the 2nd century BC.

Asfendíou Villages ③
Χωριά Ασφενδίου

14 km (9 miles) W of Kos town. 🚌

The Asfendíou villages of Zía, Asómatos, Lagoúdi, Evangelístria and Agios Dimítrios are a cluster of picturesque hamlets on the wooded slopes of Mount Dikaíos. These mountain villages have managed to retain their traditional character, with whitewashed houses and attractive Byzantine churches. The highest village, **Zía**, has become the epitome of a traditional Greek village, at least to the organizers of the many coach tours that regularly descend upon it. The more adventurous traveller can take the very rough track from the Asklepieíon via tiny Asómatos to Zía. The lowest village, **Lagoúdi**, is less commercialized and a road leads from here to Palaió Pylí.

Tigkáki ④
Τιγκάκι

12 km (7 miles) W of Kos town. 🚌 🚲 Tigkáki.

The popular resorts of Tigkáki and neighbouring Marmári have long white sand beaches ideal for windsurfing and other watersports. Boat trips are available from Tigkáki to the island of Psérimos opposite. The nearby **Alykés Saltpans** are a perfect place for birdwatching. The many wetland species here include small waders like the avocet, and the black-winged stilt with its long pink legs.

HIPPOCRATES

The first holistic healer and "father of modern medicine", Hippocrates was born on Kos in 460 BC and died in Thessaly in about 375 BC. He supposedly came from a line of healing demigods and he learned medicine from his father and grandfather: his father was a direct descendant of Asklepios, the god of healing, his mother of Herakles. He was the first physician to classify diseases and introduced new methods of diagnosis and treatment. He taught on Kos before the Asklepieíon was established, and wrote the Hippocratic Oath, to cure rather than harm, still sworn by medical practitioners worldwide.

Palaió Pylí castle perched precariously on a cliff's edge

Palaió Pylí ❺
Παλαιό Πυλί

15 km (9 miles) W of Kos town.
🚌 to Pylí.

The deserted Byzantine town of Palaió Pylí is perched on a crag 4 km (2 miles) above the farming village of Pylí, with the remains of its castle walls built into the rock. Here the Blessed Christodoulos built the 11th-century church of the Ypapandís (Presentation of Jesus), before he went to Pátmos (see p160). In Pylí lies the Classical *thólos* tomb of the mythical hero-king Chármylos. It has 12 underground crypts, which are now surmounted by the church of Stavrós.

Kardámaina ❻
Καρδάμαινα

26 km (16 miles) SW of Kos town.
🚌 🚤 Kardámaina.

Once a quiet fishing village noted for its ceramics, Kardámaina is the island's biggest resort – brash, loud and packed with young British and Scandinavian tourists. It has miles of crowded golden sands and a swinging nightlife. It is quieter further south with some exclusive developments. Sights include a Byzantine church and the remains of a Hellenistic theatre.

Antimácheia ❼
Αντιμάχεια

25 km (16 miles) W of Kos town.
✈ 🚌
The village of Antimácheia is dominated by its Venetian castle and windmills. The castle, located near the airport, was built by the Knights of Rhodes (see pp184–5) as a prison in the 14th century, and was constantly bombarded by pirates. Its massive crenellated battlements and squat tower now overlook an army base, and there are good views towards Kardámaina. The inner gateway still bears the coat of arms of the Grand Master Pierre d'Aubusson (1476–1503) and there are two small chapels within the walls.

Antimácheia castle battlements

ENVIRONS: The road north from Antimácheia leads to the charming port of **Mastichári**. There are good fish tavernas here and a long sandy beach that sweeps into dunes at the western end. On the way to the dunes, the ruins of an early Christian basilica, with good mosaics, can be seen.

Kamári ❽
Καμάρι

15 km (9 miles) SW of Kos town.
🚌 🚤 Paradise 7 km (4 miles) E.

Kamári is a good base for exploring the southwest coast, where the island's best beaches can be found. Mostly reached via steep tracks from the main road, the most famous is Paradise beach with fine white sands. Kamári beach leads to the 5th-century AD Christian basilica of Agios Stefanos which has mosaics and Ionic columns.

ENVIRONS: Kéfalos, on the mountainous peninsula inland from Kamári, is known for its thyme, honey and cheeses. Sights include the ruined Castle of the Knights, said to be the lair of a dragon. According to legend, Hippocrates' daughter was transformed into a dragon by Artemis, and awaits the kiss of a knight to resume human form. Above Kéfalos is the windmill of Papavasílis, and nearby at Palátia are the remains of **Astypálaia**, the birthplace of Hippocrates. Neighbouring Aspri Pétra cave has yielded remains. The journey to **Moní Agíou Ioánni**, 6 km (4 miles) south of Kéfalos, passes through dramatic scenery, and a track leads to the beach of Agios Ioánnis Theológos.

Music bars and clubs in the resort of Kardámaina

Chóra overlooking Astypálaia's main harbour, Skála

Astypálaia
Αστυπάλαια

🏛 1,100. ✈ 11 km (7 miles) E of
Astypálaia town. 🚢 🚌 Astypálaia
town. 🛈 near Kástro, Astypálaia
town (22430 61206).

WITH ITS DAZZLING white
fortified town of Chóra
and its scenic coastline, the
island of Astypálaia retains an
exquisite charm. A backwater
in Classical times, Astypálaia
flourished in the Middle Ages
when the Venetian Quirini
family ruled from 1207 to 1522.
  The most westerly of the
Dodecanese, it is a remote
island with high cliffs and a
hilly interior. There are many
coves and sandy bays along
the coast, which was once
the lair of Maltese pirates.
  Astypálaia town incorporates the island's original
capital, Chóra, which forms its
maze-like upper town. The
splendid Venetian kástro of
the Quirini family is on the
site of the ancient acropolis.
Houses were built into the
kástro's walls for protection,
and the Quirini coat of arms
can still be seen on the gateway. Within its walls are two
churches: the silver-domed,
14th-century Panagía Portaïtissa
(Madonna of the Castle Gates),
and the 14th-century Agios
Geórgios (St George), built on
the site of an ancient temple.
  A two-hour hike westwards
from the derelict windmills
above Chóra leads to **Agios
Ioánnis** and its gushing waterfall. **Livádi**, the main resort,
lies south of Chóra in a fertile

valley with citrus groves
and cornfields. It has a long
beach. The nudist haunt of
Tzanáki lies a short distance
to the south. From Livádi a
dirt track leads north to **Agios
Andréas**, a remote and attractive cove, an hour and a
half's trek away.
  North of Chóra, on the narrow land bridge between the
two sides of the island, lies
Maltezána (also known as
Análipsi), the fastest-growing
resort on the island. Named
after the marauding pirates
who once frequented it,
Maltezána was where the
French Captain Bigot set fire
to his ship in 1827 to prevent
it being captured.
  On the northeastern peninsula is the "lost lagoon", a deep
inlet at the hamlet of **Vathý**.
From here you can visit the
caves of Drákou and Negrí by
boat, or the Italian Kastellano
fortress, built in 1912, 3 km
(2 miles) to the south.

**A typical housefront in Mandráki
on Nísyros**

Nísyros
Νίσυρος

🏛 1,000. ✈ 🚢 🚌 Mandráki
harbour. 🚗 Gialiskári 2 km (1 mile) E
of Mandráki; Páloi 4 km (2 miles) E of
Mandráki.

ALMOST CIRCULAR, Nísyros is
on a volcanic line which
passes through Aígina, Póros,
Mílos and Santoríni. In 1422
there was a violent eruption
and its 1,400-m (4,593-ft) high
peak exploded, leaving a
huge caldera (see p172).
Everything flourishes in the
volcanic soil and there is
some unique flora and fauna.
  According to mythology,
Nísyros was formed when the
enraged Poseidon threw a
chunk of Kos on the warring
giant, Polyvotis, who was
submerged beneath it, fiery
and fuming. In ancient times,
it was famous for its millstones,
often known as the "stones
of Nísyros". Now the island
prospers from pumice
mining on the islet of Gyalí
to the north.

MANDRAKI
Boats dock at Mandráki, the
capital, with quayside tavernas,
ticket agencies and buses
shuttling visitors to the
volcano. Mandráki's narrow
two-storey houses have
brightly painted wooden
balconies, often hung with
strings of drying tomatoes and
onions. A maze of lanes
congregates at Plateía Iróön,
with its war memorial. Other
roads weave south, away from
the sea, past the *kípos* (public

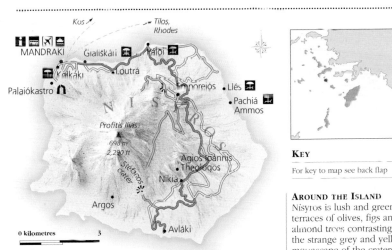

Kos
Tilos, Rhodes

MANDRÁKI
Gialiskári   Páloi
Kalkáki   Loutrá
Palaiókastro
Emporeiós   Liés
Pachiá Ammos

Profítis Ilías
698 m
2,290 ft

Stéfanos crater

Agios Ioánnis Theológos
Nikiá

Argós

Avláki

0 kilometres   3
0 miles   1

orchard) to the main square, Plateía Ilikioménon. At night, the area is bustling: shops that resemble houses are open, with traditional painted signs depicting their wares. The lanes become narrow and more winding as you approach the medieval Chóra district. In the nearby Langádi area, the balconies on the houses almost touch across the street.

The major attractions in Mandráki are the 14th-century kástro and the monastery. The former is the castle of the Knights of St John (see pp184–5), built in 1325 high up the cliff face. The monastery, **Moní Panagías Spilianís**, lies within the kástro and dates from around 1600. Inside, a finely carved iconostasis holds a Russian-style icon, decked in gold and silver offerings, of the Virgin and Child. The fame of the church grew after Saracens failed to find its treasure of silver, hidden by being worked into the Byzantine icons. The library holds rare editions and a number of ecclesiastical treasures.

The main square in Nikiá with its *choklákia* mosaic

The Historical and Folk Museum

The **Historical and Folk Museum**, on the way up to the kástro, has a reconstructed traditional island kitchen, embroideries and a small collection of local photographs.

Excursion boats offer trips from Mandráki to **Gyalí** and the tiny **Agios Antónios** islet beyond. Both destinations have white sandy beaches.

⚐ Historical and Folk Museum
Kástro. ☐ May–Sep: daily.

AROUND THE ISLAND

Nísyros is lush and green with terraces of olives, figs and almond trees contrasting with the strange grey and yellow moonscape of the craters. No visit would be complete without an excursion to the volcano and by day the island is swamped with visitors from Kos. However, it is quiet when the excursion boats have left.

Above Mandráki lies the **Palaiókastro**, the acropolis of ancient Nísyros, dating back 2,600 years. Remains include Cyclopean walls made from massive blocks carved from the volcanic rock, and Doric columns.

Nísyros is pleasant for walking. Visits to the volcano must include the pretty village of **Nikiá** (see p172), with its *choklákia* mosaic in the round "square", and abandoned **Emporeiós** which clings to the rim of the crater.

To the east of Mandráki, **Páloi** is a pretty fishing village with good tavernas and a string of dark volcanic sand beaches. Two kilometres (1 mile) west of the village, at **Loutrá**, an abandoned spa can be found.

The *meltémi* wind blows fiercely on Nísyros in high season, and the beaches east of Páloi can often be littered with debris.

View of Mandráki, the capital of Nísyros

The Geology of Nísyros

Crystals in a steam vent

Fuming and smelling of rotten eggs, the centre of Nísyros is a semi-active caldera – a crater formed by an imploded mountain. Its eruption, around 24,000 years ago, was accompanied by an outpouring of pumice, forming a blanket 100 m (328 ft) thick on the upper slopes of the island. When formed, the caldera was 3 km (2 miles) in diameter. It is now occupied by two craters and five solidified lava domes, forced upwards in the last few thousand years, including Profítis Ilías, the largest in Europe. Further eruptions in 1873 built cones of ash 100 m (328 ft) high.

Steep paths descend to the crater floor, where the surface is hot enough to melt rubber-soled shoes. Gas vents let off steam, at 98˚ C (208˚ F), which bubbles away beneath the earth's crust.

Paths lead visitors around the caldera.

Profítis Ilías dome is almost 700 m (2,300 ft) high.

Ash cones have been produced in the recent life of the caldera.

Original caldera wall

Lava dome

The Stéfanos crater, which is 300 m (985 ft) wide and 25 m (82 ft) deep, was created by an explosion of pressurized water and superheated steam.

NISYROS CALDERA

This huge caldera contains several water-filled mini craters. The largest is the still-active Stéfanos crater, which has a number of hot springs, boiling mud pots and gas vents. There is a stench of sulphur and numerous pure sulphur crystals are eagerly snapped up by would-be geologists.

Nikiá is the more appealing of Nísyros's two rim villages with its brightly painted houses and choklákia pebble mosaics. There are good views from Nikiá of the crater, and a path down to the caldera.

The oldest volcanic minerals found on Nísyros date back 200,000 years. There are vast amounts of pumice around the caldera and rich deposits of sulphur and kaoline.

Sulphur   **Kaoline**   **Pumice**

Tílos
Τήλος

300. ≡ Livádia. ℹ Megálo Chorió (22460 44320). ➤ Eristós 10 km (6 miles) NW of Livádia.

REMOTE TÍLOS is a tranquil island, with good walking and, as a resting stop on migration paths, it offers rich rewards for birdwatchers. Away from the barren beaches, Tílos has a lush heartland, with small farms growing everything from tobacco to almonds. Its hills are scattered with chapels and ruins of Crusader castles, outposts of the Knights of St John, who ruled from 1309 until 1522.

There is a strong tradition of music and poetry on the island – the poet Erinna, famous for the *Distaff*, was born here in the 4th century BC. In the 18th and 19th centuries Tílos was known for weaving cloth for women's costumes, still worn by some islanders today.

LIVÁDIA
Livádia, the main settlement, has a tree-fringed pebble beach sweeping round its bay. The blue and white church of **Agios Nikólaos** dominates the waterfront, and has an iconostasis carved in 1953 by Katasáris from Rhodes. On the beach road, the tiny, early Christian basilica of **Agios Panteleïmon kai Polýkarpos** has an attractive mosaic floor.

The pebble beach at Livádia

AROUND THE ISLAND
Buses run from Livádia to Megálo Chorió and Erystos, and mopeds can be hired; otherwise you are on foot.

Built on the site of the ancient city of Telos, **Megálo Chorió** is 8 km (5 miles) uphill from Livádia. The kástro was built by the Venetians who incorporated a Classical gateway and stone from the ancient acropolis. The **Palaeontological Museum** has midget fossilized mastodon (elephant) bones from the Misariá region, and a gold treasure trove, found in a Hellenistic tomb in the Kená region of the island.

The church of Archángelos Michaíl (1827) was built against the kástro walls. It has silver icons from the original Taxiárchis church, a gilded 19th-century iconostasis and the remains of 16th-century frescoes.

South of Megálo Chorió lies **Erystos,** a long sandy beach. **Agios Antónis** beach to the west of Megálo Chorió has the petrified remains of human skeletons. These "beach rocks" are thought to be of sailors caught in the lava when Nísyros erupted in 600 BC.

Detail of the War Memorial at Livádia

Perched on a cliff on the west coast, the Byzantine **Moní Agiou Panteleïmonos** is the island's main sight. In a cluster of trees, this fortified monastery with red pantiled roofs is famous for its sunset views. Built in 1470 it has circular chapels, a mosaic courtyard and medieval monks' cells. The dome of the church has a vision of *Christ Pantokrátor* (1776) by Gregory of Sými. Other important artifacts include 15th-century paintings of Paradise and the apostles, and a carved iconostasis that dates from 1714.

The fossilized bones of mini mastodons from 7000 BC were discovered in the **Charkadió Grotto**, a ravine in the Misariá area. The ruined fortress of Misariá marks the spot.

Mikró Chorió, below Misariá, has about 220 roofless, abandoned houses. Those residents who had stone roofs took them with them to Livádia when the population abandoned the village in the 1950s. Quiet during the day, at night the ruins are illuminated, and one house has been restored as a bar. There is also the mid-17th-century church of **Timía Zóní**, which has 18th-century frescoes, and the chapels of **Sotíros**, **Eleoúsas** and **Prodrómou**, with 15th-century paintings.

🏛 Palaeontological Museum
Megálo Chorió. **C** 22460 44212. ⚪ daily; request key at town hall.

One of many almond orchards on Tílos

Sými
Σύμη

EVER SINCE CLASSICAL TIMES, rocky, barren Sými has thrived on the success of its sponge-diving fleet and boat-building industry, which once launched 500 ships a year. By the 17th century it was the third-richest island in the Dodecanese. The Italian occupation in 1912 and the arrival of artificial sponges and steam power ended Sými's good fortunes. Its population had fallen from 23,000 to 6,000 by World War II, and the mansions built in its heyday crumbled.

A prayer in a bottle at Moní Taxiárchi

Tilos

NIMOS

Rhodes

Emporeiós · Nos · *Noúlia* · Agía Marína

Moní Agíou Michaíl Roukoumióti · SÝMI TOWN · Pédi · 250 m 820 ft · Agios Nikólaos

Agios Aimilianós

Cape Kefála · Agios Vasílios · Agios Geórgios Dissálona

· Nanoú

PIDIMA
GIALESINO
MEGALONISI

· Marathoúnta

Panormítis

Moní Taxiárchi Michaíl Panormíti

TEFTLOYSA

SÝMI TOWN

The harbour area, Gialós, is one of the most beautiful in Greece, surrounded by Neo-Classical houses and elaborate churches built on the hillside. Gialós is often busy with day trippers, particularly late morning and early afternoon.

A clock tower (1884) stands on the western side of the harbour where the ferries dock; beyond is the shingle bay of Nos beach. Next door to the town hall, the **Maritime Museum** has an interesting record of Sými's seafaring past.

Gialós is linked to the upper town, Chorió, by a road and also by 375 marble steps. Chorió comprises a maze of lanes and distinctive houses, often with traditional interiors. The late 19th-century church of **Agios Geórgios** has an unusual pebble mosaic of fierce mermaids who, in

Greek folklore, are responsible for storms that sink ships. The **Sými Museum**, high up in Chorió, has a small but interesting collection of costumes and traditional items. Beyond the museum is the ruined Byzantine **kástro** and medieval walls. Megáli Panagía church, the jewel of the kástro, has an important post-Byzantine icon

For key to map see back flap

KEY

0 kilometres   4

0 miles   2

of the *Last Judgment*, from the late 16th century, by the painter Geórgios Klontzás.

Maritime Museum
Plateía Ogdóis Maḯou. ☎ 22460 72363. ☐ Apr–Oct: daily.
● Nov–Apr. ⊘
Sými Museum
Chorió. ☎ 22460 71114.
☐ Tue–Sun. ● main public hols.

The pastel-coloured houses of Chorió on the ancient acropolis overlooking Sými's harbour

The traditional craft of boat building in Sými town

ENVIRONS: The road from Gialós to Chorió passes the hill of **Noúlia**, also known as Pontikókastro. On the hill are the remains of 20 windmills and an ancient tomb monument believed to have been erected by the Spartans in 412–411 BC.

AROUND THE ISLAND

Sými's road network is limited but there are plenty of tracks over its rocky terrain. East of Sými town, an avenue of eucalyptus trees leads down through farmland to **Pédi** bay, a beach popular with local families. From here taxi boats run to **Agios Nikólaos** beach and there are paths to Agios Nikólaos and **Agía Marína**.

The 18th-century church of **Moní Agíou Michaïl Roukounióti**, 3 km (2 miles) west of Sými town, is built like a desert fortress in Gothic and folk architecture. It houses 14th-century frescoes and a rare 15th-century, semicircular icon of the *Hospitality of Abraham* by Cretan artist Stylianós Génis.

Sými's most popular sight is **Moní Taxiárchi Michaïl Panormíti** in Panormíti bay, a place of pilgrimage for Greek sailors worldwide. Its white buildings, spanning the 18th to 20th centuries, line the water's edge. The pleasant horseshoe-shaped harbour is dominated by the elaborate mock-Baroque bell tower, a 1905 copy of the famous bell tower of Agía Foteiní in Izmir.

The monastery is famous for its icon of the Archangel Michael, Sými's patron saint and guardian of seafarers. Despite being removed to Gialós, it mysteriously kept

returning to Panormítis so the monastery was founded here. The single-nave *katholikón* was built in 1783 on the remains of an early Byzantine chapel also dedicated to the saint.

According to tradition, if you ask a favour of St Michael, you must vow to give something in return. As a result, the interior is a dazzling array of

The mock-Baroque belltower of Moní Taxiárchi Michaïl Panormíti

votive offerings, or *támata*, from pilgrims, including small model ships in silver and gold.

The intricate Baroque iconostasis by Mastrodiákis Taliadoúros is a remarkable piece of woodcarving. The walls and ceiling are covered in smoke-blackened 18th-century frescoes by the two Sými-brothers Nikítas and Michaïl Karakostís.

The sacristy museum is full of treasures, including a post-Byzantine painting of the ten saints, Agioi Déka, by the Cretan Theódoros Poulákis. There are prayers in bottles, which have floated miraculously into Panormítis, containing money for the monastery from faithful sailors. The cloister has a *choklákia* courtyard of zigzag pebble mosaics *(see p194)* and an arcaded balcony.

West of the monastery, past the taverna, is a memorial to the former abbot, two monks and two teachers executed by the Germans in 1944 for running a spy radio for British commandos. Small Panormítis beach is here and there are woodland walks to **Marathoúnta**.

Moní Taxiárchi Michaïl Panormíti

Panormíti bay. Tue–Sun.

Rhodes

Ρόδος

R HODES, THE CAPITAL of the Dodecanese, was an important centre in the 5th to 3rd centuries BC. It was part of both the Roman and Byzantine empires, before being conquered by the Knights of St John. They occupied Rhodes from 1306 to 1522, and their medieval walled city still dominates Rhodes town. Ottoman and Italian rulers followed. Fringed by sandy beaches, and with good hiking and lively nightlife, Rhodes attracts thousands of tourists each year.

KEY

For key to map see back flap

Ancient Kámeiros
The stunning ruins of this once-thriving Doric city include a 6th-century BC Temple of Athena Polias ❺

Skála Kameírou
A pleasant place to relax, Skála Kameírou is an attractive harbour that once served the ancient city of Kámeiros ❻

Kritinía castle, built by the Knights of Rhodes, was one of their larger strongholds *(see p189)*.

Emponas
The slopes around this traditional town have been cultivated with vines by the Emery winery since the 1920s ❼

Monólithos
The village is dominated by the 15th-century castle, perched high on a massive rock. It was built by the Knights of Rhodes ❽

Moní Skiádi
This monastery was built in the 18th and 19th centuries and is famous for its icon of the Panagía, or the Blessed Virgin ❾

Siána is a pretty traditional hill-village, known for its locally distilled spirit, *soúma (see p189)*.

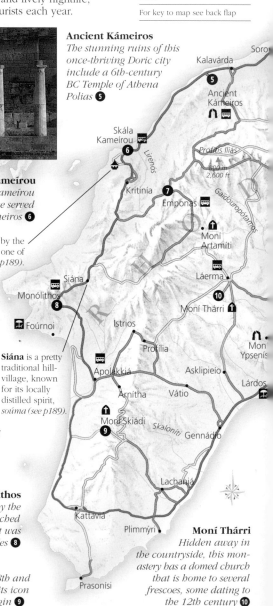

Moní Thárri
Hidden away in the countryside, this monastery has a domed church that is home to several frescoes, some dating to the 12th century ❿

Petaloúdes

Called butterfly valley, this tranquil place is, in fact, home to thousands of moths during the summer **4**

Moní Filerímou

The monastery is set on the beautiful hillsides of Mount Filérimos. The main church dates back to the 14th century **3**

VISITORS' CHECKLIST

100,000. ✈ 25 km (16 miles) SW of Rhodes town. ⚓ Commercial harbour, Rhodes town. ℹ Rhodes town (22410 22661). ⚜ Rodini Park Wine Festival, outskirts of Rhodes town: end Aug.

Chálki, Piraeus, Astypálaia ↑ *Sými, Kos*

Kastellórizo

RHODES TOWN 1

Triánda

Ancient Ialyssós **2**

Paradísi

Moní Filerímou **3**

Réni

Koskinoú

Koskinoú **15**

Thérmes Kalithéas

Kalithéa

Kalythiés

Faliráki **14**

4 Petaloúdes

Psinthos

Kadikó Bay

Afántou

Kolympia

Loútari

Eptá Pigés **13**

Moní Tsampíkas

Tsampíka

12 Archángelos

Stégna

Charáki

Líndos **11**

ardos

Péfkoi

Ancient Ialyssós

Set on a plateau with commanding views, this ancient site dates back to 2500 BC. The ruins include remains of a 3rd-century BC acropolis **2**

Faliráki

This fun-packed resort offers all sorts of nightlife and watersports, and is particularly popular with the young **14**

Faraklós

Faraklós was once used by the Knights of Rhodes as a prison. Today it overlooks Charáki village (see pp190–91).

Eptá Pigés

This is an enchanting beauty spot that takes its name from the "seven springs" that are the source for the area's central reservoir **13**

Archángelos

A popular place to visit, Archangelos is set in attractive countryside, and maintains a tradition of handicraft production **12**

★ **Rhodes Town**
Mandráki harbour is at the centre of Rhodes town, which is one of Greece's most popular tourist destinations **1**

Koskinoú

This small village offers visitors the opportunity to see traditional Rhodian houses and choklákia pebble mosaics (see p194) **15**

STAR SIGHTS

★ **Rhodes Town**

★ **Líndos**

0 kilometres   10
0 miles   6

★ **Líndos**
One of the island's most visited sites, the acropolis at Líndos towers over the town from its clifftop position **11**

Street-by-Street: Rhodes Old Town ●
Παλιά Πόλη Ρόδου

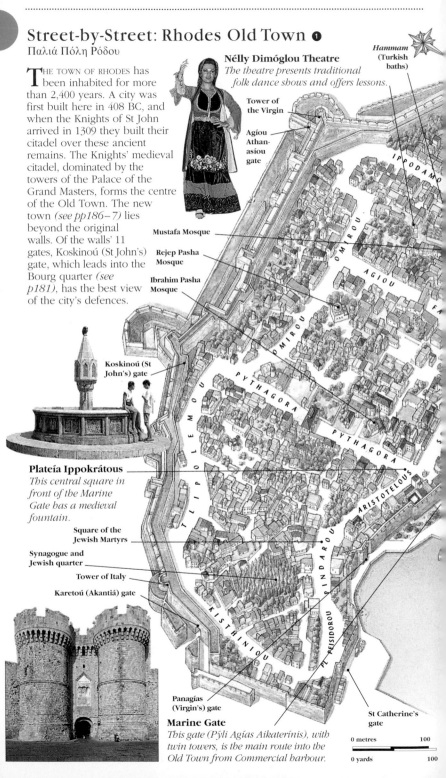

THE TOWN OF RHODES has been inhabited for more than 2,400 years. A city was first built here in 408 BC, and when the Knights of St John arrived in 1309 they built their citadel over these ancient remains. The Knights' medieval citadel, dominated by the towers of the Palace of the Grand Masters, forms the centre of the Old Town. The new town *(see pp186–7)* lies beyond the original walls. Of the walls' 11 gates, Koskinoú (St John's) gate, which leads into the Bourg quarter *(see p181)*, has the best view of the city's defences.

Nélly Dimóglou Theatre
The theatre presents traditional folk dance shows and offers lessons.

Hammam (Turkish baths)

Tower of the Virgin

Agíou Athanasíou gate

Mustafa Mosque

Rejep Pasha Mosque

Ibrahim Pasha Mosque

Koskinoú (St John's) gate

Plateía Ippokrátous
This central square in front of the Marine Gate has a medieval fountain.

Square of the Jewish Martyrs

Synagogue and Jewish quarter

Tower of Italy

Karetoú (Akantiá) gate

Panagías (Virgin's) gate

Marine Gate
This gate (Pýli Agías Aikaterínis), with twin towers, is the main route into the Old Town from Commercial harbour.

St Catherine's gate

0 metres		100
0 yards		100

Tower of Spain

Ottoman Library

Mosque of Suleiman
First built in 1523, it commemorates Suleiman's conquest of Rhodes (see p181).

Agíou Georgíou (St George's) tower

APOLLONION

IPPODAMOU

ORFEOS

SOKRATOUS

IPPOTON

APELLOU

VISITORS' CHECKLIST

🏘 42,000. ✈ Paradisi 25 km (16 miles) SW of Rhodes town. ⚓ Commercial harbour. 🚌 Mandráki. 🚌 Sat at Zéfiros, Wed at Viranes. ⚐ Rodini Park Wine Festival, Rhodes town. End Aug. ⚓ Psaropoúla 1 km (0.5 mile) SW.

Tilevólon (St Anthony's) gate

Ampouáz (d'Amboise) gate

★ Street of the Knights
Lining this street are the various Inns of the Knights. The austere gateway to the Inn of France is shown here (see pp184–5).

St Peter's tower

Temple of Aphrodite

Elefthería (Liberty) gate

St Paul's tower

Navarcheíou gate

Byzantine Museum (see p180)

Decorative Arts Museum (see p180)

Arsenal gate

The walls, dating from 1330, are up to 12 m (40 ft) thick and 4 km (2.5 miles) long. Tours start at the Palace of the Grand Masters.

★ Palace of the Grand Masters
This was the final line of defence for the Knights. The palace (see pp182–3) is now home to two permanent exhibitions about ancient and medieval Rhodes.

STAR SIGHTS

★ Palace of the Grand Masters

★ Street of the Knights

Archaeological Museum
Housed in the flamboyant Gothic Knights' hospital, completed in 1481, the museum displays a large collection, including this Hellenistic statue of a horse (see p180).

Exploring Rhodes Old Town

DOMINATED BY THE Palace of the Grand Masters, this medieval citadel is surrounded by moats and 4 km (2.5 miles) of walls. Eleven gates give access to the Old Town, which is divided into the Collachium and the Bourg. The Collachium was the Knights' quarter, and dates from 1309. The Bourg housed the rest of the population, which included Jews and Turks as well as Greeks. As one of the finest walled cities in existence, the Old Town is now a World Heritage Site.

An arched street in the Old Town

The imposing 16th-century d'Amboise gate

The Collachium

This area includes the Street of the Knights *(see pp184–5)* and the Palace of the Grand Masters *(see pp182–3)*. The main gates of entry from the new town are d'Amboise gate and the Eleftherías (Liberty) gate. The former was built in 1512 by Grand Master d'Amboise, leading from Dimokratías to the palace. The Eleftherías gate was built by the Italians and leads from Eleftherías to Plateía Sýmis. An archway leads from here into Apelloú.

🔲 Archaeological Museum

Plateía Mouseíou. 📞 *22410 27657.* ⏱ *Tue–Sun.* ⬤ *main public hols.* 📷

The museum is housed in the Gothic Hospital of the Knights, built in 1440–81. Most famous of the exhibits is the 1st-century BC marble *Aphrodite of Rhodes*. Other gems include a 2nd-century BC head of Helios the Sun God, discovered at the Temple of Helios on the nearby hill of Monte Smith. The grave *stelae* from the necropolis of Kámeiros give a good insight into 5th-century BC life. Exhibits also include *koúroi* (550–525 BC) from Kámeiros and coins, jewellery and ceramics from the Mycenaean graves at nearby Ialyssós.

🔲 Decorative Arts Museum

Plateía Argyrokástrou. 📞 *22410 75674.* ⏱ *Tue–Sun.* ⬤ *main public hols.* 📷 ♿

This is an excellent folk museum featuring Lindian plates and tiles, a wide range of island costumes and a reconstructed traditional Rhodian house.

Aphrodite of Rhodes, Archaeological Museum

🔲 Medieval Rhodes and Ancient Rhodes Exhibitions

Palace of the Grand Masters. 📞 *22410 23359.* ⏱ *Tue–Sun.* ⬤ *main public hols.* 📷 ♿

Both of these permanent exhibitions can be seen as part of a tour of the Palace of the Grand Masters *(see pp182–3)*. The Medieval Rhodes exhibition is titled: Rhodes from the 4th century AD to the Turkish Conquest (1522). It gives an insight into trade and everyday life in Byzantine and medieval times, with Byzantine icons, Italian and Spanish ceramics, armour and militaria. The Ancient Rhodes exhibition, entitled Ancient Rhodes: 2,400 years, is situated off the inner court. It details 45 years of archaeological investigations on the island with a marvellous collection of finds.

🔲 Byzantine Museum

Apéllou. 📞 *22410 27657.* ⏱ *Tue–Sun.* ⬤ *main public hols.* 📷 ♿

Dating from the 11th century, this Byzantine church became the Knights' cathedral, but was converted under Turkish rule into the Mosque of Enderum, known locally as the Red Mosque. Now a museum, it houses a fine collection of icons and frescoes. Among the exhibits are striking examples of 12th-century paintings in the dynamic Comnenian style from Moní Thárri *(see p190)* and late 14th-century frescoes from the abandoned church of Agios Zacharías on Chálki.

Courtyard at the Knights' Hospital, now the Archaeological Museum

♙ Medieval City Walls

Tours from the Palace of the Grand Masters. ○ *Tue & Fri: 2.45pm.*

A masterpiece of medieval military architecture, the huge walls run for 4 km (2.5 miles) and display 151 escutcheons of Grand Masters and Knights.

The Bourg's clocktower

The Bourg

Close to d'Amboise gate is the restored clock tower, which has excellent views. It was built in 1852 on the site of a Byzantine tower and marks the end of the Collachium. The Bourg's labyrinth of streets begins at Sokrátous, the Golden Mile of bazaar style shops, off which lie shady squares with pavement cafés and tavernas. The architecture is a mix of medieval, Neo-Classical and Levantine. Between the houses, with rickety wooden balconies, Ottoman mosques can be found.

Other than the major sights listed below, the Hospice of the Tongue of Italy (1392) on Kisthiníou is worth a visit, as is the Panagía tis Níkis (Our Lady of Victory). It stands near St Catherine's gate, and was built by the Knights in 1480 after the Virgin had appeared to them, inspiring victory over the Turks.

☪ Mosque of Suleiman the Magnificent

Orféos Sokrátous, ● *under renovation.*

The pink mosque was constructed in 1522 to commemorate the Sultan's victory over the Knights. Rebuilt in 1808, using material from the original mosque, it remains one of the town's major landmarks. Its superb, but unsafe, minaret had to be removed in 1989, and the once-mighty mosque is now crumbling. It is sadly closed to the public.

🏛 Library of Ahmet Havuz

Orféos Sokrátous. 🕻 *22410 74090.* ○ *Mar–Oct: 9:30am–4pm Mon–Sat.* ● *Nov–Feb; main public hols.*

The Library of Ahmet Havuz (1793) houses the chronicle of the siege of Rhodes in 1522. This is a collection of very rare Arabic and Persian manuscripts, including beautifully illuminated 15th- and 16th-century Korans, which were restored to the library in the early 1990s, having been stolen then rediscovered in London.

🎭 Nélly Dimóglou Theatre

7 Andrónikou. 🕻 *22410 20157.* ○ *mid-May–mid-Oct: Mon, Wed & Fri.* 🍴 ♿

The Nélly Dimóglou Theatre offers lessons in authentic Greek folk dancing. Its gardens are open all day for refreshments, and performances begin at 9:20pm every evening from Monday to Friday.

♨ Hammam

Plateía Arionos. 🕻 *22410 27739.* ● *Mon & Sun* 🍴

The *hammam*, or Turkish baths, were built by Mustapha Pasha in 1765. For decades a famous place of rest and relaxation for Eastern nobility, the *hammam* is now used by Greeks, tourists and the Turkish minority. Your own soap and towels are essential, and sexes are segregated.

☪ Mosque of Ibrahim Pasha

Plátanos. 🕻 *22410 73410.* ○ *daily.* 🍴 *donation.*

Situated off Sofokléous, the Mosque of Ibrahim Pasha was built in 1531 and refurbished in 1928. The mosque has an exquisite interior.

☪ Mosque of Rejep Pasha

Ekátonos. ● *under renovation.*

Built in 1588, Rejep Pasha is one of the most striking of the 14 or so mosques to be found in the Old Town. The mosque, which has a fountain made from Byzantine and medieval church columns, contains the sarcophagus of the Pasha. The tiny Byzantine church of Agios Fanoúrios is situated close by.

The Jewish Quarter

East from Hippocrates Square, the Bourg embraces Ovriakí. This was the Jewish Quarter from the 1st century AD until German occupation in 1944, when the Jewish population was transported to Auschwitz.

East along Aristotélous is **Plateía Evraíon Martýron** (Square of the Jewish Martyrs), named in memory of all those who perished in the concentration camps. There is a bronze sea horse fountain in the centre, and to the north is Admiralty House, an imposing medieval building. The Synagogue is on Simíou.

The dome of the Mosque of Suleiman the Magnificent

Rhodes: Palace of the Grand Masters

Παλάτι του Μεγάλου Μαγίστρου

A FORTRESS WITHIN a fortress, this was the seat of 19 Grand Masters, the nerve centre of the Collachium, or Knights' Quarter, and last refuge for the population in times of danger. Built in the 14th century, it survived earthquake and siege, but was blown up by an accidental explosion in 1856. It was restored by the Italians in the 1930s for Mussolini and King Victor Emmanuel III. The palace has some priceless mosaics from sites in Kos, after which some of the rooms are named. It also houses two exhibitions: Medieval, and Ancient Rhodes *(see p180)*.

Gilded angel candleholder

Chamber with Colonnades
Two elegant colonnades support the roof and there is a 5th-century AD early Christian mosaic.

Chamber of the Sea Horse and Nymph

Thyrsus Chamber

The Second Cross-Vaulted Chamber, once used as the governor's office, is paved with an intricately decorated, early Christian mosaic of the 5th century AD from Kos.

First Cross-Vaulted Chamber

★ Medusa Chamber
The mythical Gorgon Medusa, with hair of writhing serpents, forms the centrepiece of this important late Hellenistic mosaic. The chamber also features Chinese and Islamic vases.

Laocoön Chamber
A copy of the sculpture of the death of the Trojan, Laocoön, and his sons dominates the hall. The 1st-century BC original by Rhodian masters Athenodoros, Agesandros and Polydoros is in the Vatican.

The battlements and heavy fortifications of the palace were to be the last line of defence in the event of the city walls being breached.

★ **Central Courtyard**
The palace is built around a courtyard paved with geometric marble tiles. The north side is lined with Hellenistic statues taken from the Odeion in Kos (see p167).

Entrance to Ancient Rhodes exhibition *(see p180)*

The Chamber of the Nine Muses has a late Hellenistic mosaic featuring busts of the Nine Muses of Greek myth.

★ **Main Gate**
This imposing entrance, built by the Knights, has twin horseshoe-shaped towers with swallowtail turrets. The coat of arms is that of Grand Master del Villeneuve, who ruled from 1319 to 1346.

Entrance →

Street of the Knights *(see pp184–5)*

The First Chamber, with its 16th-century choir stalls, features a late Hellenistic mosaic.

Grand staircase

Entrance to Medieval Rhodes exhibition *(see p180)*

The Second Chamber has a late Hellenistic mosaic and carved choir stalls.

THE FIRST GRAND MASTER

The first Grand Master, or Magnus Magister, of the Knights was Foulkes de Villaret (1305–19), a French knight. He negotiated to buy Rhodes from the Lord of the Dodecanese, Admiral Vignolo de Vignoli. This left the Knights with the task of conquering the island's inhabitants. The Knights of Rhodes (see pp184–5), as they became, remained here until their expulsion in 1522. The Villaret name lives on in Villaré, one of the island's white wines.

Foulkes de Villaret

MAGNUS FRATER FULCUS 1305 — MAGISTER DE VILLARET 1319

STAR FEATURES

★ **Central Courtyard**

★ **Medusa Chamber**

★ **Main Gate**

Rhodes: Street of the Knights

ONE OF THE OLD TOWN'S most famous sights, the medieval Street of the Knights (Odos Ippotón) is situated between the harbour and the Palace of the Grand Masters *(see pp182–3)*. It is lined by the Inns of the Tongues, or nationalities, of the Order of St John. Begun in the 14th century in Gothic style, the Inns were used as meeting places for the Knights. The site of the German Inn is unknown, but the others were largely restored by the Italians in the early 20th century.

This residence was built for the head of the Tongue of Aragon, Diomede de Vilaragut.

Access to the Turkish garden

SOUTH SIDE

The Archaeological Museum *(see p180)*, was originally the New Hospital of the Knights.

← **To Inn of England**

The Inn of Provence has coats of arms set in the wall. They represent the Order of the Knights of St John, the Royal House of France, Grand Master del Carretto and the Knight de Flota.

Agía Triáda, or French Chapel

NORTH SIDE

Palace of the Grand Masters ←

Arched bridge connecting Inn of Spain and Inn of Provence

The Knights of Rhodes

Coat of arms of Foulkes de Villaret, first Grand Master

FOUNDED IN THE 11th century by merchants from Amalfi, the Order of Hospitallers of the Knights of St John guarded the Holy Sepulchre and tended Christian pilgrims in Jerusalem. They became a military order after the First Crusade (1096–9), but had to take refuge in Cyprus when Jerusalem fell in 1291. They then bought Rhodes from the Genoese pirate Admiral Vignoli in 1306, and eventually conquered the Rhodians in 1309. A Grand Master was elected for life to govern the Order, which was divided into seven Tongues, or nationalities: France, Italy, England, Germany, Provence, Spain and Auvergne. Each Tongue protected an area of city wall known as a Curtain. The Knights fortified the Dodecanese with around 30 castles and their defences are some of the finest examples of medieval military architecture.

The Knights *were drawn from noble Roman Catholic families. Those who entered the Order of the Knights of St John swore vows of chastity, obedience and poverty. Although knights held all the major offices, there were also lay brothers.*

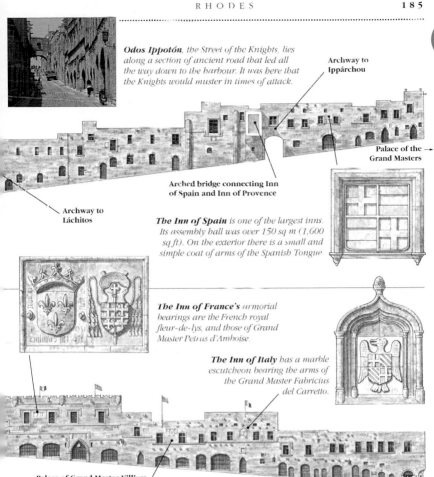

Odos Ippotón, the Street of the Knights, lies along a section of ancient road that led all the way down to the harbour. It was here that the Knights would muster in times of attack.

Archway to Ippárchou

Palace of the → Grand Masters

Arched bridge connecting Inn of Spain and Inn of Provence

Archway to Láchitos

The Inn of Spain is one of the largest inns. Its assembly hall was over 150 sq m (1,600 sq ft). On the exterior there is a small and simple coat of arms of the Spanish Tongue.

The Inn of France's armorial bearings are the French royal fleur-de-lys, and those of Grand Master Petrus d'Amboise.

The Inn of Italy has a marble escutcheon bearing the arms of the Grand Master Fabricius del Carretto.

Palace of Grand Master Villiers de l'Isle Adam (1521–34)

Inn of Auvergne →

The Great Siege of Rhodes in 1522 resulted in the Knights being defeated by the Turks. From a garrison of 650 Knights, only 180 survived. They negotiated a safe departure, although the Rhodians who fought with them were slaughtered. Seven years later, the Knights found sanctuary on the island of Malta. Their final defeat came in 1798 when Malta was annexed by Napoleon.

Pierre d'Aubusson, Grand Master from 1476 to 1503, is featured in this market scene. He oversaw a highly productive time in terms of building in Rhodes, including completion of the Hospital (now the Archaeological Museum).

Exploring Rhodes New Town

THE NEW TOWN grew steadily over the last century, and became firmly established during the Italian Fascist occupation of the 1920s with the construction of the grandiose public buildings by the harbour. The New Town is made up of a number of areas including Néa Agora and Mandráki harbour in the eastern half of town. The Italian influence remains in these areas with everything from pizzerias to Gucci shops. The town's west coast is a busy tourist centre, with lively streets and a crammed beach.

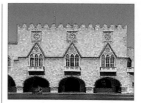

Government House, previously the Italian Governor's Palace

Mandráki harbour with the two statues of deer at its entrance

Mandráki Harbour

The harbour is the hub of life, the link between the Old and New towns where locals go for their evening stroll, or *vólta*. It is lined with yachts and excursion boats for which you can book a variety of trips in advance.

A bronze doe and stag guard the harbour entrance, where the Colossus was believed to have stood. The harbour sweeps round to the ruined 15th-century fortress of **Agios** Nikólaos, now a lighthouse, on the promontory past the three medieval windmills.

Elegant public buildings, built by the Italians in the 1920s, line Mandráki harbour: the post office, law courts, town hall, police station and the National Theatre all stand in a row. The **National Theatre** often shows Rhodian character plays based on folk customs.

Nearby, on Plateía Eleftherías, is the splendid church of the **Evangelismós** (Annunciation), a 1925 replica of the Knight's Church of St John, which has a lavishly decorated interior. The Archbishop's Palace is next door beside a giant fountain, which is a copy of the Fontana Grande in Viterbo, Italy. Further along, the mock Venetian Gothic **Government House** (Nomarchía) is ornately decorated and surrounded by fine vaulted arcades. Unfortunately there is no access for tourists or the general public.

At the north end of Plateía Eleftherías is the attractive **Mosque of Murad Reis**, with its graceful minaret. It was named after a Turkish admiral serving under Suleiman who was killed during the 1522 siege of Rhodes. Situated within the grounds is the Villa Kleoboulos, which was the home of the British writer Lawrence Durrell between 1945 and 1947. Also in the grounds is a cemetery reserved for Ottoman notables.

Heading north from the area around Mandráki harbour, a pleasant stroll along the waterfront via the crowded Elli beach leads to the northern tip of the New Town. The Hydrobiological Institute is situated on the coastal tip, housing the **Aquarium**. Set in a subterranean grotto, this is the only major aquarium in Greece, displaying nearly 40 tanks of fish. Opposite, on the north point of the island is Aquarium Beach, which is particularly good for windsurfing and paragliding.

The minaret of the Mosque of Murad Reis

🐟 **Aquarium**
Hydrobiological Institute, Kássou.
📞 22410 27308. ⬤ daily. ⬤ main public hols. 📷 ♿

THE COLOSSUS OF RHODES

Painting of the Colossus by Fischer von Erlach, 1700

One of the Seven Wonders of the Ancient World, the Colossus was a huge statue of Helios, the sun god, standing at 32–40 m (105–130 ft). Built in 305 BC to celebrate Rhodian victory over Demetrius, the Macedonian besieger, it was sculpted by Chares of Líndos. It took 12 years to build, using bronze from the battle weapons, and cost 9 tons (10 imperial tons) of silver. Traditionally pictured straddling Mandráki harbour, it probably stood at the Temple of Apollo, now the site of the Palace of the Grand Masters in the Old Town (*see pp182–3*). An earthquake in 227 BC caused it to topple over.

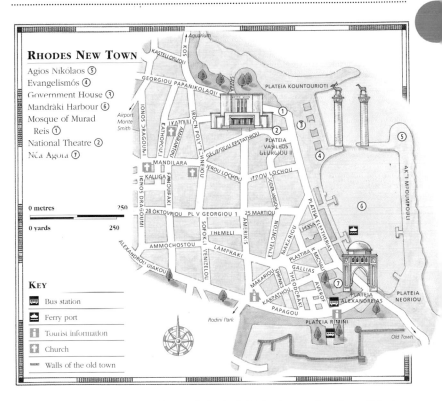

RHODES NEW TOWN

Agios Nikólaos ⑤
Evangelismós ④
Government House ③
Mandráki Harbour ⑥
Mosque of Murad
  Reis ①
National Theatre ②
Néa Agora ⑦

0 metres   250

0 yards   250

KEY

🚌 Bus station

⚓ Ferry port

ℹ️ Tourist information

✝️ Church

▥ Walls of the old town

Néa Agora

Mandráki is backed by the New Market or Néa Agora with its Moorish domes and lively cafés. Inside the market are food stalls, gift shops, small *souvláki* bars and cafés. It is popular as a meeting place for people coming from outlying villages and islands. Behind the Néa Agora, in the grounds of the Palace of the Grand Masters, a sound and light show is held. This takes place daily in one of four languages and tells the story of the over- throw of the Knights by Sulei- man the Magnificent in 1522.

Monte Smith

Monte Smith, a hill to the west of town, offers panoramic views over Rhodes town and the coast. It is named Monte Smith after the English Admiral Sir Sidney Smith who kept watch from there for Napoleon's fleet in 1802. It is also known as Agios Stéphanos.

The hill is the site of a 3rd-century BC Hellenistic city which was excavated by the Italians. They restored the 3rd- century BC stadium, the 2nd-century BC acropolis and a small theatre or odeion. This was built in an unusual square shape and is used for performances of ancient drama in the summer. Only three columns remain of the once-mighty Temple of Pythian Apollo, and there are other ruins of the temples of Athena Polias and Zeus. Near- by, on Voreíou Ipeírou, are the remains of the Asklepieíon, a temple dedicated to the god of healing, Asklepios.

Rodíni Park

The beautiful Rodíni Park, 3 km (2 miles) to the south of Rhodes town, is now home to the Rhodian deer sanctuary, and perfect for a break away from the crowded centre. It is the site where the orator Aeschines built the School of Rhetoric in 330 BC, attended by both Julius Caesar and Cassius, although there are no remains to visit. Sights include a 3rd-century BC necropolis with Doric rock tombs and sev- eral Ptolemaic, rock-cut tombs. In medieval times the Knights grew their herbs at Rodíni.

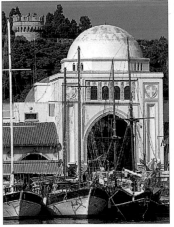

A view of the domed centrepiece of the New Market from Mandráki Harbour

Exploring Western Rhodes

THE WINDSWEPT WEST COAST is a busy strip of hotels, bars and restaurants, along shingly beaches from Rhodes town to the airport at Paradísi. But head south and the landscape becomes green and fertile, with vineyards and wooded mountain slopes, dotted with traditional farming villages.

An icon at Our Lady of Filérimos

The attractions include Moní Filerímou, Ancient Kámeiros, the wine-making village of Emponas, and the enchanting valley of Petaloúdes, the place that gives Rhodes its name as the "Island of Butterflies". Further south is a dramatic mix of scenery with castle-topped crags and sea views to the islands of Chálki and Alimiá.

Ancient Ialyssós ❷
Αρχαία Ιαλυσός

15 km (9 miles) SW of Rhodes town. 🚌 to Triánda. ☐ Tue–Sun. ⬤ main public hols.

Named after a grandson of the sun god Helios, Ialyssós fused with two other Doric city-states, Líndos and Kámeiros, to create one capital, Rhodes, in 408 BC. As this new centre grew, Ialyssós, Líndos and Kámeiros lost their former importance. However, Ialyssós proved a much fought-over site: the Byzantines were besieged by the Genoese there in 1248; the Knights *(see pp184–5)* used it as a base before taking Rhodes in 1309; and it was Suleiman's headquarters before his assault on the Knights in 1522. The Italians used it again for gun positions during World War II.

The only remnant of the acropolis is the 3rd-century BC **Temple of Athena Polias and Zeus Poliefs** by the church of Agios Geórgios. The restored lion-head fountain, to the south, is 4th century BC.

Moní Filerímou ❸
Μονή Φιλερήμου

15 km (9 miles) SW of Rhodes town. 🕻 22410 92202. 🚌 to Triánda. ☐ Tue–Sun. ⬤ main public hols.

One of Rhodes' beauty spots, the hillsides of Filérimos are home to cypresses and pines. Among the trees sits Moní Filerímou, its domed chapels decorated with the cross of the Knights and the coat of arms of Grand Master Pierre d'Aubusson. A place of worship for 2,000 years, layers of history and traditions can be seen, from Phoenician to Byzantine, Orthodox and Catholic.

The main attraction is Our Lady of Filérimos, the Italian reconstruction of the Knights' 14th-century church of the Virgin Mary. The church is a complex of four chapels: the main one, built in 1306, leads to three others. The innermost chapel has a Byzantine floor decorated with a red mosaic fish.

The Italians erected a Calvary, from the entrance of the monastery, in the form of an avenue with the Stations of the Cross illustrated on plaques. On the headland stands a giant 18-m (59-ft) cross.

Petaloúdes ❹
Πεταλούδες

26 km (16 miles) SW of Rhodes town. 🚌

Petaloúdes, or Butterfly Valley, is a narrow leafy valley with a stream crisscrossed by wooden bridges. It teems, not with butterflies, but with Jersey tiger moths from June to September. Thousands are attracted by the golden resin of the storax trees, which exude vanilla-scented gum used for incense. Cool and pleasant, Petaloúdes attracts walkers as well as lepidopterists, and is at its most peaceful in the early morning before all the tour buses arrive.

There is a walk along the valley to the **Moní Panagías Kalópetras**. This rural church, built in 1782, is a tranquil resting place, and the fine views are well worth the climb.

Jersey tiger moth

Ancient Kámeiros ❺
Αρχαία Κάμειρος

36 km (22 miles) SW of Rhodes town. 🕻 22410 40037. 🚌 ☐ Tue–Sun. ⬤ main public hols. 🅿 ♿ to lower sections only.

Discovered in 1859, this Doric city was a thriving community during the 5th century BC. Founded by Althaemenes of Crete, the city was probably destroyed in a large earthquake in 142 BC. In spite of this, it remains one of the best-preserved Classical Greek cities.

There are remains of a 3rd-century BC Doric temple, an altar to Helios, public baths and a 6th-century BC cistern, which supplied 400 families. The 6th-century BC Temple of Athena Polias is on the top terrace, below which are remains of the Doric stoa, 206 m (675 ft) long.

Moní Filerímou in its woodland setting

Monólithos castle in its precarious position overlooking the sea

Skála Kameírou 6
Σκάλα Καμείρου

50 km (30 miles) SW of Rhodes town.
🏛 100. 🚌

The fishing harbour of Skála Kameírou makes a good place for lunch. It was the Doric city of an ancient port, and the outline of a Lycian tomb remains on the cliff side. Nearby, **Kritiniá castle** is one of the Knights' more impressive ruins. Its three levels are attributed to different Grand Masters. Clinging to the hillside, a cluster of white houses form the picturesque village of **Kritiniá**.

Emponas 7
Έμπωνας

55 km (34 miles) SW of Rhodes town.
🏛 1,500. 🚌

Situated in the wild foothills of Mount Attávyros, the atmospheric village of Emponas has been home to the Cair

winery since the 1920s and is also famous for its folk dancing and festivals. Although the village is popular for organized Greek nights, Emponas has maintained its traditional ways.

Monólithos 8
Μονόλιθος

80 km (50 miles) SW of Rhodes town.
🏛 250. 🚌 🚕 Foúrni 5 km (3 miles) SW.

Named after its monolith, a crag with a dramatic 235-m (770-ft) drop to the sea, Monólithos is the most important village in the southwest.

Situated at the foot of Mount Akramýtis, the village is 2 km (1 mile) from **Monólithos castle**. This impregnable 15th-century fortress, built by Grand Master d'Aubusson, is perched spectacularly on the vast grey rock. Its massive walls enclose two small 15th-century chapels, Agios Panteleïmon

and Agios Geórgios, both decorated with frescoes. Views from the top are impressive, and the sheer drop hair-raising.

Down a rough road south from the castle is the sheltered sandy beach of **Foúrni**, which has a seasonal taverna.

ENVIRONS: Between Emponas and Monólithos, the pretty hill village of **Siána** is famous for its honey and fiery *soúma* – a kind of grape spirit, like the Cretan raki. The villagers were granted a licence by the Italians to make the spirit, and you can sample both the fire water and honey at the roadside cafés. The village houses have traditional clay roofs, and the domed church of **Agios Panteleïmon** has restored 18th-century frescoes.

Moní Skiádi 9
Μονή Σκιάδι

8 km (5 miles) S of Apolakkiá.
📞 22440 46006. 🚌 to Apolakkiá.
🕐 daily.

Moní Skiádi is famous for its miraculous icon of the Panagía or the Blessed Virgin. When a 15th-century heretic stabbed the Virgin's cheek it was supposed to have bled, and the brown stains are still visible. The present monastery was built during the 18th and 19th centuries around the 13th-century church of Agios Stavrós, or the Holy Cross. At Easter the holy icon is carried from village to village until finally coming to rest for a month on the island of Chálki.

Sunset over the village of Emponas and Mount Attávyros

Exploring Eastern Rhodes

THE SHELTERED EAST COAST has miles of beaches and rocky coves, the crowded holiday playgrounds of Faliráki and Líndos contrasting with the deserted sands in the southeast. For sightseeing purposes the way east divides into two sections: from the southern tip of the island at Prasonísi up to Péfkoi, and then from Líndos up to Rhodes town. The landscape is a rich patchwork, from the oasis of Eptá Pigés and the orange groves near Archángelos, to the stretches of rugged coastline and sandy bays.

Fountain in Lárdos village

Moní Thárri ⑩
Μονή Θάρρι

40 km (25 miles) S of Rhodes town.
to Laérma. ☐ daily.

From the inland resort of Lárdos follow signs to Láerma, which is just north of Moní Thárri, famous for its 12th-century frescoes. Reached through a forest, the domed church was hidden from view in order to escape the attention of marauding pirates.

According to legend, it was built in the 9th century by a mortally ill Byzantine princess, who miraculously recovered when it was completed.

The 12th-century north and south walls remain, and there are vestiges of the 9th-century building in the grounds. The nave, apse and dome are covered with frescoes. Some walls have four layers of paintings, the earliest dating as far back as 1100, while there are three layers in the apse dating from the 12th–16th centuries. These

Asklipieío village

are more distinct, and depict a group of prophets and a horse's head. The monastery has been extended and has basic accommodation for visitors.

About 8 km (5 miles) south along a rough track is the pleasant village of **Asklipieío**, with the frescoed church of Kímisis tis Theotókou.

Líndos ⑪
See pp192–3.

Archángelos ⑫
Αρχάγγελος

33 km (20 miles) S of Rhodes town.
🚶 3,000. 🚌 🚏 Stégna 3 km
(2 miles) E.

The island's largest village, Archángelos lies in the Valley of Aíthona, which is renowned for its oranges. The town itself is famous for pottery, handwoven rugs and leather boots. Traditionally worn as protection from snakes while in the fields working, they are made of sturdy cowhide for the feet, with soft goatskin leggings. The townspeople have their own dialect and are fiercely patriotic – some graves are even painted blue and white.

In the centre, the church of **Archángeloi Michaïl and Gavriíl**, the village's patron saints, is distinguished by a tiered bell tower and pebble-mosaic courtyard.

Above the town are ruins of the **Crusader castle**, built by Grand Master Orsini in 1467 as part of the Knights' defences against the Turks. Inside, the chapel of Agios Geórgios has a modern fresco of the saint in action against the dragon. To the east of the town, at the end of a minor road, lies the bay of **Stégna**, a quiet and sheltered stretch of sand.

ENVIRONS: South past Malónas is the castle of **Faraklós**. It was a pirate stronghold before the Knights saw them off and turned it into a prison. The fortress overlooks Charáki,

Charáki village with the castle of Faraklós in the background

The sandy beach at Tsampíka

a pleasant fishing hamlet, now growing into a holiday resort, with a pebble beach that is lined with fish tavernas.

Eptá Pigés ⑬
Επτά Πηγές

26 km (16 miles) S of Rhodes town. 🚌 to Kolýmpia. 🚉 Tsampíka 5 km (3 miles) SE.

Eptá Pigés, or Seven Springs, is one of the island's leading woodland beauty spots. Peacocks strut beside streams and water- falls, where the seven springs feed a central reservoir. The springs were har- nessed to irrigate the orange groves of Kolýmpia to the east. The lake can be reached either by a woodland trail, or you can shuffle ankle deep in water through a 185-m (605-ft) tunnel.

Peacock at Eptá Pigés

ENVIRONS: Further east along the coast, the Byzantine Moní Tsampíkas sits on a moun- tain top at 300 m (985 ft). Legend has it that the 11th- century icon in the chapel was found by an infertile couple, who later conceived a child. The chapel hence became a place of pilgrimage for child- less women, who still walk there barefoot, and pray to the icon of the Virgin. They also pledge to name their child Tsampíka or Tsampíkos, names unique to the Dodecanese.

Below the monastery lies Tsampíka beach, a superb stretch of sand that becomes very crowded in the tourist season. Various watersports are also available here.

Faliráki ⑭
Φαληράκι

15 km (9 miles) S of Rhodes town. 🏃 400. 🚌

Faliráki, the island's most popular resort, consists of long sandy beaches surround- ed by whitewashed hotels, holiday apartments and restaurants. Also a good base for families who like a lively holiday with plenty of activities, it is a brash and loud resort that caters mostly for a younger crowd. As well as a waterslide complex, there are all types of watersports to enjoy. There are bars and discos, and numerous places to eat, from fish and chips to Chinese. Other diversions include bungee-jumping or a visit to the Faliráki Snake House.

🐍 Faliráki Snake House
Faliráki. 📞 22410 85841.
🅾 Apr–Oct: daily. 🈸 &

ENVIRONS: Slightly inland, the village of Kalythiés offers a more traditional break. Its attractive Byzantine church, Agía Eleoúsa, contains some interesting frescoes. Further

southeast, rocky Ladikó Bay is worth a visit. It was used as a location for filming The Guns of Navarone.

Golfers can visit the 18 hole course at Afántou village, with its pebbly coves and beaches, popular for boat trips from Rhodes town. Set in apricot orchards, Afántou means the "hidden village", and it is noted for its hand-woven carpets.

Koskinoú ⑮
Κοσκινού

10 km (6 miles) S of Rhodes town. 🏃 1,200. 🚌 Réni Koskinoú 2 km (1 mile) NE.

The old village of Koskinoú is characterized by its traditional Rhodian houses featuring the choklákia pebble mosaic floors and courtyards. There is an attractive church of Eisódia tis Theotókou, which has a multi-tiered bell tower. Nearby, Réni Koskinoú has good hotels, restaurants and beaches.

ENVIRONS: South of Koskinoú lies Thérmes Kalithéas, Kalithea Spa, once frequented for its healing waters. Now abandoned, the domed pavilions, pink-marbled pillars and Moorish archways look quite bizarre. Often used in films, the spa is set in lovely gardens, reached through pinewoods. There is now a busy lido here, and the rocky coves are popular for scuba- diving and snorkelling.

A church with a tiered bell tower in Koskinoú village

Líndos ⑪
Λίνδος

LINDOS WAS FIRST INHABITED around 3000 BC. Its twin harbours gave it a head start over Rhodes' other ancient cities of Kámeiros and Ialyssós as a naval power. In the 6th century BC, under the benevolent tyrant Kleoboulos, Líndos thrived and grew rich from its many foreign colonies. With its dazzling white houses, Crusader castle and acropolis dramatically overlooking the sea, Líndos is a magnet for tourists. Second only to Rhodes town as a holiday resort, it is now a National Historic Landmark, with development strictly controlled.

Carved stones of stoa

A traditional Líndian doorway

EXPLORING LÍNDOS VILLAGE
Líndos is the most popular excursion from Rhodes town, and the best way to arrive is by boat. The narrow cobbled streets can be shoulder to shoulder with tourists in high summer, so spring or autumn are more relaxed times to visit. Líndos is a sun trap, and is known for consistently recording the highest temperatures on the island.

Traffic is banned so the village retains much of its charm and donkeys carry people up to the acropolis. But it is very busy, with a bazaar of gift shops and fast-food outlets. Happily there are also several good tavernas

and, at the other end of the scale, there are a number of stylish restaurants offering international cuisine.

The village's winding lanes are fronted by imposing doorways which lead into the flower-filled courtyards of the unique Líndian houses. Mainly built by rich sea-captains between the 15th and 18th centuries, these traditional houses are called *archontiká*. They have distinctive carvings on the stonework, like ship's cables or chains, and are built round *choklákia* pebble mosaic courtyards *(see p194)*. The older houses mix Byzantine and Arabic styles and a few have small captain's rooms built over the doorway. Some of the *archontiká* have been converted into apartments and restaurants.

In the centre of the village lies the Byzantine church of the **Panagía**, complete with its graceful bell tower and pantiled domes. Originally a 10th-century basilica, it was rebuilt beween 1489 and 1490. The frescoes inside were painted by Gregory of Sými in 1779.

On the road which leads up to the acropolis is the **Pántheon**, a waxwork museum of characters in mythology, including gods and heroes, such as Perseus and Herakles. There are sound and light shows accompanying each character, and a souvenir shop.

Also on the path leading to the acropolis, are a number of women selling the lace for which Líndos is renowned. Lindian stitchwork is sought after by museums throughout the world; it is said that even Alexander the Great wore a cloak stitched by Lindian

Líndos Stoa
This colonnade or stoa was built in the Hellenistic period around 200 BC.

The battlements were built in the 13th century by the Knights of Rhodes.

A trireme warship is carved into the rock.

THE ACROPOLIS AT LÍNDOS
Perched on a sheer precipice 125 m (410 ft) above the village, the acropolis is crowned by the 4th-century BC Temple of Lindian Athena, its remaining columns etched against the skyline. The temple was among the most sacred sites in the ancient world, visited by Alexander the Great and supposedly by Helen of Troy and Herakles. In the 13th century, the Knights Hospitallers of St John fortified the city with battlements much higher than the original walls.

Líndos lace seller on the steps to the acropolis

The acropolis overlooking Líndos town and bay

VISITORS' CHECKLIST

1 km (0.5 mile) E of Líndos village.
22440 31258. Jul–Sep:
8am–7pm Tue–Sun, noon–
7pm Mon; Oct–Jun: 8:30am–
3:20pm Tue–Sun. main
public hols.

women. The main beach at Líndos, **Megálos Gialós**, is where the Líndian fleet once anchored, and it sweeps north of the village round Líndos bay. It is a popular beach and it tends to get very crowded in summer, but a wide selection of watersports are available. It is also safe for children, and several tavernas can be found along the beachfront.

Pántheon
Along the road to the acropolis.
Apr–Oct: daily.

ENVIRONS: Tiny, trendy **Pallás** beach is linked to Líndos's main beach by a walkway. Nudists make for the headland, around which is the more exclusive **St Paul's Bay**, where the Apostle landed in AD 43, bringing Christianity to Rhodes. An idyllic, almost enclosed cove, it has azure waters and a white chapel dedicated to St Paul, with a festival on 28 June.

Although called the **Tomb of Kleoboulos**, the stone monument on the promontory north of the main beach at Lindos bay had nothing to do with the great Rhodian tyrant. The circular mausoleum, made from huge blocks of stone, was constructed around the 1st century BC, several centuries after his death. In early Christian times the tomb was converted into the church of Agios Aimilianós, though who was originally buried here still remains a mystery.

Péfkos, 3 km (2 miles) south of Líndos, has small sandy beaches fringed by pine trees, and is fast developing as a popular resort.

Lárdos is a quiet inland village, 7 km (4 miles) west of Líndos. **Lárdos Bay**, 1 km (0.5 mile) south of the village, has sand dunes bordered by reeds, and is being developed with upmarket village-style hotels.

RECONSTRUCTION OF THE ACROPOLIS (C. AD 300)

Vaulted structures support the terrace.

The Doric stoa was built in the 3rd century BC.

Temple of Lindian Athena, 4th century BC

Agios Ioánnis, the church of St John, was built in the 13th century.

The palace of the commander of the fortress was added in the period of the Knights.

Medieval entrance to the acropolis

Roman temple of Diocletian, 3rd century AD

Temple of Lindian Athena

Propylaia

Doric stoa

Nimporió with Agios Nikólaos church towering above the surrounding buildings

Chálki
Χάλκη

🏛 *280.* 🚢 *Nimporió.* ℹ *Piátsa, Nimporió (22460 45333).* 🎭 *Chorió: Panagía 15 Aug.* 🚢 *Nimporió.*

CHALKI WAS ONCE a thriving sponge-fishing island, but was virtually abandoned when its sponge divers emigrated to Florida in search of work in the early 1900s. Tourism has grown steadily as the island has been smartened up. Once fertile, Chálki's water table was infiltrated by sea water and the island is now barren with fresh water shipped in by tanker. Sheep and goats roam the rocky hillside, there is little cultivation and produce is imported from Rhodes.

NIMPORIO
Chálki's harbour and only settlement, Nimporió is a quiet and picturesque village with a Neo-Classical flavour.

A goat farmer in Chálki on his journey home

The main sight in Nimporió is the church of **Agios Nikólaos** with its elegant bell tower, the highest in the Dodecanese, tiered like a wedding cake. The church is also known for its magnificent black and white *choklákia* pebble mosaic courtyard depicting birds and the tree of life. The watchful eye painted over the main door is to ward off evil spirits.

A row of ruined windmills stands above the harbour, which also boasts an Italianate town hall and post office plus a fine stone clock tower. Nearby is sandy **Póntamos** beach, which is quiet and shallow and suitable for children.

AROUND THE ISLAND
The island is almost traffic-free so it is ideal for walkers. An hour's walk uphill from Nimporió is the abandoned former capital of **Chorió**. Its Crusader castle perches high on a crag, worth a visit for the coat of arms and Byzantine

---

CHOKLAKIA MOSAICS

A distinctive characteristic of the Dodecanese, these decorative mosaics were used for floors from Byzantine times onwards. An exquisite art form as well as a functional piece of architecture, they were made from small sea pebbles, usually black and white but occasionally reddish, wedged together to form a kaleidoscope of raised patterns. Kept wet, the mosaics also helped to keep houses cool in the heat.

Early examples featured abstract, formal and mainly geometric designs such as circles. Later on the decorations became more flamboyant with floral patterns and symbols depicting the lives of the householders with ships, fish and trees. Aside from Chálki, the houses of Líndos also have fine mosaics *(see pp192–3)*. On Sými the church of Agios Geórgios *(see p174)* depicts a furious mermaid about to dash a ship beneath the waves.

A *choklákia* mosaic outside Moní Taxiárchi in Sými

Circular *choklákia* mosaic in Chálki

frescoes in the ruined chapel. On a clear day you can see Crete. The Knights of St John (*see pp184–5*) built it on an ancient acropolis, using much of the earlier stone.

The Byzantine church of the **Panagía** below the castle has some interesting frescoes and is the centre for a giant festival on 15 August. Clinging to the mountainside opposite is the church of **Stavrós** (the Cross).

From Chorió you can follow the road west to the Byzantine **Moní Agíou Ioánnou Prodrómou** (St John the Baptist). The walk takes about three to five hours, or it is a one hour drive. The monastery has an attractive shaded court-yard. It is best to visit in the early morning or to stay over-night: the caretakers will offer you a cell. You can walk from Nimporió to the pebbly beaches of **Kánia** and **Dyó Gialí** or take a taxi boat.

The interior of Moní Agíou Ioánnou Prodrómou

OUTLYING ISLANDS
Excursions run east from Nimporió to deserted **Alimiá** island, where Italy berthed some submarines in World War II. There are several small chapels and a ruined castle.

Kastellórizo
Καστελλόριζο

🏘 275. ✈ 2.5 km (1.5 miles) S of Kastellórizo town. ⛴ Kastellórizo town. 🏨 500 m (1,640 ft) N of port (22460 49333).

R EMOTE Kastellórizo is the most far-flung Greek island, just 2.5 km (1.5 miles) from Turkey but 120 km (75

miles) from Rhodes. It was very isolated until the airport opened up tourism in 1987. Kastellórizo has no beaches, but clear seas full of marine life, including monk seals, and it is excellent for snorkelling. Known locally as Megísti (the biggest), it is the largest of 14 islets.

The island's population has declined from 15,000 in the 19th century to nearly 300 today. From 1920 it was se verely oppressed by the Italians who occupied the Dodecanese, and in World War II it was evacuated and looted.

Despite hardships, the water-side bustles with tavernas and sometimes impromptu music and dancing. It is a strange backwater but the indomitable character of the islanders is famous throughout Greece.

Kastellórizo town is the island's only settlement, with reputedly the best natural har-bour between Piraeus and Beirut. Above the town is the ruined fort or **kástro** with spectacular views over the islands and the coast of Turkey. It was named the Red Castle (Kastello Rosso) by the Knights of St John due to its red stone, and this name was adopted by the islanders. The **Castle Museum** contains cos-tumes, frescoes and photo-graphs. Nearby, cut into the rock, is Greece's only **Lycian Tomb**, from the ancient Lycian civilization of Asia Minor. It is noted for its Doric columns.

Most of the old Neo-Classical houses stand in ruins, blown up during World War II or destroyed by earthquakes.

A traditional housefront in Kastellórizo town

However, buildings are being restored as tourism develops. The Italian film *Mediterraneo* was set here and since then the island has attracted many Italian tourists.

Highlights worth seeing include the elegant cathedral of **Agioi Konstantínos kai Eléni**, incorporating granite columns from the Temple of Apollo in Patara, Anatolia.

From town a path leads up to four white churches and the **Palaiókastro**. This Doric fortress and acropolis has a 3rd century BC inscription on the gate referring to Megísti.

A boat trip southeast from Kastellórizo town to the spectacular **Parastá Cave** should not be missed; it is famed for its stalactites and the strange light effects on the vivid blue waters.

🏛 **Castle Museum**
Kastellórizo town. 📞 22460 49283.
🕐 Tue–Sun. ⬤ main public hols.

Kastellórizo town with Turkey in the background

Kárpathos
Κάρπαθος

WILD, RUGGED KARPATHOS is the third-largest island in the Dodecanese. Dramatically beautiful, it has remained largely unspoilt despite the recent increase in tourism. Like most of the Dodecanese, it has had a chequered history including periods of domination by both the Romans and Byzantines. Once known as Porfiris, after the red dye that is manufactured locally, the island's name today is thought to derive from the word *arpaktós* ("robbery"), as the island was a pop-

Folk reliefs on a taverna in Diafáni

ular pirate lair in medieval times.

KEY

For key to map see back flap

KARPATHOS TOWN

Kárpathos town, also known as Pigádia, is the island's main port and capital, sheltered in the southeast of Vróntis bay. Once an ordinary working town, it now has hotels strung out all around the previously deserted bay. The waterfront is bustling with pavement cafés and restaurants that serve international fare. Opposite the Italianate town hall, **Kárpathos park** has an open-air display of ancient objects. Exhibits include an early Christian marble font and objects discovered in 5th-century BC Mycenaean tombs on the island.

ENVIRONS: South of Kárpathos town there is a pretty walk through olive groves to the main resort of **Amoopí**, 7 km (4 miles) away, with its string

0 kilometres 5
0 miles 3

of sandy beaches. Above Amoopí, the village of **Menetés**, nestling at 350 m (1,150 ft) on the slopes of Mount Profitis Ilías, has quaint vine-covered streets. The traditional pastel-coloured houses have attractive courtyards and gardens. Inside the village church is a carved wooden iconostasis.

AROUND THE ISLAND

A mountainous spine divides the wild north from the softer, fertile south. On the west coast, 8 km (5 miles) from Menetés, the village of **Arkása** has been transformed into a resort. In 1923, the 4th-century church of Agía Anastasía was discovered. It contained some fine early Byzantine mosaics, the best of which depicts two deer gazing into a water jug, now in the Rhodes's Archaeological Museum (*see p180*).

Apéri, 8 km (5 miles) north of Kárpathos town, was the island's capital until 1892, and is said to be one of the richest villages in Greece. It sits 300 m (985 ft) up Mount Kalí Límni and has fountains and fine houses with exquisite gardens dating from the 1800s.

Othos, just to the west of Apéri, is the highest village on the island, at 450 m (1,500 ft) above sea level. It is also one

The white mansions of Apéri, clustered on the hillside

◁ **The historical village of Olympos, sitting high in the hills of northern Kárpathos**

Windmills in the traditional village of Olympos

of the oldest, with traditional Karpathian houses. One of the houses is a **Folk Museum** with textiles and pottery on show. There is also a family loom and tools for traditional crafts.

The west coast resort of **Lefkós** is considered to be the jewel of the island by the Karpathians, with its three horseshoe bays of white sand. On the east coast, **Kyrá Panagiá**, with its pink-domed church, is another beautiful cove of fine white sand. **Apélla**, the next beach along, is a stunning crescent of sand with azure water.

Diafáni, a small, colourful village on the northeast coast, has a handful of tavernas and hotels and both sand and shingle beaches. A 20-minute bus-ride away is the village of **Olympos**, which spills down from a bleak ridge 600 m (1,950 ft) up. Founded in 1420, and virtually cut off from the rest of the island for centuries by its remote location, this village is now a strange mix of medieval and modern. The painted houses huddle together in a maze of steps and alleys just wide enough for mules. One traditional house, with just a single room containing many embroideries and bric-a-brac, is open to visitors. Customs and village life are carefully preserved and traditional dress is daily wear for the older women who still bake their bread in outdoor ovens.

From Olympos a rough track leads north to **Avlóna**, inhabited only in the harvest season by local farmers. From here, **Vroukoúnda**, the site of a 6th-century BC city, is a short walk away. Remains of the protective city walls can be seen, as can burial chambers cut into the cliffs.

Folk Museum

Othos village. Apr–Oct: daily. Nov–Mar.

Visitors' Checklist

5,000. 17 km (11 miles) S of Kárpathos town. Kárpathos town, Diáfani. corner of 28th Oktovríou & Dimokratías, Kárpathos town. Kárpathos town (22450 22222). Panagía at Olympos: 15 Aug.

Outlying Islands

North of Avlóna is the island of **Sariá**, site of ancient Nísyros, where the ruins of the ancient city can be seen. Excursion boats go there from Diafáni.

Barely touched by tourism, **Kásos**, off the south coast of Kárpathos, was the site of a massacre by the Turks in 1824, commemorated annually on 7 June in the capital, Frý. Near the village of Agía Marína are two fine caves, Ellinokamára and Sellái, both with stalactites and stalagmites. Chélathros Bay is ideal for sun lovers, as are the quiet beaches of the tiny offshore islet of **Armáthia.**

The Traditions of Olympos

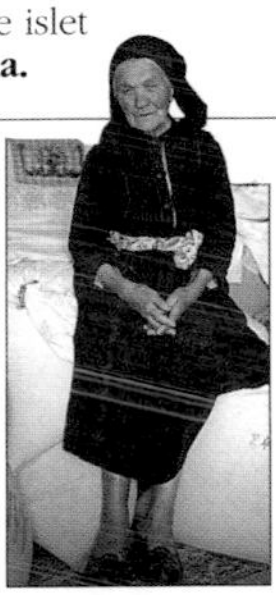

Matriarch at the Olympos windmills

The costume of the women of Olympos consists of white pantaloons with an embroidered tunic or a dark skirt with a long patterned apron. Fabrics are heavily embroidered in lime green, silver and bright pinks. Daughters wear a collar of gold coins and chains to indicate their status and attract suitors. The society was once strictly matriarchal. Today the mother passes on her property to the first-born daughter and the father to his son, ensuring that the personal fortunes of each parent are preserved through the generations.

Traditional houses in Olympos often have decorative balconies and the initials of the owners sculpted above the entrance. Consisting of one room built around a central pillar with fold-away bedding, they are full of photographs and souvenirs. People flock to Olympos from all over the world for the Festival of the Assumption of the Virgin Mary, from 15 August, one of the most important festivals in the Orthodox church. The village celebrations of music and dance last three days. Traditional instruments are played, including the *lýra*, which stems from the ancient lyre, the bagpipe-like goat-skin *tsampourás*, and the *laoúto*, which is similar to a mandolin.

Interior of an Olympos house

THE CYCLADES

ANDROS · TINOS · MYKONOS · DELOS · SYROS · KEA
KYTHNOS · SERIFOS · SIFNOS · PAROS · NAXOS · AMORGOS
IOS · SIKINOS · FOLEGANDROS · MILOS · SANTORINI

ERIVING THEIR NAME FROM THE WORD "KYKLOS", *meaning circle*, *because they surround the sacred island of Delos, the Cyclades are the most visited island group. They are everyone's Greek island ideal, with their dazzling white houses, twisting cobbled alleyways, blue domed churches, hilltop windmills and stunning beaches.*

The islands were the cradle of the Cycladic civilization (3000–1000 BC). The early Cycladic culture developed in the Bronze Age and has inspired artists ever since with its white marble figurines. The Minoans from Crete colonized the islands during the middle Cycladic era, making Akrotíri on Santoríni a major trading centre. During the late Cycladic period the Mycenaeans dominated, and Delos became their religious capital. The Dorians invaded the islands in the 11th century BC, a calamity that marked the start of the Dark Ages.

Venetian rule (1204–1453) had a strong influence, evident today in the medieval kástra seen on many islands and the Catholic communities on Tínos, Náxos and Sýros.

Traditional mule transport

There are 56 islands in the group, 24 inhabited, some tiny and undisturbed, others famous holiday playgrounds. They are the ultimate islands for sun, sea and sand holidays, with good nightlife on Mýkonos and Ios. Sýros, the regional and commercial capital, is one of the few islands in the group where tourism is not the mainstay. Cycladic life is generally centred on the village, which is typically divided between the harbour and the upper village, or Chóra, often topped with a kástro.

Most of the Cyclades are rocky and arid, with the exceptions of wooded and lush-valleyed Andros, Kéa and Náxos. This variety ensures the islands are popular with artists, walkers and those seeking quiet relaxation.

The sandy cove of Kolymbíthres beach, Páros

◁ The tiered, whitewashed houses of Triandáros village, Tínos

Exploring the Cyclades

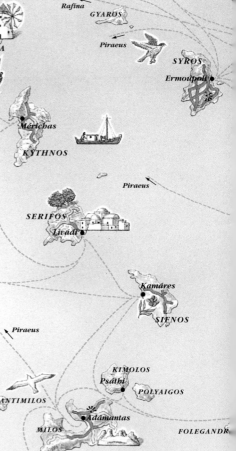

THE CYCLADES ARE BEST KNOWN for their beaches and whitewashed clifftop villages with stunning views; most famously, Firá on Santoríni. Mýkonos and Ios are well-established beach destinations, while more remote islands such as Mílos and Amorgós also have beautiful stretches of sand. Packed in July and August, these usually arid islands are beautiful in spring when they are carpeted with wild flowers. Varying in character, some of the islands, such as Síkinos, are quiet and traditional whereas others, such as Ios, are more nightlife-orientated. The Cyclades also offer a rich ancient history, evident in the ruins of ancient Delos.

GETTING AROUND

Páros and Sýros are the travel hub of the Cyclades. Ferries serve most of the islands from here and link to Crete and the Dodecanese. The islands are buffeted by the strong *meltémi* wind from July to September. It provides relief from the heat but can play havoc with ferry timetables.
   Mýkonos and Santoríni have international airports, and islands with domestic airports include Sýros, Mílos, Páros and Náxos.

SEE ALSO

- *Where to Stay* pp304–6
- *Where to Eat* pp328–30
- *Travel Information* pp356–9

ANDROS

Gávrio

Andros Town

Rafina

Skiáthos

Rafina

Lávrio

TINOS

Korissía

Rafina

GYAROS

KEA

Piraeus

SYROS

Ermoúpoli

Piraeus

Méricbas

KYTHNOS

Piraeus

SERIFOS

Liváti

Piraeus

Kamáres

SIENOS

Piraeus

KIMOLOS

Psáthi

POLYAIGOS

ANTIMILOS

Adámantas

MILOS

FOLEGANDR

Boat garages in Mandrákia, Mílos

Crete

| 0 kilometres | 20 |
| 0 miles | 10 |

Islands at a Glance

Amorgós *p229*
Andros *pp204–6*
Delos *pp214–15*
Folégandros *p231*
Ios *p230*
Kéa *p219*
Kýthnos *p220*
Mílos *pp232–3*
Mýkonos *pp210–11*

Náxos *pp226–7*
Páros *pp222–5*
Santoríni *pp234–7*
Sérifos *pp220–21*
Sífnos *p221*
Síkinos *pp230–31*
Sýros *pp216–18*
Tínos *pp208–9*

LOCATOR MAP

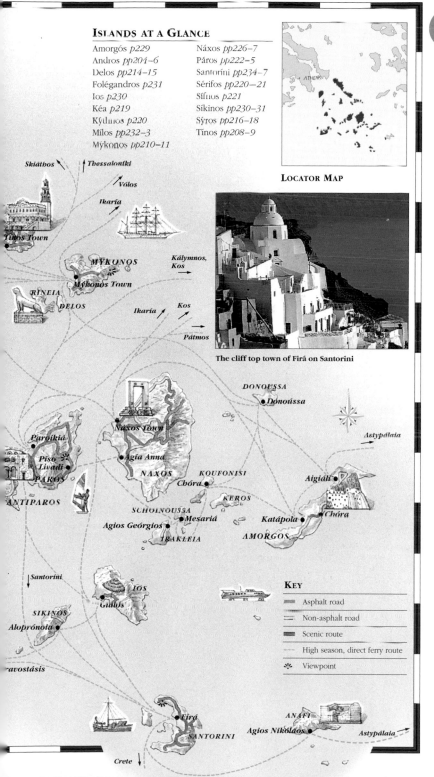

The cliff top town of Firá on Santoríni

KEY

- Asphalt road
- Non-asphalt road
- Scenic route
- High season, direct ferry route
- Viewpoint

Andros

Άνδρος

THE NORTHERNMOST OF THE CYCLADES, Andros is lush and green in the south, scorched and barren in the north. The fields are divided by distinctive dry-stone walls. The island was first colonized by the Ionians in 1000 BC. In the 5th century BC, Andros sided with Sparta during the Peloponnesian War *(see p28)*. After Venetian rule, the Turks took power in 1566 until the War of Independence. Andros has long been the holiday haunt of wealthy Athenian shipping families.

Andros Town ❶

Χώρα

🏛 *1,680.* 🚌 *Plateía Agías Olgas.* ℹ️ *22820 22316.*

The capital, Andros town, or Chóra, is located on the east coast of the island 20 km (12 miles) from the island's main port at Gávrio.

An elegant town with magnificient Neo-Classical buildings, it is the home of some of Greece's wealthiest shipowners. The pedestrianized main street is paved with marble slabs and lined with old mansions converted into public offices among the *kafeneía* and small shops.

The *Hermes of Andros*, in the Archaeological Museum

PLATEÍA KAÏRI

This is the main square in the town's Ríva district and is home to the **Archaeological Museum**, built in 1981. The museum's most famous exhibit is the 2nd-century BC *Hermes of Andros*, a fine marble copy of the 4th-century BC bronze original. Other exhibits include the *Matron of Herculaneum*, which was found with the *Hermes*, and finds from the 10th-century BC city at Zagorá. There are also finds from Ancient Palaiópoli *(see p206)* near Mpatsí, architectural illustrations and a large collection of ceramics.

The **Museum of Modern Art**, which was endowed by the Goulandrís family, has an excellent collection of paintings by 20th-century artists such as Picasso and Braque and leading Greek artists such as Alékos Fasianós. The sculpture garden has works by Michális Tómpros (1889–1974).

🏛 **Archaeological Museum**
Plateía Kaïri. ℹ️ *22820 23664.*
🕐 *Tue–Sun.* ⚫ *Mon, main public hols.* ♿

🏛 **Museum of Modern Art**
Plateía Kaïri. ℹ️ *22820 22444.*
🕐 *Wed–Mon.* ⚫ *main public hols.* ♿ *except Sun.*

KÁTO KÁSTRO AND PLATEÍA RÍVA

From Plateía Kaïri an archway leads into the maze of streets that form the medieval city, Káto Kástro, wedged between Parapórti and Nimporió bays. The narrow lanes lead to wind-swept Plateía Ríva at the end of the peninsula, jutting into the sea and dominated by the heroic statue of the *Unknown Sailor* by Michális Tómpros. Just below, a precarious stone bridge leads to the islet opposite, with the Venetian castle, **Mésa Kástro**, built in 1207–1233. The **Maritime Museum** has model ships, photographs and a collection of nautical instruments on display, is situated inside the town hall.

On the way back to the centre of the town is the church of **Panagía Theosképasti**, built in 1555 and dedicated to the Virgin Mary. Legend has it that the priest could not afford the wood for the church roof, so the ship delivering the wood set sail again. It ran into a storm and the crew prayed to the Virgin for help, promising to return the cargo to Andros. The seas were miraculously calmed and the church became known as Theosképasti, meaning "sheltered by God".

Statue of the *Unknown Sailor*

🏛 **Maritime Museum**
Plateía Ríva. ℹ️ *22820 22275.*
🕐 *Apr–Sep: Wed–Mon; Oct–Mar: Fri–Sun.* ⚫ *main public hols.* ♿

ENVIRONS: Steniés, 6 km (4 miles) northwest of Andros town, is very beautiful and popular with wealthy shipping families. Fifteen minutes' walk southwest of Steniés, the 17th-century Mpístis-Mouvelás tower is a fine example of an Andriot house.

Below Steniés lies **Giália** beach, which is shaded with eucalyptus trees and has a fish taverna. Above Steniés, 3 km (2 miles) west, in **Apoíkia**, mineral water is bottled from the Sáriza spring. You can taste the waters at the spring.

Typical white houses and a small church in Káto Kástro

Around Andros Island

Lion's head
fountain in Ménites

Pᴿᴼˢᴾᴱᴿᴼᵁˢ, neat, and dotted with many white dovecotes first built by the Venetians, Andros retains its traditional charm while playing host to international holiday-makers. There are a number of unspoiled sandy beaches, watersport facilities, wild mountains and a good network of footpaths. However, unless you are a keen trekker, car or bike hire is essential as the bus service is quite limited.

VISITORS' CHECKLIST

🏠 9,000. ⛴ Gávrio. 🚌
ℹ 22820 22215, 🎎 Agios
Panteleïmon Festival at Moni
Panachrántou: 27 Jul.

Mesariá ➋
Μεσαριά

8 km (5 miles) SW of Andros town.
🏠 850. 🚌

From Andros town the road passes through the medieval village of Mesariá with ruined tower houses and the pantiled Byzantine church of the **Taxiárchis**, built by Emperor Emanuel Comnenus in 1158 and recently restored.

Springs gush from marble lion's head fountains in the leafy village of **Ménites**, just above Mesariá. Ménites is known both for its nightingales and for the taverna overlooking a stream. Steps lead up to the pretty restored church of **Panagía i Koúmoulos** (the Virgin of the Plentiful) thought to be built on the site of an ancient Temple of Dionysos.

SIGHTS AT A GLANCE

Andros Town ➊
Gávrio ➏
Mesariá ➋
Moní Panachrántou ➌
Mpatsí ➎
Palaiókastro ➍

Moní Panachrántou ➌
Μονή Πανυχράντου

12 km (7 miles) SW of Andros town.
☎ 22020 51090. ◯ daily.

This spectacular monastery is perched 230 m (755 ft) above sea level in the mountains southwest of Andros town. It can be reached either by a two-hour steep walk from Mesariá or a three-hour trek from Andros town.

It was founded in 961 by Nikifóros Fokás, who later became Byzantine Emperor as reward for his help in the liberation of Crete from Arab occupation. The fortified monastery is built in Byzantine style and today houses just three monks. The church holds many treasures, including the skull of Agios Panteleïmon, believed to have healing powers. Visitors flock here to see the skull on the saint's annual festival day.

Moní Panachrántou overlooking the valley

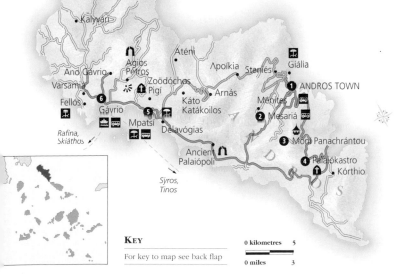

Palaiókastro ④
Παλαιόκαστρο

18 km (11 miles) SW of Andros town.
◯ *unrestricted access.*

High on a rocky plateau inland is the ruined Venetian Palaiókastro built between 1207 and 1233. Its alternative name, the Castle of the Old Woman, is after a woman who betrayed the Venetians to the Turks in the 16th century. After tricking her way inside the castle, she opened the gates for the Ottoman Turks. Appalled by the bloody massacre that followed, she hurled herself off the cliffs near Kórthio, 5 km (3 miles) to the southeast, in remorse. The rock from which she jumped is known as Tis Griás to Pídima, or Old Lady's Leap.

Mpatsí ⑤
Μπατσί

8 km (5 miles) S of Gávrio.
🚶 *200.* 🚌

Built around a sweeping sandy bay, Mpatsí is a pretty resort. It has a small fishing harbour and a maze of narrow lanes reached by white steps from the café-lined seafront. Despite the lively nightlife Mpatsí has retained its village atmosphere. The main beach is popular with families while **Delavógias** beach, south along the coastal track, is a favourite with naturists. Agía Marína, further along, has a friendly, family-run taverna.

ENVIRONS: South of Mpatsí the original capital of Andros, **Ancient Palaiópoli,** was inhabited until around AD 1000 when the people moved

to Mesariá *(see p205).* It was largely destroyed in the 4th century AD by an earthquake, but part of the acropolis is still visible, as are the remains of some of the temples under the sea.

Inland lies **Káto Katákoilos** village, known for its island music and dance festivals. A rough track leads north from here to remote **Aténi**, a hamlet at the head of a lush valley. Two beautiful beaches lie further to the windy north-east, in the bay of Aténi. The garden village of **Arnás**, high on the slopes of the Kouvára mountain range, has flowing springs and is one of the island's greenest spots. The area has many dry-stone walls and is spectacular walking country.

♘ Ancient Palaiópoli
9 km (6 miles) S of Mpatsí.
◯ *unrestricted access.* ♿ *limited.*

Gávrio ⑥
Γαύριο

🚶 *450.* ⛴ 🚌 *Fellós 4 km (2.5 miles) NW.*

Gávrio is a rather character-less port which, at weekends, becomes packed with Athenians heading for their holiday homes. There is a beach, a good campsite and plenty of tavernas. During the high season it can be the only

Agios Pétros tower near Gávrio

place with rooms available as Mpatsí is often pre-booked by package companies.

ENVIRONS: From Gávrio, it takes an hour or so to walk up to the tower of **Agios Pétros,** the island's best-preserved ancient monument. Dating from the Hellenistic era, the tower stands 20 m (66 ft) high in an olive grove below the hamlet of Káto Agios Pétros. The upper storeys of the tower were reached by footholds and an internal ladder, and its inner hall was once crowned by a corbelled dome. The purpose of the tower remains a mystery, although it may have been built to serve as a watchtower to guard the nearby mines from attack by marauding pirates.

North of Gávrio there are good beaches beyond the village of Varsamiá, which has two sandy coves. **Fellós** beach is the best, but is fast being developed with holiday villas.

A turn-off from the coastal road, 8 km (5 miles) south of Gávrio, leads to the 14th-century convent, **Zoödóchos Pigí,** the Spring of Life. Only a handful of nuns remain where there were 1,000 monks, but they are happy to show visitors their collection of icons and Byzantine tapestries.

The beach at Mpatsí Bay on Andros

Cycladic Art

WITH THEIR SIMPLE geometric shapes and purity of line, Cycladic marble figurines are the legacy of the islands' Bronze-Age civilization *(see pp24–5)* and the first real expression of Greek art. They all come from graves and are thought to represent, or be offerings to, an ancient deity. The earliest figures, from before 3000 BC, are slim and violin-shaped. By the time of the Keros-Sýros culture of 2700–2300 BC, the forms are recognizably human and usually female. They range from palm-sized up to life-size, the proportions remaining consistent. Obsidian blades, marble bowls prefiguring later Greek art, abstract jewellery and pottery, including the strange "frying pans", also survive. The examples of Cycladic art shown here are from the Museum of Cycladic Art in Athens *(see p287)*. Cycladic artefacts are also in many museums throughout the Cyclades.

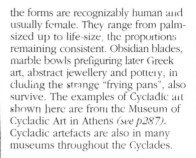

"Violin" figurines, *such as this one, date from the early Cycladic period of 3,300–2700 BC. Often no bigger than a hand, the purpose of these highly schematic representations of the human form is unknown. In some graves up to 14 of these figurines were found; other graves had none.*

"Frying pan" *pottery vessels take their name from their shape but their function is unknown. They may have been used in religious rituals. Decorated with spirals or suns, they belong to the mature phase of Cycladic art.*

Collared vases, *or* kandelas, *carved from marble, are one of the high points of Cycladic art. Probably used for food storage, the four lugs on the sides would have allowed them to be hung from a support.*

This male figurine, *found together with a female figurine, is one of the few male figures to have been found. He is also atypical in having one arm raised and a hand slung across his chest.*

This female figurine *with folded arms is typical of Cycladic sculpture. The head is slightly tipped back, with only minimal markings for arms, legs and features.*

INFLUENCE ON MODERN ART

Considered crude and ugly when first discovered in the 19th century, the simplicity of both form and decoration of Cycladic art exerted a strong influence on 20th-century artists and sculptors such as Picasso, Modigliani, Henry Moore and Constantin Brancusi.

Henry Moore's *Three Standing Figures*

The Kiss **by Brancusi**

Tínos
Τήνος

A CRAGGY YET GREEN ISLAND, Tínos was first settled by Ionians in Archaic times. In the 4th century BC it became known for its Sanctuary of Poseidon and Amphitrite. Under Venetian rule from medieval times, Tínos became the Ottoman Empire's last conquest in 1715. Tínos has over 800 chapels, and in the 1960s the military Junta declared it a holy island. Many Greek Orthodox pilgrims come to the church of the Panagía Evangelístria (Annunciation) in Tínos town. The island is also known for its many dovecotes *(peristeriónes)*, scattered across the landscape.

Archaeological Museum exhibit from Exómpourgo

Christians. Tínos becomes very busy during the festivals of the Annunciation and the Assumption when the icon is paraded through the streets *(see pp44–5)* and the devout often crawl to Panagía Evangelístria.

The church is a treasury of offerings, such as an orange tree made of gold and silver, from pilgrims whose prayers have been answered. The icon itself is so smothered in gold and jewels it is hard to see the painting. The crypt where it was found is known as the chapel of Evresis, or Discovery. Where the icon lay is now lined with silver and the holy spring here, Zoödóchos Pigí, is said to have healing powers.

The vestry has gold-threaded ecclesiastical robes, and valuable copies of the gospels.

Tínos town and the small harbourfront

TINOS TOWN
A typical island capital, Tínos town has narrow streets, whitewashed houses and a bustling port lined with restaurants and hotels.

♠ Panagía Evangelístria
Church & museums ◯ *daily.*
【 22830 22256. ♿
Situated at the top of Megalóchari, the main street that runs up from the ferry, Panagía Evangelístria, the church of the Annunciation, dominates Tínos town. The pedestrianized Evangelistrías, which runs parallel to Megalóchari, is packed with stalls full of icons and votive offerings. Built in 1830,

the church houses the island's miraculous icon. In 1822, during the Greek War of Independence, Sister Pelagía, a nun at Moní Kechrovouníou, had visions of the Virgin Mary showing where an icon had been buried. In 1823, acting on the nun's directions, excavations revealed the icon of the Annunciation of the Archangel Gabriel, unscathed after 850 years underground. Known in Greece as the Megalóchari (the Great Joy) the icon was found to have healing powers, and the church became a pilgrimage centre for Orthodox

Pilgrim crawling to the Panagía Evangelístria

Pánormos

Pýrgos

Kolympíthres

Istérnia

Kallóni

Kómi

Mýkonos, Vólos

Kámpos

Exómpourgo

Kiónia

Potamiá

Santa Margarita

Moní Kechrovouníou

Stavrós

Agios Ioánnis

TINOS TOWN

Agios-Fokás

Sýros, Páros

Andros, Skiáthos, Thessaloniki

The pretty village of Pýrgos in the north of the island

VISITORS' CHECKLIST

👤 9,000. 🚤 Tinos town. 🚌 Quay, Tinos town. 🛈 corner of Kiunion & Vlacháki, Tinos town (22830 23733). 🎉 Annunciation & Panagia at Panagia Evangelistrias, Tinos town: 25 Mar & 15 Aug.

Also within the church complex is a museum, displaying items by local sculptors and painters, including works by sculptors Antónios Sóchos, Geórgios Vitális and Ioánnis Voúlgaris. The art gallery has works of the Ionian School, a Rubens, a Rembrandt and 19th-century works by international artists.

🏛 Archaeological Museum
Megalóchari 📞 22830 22670
🕐 Tue–Sun. 🔴 main public hols. 📷
On Megalóchari, near the church, is the Archaeological Museum which has displays of sculptures of nereids (sea-nymphs) and dolphins found at the Sanctuary of Poseidon and Amphitrite. There is also a 1st-century BC sundial by Andronikos Kyrrestes, who designed Athens' Tower of the Winds (see p283), and some huge 8th-century BC storage jars from ancient Tínos on the rock of Exómpourgo.

ENVIRONS: East of town, the closest beach is shingly **Agios Fokás.** To the west is the popular beach at **Stavrós,** with a jetty that was built in Classical times. To the north near Kiónia are the foundations of the 4th-century BC **Sanctuary of Poseidon and Amphitrite,** his sea-nymph bride. The excavations here have yielded many columns, or kiónia, after which the surrounding area is named.

AROUND THE ISLAND
Tínos is easy to explore as there are plenty of taxis and a good bus service around the island. North of Tínos town is the 12th-century walled **Moní**

Kechrovouníou, one of the largest convents in Greece. You can visit the cell where Sister Pelagía had her visions and the chest where her embalmed head is kept.

At 640 m (2,100 ft) high, the great rock of **Exómpourgo** was the site of the Archaic city of Tínos and later became home to the Venetian fortress

The interior of the 12th-century Moní Kechrovouníou

of St Elena. Built by the Ghisi family after the Doge handed over the island to them in 1207, the fortress was the toughest stronghold in the Cyclades, until it surrendered to the Turks in 1714. You can see remains of a few ancient walls on the crag, medieval houses, a fountain and three churches.

From Kómi, to the north, a valley runs down to the sea at **Kolympíthres,** with two sandy bays: one is deserted; the other has rooms and tavernas.

Overlooking the harbour of Pánormos in the northwest of the island, the pretty village of **Pýrgos** is famous for its sculpture school. The area is known for its green marble, and the stonework here is among the finest in the islands. Distinctive, carved marble fanlights and balconies decorate the island villages. There are examples at the **Giannoúlis Chalepás Museum,** housed in the former home of the island's renowned sculptor (1851–1938). The old grammar school is now the School of Fine Arts, and a shop in the main square exhibits and sells works by the students.

🏛 Giannoúlis Chalepás Museum
Pýrgos. 🔲 daily. 🔴 Oct–Apr. 📷 ♿

THE PERISTERIONES (DOVECOTES) OF TINOS

The villages of Tínos are studded with around 1,300 beautiful white dovecotes (peristeriónes), all elaborately decorated. They have two storeys: the lower floor is for storage, the upper houses the doves and is usually topped with stylized winged finials or mock doves. The breeding of doves was introduced by the Venetians. Although also found on the islands of Andros and Sífnos, the peristeriónes of Tínos are considered the finest.

A dovecote in Kámpos with traditional elaborate patterns

Mýkonos
Μύκονος

Pétros the Pelican, the island mascot

Aᴸᴛʜᴏᴜɢʜ MYKONOS IS DRY AND BARREN, its sandy beaches and dynamic nightlife make this island one of the most popular in the Cyclades. Under Venetian rule from 1207, the islanders later set up the Community of Mykonians in 1615 and flourished as a self-sufficient society. Visited by intellectuals in the early days of tourism, today Mýkonos thrives on its reputation as the glitziest island in Greece.

Mýkonos harbour in the early morning

The most famous church on the island, familiar from postcards, is the extraordinary **Panagía Para-portianí**, in the Kástro. Built on the site of the postern gate *(parapórti)* of the medieval fortress, it is made up of

7th-century BC amphora in the Archaeological Museum

four chapels at ground level with another above. Part of it dates from 1425 while the rest was built in the 16th and 17th centuries.

From Kástro, the lanes run down into Venetía, or **Little Venice** (officially known as Alefkándra), the artists' quarter. The tall houses have painted balconies jutting out over the sea. The main square, Plateía Aléfkandras, is home to the large Orthodox cathedral of Panagía Pigadiótissa (Our Lady of the Wells).

The **Maritime Museum of the Aegean**, at the end of Matogiánni, features a collection of model ships from pre-Minoan times to the 19th century, maritime instruments, paintings and 5th-century BC coins with nautical themes.

Next door, **Lena's House**, a 19th-century mansion, evokes the life of a Mykonian lady, Léna Skrivánou. Everything is preserved, from her needle-work to her chamber pot.

Works of Greek and inter-national artists are on show at the **Municipal Art Gallery** on Matogiánni, and include an exhibition of works by local Mykonian painters.

MYKONOS TOWN

Mýkonos town (or Chóra) is the supreme example of a Cycladic village – a tangle of dazzling white alleys and cube-shaped houses. Built in a maze of narrow lanes to defy the wind and pirate raids, the bustling port is one of the most photographed in Greece. Many visitors still get lost around the lanes today.

Taxi boats for the island of Delos *(see pp214–15)* leave from the quayside. The island's mascot, Pétros the Pelican, may be seen near the quay, hunting for fish.

Adjacent to the harbour is Plateía Mavrogénous, over-looked by the bust of revolutionary heroine Mantó Mavrogénous (1796–1848). She was awarded the rank of General for her victorious battle against the Turks on Mýkonos during the War of Independence in 1821.

The **Archaeological Museum**, housed in a Neo-Classical building south of the ferry port, has a large

Mantó Mavrogénous

collection of Roman and Hellenistic carvings, 6th- and 7th-century BC ceramics, jewellery and gravestones, as well as many finds from the ancient site on Delos.

Kástro, the oldest part of the town, sits high up above the waterside district. Built on part of the ancient castle wall is the excellent **Folk Museum**, one of the best in Greece. It is housed in an elegant sea-captain's mansion and has a fine collection of ceramics, embroidery and ancient and modern Mykonian textiles. Among the more unusual exhibits is the original Pétros the Pelican, now stuffed, who was the island's mascot for 29 years. The 16th-century Vonís Windmill is part of the Folk Museum and has been restored to full working order. It was one of the 30 windmills that were used by families all over the island to grind corn. There is also a small threshing floor and a dovecote in the grounds around the windmill.

Working 16th-century windmill, part of the Folk Museum

The famous Paraportianí church

🔘 **Archaeological Museum**
Harbourfront. 📞 22890 22325.
🕐 Tue–Sun. 🔴 main public hols. 📷

🔘 **Folk Museum**
Harbourfront. 📞 22890 22591.
🕐 Apr–Oct: 5–8pm Mon–Sat. ♿

🔘 **Maritime Museum of the Aegean**
Enóplon Dynámeon. 📞 22890
22700. 🕐 Apr–Oct: daily. 🔴 main
public hols. ♿ 📷

🔘 **Lena's House**
Enóplon Dynámeon. 🕐 Apr–Oct:
daily. ♿ limited.

🔘 **Municipal Art Gallery**
Matogiánni. 📞 22890 22615.
🕐 Apr–Oct: daily. ♿

AROUND THE ISLAND

Mýkonos is popular primarily for its beaches; it has no lush countryside. The best ones are along the south coast. At stylish **Platýs Gialós**, 3 km (2 miles) south of the town, regular taxi boats are available to ferry sun-worshippers from bay to bay. Backed by hotels and restaurants, this is the main family beach on the island, with watersports and a long sweep of sand. Serious sun-lovers head southeast to the famous nudist beaches. First is **Parágka**, or Agía Anna, a quiet spot with a good taverna. Next is **Paradise**, with its neighbouring camping site, disco

music and water-sports. The lovely cove of **Super Paradise** is gay and nudist. **Eliá**, at the end of the boat line is also nudist and busy in high season.

In contrast to Mýkonos town, the inland village of **Ano Merá**, 7.5 km (4.5 miles) east, is traditional and largely unspoilt by tourism. The main attraction is the 16th-century **Panagía i Tourlianí**, dedicated to the island's protectress. Founded by two monks from Páros, the red-domed monastery was restored in 1767. The ornate marble tower was sculpted by Tíniot craftsmen. The monastery houses some fine 16th-century icons, vestments and

embroideries. Northwest of the village is Palaiókastro hill, once crowned by a Venetian castle. It is thought to be the site of one of the ancient cities of Mýkonos. Today it is home to the 17th-century working **Moní Palaiokástrou** To the northwest, in the pretty village of **Maráthi**, is Moní Agíou Panteleïmona, founded in 1665. From here, the road leads to **Pánormos Bay** and **Fteliá**, a windsurfers' paradise.

VISITORS' CHECKLIST

👥 4,500. ✈ 3 km (1.5 mile) SE
of Mýkonos town. 🚢 Mýkonos
town. 🚌 Polykandrióti, Mýkonos
town (for north of island); on
road to Ornós, Mýkonos town
(for south of island). ℹ Harbourfront, Mýkonos town (22890
22201). 🎉 Fishermen's Festival,
Mýkonos town: 30 Jun.

Platýs Gialós beach, one of the best on Mýkonos

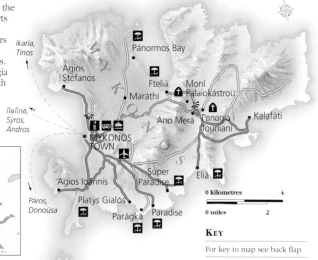

Delos

Δήλος

TINY, UNINHABITED Delos is one of the most important archaeological sites in Greece. According to legend, Leto gave birth to Artemis and Apollo here. The Ionians arrived in about 1000 BC, bringing the worship of Apollo and founding the annual Delia Festival, during which games and music were played in his honour. By 700 BC, Delos was a major religious centre. First a place of pilgrimage, it later became a thriving commercial port particularly in the 3rd and 2nd centuries BC. It is now an open-air archaeological museum with mosaics and marble ruins covered in wild flowers in spring.

Artemis of Delos

Archaeological Museum
This displays most of the finds from the island, including storage pots used for offerings and koúroi dating from the 7th century BC.

The Sanctuary of Apollo has three temples: one dating from the 6th century BC and two dating from the 5th century BC.

Stadium and Gymnasium

The Sanctuary of Dionysos has remains of huge phallic monuments dating back to 300 BC.

The Sacred Lake, now dried up, was so called because it had witnessed Apollo's birth. A wall marks the lake's Hellenistic boundaries.

★ Lion Terrace
The famous lions (now replaced by replicas) were set up to overlook and protect the Sacred Lake. They were carved from Naxian marble at the end of the 7th century BC. Originally there were nine, but now only five remain.

TIMELINE

3000 BC	1000 BC	750	500	250	AD 1

1000 BC Ionians arrive on Delos and introduce Apollo worship

422 BC Athens exiles Delians to Asia Minor; Delians return the following year

426 BC Second purification

478 BC Athenians make Delos the centre of the first Athenian League

88 BC Delos sacked by Mithridates

166 BC Romans return Delos to Athens. Trade flourishes

2000 BC Earliest settlement on Mount Kýnthos

700 BC Naxians in control of Sanctuary of Apollo

550 BC Polykrates, the tyrant of Sámos, conquers the Cyclades, but respects the sanctity of Delos

314 BC Delos declares independence from Athens

543 BC First purification (removal of tombs) of Delos by Athenians

250 BC Romans settle in Delos

69 BC Romans fortify Delos after sack by pirates

House of the Dolphins

This house of the 2nd century BC contains a mosaic of two dolphins with an elaborate Greek key design and waved borders.

VISITORS' CHECKLIST

2.5 km (1 mile) SW of Mýkonos town. 22890 22259.
8–10am daily from Mýkonos town returning 12–2pm.
8:30am 3pm Tue–Sun.
1 Jan, 25 Mar, Good Fri am, Easter Sun, Mon, 1 May, 25, 26 Dec.

Mount Kýnthos

House of the Masks

Probably a hostelry for actors, this house contains a 2nd-century BC mosaic of Dionysos, god of theatre, riding a panther.

★ Theatre

Built in 300 BC to hold 5,500 spectators, the theatre was sited in a natural amphitheatre. On its west side, a huge, vaulted cistern collected rainwater draining from the theatre and supplied part of the town.

★ Theatre Quarter

In Hellenistic and Roman times the wealthy built houses near the theatre, many with opulent, colonnaded courtyards.

House of Dioscourides and Cleopatra

Two statues represent the couple Cleopatra and Dioscourides, who lived here in the 2nd century BC.

KEY

Theatre quarter

STAR SIGHTS

★ Theatre

★ Lion Terrace

★ Theatre Quarter

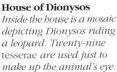

House of Dionysos

Inside the house is a mosaic depicting Dionysos riding a leopard. Twenty-nine tesserae are used just to make up the animal's eye.

Sýros
Σύρος

Rocky syros, or Sýra, is the commercial, administrative and cultural centre of the Cyclades. Archaeological digs have revealed finds of the Cycladic civilization dating from 2800 to 2300 BC. The inhabitants converted to Catholicism under the French Capuchins in the Middle Ages. The 19th century saw Sýros become a wealthy and powerful port in the eastern Mediterranean. Though Sýros does not live off tourism, more visitors arrive each year attracted by its traditional charm.

Town hall, designed by Ernst Ziller

The twin peaks of Ermoúpoli: Ano Sýros and Vrondádo

Ermoúpoli ❶
Ερμούπολη

🏛 13,000. ⛴ 🚌 Aktí Ethnikís Antistassis. 🛈 Thymáton Sperchíon 11 (22810 86725).

Elegant Ermoúpoli, named after Hermes, the god of commerce, is the largest city in the Cyclades. In the 19th century it was Greece's leading port and a major coaling station with a huge natural harbour and thriving shipyard. Crowned by the twin peaks of Catholic Ano Sýros to the north, and the Orthodox Vrondádo to the south, the city is built like an amphitheatre around the harbour.

The Lower Town
The architectural glories of central **Plateía Miaoúli** have led to the town becoming a National Historical Landmark. Paved with marble and lined with palm-shaded cafés and pizzerias, the grand square is the city's hub and meeting place, especially for the evening stroll, or *vólta*. There is also a marble bandstand and a statue dedicated to the revolutionary hero Admiral Andréas Miaoúlis. The square is dominated by the vast Neo-Classical **town hall** (1876), designed by the German architect Ernst Ziller.

The **Archaeological Museum**, up the steps to the left of the town hall, houses bronze and marble utensils from the 3000 BC Cycladic settlement of Chalandrianí. Also on display are Cycladic statuettes and Roman finds. Left of the town hall is the **Historical Archives Office**.

Nearby, on Plateía Vardáka, is the **Apollo Theatre**, designed in 1864 by French architect Chabeau as a copy of La Scala, Milan. The first opera house in Greece, it is noted for its

Statue of Andréas Miaoúlis

Sights at a Glance
Ermoúpoli ❶
Galissás ❸
Kíni ❷
Poseidonía ❹
Vári ❺

Key
For key to map see back flap

0 kilometres   4

0 miles   2

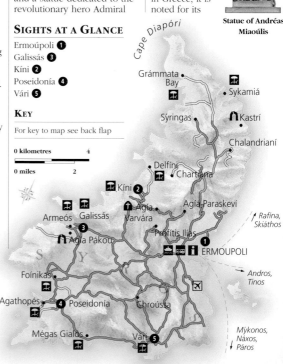

Cape Diapóri

Grámmata Bay

Sykamiá

Sýringas

Kastrí

Chalandrianí

Delfíni
Chartiána

Kíni ❷

Armeós   Galissás
Agía Varvára

Agía-Paraskeví

Rafina, Skiáthos

Agía Pákou ❸

Profítis Ilías

ERMOUPOLI ❶

Foínikas

Andros, Tínos

Agathopés   Poseidonía ❹

Chroússa

Mégas Gialós

Vári ❺

Mýkonos, Náxos, Páros

MARKOS VAMVAKARIS

One of the greatest exponents of *rempétika*, the Greek blues, Márkos Vamvakáris (1905–72) was born in Ano Sýros. Synonymous with hash dens and the low-life, *rempétika* was the music of the urban underclass. With strong Byzantine and Islamic influences, it is often played on the *baglama* or the bouzouki. Vamvakáris was a master of the bouzouki as well as a noted composer. Over 20 recordings have been made of his music, the earliest of which dates back to the 1930s. A bust of Vamvakáris looks out to sea from the small square named after him in Ano Sýros.

fine wall paintings of Mozart and Verdi and is still used for plays and concerts.

Across the street the 1871 **Velissarópoulos Mansion**, now housing the Labour Union, has an elaborate marble façade and splendid painted ceilings and murals. Beyond here is the church of **Agios Nikólaos** (1848) with a marble iconostasis by the 19th-century sculptor Vitális. Also by Vitális is the world's first monument of the unknown soldier, in front of the church.

THE UPPER TOWN

The twin bell towers and distinctive blue and gold dome of Agios Nikólaos mark the start of the **Vapória** district. Here Sýros's shipowners built their Neo-Classical mansions, with some of the finest plasterwork, frescoes and marble carvings in

Marble iconostasis by Vitális, in the church of Aglos Nikólaos

Greece. The houses cling to the coastline above the town's quays and moorings at Tálira, Evangelístria and Agios Nikólaos.

The charming district of **Vrontádo**, on the eastern peak, has a number of excellent tavernas spread out on its slopes at night. The Byzantine church of the **Anástasis** on top of the hill has views to Tínos and Mýkonos.

A ceiling in one of Ermoúpoli's mansions

A half-hour's climb along Omiroú, or a brief bus ride, is the fortified medieval quarter of **Ano Sýros**, on the western peak. It is also known as Apáno Chóra or Kástro. On the way is the Orthodox cemetery of **Agios Geórgios** with its elaborate marble mausoleums. Ano Sýros is a maze of whitewashed passages, arches and steps forming a huddle of interlinking houses. The architecture is unique, making the most of minimal space with *stegádia* (slate or straw roofs) and tight corners. The main entrance into Ano Sýros is Kamára, an ancient passageway leading into the main road, or Piatsa. The **Vamvakáris Museum**, dedicated to the life and work of Márkos Vamvakáris, is situated just off this road. At the top of Ano

Sýros, the Baroque **Aï-Giórgis**, known as the cathedral of St George, was built on the site of a 13th-century church. The basilica contains fine icons. The Jesuit cloister was founded in 1744 around the church of Our Lady of Karmilou (1581), and houses 6,000 books and manuscripts in its library. Below it, the Capuchin convent of **Agios Ioánnis** was a meeting place and a refuge from pirates. Its church was founded by Louis XIII of France as a poorhouse.

🏛 Archaeological Museum
Plateía Miaoúli. 22810 88487. ☐ Tue–Sun. ● main public hols. ♿ limited.

🏛 Historical Archives Office
Plateía Miaoúli. 22810 86891. ☐ 8:30am–2pm Mon–Fri. ● main public hols.

🏛 Vamvakáris Museum
Plateía Vamvakári, Ano Sýros. 22810 82934. ☐ Jun–Sep: daily ● main public hols.

A typical street in the Ano Sýros quarter

Around Sýros Island

S YROS HAS NUMEROUS attractive coves as well as popular resorts like Galissás and Kíni. The landscape is varied with palm trees and terraced fields. In the northern region of Apáno Meriá the traditional farms built to house both families and animals are in total contrast to the Italianate mansions and holiday homes of the south. Sýros has good roads, especially in the south, and is easy to explore by car or bike. There is a regular bus from the harbour to Ano Sýros, the main resorts and outlying villages.

Kíni Bay and the town's harbour

Kíni ❷
Κίνι

9 km (6 miles) NW of Ermoúpoli.
🚶 300. 🚌 🚤 Delfíni 3 km
(2 miles) N.

The fishing village of Kíni is set in a horseshoe-shaped bay with two good sandy beaches. Kíni is a popular meeting place for watching the sunset over an ouzo, and it has some excellent fish tavernas.

North, over the headland, is the award-winning **Delfíni** beach – the largest on Sýros and popular with naturists.

Between Ermoúpoli and Kíni, set in pine-covered hills, is the red-domed convent of **Agía Varvára**. With spectacular views to the west, the

The red-tiles roofs of Agía Varvára convent near Kíni

Orthodox convent was once a girls' orphanage. The nuns run a weaving school and their knitwear and woven goods are on sale at the convent. The frescoes in the church depict the saint's martyrdom.

ENVIRONS: Boat services run from Kíni to some of the island's remote northern beaches. **Grámmata Bay** is one of the most spectacular, a deep sheltered inlet with golden sands where sea lilies grow in autumn. Some of the rocks here have a Hellenistic inscription carved on them, seeking protection for ships from sinking.

A boat trip around the tip of the island past Cape Diapóri to the east coast takes you to **Sykamiá** beach. Here there is a cave where the Syriot philosopher Pherekydes is thought to have lived during the summer months. A physicist and astronomer, Pherekydes pioneered philosophical thought in the mid-6th century BC, and was the inventor of the heliotrope, an early sundial. From Sykamiá you

can see the remains of the Bronze-Age citadel of **Kastrí** with its six towers perched on a steep rock.

Galissás ❸
Γαλησσάς

7 km (4 miles) W of Ermoúpoli.
🚶 500. 🚌 🚤 Armeós beach 1 km
(0.5 miles) N.

Lively Galissás has the most sheltered beach on the island, fringed by tamarisk trees and, across the headland to the north, **Armeós** beach is a haven for nudists. Galissás has both the island's campsites, making it popular with backpackers. In high season it can be a noisy place to stay, and is often full of bikers. To the south of the bay lies **Agía Pákou**, which is the site of the Classical city of Galissás.

Huge **Foínikas** bay, 3 km (2 miles) further south, was originally settled by the Phoenicians, and now houses more than 1,000 people. Foínikas is a popular resort with a pier and moorings for yachts and fishing boats.

Sweeping Foínikas bay on the southwest coast of Sýros

Poseidonía ❹
Ποσειδωνία

12 km (7 miles) SW of Ermoúpoli.
🚶 700. 🚌 🚤 Agathopés 1 km
(0.5 miles) S.

Poseidonía, or Dellagrázia, is one of the largest tourist sites on the island, with cosmopolitan hotels and restaurants. The island's first main road

An Italianate mansion in Poseidonia

was built in 1855 from Ermoú-poli through Poseidonia to Foínikas. The affluent village contains some Italianate mansions, which are the country retreats of wealthy islanders. A short walk to the southwest, quieter **Agathopés** is one of the island's best beaches with safe waters protected by an islet opposite. Mégas Gialós, 3 km (2 miles) away on the west coast, is a pretty beach shaded by tamarisk trees.

Vári ❺
Βάρη

8 km (5 miles) S of Ermoúpoli.
🏘 1,150. 🚌 🚐 Vári.

Quaint, sheltered Vári has become a major resort, but it still has traditional houses. On the Chontrá peninsula, east of the beach, is the site of the island's oldest prehistoric settlement (4000–3000 BC).

Kéa
Κέα

🏘 1,600. 🚊 🚐 Korissía.
ℹ 22880 21100. 🚕 Gialiskári 6 km (4 miles) NW of Ioulis

KÉA WAS FIRST inhabited in 3000 BC and later settled by Phoenicians and Cretans. In Classical times it had four cities: Ioulís, Korissía, Poiíessa and Karthaía. The remains of Karthaía can be seen on the headland opposite Kýthnos. It is a favourite spot for rich Athenians due to its proximity to Attica. Mountainous, with fertile valleys, Kéa has been known since ancient times for its wine, honey and almonds.

IOULIS

The capital, Ioulís, or Ioulída, with its red terracotta-tiled roofs and winding alleyways, is perched on a hillside 5 km (3 miles) above Korissía. Ioulís has 26 windmills situated on the Mountain of the Mills. The town is a maze of tunnel-like alleys, and has a spectacular Neo-Classical **town hall** (1902) topped with statues of Apollo and Athena. On the west side are ancient bas-relief sculptures and in the entrance a sculpture of a woman and child found at ancient Karthaía.

The Kástro quarter is reached through a white archway, which stands on the site of the ancient acropolis. The Venetians, under the leadership of Domenico Micheli, built their castle in 1210 with stones from the ancient walls and original Temple of Apollo. There are panoramic views from here. The **Archaeological Museum**

is based in a fine Neo-Classical house. Its displays include an interesting collection of Minoan finds from Agía Eiríni; artifacts from the four ancient cities; Cycladic figurines and ceramics; and a copy of the stunning, marble, 6th-century BC *koúros* of Kéa. The smiling 6th-century BC **Lion of Kéa** is carved into the rock 400 m (1,300 ft) north of the town.

🏛 **Archaeological Museum**
☎ 22880 22079. ◯ Tue–Sun
⬤ main public hols.

AROUND THE ISLAND

The port of **Korissía** can be packed with Greek families on holiday breaks; as can **Vourkári**, an attractive and popular resort further north on the island that is famous for its fish tavernas.

The archaeological site of **Agía Eiríni** is topped by the chapel of the same name. The Bronze-Age settlement was destroyed by an earthquake in 1450 BC, and was excavated from 1960 to 1968. First occupied at the end of the Neolithic period, around 3000 BC, the town was fortified twice in the Bronze Age and there are still remains of the great wall with a gate, a tower and traces of streets. Many of the finds are displayed in the Archaeological Museum in Ioulís. The most spectacular monument on Kéa is the Hellenistic tower at Moní Agías Marínas, 5 km (3 miles) southwest of Ioulís.

A Hellenistic tower at Moní Agías Marínas on Kéa

Kýthnos
Κύθνος

🏠 *1,500.* ⚓ 🚌 *Mérichas.*
ℹ️ *22810 31201.*

BARREN KYTHNOS attracts more Greek visitors than foreign tourists, although it is a popular anchorage for flotilla holidays. Its dramatic, rugged interior and the sparsity of visitors make it an ideal location for walkers.

The local clay was traditionally used for pottery and ceramics, but is also used to make the red roofing tiles that characterize all the island's villages.

Known locally as Thermiá because of the island's hot springs, Kýthnos attracts visitors to the thermal spa at Loutrá. Since the closure of the iron mines in the 1940s, the islanders have lived off fishing, farming and basket-weaving. To celebrate festivals, such as the major pre-Lenten carnival, the islanders often wear traditional costumes.

CHORA

Also known as Messariá, the capital is a charming mix of red roofs and Cycladic cube-shaped houses. Also worth visiting is the church of **Agios Sávvas**, founded in 1613 by the Venetian Cozzadini family whose coat of arms it bears. The oldest church is **Agía Triáda** (Holy Trinity), a domed, single-aisle basilica.

Interior of the church of Panagía Kanála in Kanála town on Kýthnos

AROUND THE ISLAND

The road network is limited, but buses connect the port of Mérichas with Kanála in the south and Loutrá in the north. The remaining areas of the island are mostly within a walkable distance of these points. **Mérichas**, on the west coast, has a small marina and tree-fringed beach, lined with small hotels and tavernas. Just to the north, the sandy beach of **Martinákia** is popular with families. Further along the coast are the lovely beaches at **Episkopí** and **Apókrisi**, overlooked by **Vryókastro,** the Hellenistic ruins of ancient Kýthnos.

Potter at work in Dryopída

You can walk to **Dryopída**, a good hour south of Chóra, down the ancient cobbled way with dramatic views. The town was named after the ancient Dryopes tribe whose king, Kýthnos, gave the island its name. The charming red-roofed village is divided into two districts by the river valley: Péra Roúga is lush with crops, while Galatás was once a centre for ceramics, but only one pottery remains.

At **Kanála**, 5 km (3 miles) to the south, holiday homes have sprung up by the church of Panagía Kanála, dedicated to the Virgin Mary, the island's patron saint. Set in attractive shaded picnic grounds, the church houses Kýthnos's most venerated icon of the Virgin. It is probably by master iconographer, Skordílis, as Kýthnos was a centre for icon-painting in the 17th century. Kanála beach has views to Sérifos and Sýros and there are good beaches nearby.

Loutrá is a straggling resort on the northeast coast with windswept beaches. Its spa waters are saturated with iron, and since ancient times the springs of Kákavos and Agioi Anárgyroi have been used as a cure for ailments ranging from gout, rheumatism and eczema to gynaecological problems. The Xenía Hotel, situated next door to the excellent Hydrotherapy Centre, has late 19th-century marble baths inside. A Mesolithic settlement to the north, dating from 7500–6000 BC, is the oldest in the Cyclades.

Sérifos
Σέριφος

🏠 *1,100.* ⚓ 🚌 *Livádi.*
ℹ️ *22810 51210.*

IN MYTHOLOGY, the infant Perseus and his mother Danae were washed up on the shores of rocky Sérifos, known as "the barren one". Once rich in iron and copper mines, the island has bare hills

The red-roofed village of Dryopída on Kýthnos

The whitewashed village of Chóra on Sérifos

with small fertile valleys, and long sandy beaches.

Ferries dock at **Livádi** on the southeast coast. The town is situated on a sandy, tree-fringed bay backed by hotels and tavernas. Follow the stone steps up from Livádi, or use the sporadic bus service to reach the dazzling white **Chóra** high above on the steep hillside. It is topped by the ruins of a 15th-century Venetian kástro. Many of its medieval cube-shaped houses, some incorporating stone from the castle, have been renovated as holiday homes by Greek artists and architects. It is an attractive town with chapels and windmills perched precariously, offering breathtaking views of the island.

Near to the northern inland village of Galaní, the fortified **Moní Taxiarchón** (Archangel), built in 1500, is run by a single monk. The monastery contains fine 18th-century frescoes by Skordílis and some valuable Byzantine manuscripts.

Sífnos
Σίφνος

🏯 1,950. 🛥 🚌 Kamáres.
ℹ 22840 31210.

FAMOUS FOR its pottery, poets and chefs, Sífnos has become the most popular destination in the western Cyclades. Visitors in their thousands flock to the island in summer lured by its charming villages, terraced countryside dotted with ancient towers, Venetian dovecotes and long

sandy beaches. In ancient times Sífnos was renowned for its gold mines. The islanders paid yearly homage to the Delphic sanctuary of Apollo with a solid gold egg. One year they cheated and sent a gilded rock instead, incurring Apollo's curse. The gold mines were flooded, the island ruined and from then on was known as *sífnos*, meaning empty.

A fountain in Kástro, Sífnos

APOLLONIA
The capital is set above Kamáres port and is a Cycladic labyrinth of white houses, flowers and belfries. It is named after the 7th-century BC Temple of Apollo, which overlooked the town, now the site of the 18th-century church of the **Panagía Ouranofóra**. The **Museum of Popular Arts and Folklore** in the main square has a good collection of local pottery and embroideries.

🏛 Museum of Popular Arts and Folklore
Plateía Iróön. ⬜ Apr–Oct:
9am–10pm daily. 🅿

AROUND THE ISLAND
Sífnos is a small, hilly island, popular with walkers. Buses from Kamáres port connect it with Apollonía and Kástro, on the east coast. **Artemónas** is Apollonía's twin village, the second largest on Sífnos, with impressive Venetian houses sporting distinctive chimneys. The 17th-century church, Agios Geórgios tou Aféndi, contains several fine icons from the period. The church of Panagía Kónchi, with its cluster of domes, was built on the site of a temple of Artemis.

Kástro, 3 km (2 miles) east of Artemónas, overlooks the sea, the backs of its houses forming massive outer walls *(see pp18–19)*. Some buildings in the narrow, buttressed alleys bear Venetian coats of arms. There are ruins of a Classical acropolis in the village. The **Archaeological Museum** has a collection of Archaic and Hellenistic sculpture, and Geometric and Byzantine pottery.

The port of **Kamáres** is a straggling resort, with waterside cafés and tavernas. The north of the harbour was once lined with pottery shops making Sífnos's distinctive blue and brown ceramics, but only two remain. Taxi boats go from Kamáres to the pretty pottery hamlet of **Vathý**, in the south. An hour's walk to the east is the busy resort of **Platýs Gialós**, with its long sandy beach. This is also connected by bus to Apollonía and Kamáres.

🏛 Archaeological Museum
Kástro. ☎ 22840 31022.
⬜ Tue–Sun. ● main public hols.

A chapel with steps leading down to a small quay at Platýs Gialós, Sífnos

Páros
Πάρος

FERTILE, THYME-SCENTED Páros is the third largest Cycladic island. Since antiquity it has been famous for its white marble, which ensured the island's prosperity from the early Cycladic age through to Roman times. In the 13th century Páros was ruled by the Venetian Dukes of Náxos, then by the Turks from 1537 until the Greek War of Independence *(see pp38–9)*. Páros is the hub of the Cycladic ferry system and is busy in high season. Buffeted by strong winds in July and August, it is a wind-surfer's paradise. There are several resorts, but it retains its charm with hill-villages, vineyards and olive groves.

An ornate chandelier in the interior of Ekatontapyliani

The famous windmill beside Paroikiá's busy port

Paroikiá ❶
Παροικιά

🏘 3,000. ⛴ 🚌 harbour.
ℹ 22840 52158. ⏰ Apr–Oct.
🎭 Kriós 3 km (2 miles) N.

The port of Paroikiá, or Chóra, owes its foundations to the marble trade. Standing on the site of a leading early Cycladic city, it became a major Roman marble centre. Traces of Byzantine and Venetian rule remain, although earthquakes have caused much damage.

Today it prospers as a resort town, with its quayside wind-mill and commercialized water-front crammed with ticket agencies, cafés and bars. The area behind the harbour is an enchanting Cycladic town, with narrow paved alleys, archways dating from medieval times and white houses overhung with cascading jasmine.

🔒 Ekatontapyliani
W Paroikiá. 📞 22840 21243. ⏰ daily.
The Ekatontapylianí (Church of a Hundred Doors) in the west of town is the oldest in Greece in continuous use and

a major Byzantine monument. Its official name is the Dormition of the Virgin.

According to legend, the church was founded by St Helen, mother of Constantine, the first Christian Byzantine emperor. After having a vision here showing the path to the True Cross, she vowed to build a church on the site but died before fulfilling her promise. In the 6th century AD the Emperor Justinian carried out her wish, com-missioning the architect Ignatius to design a cathedral. He was the apprentice of Isidore of Miletus, master builder of Agía Sofía in Constantinople. The result was so impres-sive that Isidore, consumed with jealousy, pushed his pupil off the roof. Ignatius grabbed his master's foot and they both fell to their deaths. The pair are immortalized in stone in the north of the court-yard in front of the church.

Theoktísti's footprint

Ekatontapylianí is made up of three interlocking buildings. It is meant to have 99 doors and windows. According to legend, when the 100th door is found, Constantinople (Istanbul) will return to the Greeks. Many earthquakes have forced much reconstruction, and the main church building was restyled in the 10th century in the shape of a Greek cross. The sanctuary columns date from the pre-Christian era and the marble screen, capitals and iconostasis are of Byzantine origin.

On the carved wooden iconostasis is an icon of the Virgin, worshipped for its healing virtues. Nearby a foot-print, set in stone, is claimed

Fishing boats, Paroikiá harbour

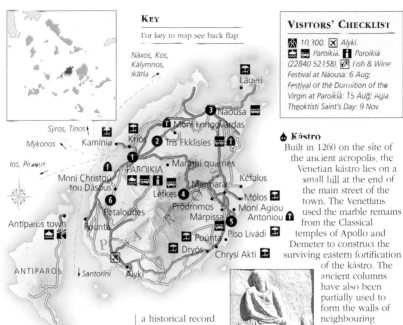

KEY

For key to map see back flap

Náxos, Kos,
Kálymnos,
Ikaría

Lágeri

Náousa

Moní Longovárdas

Trís Ekklisíes

Marathi quarries

Kéfalos

Moní Christoú
tou Dásous

PAROIKIA

Léfkes

Marmara

Mólos

Pródromos

Moní Agíou
Antoníou

Petaloúdes

Márpissa

Poúnta

Píso Livádi

Antíparos town

Dryós

Poúnta

Chrysí Aktí

ANTIPAROS

Santoríni

Alykí

Sýros, Tínos

Mýkonos

Kamínia

Kríos

Ios, Piraeus

0 kilometres 5

0 miles 2

SIGHTS AT A GLANCE

Léfkes ❹
Náousa ❸
Paroikiá ❶
Petaloúdes ❻
Píso Livádi ❺
Trís Ekklisíes ❷

VISITORS' CHECKLIST

10,300. ✈ Alykí.
🚢 🚌 Paroikiá. 🛈 Paroikiá
(22840 52158). ⛴ Fish & Wine
Festival at Náousa: 6 Aug;
Festival of the Dormition of the
Virgin at Paroikiá: 15 Aug; Agía
Theoktísti Saint's Day: 9 Nov.

Kástro

Built in 1260 on the site of the ancient acropolis, the Venetian kástro lies on a small hill at the end of the main street of the town. The Venetians used the marble remains from the Classical temples of Apollo and Demeter to construct the surviving eastern fortification of the kástro. The ancient columns have also been partially used to form the walls of neighbouring houses. Next to the site of the Temple of Apollo stands the 300-year-old blue-domed church of **Agía Eléni and Agios Konstantínos**.

ENVIRONS: Taxi boats cross the bay from Paroikiá to the popular sands of Kamínia beach and Kríos, both sheltered from the prevailing north wind. The ruins of an Archaic sanctuary of Delian Apollo stand on the hill above,

to be that of Agía Theoktísti, the island's patron saint. The Greeks fit their feet into the print to bring them luck. Also displayed is her severed hand.

From the back of the church a door leads to the chapel of Agios Nikólaos, an adapted 4th-century BC Roman building. It has a double row of Doric columns, a marble throne and a 17th-century iconostasis. Next door, the 11th-century baptistry has a marble font with a frieze of Greek crosses. Ekatontapylianí has no belltower and instead the bells are hung from a tree outside.

🏛 Archaeological Museum

W Paroikiá. ☎ 22840 21231. ◐ Tue–Sun. ● main public hols. 🖼
The museum can be found behind Ekatontapylianí. One of its main exhibits is part of the priceless Parian Chronicle,

a historical record of the artistic achievements of ancient Greece up to 264 BC. It is carved on a marble tablet and was discovered in the kástro walls during the 17th century. Also on display are finds from the Temple of Apollo including a 5th-century BC Winged Victory, a mosaic depicting Herakles hunting and a frieze of Archílochus, the 7th century BC poet and soldier from Páros.

A Greco-Roman frieze in the Archaeological Museum

THE LEGEND OF AGIA THEOKTISTI

Páros's patron saint, Theoktísti, was a young woman captured by pirates in the 9th century. She escaped to Páros and lived alone in the woods for 35 years, leading a pious and frugal life. Found by a hunter, she asked him to bring her some Communion bread. When he returned with the bread she lay down and died. Realizing she was a saint, he cut off her hand to take as a relic but found he could not leave Páros until he reunited her hand with her body.

Around Páros Island

PÁROS IS AN EASY ISLAND to explore, with an excellent bus service linking the three main towns: the capital Paroikía, the trendy fishing village resort of Náousa in the north and the central mountain town of Léfkes. There are plenty of cars and bikes for hire to get to the beaches and villages off the beaten track, and boat excursions and caïques to tour the remoter shores.

The mountain village of Léfkes, the medieval capital of Páros

Trís Ekklisíes ❷
Τρεις Εκκλησίες

3 km (2 miles) NE of Paroikiá.

North of Paroikiá the road to Náousa passes the remains of three 17th-century churches, Trís Ekklisíes, adapted from an original 7th-century basilica. That was in turn built from the marble of a 4th-century BC *heróon*, or hero's shrine, tomb of the Parian poet Archilochus.

In the mountains further north, the remote, 17th-century **Moní Longovárdas** is a hive of activity. The monks make wine and books and work in the fields, and the abbot is famous for his icon-painting. Visitors are, however, discouraged and women are banned.

Main door at Moní Longovárdas

Náousa ❸
Νάουσα

12 km (7 miles) NE of Paroikiá.
👥 2,100. 🚌 🛥 *Lageri 5 km (3 miles) NE.*

With its brightly painted fishing boats and winding white alleyways, Náousa has become a cosmopolitan destination for the jetset, with expensive boutiques and relaxed bars. It

is the island's second largest town and the place to sit and watch the rich and the beautiful parade chic designer clothes along the waterfront.

The colourful harbour has a unique breakwater in the half-submerged ruin of a Venetian castle which has slowly been sinking with the coastline.

Every year, on the evening of 23 August, 100 torch-lit fishing caïques assemble to re-enact the battle of 1536 between the islanders and the pirate Barbarossa, ending with celebrations of music and dancing.

Léfkes ❹
Λεύκες

10 km (6 miles) SE of Paroikiá.
👥 850. 🚌

The mountain road to Léfkes, the island's highest village, passes the abandoned marble quarries at Maráthi, last worked for Napoleon's tomb. It is possible to explore the ancient tunnels with a torch.

Léfkes, named after the local poplar trees, was the capital under Ottoman rule. It is a charming, unspoiled village with medieval houses, a labyrinth of alleys, *kafeneía* in shaded squares and restaurants with terraces overlooking the green valley below. Shops stock local weaving and ceramic handicrafts and the town has a tiny Folk Museum.

🏛 **Folk Museum**
⏰ *Apr–Oct: daily; Nov–Mar: key at town hall.* 🎫

ENVIRONS: From the windmills overlooking Léfkes, a Byzantine marble pathway leads 3 km (2 miles) southeast to **Pródromos**, an old fortified farming village. Walk a further 15 minutes past olive groves to reach **Mármara** village with its marble-paved streets. The pretty hamlet of **Márpissa** lies about 1.5 km (1 mile) south.

On Kéfalos hill, 2 km (1 mile) east of Márpissa, are the ruins of a 15th-century Venetian fortress and the 16th-century **Moní Agíou Antoníou**. The monastery, which is often shut, is built from Classical remains. It has a fine 17th-century fresco of the *Second Coming*.

Caïques at the attractive fishing harbour at Náousa

The convent of Moní Christoú tou Dásous near Petaloúdes

Píso Livádi ❺
Πίσω Λιβάδι

15 km (9 miles) SE of Paroikiá. 🏛 50. 🚌 to Marpissa. 🚤 Poúnta 1 km (0.5 mile) S.

Situated below Léfkes on the east coast of the island, the fishing village of Píso Livádi, with its sheltered sandy beach, has grown into a lively small resort. It was once the port for Páros's hill-villages and the island's marble quarries; today there are services operated over to nearby Agía Anna (see p226) on Náxos island. The small harbour has a wide range of bars and tavernas with a disco nearby and occasional local activities and entertainments.

The beautiful and fashionable beach at Poúnta

ENVIRONS: Mólos, 6 km (4 miles) north, has a long sandy beach with dunes, tavernas and a windsurfing centre. Just to the south lies **Poúnta** (not to be confused with the village of Poúnta on the west coast), one of the best and most fashionable beaches in the Cyclades with a trendy laid-back beach bar. The island's most famous east-coast beach,

3 km (2 miles) south, is **Chrysí Aktí** (Golden Beach). With 700 m (2,300 ft) of golden sand it is perfect for families. It is also a well-known centre for watersports and has hosted the world windsurfing championships

Dryós, 2 km (1 mile) further southwest, is an expanding resort but at its heart is a pretty village with a duck-pond, tavernas, a small harbour with a pebbly beach and a string of sandy coves.

Petaloúdes ❻
Πεταλούδες

6 km (4 miles) SW of Paroikiá. 🚌 ◻ 1 Jun – 20 Sep: daily. 🎟

Petaloúdes, or the Valley of the Butterflies, on the slopes of Psychopianá, is easily reached from Paroikiá. This lush green oasis is home to swarms of Jersey tiger moths, from May to August, which flutter from the foliage when disturbed. There are mule treks along the donkey paths that cross the valley. About 2 km (1 mile) north of Petaloúdes, the 18th-century convent of **Moní Christoú tou Dásous**, Christ of the Woods, is worth the walk, although women only are allowed into the sanctuary. Páros's second patron saint, Agios Arsénios, teacher and abbot, is also buried here.

OUTLYING ISLANDS
The island of **Antíparos** used to be joined to Páros by a causeway These days a small ferry links the two from the west-coast resort of Poúnta and there are also caïque trips from Paroikiá. Antíparos town has a relaxed and stylish café society, good for escaping from the Páros crowds. Activity centres around the quay and the Venetian **kástro** area. The kástro is a good example of a 15th-century fortress town, designed with inner courtyards and narrow streets to impede pirate attacks (see pp18–19). The village also has two 17th-century churches, Agios Nikólaos and Evangelismós.

The island has fine beaches, but the star attraction is the massive **Cave of Antíparos**, with a breathtaking array of stalactites and stalagmites, discovered during Alexander the Great's reign. In summer, boats run to the cave from Antíparos town and Poúnta on Páros. From where the boat docks, it is a half-hour walk up the hill of Agios Ioánnis to the cave mouth, then a dramatic 70 m (230 ft) descent into the cavern. Lord Byron and other visitors have carved their names on the walls. In 1673 the French ambassador, the Marquis de Nointel, held a Christmas Mass here for 500 friends. The church outside, Agios Ioánnis Spiliótis, was built in 1774.

Bougainvillea on a house in Antíparos town

Náxos
Νάξος

THE LARGEST OF THE CYCLADES, Náxos was first settled in 3000 BC. A major centre of the Cycladic civilization *(see pp24–5)*, it was one of the first islands to use marble. Náxos fell to the Venetians in 1207, and the numerous fortified towers *(pýrgoi)* were built, still evident across the island today. Its landscape is rich with citrus orchards and olive groves, and it is famous in myth as the place where Theseus abandoned the Cretan princess Ariadne.

Mosaic from the Archaeological Museum in Náxos town

The Portára gateway from the unfinished Temple of Apollo

Náxos Town ❶
Χώρα

🏠 *15,000.* 🚢 🚌 *Harbourfront* ℹ *Harbourfront (22850 25201).*

North of the port and reached by a causeway is the huge marble Portára gateway on the islet of Palátia, which dominates the harbour of Náxos town, or Chóra. Built in 522 BC, it was to be the entrance to the unfinished Temple of Apollo.

The town is made up of four distinct areas. The harbour bustles with its cafés and fishermen at work. To the south is Neá Chóra, or Agios Geórgios, a concrete mass of hotels, apartments and restaurants. Above the harbour, the old town divides into the Venetian Kástro, once home of the Catholic nobility, and the medieval Bourg, where the Greeks lived.

The twisting alleys of the Bourg market area are lined with restaurants and gift shops. The Orthodox cathedral in the Bourg, the fine 18th-century

Mitrópoli Zoödóchou Pigís, has an iconostasis, painted by Dimítrios Válvis of the Cretan School in 1786.

Uphill lies the imposing medieval north gate of the fortified Kástro, built in 1207 by Marco Sanudo. Only two of the original seven gate-towers remain. Little is left of the 13th-century outer walls, but the inner walls still stand, protecting 19 impressive houses. These bear the coats of arms of the Venetian nobles who lived there, and many of the present-day residents are descended from these families. Their remains are housed in the 13th-century Catholic **cathedral**, in the Kástro, beneath marble slabs dating back to 1619.

During the Turkish occupation, Náxos was famous for its schools. The magnificent Palace of Sanoúdo, dating from 1627, which incorporates part of the Venetian fortifications, housed the French school. The most famous pupil was Cretan novelist Níkos Kazantzákis *(see p272)* who wrote *Zorba the Greek.*

Angel from the Roman Catholic cathedral

The building now houses the **Archaeological Museum**, which has one of the best collections of Cycladic marble figurines *(see p207)* in the Greek islands, as well as some beautiful Roman mosaics.

🏛 **Archaeological Museum**
Palace of Sanoúdo. 🖀 *22850 22725.* ⏰ *Tue–Sun.* ⬤ *main public hols.* 🈲

ENVIRONS: A causeway leads to the **Grótta** area, north of Náxos town, named after its numerous sea caves. To the south the lagoon-like bay of **Agios Geórgios** is the main holiday resort, with golden sands and shallow water.

The best beaches are out of town along the west coast. **Agía Anna** is a pleasant small resort with silver sands and watersports. For more solitude, head south 3 km (2 miles) over the dunes to **Pláka**, the best beach on the island and mainly nudist. Further south down the coast the pure white sands of **Mikrí Vígla**, and **Kastráki**, named after a ruined Mycenaean fortress, are exceptionally good for both swimming and watersports.

The remote and beautiful Pláka beach south of Naxos town

Around Náxos Island

INLAND, NAXOS is a dramatic patchwork of rich gardens, vineyards, orchards and villages. These are backed by wild crags and dotted with Venetian watchtowers and a wealth of historical sites. Although there are organized tours from Náxos town and a good local bus service, a hired car is advisable to explore the island fully. The Tragaía region is, however, a walker's paradise.

VISITORS' CHECKLIST

🏃 20,000. ✈ 2 km (1 mile) S
Náxos town. 🚢 Náxos town. 🚌
🛈 Náxos town (22850 25201).
🎭 Agios Nikódimos Folk Festival,
Náxos town. 14 Jul; Dionysiac
Festival, Náxos town: 1st week of
Aug; Diorvoia Festival: Jul–Aug.

Moní village in the Tragaía valley, surrounded by olive groves

Mélanes Valley ❷
Κοιλάδα Μελάνων

10 km (6 miles) S of Náxos town.
🚌 to Kinídaros.

The road south of Náxos town passes through the Livádi valley, the heart of ancient marble country, to the Mélanes villages. In **Kournochóri**, the first village, is the Venetian Della Rocca tower. At **Mýloi**, near the ancient marble quarry at Flerió, lie two 6th-century

Koúros in a private garden in Mýloi in the Mélanes valley

KEY

For key to map see back flap

BC *koúroi*, huge marble statues. One, 8 m (26 ft) long, lies in a private garden, open to visitors. The other, 5.5 m (18 ft) long, lies in a nearby field.

ENVIRONS: Southeast of Náxos town is **Glinádo**, a market town, home to the Venetian

SIGHTS AT A GLANCE

Apeíranthos ❹
Apóllon ❻
Komiakí ❺
Mélanes Valley ❷
Náxos town ❶
Tragaía Valley ❸

Bellonias tower, first of the fortified mansions on Náxos. The chapel of Agios Ioánnis Gýroulas in **Ano Sagrí**, south of Glinádo, is built over the ruins of a temple of Demeter.

Tragaía Valley ❸
Κοιλάδα Τραγαίας

15 km (9 miles) SE of Náxos town. 🚌

From Ano Sagrí the road twists to the Tragaía valley. The first village in the valley, **Chalkí**, is the most picturesque with its Venetian architecture and the old Byzantine Fragópoulos tower in its centre.

From Chalkí a road leads up to Moní, home of the most unusual church on Náxos, **Panagía Drosianí**. Dating from the 6th century, its domes are made from field stones.

Filóti is a traditional village, the largest in the region. It sits on the slopes of Mount Zas, which, at 1,000 m (3,300 ft), is the highest in the Cyclades.

Santoríni
Irakleion, Ios
Páros, Sýros
Pátmos
Ikaria
Kos
Amorgós
Donoússa

NAXOS TOWN
Agios Geórgios ❶
Galini
Faneroménis 🛈
Agía Anna
Kournochóri ❷
Mélanes Valley ❷
Kinídaros
Glinádo   Mýloi
Pláka
Mikrí Vígla
Kástraki
Ano Sagrí
Tragaía Valley ❸
Agiá
Ormos   Apóllon ❻
Abrám
Moní
Myrsíni
Komiakí ❺
Kóronos
Moní
Chalkí
Filóti
Apeíranthos ❹
Moutsoúna
Mount Zas
▲ 🌤
1,000 m
3,300 ft

0 kilometres   5
0 miles   3

Terraced fields outside the village of Komiakí

Apeíranthos ❹
Απείρανθος

25 km (16 miles) SE of Náxos town.
🏠 1,500. 🚌

Apeíranthos was colonised in the 17th and 18th centuries by Cretan refugees fleeing Turkish oppression and coming to work in the nearby emery mine. It is the island's most atmospheric village, with marble-paved streets and 14th-century towers (*pýrgoi*) built by the Venetian Crispi family. Locals still wear traditional costume, women weave on looms and farmers sell their wares from donkeys.

The small **Archaeological Museum** has a collection of proto-Cycladic marble plaques depicting scenes from daily life as well as Neolithic finds. There is also a small **Geological Museum** on the second floor of the village school. Below the village is the port of **Moutsoúna** where ships were once loaded with emery before the industry's decline. The fine beach is now lined with holiday villas.

🏛 **Archaeological Museum**
Off main road. 📞 22850 61361.
☐ *daily.* ● *main public hols.* ♿
🏛 **Geological Museum**
Village school. 📞 22850 61361.
☐ *daily.* ● *main public hols.* 🈲

Komiakí ❺
Κωμιακή

42 km (26 miles) E of Náxos town.
🏠 500. 🚌

Approaching from Kóronos the road becomes a tortuous succession of hairpin bends before finally arriving in pretty Komiakí (also known as Koronída). This is the highest village on Náxos and a former home of the emery miners. It is covered with vines and is known for being the place where the local *kítro* liqueur originated. There are wonderful views over the surrounding terraced vineyards. The village is the start of one of the finest walks on Náxos. The walk takes you down into the lush valley and the charming oasis hamlet of **Myrsíni**.

Apóllon ❻
Απόλλων

49 km (30 miles) NE of Náxos town.
🏠 100. 🚌

Originally a fishing village that is slowly turning into a resort, Apóllon gets busy in the summer with coach trips of people coming to visit the fish tavernas and the huge *koúros* found here. Steps lead up the hillside above the village to ancient marble quarries where the vast unfinished statue has lain abandoned since 600 BC. The bearded marble figure, which is believed to represent the god Apollo, is 10.5 m (35 ft) long and weighs 30 tonnes. There is also a lively festival in the village for St John the Baptist on 28 August.

ENVIRONS: At Agiá, 10 km (6 miles) west of Apóllon, stands the **Cocco Pýrgos**, built by the Venetian Cocco clan at the beginning of their rule of northern Náxos in 1770. *Pýrgoi* are fortified watchtowers that were built during the Venetian occupation of Náxos. Further along the north coast road lies the idyllic beach at **Órmos Abrám** with a good family-run taverna.

Dating from 1606, the abandoned **Moní Faneroménis** is 13 km (8 miles) south on the road winding down the west coast from Apóllon. Slightly further south towards Galíni, a road leads up to the most famous *pýrgos,* the **High Tower** of the Cocco clan. It was built in 1660 in a commanding position overlooking a valley. During the 17th century a family feud between the Orthodox Cocco and the Catholic Barozzi

The harbour at Moutsoúna, Náxos

The huge *kouros* in Apóllon's ancient quarries

families broke out as a result of an insult. The feud led to the bombardment of the High Tower when a Barozzi woman persuaded her husband, who was a Maltese privateer, to besiege it. The Cocco clan managed to hold out but the vendetta continued to rage for another 20 years until a marriage eventually united the two families.

A Venetian fortified watchtower, or *pýrgos*, west of Apóllon

OUTLYING ISLANDS

Between Náxos and Amorgós lie **Donoússa**, **Koufoníssi**, **Irakliá** and **Schinoússa**, the "Back Islands". The islands all have rooms to rent, a post office and OTE, but no banks.

Irakliá, the largest, boasts impressive stalactites in the Cave of Aï-Giánni as well as Cycladic remains. Koufoníssi consists of two islands, Ano (upper), the most developed of the Back Islands, with good sandy beaches, and the uninhabited Káto (lower). Schinoússa has wild beaches and great walking over cobbled mule tracks. Donoússa, the most northerly of the chain, is more isolated and food can be scarce. A settlement from the Geometric era was excavated on the island, but most of its visitors come for the fine sandy beaches at **Kéntros** and **Livádi**.

Amorgós
Αμοργός

🏛 *1,800.* ⛴ *Katápola & Aigiáli.* 🚌 *Katápola & Aigiáli harbours.* 🛈 *Katápola quay (22850 71278).* 🎉 *Ormos Aigiális 12 km (7 miles) NE of Amorgós town.*

DRAMATICALLY RUGGED, the small island of Amorgós is narrow and long with a few beaches. Inhabited from as early as 3300 BC, its peak was during the Cycladic civilization, when there were three cities: Minoa, Arkesini and Egiali. In 1885 a find of ceramics and marble was taken to the Archaeological Museum in Athens *(see p282)*.

CHORA

The capital, Chóra, or Amorgós town, is a dazzling clutch of whitewashed houses with windmills standing nearby. Above the town is **Apáno Kástro**, a Venetian fortress, which was built by Geremia Ghisi in 1290. Chóra also boasts the smallest church in Greece, the tiny **Agios Fanoúrios**.

ENVIRONS: Star attraction on the island is the spectacular Byzantine **Moní Panagías Chozoviótissas**, below Chóra on the east coast. The stark white monastery clings to the 180-m (590-ft) cliffs. It is a huge fortress, built into the rock, housing

the miraculous icon of the Virgin Mary. Founded in 1088 by the Byzantine Emperor Alexios I Comnenos, the monastery has a library with a collection of ancient manuscripts.

AROUND THE ISLAND

The best way to get around the island is by boat or walking, although there is a limited bus service. The main port of **Katápola** in the southwest is set in a horseshoe-shaped bay with tavernas, *pensions*, fishing boats and a small shingly beach. The harbour area links three villages: Katápola in the middle where the ferries dock, quieter **Xylokeratídi** to the north and **Rachídi** on the hill side above. A track leads from Katápola to the hilltop ruins of the ancient city of **Minoa**. All that remains are the Cyclopean walls, the gymnasium and the foundations of the Temple of Apollo.

The northern port of **Ormos Aigiális** is the island's main resort, popular for its sandy beach. It is worth following the mule paths north to the hill-villages of **Tholária**, which has vaulted Roman *tholos* tombs, and **Lagáda**, which is one of the prettiest villages on the island, with a stepped main street that is painted with daisies.

The cliff-top Moní Chozoviótissas

The white walls and blue-domed churches of Ios town

Ios
`Ιος`

🏛 1,654. 🚢 Gialós. 🚌 Ios town.
ℹ️ Ano Chóra, Ios town (22860 91222). 🚉 Mylopótas 2 km (1 mile) E of Ios town.

IN ANCIENT TIMES Ios was covered in oak woods, later used for shipbuilding. The Ionians built cities at the port of Gialós and at Ios town, later to be used as Venetian strongholds. Ios is also known as the burial place of Homer, and 15 May is the Omíria, or Homer festival. A local speciality is its cheese, myzíthra, similar to a soft cream cheese.

Ios is renowned for its nightlife and as a result is a magnet for the young. However, it remains a beautiful island. Its mountainous coastline has over 400 chapels and some of the finest sands in the Cyclades.

Ios town, also known as the Village, is a dazzling mix of white houses and blue-domed churches fast being swamped by discos and bars. There are ruins of the Venetian fortress, built in 1400 by Marco Crispi, remains of ancient walls, and 12 windmills above the town.

The port of **Gialós**, or Ormos, has a busy harbour, with yachts and fishing boats, good fish tavernas and quieter accommodation than Ios town. The beach here is windy, although a 20-minute walk west leads to the sandy

cove at Koumpará. A bus service runs from here to Ios town and the superb **Mylopótas** beach which has two campsites. Excursion boats run from Gialós to the beach at **Manganári** bay, in the south and **Psáthi** bay in the east.

On the northeast coast the beach at **Agía Theodóti** is overlooked by the medieval ruins of Palaiókastro fortress. A festival is held at nearby **Moní Agías Theodótis** on 8 September to mark the islanders' victory over medieval pirates. You can see the door the pirates broke through only to be scalded to death by boiling oil.

Homer's tomb is supposedly in the north at **Plakotós**, an ancient Ionian town which has slipped down the cliffs over the ages. Homer died on the island after his ship was forced to dock en route to Athens. The tomb entrance, ruined houses and the remains of the Hellenistic **Psarópyrgos tower** can be seen today.

Windmill above Ios town

Síkinos
Σίκινος

🏛 300. 🚢 Aloprónoia. 🚌 Síkinos town. ℹ️ Kástro, Síkinos town (22860 51222). 🚉 Agios Geórgios 7 km (3 miles) NE of Síkinos town.

SÍKINOS IS QUIET, very Greek and one of the most ruggedly beautiful islands in the Cyclades. Known in Classical Greece as Oinoe (wine island), it has remained a traditional backwater throughout history. Fishing and farming are the main occupations of the 300 or so islanders and, although there are some holiday homes, there is little mass tourism.

Síkinos town is divided into twin villages: Kástro and the pretty and unspoilt Chóra perched high up on a ridge overlooking the sea. Kástro is a maze of lanes and kafeneía. At the entrance to the village is Plateía Kástrou where the walls of 18th-century stone mansions formed a bastion of defence. The church of the Pantánassa forms the focal point and among the ruined houses is a huge marble portico.

The partly ruined Moní Zoödóchou Pigís, fortified against pirate raids, looms down from the crag above Chóra and has icons by the 18th-century master Skordílis.

In medieval Chóra there is a private **Folk Museum**, which is in the family home of an American expatriate. It has an olive press and a wide range of local domestic and agricultural artifacts.

From Chóra a path leads past the ruined ancient Cyclopean walls southwest to **Moní Episkopís**, a good hour's trek. With Doric

The golden sands of Mylopótas beach, Ios

columns and inscriptions it is thought to be a 3rd-century AD mausoleum, converted in the 7th century to the Byzantine church of Koímisis Theotókou. A monastery was added in the 17th century, but is now disused.

On the east coast 3 km (2 miles) southeast of Síkinos town, the port of **Aloprónoia**, also known as Skála, has a few small cafés that double as shops, a modern hotel complex and a wide sandy beach that is safe for children.

⏹ Folk Museum
Ano Chorio, Síkinos town.
◻ May–Sep: daily.

Koímisis tis Theotókou in Folégandros town

The sleepy port of Aloprónoia

Folégandros
Φολέγανδρος

🏘 650. ⛴ 🚌 Karavostásis.
ℹ Chóra (22860 41249).
🚌 Agáli 2 km (1 mile) W of Folégandros town.

B LEAK AND ARID, Folégandros is one of the smallest inhabited islands in the Cyclades. It aptly takes its name from the Phoenician for rocky. Traditionally a place of exile, this remote island passed quietly under the Aegean's various rulers, suffering only from the threat of pirate attack. Popular with photographers and artists for its sheer cliffs, terraced fields and striking Chóra, it can be busy in peak season, but is still a good place for walkers, with a wild

beauty and unspoiled beaches. **Folégandros town** or Chóra, perched 300 m (985 ft) above the sea to avoid pirates, is spectacular. It divides into the fortified Kástro quarter (see p18) and Chóra, or main village. Kástro, built in the 13th century by Marco Sanudo, Duke of Náxos, is reached through an arcade. The tall stone houses back on to the sea, forming a stronghold along the ridge of the cliff with a sheer drop below. Within its maze of crazy-paved alleys full of geraniums are the distinctive two-storey cube houses with brightly painted wooden balconies.

In Chóra village life centres on four squares with craft shops and lively tavernas and bars. The path from the central bus stop leads to the church of Koímisis tis Theotókou, (Assumption of the Virgin Mary). It was built after a silver icon was miraculously saved by an islander from medieval pirates who drowned in a storm. Forming part of the ancient town walls, it is thought to have once been the site of a Classical temple of Artemis.

Ferries dock at **Karavostási** on the east coast, a tiny harbour with a tree-fringed pebble beach, restaurants, hotels and rooms. There is a bus to Chóra, and **Livádi** beach is a short walk from the port. In season there are excursions available to the western beaches at **Agáli**, **Agios**

Nikólaos and **Latináki**, as well as to the island's most popular sight, the **Chrysospiliá** or Golden Cave. Named after the golden shade of its stalactites and stalagmites, the grotto lies just below sea level in the northeast cliffs.

Ano Meriá, 5 km (3 miles) to the west of Folégandros town, is a string of farming hamlets on either side of the road, surrounded by terraced fields. There are wonderful sunset views from here and on a clear day it is possible to see Crete in the distance. There is a good **Ecology and Folk Museum** with a display of farming implements, and reconstructions of traditional peasant life. On 27 July a major local festival is held for Agios Panteleïmon.

From Ano Meriá steep paths weave down to the remote beaches at **Agios Geórgios** bay and **Vígla**.

⏹ Ecology and Folk Museum
Ano Meriá. ◻ Jul–mid-Sep: daily.

Traditional houses in Kástro, Folégandros town

Mílos
Μήλος

VOLCANIC MILOS is the most dramatic of the Cyclades with its extraordinary rock formations, hot springs and white villages perched on multicoloured cliffs. Under the Minoans and Mycenaeans the island became rich from trading obsidian. However, the Athenians brutally captured and colonized Mílos in the 4th century BC. Festooned with pirates, the island was ruled by the Crispi dynasty during the Middle Ages and was claimed by the Turks in 1580. Minerals are now the main source of the island's wealth, although tourism is growing.

View across the houses of Pláka in the mid-morning sun

Museum in Athens *(see p282)*. There are also finds from the neighbouring island of Kímolos. The **History and Folk Museum** is housed in a 19th-century mansion in the centre of Pláka. It has costumes, four-poster beds and handicrafts.

The *Lady of Phylakopí* in the Archaeological Museum

Steps lead to the ruined **kástro** which was built by the Venetians on a volcanic plug 280 m (920 ft) above sea level. Only the houses that formed the outer walls of the fortress remain.

Above the kástro, the church of Mésa Panagía was bombed during World War II. It was rebuilt and renamed **Panagía Schiniótissa** (Our Lady of the Bushes) after an icon of the Virgin Mary appeared in a bush where the old church used to stand.

Just below, the church of **Panagía Thalassítra** (Our Lady of the Sea), built in 1728, has icons of Christ, the Virgin Mary and Agios Elefthérios.

The massive stone blocks of the Cyclopean walls that formed the city's East Gate in 450 BC remain, while 15 m (50 ft) west there are marble

PLAKA

On a clifftop 4 km (2.5 miles) above the port of Adámas, Pláka is a pretty mix of churches and white cube houses. These blend into the suburb of Trypití which is topped by windmills.

It is believed that Pláka is sited on the acropolis of ancient Mílos, built by the Dorians between 1100 and 800 BC. The town was then destroyed by the Athenians and later settled by the Romans.

The principal sight is the **Archaeological Museum**, its entrance hall dominated by a plaster copy of the *Venus de Milo*, found on Mílos. The collection includes Neolithic finds, particularly obsidian, Mycenaean pottery, painted ceramics, and terracotta

animals from 3500 BC, found at the ancient city of Philakopí. The most famous of the ceramics is the *Lady of Phylakopí*, an early Cycladic goddess decorated in Minoan style. However, the Hellenistic 4th-century BC statue of Poseidon and the *koúros* of Mílos (560 BC) are now in the National Archaeological

Sífnos,
Kímolos

Folégandros

Apollonía
Voúdia
Papafrágkas
Ancient Phylakopi
Mandrákia
Akradiés
Sarakíniko
Piraeus
PLAKA
Trypití
Adámas
Crete
Langáda
Zefyriá
Emporeiós
Chivadolímni
Ralaki
Agía
Kyriakí
Provátás

M Í L O S

KEY

For key to map see back flap

0 kilometres   5

0 miles   3

The twin rocks, known as The Bears, on the approach to Adámas

relics and a Christian baptismal font from a Byzantine basilica. A Roman amphitheatre nearby is still used for performances.

🏛 Archaeological Museum
Main square. **§** 22870 21620. ☐ Tue–Sun. ● 1 May. 🎟

🏛 History and Folk Museum
Pláka. **§** 22870 21292. ☐ Tue–Sat & Sun am. ● main public hols. ♿ 🎟

Inside the Christian Catacombs

ENVIRONS: In the nearby town of Trypití are the well-preserved 1st-century AD **Christian Catacombs**, which are unique in Greece. Carved into the hillside, the massive complex of galleries has tombs in arched niches, each one containing up to seven bodies. The catacomb network is 184 m (605 ft) long, with 291 tombs. Archaeologists believe that as many as 8,000 bodies were interred here.

From the catacombs, a track leads to the place where the *Venus de Milo* was discovered, now marked by a plaque. It was found on 8 April 1820, by a farmer, Geórgios Kentrótas. He uncovered a cave in the corner of his field with half of the ancient marble statue inside. The other half was found by a visiting French

officer and both halves were bought as a gift for Louis XVIII, on 1 March 1821. The statue is now on show in the Louvre, Paris. The missing arms are thought to have been lost in the struggle for possession.

⛪ Christian Catacombs
Trypití, 2 km (1 mile) SE of Pláka. **§** 22870 21625. ☐ Tue–Sun.

AROUND THE ISLAND
The rugged island is scattered with volcanic relics and long stretches of beach. The vast Bay of Mílos, the site of the volcano's central vent, is one of the finest natural harbours in the Mediterranean, and has some of Milos's best sights.

West of Adámas, the small and sandy **Langáda** beach is popular with families. On the way to the beach are the municipal baths with their warm mineral waters.

South of Adámas, the Bay of Mílos has a succession of attractive beaches, including **Chivadolímni**, backed by a turquoise saltwater lake. On the south coast is the lovely beach of Agía Kyriakí, near the village of Provatás.

Situated on the northeast tip of the island is **Apollonía**, a popular resort with a tree-fringed beach. Water taxis leave here for the island of **Kímolos**, named after the chalk (*kimolía*) mined there.

Once an important centre of civilization, little remains now of **Ancient Phylakopi**, just southwest of Apollonía. You can make out the old Mycenaean city walls, ruined houses and grave sites, but a large part of the city has been submerged beneath the sea.

GEOLOGY OF MILOS
Due to its volcanic origins, Mílos is rich in minerals and has some spectacular rock formations. Boat tours from Adámas go to the eerie pumice moonscape of Sarakíniko, formed two to three million years ago, the lava formations known as the "organ-pipes" of Glaronísia (offshore near Philakopí), and the sulphurous blue water at Papáfragkas. Geothermal action has provided a wealth of hot springs; in some areas, such as off the Mávra Gkrémna cliffs, the sea can reach 100° C (212° F) only 30 cm (12 inches) below the surface.

Mineral mine at Voúdia, still in operation

The white pumice landscape at Sarakíniko

The sulphurous blue water at Papáfragkas

Santoríni
Σαντορίνη

One of the many cliffside bars in Firá, with views over the caldera

COLONIZED BY THE Minoans in 3000 BC, this volcanic island erupted in 1450 BC, forming Santoríni's crescent shape. The island is widely believed to be a candidate for the lost kingdom of Atlantis. Named Thíra by the Dorians when they settled here in the 8th century BC, it was renamed Santoríni, after St Irene, by the Venetians who conquered the island in the 13th century. Despite tourism, Santoríni remains a stunning island with its white villages clinging to volcanic cliffs above black sand beaches.

Early Cycladic figurine

Firá ❶
Φηρά

🚶 1,550. 🚢 🚌 50 m (165 ft) S of main square. 🛈 28860 22231. ✈ Monólithos 5 km (2.5 miles) E.

Firá, or Thíra, overlooking the caldera and the island of Néa Kaméni, is the island's capital. It was founded in the late 18th century when islanders moved from the Venetian citadel of Skáros, near present day Imerovígli, to the clifftop plains for easier access to the sea.

Devastated by an earthquake in 1956, Firá has been rebuilt, terraced into the volcanic cliffs with domed churches and barrel-roofed cave houses (skaftá). The terraces are packed with hotels, bars and restaurants in good positions

along the lip of the caldera to enjoy the magnificent views, especially at sunset. The tiny port of Skála Firón is 270 m (885 ft) below Firá, connected by cable car or by mule up the 580 steps. Firá is largely

pedestrianized with winding cobbled alleys. The town's main square, Plateía Theotokopoúlou, is the bus terminal and hub of the road network. All the roads running north from here and the harbour eventually merge in Plateía

SIGHTS AT A GLANCE

Akrotíri ❹
Ancient Thíra ❸
Firá ❶
Oía ❷

KEY

For key to map see back flap

0 kilometres   5

0 miles   3

Firá's whitewashed buildings lining the clifftop

THIRASIA

Náxos, Anáfi
Síkinos, Páros, Ios
Baxédes
Oía
Ammoúdi
Arméni
Imerovígli
Kanakári
FIRA
Skála Firón
Monólithos
NEA KAMENI
Folégandros, Crete
PALAIA KAMENI
Athiniós
Kamári
ASPRO NISI
Ancient Thíra
Moní Profítou Ilía
Mount Profítis
565 m 1,855 ft
Akrotíri
Emporeió
Períssa
Kókkini Ammos
Almyrá
Vlycháda

Firostefáni. The most spectacular street, Agíou Miná, runs south along the edge of the caldera to the 18th-century church of **Agíos Minás**. With its distinctive blue dome and its white belltower, it has become the symbol of Santoríni. The **Archaeological Museum** houses finds from Akrotíri *(see p237)* and the ancient city of Mésa Vounó *(see p236)*, including early Cycladic figurines found in local pumice mines. The **New Archeological Museum** contains the colourful Firá frescoes orginally thought to be from the mythical city of Atlantis.

Housed in a beautiful 17th-century mansion, the **Mégaro Ghísi Museum**, in the northern part of the town, holds manuscripts from the 16th to 19th centuries, maps, paintings, and photographs of Firá before and after the earthquake.

Despite the 1956 earthquake you can still see vestiges of Firá's architectural glory from the 17th and 18th centuries, on Nomikoú and Erythroú Stavroú where several mansions have been restored.

The pretty ochre chapel of **Agios Stylianós**, clinging to the edge of the cliff, is worth a visit on the way to the Frangika, or Frankish quarter, with its maze of arcaded streets. To the south, the Orthodox **cathedral** is dedicated to the Ypapantí (the Presentation of Christ in the Temple). Built in 1827, it is an imposing

Detail of bright orange volcanic cliff in Firá

ochre building with two belltowers and murals by the artist Christóforos Asimís. The belltower of the **Dómos** dominates the north of town on Agíou Ioánnou. Though severely damaged in the earthquake, much of its Baroque interior has now been restored.

VISITORS' CHECKLIST

🏠 12,500. ✈ 5 km (3 miles) SE of Firá. ⛴ Skála Firón. 🚌 🚻 Firá (22860 22231). 🎵 Classical Music, Firá: Aug & Sep.

🏛 **Archaeological Museum** Opposite cable car. ☎ 22860 22217. ○ 8:30am–3pm Tue–Sun. ● main public hols.

🏛 **Mégaro Ghísi Museum** Near cable car ☎ 22860 23077. ○ May–late Oct: daily. 💰

🏛 **New Archaeological Museum** Near Firá central square. ☎ 22860 23217. ○ 8:30am–3pm Tue–Sun. ● main public hols.

GEOLOGICAL HISTORY OF SANTORINI

Santoríni is one of several ancient volcanoes lying on the southern Aegean volcanic arc. During the Minoan era, around 1450 BC, there was a huge eruption which began Santoríni's transformation to how we see it today.

1 *Santoríni was a circular volcanic island before the massive eruption that blew out its middle.*

The volcano was active for centuries, building up to the 1450 BC explosion.

Clouds containing molten rock spread over 30 km (19 miles).

Crater of 22 sq km (8.5 sq miles)

2 *The eruption left a huge crater, or caldera. The rush of water into the void created a tidal wave, or tsunami, which devastated Minoan Crete.*

A huge volume of lava was ejected, burying Akrotíri *(see p237)*.

Néa Kaméni and its active volcanic cone

Volcano walls up to 300 m (985 ft) high

Thirasía

3 *The islands of Néa Kaméni and Palaiá Kaméni, visible today, emerged after more recent volcanic activity in 197 BC and 1707. They are still volcanically active.*

Aspro Nisí   **Palaiá Kaméni**

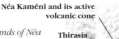

A donkey ride up the steps from Skála Firón to Firá

Around Santoríni Island

SANTORINI HAS MUCH TO OFFER apart from the frequently photographed attractions of Firá. There are some charming inland villages, and excellent beaches at Kamári and Períssa with their long stretches of black sand. You can also visit some of Santoríni's wineries, or take a ferry or boat to the smaller islands. There are good bus services but a car or bike will allow you more freedom to explore. Major sites such as Ancient Thíra and Akrotíri have frequent bus or organized tour services.

Ancient Thíra, situated at the end of the Mésa Vounó peninsula

A blue and ochre painted housefront in Oía

Oía ❷
Οία

11 km (7 miles) NW of Firá.
🚶 400. 🚌

At the northern tip of the island, the beautiful town of Oía is famous for its spectacular sunsets. A popular island excursion is to have dinner in one of the many restaurants at the edge of the abyss as the sun sinks behind the caldera. According to legend, the atmospheric town is haunted and home to vampires.

Reached by one of the most tortuous roads in the Cyclades, Oía is the island's third port and was an important and wealthy commercial centre before it was badly damaged in the 1956 earthquake.

Today Oía is designated a traditional settlement, having been carefully reconstructed after the earthquake. Its white and pastel-coloured houses with red pebble walls cling to the cliff face with the famous *skaftá* cave houses and blue-domed churches. Some of the Neo-Classical mansions built by shipowners can still be seen. A marble-paved pathway skirts the edge of the caldera to Firá. Staircases lead down to Arméni and the nearby fishing harbour at **Ammoúdi** with its floating pumice stones and red pebble beach. The tradition of boat-building continues at Arméni's small ferry dock at the base of the cliff, although the port is now mainly used by tourist boats departing daily for the small island of Thirasía.

Rock carving in Ancient Thíra

Ancient Thíra ❸
Αρχαία Θήρα

11 km (7 miles) SW of Firá.
🚌 to Kamári. ⏰ 8am–2pm Tue–Sun. ⚫ main public hols. 🏖 Períssa 200 m (600 ft) below.

Commanding the rocky headland of Mésa Vounó, 370 m (1,215 ft) up on the southeast coast, the ruins of the Dorian town of Ancient Thíra are still visible. Recolonized after the great eruption (*see p235*), the ruins stand on terraces overlooking the sea.

Excavated by the German archaeologist Hiller von Gortringen in the 1860s, most of the ruins date from the Ptolemies, who built temples to the Egyptian gods in the 4th and 3rd centuries BC. There are also Hellenistic and Roman remains. The 7th-century Santoríni vases that were discovered here are now housed in Firá's Archaeological Museum (*see p235*).

A path through the site passes an early Christian basilica, remains of private houses, some with mosaics, the agora (or market) and a theatre, with a sheer view down to the sea. On the far west is a 3rd-century BC sanctuary cut into the rock, founded by Artemídoros of Perge, an admiral of the Ptolemaic fleet. It features relief carvings of an eagle, a lion, a dolphin and a phallus symbolizing the gods Zeus, Apollo, Poseidon and Priapus. To the east, on the Terrace of Celebrations, you can find

Ammoúdi fishing village overlooked by Oía on the clifftop above

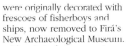

The view from ancient Thíra down to Kamári

though it was Professor Spyrídon Marinátos who, digging in 1967, unearthed the complete city; it was wonderfully preserved after some 3,500 years of burial under tonnes of volcanic ash. The highlight was the discovery of frescoes which are now displayed at the National Archaeological Museum in Athens *(see p282)*. Marinátos was killed in a fall on the site in 1974 and his grave is beside his life's work. Covered by a modern roof, the excavations include late 16th century BC houses on the Telchínes road, two and three storeys high, many still containing huge *pithoi*, or ceramic storage jars. The lanes were covered in ash and it was here that the well-known fresco of the two boys boxing was uncovered. Further along there is a mill and a pottery. A flyover-style bridge enables you to see the town's layout including a storeroom for *pithoi* which held grain, flour and oil. The three-storey House of the Ladies is named after the fresco of two voluptuous dark women. The Triangle Square has large houses that

were originally decorated with frescoes of fisherboys and ships, now removed to Firá's New Archaeological Museum.

The city's drainage system demonstrates how sophisticated and advanced the civilization was. No human or animal remains or treasure were ever found, suggesting that the inhabitants were probably warned by tremors before the catastrophe and fled in good time.

OUTLYING ISLANDS

From Athiniós, 12 km (7 miles) south of Firá, excursion boats run to the neighbouring islands. The nearest are **Palaiá Kaméni** and **Néa Kaméni**, known as the Burnt Islands. You can take a hot mud bath in the springs off Palaiá Kaméni and walk up the volcanic cone and crater of Néa Kaméni. **Thirasía** has a few tavernas and hotels. Its main town, the picturesque Manolás, has fine views across the caldera to Firá. Remote **Anáfi** is the most southerly of the Cyclades and shares the history of the other islands in the group. It is a peaceful retreat with good beaches. There are a few ancient ruins but nothing remains of the sanctuaries of Apollo and Artemis that once stood here.

graffiti which dates back as far as 800 BC. The messages praise the competitors and dancers of the *gymnopediés* – festivals in which boys danced naked and sang hymns to Apollo, or competed in feats of physical strength.

ENVIRONS: The headland of Mésa Vounó, which rises to the peak of Mount Profítis, juts out into the sea between the popular beaches of Kamári and Veríssa. **Kamári** is situated below Ancient Thíra to the north, and is the island's main resort. The beach is a mix of stone and black volcanic sand, and is backed by bars, tavernas and apartments. **Veríssa** has 8 km (5 miles) of black volcanic sand, a wide range of watersports and a campsite. A modern church stands on the site of the Byzantine chapel of Irene, after whom the island is named.

Akrotíri 1
Ακρωτήρι

12 km (7 miles) SW of Firá.
350. Kókkini Ammos 1 km (0.5 miles) S.

Akrotíri was once a Minoan outpost on the southwest tip of the island and is one of the most inspiring archaeological sites in the Cyclades. After an eruption in 1866, French archaeologists discovered Minoan pots at Akrotíri,

Storage jars found at Akrotíri

FRESCOES OF AKROTÍRI

Painted around 1500 BC, these Minoan-style murals are similar to those found at Knossós *(see pp268–71)*. The best known are *The Young Fisherman*, depicting a youth holding blue and yellow fish, and *The Young Boxers*, showing two young sparring partners with long black hair and almond-shaped eyes. Preserved by the lava, the frescoes have kept their colour. They are now on show in the New Archaeological Museum in Firá *(see p235)*.

The dramatic setting of Firá on the cliffs of Santoríni ▷

CRETE

···

CHANIA · RETHYMNO · IRAKLEIO · LASITHI

T HE ISLAND OF CRETE *is dominated by harsh, soaring mountains whose uncompromising impregnability is etched deep into the Cretan psyche. For centuries, cut off by these mountains and isolated by sea, the character of the island people has been proudly independent. Many conquerors have come and gone but the Cretan passion for individuality and freedom has never been extinguished.*

For nearly 3,000 years the ruins of an ancient Minoan civilization lay buried and forgotten beneath the coastal plains of Crete. It was not until the early 20th century that the remains of great Minoan palaces at Knosós, Phaestos, Mália and Zákros were unearthed. Their magnificence demonstrates the level of sophistication and artistic imagination of the Minoan civilization, now considered the wellspring of European culture.

Rug detail, Anógeia

Historically, the island and its people have endured occupation by foreign powers and the hardships of religious persecution. The Romans brought their administrative expertise to the island, and the ancient city-state of Górtys became capital of the Roman province of Crete in 65 BC. Byzantine rule was followed by the Venetians (1204–1669), whose formidable fortresses, such as Frangokástello, and elegant buildings in cities such as Réthymno and Chaniá testify to 400 years of foreign rule. Oppression and religious persecution by the Ottoman Turks (1669–1898) encouraged a strong independence movement. By 1913, led by Elefthérios Venizélos (1864–1936), Crete had become a province of Greece. The island was again occupied by German forces during World War II despite valiant resistance.

Today, mountains, sparkling seas and ancient history combine with the Cretans' relaxed nature to make the island an idyllic holiday destination.

A local in Réthymno wearing traditional Cretan boots and headdress

◁ A palm-fringed estuary meets the sea at Préveli Beach on Crete's southern coast

The Flora and Fauna of Crete

CRETE'S WILDLIFE is as varied as its landscape. In spring, flowers cover the coastal strip and appear inland in the patchwork of olive groves, meadows and orchards. Stony, arid *phrygana* habitat is widespread and pockets of native evergreen forests still persist in remote gorges. Freshwater marshes act as magnets for waterbirds, while Crete's position between North Africa and the Greek mainland makes it a key staging post for migrant birds in spring and autumn. Its comparative isolation has meant that several unique species of plant have evolved.

The Samariá Gorge (see pp250–51) *has been carved out by winter torrents washing down from the Omalós Plateau. Visitors should look out for peonies, cyclamens and Cretan ebony. Watch out as well for wild goats, called* kri-kri, *whose sure-footed confidence enables them to scale the precipitous slopes and cliffs.*

The Akrotíri peninsula offers sightings of chameleons.

Chaniá

OMALOS PLATEAU

Réthymno

The Omalós Plateau (see p250) *is home to the lammergeier, one of Europe's largest birds of prey. With narrow wings and distinctive wedge-shaped tail, it can be seen soaring over mountains and ravines.*

Kourtaliótiko gorge is a good spot to look for clumps of Jerusalem sage.

Moní Préveli

Agía Galíni

Mo
Ic
2,4
8,0

| 0 kilometres | 20 |
| 0 miles | 10 |

Marlin and swordfish are the largest fish in the seas around Crete.

Agía Triáda

Agía Triáda's wetlands are the haunt of black-winged stilts.

The Gulf of Mesará has a rough, grassy shoreline that is home to butterflies like the swallowtail.

Moní Préveli (see p256) *is visited by the migrant Ruppell's warbler between May and August. With his bold black and white head markings and beady red eyes, the male is a striking bird.*

Agía Galíni (see p259) *is an excellent spot for spring flowers, and in particular the striking giant orchid. It stands more than 60 cm (24 inches) tall and can bloom as early as February or early March.*

The colourful yellow bee orchid

The catchfly with its sticky stems

Cretan ebony, endemic to Crete

WILD FLOWERS ON CRETE

Botanists visit Crete in their thousands each year to enjoy the spectacular display of wild flowers. They are at their best, and in greatest profusion, from February to May. By late June, with the sun at its highest in the sky, many have withered and turned brown. Most of those that undergo this transformation survive the summer as underground bulbs or tubers.

WILDLIFE TOUR OPERATORS

Honeyguide Wildlife Holidays
36 Thunder Lane, Norwich, Norfolk NR7 0PX.
☎ 01603 300552.

Naturetrek
Cheriton Mill, Cheriton, Alresford, Hampshire SO24 0NG.
☎ 01962 733051.
W www.naturetrek.co.uk

Pure Crete
79 George St, Croydon, Surrey CR0 1LD.
☎ 020-8760 0879.
W www.pure-crete.com

Wildlife Travel
Green Acre, Wood Lane, Oundle, Northants PE8 5TP.
☎ 01832 274892.

Mália (see p273) *is one of the many coastal resorts on Crete that provide a temporary home for migrant waders in spring and autumn. This wood sandpiper will stay and feed for a day or so around the margins of pools and marshes.*

Dolphins can be spotted from northern headlands.

Mount Díkti's slopes are covered in wild flowers in spring, including Cretan bee orchids.

Eloúnta has saltpans that are much favoured by avocets.

Siteía's precipitous cliffs (see p276) *are the habitat for Cretan ebony, a shrub unique to the island, which produces pinkish-purple spikes of flowers in the spring.*

Lasíthi's fields are feeding grounds for colourful hoopoes.

Agios Nikólaos is a stopping-off place for migrants such as wagtails.

Ierápetra (see p275) *attracts the migrant woodchat shrike in summer. Woodchats feed on insects and small lizards, which they sometimes impale on thorns to make them easier to eat.*

Geckos can be found on stone walls beside many roads in eastern Crete.

Zákros (see p277), *with its high cliffs, is where you find Eleonora's falcons performing aerobatic displays in summer.*

Exploring Crete

The most southerly of the Greek islands, Crete boasts clear blue seas, sandy beaches and glorious sunshine. Its north coast bustles with thriving resorts as well as historic towns such as Réthymno and Chaniá. Its rugged southern coast, in particular the southwest, is less developed. Four great mountain ranges stretch from east to west, forming the spine of the 250-km (155-mile) long island. A hiker's paradise, they offer magnificent scenery and some spectacular gorges. The island's capital, Irákleio, is famous for its Archaeological Museum and is also a good base for exploring the greatest of Crete's Minoan palaces, Knosós.

Card players in the vine-canopied streets of Réthymno's old town

Kýthira, Gýtheio

GRAMVOUSA
RODOPOS

AKROTIRI PENINSULA ⑤

Piraeus

CHANIA ④

KASTELI KISSAMOU ①
MALEME
SOUDA

FALASARNA
POLYRINIA

Piraeus

GEORGIOUPOLI
RETHYMNO ⑦
MONI ARKADIOU
ARCHAIA ELEFTHERNA

AGIA EIRINI GORGE
LAKE KOURNAS
⑫
ANOGEL

MONI CHRYSOSKALITISSAS
SAMARIA GORGE ⑥
ARMENOI CEMETERY
MOUNT IDI ⑭

ELAFONISI BEACH
SOUGIA ③
IMPROS GORGE
AMARI VALLEY ⑬
IDEO ANTRO

②
PALAIOCHORA
AGIA ROUMELI
SFAKIA
LOUTRO ⑧
⑨
⑩ PLAKIAS
AGIA GALINI ⑯
AGIA TRIADA ⑰

FRANGOKASTELLO
⑪
MONI PREVELI

PHAESTOS ⑲

PAXIMADIA
⑱

MATALA

GAVDOPOULA

GAVDOS

See Also

• *Where to Stay* pp306–8
• *Where to Eat* pp330–32
• *Travel Information* pp356–9

View of the harbour, Sfakiá

Getting Around

The provincial capitals of Chaniá, Réthymno, Irákleio and Agios Nikólaos act as the main transport hub for each region. Crete's bus service is quite well developed, with regular buses running along the north coast road. For touring the island a car is the most convenient mode of transport, though taxi fares are reasonable. Mountain roads between villages are now largely paved.

Large domed mosque inside Réthymno's Venetian Fortétsa

SIGHTS AT A GLANCE

Agía Galíni **16**
Agía Triáda **17**
Agios Nikólaos **28**
Akrotíri Peninsula **5**
Anógeia **15**
Archánes **23**
Chaniá **4**
Chersónisos **24**
Eloúnta **27**
Frangokástello **9**
Górtys **20**
Gourniá **31**
Ierápetra **30**
Irákleio pp264–5 **21**
Kritsá **29**
Lasíthi Plateau **26**
Mália **25**
Mátala **18**
Moní Arkadíou **12**

Moní Préveli **11**
Moní Toploú **33**
Mount Idi **14**
*Palace of Knosós
pp268–71* **22**
Palaióchora **2**
*Phaestos
pp262–3* **19**
Plakiás **10**
Réthymno **7**
*Samariá Gorge
pp250–51* **6**
Sfakiá **8**
Siteia **32**
Soúgia **3**
Vaï Beach **34**
Zákros **35**

Tours
Amári Valley **13**

LOCATOR MAP

The north entrance to the Palace of Knosós

A pelican in the picturesque harbour at Siteía

A stone windmill at the entrance
to the Lasíthi Plateau

KEY

For key to map see back flap

The magnificent beach of Falásarna with its long stretch of sand and turquoise waters

Kastélli Kissámou ❶

Καστέλλι Κισσάμου

Chaniá. 🤼 3,000. 🚌 ⛴ 🚖 *Kastélli Kissámou.*

THE SMALL, UNASSUMING town of Kastélli Kissámou, also known simply as Kastélli, sits at the eastern base of the virtually uninhabited Gramvoúsa Peninsula, once a stronghold of pirates. While not a tourist-oriented town, it has a scattering of hotels and restaurants along its pebbly shore and is a good base from which to explore the west coast of Crete. Boat trips run to the tip of the **Gramvoúsa Peninsula**, where there are some isolated and beautiful sandy beaches.

ENVIRONS: Some 7 km (4 miles) south of Kastélli, the ruins of the ancient city of **Polyrínia** (City with many flocks) are scattered above the village of Ano Palaiókastro (also known as Polyrínia). Dating from the 6th century BC, the fortified city-state was developed by the Romans and later the Byzantines and Venetians. Post-Roman walls, towers and foundations can still be seen. The present church of **Enenínta ennéa Martýron** (Ninety-Nine Martyrs), built in 1894, stands on the site of a large Hellenistic building.
  On the west coast of the Gramvoúsa Peninsula, 16 km (10 miles) west of Kastélli, a winding road descends to the spectacular and isolated beach at **Falásarna**. Once the site of a Hellenistic city-state of that name, earthquakes have obliterated almost all trace of the once-thriving harbour and town. Today a few small guesthouses and tavernas are scattered along the northern end of the beach. Small roads zigzag south from here, linking some of the isolated fishing villages along the island's spectacular west coast.
  About 20 km (12 miles) east of Kastélli, at the base of the massive Rodopós Peninsula, lies the picturesque fishing village of **Kolympári**. Head1 km (0.5 miles) north of Kolympári for the impressive 17th-century **Moní Panagías Goniás**, with a magnificent seaside setting and a fine collection of 17th-century icons. Every year on 29 August (Feast of St John the Baptist), hundreds of pilgrims make the three-hour walk up the peninsula to the church of **Agios Ioánnis** to witness the mass baptism of boys named John (Ioánnis).

Palaióchora ❷

Παλαιόχωρα

Chaniá. 🤼 1,800. ⛴ 🚌
ℹ️ *Venizélou (28230 41507).*
🚢 *Elafónisos 14 km (9 miles) W.*

FIRST DISCOVERED in the 1960s by the hippie community, Palaióchora has become a haven for backpackers and package holiday-makers. This small port began life as a castle built by the Venetians in 1279. Today the remains of the fort, destroyed by pirate attacks in 1539, stand guard on a little headland dividing the village's two excellent beaches. To the west is a wide sandy beach with a windsurfing school, while to the east is a rocky but sheltered beach.

ENVIRONS: Winding up through the Lefká Ori (White Mountains), a network of roads passes through a stunning

Moní Chrysoskalítissas near Palaióchora

THE BATTLE OF CRETE (1941)

Following the occupation of Greece in World War II, German forces invaded Crete. Thousands of German troops were parachuted into the Chaniá district, where they seized Máleme airport on 20 May 1941. The Battle of Crete raged

fiercely for ten days, with high casualties on both sides. Allied troops retreated through the Lefká Ori (White Mountains) to the south where, with the help of locals, they were evacuated from the island. Four years of German occupation followed, during which time implacable local resistance kept up the pressure on the invaders, until their final surrender in 1945.

German parachutists in Crete, 1941

---

landscape of terraced hills and mountain villages, noted for their Byzantine churches. The closest of these is **Anýdri**, 5 km (3 miles) east of Palaióchora, with the 14th-century double-naved church of **Agios Geórgios** containing frescoes by Ioánnis Pagoménos (John the Frozen) from 1323.

In summer, a daily boat service runs to **Elafonísi**, a lagoon-like beach of golden sand and brilliant blue water. From here, a 5-km (3-mile) walk north takes you to **Moní Chrysos-kalítissas** (Golden Step), named for the 90 steps leading up to its church, one of which is said to appear golden, at least in the eyes of the virtuous. It can also be reached by road 28 km (17 miles) south of Kastélli Kissámou. From Palaióchora, boat trips make the rough, 64-km (40-mile) crossing to **Gávdos** island, Europe's southernmost point.

Fresco by Ioánnis Pagoménos, Agios Geórgios

Still growing as a resort, the village has rooms to rent, and a few tavernas and bars. The beach is long and pebbly. It is overlooked by the village church which is built on top of a Byzantine structure, whose mosaic floors have been largely removed.

ENVIRONS: Just over an hour's walk west of Soúgia, the ancient city-state of **Lissós** was a flourishing commercial centre in Hellenistic and Roman times. Among the remains are two fine 13th-century Christian basilicas, a 3rd-century BC Asklepieion (temple of healing) and a sanctuary. The route to Lissós leads up through the **Agía Eiríni Gorge**. Popular with experienced hikers, plans are under way to develop the gorge along the lines of the Samariá Gorge.

Soúgia ❸
Σούγια

Chaniá. 👥 270. 🚌 🚐 🚕 Soúgia; Lissós 3 km (1.5 miles) W.

ONCE ISOLATED from the rest of the world at the mouth of the Agía Eiríni Gorge, the hamlet of Soúgia is now linked with Chaniá and the north coast by a good road.

Chaniá ❹

See pp248–9.

Akrotíri Peninsula ❺
Χερσόνησος Ακρωτηρίου

6 km (3.5 miles) NW of Chaniá. 🚐 Soúda 🚌 Chaniá & Soúda. 🚕 Stavrós 14 km (9 miles) N of Chaniá. Maráthi 10 km (6 miles) E of Chaniá.

RELATIVELY FLAT by Cretan standards, the Akrotíri Peninsula lies between Réthymno (see pp254–5) and Chaniá (see pp248–9). At its base, on top of Profítis Ilías hill, is a shrine to Crete's national hero, Elefthérios Venizélos (see p39). His tomb is a place of pilgrimage, for it was here that Cretan rebels raised the Greek flag in 1897 in defiance of the Great Powers.

There are several monasteries in the northeastern hills of the peninsula. **Moní Agías Triádas**, which has an impressive multidomed church, is 17th century, while **Moní Gouvernétou** dates back to the early Venetian occupation. Monks still inhabit both. Nearby, but accessible only on foot, the abandoned **Moní Katholikoú**, is partly carved out of the rock.

Situated at the neck of the peninsula is a military base and the **Commonwealth War Cemetery**, burial ground of over 1,500 British, Australian and New Zealand soldiers killed in the Battle of Crete.

🏛 **Commonwealth War Cemetery**
4 km (2.5 miles) SE of Chaniá
🕐 daily.

Goats grazing on the Akrotíri Peninsula

Chaniá ❹

Χανιά

Olive oil tin,
Chaniá
covered
market

Sᴇᴛ ᴀɢᴀɪɴꜱᴛ ᴀ ꜱᴘᴇᴄᴛᴀᴄᴜʟᴀʀ backdrop of majestic mountains and aquamarine seas, Chaniá is one of the island's most appealing cities and a good base from which to explore western Crete. Its stately Neo-Classical mansions and massive Venetian fortifications testify to the city's turbulent and diverse past. Once the Minoan settlement of ancient Kydonia, Chaniá has been fought over and controlled by Romans, Byzantines, Venetians, Genoese, Turks and Egyptians. Following unification with Greece in 1913, the island saw yet another invasion during World War II – this time by the German army in 1941, when the Battle of Crete raged around Chaniá (see p247).

The Mosque of the Janissaries

public but clearly visible from the road, is approached along Líthinon, a street lined with ornate Venetian doorways. Many of the finds from the site are on display in Chaniá's Archaeological Museum, including a collection of clay tablets inscribed with Minoan Linear A script.

By the inner harbour stand the now derelict 16th-century Venetian arsenals, where ships were once stored and repaired. The Venetian lighthouse, at the end of the sea wall, offers superb views over Chaniá.

The Venetian Fort Firkás overlooking Chaniá's outer harbour

The Harbour

Most of the city's interesting sights are to be found in the old Venetian quarter, around the harbour and surrounding alleyways. At the northwest point of the outer harbour, the **Naval Museum**'s collection of model ships and other maritime artifacts is displayed in the well-restored Venetian Fort Firkás – also the setting for theatre and evenings of traditional dance in summer.

On the other side of the outer harbour, the **Mosque of the Janissaries** dates back to the arrival of the Turks in 1645 and is the oldest Ottoman building on the island. It was damaged during World War II and reconstructed soon after. Behind the mosque rises the hilltop quarter of Kastélli, the oldest part of the city, where the Minoan settlement of **Kydonia** is undergoing excavation. The site, closed to the

🅘 **Naval Museum**
Fort Firkás, Aktí Kountourióti.
📞 28210 91875. ⏱ daily.
● main public hols. 🎫

Around the Covered Market

Connected to the harbour by Chálidon, this turn-of-the-century covered market has a wide variety of local fruit and vegetables on sale each day, as well as Cretan souvenirs. Alongside the covered market, the bustling Skrýdlot, or Stivanádika, abounds in shops

A tranquil view of Chaniá's old harbour at dawn

The atmospheric backstreets of the old Splántzia quarter

VISITORS' CHECKLIST

Chaniá. 🏛 50,000. ✈ 16 km
(10 miles) E of Chaniá. ⚓ Soúda
bay. 🚌 Kydonías (long distance),
Plateía Agorás (around Chaniá).
🚶 Kriári 40 (28210 92943). 🛒
Mon–Thu, Sat (veg & clothes).
🎭 Nautical Week (end June).
🛳 Agía Marína 9 km (6 miles)
W; Plataniás 11 km (7 miles) W.

selling a miscellany of leather goods, including traditional Cretan boots and made-to-measure sandals. The nearby **Archaeological Museum** is housed in the Venetian church of San Francesco and displays artifacts from western Crete including pottery, sculpture, mosaics and coins that date from Neolithic times to the Roman era. Situated next to the museum is a small garden that contains a Turkish fountain. Set back in the square on the opposite side to the museum is the 19th-century cathedral of **Agía Triáda**.

Dionysos and Ariadne mosaic, Chaniá Archaeological Museum

📍
Archaeological Museum
Chálidon 21. 📞 28210 90334,
🕐 8:30am–3pm Tue–Sun.
⚫ main public hols. ♿ ♿

The Splántzia Quarter
Northeast of the market, the Splántzia quarter is a picturesque area of the old town, where houses with wooden balconies overhang the cobbled backstreets. The tree-lined square known as **Plateía 1821** commemorates a rebellion against the occupying Turks, during which an Orthodox bishop was hanged on the spot. Overlooking the square stands the Venetian church of **Agios Nikólaos** with its truncated

minaret, and, nearby, are the 16th-century church of **Agioi Anárgyroi**, with its beautiful icons and paintings, and the church of **San Rocco** which was built in 1630.

Outside the City Walls
South of the covered market along Tzanakáki are the **Public Gardens**. They were laid out in the 19th century by a Turkish *pasha* (governor). The gardens include a modest zoo which houses a few animals, including the *kri-kri* (the Cretan wild goat). The gardens also offer a children's play area, a café and an open-air auditorium, which is often used for local ceremonies and cultural performances. The nearby **Historical Museum and Archives** is housed in a Neo-Classical building, and is devoted to the Cretan pre-

occupation with rebellions and invasions. Its exhibits include photographs and letters of the famous statesman Elefthérios Venizélos (1864–1936), as well as many other historical records.

📍 **Historical Museum and Archives**
Sfakianáki 20. 📞 28210 52606.
🕐 Mon–Fri. ⚫ main public hols.

ENVIRONS: A series of sandy beaches stretches west from Chaniá all the way to the agricultural town of Tavronítis, 21 km (13 miles) away. A short walk west of Chaniá, the sandy beach of **Agioi Apóstoloi** is quieter and less developed than the city beaches.
Further west, the well-tended **German War Cemetery** stands witness to the airborne landing at Máleme of the German army in 1941 (*see p247*). Built into the side of a hill, the peaceful setting is home to over 4,000 graves whose simple stone markers look out over the Mediterranean. A small pavilion by the entrance to the cemetery houses a display commemorating the event.

🏛 **German War Cemetery**
19 km (12 miles) W of Chaniá.
📞 28210 62296. 🕐 daily.

The sandy beach of Agioi Apóstoloi, a short walk west of Chaniá

Samariá Gorge ❻
Φαράγγι της Σαμαριάς

THE MOST spectacular land-scape in Crete lies along the Samariá Gorge, the longest ravine in Europe. When the gorge was established as a national park in 1962, the inhabitants of pastoral Samariá village moved elsewhere, leaving behind the tiny chapels seen today.

Paeonia clusii, Samariá Gorge

Starting from the Xylóskalo, 44 km (27 miles) south of Chaniá, a well-trodden trail leads down a tortuous 18-km (11-mile) course to the seaside village of Agía Rouméli. The walk takes from five to seven hours. Water fountains can be found en route and sturdy shoes should be worn.

Facing east across the spectacular Samariá Gorge

Omalós Plateau

★ Xylóskalo (Wooden Stairs)
The Samariá Gorge is reached via the Xylóskalo, a zigzag path with wooden handrails which drops a staggering 1,000 m (3,280 ft) in the first 2 km (1 mile) of the walk.

Agios Nikólaos
This tiny chapel nestles under the shade of pines and cypresses near the bottom of the Xylóskalo.

THE KRI-KRI (CRETAN WILD GOAT)

Found in only a few areas of Crete, notably the Samariá Gorge, the Cretan wild goat is thought to be a truly wild relative of the all-too-numerous feral goats that are found throughout the Mediterranean region, as well as in other parts of the world. A protected species, the Cretan wild goat is nimble and sure-footed on rugged terrain, attributes that help guard against attacks by other predators. Mature adults have attractively marked coats and horns with three rings along their length.

A kri-kri on rocky terrain

0 kilometres 2

0 miles 1

★ **Samariá Village**
*Once inhabited,
the village was
abandoned in 1962
when the gorge was
designated as a
national park.*

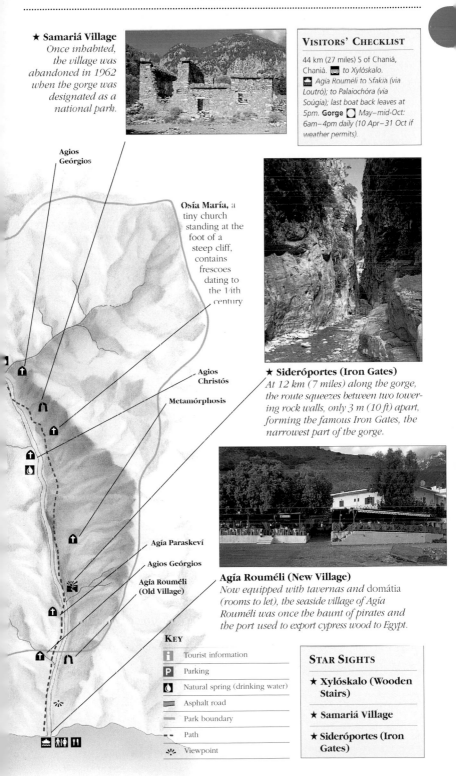

VISITORS' CHECKLIST

44 km (27 miles) S of Chaniá,
Chaniá. 🚌 to Xylóskalo.
🚢 Agia Rouméli to Sfakiá (via
Loutró); to Palaiochóra (via
Soúgia); last boat back leaves at
5pm. **Gorge** 🕓 May–mid-Oct:
6am–4pm daily (10 Apr–31 Oct if
weather permits).

Agios
Geórgios

Osía María, a
tiny church
standing at the
foot of a
steep cliff,
contains
frescoes
dating to
the 14th
century

Agios
Christós

Metamórphosis

★ **Sideróportes (Iron Gates)**
*At 12 km (7 miles) along the gorge,
the route squeezes between two towering rock walls, only 3 m (10 ft) apart,
forming the famous Iron Gates, the
narrowest part of the gorge.*

Agía Paraskeví

Agios Geórgios

Agía Rouméli
(Old Village)

Agía Rouméli (New Village)
Now equipped with tavernas and domátia
*(rooms to let), the seaside village of Agía
Rouméli was once the haunt of pirates and
the port used to export cypress wood to Egypt.*

KEY

🛈	Tourist information
🅿	Parking
🔵	Natural spring (drinking water)
	Asphalt road
	Park boundary
--	Path
🔆	Viewpoint

STAR SIGHTS

★ **Xylóskalo (Wooden
Stairs)**

★ **Samariá Village**

★ **Sideróportes (Iron
Gates)**

Réthymno ⓮
Ρέθυμνο

ONCE THE GRECO-ROMAN TOWN of Rithymna, the site of today's Réthymno has been occupied since Minoan times. The city flourished under Venetian rule during the 16th century, developing into a literary and artistic centre, and becoming a haven for scholars fleeing Constantinople. Despite modern development and tourism, the city today has retained much of its charm and remains the intellectual capital of Crete. The old quarter is rich in elegant, well-preserved Venetian and Ottoman architecture. The huge Venetian Fortétsa, built in the 16th century to defend the island against the increasing attacks by pirates, overlooks the picturesque harbour with its charming 13th-century lighthouse.

The 17th-century Nerantzés Mosque

Exploring Réthymno

Réthymno's bustling harbour-front serves as one great out-door cafeteria, catering almost exclusively for tourists. It is skirted along most of its length by a good, sandy beach, but at its western end lies a small inner harbour. A restored 13th-century **lighthouse** stands on its breakwater.

The **Fortétsa** dominates the town, above the inner harbour. Designed by Pallavicini in the 1570s, it was built to defend the port against pirate attacks (Barbarossa had devastated the town in 1538) and the threat of expansionist Turks. The ramparts are still largely intact. Within them, a mosque, a small church and parts of the governor's quarters can still be seen, though most are now in ruins. During the summer there are open-air concerts.

Traditional weaving in the Historical and Folk Art Museum

Directly opposite the main entrance to the Fortétsa, the **Archaeological Museum** occupies a converted Turkish bastion. Its collection is set out chronologically from Neolithic through Minoan to Roman times and includes artifacts from cemeteries, sanctuaries and caves in the region. Highlights include the late Minoan burial caskets (*larnakes*) and grave goods.

The old town clusters behind the Fortétsa, charac-terized by a maze of narrow vine-canopied streets and its Venetian and Ottoman houses with wrought-iron bal-conies. Off Plateía Títou Peocháki is the **Nerantzés Mosque.** This is the best-preserved mosque in the city. Built as a church by the Venetians, it was converted in 1657 into a mosque by the Turks. It now serves as the city's concert hall.

On Palaiológou, the 17th-century Venetian **Rimóndi Fountain**, with lion-headed spouts, stands alongside busy cafés and shops selling fresh produce. The elegant 16th-century Venetian **Lótzia** (Loggia) can also be seen here.

The small **Historical and Folk Art Museum** is housed in a Venetian mansion. On display here are local crafts, including some brilliantly coloured weaving, pottery, lace and jewellery.

♣ **Fortétsa**
Katecháki. [28310 28101.] May–Oct: daily. ● main public hols. ▨

🔾 **Archaeological Museum**
Cheimárras. [28310 54668.] Tue–Sun. ● main public hols. ▨

🏛 **Lótzia**
Palaiológou & Arkadíou. [28310 53270.] Mar–Sep: Mon–Fri. ● main public hols. ▨

🔾 **Historical and Folk Art Museum**
Vernárdou 30. [28310 23398.] May–Oct: Mon–Sat. ● main public hols. ▨

Tavernas and bars along Réthymno's waterfront, the focus of the town's activity

◁ Fishing boats lining the picturesque Venetian harbour of Réthymno

The magnificent shell of Frangokástello set against a dramatic backdrop

ENVIRONS: East of Réthymno, towards Pánormos, the resort developments flow one into another, while west of the city a 20-km (12-mile) stretch of relatively uncrowded beach culminates in the village of **Georgioúpoli**. Despite wholesale tourist development, this small community still retains some of its traditional atmosphere. Massive eucalyptus trees line the streets and a picturesque, turtle-inhabited river flows placidly down to the sea. **Lake Kournás**, 5 km (3 miles) inland from Georgioúpoli, is set in a hollow among the steeply rising hills. Pedaloes, windsurfs and canoes can be hired at the lake and a few shady tavernas offer refreshments.

In Arménoi, on the main Réthymno–Agía Galíni road, there is an extensive late **Minoan cemetery** where a large number of graves have been excavated, some with imposingly long entrances. Among the contents unearthed are bronze weapons, vases and burial caskets *(larnakes)*, now on view in the archaeological museums of Chaniá *(see p249)* and Réthymno.

A Sfakiot in traditional dress

🏛 **Minoan Cemetery**
9 km (6 miles) S of Réthymno.
Tue-Sun. main public hols.

Sfakiá ❽
Σφακιά

Chaniá. 400. 28250 91205. Sweetwater 3 km (2 miles) W of Loutró.

OVERLOOKING the Libyan Sea at the mouth of the breathtaking Impros Gorge, Sfakiá (also known as Chóra Sfakíon) enjoys a commanding position as the last coastal community of any size until Palaióchora *(see pp246–7)*. Cut off from the outside world until recently, it is little wonder that historically the local Sfakiot clansmen enjoy their reputation for rugged self-sufficiency and individualism, albeit accompanied by the notorious feuding. The village today is largely devoted to tourism and makes a good stepping-off point for the southwest coast.

ENVIRONS: West of Sfakiá, almost impregnable mountains plummet into the Libyan Sea, allowing space for just a couple of tiny settlements accessible only by boat or on foot along the E4 coastal path. The closest of these is **Loutró**, a charming and remote spot whose sheltered cove, curving beach and little white houses with blue shutters fulfil every

The quiet bay and whitewashed houses of Loutró

traveller's fantasy of a "real" Greek village. In summer a dozen tavernas and houses provide rooms and meals for tourists. Small boats are available to take tourists to nearby Gávdos island and the breathtaking bay around Sweetwater beach.

Frangokástello ❾
Φραγκοκάστελλο

14 km (9 miles) E of Sfakiá, Chaniá. daily.

BUILT BY THE Venetians as a bulwark against pirates and unruly Sfakiots in 1371, little remains of the interior of Frangokástello. However, its curtain walls are well preserved and from above the south entrance, the Venetian Lion of St Mark looks out to sea.

Ioánnis Daskalogiannis, the Sfakiot leader, surrendered here in 1770 and was flayed alive in Irákleio by his Turkish captors. Fifty years later Chatzimichális Daliánis, a Greek freedom fighter, wrested the fort from the Turks and tried to hold it with an army of just 385 men. Hopelessly outnumbered, he and all his followers were massacred by the pitiless Turks. Legend has it that at the end of May at dawn, their solemn shadows can be seen climbing up to the castle.

Directly below the fortress is a sandy beach whose waters are shallow and warm, an ideal spot for families with young children. A scattering of hotels and tavernas cater for holidaymakers and passing motorists.

Boats lining the small harbour at Plakiás

Plakiás ⑩
Πλακιάς

Réthymno. 🏠 100. 🚌 🚕 Damnóni
3 km (2 miles) E.

UNTIL RECENTLY just a simple
fishing harbour serving
the villages of Mýrthios and
Selliá, Plakiás has grown into a
full-scale resort with all the
usual facilities. Its grey sandy
beach is nearly 2 km (1 mile)
long. Sited at the mouth of the
Kotsyfoú Gorge, Plakiás makes
an excellent base for exploring
the region, as it has good road
connections in all directions.

ENVIRONS: A 5-minute drive,
or a scenic walk around the
headland, leads east to the
beach of **Damnóni**. Tiny
coves beyond it offer good
swimming. Holiday apartments
are being built on the adjoining
hill. Quiet **Soúda** beach lies 3
km (2 miles) west of Plakiás.

Moní Préveli ⑪
Μονή Πρέβελη

14 km (9 miles) E of Plakiás, Réthymno.
📞 28320 31246. 🚌 ⭕ daily.
🏛 museum only. ♿

ACCESSIBLE BY road through
the Kourtaliótiko Gorge,
the working monastery of
Préveli stands in an isolated but
beautiful spot overlooking the
sea. It played a prominent role
in the evacuation of Allied
forces from nearby beaches
during World War II *(see p247)*.
  The buildings cluster around
a large central courtyard dating
from 1731. There is a 19th-
century church and a small
museum displaying religious
artifacts, including silver
candlesticks and some highly

decorative robes. Further
inland, the original 16th-
century **Moní Agíou
Ioánnou** (now known
as Káto Préveli) was
founded by Abbot
Préveli and aban-
doned in the 17th
century in favour
of the more
strategic position
of the present
monastery. About
1 km (0.5 mile) east
of Moní Préveli, a
steep path leads to **Préveli**
beach (also known as Kourtaliótiko or Palm Beach), a
crystal-clear, palm-fringed oasis.

**Venetian façade of the
church at Moní Arkadíou**

Moní Arkadíou ⑫
Μονή Αρκαδίου

24 km (15 miles) SE of Réthymno,
Réthymno. 🚌 to Réthymno.
⭕ daily. 🏛 museum only.
♿ monastery only.

THE 5TH-CENTURY monastery
of Arkadíou stands at the
top of a winding gorge, at the
edge of a fertile region of fruit

trees and cypresses. Largely
rebuilt at the end of the 16th
century, the most impressive
of its buildings is the double-
naved church with an ornate
Venetian façade which dates
back to 1587.
  The monastery provided a
safe haven for its followers in
times of religious persecution
by local Muslims. On 9 November 1866, when its buildings
were crowded with hundreds
of refugees, it came under
attack by the Ottoman army.
Choosing death over surrender
the Cretans torched the gunpowder storeroom, killing
Christian and Muslim
alike. The ensuing
carnage created
instant martyrs for
freedom whose
sacrifice is not
forgotten. A
sculpture outside
the monastery
depicts the only
surviving girl and
the abbot who lit
the gunpowder. Today, a
small museum displays
sacramental vessels, icons,
prayer books, vestments and
tributes to the martyrs.

ENVIRONS: At Archaía
Eléftherna, 10 km (6 miles)
northeast of Moní Arkadíou,
lie the ruins of the ancient
city-state of **Eléftherna**.
Founded in 700 BC, all that
remains is a tower on a rocky
ridge and a derelict Hellenistic
bridge in the valley below.
Northeast of Eléftherna the
village of **Margarítes** is well
known for its pottery.

The isolated buildings of Moní Préveli, nestled into the rocks

Tour of the Amári Valley 🔞

DOMINATED BY THE PEAKS of Mount Idi to its east, the Amári Valley offers staggering views over the region's rock-strewn peaks, broad green valleys and dramatic gorges. Twisting but well-paved roads link the many small agricultural communities of the Amári where, even today, moustachioed

Detail from the church of the Panagía at Méronas

men in knee-high boots and baggy trousers *(vrákes)* can be seen outside the local tavernas. The area is dotted with shrines, churches and monasteries harbouring Byzantine frescoes and icons. Traditionally an area of Cretan resistance, many of the Amári villages were destroyed during World War II.

Olive groves in the Amári Valley

Méronas ⑧
At the centre of Méronas is the Venetian-style church of the Panagía with its early 14th-century frescoes.

Gerakári ⑦
Gerakári is famous for its fresh and bottled cherries and cherry brandy.

Thrónos ①
The beautifully frescoed church of the Panagía at Thrónos dates back to the 14th century. It still bears traces of mosaics from an early Christian basilica built in the 4th century.

Moní Asomáton ②
The Venetian buildings of **Moní Asomáton**, now an agricultural college, stand in a lush oasis of palm, plane and eucalyptus trees.

Amári ③
Sweeping views of Mount Idi can be seen from the Venetian clock tower in the centre of Amári. Just outside the village, the church of Agía Anna shelters the island's oldest frescoes, dated 1225.

Vizári ④
Just west of the village of Vizári are the ruins of an early Christian basilica dating from the 6th century.

Kardáki ⑥
The 13th-century ruined church of Agios Ioánnis Theológos stands by the roadside north of Kardáki.

Ano Méros ⑤
A large marble war memorial just outside Ano Méros depicts a woman hewing out the names of World War II Resistance heroes.

Map labels: RETHYMNO, Agía Foteini, Monastiráki, Opsigiás, Platania, SPILI, Vrýses, Fourfourás, Platýs, AGIA GALINI, Apodoúlou

TIPS FOR DRIVERS

Length: 92 km (57 miles).
Stopping-off points: There are local tavernas in every village en route. The taverna at Ano Méros offers spectacular views over the valley. Opposite the ruined church outside Kardáki is a shaded area and water fountain, an ideal stop in the heat of summer (see also p360).

KEY

- ▬ Tour route
- ═ Other roads
- ✳ Viewpoint

0 kilometres 5
0 miles 2

Mount Idi ⑭
Ψηλορείτης

Réthymno. 🚌 to Anógeia & Kamáres.

At 2,456 m (8,080 ft) the soaring peaks of Mount Idi (or Psiloreítis) are the crowning glory of the massive Psiloreítis range. The highest mountain in Crete, it is home to many sanctuaries including the famous Idaian Cave.

From Anógeia, a paved road leads to the **Nída Plateau**, a journey of 23 km (14 miles) through rocky terrain, punctuated by the occasional stone shepherd's hut. Here a lone taverna caters to visitors en route to the **Idaian Cave**, a further 20-minute hike up the hill. This huge cavern, where Zeus was reared, has yielded artifacts, including some remarkable bronze shields, dating from c.700 BC. Some of the artifacts can be seen in the Irákleio Archaeological Museum (see pp266–7). From the plateau, marked trails lead up to the peak of **Mount Idi**, while a short distance away a tiny ski resort operates at weekends, conditions permitting, from December to March.

On the mountain's southern face, a 3-hour scramble from Kamáres village leads to the **Kamáres Cave**. Here the famous Minoan pottery known as Kamáres ware was discovered and examples are now on display in the Irákleio Archaeological Museum.

CRETAN CAVES AND THE MYTH OF ZEUS

The island of Crete is home to 4,700 caves and potholes of which some 2,000 have been explored. Since Neolithic times, caves have been used as cult centres by successive religions and have yielded many archaeological treasures. Bound up with ancient Cretan mythology, the Diktian (see p273) and Idaian caves are two of the island's most visited. According to legend, Rhea gave birth to the infant god Zeus

in the Diktian Cave where he was protected by *kourítes* (warriors) and nurtured by a goat. He was then concealed and raised in the Idaian Cave to protect him from his father, Kronos, who had swallowed his other offspring after a warning that he would be dethroned by one of his sons. The Idaian Cave was an important pilgrimage centre during Classical times.

Stalagmites in the Diktian Cave (see p273), Lasíthi

Anógeia ⑮
Ανώγεια

Réthymno. 🏃 2,300. 🚌

High up in the Psiloreítis mountain range, the small village of Anógeia dates back to the 13th century. The village has suffered a turbulent past, having been destroyed by the Turks in 1821 and 1826, and then completely rebuilt after destruction by the German army in 1944.

Modern Anógeia runs along a rocky ridge, with its own square and **war memorial** – a bronze statue of a Cretan hero in traditional dress. Inscribed on the memorial are the most significant dates in Crete's recent past: 1821, Greek Independence; 1866, slaughter of Christian refugees at Moní Arkadíou (see p256); 1944, liberation from German occupation. Tavernas, shops and banks are also situated in this part of town.

The old village tumbles down the steep slopes into a warren of narrow stepped alleys, ultimately converging on a little square of stalls and tavernas. Here, a marble bust

The Nída Plateau between Anógeia village and the Idaian Cave, Mount Idi

Woman selling locally made rugs and lace in Anógeia

of local politician Vasíleios Skoulás stands next to a less formal woodcarving of his friend Venizélos *(see p39)*, by local artist Manólis Skoulás.

The stalls in the old part of the village abound in locally made embroidery, lace and brightly coloured rugs, forming one of Crete's main centres for woven and embroidered goods. Nearby tavernas serve grilled goats' meat and other Cretan specialities. Music enthusiasts can pay their respects at the shrine of Níkos Xyloúris, a 1970s folk singer who died at an early age and whose little whitewashed house overlooks the main square.

Agía Galíni ⑯
Αγία Γαλήνη

Réthymno. 🏛 1,040. 🚌 🚢 *Agía Galíni.*

FORMERLY A FISHING village situated at the southern end of the Amári Valley, Agía Galíni is today a full-blown tourist resort. The original village, now only a handful of old houses and narrow streets, is dwarfed by the mass of holiday apartments stretching up the coast. The harbourfront is alive with busy tavernas snuggled between the water and cliffs. Just beyond the harbour, the small sandy beach is popular with sunbathers.

ENVIRONS: Taxi boat trips sail daily from Agía Galíni's harbour to the neighbouring beaches of **Agios Geórgios** and **Agios Pávlos** and, further still, to **Préveli** beach at Moní

Préveli *(see p256)*. There are also daily excursions to the **Paximádia islands** where there are good sandy beaches.

Agía Triáda ⑰
Αγία Τριάδα

3 km (2 miles) W of Phaestos, Irákleio. 🚌 *to Phaestos.* 📞 *28920 91564.* 🕐 *daily.* ⚫ *main public hols.* 💷
🚢 *Kómo 10 km (6 miles) SW; Mátala 15 km (9 miles) SW.*

THE MINOAN VILLA of Agía Triáda was excavated by the Italians from 1902 to 1914. An L-shaped structure, it was built around 1700 BC, the time of the Second Palace period *(see p271)*, over earlier houses. Its private apartments and public reception rooms are located in the angle of the L, overlooking a road that may have led to the sea. Gypsum facing and magnificent frescoes used to adorn the walls of these rooms. Rich Minoan treasures, including the carved stone Harvester Vase, Boxer Rhyton (jug) and Chieftain Cup, were all found in this

area and are on display at the Irákleio Archaeological Museum *(see pp266–7)*. Evidence of the villa's importance is provided by a find of clay seals and rare tablets bearing the undeciphered Minoan Linear A script.

Following the villa's destruction by fire in around 1400 BC, a Mycenaean megaron (hall) was built on the site. The ruined settlement to the north, with its unique porticoed row of shops, dates mostly from this period, as does the magnificent painted sarcophagus that was found in the cemetery to the north. The paintwork on the sarcophagus depicts a burial procession; it can be seen in the Irákleio Archaeological Museum.

Agía Triáda archaeological site

ENVIRONS: At the village of Vóroi, 6 km (4 miles) northeast of Agía Triáda, is the fascinating **Museum of Cretan Ethnology**. Displayed here is a well-labelled collection of tools and materials used in the everyday life of rural Crete up to the early 20th century.

🏛 Museum of Cretan Ethnology
📞 *28920 91394.* 🕐 *Apr–Oct. daily; Nov–Mar: Mon–Fri* ⚫ *main public hols.* 💷

Agía Galíni resort, nestled into the rocks at the foot of the Amári Valley

Mátala's town beach flanked by sandstone cliffs

Mátala ⓲
Μάταλα

Irákleio. 🚶 132. 🚌 🚂 Kalamáki 5 km
(3 miles) N; Léntas 24 km (15 miles) SE.

C LUSTERED AROUND an idyllic
sweeping bay, Mátala re-
mained a small fishing hamlet
until the tourist boom of the
1960s, when it was transformed
into a pulsating resort. Hotels,
bars and restaurants abound
in the lively town centre and
development here is steadily
on the increase.

Despite present appearances,
Mátala has not passed un-
touched by history. Homer
described Menelaos, husband
of Helen of Troy (see p50),
being shipwrecked here on
his way home from Troy.
During Hellenistic times,
around 220 BC, Mátala served
as the port for the ancient
city-state of Górtys. The
resort's pitted
sandstone cliffs,
looming drama-
tically over the town
beach, were origi-
nally carved out for
use as tombs in the
Roman era. Later
they were extended
as cave dwellings
for early Christians,
shepherds and
recently hippies.

ENVIRONS: The area
around Mátala has
some beautiful
beaches including
the bay of **Kaloí
Liménes** to the
southeast. This was

said to have been the landing
place of St Paul the Apostle
on his way to Egypt. To
the north, a sandy track
leads to **Kommós**,
one of the best sandy
beaches on the south
coast. In this magnifi-
cent setting lay the
Minoan settlement of
Kommós, thought to
have been a major
port serving Phaestos
(see pp262–3). The
extensive site is
currently under
excavation.

Boat excursions run
daily from Mátala to the
Paximádia islands in the
bay and to palm-fringed
Préveli beach (see p256)
further west. There are also
several bus tours to the important archaeological sites
of Phaestos, Agía Triáda (see
p259) and Górtys.

Phaestos ⓳

See pp262–3.

Górtys ⓴
Γόρτυς

Irákleio. 📞 28920 31144. 🚌
🕐 8am–7pm daily. ● main public
hols. 📷 ♿

A SETTLEMENT from Minoan
through to Christian times,
the ancient city-state of Górtys
began to flourish under Dorian
rule during the 6th century
BC. Following its defeat of
Phaestos in the 2nd century
BC, Górtys became the most
important city on Crete. Its
pre-eminence was sealed
following the Roman in-
vasion of 65 BC, when
Górtys was appointed
capital of the newly
created Roman prov-
ince of Crete and
Cyrene (modern-day
Libya). Górtys con-
tinued to flourish
under Byzantine
rule, strategically
sited at the point
where a tributary of
the ancient river Lethe
(today's Mitropolianós)
flowed into the fertile
Messará Plain, with
coastal ports to the
west and south. It was
not until the late 7th
century AD that the great city
was destroyed by Arab invaders. Today, the most visited
ruins of this extensive site lie
to the north of the main road.

**Statue at the
ancient site
of Górtys**

**Section of the Law Code of Górtys,
housed in the odeion, Górtys**

THE LAW CODE OF GORTYS

The most extensive set of early
written laws in the Greek world was
found at the archaeological site of
ancient Górtys and dates from c.500
BC. Each stone slab of the Górtys
Code contains 12 columns of inscriptions in a Doric Cretan dialect. There
is a total of 600 lines which read
alternately from left to right and from
right to left (a style known as
boustrophedon, literally "as the ox-
plough turns"). The laws were on
display to the public and related to
domestic matters including marriage,
divorce, adoption, the obligations
and rights of slaves, and the sale
and division of property.

The *bema* (area behind altar) of Agios Títos basilica, Górtys

Exploring the Ruins

A car park, ticket booth and café are located near the entrance to the site. Immediately beyond stand the remains of the 6th-century basilica of **Agios Títos**, once an impressive, three-aisled edifice whose floorplan is still clearly visible. In its heyday it was the premier Christian church of Crete, traditionally held to be the burial place of St Titus, first bishop and patron saint of Crete, who was sent by St Paul to convert the heathens. Behind the basilica is an area thought to be a Greek **agora** (market place). Beyond this stand the semicircular tiered benches of the Roman **odeion**, originally used for concerts and now home to the famous stone slabs inscribed with the Law Code of Górtys.

Behind the odeion, a path leads up to the **acropolis** hill above Górtys, where a post-Minoan settlement was built

around 1000 BC. Parts of the fortifications still remain. On the east slope of the hill are the foundations of the 7th-century BC **Temple of Athena**. A statue and other votive objects found at a sacrificial altar lower down are in Irákleio Historical Museum (*see p264*).

To the south of the main road, an extensive area of Roman Górtys remains only partially excavated. Standing in a grove of old olive trees is the 7th-century BC **Temple of Pythian Apollo**, to which a monumental altar was added in Hellenistic times. The temple was converted into a Christian basilica in the 2nd century AD and remained important until AD 600, when it was superseded by the basilica of Agios Títos. At the far end of the site are the ruins of the 1st-century AD **praetorium**, the grand palace of the Roman provincial governor.

ENVIRONS: East of Górtys, in the nearby village of **Agioi Déka**, is the 13th-century Byzantine church of the same name. It was built on the spot where ten early Christian Cretans were martyred in AD 250 for their opposition to the Roman Emperor Decius. In the nave of the church is an icon portraying the ten martyrs,

13th-century icon of the ten martyrs, Agioi Déka church

North of Górtys, a scenic drive heads to the mountain village of **Zarós**, a surprisingly green oasis famous for its clear spring water. From here, a clearly marked trail leads north through the spectacular **Zarós Gorge**. About 3 km (2 miles) northwest of Zarós lies **Moní Vrontisíou**. The monastery's icons by Michaíl Damaskínós (c.1530–91), a famous painter of the Cretan School, are now on display in the Museum of Religious Art in Irákleio (*see p264*).

The ruins of the *praetorium*, the once-grand palace complex of the governor of the province, Górtys

Phaestos ⑲
Το Ανάκτορο της Φαιστού

Sᴘᴇᴄᴛᴀᴄᴜʟᴀʀʟʏ situated on a ridge overlooking the fertile Messará Plain, Phaestos was one of the most important Minoan palaces in Crete. Excavations by the Italian archaeologist Frederico Halbherr, in 1900, unearthed two palaces. Remains of the first palace, constructed around 1900 BC and destroyed by an earthquake in 1700 BC, are still visible. However, most of the present ruins are of the second palace which was severely damaged around 1450 BC, possibly by a tidal wave. The city-state was finally destroyed by Górtys *(see pp260–61)* in the 2nd century BC. Today, the superimposed ruins of both palaces make interpretation of the site difficult.

View of the Messará Plain from the north court

The archives room consists of a series of mudbrick chests. It was here that the famous Phaestos disc was discovered.

The peristyle hall, a colonnaded courtyard, bears traces of an earlier structure dating from the Prepalatial period (3500–1900 BC).

North court

First Palace shrine complex

★ **Grand Staircase**
This monumental staircase, which leads up to a propylon (porch) and colonnaded light-well, was the main entrance to the palace.

Tʜᴇ Pʜᴀᴇsᴛᴏs Dɪsᴄ

This round clay disc, 16 cm (6 inches) in diameter, was discovered at Phaestos in 1903. Inscribed on both sides with pictorial symbols that spiral from the circumference into the centre, no one has yet been able to decipher its meaning or identify its origins, though it is possibly a sacred hymn. The disc is one of the most important exhibits at the Irákleio Archaeological Museum *(see pp266–7)*.

West Courtyard and Theatre Area
The ruins of the west court date to c.1900 BC, the First Palace period. The seats on its north side were used for viewing rituals and ceremonies.

Royal Apartments
Now fenced, these rooms were the most elaborate, consisting of the Queen's Megaron or chamber (left), the King's Megaron, a lavatory and a lustral basin (covered pool).

Northeast quarter

Workshops

The main hall is where clay seals dating to c.1900 BC were found.

★ **Central Court**
This paved courtyard with views over the Psiloreítis range was formerly flanked on two sides by covered walkways. Its once grand north façade has a central doorway and recesses thought to be sentry boxes.

First Palace remains, dating from c.1900 BC, are concentrated in the southeast of the site, fenced off for protection.

A Classical temple shows that the site was still occupied after Minoan times.

STAR SIGHTS

★ **Grand Staircase**

★ **Central Court**

Storerooms

RECONSTRUCTION OF SECOND PALACE

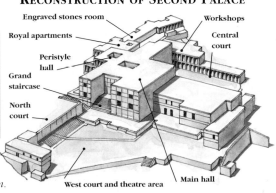

Engraved stones room — Workshops

Royal apartments — Central court

Peristyle hall

Grand staircase

North court

West court and theatre area — Main hall

Storage Pits
Dating from around 1900 BC, these circular walled pits were used for storing the palace's grain.

Irákleio ㉑

Ηράκλειο

A SETTLEMENT SINCE the Neolithic era, Irákleio served as the port for Knosós in Roman times. Under Venetian rule in the 13th century, it became known as Candia, the capital of the Aegean territories. Today the sprawl of traffic-jammed streets and concrete apartment buildings detracts from Irákleio's appeal. Yet, despite first impressions, the island's capital harbours a wealth of Venetian architecture, including the city walls and fortress. Its Archaeological Museum houses the world's greatest collection of Minoan art, and the city provides easy access to the Palace of Knosós *(see pp268–71).*

Façade of the Venetian church of Agios Títos

Exploring Irákleio

At the heart of Irákleio is Plateía Eleftheríou Venizélou, a pedestrian zone with cafés and shops grouped around the ornate 17th-century **Morosini fountain**. Facing the square, the restored church of **Agios Márkos** was built by the Venetians in 1239 and is now used as a venue for concerts and exhibitions. From here, 25 Avgoústou (25 August Street) leads north to the Venetian harbour. On this street, the elegantly restored 17th-century **Loggia** was a meeting place for the island's nobility and now serves as Irákleio's city hall. Beyond the Loggia, in a small square set back from the road, is the refurbished 16th-century church of **Agios Títos**, dedicated to the island's patron saint. On the other side of 25 Avgoustou, the tiny **El Greco Park** is named after Crete's most famous painter.

At the northern end of 25 Avgoustou, the old harbour is dominated by the Venetian **fortress**, whose dauntingly massive structure successfully repulsed prolonged assaults by the invading Turks in the 17th century. Named the *Rocca al Mare* (Fort on the Sea) by

Lion of St Mark detail, fortress

the Venetians and *Koulés* by the Turks, it was erected by the Venetians between 1523 and 1540. Opposite the fortress are the arcades of the 16th-century Venetian **Arsenáli** where ships were built and repaired. West along the waterfront, the **Historical Museum** traces the history of Crete since early Christian times. Its displays include Byzantine icons and friezes, sculptures, and archives of the Battle of Crete *(see p247).* Pride of place is given to the only El Greco painting in Crete, *The Landscape of the Gods-Trodden Mount Sinai* (c.1570).

A short walk two blocks southwest of Plateía Venizélou, on Plateía Agías Aikaterínis, is the 16th-century Venetian church of Agía Aikateríni of Sinai. Once a monastic foundation famous as a centre of art and learning, it now houses the **Museum of Religious Art**, a magnificent collection of

Byzantine icons, frescoes and manuscripts. The most significant exhibits are six icons by Michaíl Damaskinós, a 16th-century Cretan artist who learnt his craft here at Agía Aikateríni and taught El Greco. Next door, the 19th-century cathedral of **Agios Minás** towers over the square.

To the east, the street market in 1866 Street leads south to Plateía Kornárou. Here, coffee is served from a charming converted Turkish pump-house, next to which a headless Roman statue graces the

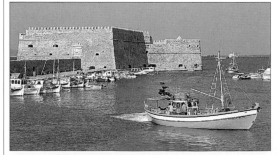

Irákleio's boat-lined harbour, dominated by the vast Venetian fortress

The Bembo drinking fountain, Plateía Kornárou

VISITORS' CHECKLIST

Irákleio. 🏛 116,000. ✈ 5 km
(3 miles) E. 🚢 E of Venetian
harbour. 🚌 Leofóros Papa-
dimitriou (for Réthymno, Chaniá,
Agios Nikólaos and Ierápetra);
Plateía Kóraka (for Mátala).
ℹ Xanthoudídou 1 (2810
228225). 🏪 Sat. 🎭 Summer
Festival: Jul–Sep. 🏖 Amoudára
10 km (6 miles) W.

16th-century **Bembo fountain**.
East, along Avérof, Plateía
Eleftherías (Freedom Square)
is dominated by a statue of
Eleuthérios Venizélos (1864–
1936), the politician central to
Crete's union with Greece. Off
the square, the pedestrianized
Daidálou is good for shops and
restaurants. Just to the north is
the **Irákleio Archaeological
Museum** (see pp266–7) and
main tourist office. The east
side of the square abuts the
Venetian ramparts, from which
there are good views.

South of the town, beyond
the old city walls, the small
Museum of Natural History
deals with the natural environment of the Aegean. Exhibits
include fossils, vegetation, and
live and stuffed animals.

🏛 **Loggia**
25 Avgoústou. ⊠ 2810 245245.
◯ Mon–Sat. ● main public hols.
⚓ **Fortress**
Venetian harbour. ◯ Tue–Sun.
● main public hols. 🌀
🏛 **Historical Museum**
Lysimáchou Kalokairinoú 7. ⊠ 2810
283219. ◯ Apr–Nov: Mon–Sat.
● main public hols 🌀 ♿
🏛 **Museum of Religious Art**
Agía Aikateríni of Sinai, Plateía Agías
Aikaterínis. ⊠ 2810 288825. ◯
Mon–Sat. ● main public hols. 🌀 ♿

🏛 **Museum of Natural
History**
Neória. ⊠ 2810 324711.
◯ daily.

ENVIRONS: Travelling west by
the main Irákleio–Réthymno
road, a turn-off to Anógeia
(see pp258–9) climbs to the
village of **Týlissos**, where the
remains of three Minoan villas
were found in 1902. West of
Irákleio, the road hugs the
coast, passing above **Agía
Pelagía**, a small resort on a
sandy cove. Further along, the
picturesque village of **Fódele**
claims to be the birthplace of
El Greco. His house lies
above the Byzantine church
just northwest of the village.

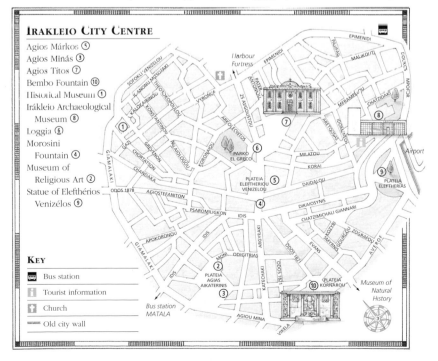

IRAKLEIO CITY CENTRE

Agios Márkos ⑤
Agios Minás ③
Agios Títos ⑦
Bembo Fountain ⑩
Historical Museum ①
Irákleio Archaeological
    Museum ⑧
Loggia ⑥
Morosini
    Fountain ④
Museum of
    Religious Art ②
Statue of Eleuthérios
    Venizélos ⑨

KEY

🚌 Bus station

ℹ Tourist information

🕇 Church

▬▬ Old city wall

Bus station
MATALA

Museum of
Natural
History

Irákleio Archaeological Museum
Αρχαιολογικό Μουσείο Ηρακλείου

THE IRAKLEIO ARCHAEOLOGICAL museum houses the world's most important collection of Minoan artifacts, giving a unique insight into a highly sophisticated civilization that existed on Crete over 3,000 years ago. On display are exhibits from all over Crete amassed since 1883, including the famous Minoan frescoes from Knosós *(see pp268–71)* and the Phaestos Disc *(see p262)*. Finely carved stone vessels, exquisite jewellery, Minoan double axes, and other artifacts make up only part of the museum's vast collection. Parts of the museum may be closed from 2003 for renovation.

Gold Bee Pendant
Found in the Chrysólakkos cemetery at Mália (see p273), this exquisite gold pendant of two bees joined together dates from the 17th century BC.

★ Bull's Head Rhyton
This 16th-century BC vessel (see p59) was used for the pouring of ritual wines. Found at Knosós, it is carved from steatite, a black stone, with inset rock crystal eyes and a mother-of-pearl snout.

★ Phaestos Disc
Made of clay, the disc was found at the Palace of Phaestos in 1903.

Ground floor

6
5
7
4
8
3
9
10
11

STAR EXHIBITS

- ★ The Hall of the Frescoes
- ★ Phaestos Disc
- ★ Bull's Head Rhyton
- ★ Snake Goddesses

Octopus Vase
This fine late Minoan vase from Palaíkastro (see p277) is decorated with images from the sea.

Stairs to first floor

THE MINOAN DOUBLE AXE

The Minoan double axe served both as a common tool used by carpenters, masons and ship-builders, and as an extremely powerful sacred symbol thought to have been a cult object connected with the Mother Goddess. The famous Labyrinth at Knosós *(see pp268–71)* is believed to have been the "dwelling place of the double axe", the word *labrys* being the ancient Greek name for double axe. Evidence of the importance of the axe for the Minoans is clear from the many vases, *larnakes* (clay coffins), seals, frescoes and pillars that were inscribed or painted with the ceremonial double axe, including the walls of the Palace of Knosós. The ceremonial axe is often depicted between sacred horns or in the hands of a priest. Votive axes (ritual offerings) were highly decorated and made of gold, silver, copper or bronze. A stylized version of the double axe also features in early Linear A and B scripts.

Minoan vase with double axe motif

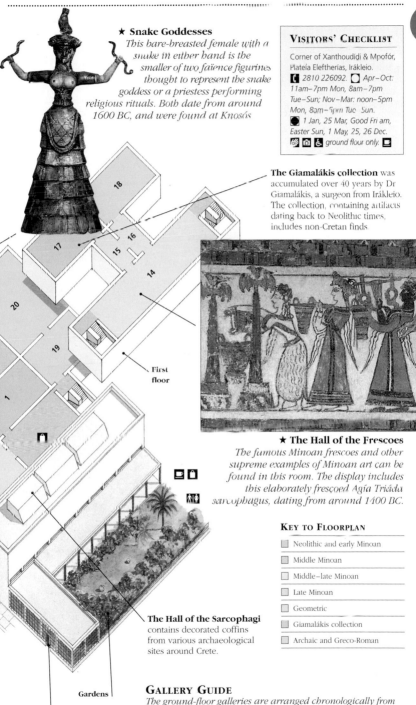

★ **Snake Goddesses**
This bare-breasted female with a snake in either hand is the smaller of two faïence figurines thought to represent the snake goddess or a priestess performing religious rituals. Both date from around 1600 BC, and were found at Knosós

The Giamalákis collection was accumulated over 40 years by Dr Giamalákis, a surgeon from Irákleio. The collection, containing artifacts dating back to Neolithic times, includes non-Cretan finds

First floor

★ **The Hall of the Frescoes**
The famous Minoan frescoes and other supreme examples of Minoan art can be found in this room. The display includes this elaborately frescoed Agía Triáda sarcophagus, dating from around 1400 BC.

KEY TO FLOORPLAN

☐	Neolithic and early Minoan
☐	Middle Minoan
☐	Middle–late Minoan
☐	Late Minoan
☐	Geometric
☐	Giamalákis collection
☐	Archaic and Greco-Roman

The Hall of the Sarcophagi contains decorated coffins from various archaeological sites around Crete.

Gardens

Entrance

GALLERY GUIDE
The ground-floor galleries are arranged chronologically from Neolithic through to Roman times. Gallery 5 contains clay tablets inscribed in Linear A and B. Stairs from gallery 13 lead to the first floor where the Minoan frescoes are exhibited in galleries 14, 15 and 16. Gallery 14, known as the Hall of the Frescoes, houses a model of the Palace of Knosós.

The Palace of Knosós ⓕ

Ανάκτορο της Κνωσού

BUILT AROUND 1900 BC, the first palace of Knosós was destroyed by an earthquake in about 1700 BC and was soon completely rebuilt. The restored ruins visible today are almost entirely from this second palace. The focal point of the site is its vast north–south aligned Central Court, off which lie many of the palace's most important areas (*see pp270–71*). The original frescoes are in the Archaeological Museum of Irákleio (*see pp266–7*).

View across the Central Court towards the northeast

To Theatre and Royal Road

Stairs to Piano Nobile (upper floor)

The Tripartite Shrine, formerly protected by a roof, was one of many shrines facing on to the Central Court.

Kouloúres (storage pits)

West Court

West Magazines

Modern entrance

Bust of Sir Arthur Evans

Horns of Consecration
Sitting on the south façade, these restored horns are a symbol of the sacred bull, and would once have adorned the top of the palace.

The South House, partly restored, was once three storeys high. It was probably the residence of a palace official.

Corridor of the Procession

South Propylon
Entrance to the palace was through this monumental, pillared gateway, decorated with a replica of the Cup-Bearer figure, a detail from the Procession fresco.

★ **Priest-King Fresco**
This replica of the Priest-King *fresco, also known as the* Prince of the Lilies, *is a detail from the* Procession *fresco and depicts a figure wearing a crown of lilies and feathers.*

VISITORS' CHECKLIST

5 km (3 miles) S of Irákleio, Irákleio.
📞 28120 231940. 🚌 🚗 May–
Oct: 8am–7pm daily; Nov–Apr:
8am–6pm daily. 🚫 1 Jan, 25
Mar, Good Fri am, Easter Sun, 1
May, 25, 26 Dec. 🎫 📷 🚻 🛒

★ **Throne Room**

With its adjoining antechamber and lustral basin, the Throne Room is believed to have served as a shrine. The original stone throne, thought to be that of a priestess, is guarded by a restored fresco of griffins, sacred symbols in Minoan times.

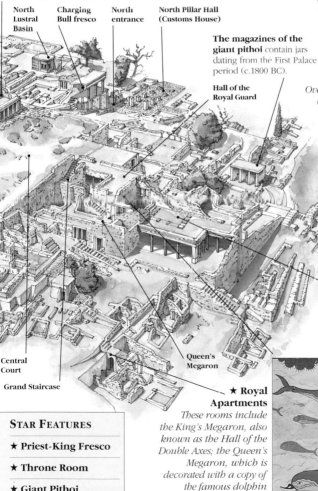

North Lustral Basin

Charging Bull fresco

North entrance

North Pillar Hall (Customs House)

The magazines of the giant pithoi contain jars dating from the First Palace period (c.1800 BC).

Hall of the Royal Guard

★ **Giant Pithoi**

Over 100 giant pithoi (storage jars) were unearthed at Knosós. The jars were used to store palace supplies.

King's Megaron (Hall of the Double Axes)

Central Court

Grand Staircase

Queen's Megaron

★ **Royal Apartments**

These rooms include the King's Megaron, also known as the Hall of the Double Axes; the Queen's Megaron, which is decorated with a copy of the famous dolphin fresco and has an en suite bathroom; and the Grand Staircase.

STAR FEATURES

★ Priest-King Fresco

★ Throne Room

★ Giant Pithoi

★ Royal Apartments

Exploring the Palace of Knosós

U NLIKE OTHER Minoan sites, the Palace of Knosós was imaginatively restored by Sir Arthur Evans between 1900 and 1929. While his interpretations are the subject of academic controversy, his reconstructions of the second palace do give the visitor an impression of life in Minoan Crete that cannot so easily be gained from the other palaces on the island.

AROUND THE SOUTH PROPYLON

T HE PALACE complex is entered via the **West Court**, the original ceremonial entrance now marked by a bust of Sir Arthur Evans. To the left are three circular pits known as *kouloúres*, which probably served as granaries. Ahead, along the length of the west façade, are the **West Magazines**. These contained numerous large storage jars *(pithoi)*, and, along with the granaries, give an impression of how important the control of resources and storage was as a basis for the power of the palace.

At the far right-hand corner of the West Court the west entrance leads to the **Corridor of the Procession**. Now cut short by erosion of the hillside, the corridor's frescoes, depicting a series of gift-bearers, seem to reflect the ceremony that accompanied state and religious events at the palace. This is further revealed in the frescoes of the **South Propylon**, to which one branch of the corridor led. From the South Propylon,

Shield motif, Knosós

steps lead up to the reconstructed **Piano Nobile**, the name given by Sir Arthur Evans to the probable location of the grand state apartments and reception halls. Stone vases found in this part of the palace were used for ritual purposes and indicate the centrality of religion to palace life. The close link between secular and sacred power is also reinforced by the **Throne Room**, where ritual bathing in a lustral basin (sunken bath) is thought to have taken place. Steps lead from the Throne Room to the once paved **Central Court**. Now open to the elements, this would have once been flanked by high buildings on all four sides.

THE ROYAL APARTMENTS

O N THE EAST SIDE of the Central Court lie rooms of such size and elegance that they have been identified as the Royal Apartments. The apartments are built into the side of the hill and accessed by the **Grand Staircase**, one of the most impressive surviving architectural features of the

Restored clay bath tub adjacent to the Queen's Megaron

palace. The flights of gypsum stairs descend to a colonnaded courtyard, providing a source of light to the lower storeys. These light-wells were a typical feature of Minoan architecture.

A drainage system was provided for the toilet beside the **Queen's Megaron**, which enjoyed the luxury of an *en suite* bathroom complete with clay bathtub. Corridors and rooms alike in this area were decorated with frescoes of floral and animal motifs. The walls of the **Hall of the Royal Guard**, a heavily guarded landing leading to the Royal Apartments, were decorated with a shield motif. The **King's Megaron**, also known as the Hall of the Double Axes, takes its name from the fine double-axe symbols incised into its stone walls. The largest of the rooms in the Royal Apartments, the King's Megaron could be divided by multiple doors, giving it great flexibility of space. Remains of what may have been a plaster throne were found here, suggesting that the room was also used for some state functions.

NORTH AND WEST OF THE CENTRAL COURT

T HE NORTH ENTRANCE of the Central Court was adorned with remarkable figurative decoration. Today, a replica of the *Charging Bull* fresco can be seen on site. The north

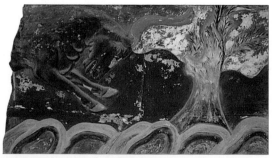

Replica of the celebrated *Charging Bull* fresco

entrance leads to the **North Pillar Hall**, named as the Customs House by Sir Arthur Evans who believed merchandise was inspected here. The hall is an addition of the Second Palace period (c.1700 BC). Immediately to the west is a room with restored steps leading into a pool, known as the **North Lustral Basin**. Traces of burning and finds of oil jars suggest that those coming to the palace were purified and annointed here before entering. Further west is the **Theatre**, a stepped court whose position at the end of the Royal Road suggests that rituals connected with the reception of visitors

The stepped court of the theatre

may have occurred here. The **Royal Road**, which leads away from the Palace to the Minoan town of Knosós, was lined with houses. Just off the Royal Road lies the so-called

Little Palace. This building has been excavated, but is not open to the public. It is architecturally very similar to the main palace and was destroyed at the same time.

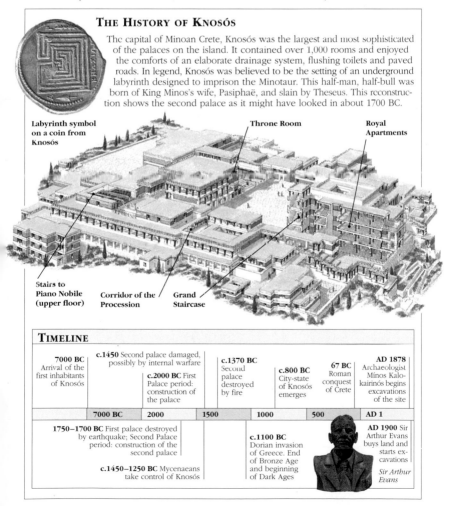

THE HISTORY OF KNOSÓS

The capital of Minoan Crete, Knosós was the largest and most sophisticated of the palaces on the island. It contained over 1,000 rooms and enjoyed the comforts of an elaborate drainage system, flushing toilets and paved roads. In legend, Knosós was believed to be the setting of an underground labyrinth designed to imprison the Minotaur. This half-man, half-bull was born of King Minos's wife, Pasiphaë, and slain by Theseus. This reconstruction shows the second palace as it might have looked in about 1700 BC.

Labyrinth symbol on a coin from Knosós

Throne Room

Royal Apartments

Stairs to Piano Nobile (upper floor)

Corridor of the Procession

Grand Staircase

TIMELINE

7000 BC Arrival of the first inhabitants of Knosós	**c.1450** Second palace damaged, possibly by internal warfare	**c.1370 BC** Second palace destroyed by fire	**c.800 BC** City-state of Knosós emerges	**67 BC** Roman conquest of Crete	**AD 1878** Archaeologist Mínos Kalokairinós begins excavations of the site
	c.2000 BC First Palace period: construction of the palace				

7000 BC	2000	1500	1000	500	AD 1

1750–1700 BC First palace destroyed by earthquake; Second Palace period: construction of the second palace			**AD 1900** Sir Arthur Evans buys land and starts excavations
c.1450–1250 BC Mycenaeans take control of Knosós	**c.1100 BC** Dorian invasion of Greece. End of Bronze Age and beginning of Dark Ages		*Sir Arthur Evans*

The modern seafront of Chersónisos, the busiest of Crete's package-holiday resorts

Archánes ㉓
Αρχάνες

Irákleio. 🏠 4,000. 🚌 🚊 ℹ 28170 51488.

AWAY FROM Crete's coastal holiday resorts, Archánes is a down-to-earth farming centre, where olive groves and small vineyards chequer the rolling landscape. Lying at the foot of the sacred **Mount Gioúchtas** (burial place of Zeus according to local tradition), Archánes was a thriving and important settlement in Minoan times.

In 1964, the remains of a Minoan **palace** were found in the town of Tourkogeitoniá. A short walk out of town, on Fourní hill to the north, lies an extensive **Minoan cemetery**. Among the treasures unearthed here was the tomb of a princess with mirror and gold diadem in place, as well as exquisitely engraved signet rings. Some of these are now on display at the **Archaeological Museum** of Archánes.

---

fff Minoan cemetery
Fourní hill. ☐ Mon, Wed–Sun. ● main public hols.

📷 Archaeological Museum
Kalochristianáki. ☐ Mon, Wed–Sun. ● main public hols. ♿

ENVIRONS: On the north slope of Mount Gioúchtas is the site of a Minoan sanctuary at **Anemospiliá**. Excavations unearthed a shocking scene of human sacrifice here, seemingly interrupted by an earthquake around 1700 BC which killed all four participants. Though little remains to be seen today, sensational views of Mount Idi (see p258) can be enjoyed from the sanctuary.

The **Kazantzákis Museum** at Myrtiá displays memorabilia of the author of Zorba the Greek.

📷 Kazantzákis Museum
Myrtiá, 14 km (9 miles) E of Archánes. (28170 742451. ☐ Mar–Oct: daily; Nov–Feb: Sun. ● main public hols. 📷

Hard Rock Café sign at Chersónisos

Chersónisos ㉔
Χερσόνησος

Irákleio. 🏠 4,050. 🚌 🚊 ℹ 28170 22764. 🚕 Chersónisos.

A FLOURISHING and busy port from Classical to early Byzantine times, Chersónisos (strictly Liménas Chersonísou) is today the centre of the package-holiday business. Amid the plethora of tavernas, souvenir shops and discos the harbour still retains faint intimations of the old Chersónisos. Along the waterfront a pyramid-shaped Roman **fountain** with fish mosaics dates from the 2nd–3rd century AD. Some remains of the **Roman harbour**, now mostly submerged, can also be seen here. Traditional Cretan life is recreated at the **Cretan Open-Air Museum** or "Lychnostátis", where exhibits include a windmill, a stone house and a gallery. The **Museum of Rural Life**, housed in a 19th-century olive oil mill, displays a range of traditional farming tools used before the introduction of modern technology. To cool off, the **Aqua Splash Water Park** is a playground of pools, waterslides and waterfalls.

📷 Cretan Open-Air Museum
Lychnostátis. (28970 23660. ☐ Apr–Oct: Mon–Fri & Sun. ● main public hols. 📷 ♿
📷 Museum of Rural Life
Piskopianá. (28970 23303. ☐ Apr– Oct: daily. 📷 ♿
💦 Aqua Splash Water Park
5 km (3 miles) S of National Highway. (28970 24950. ☐ May–Oct: daily. 📷 ♿

NIKOS KAZANTZAKIS

From the village of Myrtiá, Níkos Kazantzákis (1883–1957) was Crete's greatest writer. Dedicated to the Cretan struggle for freedom from Turkish rule, he wrote poems, philosophical essays, plays and novels including Zorba the Greek and

The Last Temptation of Christ (both made into films). Excommunicated by the Orthodox church, the epitaph on his grave in Irákleio consists of his own words: "I hope for nothing. I fear nothing. I am free."

Poster of the 1960s film version of Zorba the Greek

Mália
Μάλια

36 km (22 miles) E of Irákleio.
🏛 *2,700*. 🚌 🚆 *Stalida 3 km (2 miles) NW.*

THE MÁLIA of package-holiday fame bustles noisily with sun-seekers hellbent on enjoying the crowded beaches by day and the cacophony of competing discos by night.

In marked contrast, the less visited Minoan **Palace of Mália** lies in quiet ruins along the coastal plain to the east. The first palace was built in 1900 BC but, like all the other major palaces, It suffered destruction in 1700 BC and again in 1450 BC *(see p271)*. The site incorporates many features characteristic of other Minoan palaces – the great central court with its sacrificial altar, royal apartments, lustral basins (water pools) and light-wells (courtyards). In a small sanctuary in the west wing of the palace, the Minoan religious symbol of the double axe *(labrys)* can be seen inscribed on twin pillars.

Giant *pithos* at the Palace of Mália

Beyond the palace, remains thought to be of a town are currently under excavation while further north lies the burial site of **Chrysolakkos** (pit of gold). Important treasures were recovered here, including the famous gold bee pendant displayed in the Irákleio Archaeological Museum *(see pp266–7)*.

The chequered landscape of the agricultural plateau of Lasíthi

🏛 Palace of Mália
3 km (2 miles) E of Mália. ☎ 28970 31597. 🕐 *Tue–Sun; Jul–Oct. daily.* ● *28 Oct, main public hols.* 🅿 👤

ENVIRONS: The fast developing village of **Sísi** is situated 6.5 km (4 miles) east of Mália. Continuing eastwards, stunning views mark the descent to Mílatos. From here a well-signposted trail leads to the **Mílatos Cave** where a shrine and glass-fronted casket of bones are a memorial to those massacred here by the Turks in 1823 during the Greek War of Independence.

Lasíthi Plateau 26
Ωροπέδιο Λασιθίου

Díkti mountains, Irákleio. 🚌 *to Tzermiádo.*

HIGH UP in the formidable Díkti mountains, the bowl-shaped plain of Lasíthi was for centuries shut off from the outside world. A row of stone windmills at the

Séli Ampélou Pass marks the main entry to the plateau, a flat agricultural area lying 800 m (2,600 ft) above sea level and encircled by mountains. Fruit, potatoes, and cereals are the main crops produced here, thanks to the fertile alluvial soil washed down from the mountains. A few cloth-sailed windmills are still used today to pump irrigation water.

Along the perimeter of the plain are several villages, the largest of which is **Tzermiádo** with good tourist facilities. A path from Tzermiádo to the **Trápeza Cave** (also known as Kronion Cave) is signposted from the village centre. At the west end of the village a rough road (just over an hour's walk) leads up to the archaeological site of **Karfí**, the last retreat of Minoan civilization. On the southern edge of the plain, the village of **Agios Geórgios** has a small **Folk Museum** set in two old village houses and displaying a collection of embroidery, paintings and Kazantzákis memorabilia.

The highlight of a visit to Lasíthi is the climb to the **Diktian Cave** at Psychró, birthplace of Zeus *(see p258)*. A wealth of artifacts have been unearthed here including votive offerings, double axes and bronze statuettes, now in the Irákleio Archaeological Museum *(see pp266–7)*.

🏛 Folk Museum
Agios Geórgios.
🕐 *Mar–Oct: daily.* 🅿 👤
🏛 Diktian Cave
Psychró. ☎ 28440 31316. 🕐 *daily.* ● *27 Sep, 28 Oct, public hols.* 🅿

A small shrine in the multichambered Mílatos Cave

The fortified islet of Spinalónga off the coast of Eloúnta

Eloúnta ⓧ
Ελούντα

Lasíthi. 👥 1,500. 🚌 🛈 28410
42464. 🚢 Tue. 🚉 Eloúnta.

Once the site of the ancient city-state of Oloús, the town of Eloúnta was developed by the Venetians in 1579 as a fortified port. Today, the town is a well-established holiday resort idyllically situated on the Mirabéllou Bay. The town is blessed with attractive sandy coves and offers a good range of accommodation.

East of the village an isthmus joins the mainland to the long strip of land forming the Spinalónga peninsula. Here, remains of the Greco-Roman city-state of **Oloús**, with its temples of Zeus and Artemis, can be discerned just below the water's surface. To the north of the peninsula is the small island of **Spinalónga** where a forbidding 16th-century Venetian fortress now stands deserted. Having withstood assault from the Turks for many years, its last function was as a leper colony until the mid-1950s. Today, boats regularly ferry tourists to the island from Eloúnta and elsewhere.

Environs: The small hamlet of **Pláka**, 5 km (3 miles) north of Eloúnta, makes for a pleasant retreat from the bustle of Eloúnta. Fresh fish is served at small tavernas on the waterfront, where boat trips are available to Spinalónga island.

Skull and wreath, Archaeological Museum, Agios Nikólaos

Agios Nikólaos ⓧ
Άγιος Νικόλαος

Lasíthi. 👥 10,000. ✈ 🚌
🛈 Koundoúrou 21 (28410 22357).
🚢 Wed. 🚉 Almyrós 2 km (1.5 miles)
E; Chavánia 3 km (2 miles) W.

One of the most delightful holiday centres in Crete, Agios Nikólaos boasts a superb setting on the Mirabéllou Bay. In Hellenistic times, according to inscriptions dating back to 193 BC, this was one of two flourishing cities called Lató: Lató pros Kamára (towards the arch) and Lató Etéra (Other Lató). Having declined in importance under Venetian rule, it was not until the 19th century that modern Agios Nikólaos began to develop.

Now a thriving resort, its centre is the harbour and, with a depth of 64 m (210 ft), the Almyrí Lake or Voulisméni. Overlooking the lake, the **Folk Museum** houses a colourful display of traditional Cretan crafts and domestic items. Just north of town, in the grounds of the Mínos Palace Hotel, is the tiny 10th–11th-century church of **Agios Nikólaos** after which the town is named.

Close to several important Minoan sites, the **Archaeological Museum** at Agios Nikólaos possesses a treasure-trove of artifacts from Lasíthi Province. Pieces housed here include carved stone vases, gold jewellery from the Minoan site of Móchlos near Gourniá and pottery, including the drinking vessel known as the Goddess of Mýrtos. One unique exhibit is the skull of a man thought to be an athlete, complete with a wreath made of gold laurel leaves and a silver coin for his fare across the mythical River Styx.

In summer, boat trips run to Spinalónga island and Agioi Pántes, an island refuge for the Cretan wild goat, the *kri-kri (see p250)*.

🏛 **Folk Museum**
Koúndourou 23. 📞 28410 25093.
🕐 May–Oct: Sun–Fri. ⬤ main
public hols. 📷 ♿
🏛 **Archaeological Museum**
Palaiológou 68. 📞 28410 24943.
🕐 Tue–Sun. ⬤ main public hols. 📷

The attractive inner harbour of Agios Nikólaos, with Lake Voulisméni in the foreground

Section of the *Paradise* fresco at
Panagía Kerá in Krítsá

Krítsá 🜨

Κριτσά

Lasíthi. 🜨 2,500. 🚌 🅿 Mon.
🚉 Ammoudára 11 km (7 miles) E;
Ístro 15 km (9 miles) SE.

SET AT THE FOOT of the Lasíthi
mountains, Krítsá is a small
village known throughout
Crete for its famous Byzantine
church. Also a popular centre
for Cretan crafts, its main street
is awash with lace, elaborately
woven rugs and embroidered
tablecloths during the summer
months. From the cafés and
tavernas along the main
street, fine views of the valley
leading down to the coast can
be enjoyed. By November,
Krítsá reverts back to life as a
workaday Greek village.

East of Krítsá, situated just
off the road among olive
groves, the hallowed 13th-
century church of **Panagía
Kerá** contains some of the
finest frescoes in Crete, dating
from the 13th to mid-14th
century. The building is triple-
aisled with the central aisle
being the oldest. Beautiful
representations of the life of
Christ and the Virgin Mary
cover the interior.

ENVIRONS: North of Krítsá lie
the ruins of a fortified city
founded by the Dorians in the
7th century BC. **Lató Etéra**
flourished until Classical times
when its fortunes declined
under Roman rule: it was
superseded by the more

easily reached
port of Lató pros
Kamara (today's
Agios Nikólaos).
Sitting perched
on a saddle
between two
peaks, the site
offers fine views
of the Mirabéllou
Bay. A paved
road, with work-
shops and
houses clustered
on the right,
climbs up to a
central agora, or
marketplace, with
a cistern to collect
rainwater and a
shrine. On the north side
of the agora, a staircase
flanked by two towers leads
to the place where the city's
archives would once have
been stored. To the south of
the agora a temple and a
theatre can be seen.

🏛 Lató
4 km (2 miles) N of Krítsá.
🔲 Tue–Sun. 🔘 main public hols.

Lace shop on Krítsá's main street

Ierápetra 🜩

Ιεράπετρα

Lasíthi. 🜨 15,000. 🚌 🔢 Adrianoú
(28420 22246). 🅿 Sat. 🚉 Agiá
Fotiá 17 km (11 miles) E; Makrýs
Gialós 30 km (19 miles) E.

SITUATED ON THE southeast
coast of Crete, Ierápetra
boasts of its position as the
most southerly city in Europe.
A settlement since pre-Minoan
times, trade and cultural connections with North Africa
and the Middle East were an
important basis of the city's
existence. Sir Arthur Evans
(see p270) declared it the
"crossroads of Minoan and
Achaian civilizations". Once a

flourishing city with villas,
temples, amphitheatres, and
imposing buildings, the town
today has an air of decline.
Gone are all signs of its ancient
history, thanks partly to past
pillage and, more recently,
to modern "development".

The entrance to the old harbour is guarded by an early
13th-century Venetian **fortress**.
West of the fortress is the
attractive Turkish quarter
where a restored **mosque**
and elegant Ottoman fountain
can be seen. Also in this area,
on Kougioumtzáki, is the 14th-
century church of **Aféntis
Christós** and, off Samouíl,
Napoleon's House, where he
is said to have spent a night en
route to Egypt in 1798. Today
it is not open to the public.

The small **Archaeological
Museum** in the centre of town
displays a collection of local
artifacts that managed to survive marauders and various
archaeological predators. The
exhibits date from Minoan to
Roman times and include *lar
nakes* (burial caskets), *pithoi*
(storage jars), statues, bronze
axes and stone carvings.

An almost unbroken line
of sandy beaches stretches
eastwards from Ierápetra,
overlooked by the inevitable
plethora of hotels and restaurants. From Ierápetra's
harbour, a daily boat service
runs to the idyllic white sands
and cedar forests of the
uninhabited **Chrysí** island.

🏛 Fortress
Old port. 🔲 daily. 🔘 main public
hols. 🛐

🏛 Archaeological Museum
Adrianoú Koustoúla. 🔳 28420 28721.
🔲 Tue–Sun. 🔘 main public hols. ♿

**Mosque and Ottoman fountain in
Ierápetra's old Turkish quarter**

Gourniá archaeological site

Gourniá ③
Γουρνιά

18.5 km (11 miles) E of Agios
Nikólaos, Lasíthi. ▦ ○ *Tue–Sun.*
● *main public hols.* ▨ ▩ *Istro 8 km
(5 miles) W.*

THE MINOAN SITE of Gourniá
stands on a low hill overlooking the tranquil Mirabéllou
Bay. Excavated by the
American archaeologist Harriet
Boyd-Hawes between 1901
and 1904, Gourniá is the best-
preserved Minoan town in
Crete. A mini-palace (one-tenth
the size of Knosós) marks its
centre, surrounded by a labyrinth of narrow, stepped streets
and one-room dwellings. The
site was inhabited as early as
the 3rd millennium BC, though
what remains dates from the
Second Palace period, around
1700 BC *(see p271)*. A fire,
caused by seismic activity in
around 1450 BC, destroyed
the settlement at Gourniá.

ENVIRONS: Along the National
Highway, 2 km (1.5 miles)
west of Gourniá, an old concrete road turns left up a
spectacular 6-km (4-mile)
climb to **Moní Faneroménis**.
Here, the 15th-century chapel
of the **Panagía** has been built
into a deep cave and is the
repository for sacred (and
some say miraculous) icons.
East along the National
Highway, a left turning from
Sfáka leads down to the
delightful fishing village of
Móchlos. The small island of
Móchlos, once joined to the
mainland by a narrow
isthmus, is the site of a Minoan
settlement and cemetery.

Siteía ③
Σητεία

Lasíthi. ▦ *7,500.* ✕ ▭ ▭
▣ *Tue.* ▤ *Siteía.*

SNAKING ITS WAY through the
mountains between Gourniá
and Siteía, the National Highway traverses some of the
most magnificent scenery
in Crete. Towards Siteía,
the landscape gives way to
barren hills and vineyards.
Although there is evidence
of a large Greco-Roman city in
the region, modern Siteía dates
from the 4th century AD. It
flourished under Byzantine
and early Venetian rule but its
fortunes took a downturn in
the 16th century as a result of
earthquakes and pirate attacks.
When rebuilding took place
in the 1870s Siteía began to
prosper once again.
Today, the production of
wine and olive oil is important to the town's economy
and the mid-August Sultana
Festival celebrates its success
as a sultana exporter.
At the centre of Siteía's old
quarter lies a picturesque
harbour, with tavernas and
cafés clustering around its
edges. Above the north end
of the harbour the restored
Venetian **fort** (now used as
an open-air theatre) is all that
remains of the once extensive
fortifications of the town.
Occupying a renovated old
house near the harbourfront,
the **Folk Museum** displays an
interesting collection of local
costumes and weaving.
On the southern outskirts
of town, the **Archaeological
Museum** displays artifacts
from the Siteía district. Exhibits
range from Neolithic to Roman
times and include an exquisite
Minoan ivory statuette known
as the *Palaíkastro Koúros.*
There are pottery finds from
all over the region including a
large collection of material
from Zákros Palace.

⌂ Folk Museum
Kapetán Sífi 33. ℃ *28430 22861.*
○ *May–Sep: Mon–Fri.* ● *main
public hols.* ▨ ৬ *ground floor.*
⌂ Archaeological Museum
Piskokefálou 3. ℃ *28430 23917.*
○ *Tue–Sun.* ● *main public hols.*
▨ ৬

Siteía's old quarter on the hillside overlooking the tree-lined harbour

Moní Toploú 🔞
Μονή Τοπλού

16 km (10 miles) W of Siteía, Lasíthi.
C *28430 61226.* 🚌 *to Váï.*
Site & Museum ⭕ *daily.* 📷
🚗 *Itanos 7.5 km (4.5 miles) NE.*

FOUNDED IN THE 14th century,
Moní Toploú is now one of
the wealthiest and most influential monasteries in Crete.
The present buildings date
from Venetian times, when the
monastery was fortified against
pirate attacks. The Turkish
name "Toplou" refers to the
cannon installed here. During
World War II, Resistance radio
broadcasts were transmitted
from the monastery, an act for
which Abbot Siligknakis was
executed by German forces
near Chaniá.

Three levels of cells overlook
the inner courtyard, where a
small 14th-century church
contains frescoes and icons.
The most famous of these
is the *Lord, Thou
Art Great* icon,
completed in
1770 by the
artist Ioánnis
Kornáros. On
the façade of
the church,
an inscription
records the
Arbitration
of Magnesia in 132
BC. This was an
order that settled
a dispute between
the rival city-states of Ierapytna
(today's Ierápetra) and Itanos,
over the control of the Temple
of Zeus Diktaios at Palaíkastro.
The inscription stone was used
originally as a tombstone. The
monastery's small museum
houses etchings and 15th- to
18th-century icons.

Lord, Thou Art Great
icon by Ioánnis
Kornáros, Moní Toploú

Váï Beach 🔞
Παραλία Βάι

28 km (17 miles) NE of Siteía,
Lasíthi. 🚌

THE EXOTIC VAI BEACH is a
tropical paradise of dense
palm trees known to have
existed in Classical times and
reputedly unique in Europe.
This inviting sandy cove is
tremendously popular with
holiday-makers. Although
thoroughly commercialized,
with overpriced tavernas and
the constant arrival of tour
buses, great care is taken to
protect the palm trees.

ENVIRONS: In the desolate
landscape 2 km (1 mile) north
of Váï, the ruins of the ancient
city-state of **Itanos** stand on
a small hill between
two sandy coves.
Minoan, Greco-
Roman and
Byzantine
remains
have been
excavated
(the scant
traces of
which
can be seen today),
including a Byzan-
tine basilica and
the sparse ruins
of some Classical temples.
The agricultural town of
Palaíkastro, 10 km (6 miles)
south of Váï, is the centre of an
expanding olive business. At
the south end of Chióna beach,
2 km (1 mile) to the east, the
Minoan site of Palaíkastro is
presently under excavation.

Zákros archaeological site, situated behind the hamlet of Káto Zákros

Zákros 🔞
Ζάκρος

Káto Zákros, Lasíthi. **C** *28430
93338.* 🚌 ⭕ *Tue–Sun.* ⭕ *main
public hols.* 📷 🚗 *Káto Zákros;
Xerókampos 13 km (8 miles) S.*

IN 1961, CRETAN archaeologist
Nikólaos Pláton discovered
the unplundered Minoan
palace of Zákros. The fourth
largest of the palaces, it was
built around 1700 BC and
destroyed in the island-wide
disaster of 1450 BC. Its ideal
location made it a centre of
trade with the Middle East.

The two-storied palace was
arranged around a central
courtyard, the east side of
which contained the royal
apartments. Remains of a
colonnaded cistern hall can still
be seen, and a stone-lined
well in which some perfectly
preserved 3,000-year-old olives
were found in 1964. The main
hall, workshops and storerooms are in the west wing.
Finds from the palace include
an exquisite rock crystal jug
and numerous vases, now in
the Irákleio Archaeological
Museum (*see p266–7*).

Váï Beach with its calm waters and native palms

A SHORT STAY IN ATHENS

A VAST, SPRAWLING METROPOLIS *surrounded by rocky mountains, Athens covers 457 sq km (176 sq miles) and has a population of four million people. The city prides itself on being home to the 2,500-year-old temple of Athena – the Parthenon – as well as some superb museums. A stopover in Athens en route to the islands offers the ideal opportunity to visit the best sights in the city.*

The birthplace of European civilization, Athens has been inhabited for 7,000 years, since the Neolithic era. Ancient Athens reached its high point in the 5th century BC, when Perikles commissioned many fine new buildings, including some of the temples on the Acropolis. Other relics from the Classical period can be seen in the Ancient Agora, a complex of public buildings dominated by the reconstructed Stoa of Attalos, a long, covered colonnade.

Evzone in Plateía Syntágmatos

There is little architectural evidence of the city's more recent history of occupation. With the exception of some fine Byzantine churches, particularly those in historic Plaka, one of the oldest areas of Athens, nothing of importance has survived from the years of Frankish, Venetian and Ottoman rule. In 1834, inspired by the Classical buildings of the Acropolis, King Otto declared Athens the new capital of Greece, and his Greek, German and Danish town-planners and architects created a modern city of Neo-Classical municipal buildings, wide boulevards and elegant squares around the ancient "Sacred Rock".

The rich cultural heritage of Athens can be appreciated in some magnificent museums, including the National Archaeological Museum, where an unrivalled collection beautifully illustrates the glories of ancient Greece. The National Gallery of Art includes well-known works by both Greek and European artists.

The nightlife in Athens is excellent, with tavernas, clubs and bars open until the early hours. Open-air cinemas and theatres, such as the Theatre of Herod Atticus at the foot of the Acropolis, are popular in summer. There is music for every taste, from traditional Greek to pop, jazz and classical concerts. Shopping ranges from the flea market and antique and bric-a-brac shops in Monastiráki, to designer boutiques in Kolonáki. Pedestrianization of the city centre makes Athens a pleasant place to explore on foot.

View of the Acropolis from Filopáppos Hill

◁ Lykavittós Hill rising above the spread of concrete apartment blocks and Byzantine churches, in Athens

Exploring Athens

E VEN WITH ONLY AN AFTERNOON to spend in Athens, it is possible to visit a few of the main sights. The Acropolis is the most popular attraction, along with the Ancient Agora. The National Archaeological Museum houses many finds from these sites in its fine collection of ancient Greek art. The renovated Benáki Museum houses a glittering array of jewellery, costumes and ceramics from Greece and the Middle East, as well as many temporary exhibitions. Shopping provides an alternative to sightseeing, from the bric-a-brac in Pláka to the designer stores in Kolonáki. For information on getting around Athens, see pp288–91.

Avyssinías in Monastiráki *(see p282)*

The Central Market has a fine array of foods, herbs and spices.

Figure from the Museum of Cycladic Art *(see p287)*

Mitrópoli is Athens' cathedral. It towers over the tiny Byzantine Panagía Gorgoepíkoös (or Little Cathedral) next to it.

0 metres   250

0 yards   250

The Tower of the Winds (*see p283*)

Panepistimíou is lined with some of the best examples of Neo-Classical architecture in Athens

LOCATOR MAP

ATHENS' TOP SIGHTS

Museums and Galleries
Benáki Museum **7**
Museum of Cycladic Art **8**
National Archaeological
Museum **1**
National Gallery of Art **9**

Historic Districts
Monastiráki **2**
Pláka **6**
Psyrrí **3**

Ancient Sites
Acropolis pp284–6 **5**
Ancient Agora **4**

KEY

▢	Sight and place of interest
Ⓜ	Metro station
🚎	Main trolley bus stop
🚗	Taxi rank

Kolonáki is a fashionable district, with designer stores.

Plateía Syntágmatos is the home of the Tomb of the Unknown Soldier. The famous *évzones* (national guard) are on parade in front of the tomb.

The National Gardens were planted by order of Queen Amalía in the 19th century. Semi-tropical, they provide pleasant relief from the heat of the city.

P	Parking
🛈	Tourist information
✚	Hospital with casualty unit
🚓	Police station
✝	Church
⊠	Post office
▬	Pedestrianized street

National Archaeological Museum ❶
Εθνικό Αρχαιολογικό Μουσείο

Patission 44, Exárcheia.
📞 *210 821 7717.*
Ⓜ *Omónoia, Viktória.*
⚫ *for renovation until May 2004.*
🖼️ 📷 ♿ 🚻

Shoppers browsing in Athens' lively Monastiráki market

W HEN IT WAS OPENED in 1891, this museum brought together a collection that had previously been stored all over the city. New wings were added in 1939, but during World War II this priceless collection was dispersed and buried underground to protect it from any possible damage. The museum reopened in 1946, but it has taken another 50 years of renovation and reorganization to finally do justice to its formidable collection. With its comprehensive assembly of pottery, sculpture and jewellery, it definitely deserves ranking as one of the finest museums in the world. It is a good idea to plan ahead and be selective when visiting the museum and not attempt to cover everything in one visit.

The museum's exhibits can be divided into five main collections: Neolithic and Cycladic, Mycenaean, Geometric and Archaic, Classical sculpture, Roman and Hellenistic sculpture and the pottery collections. There are also other smaller collections that are well worth seeing. These include the stunning Eléni Stathátou jewellery collection and the recently opened Egyptian rooms.

High points of the museum include the unique finds from the grave circle at Mycenae, in particular the gold *Mask of Agamemnon.* Also not to be missed are the Archaic *koúroi* statues and the unrivalled collection of Classical and Hellenistic statues. Two of the most important and finest of the bronzes are the *Horse with the Little*

Jockey and the *Poseidon.* Also housed here is one of the world's largest collections of ancient ceramics comprising elegant figure vases from the 6th and 5th centuries BC (*see pp58–59*) and some Geometric funerary vases that date back to 1000 BC. The collection is currently closed due to earthquake damage.

The *Mask of Agamemnon* in the National Archaeological Museum

Monastiráki ❷
Μοναστηράκι

Ⓜ *Monastiráki.* **Market** ⬜ *daily.*

T HIS AREA, named after the little monastery church in Plateía Monastirakíou, is synonymous with Athens' famous fleamarket. Located next to the Ancient Agora, it is bounded by Sari in the west and Aiólou in the east. The streets of Pandrósou, Ifaístou and Areos leading off Plateía Monastirakíou are full of shops, selling a range of goods from antiques, leather and silver to tourist trinkets.

The heart of the flea market is in Plateía Avyssinías, west of Plateía Monastirakíou, where

every morning junk dealers arrive with pieces of furniture and various odds and ends. During the week and on Sunday mornings the shops and stalls are filled with antiques, second-hand books, rugs, leatherware, taverna chairs, army surplus gear and tools.

The market flourishes particularly along Adrianoú and in Plateía Agíou Filíppou. There are always numerous bargains to be had. Items particularly worth investing in include some of the colourful woven and embroidered cloths and an abundance of good silver jewellery.

Psyrrí ❸
Ψυρρί

Ⓜ *Monastiráki.*

F OR A TASTE OF Athens as it was through most of its modern history, wander the warren of streets comprising the Psyrrí district. Bordered by the Central Market, Athinas and Ermou Streets, this neighbourhood is becoming the city's trendiest area. Many of the handsome Neo-Classical buildings have been renovated for art galleries and restaurants while theatres, wine bars and boutiques pop up daily. Tiny stores specialize in unique, handmade items like copper kitchenware, belt buckles, wickerwork and icons. At night the district's transformed, commercial buzz is replaced by the gentle pleasures of cafés, restaurants and wine bars. The food here is some of the most interesting in the city and prices are reasonable. This is very much an Athenian part of town.

Ancient Agora ❹
Αρχαία Αγορά

Main entrance at Adrianoú, Monastiráki. **(** 210 321 0185. **M** *Thiseío, Monastiráki.* **Museum and site** ☐ *8am–7pm Tue–Sun, noon–3pm Good Fri.* ● *main public hols.* 🎞 📷 ♿ *limited.*

The rooftop of the church of Agios Nikólaos Ragavás, Pláka

THE AMERICAN SCHOOL of Archaeology commenced excavations of the Ancient Agora in the 1930s, and since then a complex array of public buildings and temples has been revealed. The democratically governed Agora was the political and religious heart of Ancient Athens. Also the centre of commercial and daily life, it abounded with schools and elegant stoas filled with shops. The state prison was here, as was the mint, which was used to make the city's coins inscribed with the famous owl symbol. Even the remains of an olive oil mill have been found here.

The main building standing today is the impressive two-storey stoa of Attalos. This was rebuilt between 1953 and 1956 on the original foundations and using ancient building materials. Founded by King Attalos of Pergamon (ruled 159–138 BC), it dominated the eastern quarter of the Agora until it was destroyed in AD 267. It is used today as a museum, exhibiting the finds from the Agora. These include legal finds, such as a *klepsydra* (a water clock that was used for timing plaintiffs' speeches),

bronze ballots and items from everyday life such as some terracotta toys and leather sandals. The best-preserved ruins on the site are the Odeion of Agrippa, a covered theatre, and the Hephaisteion, a temple to Hephaistos, which is also known as the Theseion.

Acropolis ❺

See pp284–6.

Pláka ❻
Πλάκα

M *Monastiráki.* 🚌 *1, 2, 4, 5, 9, 10, 11, 12, 15, 18.*

THE AREA OF PLAKA is the historic heart of Athens. Even though only a few buildings date back further than the Ottoman period, it remains the oldest continuously inhabited area in the city.

One probable explanation of its name comes from the word used by Albanian soldiers in the service of the Turks who settled here in the 16th century – *pliaka* (old) was how they used to describe the area. Despite the constant swarm of tourists and Athenians, who come to eat in old-fashioned tavernas or browse in the antique and icon shops, Pláka still retains the atmosphere of a traditional neighbourhood. The only Byzantine monument still intact in Athens is the **Lysikrates Monument** in Plateía Lysikrátous. Built to commemorate the victors at the annual choral and dramatic festival at the Theatre of Dionysos, these monuments take their name from the sponsor *(choregos)* of the winning team.

Detail from a terracotta roof, Pláka

Many churches are worth a visit: the 11th-century **Agios Nikólaos Ragavás** has ancient columns built into the walls.

The **Tower of the Winds**, in the far west of Pláka, lies in the grounds of the Roman Agora. It was built by the Syrian astronomer Andronikos Kyrrestes around 100 BC as a weather vane and water-clock. On each of its marble sides one of the eight myth-ological winds is depicted.

🏛 **Tower of the Winds**
Plateía Aéridon. **(** 210 324 5220. ☐ *daily.* ● *main public hols.* 🎞

The façade of the Hephaisteion in the Ancient Agora

Acropolis ❺
Ακρόπολη

I N THE MID-5TH CENTURY BC, Perikles persuaded
the Athenians to begin a grand programme of
new building work in Athens that has come to
represent the political and cultural achievements
of Greece. The work transformed the Acropolis
with three contrasting temples and a monumental
gateway. The Theatre of Dionysos on the south
slope was developed further in the 4th century
BC, and the Theatre of Herodes Atticus was
added in the 2nd century AD.

**The Acropolis with the Temple of
Olympian Zeus in the foreground**

**★ Porch of the
Caryatids**
*These statues of
women were used
in place of columns
on the south porch
of the Erechtheion.
The originals, four
of which can be
seen in the Acropolis
Museum, have been
replaced by casts.*

An olive tree now
grows where Athena
first planted her tree
in a competition
against Poseidon.

The Propylaia was built
in 437–432 BC to form a
new entrance to the
Acropolis.

★ Temple of Athena Nike
*This temple to Athena of
Victory is on the west side
of the Propylaia. It was
built in 427–424 BC.*

The Beulé Gate
was the first
entrance to
the Acropolis.

**Pathway to
Acropolis
from ticket
office**

STAR SIGHTS

★ **Parthenon**

★ **Porch of the
Caryatids**

★ **Temple of
Athena Nike**

Theatre of Herodes Atticus
*Also known as the Odeion of
Herodes Atticus, this superb
theatre was originally built
in AD 161. It was restored in
1955 and is used today for
outdoor concerts.*

★ Parthenon

Although few sculptures are left on this famous temple to Athena, some can still be admired, such as this one from the east pediment (see p286)

Acropolis Museum (p286)

VISITORS' CHECKLIST

Dionysíou Areopagítou (main entrance), Pláka. **Map** 6 D2.
Site ☎ 210 321 0219.
Museum ☎ 210 323 6665.
Ⓜ Acropolis. 🚌 230, 231.
Site & Museum
🕐 Apr–Oct: 8am–6:30pm daily.
Nov–Mar: 8am–2:30pm daily.
⬤ 1 Jan, 25 Mar, Easter Sun,
1 May, 25, 26 Dec.
📷 🎫
🆆 www.culture.gr

Two Corinthian columns are the remains of *choregic* monuments erected by sponsors of successful dramatic performances.

Panagía Spiliótissa is a chapel cut into the Acropolis rock itself.

Shrine of Asklepios

Stoa of Eumenes

The Acropolis rock was an easily defended site. It has been in use for nearly 5,000 years.

Theatre of Dionysos

This figure of the comic satyr, Silenus, can be seen here. The theatre visible today was built by Lykourgos in 333–330 BC.

TIMELINE

3000 BC First settlement on the Acropolis during Neolithic period			**AD 51** St Paul delivers sermon on Areopagos hill	**AD 267** Germanic Heruli tribe destroy Acropolis	*St Paul*
	480 BC All buildings of Archaic period destroyed by the Persians				
3000 BC	**2000 BC**	**1000 BC**	**AD 1**	**AD 1000**	
	1200 BC Cyclopean wall built to replace original ramparts		**417–438 BC** Construction of the Parthenon under Perikles	**AD 1687** Parthenon damaged by Venetians	
	510 BC Delphic Oracle declares Acropolis a holy place of the gods, banning habitation by mortals		*Perikles (495–429 BC)*	**AD 1987** Restoration of the Erechtheion completed	

Exploring the Acropolis

ONCE THROUGH THE PROPYLAIA, the grand entrance to the site, the Parthenon exerts an overwhelming fascination. The other fine temples on "the Rock" include the Erechtheion and the Temple of Athena Nike. Since 1975, access to all the temple precincts has been banned. However, it is a miracle that anything remains at all. The ravages of war, the removal of treasures and pollution have all taken their irrevocable toll on the Acropolis.

The *Moschophoros* (or Calf-Bearer) in the Acropolis Museum

A section from the north frieze of the Parthenon

The Parthenon

One of the world's most famous buildings, the Parthenon was commissioned by Perikles as part of his rebuilding plan. Work began in 447 BC when the sculptor Pheidias was entrusted with supervising the building of a magnificent new Doric temple to Athena, the patron goddess of the city. It was built on the site of earlier Archaic temples, and was designed primarily to house the *Parthenos*, Pheidias's impressive 12-m (39-ft) high cult statue of Athena covered in ivory and gold.

Taking nine years to complete, the temple was dedicated to the goddess during the Great Panathenaia festival of 438 BC. Designed and constructed in Pentelic marble by the architects Kallikrates and Iktinos, the complex architecture of the Parthenon replaces straight lines with slight curves. This is generally thought to have been done to prevent visual distortion or perhaps to increase the impression of grandeur. All the columns swell in the middle and all lean slightly inwards, while the foundation platform rises towards the centre.

For the pediments and the friezes which ran all the way round the temple, an army of sculptors and painters was employed. Agorakritos and Alkamenes, both pupils of Pheidias, are two of the sculptors who worked on the frieze, which represented the people and horses in the Panathenaic procession.

Despite much damage and alterations made to adapt to its various uses, which include a church, a mosque, and even an arsenal, the Parthenon remains a powerful symbol of the glories of ancient Greece. It is currently being restored.

Acropolis Museum

Built below the level of the Parthenon, this museum is located in the southeast corner of the site. Opened in 1878, it was reconstructed after World War II to accommodate a collection that was devoted solely to finds from the Acropolis. Among the treasures are some beautiful statues dating from the 5th century BC and segments of the Parthenon frieze.

The collection begins chronologically with 6th-century BC works in **Rooms I**, **II** and **III** where the *Moschophoros* or Calf-Bearer (c.570 BC) is displayed along with fragments of pedimental statues of mythological scenes. In **Room V** there is a pediment from the old Temple of Athena. **Rooms IV** and **VI** display a unique collection of *korai* (550–500 BC), votive statues of maidens offered to the goddess Athena.

Rooms VII and **VIII** contain, among other exhibits, fragments from the Erechtheion frieze and a well-preserved *metope* from the south side of the Parthenon. The collection ends in **Room IX** with the four remaining caryatids from the Erechtheion, carefully kept behind glass in a temperature-controlled environment.

View of the Parthenon from the southwest at sunrise

Benáki Museum ❼
Μουσείο Μπενάκη

Corner of Koumpári & Vasilíssis
Sofías, Kolonáki. 📞 210 367 1000.
🚊 3, 7, 8, 13. ⏰ ring for opening
hours. ⬤ main public hols. 🎫 (free
Thu). 📷 ♿ limited.

THIS OUTSTANDING museum
contains a diverse collection of Greek art and crafts,
jewellery, regional costumes
and political memorabilia from
the 3rd century BC to the 20th
century. It was founded by
Antónios Benákis (1873–1954),
the son of Emmanouíl Benákis,
a wealthy Greek who made
his fortune in Egypt. Antónios
Benákis was interested in
Greek, Persian, Egyptian and
Ottoman art from an early age
and started collecting while
living in Alexandria. When he
moved to Athens in 1926, he
donated his collection to the
Greek State, using the family
house as a museum which was
opened to the public in 1931.
The elegant Neo-Classical
mansion was built towards
the end of the 19th century
by Anastásios Metaxás, who
was also the architect of the
Kallimármaro stadium.

The Benáki collection is
made up of gold jewellery,
some dating from as far back
as 3000 BC, as well as icons,
pieces of liturgical silverware,
Egyptian artifacts, Greek
embroideries and the work of
the late artist Chatzikyriákos-
Gkíkas. The museum also
houses temporary exhibitions
of cultural interest.

Museum of Cycladic Art ❽
Μουσείο Κυκλαδικής
και Αρχαίας Ελληνικής
Τέχνης

Neofýtou Doúka 4 (new wing at
Irodótou 1), Kolonáki. 📞 210 722
8321. 🚊 3, 7, 8, 13. ⏰ 10am–4pm
Mon & Wed–Fri, 10am–3pm Sun.
⬤ main public hols. 🎫 📷 ♿ 🖥

OPENED IN 1986, this modern
museum offers the visitor
the world's finest collection of
Cycladic art. Assembled by
Nikólaos and Dolly Goulandrís
and helped by the donations
of other Greek collectors, it

has brought together a fine
selection of ancient Greek art,
spanning 5,000 years of history.

The museum is clearly laid
out and provides a relaxed
atmosphere in which to view
the exhibits. Spread over five
floors, the displays start on the
first floor, which is home to
the Cycladic collection. Dating
back to the 3rd millennium
BC, the Cycladic figurines
were found mostly in graves,
although their exact
usage remains a
mystery. One of the
finest examples is the
Harp Player. Ancient
Greek art is exhibited
on the second floor
and the Charles Polítis
collection of Classical
and Prehistoric art on
the fourth floor,
high-lights of which
include some terra-
cotta figurines of
women from Tanágra,
central Greece. The third
floor of the museum is used for
temporary, visiting exhibitions.

A new wing was opened in
the adjoining Stathátos Mansion
in 1992, named after its original inhabitants, Otto and
Athiná Stathátos. It houses the
Greek Art Collection of the
Athens Academy. Temporary
exhibitions are also
on display on the
first floor of the
Stathátos
Mansion.

**Seated
Cycladic figure**

National Gallery of Art ❾
Εθνική Πινακοθήκη

Vasiléos Konstantínou 50, Ilísia. 📞 210
723 5937. 🚊 3, 13. ⏰ 9am–3pm,
Mon, Wed–Sat (also 6–9pm Mon &
Wed), 10am–2pm Sun. ⬤ main
public hols. 🎫 ♿

THIS MODERN, low-
rise building holds
a permanent collection
of European and
Greek art. The first
floor is devoted
mainly to European art
and includes works by
Van Dyck, Cézanne,
Dürer and Rembrandt,
as well as Picasso's
*Woman in a White
Dress* (1939) and Carav-
aggio's *Singer* (1620).
Most of the collection
is made up of Greek
art from the 18th to
20th centuries. The
1800s feature paintings of the
War of Independence (*see
pp38–9*). There are also some
excellent portraits including
The Loser of the Bet (1878) by
Nikólaos Gýzis (1842–1901),
Waiting (1900) by Nikifóros
Lýtras (1832–1904) and *The
Straw Hat* (1925) by Nikólaos
Lýtras 1883–1927).
Temporary exhi-
bitions are on
the ground
floor.

Icon of the *Adoration of the Magi* from the Benáki Museum

Getting Around Athens

Trolleybus stop sign

THE SIGHTS OF ATHENS' city centre are closely packed, and almost everything of interest can be reached on foot. This is the best way of sightseeing, especially in view of the appalling traffic congestion, which can make both public and private transport slow and inefficient. The expansion of the metro system should go some way to relieve these traffic problems but, until its completion, the bus and trolleybus network provides the majority of public transport in the capital for Athenians and visitors alike. Taxis are a useful alternative and, with the lowest tariffs of any EU capital, are worth considering even for longer journeys.

Orange and white regional bus for the Attica area

One of the large fleet of blue and white buses

BUS SERVICES IN ATHENS

ATHENS IS SERVED by an extensive bus network. Bus journeys are inexpensive, but can be slow and uncomfortably crowded, particularly in the city centre and during rush hours; the worst times are from 7am to 8:30am, 2pm to 3:30pm and 7:30pm to 9pm.

Tickets can be bought individually or in a book of ten, but either way, they must be purchased in advance from a *períptero* (street kiosk), a transport booth, or certain other designated places. The brown, red and white logo, with the words *eisitíria edó*, indicates where you can buy bus tickets. The same ticket can be used on any bus or trolleybus, and must be stamped in a special ticket machine to cancel it when you board. There is a penalty fine for not stamping your ticket. Tickets are valid for one ride only, regardless of the distance and, within the central area, are not transferable from one vehicle to another.

Athens bus ticket booth

USEFUL ROUTES IN ATHENS

Work continues on the metro extension to Kerameikós. The metro station for the site will be Botanikós and it is due to be in operation by 2006.

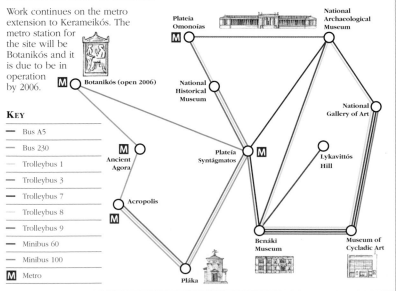

KEY

— Bus A5
— Bus 230
— Trolleybus 1
— Trolleybus 3
— Trolleybus 7
— Trolleybus 8
— Trolleybus 9
— Minibus 60
— Minibus 100
M Metro

Plateía Omonoías
National Archaeological Museum
Botanikós (open 2006)
National Historical Museum
National Gallery of Art
Ancient Agora
Plateía Syntágmatos
Lykavittós Hill
Acropolis
Benáki Museum
Museum of Cycladic Art
Pláka

ΜΟΝΑΣΤΗΡΙΟΝ
Monastirion

Monastiráki metro sign

ATHENS BUS NETWORKS

THERE ARE FOUR principal bus networks serving greater Athens and the Attica region. They are colour coded: blue and white; red; orange and white; and green. Blue and white buses cover an extensive network of over 300 routes in greater Athens, connecting districts to each other and to central Athens. In order to reduce Athens' smog, some of these are being replaced with green and white "ecological" buses running on natural gas. A small network of minibuses with red stop signs operates in the city centre only.

Orange and white buses serve the area around Athens. On these you pay the conductor and, as distances are greater, fares are also more expensive. The two terminals for orange and white buses are both situated on Mavrommataíon, by Pedío tou Areos (Areos Park). Though you can board at any designated orange stop, usually you cannot get off until you are outside the city area. These buses are less frequent than the blue and white service, and on some routes stop running in the early evening.

Green express buses, the fourth category, travel between central Athens and Piraeus. Numbers 040 and 049 are very frequent – about every 6 minutes – running from Athinas, by Plateía Omonoías, to various stops in Piraeus, including Plateía Karaïskáki, at the main harbour.

TROLLEYBUSES IN ATHENS

ATHENS HAS a good network of trolleybuses, which are orange-yellow or purple and yellow in colour. There are about 19 routes that crisscross the city. They provide a good way of getting around the central sights. All routes pass the Pláka area. Route 3 is useful for visiting the National Archaeological Museum from Plateía Syntágmatos, and route 1 links Lárissis railway station with Plateía Omonoías and Plateía Syntágmatos.

Front view of an Athens trolleybus

ATHENS' METRO

THE METRO, which has three lines, is a fast and reliable means of transport in Athens.

Line 1, the original line, runs from Kifissiá in the north to Piraeus in the south, with central stations at Thiseío, Monastiráki, Omónoia and Victoria. The majority of the line is overland and only runs underground between Attikí and Monastiráki stations through the city centre. The line is used mainly by commuters, but offers visitors a useful alternative means of reaching Piraeus.

Lines 2 and 3 form part of a huge expansion of the system, due to be completed in time for the 2004 Olympic Games. The new lines have been built 20 m (66 ft) underground to avoid material of archaeological interest. Syntágma and Acropolis stations have displays of archaeological finds.

From June 2004 onwards line 2 will run from Agios Antónios in northwest Athens to Ilioúpoli in the southeast. Line 3 currently runs from Syntágma to Ethnikí Amyna in the northeast but is being extended to the Elefthérios Venizélos airport by June 2004. Its extension from Syntágma to Monastiráki is also due for completion by June 2004.

One ticket allows travel on any of the three lines and is valid for 90 minutes in one direction. This means you can exit the station, then go back and continue your journey within the time limit. An alternative, slightly cheaper, ticket is sold for single journeys on Line 1. All tickets can be bought at any metro station and must be validated before entering the train – use the machines at the platform entrances.

Trains run every five minutes from 5am to 12:30am on Line 1, and from 5:30am to midnight on Lines 2 and 3.

Archaeological remains on display at Syntágma metro station

DRIVING IN ATHENS

DRIVING IN ATHENS can be a nerve-racking experience, especially if you are not accustomed to Greek road habits. Many streets in the centre are pedestrianized and there are also plenty of one-way streets, so you need to plan routes carefully. Finding a parking space can also be very difficult. Despite appearances to the contrary, parking in front of a no-parking sign or on a single yellow line is illegal. There are small car parks at street level for legal parking, as well as under-ground car parks, though these usually fill up quickly.

In an attempt to reduce dangerously high air pollution levels, there is an "odd-even" driving system in force. Cars that have an odd number at the end of their licence plates can enter the central grid, also called the *daktýlios,* only on dates with an odd number, and cars with an even number at the end of their plates are only allowed on dates with an even number. To avoid this, some people have two cars – with an odd and even plate. The rule does not apply to foreign cars but, if possible, it is better to avoid taking your car into the city centre.

No parking on odd-numbered days of the month

No parking on even-numbered days of the month

Yellow Athens taxi

ATHENIAN TAXIS

SWARMS OF YELLOW taxis can be seen cruising around Athens at most times of the day or night. However, trying to persuade one to stop for you can be difficult, especially between 2pm and 3pm when taxi drivers usually change shifts. Then, they will only pick you up if you happen to be going in a direction that is convenient for them.

To hail a taxi, stand on the edge of the pavement and shout out your destination to any cab that slows down. If a cab's "TAXI" sign is lit up, then it is definitely for hire, (but often a taxi is also for hire when the sign is not lit). It is also common practice for drivers to pick up extra passengers along the way, so do not ignore the occupied cabs. If you are not the first passenger, take note of the meter reading immediately: there is no fare-sharing, so you should be charged for your portion of the journey only, (or the minimum fare of 1.5 euros, whichever is greater).

Athenian taxis are extremely cheap by European standards – depending on traffic, you should not have to pay more than 2.5 euros to go anywhere in the downtown area, and between 4.5 and 7.5 euros from the centre to Piraeus. Double tariffs come into effect between midnight and 5am, and for journeys that exceed certain distances from the city centre. Fares to the airport, which is out of town at Spáta, are between 12 and 15 euros. There are also small surcharges for extra pieces of luggage weighing over 10 kg (22 lbs), and for journeys from the ferry or railway terminals. Taxi fares are increased during holiday periods, such as Christmas and Easter.

For an extra charge, (1–2.5 euros), you can make a phone call to a radio taxi company and arrange for a car to pick you up at an appointed place and time. Radio taxis are plentiful in the Athens area. Listed below are the telephone numbers of a few companies:

Express
[01 993 4812.
Kosmos
[1300.
Hellas
[01 645 7000.

WALKING

THE CENTRE OF ATHENS is very compact, and almost all major sights and museums are to be found within a 20- or 25-minute walk of Plateía Syntágmatos, which is generally regarded as the city's centre. This is worth bearing in mind, particularly when traffic is

Sign for a pedestrianized area

congested, all buses are full, and no taxi will stop. Athens is still one of the safest European cities in which to walk around, though, as in any sizeable metropolis, it pays to be vigilant, especially at night.

Visitors to Athens, walking up Areopagos Hill

ATHENS TRANSPORT LINKS

THE HUB OF ATHENS' city transport is the area around Plateía Syntágmatos and Plateía Omonoías. From this central area trolleybuses or buses can be taken to the airport, the sea port at Piraeus, Athens' two train stations, and its domestic and international coach terminals.

Bus E95 runs between the airport and Syntágmatos and bus E96 between the airport and Piraeus.

Buses 040 and 049 link Piraeus harbour with Syntágmatos and Omonoías in the city centre. The metro also extends to Piraeus harbour and the journey from the city centre to the harbour takes about 90 minutes.

Trolleybus route 1 goes past Lárissis metro station, as well as Lárissis train station (with the Peloponnísou station a short walk away from them both), while bus 024 goes to coach terminal B, on Liosíon, and bus 051 to coach terminal A, on Kifisoú.

Though more expensive than public transport, the most convenient way of getting to and from any of these destinations is by taxi. The journey times vary greatly but, if traffic is free flowing, from the city centre to the airport takes about 40 minutes; the journey from the city centre to the port of Piraeus takes around 40 minutes; and the journey from Piraeus to the airport takes about 90 minutes.

Bus from the port of Piraeus to Athens' city centre

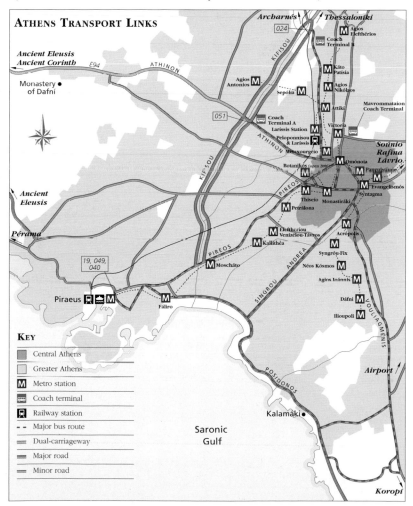

TRAVELLERS' NEEDS

WHERE TO STAY 294-311
WHERE TO EAT 312-333

WHERE TO STAY

Accommodation in the Greek islands is functional in most cases, and occasionally inspired. It is almost always abundant in a country that depends so heavily on tourism, and consequently is good value compared with most other European destinations. Despite inroads of commercialization in the busier resorts, hospitality off the beaten track

Holiday apartment sign, Ionian Islands

can still be warm and heartfelt. Various types of accommodation are described over the next four pages. Information is also given for camping and hostelling. The listings section on pages 298–311 includes over 150 places to stay, ranging from informal *domátia* (rooms) and alpine refuges, to luxurious hotels and accommodation in restored buildings.

HOTELS

MOST GREEK HOTELS are of standard Mediterranean concrete architecture, though in coastal resorts height limits restrict the building of vast towering structures. Many surviving hotels date from the 1967–74 Junta era, when massive investment in "modern" tourism was encouraged. A very few Neo-Classical, or older, hotels remain – now benefiting from government preservation orders.

Hotels built since the 1980s are generally designed with greater imagination and

sensitivity to the environment. The more expensive hotels will have a correspondingly higher level of service, offered by trained personnel.

CHAIN HOTELS

GREECE, with its tradition of family business ownership, has not taken to the idea of chain hotels. Among the few that operate on the islands, the oldest is the formerly state-run Xenía, founded during the 1950s. Most of their hotels, with well-worn facilities and indifferent service, are worth avoiding. Newer chains, such

as **Grecotel** on Crete and **Chandris Hotels** on Corfu and Chíos, are a better bet. Grecotel have essentially consolidated the management of previously existing hotels.

RESTORED SETTLEMENTS AND BUILDINGS

DURING THE 1970s, the EOT (Greek Tourist Office) began sponsoring the restoration of derelict buildings in vernacular style for accommodation. They usually offer good value for money and an exceptionally atmospheric environment. Preservation considerations, however, often mean that bathrooms must be shared rather than *en suite*. Such developments are found at Psará and at Mestá, on the island of Chíos. The complex at Mestá, however, has now been privatized, reflecting the growing commercial interest in such developments.

Private entrepreneurs have also successfully installed many small and medium-sized hotels in centuries-old buildings. Ventures that have worked well can be found on the islands of Ydra, Crete (at Chaniá and Réthymno), Sými, Mýkonos, Sýros, Lésvos, Folégandros and Kálymnos.

DOMATIA

A LARGE PROPORTION of Greek accommodation, especially on the small islands, is in *domátia*, or rented rooms. Formerly these would often be in the home of the managing family, but nowadays they

Hotel Alykí (see p304), with boats at the waterfront, on Sými

◁ Stení Valá Taverna on the island of Alónnisos

Skiáthos Palace Hotel *(see p300)*

are far more likely to be in a separate, purpose-built, modern structure. They are generally good value compared to hotels of the same comfort. Increasingly they have *en suite* bathrooms, are well appointed with neutral pine furniture, and often have a kitchen for guests' use. There is usually no communal area, however, and hot water is either provided by an electric immersion heater, or by a solar energy device.

GRADING

Hotels and domatia are graded by the EOT. Hotel categories range from E-class up to A-class, plus de luxe. *Domátia* range from C-class to A-class. There is supposed to be a direct correlation between amenities and the classification, but there are often deviations – usually the result of a dispute with the local authorities.

E-class hotels, with the most basic facilities and narrow profit margins, are almost extinct. D-class still survive, and these should have at least some rooms *en suite*. In a C-class hotel, all rooms must have *en suite* bathrooms, and the hotel must have some sort of common area, if only a small combination bar and breakfast area where a basic continental breakfast can be served. B-class hotels must have extra amenities such as a full-service restaurant, a more substantial breakfast, and at least one sports facility, such as a pool or tennis court. A-class hotels are usually at beachfront locations, and offer all conceivable diversions, as well as aids for the business traveller, such as

conference halls or telecommunications facilities. De luxe hotels are the same, only more so – effectively self-contained resort complexes.

C-class *domátia*, offering baths down the hall and "jail-like" decor, are on the way out, supplanted by B-class blocks with guaranteed *en suite* plumbing and often a shared kitchen. A-class rooms are nearly synonymous with apartments; landscaping is usually superior and kitchens are built into each unit.

PRICES

The price of hotel rooms and *domátia* should correspond to their official category, though rates are variable, depending on high or low season and location. For around 25 euros, it is possible to find a C-class *domátio* for two without bathroom, or an E/D-class hotel; 35–45 euros covers a B-class double *domátio*, while A-class *domátia* cost up to 90 euros and C-class hotels charge between 60 and 120 euros. B-class hotels ask 90 to 135 euros per double room, while A-class hotels typically cost from 130 to 180 euros. De luxe resorts are exempt from the EOT price control scheme and can easily run in excess of

Dodecanese window

180 euros per night. These rates are only the official EOT rates, including VAT and municipal taxes; prices can drop by up to 50 per cent in early spring or late autumn. Rates include breakfast, but stays of less than three nights can incur surcharges in high season.

OPENING SEASONS

Most island hotels, and all island *domátia*, operate only during peak season (late April to late October). But if Orthodox Easter falls early in April, many facilities may open then. *Domátia* are in fact forbidden by law to be open during winter. At such times your options may be limited to a single hotel at an island's main port. The listings in this guide indicate when hotels are closed.

BOOKING

The most common and cost-effective method of booking accommodation is by reserving in advance through a package holiday or travel agency. If, however, you contact a hotel direct, it is better to do so by fax so that the transaction is properly recorded in writing.

You may also be asked to provide a credit card number, or forward travellers' cheques equivalent to the value of the first night's stay in advance. If you fail to show up this sum is forfeitable.

Stélla Tsakíri *(see p300)* at Volissós, Chíos

SELF-CATERING APARTMENTS AND VILLAS

SELF-CATERING apartments or villas are known as studios or *garsonières*, and are the logical outgrowth of *domátia*. The main differences are that kitchens are built into each studio or multi-bedroom unit, and many have swimming pools and landscaped gardens.

With few exceptions, these are far better equipped and easy to reserve through overseas package holiday companies. Many villas are block-booked yearly by particular companies and are essentially not available to independent travellers. But in slow years, where this is not the case, the best strategy is personally to visit travel agencies in the island town concerned – they will know of any current vacancies and place you in a villa for a modest commission. In the low season it is sometimes possible to get a villa or apartment long term, by direct negotiation with the owners.

YOUTH HOSTELS

THE GREEK ISLANDS have seven youth hostels *(xenón neótitos)* recognized by the IYHF (International Youth Hostel Federation). The hostels are found on Santoríni, Corfu and on Crete at Irákleio, Réthymno, Plakiás, Siteía and Myrtiá. Greek hostels are not nearly as regimented as their northern European equivalents. Even without an IYHF membership card, it is usually

Monastery of Agios Geórgios on Skýros *(see pp112–13)*

possible to stay at a hostel, providing a vacancy is available, by paying a supplement.

There are also a handful of unofficial hostels that operate on the islands. These can be very good, and are often better equipped than the IYHF-recognized hostels.

ALPINE REFUGES

AMONG THE ISLANDS, only Crete has bona fide alpine refuges, or *katafýgia*. There are three on the island: one on Mount Psiloreítis and two in Chaniá's White Mountains. The refuge at Kallérgi, above the Samariá Gorge in the White Mountains, is the only one staffed most of the year round. For the other two, keys must be rented from Irákleio and Chaniá respectively, at branches of the **EOS** (Greek Alpine Club). This will, however, prove an expensive undertaking unless you are part of a large group.

RURAL TOURISM

CONCEIVED DURING the 1980s to give women in the Greek provinces a measure of financial independence, rural tourism allows foreigners to stay on a bed-and-breakfast basis in a village house, and also provides the opportunity to participate, if desired, in the daily life of a farming community. There is one such programme on the Greek islands, at Pétra (Lésvos), which is managed by a **Women's Rural Tourism Cooperative**. The Pétra cooperative runs a centrally located, good-value restaurant, featuring regional cuisine. Booking is made to each local cooperative directly.

MONASTERIES

THE LESS-TOURISTED monasteries and convents in Greece operate *xenónes* or hostels, intended primarily for Greek Orthodox pilgrims on weekend visits. They will always have priority, but it is often possible to find a vacancy at short notice.

Accommodation is of the spartan-dormitory variety, with a frugal evening meal and morning coffee also provided; it is customary to leave a donation in the *katholikón* (main church).

On the islands the tradition of hospitality, dating back to medieval times, is on the wane – a victim of mass tourism and its attendant commercialization. However, especially in the remoter parts of Rhodes, Crete and other large islands, it is possible to stay in staffed monasteries.

CAMPING

THE GREEK ISLANDS have nearly 80 officially recognized campsites. Most of these are in attractive beachfront settings, and also cater to caravanners. A small minority are owned and managed by the EOT (although they are soon to be privatized), or by the local municipality; the rest are privately run. All but the most primitive sites have solar-heated hot showers, shady

Self-catering apartment on Santoríni

landscaping, a snack bar or café, and power hookups available for an extra fee. The most luxurious campsites are miniature holiday villages, with swimming pool, tennis courts, laundry rooms, banking and postal facilities and bungalows for the tentless. The ground at the sites is generally hard, so short pegs are best. For a regularly updated booklet on campsites and their amenities, contact the **Greek Camping Association**.

Green hotel *(see p308)* in Spíli, Crete

DISABLED TRAVELLERS

THE GUIDE *Holidays and Travel Abroad*, which is published by **RADAR** (Royal Association for Disability and Rehabilitation) provides

Lakka Paxi Camping, on the Ionian Islands

details on wheelchair access to the more established hotels, and is worth contacting for advice. Other organizations which provide useful information for disabled travellers about access to hotels and places of interest in Greece include **Holiday Care Service** and **Tripscope**. In the hotel listings of this guide we have indicated which establishments have facilities, such as lifts, for the disabled.

Greek information sources for disabled travellers tend to be rudimentary: the EOT only publishes a questionnaire, which can be sent to specific establishments to assess the suitability of their facilities.

FURTHER INFORMATION

THE INVALUABLE *Guide to Hotels* is published by, and available from, the EOT (Greek Tourist Office). It covers all officially registered hotels – though not villas or *domátia* – indicating prices, facilities and the operating season. *Camping in Greece*, published free by the Greek Camping Association is also available from EOT offices. There are two other, privately issued, publications, the monthly *Greek Travel Pages* (GTP) and the quarterly *Tourist Guide of Greece*. Both offer skeletal information, unless the hotel concerned has purchased advertising space.

DIRECTORY

CHAIN HOTELS

Chandris Hotels
Syngroú 385, 17564 Paléo Fáliron, Athens.
(210 947 1000.

Club Méditerranée Hellas SA
Syngroú 143, 11721 Athens.
(210 930 1191/2
W www.clubmed.com

Divani Hotels
Parthenónos 19–25, 11742 Athens.
(210 922 9650.

Grecotel
Emanoúil Portalioú 23, 74100 Réthymno, Crete.
(28310 71002 (Crete).
(210 725 0920 (Athens).

Mamidakis Hotels of Greece

Panepistimíou 56, 106/8 Athens.
(210 381 9781-6.

Zante Hotels
PO Box 191, Laganás 29100, Zákynthos.
(26950 52310.
W www.zanteweb.gr

HOSTELS

IYHF (UK)
1st floor, Fountain House, Parkway, Welwyn Garden City, Herts AL8 6JH, England.
(01707-324170.

IYHF (Greece)
Víktoros Ougó 16, 10438 Athens.
(210 523 2049.

ALPINE REFUGES

EOS (Ellinikós Orivatikós Sýndesmos)

(Greek Alpine Club)
Filadelfías 126, 13671 Acharnés, Attica.
(210 246 1528.

WOMEN'S RURAL TOURISM COOPERATIVE

Pétra, Lésvos
(22530 41238.

CAMPING

Greek Camping Association
Sólonos 102, 10680 Athens. (210 362 1560.

DISABLED TRAVELLERS

Holiday Care Service
2nd floor, Imperial Buildings, Victoria Rd, Horley RH6 7PZ.
(01293 774535.

RADAR
12 City Forum, 250 City Rd, London EC1V 8AF.
(020 725 03222.

Tripscope
The Courtyard, Evelyn Rd, London W4 5JL.
(08457 585641.
W www.tripscope.org.uk

FURTHER INFORMATION

Greek Travel Pages
Psýlla 6, 10557 Athens.
(210 324 7511.
W www.gtp.gr

Hellenic Chamber of Hotels
Stadíou 24, 10564 Athens.
(210 331 0022.
@ grhotels@otenet.gr

Tourist Guide of Greece
Patission 137, 11251 Athens.
(210 864 1688.

Choosing a Hotel

Tнеse нотеls have been selected across a wide price range for their good value, facilities and location; they are listed by area, starting with the Ionian Islands. Use the colour-coded thumb tabs, which indicate the regions covered on each page, to guide you to the relevant section of the chart. For more information on hotels see pages 294–7.

	NUMBER OF ROOMS	RESTAURANT	CLOSE TO BEACH	SWIMMING POOL	AIR-CONDITIONING
THE IONIAN ISLANDS					
CORFU: *Akrotíri Beach* €€€€€ T Desýlla 155, Palaiokastrítsa, 49083. 26630 41237. FAX 26630 41277. One of the best hotels in this popular resort, the Akrotíri Beach enjoys a lovely setting on a headland. ● Nov–Apr.	127	●	■	●	■
CORFU: *Bella Venezia* @ belvenht@hol.gr €€€€€ N Zampéli 4, Corfu town, 49100. 26610 46500. FAX 26610 20708. Close to the town centre, this Neo-Classical mansion has high- ceilinged rooms which are comfortable and tasteful without being extravagant. Hospitable and courteous staff.	32		■		■
CORFU: *Corfu Palace* €€€€€ Leofóros Dimokratías 2, Corfu town, 49100. 26610 39485-7. FAX 26610 31749. This luxury hotel is set in beautiful tropical gardens, with a peaceful, seafront location and views to the Greek mainland.	106	●	■	●	■
CORFU: *Divani Palace* €€€€€ Nafsikás 20, Corfu town, 49100. 26610 38996-8. FAX 26610 35929. A smart hotel, situated 3 km (2 miles) outside Corfu town, on a wooded hillside overlooking the lagoon of Kanóni. ● Nov–Mar.	164	●	■	●	■
CORFU: *San Stéfano* €€€€€ Seafront, Benítses, 49081. 26610 71118. FAX 26610 71124. @ sanstefano@hol.gr This smart hotel was once used to accommodate European politicians at a conference, so facilities are excellent. ● Nov–Mar.	259	●	■	●	■
ITHACA: *Méntor* €€€€€ Vathý harbourfront, 28300. 26740 33033. FAX 26740 32293. A small, smart hotel, it is kept spotless by family owners. There is a bar in the roof garden, ideal for watching the sun go down.	36	●	■		■
KEFALLONIA: *Kefalloniá Star* €€€€ Ioánnou Metaxá 60, Argostóli, 28100. 26710 23181. FAX 26710 23180. A long-established hotel on the main harbour road, it has some balconied front rooms and fine sea views. A comfortable place to stay.	42		■		
KEFALLONIA: *Rosa's Studios* €€€€€ Lourdata Beach, 28083. 26710 31105. FAX 26710 23469. These well-equipped studios have balconies overlooking the sea. With steps leading down to the pretty beach below, the sea couldn't be more accessible. Note that breakfast is not provided. ● Oct–Apr.	15		■		
KEFALLONIA: *Tourist* €€€€€ Antonis Tritsi 109, Argostóli, 28100. 26710 22510. FAX 26710 22510. Blue and white décor gives a very Greek look to this pleasant hotel on the waterfront. The rooms are comfortable and reasonably priced.	22	●	■		
LEFKADA: *Lefkás* €€€€€ Panágou 2, Lefkáda town, 31100. 26450 23916. FAX 26450 24579. A large, centrally located hotel, with friendly staff and a relaxed atmosphere. All the rooms are airy and spacious. ● Nov–Feb.	93	●	●		■
LEFKADA: *Nydrí* €€€€€ Seafront, Nydrí, 31100. 26450 92400. FAX 26450 92151. Situated on the waterfront, overlooking the nearby islands, this hotel offers well-equipped rooms with balconies. There is also a beach bar.	18		■		■
MEGANISI: *Meganísi* €€€€€ North of main square, Katoméri, 31083. 26450 51240. FAX 26450 51639. This family-run hotel is the only one on the island. It offers simple but comfortable accommodation in a rural setting.	25	●		●	■

	Price categories are for a standard double room for one night in peak season, including tax, service charges and breakfast: € under 25 euros €€ 25–35 euros €€€ 35–45 euros €€€€ 45–60 euros €€€€€ over 60 euros.	RESTAURANT — Restaurant within the hotel sometimes reserved for residents only. CLOSE TO BEACH — Within walking distance of the beach. SWIMMING POOL — Hotel swimming pools are usually quite small and outdoors unless otherwise stated. AIR-CONDITIONING — Hotel with air-conditioning in all the rooms.	NUMBER OF ROOMS	RESTAURANT	CLOSE TO BEACH	SWIMMING POOL	AIR-CONDITIONING
ZAKYNTHOS: *Montreal* €€€€€ Alykés, 29090. **(** 26950 83241. FAX 26950 83342. Right on the busy beach of this popular holiday resort, all of the rooms have sea views and are modern and well kept. ● *Nov–Apr.*			35	●	■		■
ZAKYNTHOS: *Strada Marína* €€€€€ Lomvárdou 14, Chóra, 29090. **(** 26950 42761. FAX 26950 28733. @ stradamarina@aias.gr The town's smartest hotel is right on the waterfront and its rooms offer all modern facilities. There is also a relaxing roof garden.			112	●	■	●	■

THE ARGO-SARONIC ISLANDS

			NUMBER OF ROOMS	RESTAURANT	CLOSE TO BEACH	SWIMMING POOL	AIR-CONDITIONING
AIGINA: *Aiginítiko Archontikó* €€€€€ Thomaídon 1, Aígina town, 18010. **(** 22970 24968. FAX 22970 26716. A Neo-Classical mansion with two courtyards and a roof garden. The public rooms are beautifully restored and the simple guest rooms contain brass beds and antique furniture. ● *Nov–Mar.*			10.				■
AIGINA: *Nafsiká* €€€€€ N Kazantzáki 55, Aígina town, 18010. **(** 22970 22333. FAX 22970 22477. This small, quiet family-run hotel is situated by the sea just outside town. It provides easy access to the archaeological site. ● *Nov–Mar.*			36	●	■		■
KYTHIRA: *Margaríta* €€€€€ Town centre, Chóra, 80100. **(** 27360 31711. FAX 27360 31325. Housed in a converted 19th-century mansion, this is Chóra's most elegant accommodation. Rooms do not have balconies. ● *Nov–Mar.*			12				
KYTHIRA: *Rigas Apartments* €€€€€ Kapsáli bay, 80100. **(** 27360 31265 FAX 27360 31265 These modern, self-sufficient apartments are built in the traditional island style, each with a kitchen, bathroom and balcony. ● *Nov–Mar.*			15		■		■
YDRA: *Hydra* €€€€€ Voúlgari 8, Ydra town, 18040. **(** 22980 52102. FAX 22980 52091. A converted mansion, set on the top of a hill in the west of the town. The most attractive rooms are those facing the harbour.			13				
YDRA: *Mistral* €€€€€ Ydra town, 18040. **(** 22980 52509. FAX 22980 53412 Situated at the southeast corner of town, the hotel does not have port views, but it is quiet with friendly staff and hearty breakfasts. ● *Nov–Feb.*			20				■
YDRA: *Neféli* €€€€€ Tsamadoú 8-14, Ydra town, 18040. **(** 22980 53297. FAX 22980 53297. This western hillside conversion has three terraces on which breakfast is served. The climb up is steep but the views are rewarding. ● *Nov–Feb.*			10		■		
YDRA: *Ydroússa* €€€€€ Behind park, Ydra town, 18040. **(** 22980 52400. FAX 22980 52161. Formerly the state-run Xenía, this rambling mansion has benefited from privatization. It is situated in the town centre.			36	●			■
SPETSES: *Poseidónion* €€€€€ On waterfront, Ntápia, Spétses town, 18050. **(** 22980 72308. FAX 22980 72208. This Edwardian hotel offers somewhat faded elegance especially in its ground-floor common areas. Insist on a seaward room with tall windows and views across to the Peloponnese. ● *Nov–Mar.*			52		■		
SPETSES: *Spétses* €€€€€ West of Ntápia, Spétses town, 18050. **(** 22980 72602. FAX 22980 72494. One of few high-quality hotels on the island at only a fraction more than most hotels here. All the rooms have views of the sea. ● *Nov–Mar.*			77	●	■		

For key to symbols see back flap

		Number of Rooms	Restaurant	Close to Beach	Swimming Pool	Air-Conditioning
Price categories are for a standard double room for one night in peak season, including tax, service charges and breakfast: € under 25 euros €€ 25–35 euros €€€ 35–45 euros €€€€ 45–60 euros €€€€€ over 60 euros.	**Restaurant** Restaurant within the hotel sometimes reserved for residents only. **Close to Beach** Within walking distance of the beach. **Swimming Pool** Hotel swimming pools are usually quite small and outdoors unless otherwise stated. **Air-Conditioning** Hotel with air-conditioning in all the rooms.					

THE SPORADES AND EVVOIA

	Number of Rooms	Restaurant	Close to Beach	Swimming Pool	Air-Conditioning
ALONNISOS: *Charavgí* €€€€€ Harbourfront, Patitíri. 📞 24240 65090. FAX 24240 65189. Wonderful views of the whole village can be enjoyed from this reasonably priced hotel. All rooms have balconies. ● *Nov–Mar.* 🛏 ♿ ▮	19		▨		▨
EVVOIA: *Béis* €€€€ Kými beach, 34003. 📞 22220 22604. FAX 22220 29113. This comfortable hotel offers rooms with a view of the port. There is also an excellent restaurant serving freshly caught fish. 🛏 ♿ ▮	38	●	▨		
EVVOIA: *Apollon* €€€€€ Kárystos bay, 34001. 📞 24240 22045-8. FAX 24240 22049. Situated on the edge of a lush bay, this modern hotel consists of suites overlooking the sea. Suites sleep five comfortably. ● *Nov–Mar.* 🛏 ▮ ▮ ▮	36	●	▨	●	▨
EVVOIA: *Candíli* W www.candili.co.uk €€€€€ 1 km (0.5 miles) from seafront, Prokópi, 34004. 📞 69740 62100. Set in a splendid estate, this hotel and seminar centre offers various courses such as mosaics and painting. A Landrover is available for use. 🛏 ▮ ▮	12			●	
SKIATHOS: *Atrium Hotel* €€€€€ Plataniás beach, Agía Paraskeví, 73002. 📞 24270 49376. FAX 24270 49444. A smart, newly built hotel set on a wooded hill above the sandy beach of Plataniás. All rooms have private balconies. ● *Oct–Mar.* 🛏 ▮ ▮ ▮	75	●	▨	●	▨
SKIATHOS: *Esperídes* €€€€€€ Achladiá, 6 km (4 miles) S of Skiathos town, 73002. 📞 24270 22245. FAX 24270 21580. Achladiá bay's resort hotel has excellent facilities including tennis courts. The spacious rooms overlook a sandy beach. ● *Nov–Mar.* 🛏 ▮	180	●	▨	●	▨
SKIATHOS: *Palace* €€€€€ Koukounariés beach, 37002. 📞 24270 49700. FAX 24270 49666. Situated on a sandy beach backed by pine trees, the rooms of this resort-type hotel all enjoy good sea views. ● *Nov–Mar.* 🛏 ♿ ▮ ▮ ▮	220	●	▨	●	▨
SKOPELOS: *Thea Home* €€€€ Waterfront, Skópelos town, 37003. 📞 24240 22859. FAX 24240 23556. This small, family-run hotel has a warm atmosphere and friendly staff. Rooms have balconies overlooking Skópelos bay. ● *Oct–Apr.* 🛏 ▮	12		▨		
SKOPELOS: *Zanétta* €€€€€ 300 m (990 ft) from the seafront, Elios, 37003. 📞 24240 33140. FAX 24240 33717. Consisting of 60 well-furnished apartments with kitchen units, the Zanétta is surrounded by beautiful woodland. ● *Oct–Apr.* 🛏 ♿ ▮	60	●		●	
SKYROS: *Neféli* €€€€€ Plagiá area, Skýros town, 34007. 📞 22220 91964. FAX 22220 92061. This traditional-style hotel situated on the edge of Skýros town, has ten independent rooms and nine separate flats. 🛏 ▮	22		▨		▨

THE NORTHEAST AEGEAN ISLANDS

	Number of Rooms	Restaurant	Close to Beach	Swimming Pool	Air-Conditioning
CHIOS: *Stélla Tsakíri* €€€ Plateía Pýrgou, Volissós, 82103. 📞 22740 21421. FAX 22740 21521. A cluster of traditional stone houses, meticulously renovated by an Athenian sculptor. They all have terraces, full kitchens and original features. 🛏 ▮	9				
CHIOS: *Kýma* @ kyma@chi.forthnet.gr €€€€€ Evgeníou Chandrí 1, Chíos town, 82100. 📞 22710 44500. FAX 22710 44600. A friendly, efficient, family-run hotel, overlooking the beach. It was originally built as a waterside villa for a Greek shipping magnate. 🛏 ▮	59		▨		▨

LESVOS: *Clára Hotel and Bungalows* €€€€€ 41
Avláki district, Pétra, 81109. **☎** 22530 41532-3. **FAX** 22530 41535.
A pastel-painted, well-landscaped, hillside complex, looking north
to Pétra and Mólyvos. All rooms have balconies and post modern,
minimalist decor. There are also tennis courts. ● *Oct–Mar.*

LESVOS: *Laureate* €€€€€ 35
Vareiá beach, 81100. **☎** 22510 43111. **FAX** 22510 41629.
This luxurious hotel is housed in a restored villa with private rooms,
studios and flats. It is set in a beautiful garden with avenues of
bay trees and wonderful giant pines.

LESVOS: *Olive Press* €€€€€ 41
Behind Mólyvos beach, 81108. **☎** 22530 71205. **FAX** 22530 71647.
A charming, characterful hotel, converted from an old olive press. The rooms
are arranged around an inner courtyard and are all spacious. There are
also 12 self-contained studios with kitchens. ● *15 Oct; Nov–Mar.*

LESVOS: *Vaterá Beach* €€€€€ 24
Vaterá beach, 81300. **☎** 22520 61212. **FAX** 22520 61164. **@** hovatera@otenet.gr
A modern and friendly, family-run establishment, overlooking a sandy
beach. All rooms have spacious balconies commanding wonderful
views of the Aegean and the mountains. ● *Nov–Apr.*

LIMNOS: *Akti Mýrina* €€€€€ 125
2 km (1 mile) N of Myrína, 81400. **☎** 22540 22681. **FAX** 22540 22947.
A luxury hotel comprising stone cottages with gardens, set on
terraces overlooking a private beach. The hotel is well-equipped
and offers tennis courts, a fitness centre and watersports facilities.
● *Oct–mid-May.*

LIMNOS: *Villa Afroditi* €€€€€ 12
Behind Platí beach, Platí, 81400. **☎** 22540 23141. **FAX** 22540 25031.
One of the cleanest hotels on the island and always busy. The attached
restaurant is popular and facilities are good. ● *Oct–Apr.*

SAMOS: *Fytó Bungalows* €€€€€ 87
800 m (2,600 ft) W of Pythagóreio, 83103. **☎** 22730 61314. **FAX** 22730 62045
A modern and comfortable hotel with a delightful garden and shaded
terrace. Ideally placed for exploring the local beaches and the
archaeological sites of Sámos. ● *Nov–Apr.*

SAMOS: *Olympia Beach* €€€€€ 12
On the beach, Kokkári, 83100. **☎** 22730 92353. **FAX** 22730 92457.
This quiet, family-run hotel enjoys a seafront setting with good views.
A traditional-style building with timber and marble interior. All rooms
have balconies. Close to all amenities. ● *Nov–Mar.*

SAMOS: *Sámaina Bay Hotel* €€€€€ 75
Karlóvassi beach, 83200. **☎** 22730 34004-8. **FAX** 22730 34009.
A comfortable hotel, not in an ideal location but well-run and long-
established. Some rooms have a sea view and the hotel has good facilities
including a sauna and large lounge area. ● *Nov–Mar.*

SAMOTHRAKI: *Kastro* w www.kastrohotel.gr €€€€€ 50
Paleópolis, 3 km (2 miles) N of Chóra, 68002. **☎** 25510 89400. **FAX** 25510 41000.
This is an upmarket hotel offering fine sea views. The hotel serves as a
convenient base for exploring the Sanctuary of the Great Gods.

THASOS: *Alkyón* €€€€€ 11
18 Octovriou, Harbourfront, Thásos town, 64004. **☎** 25930 22148. **FAX** 25930
23662. This highly recommended, small hotel is run by a team of botanical
and culinary experts. Botanical walking tours are on offer. ● *Nov–Apr.*

THASOS: *Miramáre* €€€€€ 30
Skála Potamiás, 64004. **☎** 25930 61040. **FAX** 25930 61043.
A modern hotel situated in a leafy ravine at the southern end of the
spectacular Chryssi Ammoudiá beach. ● *Nov–Apr.*

THASOS: *Alexándra Beach Hotel* **@** alexandra@tha.forthnet.gr €€€€€ 124
Potós beach, 64004. **☎** 25930 52391-8. **FAX** 25930 51185.
Perched on a headland above a 2 km (1 mile) beach, this hotel comprises
a large complex with all amenities. Tennis courts, fitness centre and
watersport gear hire are on offer. ● *Nov–Mar.*

Price categories are for a standard double room for one night in peak season, including tax, service charges and breakfast: € under 25 euros €€ 25–35 euros €€€ 35–45 euros €€€€ 45–60 euros €€€€€ over 60 euros.	**RESTAURANT** Restaurant within the hotel sometimes reserved for residents only. **CLOSE TO BEACH** Within walking distance of the beach. **SWIMMING POOL** Hotel swimming pools are usually quite small and outdoors unless otherwise stated. **AIR-CONDITIONING** Hotel with air-conditioning in all the rooms.	

THE DODECANESE

	NUMBER OF ROOMS	RESTAURANT	CLOSE TO BEACH	SWIMMING POOL	AIR-CONDITIONING
ASTYPALAIA: *Australía* €€€€ Opposite kástro, Astypálaia town, 85900. ☎ 22430 61275. ℻ 22430 61067. A modern, open-plan hotel situated on the seafront overlooking the castle. Balconies have sea views and there is a tree-shaded garden. Below the hotel is a restaurant offering fresh fish and meat grills. 🛏 🔧 ⛰	15	●	■		■
CHALKI: *Argyrénia* €€ Póntamos beach, Nimporió, 85110. ☎ 22460 45205. Set in lovely gardens off the road to Póntamos beach, the Argyrénia consists of chalet-style rooms with terraces. There are no cooking facilities but tavernas can be found nearby. 🛏 ♿ 🔧 ✉	9		■		
CHALKI: *Captain's House Pension* €€€ Off main square, Nimporió, 85110. ☎ 22460 45201. A delightful *pension* in a Neo-Classical mansion, run by an ex-Greek naval officer. Breakfast is served on the shady terrace. ● *Nov–Mar.* 🛏 🔧	3				■
KALYMNOS: *Galíni* €€ Main square, Vathý, 85200. ☎ 22430 31241. ℻ 22430 31100. Family-run *pension* overlooking the boatyard and Vathý bay. Rooms are simple but comfortable. Breakfast is served on the terrace. 🛏 🔧 ⛰ ✉	14	●	■		■
KALYMNOS: *Olympic Hotel* €€€€ Agios Nikolaos, 85200. ☎ 22430 28801. ℻ 22430 51713. Recently renovated, this hotel is located right at the heart of the marina, close to all amenities, and only minutes from the beach. 🛏 🔧 ✉	42		■		■
KALYMNOS: *Panórama* €€€€ Harbourfront, Póthia, 85200. ☎ 22430 23138. ℻ 22430 23138. This small hotel is set back from the bustling seafront. It is beautifully decorated and offers magnificent views of the sea. 🛏	13		■		■
KARPATHOS: *Amoopí Bay* €€€€ Amoopí beach, 85700. ☎ 22450 81184. ℻ 22450 81105. Situated right on the beach, the rooms are basic but all have balconies, and the price includes breakfast and dinner. ● *Nov–Mar.* 🔧	65		■		
KASOS: *Anagénnisis* €€€€ Town centre, Frý, 85855. ☎ 22450 41495. ℻ 22450 41036. A comfortable American-Greek run establishment. Expect to pay more for rooms enjoying sea views. 🛏	12		■		
KASTELLORIZO: *Mavrothalassítis* 🌐 www.kastellorizo.de €€€ Behind harbour, Kastellórizo town, 85111. ☎ 22460 49028. ℻ 22410 49208. A restored mansion hotel, run by Australian-Greek brothers, with *en suite* facilities and cool bedrooms. 🛏	6		■		
KASTELLORIZO: *Megísti* €€€€€ Harbourfront, Kastellórizo town, 85111. ☎ 22410 49272. ℻ 22410 67062. A municipal hotel, overlooking the harbour. Probably the most comfortable accommodation in the town. ● *Nov–Mar.* 🛏 ✉	17		■		
KOS: *Afentoúlis* €€€ Evripídou 1, Kos town, 85300. ☎ 22460 25321. ℻ 22460 25797. A small family-run hotel with very friendly management, in a quiet spot close to the sea. There is a lovely jasmine-filled garden. ● *Oct–Mar.* 🛏 🔧	17		■		
KOS: *Karávia Beach* @ karavia@kos.forthnet.gr €€€€€ Karávia beach, 2 km (1 mile) N of Pylí, 85300. ☎ 22420 41291-4. ℻ 22420 41215. A luxury holiday complex, where the emphasis is on organized entertainment, including boat trips to the nearby islands. ● *Nov–Apr.* 🛏 ♿ 🔧 ⛰ ✉	300	●	■	●	■

Kos: *Porto Bello Beach* €€€€€ | 350
Seafront, 2 km (1 mile) W of Kardamaína, 85300. (22420 01217. FAX 22420 91168.
Situated right on the beach, this resort hotel consists of whitewashed bunga-
lows. Sea views and a children's playground. ● *Nov–Apr.* 🖼 🖼 🖼 🖼 🖼

Leros: *Kávos* €€ | 10
Harbourfront, Pantéli, 85400. (22470 23247. FAX 22470 23247
This excellent, inexpensive guesthouse overlooks the picture-postcard
fishing harbour at Panteli. Some rooms have balconies. 🖼 🖼

Leros: *Archontikó Angélou* €€€€ | 17
Waterfront, Alinda, 85300. (22470 22749. FAX 22470 24403.
This hotel is housed in a traditional mansion built in 1895 during the
Turkish occupation. It is set in its own lovely grounds. ● *Nov–Mar* 🖼 🖼 🖼

Leros: *Voulaféntdis Bungalows* €€€€€ | 38
Seafront, Alinda, 85400. (22470 23515. FAX 22470 24533.
This luxury studio development is built around a traditional mansion.
There are good facilities and a piano bar. ● *Oct–Apr.* 🖼 🖼 🖼

Nisyros: *Porfýris* €€ | 15
Mandráki, 85111. (22420 31376. FAX 22420 31176
A pleasant, reasonably priced hotel overlooking the public orchards. There
are good views of the islet of Gyalí from the terrace. ● *Nov–Apr.* 🖼 🖼

Nisyros: *Charítos* €€€€ | 11
Behind harbourfront, Mandráki, 85111. (22420 31322. FAX 22420 31122.
Set back from Mandráki harbour, the Charítos is handy for the ferries. A
friendly *pension* with spacious rooms and balconies with sea views. 🖼 🖼

Patmos: *Artemis* €€€€€ | 24
At entrance to Gríkos resort, 85500. (22470 31555. FAX 22470 34016.
This resort hotel, comprising traditional island-style accommodation, enjoys
sea views and good facilities, including an athletic centre. ● *Nov–Mar.* 🖼 🖼

Patmos: *Astéri* €€€€€ | 26
Mérichas bay, Skála, 85500. (22470 32465. FAX 22470 31347.
This family-run hotel is in a quiet spot, overlooking Mérichas bay. The
owner keeps bees and serves honey for breakfast. ● *Nov–Feb.* 🖼 🖼 🖼 🖼

Patmos: *Australis* €€€€€€ | 24
500 m (1,650 ft) above town, Skála, 85500. (22470 31576. FAX 22470 32284.
Located in a peaceful area, this family-run *pension* is set in beautiful gardens.
Breakfast is served on the jasmine-scented terrace. ● *Nov–Mar.* 🖼 🖼

Patmos: *Golden Sun* €€€€€ | 24
Off Chóra–Gríkos road, 85500. (22470 32318. FAX 22470 34019.
A traditional hotel situated in a small fishing village overlooking the bay of
Gríkos. The roof terrace commands fine sea views. ● *Nov–Mar.* 🖼 🖼 🖼

Rhodes: *Spartális* €€€€ | 79
N Plastira 2, Rhodes town, 85100. (22410 24371. FAX 22410 20406.
A basic but friendly hotel, handily placed close to the harbour for ferries
and boat trips. There is a lovely breakfast terrace. 🖼 🖼 🖼 🖼

Rhodes: *Nikolís* @ nikoliss@hol.gr €€€€€ | 25
Ippodámou 61, Rhodes town, 85100. (22410 34561. FAX 22410 32034.
Housed in an atmospheric medieval building in the heart of the old town,
this luxurious hotel offers jacuzzis in some of its suites. 🖼 🖼 🖼 🖼

Rhodes: *Hilton Rhodes Resort* @ sales_rhodes@hilton.com €€€€€ | 404
Leofóros Ialyssoú, Ixiá, 85101. (22410 75000. FAX 22410 76690.
The town's most lavish five-star hotel, set in beautiful gardens by Ixiá beach,
4 km (3 miles) southwest of Rhodes town. ● *Nov–Feb.* 🖼 🖼 🖼 🖼 🖼

Rhodes: *Rhodos Palace* €€€€€ | 785
Ialyssós bay, Ixiá, 85101. (22410 25222. FAX 22410 25350.
A luxury hotel with apartments and bungalows in extensive grounds.
Facilities include indoor and outdoor pools. ● *Dec–Feb.* 🖼 🖼 🖼 🖼 🖼

Symi: *Alykí* €€€€€ | 15
Waterfront, Sými town, 85600. (22460 71665. FAX 22460 71655.
This restored sea-captain's mansion has an elegant interior. It is set in
picturesque surroundings, the rooms enjoying sea views. ● *Nov–Mar.* 🖼 🖼

Price categories are for a standard double room for one night in peak season, including tax, service charges and breakfast:
€ under 25 euros
€€ 25–35 euros
€€€ 35–45 euros
€€€€ 45–60 euros
€€€€€ over 60 euros.

RESTAURANT
Restaurant within the hotel sometimes reserved for residents only.

CLOSE TO BEACH
Within walking distance of the beach.

SWIMMING POOL
Hotel swimming pools are usually quite small and outdoors unless otherwise stated.

AIR-CONDITIONING
Hotel with air-conditioning in all the rooms.

	NUMBER OF ROOMS	RESTAURANT	CLOSE TO BEACH	SWIMMING POOL	AIR-CONDITIONING
SYMI: *Chorió* €€€€€ Chorió area, Sými town, 85600. (22460 71800. FAX 22460 71802. This modern, stylish hotel is situated opposite the village windmills and enjoys views over the town. All rooms have balconies. ● *Nov–Mar.*	17				
SYMI: *Niréfs* €€€€€ Akti Georgiou, Sými town, 85600. (22460 72400. FAX 22460 72404. Housed in a beautifully restored municipal hotel, this traditional island-style hotel has a cosmopolitan feel and is the island's finest. ● *Oct–Apr.*	40	●	■		
TILOS: *Eiríni* €€€ Seafront, Livádia, 85002. (22460 44293. FAX 22460 44238. A family-run hotel with plain and tasteful décor, set in beautiful, lush gardens with hibiscus plants and banana trees. ● *Nov–Mar.*	28		■		
TILOS: *Panórama Studios* €€€€€ Livádia bay, 85002. (22460 44365. FAX 22460 44365. Smart and stylish studios with a shared terrace, set in a peaceful spot on a hillside overlooking the bay of Livádia. The terrace has a vine-covered canopy, draped with bougainvillea and geraniums. ● *Oct–Mar.*	22				■
THE CYCLADES					
AMORGOS: *Aegiáli* €€€€€ On hillside above port, Aigiáli, 84008. (22850 73393. FAX 22850 73395. This smart hotel complex with good facilities, including a taverna and large pool, offers lovely sea views from its veranda.	30	●	■	●	■
ANDROS: *Paradise* €€€€€ 700 m (2,300 ft) from beach, Andros town, 84500. (22820 22187. FAX 22820 22340. This elegantly appointed hotel in a Neo-Classical mansion has a snack bar, and minibus service for transfers and tours. ● *Nov–Mar.*	41		■	●	
FOLEGANDROS: *Anemómylos Apartments* €€€€€ Seafront, Chóra, 84011. (22860 41309. FAX 22860 41407. A fully equipped complex built in traditional Cycladic style around a courtyard with balconies overhanging the sea. ● *mid-Oct–Apr.*	18				
FOLEGANDROS: *Kástro* €€€€€ North end of Chóra, 84011. (22860 41230. FAX 22860 41230. Rooms look down sheer cliffs to the sea from this 500-year-old traditional house. It is part of the ancient Kástro walls, with its pebble mosaic floors and barrel ceilings. Handy for the central squares. ● *Nov–Mar.*	13				
IOS: *Diónysos* €€€€€ Mylopótas, 2 km (1 mile) SE of Ios town, 84001. (22860 91215. FAX 22860 91633. This luxury, traditional-style hotel is situated right on the beach. There are good facilities and a transfer service. ● *Nov–Apr.*	40	●	■	●	■
IOS: *Pétra Holiday Village* €€€€€ Ios bay, Ios town, 84001. (22860 91409. FAX 22860 91049. A group of traditional-style houses overlooking Ios bay. Tastefully decorated with whitewashed interiors and private terraces. ● *Oct–Apr.*	18		■		
KEA: *Kéa Beach* €€€€€ Koúndouros bay, 5 km (3 miles) S of Pisses, 84002. (22880 31230-3. FAX 22880 31234. A luxury bungalow complex built in traditional Cycladic style and offering all facilities from a nightclub to watersports. ● *Nov–Apr.*	80	●	■	●	■
KYTHNOS: *Kýthnos* €€€ Mérichas bay, 84006. (22810 32247. FAX 22810 32092. A basic but friendly hotel, situated right on the waterfront. Rooms at the front have balconies overlooking the sea.	15		■		

KYTHNOS: *Porto Klaras*   €€€€€   24
Loutrá beach, Loutrá, 84006. **(** 22810 31276. **FAX** 22810 31355.
Very well-appointed new apartments near the beach and hot springs,
with a wide range of accommodation from family suites to doubles with
sea views and a pretty garden bar area. ● *Dec–Apr.*

MILOS: *Delfíni*   €€€€€   23
Behind the harbour, Adámas, 84801. **(** 22870 22001. **FAX** 22870 22294.
This small, friendly hotel, set back from the harbour at Adámas, is run by a
local sea captain. Quiet location with breakfast terrace. ● *Nov–Mar.*

MILOS: *Pópi's Windmill*   €€€€€   8
Off main square, Trypití, 84801. **(** 22870 22286. **FAX** 22870 22396.
Pópi's Windmill is a luxuriously converted windmill with lovely views
towards Adámas port ● *Nov–Apr.*

MYKONOS: *Cavo Tagoo*   €€€€€   72
500 m (1,650 ft) N of port, Mýkonos town, 84100. **(** 22890 23692. **FAX** 22890
24923. One of the island's most stylish yet friendly hotels. Winner of the
Aegean architectural award, it features a range of Cycladic maisonettes
with lovely furnishings, overlooking the bay at Tagoo. ● *Nov–Mar.*

MYKONOS: *The Princess of Mýkonos*   €€€€€   38
Agios Stéfanos beach, 84600. **(** 22890 23806. **FAX** 22890 23031
Favourite of stars like Jane Fonda, this is another Cycladic-style hotel in
traditional blue and white. It has all the luxury facilities, from gym to
conference rooms and satellite TV. ● *Nov–Mar.*

NAXOS: *Grotta* @ grotta@naxos_island.com   €€€€   40
Aplómata area, behind port, Náxos town, 84300. **(** 22850 22215. **FAX** 22850 22646.
Beautifully situated on a headland, this hotel enjoys good views of both
the town and the sea. Rooms are clean with balconies.

NAXOS: *Nissaki Beach Hotel* @ nissaki@naxos_island.com   €€€€€   40
Agios Geórgios, Náxos town, 84300. **(** 22850 25710. **FAX** 22850 23876.
Recently renovated in traditional Cycladic décor, this hotel is situated next to
the beach. Some rooms have views of the sea, others the pool.

PAROS: *Dína*   €€€€   8
On main through road, Paroikiá, 84400. **(** 22840 21325. **FAX** 22840 23525.
A small and friendly establishment, centrally placed and beautifully kept,
with spotless rooms and plain but attractive interiors. ● *Nov–Apr.*

PAROS: *Astir of Paros*   €€€€€   57
Kolympíthres, 11 km (7 miles) N of Paroikiá, 84400. **(** 22840 51976. **FAX** 22840
51985. A de luxe resort hotel offering well-equipped rooms with balconies.
Facilities include horseback riding. ● *Nov–Mar.*

PAROS: *Hotel Asterías*   €€€€€   36
Paroikiá, 84400. **(** 22840 21797. **FAX** 22840 22172.
By the sea, most of the rooms have been refurbished, and all have balconies.
The bar outside offers breakfast, snacks and drinks. ● *Oct–Mar.*

SANTORINI: *Erevos*   €€€€€   8
Overlooking the caldera, Imerovigli, 84700. **(** 22860 24250 **FAX** 22860 23110.
Built into the rock face in one of the quietest locations on the island, the
Erevos is housed in an 18th-century building. Rooms have traditional
furniture and patios with views of the volcano

SANTORINI: *Fanári Villas*   €€€€€   19
Ammoúdi bay, 84700. **(** 22860 71008. **FAX** 22860 71235.
These are traditional *skaftá* cave houses which have been given the luxury
touch. There is a bar and steps to Ammoúdi bay below. ● *Nov–Mar.*

SANTORINI: *Hermes* Ⓦ www.hermeshotel-santorini.com   €€€€€   36
Kamári beach, 84700. **(** 22860 31664. **FAX** 22860 32240.
Set among beautiful gardens, this friendly, family-run hotel offers well-
appointed rooms, not far from the town centre. ● *Nov–Apr*

SANTORINI: *Kavalári* @ info@kavalari.com   €€€€€   18
Near bus station, Firá, 84700. **(** 22860 22455. **FAX** 22860 22603.
Formerly a sea captain's home, this unusual hotel is terraced into the
rock face. It has spectacular views over the caldera and is a great spot
from which to enjoy the sunset. ● *Nov–Mar.*

Price categories are for a standard double room for one night in peak season, including tax, service charges and breakfast: € under 25 euros €€ 25–35 euros €€€ 35–45 euros €€€€ 45–60 euros €€€€€ over 60 euros.	**RESTAURANT** Restaurant within the hotel sometimes reserved for residents only. **CLOSE TO BEACH** Within walking distance of the beach. **SWIMMING POOL** Hotel swimming pools are usually quite small and outdoors unless otherwise stated. **AIR-CONDITIONING** Hotel with air-conditioning in all the rooms.	NUMBER OF ROOMS	RESTAURANT	CLOSE TO BEACH	SWIMMING POOL	AIR-CONDITIONING

SANTORINI: *Palace* @ spalace@otenet.gr €€€€€ 500 m (1,640 ft) from main square, Firá, 84700. 22860 22771. FAX 22860 23705. Fine views of the Aegean sea can be enjoyed from this smart hotel with spacious rooms and good facilities. ● *Nov–Mar.*		106	●		●	■
SERIFOS: *Aretí* €€€€€ Waterfront, Livádi, 84005. 22810 51479. FAX 22810 51547. A convenient place to stay for the ferry, this family-run hotel and cake shop has comfortable rooms with terraces and a peaceful tiered garden overlooking the sea. ● *Nov–Mar.*		13		■		
SIFNOS: *Artemón* €€€€€ Agiou Konstantinou 3, Artemónas, 84003. 22840 31303. FAX 22840 32385. Situated in Artemónas, 1.5 km (1 mile) from the capital Apollonía, the Artemón is a smart and tasteful hotel within walking distance of quiet beaches. There is a terrace with sea views. ● *Nov–Mar.*		23	●	■		■
SIFNOS: *Aléxandros* €€€€€ Seafront, Platýs Gialós, 84003. 22840 71333. FAX 22840 71303. Situated on the hillside above the beach, this pleasant hotel has a restaurant, terraces and a pool overlooking Gialós beach. ● *Oct–Apr.*		56		■	●	
SIKINOS: *Flóra* €€€ Overlooking the harbour, Aloprónia, 84010. 22860 51214. FAX 22860 51100. Excellent, modestly priced, Cycladic-style development on the hillside above the port. There are eight self-contained chalet-style rooms built around courtyards with wonderful sea views.		10				
SYROS: *Villa Nostos* €€€€ Spathation 2, Ermoúpoli, 84100. 22810 84226. Housed in a Neo-Classical building, this hotel offers clean, basic accommodation. Breakfast is not provided but there is a kitchen for guest use. ● *Nov–Mar.*		5	●	■		■
SYROS: *Omiros* €€€€€ Omirou 43, Ermoúpoli, 84100. 22810 84910. FAX 22810 86266. The former home of the renowned sculptor, Vitális, this 150-year-old Neo-Classical mansion has been tastefully converted. It has a spacious roof terrace overlooking the port.		15				■
TINOS: *Aeolos Bay Hotel* €€€€€ Agios Fokas beach, 84200. 22830 23339. FAX 22830 23086. A short walk out of town, overlooking the beach, this smart, comfortable hotel has pool and friendly resident parrot. Well appointed and set in pleasant gardens with a breakfast terrace. ● *Nov–Mar.*		69	●	■	●	
CRETE						
AGIA PELAGIA: *Alexander House* €€€€€ On seafront. 2810 811303. FAX 2810 811381. @ alexhh@otenet.gr Situated in Agía Pelagía, 20 km (12 miles) west of Irákleio, this is a very pleasant, tasteful hotel arranged around a courtyard and swimming pool, a minute's walk from the beach. ● *Nov–Mar.*		79	●	■	●	■
AGIA PELAGIA: *Kapsís Beach Hotel and Bungalows* €€€€€ On seafront, 100m (330 ft) before the village. 2810 811112. FAX 2810 811314. @ capsis.crete@capsis.gr One of the best luxury hotels on the island. Superbly situated on a promontory, surrounded by sandy beaches.		664	●	■	●	■
AGIOS NIKOLAOS: *Istron Beach* €€€€€ 13 km (8 miles) E of Agios Nikólaos. 28410 61303. FAX 28410 61383. This delightfully secluded resort hotel overlooks a cove and has the luxury of its own sandy beach. Friendly atmosphere.		117	●	■	●	■

AGIOS NIKOLAOS: *Mínos Beach* €€€€€ 118
Ammoúdi, 72100. 28410 22345. FAX 28410 22548.
This exclusive resort hotel, with whitewashed bungalows, is set
in handsomely landscaped gardens on the Gulf of Mirampello.
The hotel has its own private beach. Nov–Mar.

CHANIA: *Terésa* €€€ 8
Angélou 8, 73100. 28210 92798. FAX 28210 92798.
Renovated Venetian house with fabulous views of the harbour from its
roof terrace and some of the rooms. Excellent value for money.

CHANIA: *Amforá* €€€€€ 20
B Párodos Theotokopoúlou 20, 73131. 28210 93224. FAX 28210 93226.
Beautifully restored 13th-century Venetian mansion with tastefully appointed
rooms and a charming roof terrace overlooking the harbour.

CHANIA: *Villa Androméda* €€€€€ 8
Eleftheríou Venizélou 150, 73133. 28210 28300 FAX 28210 28303.
This elegantly restored Neo-Classical mansion was built in 1870 and was
once home to the German consulate. The hotel comprises eight
luxuriously decorated suites. 20 Nov–20 Dec, 25 Jan–25 Feb.

CHERSONISOS: *Creta Maris* €€€€€ 297
Seafront, 800m (2,600 ft) W of Chersónisos, 70014. 28970 22115. FAX 28970
22130. A luxury hotel consisting of individual bungalows close to Chersónisos, with an outdoor theatre and open-air cinema. Nov–Mar.

CHERSONISOS: *Silva Maris* €€€€€ 300
Chersónisos beach, 70014. 28970 22850. FAX 28970 21404.
Built in the style of an Aegean village, the hotel is situated on the east side of
Chersónisos. Rooms have balconies with sea views. Nov–Feb.

ELOUNTA: *Eloúnta Beach Hotel* €€€€€ 268
2 km (1 mile) N of Eloúnta, 72053. 28410 41412. FAX 28410 41373.
The Eloúnta, Crete's grande dame of resort hotels, offers every amenity
imaginable from jacuzzis, Turkish baths and saunas, to scuba diving,
jet-skiing and parasailing. Nov–Feb.

ELOUNTA: *Eloúnta Mare* €€€€€ 156
2 km (1 mile) N of Eloúnta, 72053. 28410 41102. FAX 28410 41307.
A resort hotel on the Gulf of Mirampello comprising a central building
and 47 traditional whitewashed bungalows, each with its own pool and
garden. Private beach and full range of amenities. Nov–Mar.

IERAPETRA: *Astron* €€€€€ 66
Michaíl Kóthri 56, 72200. 28420 25114. FAX 28420 25917.
Comfortable, new hotel on the outskirts of Ierápetra. Balconied rooms
with sea views and a sandy beach just 20 m (65 ft) away.

IRAKLEIO: *Atlantís* €€€€€ 160
Ygeías 2, 71202. 2810 229103. FAX 2810 226265. @ atlantis@atl.grecotel.gr
Tucked away in a quiet street this large, modern hotel enjoys panoramic
views over the ferry port and city of Irákleio.

IRAKLEIO: *Galaxy* €€€€€ 140
Dimokratías 67, 71306. 2810 238812. FAX 2810 211211. @ galaxyer@otenet.gr
This attractive, modern hotel is set around a central court and swimming
pool. The rooms are tastefully decorated.

IRAKLEIO: *Lató* €€€€€ 50
Epimenídou 15, 71202. 2810 228103. FAX 2810 240350. @ lato@her.forthnet.gr
Pleasant hotel with superb views over the Venetian harbour and in a
good central location below the Archaeological Museum.

KASTELLI KISSAMOU: *Kíssamos* W www.hotelkissamos.gr €€€ 30
Iróon Polytechníou, 73400. 28220 22086. FAX 28220 22475.
A friendly, well-run hotel in the centre of town. The only lodgings in town
with heating and water throughout winter.

LOUTRO: *The Blue House* €€€ 20
Harbourfront, 73011. 28250 91127. FAX 28250 91035.
A traditional whitewashed house with blue shutters in one of Crete's most
magical spots. Each room has its own balcony overlooking the tiny
harbour. A 15-minute ferry ride from Sfakiá. Nov–Mar.

For key to symbols see back flap

Price categories are for a standard double room for one night in peak season, including tax, service charges and breakfast:
€ under 25 euros
€€ 25–35 euros
€€€ 35–45 euros
€€€€ 45–60 euros
€€€€€ over 60 euros.

Restaurant
Restaurant within the hotel sometimes reserved for residents only.

Close to Beach
Within walking distance of the beach.

Swimming Pool
Hotel swimming pools are usually quite small and outdoors unless otherwise stated.

Air-Conditioning
Hotel with air-conditioning in all the rooms.

	Number of Rooms	Restaurant	Close to Beach	Swimming Pool	Air-Conditioning
MATALA: *Oríon* — €€€€€	46			●	
PALAIOCHORA: *Réa* — €€€€€	14				
PLAKIÁS: *Plakiás Bay* — €€€€	28	●			
RETHYMNO: *Liberty* — €€€€	24	●			
RETHYMNO: *Fortétsa* — €€€€	54	●			
RETHYMNO: *Grecotel Creta Palace* — €€€€€	355	●	●	●	
SITEIA: *Archontikó* — €€	10	●			
SPILI: *Green* — €€€	13				
ZARÓS: *Idi Hotel* — €€€	52	●		●	
AREOS: *Park Hotel Athens* — €€€€€	146	●		●	
EXARCHEIA: *Exarcheíon* — €€	54				
EXARCHEIA: *Museum* — €€€€	58				

MATALA: *Oríon* — €€€€€ — 46
1 km (0.5 miles) S of Mátala, 70200. (28920 45129. FAX 28920 45329.
A smart, reasonably priced hotel in a wonderfully secluded position just outside Mátala on the south coast of Crete. Large swimming pool and several outstanding beaches within easy striking distance. ● Nov–Apr.

PALAIOCHORA: *Réa* — €€€€€ — 14
Antoníou Peráki, 73001. (28230 41307. FAX 28230 41605.
A friendly, family-run hotel with a shady, flower-decked terrace. There is a sandy beach only five minutes' walk away. ● Nov–Feb.

PLAKIÁS: *Plakiás Bay* — €€€€ — 28
Plakiás bay, 74060. (28230 31215. FAX 28230 31951.
A small, whitewashed hotel bedecked with flowers and enjoying a superb position overlooking Plakiás bay. ● Nov–Mar.

RETHYMNO: *Liberty* — €€€€ — 24
Corner of Moátsou & Preveláki, 74100. (28310 55851. FAX 28310 55850.
A comfortable hotel with a central location near the Municipal Gardens and close to the waterfront. ● Nov–Mar.

RETHYMNO: *Fortétsa* — €€€€ — 54
Melisinoú 16, 74100. (28310 55551. FAX 28310 54073. @ mliodak@ret.forthnet.gr
One of the nicest hotels in Réthymno, on a quiet backstreet just behind the Fortétsa, one minute's walk from the seafront. ● Dec–Feb.

RETHYMNO: *Grecotel Creta Palace* — €€€€€ — 355
Missyria, 74100. (28310 55181. FAX 28310 54085.
Resort hotel with its own beach in Misiría, 4 km (2 miles) east of Réthymno. Full range of facilities including a fitness club. ● Nov–Mar.

SITEIA: *Archontikó* — €€ — 10
Kondyláki 16, 72300. (28430 28172.
This hotel is housed in an elegant, old building with high ceilings and a tiny garden. There is a friendly, relaxed atmosphere. ● Nov–Feb.

SPILI: *Green* — €€€ — 13
Off main square, 74100. (28320 22225. @ maravelh@otenet.gr
Situated in the mountain town of Spíli, 20 km (12 miles) south of Réthymno, this hotel is recognized by a forest of geraniums. ● Nov–Mar.

ZARÓS: *Idi Hotel* — €€€ — 52
North of Zarós, at the foot of Mount Idi, 70002. (28940 31302. FAX 28940 31511.
A delightful hotel with an alpine setting just outside Zarós, 38 km (24 miles) south of Irákleio. Zarós is famous for its spring waters.

ATHENS

AREOS: *Park Hotel Athens* — W www.park.hotel.gr — €€€€€ — 146
Leofóros Alexándras 10, 10682. (210 6466 362. FAX 210 823 8420.
Situated opposite the relaxing Areos Park, this hotel has spacious rooms. There is also a good rooftop bar and a 24-hour coffee shop.

EXARCHEIA: *Exarcheíon* — €€ — 54
Themistokléous 55, 10683. (210 380 0731. FAX 210 380 3296.
This hotel is close to the late-night action of Plateía Exarcheíon. The rooms are basic, and there is a good pavement café.

EXARCHEIA: *Museum* — €€€€ — 58
Mpoumpoulínas 16, 10682. (210 380 5611. FAX 210 380 0507.
The modern façade of this building hides a genteel interior. Situated opposite the National Archaeological Museum, it is frequented by academics. The rooms are clean and quiet.

ILISIA: *Hilton* €€€€€ 517
Leofóros Vasilíssis Sofías 46, 11528. 210 728 1000. FAX 210 728 1111.
Athens' best-known modern hotel. All the rooms have large balconies,
providing stunning views across the city. 🔲 🔥 🛢 🖴

KOLONAKI: *Athenian Inn* €€€€€ 25
Cháritos 22, 10675. 210 723 9552. FAX 210 724 2268.
This hotel offers clean, basic rooms and friendly management. Situated in the
heart of Kolonáki, amongst a choice of shops, restaurants and cafés. 🔲 🖴

KOLONAKI: *St George Lycabettus* €€€€€ 167
Kleoménous 2, 10675. 210 729 0711. FAX 210 729 0439. @ info@sglycabettus.gr
Situated beneath Lykavittós Hill, this small, luxury hotel offers large rooms
with a good views. The rooftop restaurant is excellent. 🔲 🔥 🖴

KOUKAKI: *Marble House* w www.marblehouse.gr €€€ 16
Anastasíou Zínni 35, 11741. 210 923 4058. FAX 210 922 6461.
At the end of a quiet cul de-sac, this is a firm favourite among mid-range
pensions for its cleanliness and helpful management. Most rooms are *en
suite* and many have vine-covered balconies. 🔲 🛢

MAKRYGIANNI: *Athens Gate* €€€€€ 100
Leofóros A Syngroú 10, 11742. 210 923 8302. FAX 210 923 7493.
This centrally located, modern hotel offers comfortable rooms and a roof
top garden with views of the Acropolis and Hadrian's Arch. 🔲 🔥 🛢 🖴

MAKRIGIANNI: *Divani Palace Acropolis* @ acropol@otenet.gr €€€€€ 251
Parthenónos 19–25, 11742. 210 928 0100. FAX 210 921 4993.
Beautifully upgraded to de luxe standard, this hotel is just a short stroll
from the Acropolis. An original section of the Themistoklean Long Walls
is on view in the hotel lobby. 🔲 🔥 🛢 🖴

MAKRYGIANNI: *Iródeion* @ herodeion@otenet.gr €€€€€ 90
Rovértou Gkálli 4, 11742. 210 923 6832. FAX 210 921 1650.
This hotel has large modern rooms, a patio shaded by pistachio
trees and a roof terrace with views of the Acropolis. 🔲 🔥 🛢 🖴

MAKRYGIANNI: *Royal Olympic* w www.royalolympic.com €€€€€ 304
Athanasíou Diákou 28–34, 11743. 210 922 6411. FAX 210 923 3317.
The Royal Olympic has large rooms, all with superb views of the Temple
of Olympian Zeus. Good grill restaurant. 🔲 🔥 🛢 🖴

METAXOURGEIO: *Stanley* €€€€€ 389
Odysséos 1, Plateía Karaiskáki, 10437. 210 524 1611. FAX 210 524 4611.
The Stanley hotel has large fully equipped rooms with balconies. Facilities
include a rooftop garden and pool, a restaurant and busy bar. 🔲 🔥 🛢 🖴

MONASTIRAKI: *Témpi* €€€ 24
Aiólou 29, 10551. 210 321 3175. FAX 210 325 4179.
Overlooking the flower market and Agía Eiríni church, this hotel is ideal
for those who want to explore Athinás market's food and stalls. 🔲 🛢

MONASTIRAKI: *Attalos* €€€€€ 80
Athinás 29, 19554. 210 321 2801. FAX 210 324 3124.
Ideally situated for shopping, near Monastiráki and Athinás, the Attalos
offers adequate rooms, some with balconies. The hotel also has a roof
garden with good views of the Acropolis. 🔲 🔥 🛢 🖴

NEOS KOSMOS: *Athenian Kallirhoe* €€€€€ 68
Petmezá 15, 11743. 210 921 5353. FAX 210 921 5342.
This is a small, luxurious hotel just a short walk from the Acropolis. The
rooms are modern and comfortable. 🔲 🔥 🖴

NEOS KOSMOS: *Athenaeum Inter-Continental* €€€€€ 520
Leofóros Andrea Syngroú 89–93, 11745. 210 920 6000. FAX 210 920 6500.
Decorated throughout by modern Greek artists, this luxurious hotel
offers a choice of fine restaurants and bars and shops. Facilities also
include a fully equipped gymnasium. 🔲 🔥 🖴

NEOS KOSMOS: *Ledra Marriott* €€€€€ 259
Leofóros Andrea Syngroú 115, 11745. 210 934 7711. FAX 210 935 8603.
As well as all the amenities expected from a luxury hotel, the Marriot's
rooms are large and spacious and the hotel boasts superb restaurants,
particularly the trendy Polynesian Kona Kai. 🔲 🔥 🖴

For key to symbols see back flap

				NUMBER OF ROOMS	RESTAURANT	CLOSE TO BEACH	SWIMMING POOL	AIR-CONDITIONING

Price categories are for a standard double room for one night in peak season, including tax, service charges and breakfast:
€ under 25 euros
€€ 25–35 euros
€€€ 35–45 euros
€€€€ 45–60 euros
€€€€€ over 60 euros.

RESTAURANT
Restaurant within the hotel sometimes reserved for residents only.

CLOSE TO BEACH
Within walking distance of the beach.

SWIMMING POOL
Hotel swimming pools are usually quite small and outdoors unless otherwise stated.

AIR-CONDITIONING
Hotel with air-conditioning in all the rooms.

Hotel	Price	Rooms	Restaurant	Close to Beach	Swimming Pool	Air-Conditioning
OMONOIA: *La Mirage* Maríkas Kotopoúli 3, 10431. 210 523 4071. FAX 210 523 3992. A favourite for those who want to be close to the 24-hour hustle and bustle of Plateía Omonoías. All rooms are double-glazed.	€€€	208	●			■
OMONOIA: *Dorian Inn* Peiraiós 17, 10552. 210 523 9782. FAX 210 522 6196. @ dorianho@otenet.gr Situated in the heart of the city centre, the roof garden of this smart hotel offers spectacular views over Athens and the Acropolis.	€€€€€	146	●		●	■
OMONOIA: *King Minos* Peiraiós 1, 10552. 210 523 1111-8. FAX 210 523 1361. The hotel's large and comfortable public lounge areas, including the restaurant and the bar, are good places in which to unwind. All the rooms are quiet.	€€€€€	194	●			■
OMONOIA: *Titánia* Panepistimíou 52, 10678. 210 330 0111. FAX 210 330 0700. The entrance to this well-appointed hotel is through a shopping arcade close to Plateía Omonoías. Rooms are well equipped and the rooftop terrace bar and ground-floor café are always busy.	€€€€€	396	●			■
PLAKA: *Faídra* Chairefóntos 16, 10558. 210 323 8461. FAX 210 322 795. The hotel's location next to the Lysikrates monument more than makes up for the slightly tacky quality of its rooms and public areas.	€€€€	21				
PLAKA: *John's Place* Patróou 5, 10557. 210 322 9719. One of the better bargain backpacking hotels. The rooms are small but very clean, and bathrooms are shared.	€€€€	15				
PLAKA: *Koúros* Kódrou 11, 10557. 210 322 7431. Situated in the heart of Pláka, this cheerful small *pension* is housed in a converted Neo-Classical mansion house. Rooms are basic but clean and have balconies.	€€€€	10				
PLAKA: *Acropolis House Pension* Kódrou 6–8, 10557. 210 322 2344. Housed in a converted 19th-century building, the rooms in this *pension* are large and airy. All rooms have private balconies.	€€€€€	19				■
PLAKA: *Adónis* Kódrou 3, 10557. 210 324 9737. FAX 210 323 1602. The Adónis is a modern hotel offering decent, basic accommodation and panoramic views across Athens from its roof garden. All the rooms have balconies.	€€€€€	26				
PLAKA: *Myrtó* Níkis 40, 10558. 210 322 7237. FAX 210 323 4560. Close to the central areas of Plateía Syntágmatos and Pláka, this small hotel is ideal for short stays and is popular with young couples.	€€€€€	12				■
PLAKA: *Omiros* Apóllonos 15, 10557. 210 323 5486. FAX 210 322 8059. A lovely roof garden distinguishes this otherwise basic hotel which is located in a quiet area of Pláka.	€€€€€	37				
PLAKA: *Adrian* Adrianoú 74, 10556. 210 325 0461. FAX 210 325 0461. Situated in central Pláka, this hotel has simple, comfortable rooms as well as a quiet terrace to escape the bustle of the city.	€€€€€	22				■

PLAKA: *Aphrodite* 　　　　　€€€€€　84
Apóllonos 21, 10557. 📞 *210 323 4357.* FAX *210 322 5244.*
This hotel is well located and offers clean, good-value rooms, some of
which enjoy wonderful views of the Acropolis

PLAKA: *Byron* 　　　　　€€€€€　20
Vyronos 19, 10558. 📞 *210 323 0327.* FAX *210 322 0276*
Situated on the southern fringe of Pláka, this small and somewhat basic
hotel is close to the Acropolis. Some rooms have balconies.

PLAKA: *Ermís* 　　　　　€€€€€　45
Apóllonos 19, 10557. 📞 *210 323 5514.* FAX *210 322 2412.*
The rooms of this newly-renovated hotel are large, and
some have balconies overlooking a playground.

PLAKA: *Neféli* 　　　　　€€€€€　18
Angelikis Chatzimicháli 2, 10558. 📞 *210 322 8044.*
A modern hotel, hidden away in a peaceful backwater in Pláka.
The rooms are clean and of a good, basic standard.

PLAKA: *Pláka* 　　　　　€€€€€　67
Mitropoleos & Kapnikareas 7, 10556. 📞 *210 322 2096.* FAX *210 322 2412.*
Set in the heart of Pláka, with a superb view of the Acropolis, this is a
comfortable hotel with a friendly atmosphere.

STATHMOS LARISSIS: *Novotel Athens* 　　€€€€€　195
Michaíl Vóda 4 6, 10439. 📞 *210 825 0422.* FAX *210 883 7816.*
Run by the French group, Novotel, this smart, centrally located
hotel has modern, well-equipped rooms and a stunning rooftop
garden and swimming pool.

STREFI HILL: *Oríon* 　　　　　€€€€€　38
Anexartisías 5 & E Mpenáki 105, 11473. 📞 *210 382 7362.* FAX *210 380 5193.*
Besides Stréfi Hill, just above the bustling Exárcheia area, this quiet hotel
is popular with students looking for short-term accommodation.

SYNTAGMA: *Amalía* 　　　　　€€€€€　98
Leofóros Vasilíssis Amalías 10, 10557. 📞 *210 607 2135.* FAX *210 322 3872.*
Although the rooms are fairly small, all the bathrooms are marble.
The hotel is centrally located and has good views of both the
Parliament building and the National Gardens.

SYNTAGMA: *Aretoúsa* 　　　　　€€€€€　87
Mitropóleos 6–8 & Níkis 12, 10563. 📞 *210 322 9431.* FAX *210 322 9439.*
Decent value characterizes this centrally located hotel. The rooms are
modern and there is a roof garden as well as a lively bar.

SYNTAGMA: *Astor* 　　　　　€€€€€　130
Karageórgi Servías 16, 10562. 📞 *210 335 1000.* FAX *210 325 5115.*
The popular all-year-round rooftop restaurant of this hotel boasts
stunning views over Athens. The double rooms from the sixth floor
upwards share this impressive view of the city.

SYNTAGMA: *Athens Plaza* 　　　　€€€€€　177
Vasiléos Georgíou & Stadíou, 10564. 📞 *210 325 5301.* FAX *210 323 5856.*
This grand hotel offers luxurious blue and white rooms, all of which
are soundproofed. There are good facilities and its Explorers' Lounge and
Marco Polo restaurant are always busy.

SYNTAGMA: *Electra* 　　　　　€€€€€　110
Ermoú 5, 10557. 📞 *210 322 3223.* FAX *210 322 0310.*
This centrally located hotel is ideally situated for shopping expeditions
to Monastiráki. All the rooms are clean and pleasant.

SYNTAGMA: *Esperia Palace* 　　　　€€€€€　184
Stadíou 22, 10564. 📞 *210 323 8001.* FAX *210 323 8100.* W www.greekhotel.com
A smart city hotel with marble lobbies and tastefully decorated rooms.
Its restaurant and bar are popular with Athenians.

SYNTAGMA: *Grande Bretagne* 　　　€€€€€　450
Plateía Syntágmatos, 10563. 📞 *210 323 0000.* FAX *210 322 8034.*
This luxurious hotel was built in 1852 and is the landmark of Plateía
Syntágmatos, the most desirable hotel location in Athens. The lobby
and rooms are beautiful and the service is excellent.

For key to symbols see back flap

WHERE TO EAT

To EAT OUT IN GREECE is to experience the democratic tradition at work. Rich and poor, young and old, all enjoy their favourite local restaurant, taverna or café. Greeks consider the best places to be where the food is fresh, plentiful and well cooked, not necessarily where the setting or cuisine is the

Tsikoudiá, a strong spirit from Crete

fanciest. Visitors too have come to appreciate the simplicity and health of the traditional Greek kitchen – olive oil, yoghurt, vegetables, a little meat or fish and some wine, always shared with friends. The traditional three-hour lunch and siesta is still the daily rhythm of the islands, and only in the main tourist areas will you find the Western European routine of a substantial breakfast, a larger and briefer lunch (1pm–2:30pm) and an earlier dinner (7:30–11pm). Greeks prefer a quick breakfast coffee, heavy lunch, and an evening *mezédes* selection, before a long, late dinner that can stretch well into the night.

TYPES OF RESTAURANT

OFTEN DIFFICULT to find in more developed tourist resorts, the *estiatórion*, or traditional Greek restaurant, is one of Europe's most enjoyable places to eat. Friendly, noisy, and sometimes in lovely surroundings, *estiatória* are reliable purveyors of local recipes and wines, particularly if they have been owned by the same family for decades. Foreigners unfamiliar with Greek dishes may be invited into the kitchen to choose their fare. In Greece, the entire family dines together and takes plenty of time over the meal, especially at the weekends.

Many traditional restaurants specialize in either a regional cuisine, a method of cooking, or a certain type of food. In some Northeast Agean islands such as Lésvos, where a small minority of Greeks from Asia Minor have settled, food may be spicier than the Greek norm, with lots of red peppers and such dishes as *giogurtlú* (kebabs drenched in yoghurt and served on pitta bread).

The menu (*see pp316–17*) in a traditional restaurant tends to be short, comprising at most a dozen *mezédes* (appetizers or snacks), eight main dishes, four or five vegetable dishes and salads, plus a dessert of fresh or cooked fruit, and a selection of local and national wines.

Restaurants vary from very expensive in the main island towns to the magnificently inexpensive. The cheapest of the traditional restaurants is known as a *mageirió*, though they are becoming increasingly rare. Here there is little choice in either wines or dishes, all of which will be *mageireftá* (ready-cooked), but the food is home-made and tasty and the barrel wine is at the very least drinkable and is often good if it comes from the owner's village.

Many hotels have restaurants

Traditional restaurant on Pátmos

open to non-residents. Large island hotels generally offer more expensive, international cuisine. Some will also offer a Greek menu, which tends to be a more elaborate presentation of traditional dishes. Smaller country hotels, however, occasionally have excellent kitchens, and serve good local wines; it is worth checking on any close by.

In the last few years a new breed of young Greek chefs has emerged in "*kultúra*" restaurants, developing a style of cooking that encompasses the country's magnificent raw materials, flavours and colours. These dishes are served with exciting new Greek wines such as Erodios (a rosé), Mackedon (a sauvignon/roditis blend) or a Chardonnay.

TAVERNAS

ONE OF THE GREAT pleasures for the traveller in Greece is the tradition of the taverna, a place to eat and drink, even if you simply snack on some *mezédes*. Traditional tavernas open mid-evening and stay open late; occasionally they are also open for lunch.

Windmill restaurant (*see p324*), Skiáthos town

Outside diners at a taverna in Plakiás, Crete

Menus are short and seasonal – perhaps six or eight *mezédes* and four main courses comprising casseroles and dishes cooked *tis óras* (to order), along with the usual accompaniments of vegetables, salads, fruit and wine.

Some tavernas specialize in the foods and wines of the owner's home region, some in a particular cooking style and others in certain foods.

A *psarotavérna* is the place to find good fish dishes. In small fishing villages you may find the rickety tables of a *psarotavérna* literally on the beach. Close to the lapping waves the owner may serve fish, such as red mullet, bass and octopus, that he himself caught that morning. The large fish restaurants in the tourist areas may serve frozen or imported fish, although the law stipulates that menus must state whether fish is fresh or frozen. For delicious grills try a *psistariá*, a taverna that specializes in spit-roasts and chargrilling *(sta kárvouna)*. In the countryside, you may find lamb, kid, pork, chicken, game, offal, lambs' heads and even testicles char-grilled, and whole lamb is roasted on the spit. At the harbourside, fish and shellfish are grilled (broiled) and served with fresh lemon juice and olive oil. Family-run country tavernas and cafés provide simple meals, such as omelettes and

Accordian player in a taverna on Sými

salads at any time of day, but many close quite early in the evening. After your meal in the taverna, follow the Greeks and enjoy a visit to the local *zacharoplasteío (see p314)* for a range of desserts.

CAFES AND BARS

CAFES, KNOWN AS *kafeneía*, are the pulse of Greek life and even the tiniest hamlet has a place to drink coffee and wine. Equally important is its function as the centre of communication – mail is collected here, telephone calls made, and newspapers read, dissected and discussed. All *kafeneía* serve Greek coffee, sometimes *frappé* (instant coffee served cold, in a tall glass), soft drinks, beer, ouzo and local wine. Most also serve some kind of snack to order. All open early in the morning and remain open until late at night. As the social hub of their communities, country *kafeneía*, as well as many in island towns, open seven days a week.

A *galaktopoleío*, or "milk shop", has a seating area where you can enjoy fine yoghurt and honey. A *kapileió* (wine shop with a café-bar attached) is the place to try local wines from the cask, and you may find a few bottled wines as well. The owner is invariably from a wine village or family, and will often cook some simple regional specialities to accompany the wine.

In a *mezedopoleío*, or *mezés* shop, the owner will not only serve the local wine and the *mezédes* that go with it, but also ouzo and the infamous spirit raki, both distilled from the remnants of the grape harvest. Their accompanying *mezédes* are less salty than those served with wine.

No holiday in Greece is complete without a visit to an *ouzerí*. You can order a dozen or more little plates of savoury meats, fish and vegetables and try the many varieties of ouzo, served in small jugs, with a glass of water to wash the ouzo down. It is a noisy and fun place to eat and drink.

Artemónas restaurant *(see p330)* on the island of Sífnos

A waterside restaurant at Skála Sykaminiás, Lésvos

FAST FOOD AND SNACKS

VISITORS can be forgiven for thinking Greeks never stop eating, for there seem to be snack bars on every street and vendors selling sweets, nuts, rolls, seasonal corn and chestnuts at every turn.

Although American-style fast-food outlets dominate tourist centres, it is easy to avoid them by trying the traditional Greek eateries. Try the food of the extremely cheap *souvlatzídiko*, which offers a mostly take-away service of *souvláki* – chunks of meat, fish or vegetables, grilled (broiled) or roasted on a skewer – with fresh bread. The *ovelistírio* serves *gýros* – meat from a revolving spit in a pitta bread pocket. The food is sold "*sto chéri*" (in the hand, or to take away).

Many bakeries sell savoury pies and an array of flavourful bread rolls, and in busy areas you will always be able to find a café serving substantial snacks and salads.

If you have a sweet tooth you will love the *zacharo-plasteío* (literally, "shop of the sugar sculptor"). The baker prepares traditional sweet breads, tiny sweet pastries and a whole variety of fragrant honey cakes.

BREAKFAST

FOR GREEKS, this is the least important meal of the day. In traditional homes and *kafeneía* a small cup of Greek coffee accompanies *paximádia* (slices of bread rusks) or

koulourákia (firm, sesame-covered, or slightly sweet, rolls in rings or s-shapes) or pound cakes, filled with traditional home-made jam.

Elsewhere, and in many tourist cafés, this has been replaced by a large cup of brewed coffee and French-style croissants or delicious brioche-style rolls. During summer, some *kafeneía* will still serve fresh figs, thick yoghurt, pungent honey and slightly sweet currant bread, as well as a variety of English and continental breakfasts to cater for visitors' tastes.

Baklavás, a sweet cake of wheat, honey and nuts

RESERVATIONS

ALTHOUGH ISLAND restaurants generally have a casual atmosphere, they can, of course, be very popular; if it is possible to make a reservation, it is probably best to do so. Also, it is local practice to visit the restaurant or taverna earlier in the day to check on the dishes to be served. The proprietor will then take your order and reserve any special dish that you request.

WINE

THE GRAPE VARIETIES that abound in Greece today produce wines that are quite distinct from those of Western Europe. However, restaurateurs are only now learning to look after bottled wines. If the wine list contains the better wines, such as Ktima Merkoúri, Seméli or Strofiliá, the proprietor probably knows how to look after them and it will be safe to order a more expensive bottle. For a little less, good-value bottles include the nationally known Cambás and Boutári wines.

Traditional restaurants and tavernas may only stock carafe wine, which is served straight from the barrel and is always inexpensive. Carafe wines are often of the region, and the Greek rosé in particular is noted for having an unusual but pleasing flavour.

Wine from Límnos

HOW TO PAY

GREECE IS very much a cash society. If you need to pay by credit card, check first that the restaurant takes your credit card – many proprietors do not accept the whole range. *Kafeneía* almost never take credit cards, and café-bars very rarely do, although many will be happy to take travellers' cheques. Country restaurants, tavernas, *kafeneía* and bars will only accept cash.

The restaurant listings in this guide on pages 322–33 indicate whether or not credit cards are accepted at each establishment.

Kástro's bar *(see p329)* in the town of Mýkonos

Bright lights of Ouzeri To Kamaki (see p324) on Alónissos

SERVICE AND TIPPING

GREEKS TAKE PLENTY of time when they eat out and expect a high level of attention. This means a great deal of running around on the part of the waiter, but in return they receive good tips – 15 per cent if the service has been especially attentive, though more often a tip is about 10 per cent. Prices in traditional establishments do include service, but the waiters still expect a tip so always have coins ready to hand. Tap water is offered free with the meal.

Basket of local bread from Rhodes

Western-style restaurants and tourist tavernas sometimes add a service charge to the bill, their prices can be considerably higher because of additional trimmings, such as air-conditioning and phones.

DRESS CODE

THE GREEKS DRESS quite formally when dining out. Visitors should wear whatever is comfortable, but skimpy tops and shorts, and active sportswear are usually only acceptable near the beach – though most tourist establishments rarely turn away custom. Some hotel restaurants have policies requesting formal dress; in the listings we indicate which restaurants fall into this category.

In summer, if you dine outside, take a jacket or sweater for later in the evening.

CHILDREN

CHILDREN become restaurant and taverna habitués at a very early age in Greece – it is an essential part of their education. Consequently, children are welcome everywhere in Greece except the drinking bars. In formal restaurants children are expected to be well behaved, but in summer, when the Greeks enjoy long hours eating outside, it is perfectly acceptable for the children to play and enjoy themselves too. Special facilities, such as high chairs, are unknown in all but the most considerate hotel dining rooms, but generally, casual restaurants and tavernas are perfect for dining with children of any age.

SMOKING

SMOKING is commonplace in Greece and until recently establishments maintaining a no-smoking policy have been difficult to find. However, new EU regulations make it obligatory for all restaurants to have no-smoking areas. In practice, of course, change is slow but for at least half the year you can always dine outdoors.

WHEELCHAIR ACCESS

IN COUNTRY AREAS, where room is plentiful, there are few problems for wheelchair users. But in crowded tourist restaurants access is often restricted. The streets themselves can have uneven pavements (sidewalks) on the islands, and many restaurants have narrow doorways and steps. There are several organizations for assisting disabled vacationers, and those listed on pages 297 and 337 provide specific information for visitors travelling to the Greek islands.

VEGETARIAN FOOD

GREEK CUISINE provides plenty of choice for vegetarians. Greeks enjoy a variety of dishes for each course, so it is easy to order just vegetable dishes in any traditional restaurants, tavernas or *kafeneía*. Greek vegetable dishes are substantial, inexpensive and very satisfying. Usually they are prepared in imaginative ways to complement or enhance their flavour.

Vegans may have a little more difficulty but, as Greek cooking relies very little on dairy products, it is possible to follow a vegan diet on any of the Greek islands.

PICNICS

THE BEST TIME to picnic in Greece is in spring, when the countryside is at its most beautiful and temperatures are not too hot. Traditional seasonal foods, such as Lenten olive oil breads, sweet Easter breads, pies filled with wild greens, fresh cheese and young retsina wine, make perfect picnic fare. In summer, peaches and figs, yoghurt, hard cheese, tomatoes, bread and olives are the ideal beach snacks.

People drinking coffee at the Liston in Corfu town

The Classic Greek Menu

THE TRADITIONAL FIRST COURSE is a selection of *mezédes*, or snacks; these can also be eaten in *ouzerís*, or bars, throughout the day. Meat or fish dishes follow next, usually served with a salad. The wine list tends to be simple, and coffee and cakes are generally consumed after the meal in a nearby pastry shop. In rural areas traditional dishes can be chosen straight from the kitchen.

Mezédes are both a first course and a snack with wine or other drinks.

Taramosaláta *is a purée of salted mullet roe and breadcrumbs or potato. Traditionally a dish for Lent, it is now on every taverna menu.*

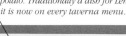

Souvlákia *are tiny chunks of pork, flavoured with lemon, herbs and olive oil, grilled (broiled) on skewers. Here they are served with* **tzatzíki***, a mixture of yoghurt, cucumber, garlic and mint.*

Olives

Fish are at their best around the coast and on the islands.

Melitzanosaláta and revithosaláta *are purées. Melitzanosaláta is grilled (broiled) aubergines (eggplants) and herbs; revithosaláta is chickpeas, coriander and garlic.*

Melitzánes imám baïldí *are aubergines (eggplants) filled with a ragout of onions, tomatoes and herbs.* **Ntolmádes** *are parcels of vine leaves stuffed with currants, pine nuts and rice.*

Fried squid

ΜΕΖΕΣ
Mezés

Ελιές
Eliés

Ταραμοσαλάτα
Taramosaláta

Τζατζίκι
Tzatzíki

Σουβλάκια
Souvlákia

Ρεβυθοσαλάτα
Revythosaláta

Μελιτζανοσαλάτα
Melitzanosaláta

Ντολμάδες
Ntolmádes

Μελιτζάνες ιμάμ μπαΪλντί
Melitzánes imám baïldí

Χωριάτικη σαλάτα
Choriátiki saláta

ΨΑΡΙΑ
Psária

Πλακί
Plakí

Σχάρας
Scháras

Τηγανιτά καλαμάρια
Tiganitá kalamária

Choriátiki saláta*, Greek salad, combines tomatoes, cucumber, onions, herbs, peppers and feta cheese.*

Scháras *means "from the grill". This summer dish of grilled (broiled) swordfish is served with salad leaves.*

Psária plakí *is a whole fish baked in an open dish with carrots, leeks and potatoes in a tomato, fennel and olive oil sauce.*

BREAD IN GREECE

Bread is considered by Greeks to be the staff of life and is served at every meal. Village bakers vary the bread each day with flavourings of currants, herbs, wild greens or cheese. The many Orthodox festivals are celebrated with special breads.

Olive rolls with herbs   **Pitta bread, unleavened**

Paximádia (twice-baked bread)   *Koulourákia* (sweet or plain rolls)   *Tsouréki* (festival bread loaf)

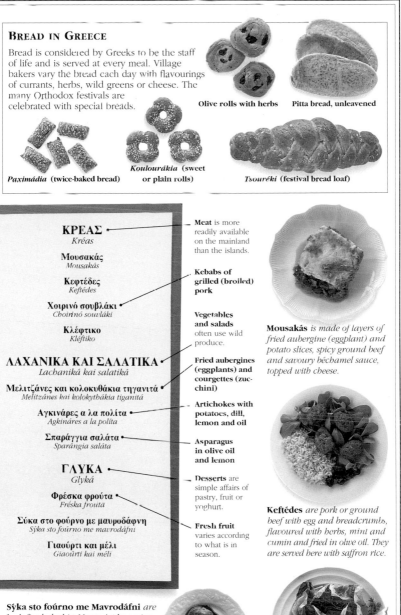

ΚΡΕΑΣ
Kréas

Μουσακάς
Mousakás

Κεφτέδες
Keftédes

Χοιρινό σουβλάκι
Choirinó souvláki

Κλέφτικο
Kléftiko

ΛΑΧΑΝΙΚΑ ΚΑΙ ΣΑΛΑΤΙΚΑ
Lachaniká kai salatiká

Μελιτζάνες και κολοκυθάκια τηγανιτά
Melitzánes kai kolokythákia tiganitá

Αγκινάρες α λα πολίτα
Agkináres a la políta

Σπαράγγια σαλάτα
Sparángia saláta

ΓΛΥΚΑ
Glyká

Φρέσκα φρούτα
Fréska froúta

Σύκα στο φούρνο με μαυροδάφνη
Sýka sto foúrno me mavrodáfni

Γιαούρτι και μέλι
Giaoúrti kai méli

Meat is more readily available on the mainland than the islands.

Kebabs of grilled (broiled) pork

Vegetables and salads often use wild produce.

Fried aubergines (eggplants) and courgettes (zucchini)

Artichokes with potatoes, dill, lemon and oil

Asparagus in olive oil and lemon

Desserts are simple affairs of pastry, fruit or yoghurt.

Fresh fruit varies according to what is in season.

Mousakás *is made of layers of fried aubergine (eggplant) and potato slices, spicy ground beef and savoury béchamel sauce, topped with cheese.*

Keftédes *are pork or ground beef with egg and breadcrumbs, flavoured with herbs, mint and cumin and fried in olive oil. They are served here with saffron rice.*

Sýka sto foúrno me Mavrodáfni *are fresh figs baked in Mavrodaphne wine sauce, served as a dessert or sweet treat. The sauce, of wine, spices and honey, is flavoured with orangeflower water.*

Giaoúrti kai méli *(yoghurt with honey) is the most wonderful snack in Greece, served in speciality "milk shops", to be eaten there or taken home.*

Kléftiko *is usually goat meat wrapped in parchment paper and cooked so that the juices and flavours are sealed in.*

Eating Fish on the Islands

GREEK COOKS HAVE ENJOYED a wealth of fish and seafood since ancient times. The warm and sheltered waters of the Aegean are the migratory path for tuna and swordfish, and a feeding ground for tasty anchovies and the ubiquitous sardine. Coves and caves around the hundreds of rocky islands shelter highly prized red mullet, dentex and parrot fish, while the long shoreline is home to a variety of shellfish and crustaceans. There is nothing better than eating simply prepared fish or seafood, fresh from the sea, in a harbourside taverna with the Aegean shimmering in the brilliant sunshine. Fish are grilled (broiled), pan-fried or baked, then served complete with their heads: to Greeks this is the tastiest part, and it helps to identify the variety.

Keeping fish fresh at the Lésvos port of Skála Sykaminiás

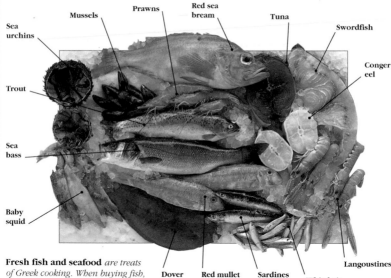

Sea urchins

Mussels

Prawns

Red sea bream

Tuna

Swordfish

Conger eel

Trout

Sea bass

Baby squid

Dover sole

Red mullet

Sardines

Whitebait

Langoustines

Fresh fish and seafood *are treats of Greek cooking. When buying fish, check for bright eyes, moist red gills, a firm body and a fresh, salty smell.*

Tsirosaláta *is a typical year-round mezés. Thin strips of smoked fish, baked beetroot and fresh herbs are served with olive oil and lemon juice.*

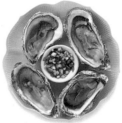

Streídia, *or oysters, were first "farmed" by the ancient Greeks. They are served with shallot, red-wine vinegar and parsley sauce.*

Achinoí *are sea-urchin roes. Gathered at full moon, when the roes are fattest, achinoí are a late-night speciality of many Cretan fish tavernas.*

Psarósoupa, *or fish soup, is served as a first course. Mussels, shellfish, prawns, scorpion fish, sea bass and other fish are cooked in a leek and herb broth.*

Astakós *is a rare and expensive treat. The lobsters, gathered by sponge divers, are served with olive oil and lemon juice.*

Tónnos psitós *is pan-fried tuna steak with a medley of carrots, leeks, potatoes and dill. It is served during the spring and autumn tuna migrations.*

Marídes *are tiny whitebait dipped in flour and fried in olive oil. A first or main course, they are served with a Kos lettuce, dill and spring onions.*

Barboúnia, *or red mullet, has been the most esteemed fish in Greece since antiquity. It is usually fried whole.*

Bourthéto *are the small fish of the catch baked in a thick tomato sauce spiced with cayenne pepper.*

Garídes saganáki *is a modern dish of large shrimps or prawns baked in a tomato, olive oil and parsley sauce and topped with féta cheese.*

Kavoúras *is a late summer dish of simply boiled crab served with sharp, juicy, Ionian green olives and an olive oil and lemon juice sauce.*

Kalamáres, *a Greek favourite, is small pieces of barbecued squid, often served in red-wine vinegar and olive oil, as here, or deep fried.*

Sardélles *are sardines wrapped in vine leaves and grilled (broiled). The leaves are discarded and the fish served with lemon and dill.*

Chopped
aubergines

Rosemary

Sea bass

Green
salad

Lavráki *is a whole sea bass baked in olive oil, red-wine vinegar and fresh rosemary. The head is considered the source of the fish's flavour, which then filters through to the rest of the body. Sharp salad greens are the perfect complement to this delicate, sweet fish.*

What to Eat on the Islands

EACH GROUP OF ISLANDS has a distinct culinary identity reflecting geographical location and history. Many Ionian dishes are pasta based, a legacy of the era of Venetian occupation.

Bunch of grapes

Those of the rocky and dramatic Cyclades are intensely flavoured. The cooks of the Dodecanese and Northeast Aegean benefit from the rich harvest of the surrounding sea. Crete is unique in its long Turkish occupation and taste for highly spiced dishes. Some beautiful kitchen utensils and unusual ingredients from Minoan times have been excavated by archaeologists on Crete.

Customers at a banana stall by the edge of the road near Vái, Crete

Saláta limniótiki *is an Aegean* mezés *of new potatoes, dill and capers.*

Agkináres a la políta *are artichoke hearts in olive oil and lemon juice.*

Fáva *is a purée of yellow Santoríni lentils, capers and oil.*

Prása me sousámi *is baked leeks with sesame seeds.*

Mpriám *is a casserole of late-summer vegetables topped with a crust of breadcrumbs and cheese.*

Sofríto, *a speciality of Corfu, is a stew of meat, olive oil, wine vinegar and tomatoes, flavoured with fresh garlic.*

Pastítsio, *a speciality of Corfu, is a pie with layers of macaroni, a meat and tomato filling, and béchamel sauce, topped with cheese.*

Candied pistachio nuts

Oranges

Morello cherries

Sweet bread

Glyká *are fruits preserved in heavy syrup. Here, pistachio nuts, morello cherries and oranges are served with sweet bread.*

CHEESES

Greece produces several types of sheep's, cow's and goat's cheeses. Each is manufactured according to local traditions.

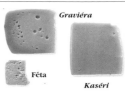

Féta in olive oil   *Kefalotýri*   *Féta*   *Graviéra*   *Kaséri*

CRETE

Cretan cooking has a number of dishes unique to the island. The use of pork, a legacy of antiquity, is more popular here than anywhere else in Greece.

Chórta *are wild greens, here boiled, and served with olive oil and vinegar or lemon juice.*

Choirinó kritikó, *the classic dish of inland Crete villages, is thick pork cutlets baked until tender.*

Saligkária, *or snails, are a* mezés *served with the local spirit* tsigouthiá.

Saláta kritikí, *a watercress salad, here mixed with féta cheese and oranges, is served in spring as a* mezés *or with grilled (broiled) meat.*

Arnáki psitó *is grilled (broiled) lamb cutlet flavoured with lemon, olive oil, oregano and sea salt, served with peppers.*

Stifádo *is a hearty casserole made with beef or rabbit, baked with shallots, herbs, tomatoes, olive oil and vinegar.*

Loukoumádes *are a snack of small deep-fried doughnuts soaked in honey-syrup and sprinkled with cinnamon.*

DRINKS IN GREECE

The three distinct areas of wine production in the islands are Ionian, Crete and Aegean. Greek specialities include retsina (wine flavoured with pine resin), the spirit ouzo, and dessert wines from the north Aegean. Small cups of Greek coffee are drunk for breakfast.

Strong Greek coffee

Bougátsa *is a pastry of sweet custard or savoury cheese dusted with cinnamon and sugar.*

Sýka me tyrí *is a summer* mezés, *dessert or snack, of fresh figs with* mizýthra, *a cheese, made from whey.*

Retsina, made by Kourtaki

Bottle of the spirit ouzo

Gentilini, a white wine from Crete

Red wine from Crete

A dish of seasonal fruits, often including watermelon, is served after every meal.

Choosing a Restaurant

THE RESTAURANTS in this guide have been selected across a wide range of price categories for their good value, traditional food and interesting location. This chart lists the restaurants by area, starting with the Ionian Islands, and highlights some of the factors which may influence your choice. For more details on restaurants, see pages 312–315.

	AIR-CONDITIONING	OUTDOOR TABLES	LIVE ENTERTAINMENT	LOCAL WINES

THE IONIAN ISLANDS

CORFU: *Nikólas* €€ Seafront, Gimári. (26630 91136. In Gimári, 2 km (1 mile) west of Kalámi, this taverna is delightfully situated on a quiet beach. Traditional Greek cuisine such as *mousakás*, grilled meats and fresh fish is on offer here. ● *Nov–Mar.* ⬛		■	●	■
CORFU: *Vráchos* €€ Palaiokastrítsa beach. (26630 41233. This well-situated taverna offers good, reliable food. The restaurant specializes in seafood, from lobster and swordfish to mullet. ○ *weekends only.* ● *Nov–Mar.* ⬛		■		■
CORFU: *Rex* €€ Kapodistríou 66, Corfu town. (26610 39649. Housed in a mid 19th-century town house, the Rex is a truly traditional Greek restaurant serving genuine Greek and Corfiot food. Specialities include swordfish *mpourdétto*, a spicy fish stew with peppers and potatoes. ⬛	●	■		
CORFU: *Tría Adélfia* €€ Harbourfront, Kassiópi. (26630 81211. Despite the increasing tourist trade, this restaurant manages to retain its Greek atmosphere. The menu includes standard Greek fare such as *mousakás* and salads, while its fish is genuinely fresh, caught daily by the owner. ● *Nov–Mar.* ⬛		■	●	■
ITHACA: *Fatoúro* € Main square, Stavrós. (26740 31385. Situated in a pleasant hill-village, this simple taverna serves good, home-made, traditional dishes. There is no menu as the owner cooks what is fresh, including good vegetable stews and herb-covered salads.		■		■
ITHACA: *Trechantíri* € Behind Plateía Doureíou Ippou, Vathý. (26740 33066. A well-established family taverna in the market area where a husband-and- wife team provide good examples of traditional dishes such as *mousakás* or roast lamb, accompanied by generous salads and retsina. ● *lunch; Dec–Jan.*	●	■		■
KEFALLONIA: *Anonymous* €€ Antóni Trítsi 47, Argostóli. (26710 22403. Three or four daily specials are always on offer at this welcoming taverna. Dishes often include fresh fish and other typical Greek specialities. ● *Nov–Feb.*		■		■
KEFALLONIA: *Dásos* €€ Harbourfront, Fiskárdo. (26740 41276. This restaurant serves fresh fish as well as a good example of the island speciality, Kefalloniá meat pie *(kreatópita)*. This consists of beef chunks with a pastry topping, served with rice and tomato sauce. ● *Oct–Mar.* ⬛		■		■
KEFALLONIA: *Patsoúras* €€ Ioánnou Metaxá 40, Argostóli. (26710 22779. This small, family-run restaurant has a pleasant garden, and serves authentic island dishes such as *krasáto* (pork in wine) and the ubiquitous Kefalloniá meat pie. ● *Nov; Easter day, Christmas day.* ⬛	●	■		■
LEFKADA: *Káto Vrýsi* € Dórpfeld, Lefkáda town. (26450 22722. This traditional taverna provides classic Greek dishes such as *mousakás*, chicken, salads and the popular pasta dish, *pastítsio*. ● *Oct–Mar.*		■		■
LEFKADA: *Oscar* €€ Habourfront, Nydri. (26450 92520. This smart but casual taverna caters mainly for tourists and offers a wider range of salads, grilled fish and meat than other local restaurants. ● *Nov–Mar.* ⬛		■	●	■

	AIR-CONDITIONING	OUTDOOR TABLES	LIVE ENTERTAINMENT	LOCAL WINES
Average prices for a three-course meal for one, including a half-bottle of house wine, tax and service: € up to 12 euros €€ 12–18 euros €€€ 18–24 euros €€€€ 24–32 euros €€€€€ over 32 euros	**AIR-CONDITIONING** Restaurant with air-conditioning. **OUTDOOR TABLES** Tables for eating outdoors, often with a good view. **LIVE ENTERTAINMENT** Dancing or live music performances on various days of the week. **LOCAL WINES** A specialized selection of local Greek wines.			

		AIR-CONDITIONING	OUTDOOR TABLES	LIVE ENTERTAINMENT	LOCAL WINES
PAXOS: *Táka Táka* €€ Gáios, 50m (165 ft) from the main square (look for signs). ☎ 26620 32329. This delightful vine-covered garden restaurant is a long-standing favourite with the locals. The menu specializes in grilled meat and fish dishes. ● *Nov–Mar.*			■		■
ZAKYNTHOS: *I Mantaléna* € Seafront, 1 km (0.5 miles) E of Alykés. ☎ 26950 83487. A superb family-run restaurant which serves a welcoming drink, water from its own well, wine from the family vines and wonderful home-cooked dishes – the stuffed vine leaves are delicious. ● *main public hols; weekends Oct–Apr.*			■		■
THE ARGO SARONIC ISLANDS					
AIGINA: *Avra* €€ Kazantzákis, Aigina town. ☎ 22970 24493. A stone exterior and wooden furniture give this fish taverna a rustic feel. Beautifully situated by the sea, it offers specialities such as cuttlefish in wine.			■		■
AIGINA: *Kóstas* €€ Close to Agía Marína beach, Agía Marína. ☎ 22970 32424. Greek specialities including rabbit *stifádo* (casserole) are cooked by the chef, who is also the owner. There is a garden with mulberry trees. ✍			■		■
AGKISTRI: *To Konaki* € Milos. ☎ 22970 91321. This traditional taverna serves standard Greek fare and is popular with locals and tourists alike. There is live entertainment on Thursdays. ● *Oct–Apr: Mon–Fri.*			■	●	
KYTHIRA: *Sotíris* €€ Main square, Avlémonas. ☎ 27360 33722. This fish taverna is deservedly popular with the islanders, serving the catch of the day. Seafood is accompanied by the house white wine. ● *Oct–Apr: Mon–Fri.*			■		■
KYTHIRA: *Taverna Magos* €€ Harbourfront, Kapsáli, 1.5km (1 mile) E of Chóra. ☎ 27360 31407. This traditional taverna, situated in the heart of the picturesque harbour, overlooks the sea and offers fresh seafood and vegetable dishes. ● *Nov–Feb.*			■		■
POROS: *O Karavolos* € Behind the cinema, Póros town. ☎ 22980 26158. Hidden away in a little alley, this traditional, family-run taverna offers typical Greek cuisine and fresh fish at excellent prices.			■		■
SPETSES: *O Pánas* € Harbour, Agia Marina. ☎ 22980 73030. A genuine *ouzeri* run by a Greek-American woman and her husband. Vegetarian *mezédes*, grilled meat and seafood are on offer. ● *Oct–Apr: Mon–Thu.*			■	●	
SPETSES: *Exedra* €€ Palió Limáni, Spétses town. ☎ 22980 73497. Situated on the waterfront, this traditional Greek taverna offers good local dishes, such as shrimps *saganaki* and fish *á la spetsiota*. ● *Nov–Dec.* ✍			■		
YDRA: *Kondylénia's* €€ On coast road towards Kamíni, 1 km (0.5 miles) W of Ydra town. ☎ 22980 53520. A lunch-time favourite for its stunning sea views to the Peloponnese, this taverna offers interesting recipes such as spinach, squid and prawn casserole. ● *Oct–Mar.*			■		
YDRA: *Xerí Eliá* €€€ Off main square, Ydra town. ☎ 22980 52886. A wonderful old taverna with traditional stone walls and wooden ceiling. Lamb *kapamá*, fresh fish and *mpaklavás* can be enjoyed in a large garden. ✍		●	■	●	

For key to symbols see back flap

Average prices for a three-course meal for one, including a half-bottle of house wine, tax and service:

- € up to 12 euros
- €€ 12–18 euros
- €€€ 18–24 euros
- €€€€ 24–32 euros
- €€€€€ over 32 euros

AIR-CONDITIONING
Restaurant with air-conditioning.

OUTDOOR TABLES
Tables for eating outdoors, often with a good view.

LIVE ENTERTAINMENT
Dancing or live music performances on various days of the week.

LOCAL WINES
A specialized selection of local Greek wines.

THE SPORADES AND EVVOIA

Name / Details	Price	AIR-CONDITIONING	OUTDOOR TABLES	LIVE ENTERTAINMENT	LOCAL WINES
ALONNISOS: *To Kamáki* Ikion Dolópon, Patitíri. 24240 65245. All variety of seafood *mezédes*, such as baked mussels, stuffed squid and red mullet, are served at this popular *ouzerí*. ● Nov–Mar.	€€	■			
EVVOIA: *Gkoúveris* Leofóros Mpoudoúri 20, Chalkída. Sole, sea bream and mackerel are grilled outside at this waterfront taverna. Dishes such as salads and boiled vegetables are also on offer. ● Easter day, 1 Jan.	€€	●	■		■
EVVOIA: *Kávo d'Oro* Párodos Sachtoúri, Kárystos. 22240 22326. This established taverna serves good home cooking. The olive oil based vegetable and meat stews, *ntolmádes* and aubergines are all worth trying. ● Oct–Dec.	€€		■		■
EVVOIA: *Skýros* Harbourfront, Kými. 22220 22624. A seafront setting and friendly service characterize this excellent taverna. Local grilled shrimps, octopus and baby red mullet are on offer. ● Nov–Apr.	€€		■	●	■
EVVOIA: *To Pyrofáni* Next to Agía Triáda, Límni. 22270 31640. Freshly caught fish, lobster and crayfish are available at this fish taverna. Try the *garídes saganáki* (baked shrimps), a particularly good house speciality.	€€		■	●	■
SKIATHOS: *I Mouriá* Behind the National Bank, Skiáthos town. 24270 23069. This old stone town house produces some of the best food on the island. Favourites here are rich rabbit *stifádo*, fried squid and boiled wild greens, all accompanied by carafes of pungent retsina. ● lunch; Nov–Apr.	€		■		■
SKIATHOS: *Troúllos* Troúllos beach, Troúllos. 24270 49255. Tables almost spill out on to the sandy beach at this well-established taverna. Swordfish *souvláki* and whitebait are always good here. ● mid-Oct–mid-Apr.	€€		■		
SKIATHOS: *Ta Psarádika* Next to fish market, Skiáthos town. 24270 23412. This taverna is popular with locals, who come for warming tripe soup (*pastsás*) in the winter, and a variety of delicious fish and *mezédes* in the summer.	€€		■		■
SKIATHOS: *Windmill* Kotróni Hill, Skiáthos town. 24270 24550. Housed in an old windmill with wonderful views over the harbour and town, this restaurant offers mainly international cuisine. ● lunch; Oct–Apr.	€€€		■		
SKOPELOS: *Finikas* Yifteroma, Skópelos town. 24240 23247. Situated in the old part of Skópelos town, this taverna offers unusual dishes such as pork braised with plums and chicken stuffed with cheese. ● lunch; Nov–Apr.	€€		■		■
SKYROS: *Asterias* Off main square, Skýros town. 22220 91380. Traditional Greek cuisine as well as lobster with spaghetti, the local speciality, can be enjoyed at this quiet, family-run restaurant. ● Oct–Jun.	€€		■		
SKYROS: *O Liakós* Skýros town centre. 22220 93509. This roof garden taverna serves traditional Greek dishes with imaginative touches. Specialities include *tomatakeftédhes* (tomato fritters) and homemade cheese pies. Fine views over Skýros town. ● lunch Sun.	€€		■		■

THE NORTHEAST AEGEAN ISLANDS

CHIOS: *O Dólomas* €
Near Morning Star Hotel, Kondári, 2 km (1 mile) N of Karfás. **[** *22710 ∕1040.*
Despite the tacky decor and often perfunctory service, the *mezédes* are excellent.
Meals can be enjoyed in a pleasant, tree-shaded garden. ● *Mon; Tue–Sat lunch; Oct.*

CHIOS: *O Mórias sta Mestá* €
Main square, Mestá. **[** *22710 76400.*
Tasty rural specialities are on offer at this grill-house, including pickled
krítamo (samphire). The local raisin wine is heavy and sherry-like.

CHIOS: *Apolafsi* €€
Aqía Ermióni, 7km (4 miles) S of Chíos town. **[** *22710 31359.*
Located right on the seafront, this recently refurbished taverna offers a range of
seafood and *mezédes*. Enjoy your meal at a table by the water's edge. ● *Nov–Mar.*

FOURNOI: *Nikos's* €€
Waterfront, Port town. **[** *22750 51253.*
Also known as the Reméntzo, this is the spot for succulent *skathári*
(black bream) or *astakós* (the local lobster variant). Customers pick
their own fish which is then grilled.

LESVOS: *I Sykaminiá* €
Habourfront, Skála Sykaminiás **[** *22530 55319.*
The longest-running of three eateries in the area, the taverna functions as the
locals' *kafeneío* in winter. Specialities include local sardines, anchovies, squid
and stuffed squash flowers. You can sit out under the mulberry tree.

LESVOS: *Jay's* €
Seafront, Skála Eresoú. **[** *22530 53624.*
A British-run restaurant serving mainly Chinese, Thai and Indian cuisine as
well as a wide variety of vegetarian dishes. ● *Nov–Apr.*

LESVOS: *To Ammoudéli* €
On Plomári–Melínta road **[** *22520 31333.*
With terrace seating overlooking the sea, this cheap and cheerful establishment
features seafood (the octopus is a speciality) and meat grills. There is also a
limited choice of *mezédes* and locally produced ouzo. ● *15 Aug, Nov–Apr.*

LESVOS: *Captain's Table* €€
Harbourfront, Mólyvos. **[** *22530 71241.*
Live music and family ownership ensure this restaurant has a lively,
welcoming atmosphere. Fresh fish and a wide choice of *mezedes*
are on offer. ● *lunch; Oct–Apr.* ☑

LESVOS: *Vafeiós* €€
On road to Kaminía, Vafeiós, 5 km (3 miles) SE of Mólyvos. **[** *22530 71/52.*
An extensive menu of local dishes, reasonable prices, and a lovely terrace
setting make this a firm favourite with both islanders and tourists from nearby
Mólyvos. The cuisine is rich, so come with an appetite. ● *Nov–Mar.* ☑

LIMNOS: *Nasos Kotsinadelis Taverna* €
Tsimántria, 1.5km (1 mile) E of Kontiás. **[** *22540 51277.*
In an old, traditional-style building in the village square, providing ample
seating outside. The menu ranges from grilled meats such as *kokoretsí* (offal
kebab), to grilled octopus. The owner entertains diners on the lyre.

LIMNOS: *O Plátanos* €
Central market area, Myrína. **[** *22540 22070.*
Situated on an atmospheric little square hemmed in by old houses and the
century old plane tree, this restaurant offers traditional oven-cooked food,
such as *pastítsio* (macaroni pie) and vegetable casseroles.

SAMOS: *Anna's Garden Café* €€
Pythagora and Aristarchou, Pythagóreio. **[** *22730 61635.*
In a cool and tranquil garden setting, this family run restaurant serves a
mouthwatering array of Greek cuisine. Good desserts. ● *Nov–Apr.*

SAMOS: *Oi Psarádes* €€
Waterfront, Kondakaíika village, 5 km (3 miles) E of Karlóvasi. **[** *22730 32489.*
Abundant fish dishes, accompanied by a limited selection of *mezédes* and
salads, are served on a terrace overlooking the sea. The taverna is at its best
in May, just before the net-fishing season closes. ● *Nov–Mar.*

Average prices for a three-course meal for one, including a half-bottle of house wine, tax and service:
€ up to 12 euros
€€ 12–18 euros
€€€ 18–24 euros
€€€€ 24–32 euros
€€€€€ over 32 euros

AIR-CONDITIONING
Restaurant with air-conditioning.

OUTDOOR TABLES
Tables for eating outdoors, often with a good view.

LIVE ENTERTAINMENT
Dancing or live music performances on various days of the week.

LOCAL WINES
A specialized selection of local Greek wines.

	AIR-CONDITIONING	OUTDOOR TABLES	LIVE ENTERTAINMENT	LOCAL WINES
SAMOS: *To Kýma* €€ Karlóvasi shore road. 22730 34017. Opened in 1984, this *ouzerí*, operating out of a small white house, offers consistent quality in its food. Generous seafood medleys and some of the best sunset views on the island are on offer. ● *Nov–Mar: lunch.*		▪		▪
SAMOTHRAKI: *I Plateía* €€ Main square, Chóra. 25510 41224. Of the two excellent tavernas on Chóra's main square, this has sea views and a more daring menu than most establishments. Items such as stuffed squid complement old standards like *mýdia saganáki* (mussels with cheese). ● *Oct–May.*		▪	●	▪
THASOS: *O Gláros* € Alykí bay. 25930 31547. This is the oldest and arguably the best-value of several tavernas in this area. Fish, meat grills and salads can be enjoyed on a vine-shaded terrace with views across Alykí bay. ● *Oct–May.*		▪		
THASOS: *Ta Platánia* € 4km from Skála Potamiás, on road to Tsímia. 25930 41340. This is a simple grill house serving all the standard Greek fare. Enjoy a steak and salad under the Plane trees from which it takes its name. ● *Nov–Apr.*		▪		
THASOS: *Kleoníki* €€ Near bus terminus, Theológos village. 25930 31000. The Kleoníki, also known as Taverna Iatroú is a traditional grill-house specializing in locally raised suckling pig, goat, skewered lamb and *kokorétsi* (offal kebab).		▪		
THE DODECANESE				
ASTYPALAIA: *Astrópalos* € Livádi beach. 22430 61473. Situated right on the beach, this traditional taverna serves typical Greek cuisine and fresh seafood at excellent prices. ● *Nov–Apr.*		▪	●	▪
CHALKI: *Pontamos* € Póntamos beach, Nimporió. 22460 45295. Cool off under the shady carob tree at this atmospheric taverna perched above the sands. A bustling lunch-time favourite offering a good selection of Greek dishes and snacks. ● *Oct–Apr.*		▪		
KALYMNOS: *Iliovasílema* € Next to Plaza Hotel, Masouri beach. 22430 47683. Run by the local butcher, the furniture here may be garish but the meat is wonderful. Excellent rabbit *stifádo* and roasts are on offer as well as vegetarian dishes. The friendly atmosphere makes it a popular family choice. ● *Nov–Apr.*		▪		
KALYMNOS: *Xeftéris* €€ Next to Moní Christou, Póthia. 22430 28642. Considered by the locals to be the town's best taverna, Xeftéris has been run by the same family for more than 85 years. The restaurant is tucked away in an alley and the menu features fresh fish, roast lamb, and vegetable dishes.		▪		▪
KARPATHOS: *Kalí Kardiá* € On road to Vróntis beach, Kárpathos town. 22450 22256. This friendly Greek/American, family-run taverna is situated at the water's edge and offers a good selection of oven dishes as well as fresh fish. ● *Oct–Mar.*		▪	●	▪

Kasos: *Emporeiós*   €
Emporeió harbour, 1 km (0.5 miles) from Frý. 22450 41586.
In a quiet setting with a pleasant garden, this traditional fish taverna always serves
fresh seafood and barbecued meats at reasonable prices. ● *Nov–Apr.*

Kastellorizo: *Ta Platánia*   €
Plateía Choráfia, Kastellórizo town. 22460 49206.
Above the harbour, this restaurant specializes in food such as *revythokeftédes*
(chickpea fritters) and oven-cooked dishes. Enjoy the free *chalvá*. ● *Oct–Apr.*

Kos: *Frangolis*   €€
Plateía Arístonis, Kakó Prinári, Kos town. 22420 28761.
Deemed to be one of the island's best traditional tavernas, the Frangolis has
an authentic Greek menu – rare in Kos town. Barbecued meat and oven dishes
can be enjoyed in the tree-shaded garden

Kos: *Olympiáda*   €€
Kleopátras 2, Kos town. 22420 23031.
Away from the bustle, this traditional taverna serves all the standard oven fare.
Good value and very Greek with a cheerful service. ● *Easter, 15 Dec–15 Jan.*

Kos: *O Plátanos*   €€€
Plateía Plátanou, Kos town. 22420 28991.
Named after Hippocrates' plane tree, this café overlooks the ancient agora.
Classical music and cakes are enjoyed under a shady canopy. ● *Nov–Apr.*

Leros: *María*   €€
On the waterfront, Pantéli. 22470 22967.
An atmospheric and authentic fish taverna, the María serves a wide range of
fresh fish from tiny crisp whitebait to *kalamári* (squid). ● *Oct–May.*

Leros: *Da Giusi Marcello*   €€€
Next to the church behind the harbour, Agía Marína. 22470 24888.
This tiny Italian restaurant uses only the finest, organic ingredients. Good
vegetarian choices and specially imported wines from Italy. ● *Jan & Feb.*

Lipsi: *Kalypsó*   €
Kalypsó Hotel, on the waterfront, Lipsí town. 22470 41242.
Attached to the hotel, this vine-covered restaurant, also known as Mr Maungo's
after the characterful proprietor, serves all the usual Greek favourites. Look
out for delicious grilled octopus and stuffed baby goat.

Nisyros: *Hellenis*   €
Hotel Hellenis, Páloi beach. 22420 31453.
Linked to the hotel of the same name, this traditional taverna specializes in local
fare such as *revythokeftédes* (chickpea fritters) and skewered lamb.

Nisyros: *Nísyros*   €
On main road, Mandráki. 22420 31460.
With tables spilling across a narrow alley under a vine-clad canopy, the Nísyros
is popular for lunch or dinner with all the usual Greek favourites.

Patmos: *Balcony View*   €
Chóra. 22470 32115.
Taverna specialising in seafood and traditional dishes such as *moussakás*
(potatoes, aubergines and minced lamb) baked in a clay pot. Excellent
views over the harbour. ● *Nov–May.*

Patmos: *Arion Cafe*   €€
On the waterfront, Skála. 22470 31595.
This pavement café is a popular meeting place. It has a Neo-Classical façade and
cavernous music bar inside. Serves coffees, cocktails, and snacks. ● *Oct–Mar.*

Patmos: *Villa Zabaro*   €€
Harbour, Skála. 22470 31529.
Situated 100m (300 ft) from the harbour, this atmospheric restaurant serves
classical Greek and Mediterranean cuisine.

Rhodes: *Bombay*   €€
Agiou Fanouríou 14, Rhodes town. 22410 70527.
This restaurant is situated off a quiet cobbled street in the heart of the old
town. Authentic Indian dishes created by the Bangladeshi chef are served in
atmospheric surroundings. ● *lunch; Dec–Mar.*

	AIR-CONDITIONING	OUTDOOR TABLES	LIVE ENTERTAINMENT	LOCAL WINES

Average prices for a three-course meal for one, including a half-bottle of house wine, tax and service:
€ up to 12 euros
€€ 12–18 euros
€€€ 18–24 euros
€€€€ 24–32 euros
€€€€€ over 32 euros

AIR-CONDITIONING
Restaurant with air-conditioning.

OUTDOOR TABLES
Tables for eating outdoors, often with a good view.

LIVE ENTERTAINMENT
Dancing or live music performances on various days of the week.

LOCAL WINES
A specialized selection of local Greek wines.

RHODES: *L'Auberge Bistro*   €€
Praxitelous 21, Rhodes Old Town. **[** 22410 34292.
This charming bistro is housed in a beautifully restored medieval building with a courtyard. French cuisine with a twist and excellent desserts. ● *lunch; Mon; Dec–Mar.*

| | | ■ | | ■ |

RHODES: *Sandy Beach*   €€
Next to Sun Beach Hotel, Ialyssós bay, 5 km (3 miles) N of ancient site. **[** 22410 94600.
Situated right on the beach, this lunch-time favourite excels at Greek classics such as *kopanistí* (a purée of cracked olives, strong cheese and paprika) and *skordaliá* (potato and garlic purée). There is also a range of ouzos. ●

| | | ■ | | ■ |

RHODES: *Paliá Istoría*   €€€
Mitropóleos 108, Ammos district, Rhodes town. **[** 22410 32421.
This award-winning eatery offers Greek and Mediterranean dishes with a twist. The imaginative and healthy creations range from beetroot with walnuts to lobster spaghetti. Dine beneath the shady pergola. Reservations advisable. ● *lunch.* ●

| | | ■ | | ■ |

SYMI: *O Meraklís*   €
Next to Agios Ioánnis, Gialós area, Sými town. **[** 22460 71003.
Tucked away behind the bank, this traditional taverna is the nearest you will get to good home cooking. Excellent vegetable dishes, fresh fish, and all the usual Greek favourites are available. Reasonable prices and friendly service. ●

| | ● | ■ | | ■ |

SYMI: *Tólis*   €€
Pédi bay. **[** 22460 71601.
Situated right at the water's edge, this friendly, family-run taverna is a popular lunch-time haunt offering a small but appetizing menu including fresh fish of the day and local vegetable dishes. ● *Nov–Apr.*

| | | ■ | ● | ■ |

TELENDOS: *Telendos*   €€
Waterfront, Télendos harbour. **[** 22430 47502.
This reasonably priced, harbourside taverna, offers a wide range of starters, excellent fresh seafood, home-cooked dishes and salads. Good views of nearby Kálymnos can be enjoyed from the tables along the seafront. ● *Nov–mid-Apr.* ●

| | | ■ | ● | ■ |

TILOS: *Eirína*   €
Waterfront, Livádia. **[** 22460 44206.
With tables at the water's edge, this traditional taverna serves up good Greek fare. Vegetable dishes such as *fasoláda* (bean soup) and *gígantes* (haricots) are especially good. Everything has a home-cooked touch. ● *Nov–Apr.*

| | | ■ | | |

THE CYCLADES

AMORGOS: *Ambrosia*   €€
On Aigiáli–Tholária road. **[** 22850 73107.
Traditional Greek cuisine and panoramic views of the sea are on offer at this popular restaurant. Fresh fish and lobster are always available. ●

| | ● | ■ | ● | ■ |

AMORGOS: *Vitséntsos*   €€€
Harbourfront, Katápola. **[** 22850 71518.
This popular but pricey harbourside taverna serves island specialities such as kid and potato casserole. Fresh fish is also available daily. ● *mid-Oct–mid-Mar.*

| | | ■ | | |

ANDROS: *Archipélagos*   €€
Seafront, Andros town. **[** 22820 24430.
Situated on the beach, this modern taverna is decorated in a traditional Greek style with a stone exterior. Standard Greek dishes and fresh fish are on offer.

| | | ■ | | ■ |

ANDROS: *Siróco*   €€
Behind main square, Mpatsí. **[** 22820 41023.
Housed in a 100-year-old building with a wooden interior, this restaurant offers traditional Greek cuisine as well as European food such as pizza and spaghetti. Service is good and there are nice sea views. ● *lunch.*

| | | ■ | | ■ |

FOLEGANDROS: *Kalimnios* €€
Waterfront, Karavostásis. 22860 41146.
This simple taverna set at the water's edge specializes in fresh fish
and traditional Greek dishes. ● Nov–Apr.

IOS: *Fiesta* €
Páno Foúrnos, Ios town. 22860 91766.
Situated in "The Village", this restaurant serves pizza as well as grilled meats.
● Christmas period.

IOS: *Pithári* €
Plateía Evangelismoú, Ios town. 22860 91379.
This friendly taverna is one of the island's best. Excellent traditional Greek
cuisine is on offer along with barrel wines. ● 20 Oct–20 Apr.

KYTHNOS: *To Kantoúni* €
Mérichas bay. 22810 32220.
Perched at the water's edge with a view across the bay, this simple eatery
specializes in grills and *sfougáta* (fried cheese balls).

KYTHNOS: *Ostria* €
Harbourfront, Mérichas. 22810 32263.
This restaurant, overlooking the water, serves traditional Greek dishes
as well as good seafood. Specialities include cheese croquettes and
locally-produced *loukániko* (spicy sausage). ● Dec–Jan.

MILOS: *Varco* €
Chiovasalos (near the harbour), Adámas. 22870 22660.
This cheap and cheerful waterfront taverna offers tasty, traditional Greek
dishes and a good barrel wine. Fresh fish is also available. ● lunch; Dec–Jan.

MILOS: *Kyma* €€
Adámas shore road. 22870 22522.
As well as the standard Greek fare, this restaurant also serves a variety of
generously topped pizzas. ● Nov–May.

MYKONOS: *Antoníni's* €
Plateía Mantó, Mýkonos town. 22890 22319.
For many this is the island's best eating place serving authentic Greek
dishes at palatable prices. Enjoy the excellent *mezédes* followed by
stámnas, a delicious veal casserole. ● Nov–Mar.

MYKONOS: *Kástro* €€€
Kástro area, Little Venice, Mýkonos town. 22890 23072.
This legendary gay bar, overlooking the Kástro district, is a relaxing place to
sip strawberry daiquiris and listen to classical music. ● lunch; mid-Oct–Apr.

MYKONOS: *Chez Katrin* €€€€
Nikíou, Mýkonos town. 22890 22169.
Commonly known as Bobby's and beloved by the locals, this is one of the
island's oldest international restaurants, known for its French cuisine and
delicious chocolate mousse. Booking advisable. ● Nov–Apr.

NAXOS: *Manólis* €€
Old town centre, Náxos town. 22850 25168.
Traditional Greek cuisine can be enjoyed at this garden taverna in the heart of
the old town. Dishes on offer include *melitzánes* (fried aubergines), *skordaliá*
(potato and garlic purée) and other well-known favourites. ● lunch; Nov–Mar.

NAXOS: *Oneiro* €€€
Parapórti area, Náxos town. 22850 23846.
Fine views from the roof garden, romantic candle-lit tables and an international
menu make the Oneiro a good choice. ● lunch; Nov–Apr.

PAROS: *Páros* €€
Off Agorá, Paroikiá. 22840 21319.
Traditional Greek cuisine and Páros specialities such as cheese
pies can be enjoyed at this family-run restaurant situated on the seafront.
● mid-Oct–May.

PAROS: *Tamarísko* €€€
Off Agorá, Paroikiá. 22840 24689.
Considered the best restaurant on the island, the international cuisine is good
value and served in a peaceful, secluded garden. ● lunch; Sep–Jun Mon; Jan.

Average prices for a three-course meal for one, including a half-bottle of house wine, tax and service: € up to 12 euros €€ 12–18 euros €€€ 18–24 euros €€€€ 24–32 euros €€€€€ over 32 euros	**AIR-CONDITIONING** Restaurant with air-conditioning. **OUTDOOR TABLES** Tables for eating outdoors, often with a good view. **LIVE ENTERTAINMENT** Dancing or live music performances on various days of the week. **LOCAL WINES** A specialized selection of local Greek wines.	AIR-CONDITIONING	OUTDOOR TABLES	LIVE ENTERTAINMENT	LOCAL WINES
SANTORINI: *Camille Stefaní* €€€ Kamári beach. 🅒 22860 31716. This elegant restaurant is situated by the beach and offers French-influenced cuisine. The restaurant also has its own wine label. ● *Nov–Mar.* 🄴				■
SANTORINI: *Nikólas* €€€ Above central square, Firá. 🅒 22860 24550. Old-established traditional taverna in the heart of Firá with authentic Greek menu, fresh fish and wines from the barrel.				■
SERIFOS: *Tákis* €€€ On the waterfront, Livádi. 🅒 22810 51159. Occupying a good location, right on the seafront, Tákis has a large menu including fish dishes and salads. There is also an extensive wine list. ● *Dec–Mar.*		■		
SIFNOS: *Artemónas* €€ Agíou Kostantínou 3, Artemónas. 🅒 22840 31303. Situated in the peaceful garden of the Artemónas hotel, this restaurant offers good home-made dishes. All vegetables are organic. ● *Oct–May.* 🄴		■		
SIFNOS: *Liotrívi Maganas* €€ Next to bus terminus, Artemónas. 🅒 22840 31246. One of the best-known tavernas in the Cyclades, Liotrívi is famous for its local specialities. Greeks queue up for the *revýthia* (chickpea stew), a Sifniot Sunday special. There is a lively traditional atmosphere and good barrel wines. ● *Dec.*	●	■	●	■
SYROS: *I Folia* €€ Athanasíou Diákou 1, Ermoúpoli. In the Vrontádo district, this is rated one of the finest tavernas in the Cyclades. Basic and unpretentious, it specializes in classic dishes like casseroled pigeon and rabbit and cauliflower *keftédes* (meatballs).	●	■		■
SYROS: *Lilís'* €€ Piátsa, Ano Sýros area. 🅒 22810 88087. Famous for its stunning views over the bay and wide range of imaginative Greek, *nouvelle cuisine* style dishes. There is live music at weekends. ● *winter: lunch.*	●	■	●	■
SYROS: *To Iliovasílema* €€ Kíni beach, Kíni. 🅒 22810 71211. Named after the marvellous sunset, this popular beach-side taverna has a wide menu and is run by a famous family of Syriot musicians and singers. ● *Nov–Mar.*		■		■
TINOS: *Palaiá Pallláda* € Pallláda area, behind the port, Tínos town. 🅒 22830 23516. Situated in the Pallláda area, this restaurant offers traditional Greek taverna cuisine as well as fresh fish, meat grills and a barrel wine. ● *1–20 Jan.* 🄴		■		
TINOS: *Taverna O Kípos* € Trión Ierarchón, Tínos town. 🅒 22830 23138. This traditional Greek taverna offers good local food, including beef *stifado*, and a range of local cheeses. Enjoy your meal outside in the pretty garden. 🄴		■	●	
CRETE				
AGIA ROUMELI: *To Farángi* € Main square. 🅒 28250 91225. Specialities at this family-run taverna include stuffed cabbage leaves, peppers and vine leaves. Try the *sfakianés pítes*, pies with honey. ● *15 Nov–Mar.*		■	●	■
AGIOS NIKOLAOS: *Itanos* € Kýprou 1. 🅒 28410 25340. This popular taverna, situated off Plateía Venizélou, serves traditional Cretan cuisine such as charcoal-grilled goat meat. Pavement seating is available.		■		■

AGIOS NIKOLAOS: *I Tráta* €€
Akti Pangálou 17. 28410 22028.
A fish taverna and grill-house, the I Tráta offers fresh fish and meat grills as
well as most traditional Greek dishes and Italian food such as pizza.

CHANIA: *Akrogiáli* €€
Akti Papanikolí 19, Néa Chóra area. 28210 73110.
The busiest and trendiest fish restaurant in Néa Chóra, 18km (11 miles) from
Chaniá, the Akrogiáli always offers a wide selection of fish and good service.
Try the barbecued cuttlefish. Nov–Apr: Mon–Sat: lunch; Easter day & 25 Dec: eve.

CHANIA: *O Anemos* €€
Sourmelí 40–42, Aktí Tompázi. 28210 58330.
This smart restaurant, situated on the waterfront and below the city's old
Venetian wall, specializes in seafood dishes and offers interesting choices such
as squid cooked in ouzo. Fish is always fresh and meat grills are also available.

CHANIA: *Mylos* €€€
Platánias. 28210 68578.
This charming restaurant is set in an old watermill. Enjoy traditional Cretan
and Mediterranean cuisine in its shady garden. lunch; Nov–Mar

CHANIA: *Thólos* €€€
Agíon Déka 36, Old town. 28210 46725.
Housed in a 14th-century building, this open-air restaurant has tables on three
levels. All food is carefully prepared and made from the best local produce.
The restaurant also offers an extensive wine list. Nov–Apr.

CHANIA: *The Well of the Turk* €€€
1–3 Kaliníkou Zarpáki. 28210 54547.
This cosy restaurant, with candle-lit tables and eastern music, is set in a stone
built cellar. Spicy, original-tasting food is on offer including aubergine meatballs and stuffed *kalamári* (squid). Sunday lunch; Tue; mid-Nov–mid-Dec: lunch.

CHORAFAKIA: *Eiríni* €
At entrance to village. 28210 39470.
Situated in Chorafákia, 8 km (5 miles) north of Chaniá, this bustling taverna
offers simple home cooking. Especially good are the *agkináres me koukiá*
(artichokes with broad beans), and the oven-cooked goat or lamb in lemon sauce.

IRAKLEIO: *I Erganos* €
G Georgiádou 5. 2810 285629.
Traditional Cretan cuisine is on offer at this family-run restaurant which is
situated in an old house with four rooms. Specials such as *sygoúri* (meat
soup) make this a winter rather than a summer choice. lunch; Aug.

IRAKLEIO: *O Kyriákos* €€
Leofóros Dimokratías 53. 2810 222464.
Traditional Cretan food can be enjoyed at this old restaurant with a
wooden interior. Customers select their dishes in the kitchen and
see how they are prepared. Wed evening; Jun–Sep.

IRAKLEIO: *Loukoulos* €€€
Odos Korai 5. 2810 224435.
Classic architecture and luxurious décor make this an elegant restaurant. Listen
to classical music on the terrace whilst sampling the Mediterranean cuisine.

KOUNOUPIDIANA: *O Mítsos:* €
Main square. 28210 64331
Situated in Kounoupidianá, 4 km (2 miles) northeast of Chaniá, this old, family-
run, grill-house offers the best grilled chickens in the Chaniá area. The service
is quick, the food simple and the atmosphere friendly. lunch.

KOUTSOURAS: *Kalliontzís* €
On the seafront, at entrance to village. 28430 51207.
Situated in Koútsouras, 18 km (11 miles) east of Ierápetra, the Kalliontzís
offers excellent home cooking and a warm, friendly atmosphere. The tables
outside are under the shade of tamarisk trees. Oct–May.

KOUTSOURAS: *Rodisson* €
Seafront, 18 km (11 miles) E of Ierápetra. 28430 51026.
Situated in Koútsouras, this atmospheric restaurant is run by a young
couple. Specialities here are *pítes* (stuffed pastry rolls filled with cheese,
tomatoes, peppers and spices). lunch; Nov–Feb.

<table>
<tr><td>

Average prices for a three-course meal for one, including a half-bottle of house wine, tax and service:
€ up to 12 euros
€€ 12–18 euros
€€€ 18–24 euros
€€€€ 24–32 euros
€€€€€ over 32 euros

</td><td>

AIR-CONDITIONING
Restaurant with air-conditioning.

OUTDOOR TABLES
Tables for eating outdoors, often with a good view.

LIVE ENTERTAINMENT
Dancing or live music performances on various days of the week.

LOCAL WINES
A specialized selection of local Greek wines.

</td></tr>
</table>

	AIR-CONDITIONING	OUTDOOR TABLES	LIVE ENTERTAINMENT	LOCAL WINES

RETHYMNO: *O Goúnos*   € | ● | | ● | ▦
Koronaíou 6. 28310 28816.
Traditional Greek dishes such as rabbit *stifádo* and goat soup are on offer at this taverna, a 150-year-old building. There is traditional dance in summer.

RETHYMNO: *Mourayio Maria*   €€ | ● | ▦ | ● | ▦
Neárchou 45. 28310 26475.
Situated in the old Venetian part of the harbour, this traditional restaurant is housed in a building which dates from the 16th century. Established for 25 years, the speciality is seafood, and in particular lobster. ● *Nov–Mar.* ▤

RETHYMNO: *Tavérna tou Kómpou*   € | | ▦ | | ▦
On Réthymno–Chaniá road. 28310 29725.
Cretan specialties such as *apátzia* (smoked pork sausages) and *glykádia* (goat meat) can be enjoyed at this traditional taverna with cosy alcoves and a fireplace. Meats are charcoal-grilled and there is a tree-filled garden. ● *lunch; Nov–Apr: Mon.*

SFAKIA: *Livykón*   €€ | | ▦ | | ▦
Seafront. 28250 91211.
Part of the Livikón hotel, this family-run restaurant, overlooking the sea, offers copious amounts of basic Greek food at reasonable prices. Dishes include fresh fish and *sfakianés pítes* (pies with honey). ● *Nov–Mar.* ▤

SITEIA: *Zorbás*   €€ | | ▦ | | ▦
Harbourfront. 28430 22689.
Eat *mezédes*, drink coffee or have a full meal at this old-fashioned Greek taverna. Dishes such as *mousakás* and *fasólia* (green beans) are on the menu. ▤

SOUDA: *O Mantás*   €€ | ● | ▦ | | ▦
Ellis 12. 28210 89413.
Decorated in a traditional and simple Greek style, this famous fish taverna serves excellent fish. The service is good and the food value for money. ● *20 Aug–10 Sep, Easter period, 25, 26 Dec.*

ZAKROS: *Káto Zákros Bay*   €€ | | ▦ | ● | ▦
Seafront, close to Zákros archaeological site.
Guests are well looked after in this family-run taverna. Traditional dishes such as *mousakás* are available and fish is freshly barbecued. The food is always well prepared and all vegetables, fruits and meats are home grown. ● *Oct–Apr.*

ATHENS

ACROPOLIS: *Strofí*   €€ | ● | ▦ | | ▦
Rovértou Gkálli 25, 11742. 210 921 4130.
The rooftop views of the Acropolis attract a constant stream of diners. The menu features all the mainstays of a Greek taverna including fried courgettes, octopus and roast lamb. ● *lunch; Sun.* ▤

EXARCHEIA: *Ama Lachei*   €€ | | ▦ | | ▦
Kallidromíon 69, 10681. 210 384 5978.
This well-known *mezedopoleío* is about as authentic as they get. It is situated in the heart of Exárcheia, well off the usual tourist track. ● *lunch; Sun.*

EXARCHEIA: *Yiantes*   €€ | ● | ▦ | | ▦
Valtetsíou 44, 10681. 210 330 1369.
Set in a beautiful garden, this taverna offers wonderful dishes such as chicken stuffed with grapes.

KOLONAKI: *Filíppos*   €€ | | ▦ | | ▦
Xenokrátous 19, 10675. 210 721 6390.
This Kolonáki favourite offers all the standard taverna fare. Roast chicken with lemon potatoes and *ntolmádes* are particularly good. ● *Sat dinner; Sun; 15 Aug.*

KOLONAKI: *To Kafeneío*   €€
Loukianoú 26, 10675. **[** *210 722 9056.*
Excellent *mezédes* are served at this up-market Kolonáki *mezedopoleío*. Also
featured are some of the better new-generation Greek wines. ● *Sun; Aug.*

KOLONAKI: *Dódeka Apóstoloi*   €€€€
Kanári 17, 10671. **[** *210 361 9358.*
Typical *mezédes* are served in the downstairs wine bar at lunch times whilst in
the evenings international cuisine is on offer upstairs. ● *Sun; May–Sep: lunch.*

KOLONAKI: *Academy of Food and Wine*   €€€€
Akadamias 24, 10673. **[** *210 364 1434*
Good quality food and wines, presented with great flair and attention to
detail, are served here. ● *lunch; Sun.*

MONASTIRAKI: *Oinothíki*   €€€
Plateía Avissynías, 10555. **[** *210 321 5465.*
This tiny wine bar offers one of the best wine lists in the city and a limited
selection of *mezédes* to complement the wines. ● *Jul–Aug.*

MONASTIRAKI: *Cafe Avissynía*   €€€€
Plateía Avissynías, 10555. **[** *210 321 7047.*
Tables are always packed for the accordionist and singer who perform
every weekend. During the week, when the café is quieter, is a better time
to sample the unusual Macedonian dishes. ● *Aug.*

MONASTIRAKI: *Koutí*   €€€€
Adrianoú 23, 10555. **[** *210 321 2836.*
Set in a well-restored 19th-century house overlooking the Ancient Agora, this
restaurant serves fresh Mediterranean food. ● *Mon evening; Aug.*

OMONOIA: *Athinaikón*   €€
Themistokléous 2, 10678. **[** *210 383 8485.*
This old establishment serves a wide range of well-executed and
delicious fish and meat *mezédes*. Meals are accompanied by
carafes of ouzo and wine. ● *Sun; Aug.*

OMONOIA: *Ideal*   €€€
Panepistimíou 46, 10678. **[** *210 330 3000.*
Since 1922, this much-loved institution has been serving excellent Greek and
international cuisine. Specials include milk-fed veal with aubergine, stuffed
courgettes and *agkináres a la políta* (artichokes in lemon juice). ● *Sun.*

PLAKA: *O Damígos*   €€
Kydathinaíon 41, 10558. **[** *210 322 5084.*
This basement taverna specializes in salt cod and garlic sauce, chunky chips
and salad. The chilled retsina is excellent. ● *Jun–Aug.*

PLAKA: *Tsekoúras*   €€
Corner of Tripódon & Epicharmou 2, 10558. **[** *210 323 3710.*
Distinguished by its indoor fig tree, this cheap and cheerful taverna serves
delicious fava beans, stewed snails, salads and grills. ● *lunch; Aug*

PLAKA: *Dáfni*   €€€€
Lysikrátous 4, 10557. **[** *210 322 7971.*
Garish frescoes adorn the walls of this converted Neo-Classical
mansion. Stick to the simple dishes, such as swordfish or *keftédes*
(pork or beef meatballs). ● *lunch; Nov–Apr: Sun.*

SYNTAGMA: *Strofiliá*   €€€
Plateía Karýtsi 6, 10561. **[** *210 323 4803.*
Named after the owner's excellent wine made in Attica, this bar offers a wide
range of wines by the glass, and a few interesting *mezédes*. ● *Jun–mid-Sep.*

THISEIO: *Iródeion*   €€
Apostólou Pávlou 29, 11851. **[** *210 346 1585*
Unusual *mezédes* such as fried chicken breast and stuffed *kalámari* are served at
this traditional *mezedopoleío*. A warm atmosphere and Acropolis views.

THISEIO: *Pil Poul*   €€€€€
Corner of Apostólou Pávlou & Poulopoúlou, 11851. **[** *210 342 3665.*
Fashionable Mediterranean cooking and views of the Acropolis draw the
crowds to this busy and expensive restaurant. ● *lunch; Sun.*

SURVIVAL
GUIDE

PRACTICAL INFORMATION 336-351
TRAVEL INFORMATION 352-361

PRACTICAL INFORMATION

GREECE'S APPEAL is both cultural and hedonistic. Its physical beauty, hot climate and warm seas, together with the easy-going outlook of its people, are all conducive to a relaxed holiday. It does pay, however, to know something about the nuts and bolts of Greek life to avoid unnecessary frustrations – when to visit, what to bring, how to get around and what to do if

Soldier in ceremonial dress

things go wrong. Greece is no longer the cheap holiday destination it once was, though public transport, vehicle hire, eating out and hotel accommodation are still relatively inexpensive compared with most other European countries. Tourist information is available through the many EOT offices *(see p338)*, which offer plenty of advice on the practical aspects of your stay.

WHEN TO VISIT

HIGH SEASON in the Greek islands – from late June to early September – is the hottest *(see p47)* and most expensive time to visit, as well as being very crowded. December to March are the coldest and wettest months everywhere, with reduced public transport, and many hotels and restaurants closed throughout the winter.

Spring (from late April to May) is one of the loveliest times to visit the islands – the weather is sunny but not yet debilitatingly hot, there are relatively few tourists about, and the countryside is ablaze with brightly coloured wild flowers, against a backdrop of fresh, verdant vegetation.

WHAT TO BRING

MOST OF LIFE'S comforts are available in Greece, but a few items that are advisable to take include: a good map of the area in which you intend to stay *(see p360)*; an AC adaptor for your electrical gadgetry *(see p339)*; sunglasses

and a sun hat, mosquito repellent, any medical supplies you might need and a high-factor suntan lotion.

Apart from swimwear, light clothing is all you need for most of the year, although a sweater or light jacket for the evening is also recommended, and is essential either side of high season, in May and October. During winter and spring, rainwear should be taken, as well as warm clothes.

Many religious buildings have dress codes (usually signposted) that should be adhered to *(see p339)*.

ΕΛΕΓΧΟΣ ΔΙΑΒΑΤΗΡΙΩΝ PASSPORT CONTROL

Passport control sign at a Greek airport

VISA REQUIREMENTS

VISITORS FROM EU countries, the US, Canada, Australia and New Zealand need only a valid passport for entry to Greece (no visa is required), and can stay for a period of up to 90 days. For longer stays a resident's permit must be

obtained from the **Aliens' Bureau** in Athens, or the local police in remoter areas.

Non-EU citizens planning to work or study in Greece should contact their local Greek consulate a few months in advance about visa requirements and work permits.

CUSTOMS

VISITORS ENTERING Greece from within the EU are no longer subject to any customs controls or other formalities. Limits for duty-paid goods have been similarly relaxed in recent years, though anything valuable should be recorded in your passport upon entry if it is to be re-exported. Visitors coming from non-EU countries may be subject to the occasional spot check on arrival in Greece.

The unauthorized export of antiquities and archaeological artifacts from Greece is treated as a serious offence, and penalties range from hefty fines to prison sentences.

Any prescription drugs that are brought into the country should be accompanied by a copy of the prescription for the purposes of the customs authorities *(see p341)*.

Restrictions on the import and export of money are covered on page 343.

On 30 June 1999, the intra-EU Duty and Tax Free Allowances, better known as Duty Free and mainly affecting such luxury items as alcohol, perfumes and tobacco, were abolished. EU residents can now import greater amounts of these goods, as long as they are for personal use.

Visitors on the beach in high summer

◁ **Fisherman at Skála Sykaminiás on Lésvos**

A family arriving at a Greek airport

TRAVELLING WITH CHILDREN

CHILDREN ARE much loved by the Greeks and welcomed just about everywhere. Baby-sitting facilities are provided by most hotels on request, though check before you book in *(see p295)*.

Concessions of up to 50 per cent are offered on most forms of public transport for children aged 10 and under, but in some cases it is 8 and under.

Swimming in the sea is generally safe for kids, but keep a close eye on them as lifeguards are rare in Greece. Also be aware of the hazards of overexposure to the sun and dehydration.

WOMEN TRAVELLERS

GREECE IS A VERY SAFE country and foreign women travelling alone are usually treated with respect, especially if dressed modestly *(see p339)*. However, in tourist areas lone women may draw unwanted attention from young Greek men. Hitchhiking alone in Greece is not advisable.

STUDENT AND YOUTH TRAVELLERS

WITHIN Greece itself, no concessions are offered on ferry, bus or train travel, except to students actually studying in Greece. However, there are plenty of deals to be had getting to Greece, especially during low

season. There are scores of agencies for student and youth travel, including **STA Travel**, which has 120 offices worldwide. IYHF (International Youth Hostel Federation) membership cards are rarely asked for in Greek hostels, but to be on the safe side it is worth joining before setting off. Most staterun museums and archaeological sites are free to EU students holding a valid International Student Identity Card (ISIC); non-EU students with an ISIC card are usually entitled to a 50 per cent reduction. There are no youth concessions available for these entrance fees, but occasional discounts are possible with a "Go 25" card, which can be obtained from any STA office by travellers who are under 26.

International student identity card

FACILITIES FOR THE DISABLED

THERE ARE FEW facilities in Greece for assisting the disabled – sights with wheelchair access are indicated for entries in this guide. In the UK, organizations such as **Holiday Care Service**, **Tripscope** and **RADAR** *(see p297)* give advice. In the US, **SATH** also has useful information for travellers with disabilities. Agencies such as **The Assisted Travel Service** organize holidays specifically for the disabled.

A sign directing access for wheelchairs at a Greek airport

DIRECTORY

GREEK TOURIST OFFICES (EOT)

Greek National Tourist Board Internet Site
W www.gnto.gr

Athens
Tsocha 7, Ambelokipi, 11521 Athens.
(210 870 7502
or 210 870 7000.

Australia
51-57 Pitt St, Sydney, NSW 2000.
((612) 9241 1663.

Canada
91 Scollard St, 2nd Floor, Toronto, Ontario M5R 1G4.
((416) 968-2220.

United Kingdom and Republic of Ireland
4 Conduit St, London W1S 2DJ.
(020-7495 9300.

USA
Olympic Tower, 645 Fifth Ave, New York, NY 10022.
((212) 421-5777.

USEFUL ADDRESSES

Aliens' Bureau
Leofóros Alexándras 173, Athens.
(210 647 6000.

Hostelling International USA
8401 Colesville Road, Suite 600, Silver Spring, MD 20910.
((301) 495-1240.

Pacific Travel
Nikis 26, 10557 Athens.
(210 324 1007
or 210 322 3213.

STA Travel
86 Old Brompton Rd, London SW7 3LQ.
(020-7361 6161.
W www.statravel.co.uk

10 Downing St, New York, NY 10014.
((212) 627-3111.

SATH (Society for the Advancement of Travel for the Handicapped)
347 Fifth Ave, Suite 610, New York, NY 10016.
((212) 447-7284.

The Assisted Travel Service
1 Tank Lane, Purfleet, Essex RM19 1TA.
(01708 863198.
W www.assistedholidays.com

Holiday Essentials

The EOT's Greek tourism emblem

FOR A CAREFREE holiday in Greece, it is best to adopt the philosophy *sigá, sigá* (slowly, slowly). Within this principle is the ritual of the afternoon siesta, a practice that should be taken seriously, particularly during the hottest months when it is almost a physiological necessity. Almost everything closes for a few hours after lunch, reopening later in the day when the air cools and Greece comes to life again. The shops reopen their doors, the restaurants start filling up and, at seafront locales, practically everyone partakes in the *vólta*, or evening stroll – a delightful Greek institution.

TOURIST INFORMATION

TOURIST INFORMATION is available in many towns and villages in Greece, either in the form of government-run **EOT** offices (Ellinikós Organismós Tourismoú, or the Hellenic Tourism Organization), municipally run tourist offices, the local tourist police *(see p340)*, or privately owned travel agencies. The EOT publishes an array of tourist literature, including maps, brochures and leaflets on transport and accommodation – be aware though that not all of their information is up to date and reliable. The addresses and phone numbers of the EOT and municipal tourist offices, as well as the tourist police, are listed throughout this guide.

GREEK TIME

GREECE IS ALWAYS 2 hours ahead of Britain (GMT), 1 hour ahead of European countries on Central European Time (such as France), 7 hours ahead of New York, 10 hours ahead of Los Angeles and 8 hours behind Sydney.

As Greece is now part of the EU, it follows the rule that all EU countries must put their clocks forward to summertime, and back again to wintertime on the same days, in order to avoid any confusion when travelling between countries. This should lessen the chance of missing a ferry or flight due to confusion over the time!

Entry ticket to an archaeological site

OPENING HOURS

OPENING HOURS tend to be vague in Greece, varying from day to day, season to season and place to place. It is therefore advisable to use the times given in this book as rough guidelines only and to check with local information centres for accurate times.

State-run museums and archaeological sites generally open from around 8:30am to 2:45pm (the major ones stay open as late as 8 or 9pm in the summer months).

Mondays and main public holidays *(see p46)* are the usual closing days for most tourist attractions. Locally run and private museums may be closed on additional public holidays and also on local festival days.

A *períptero*, or kiosk, with a wide array of papers and periodicals

Monasteries and convents are open during daylight hours, but will close for a few hours in the afternoon.

Opening times for shops are covered on page 346, pharmacies on page 341, banks on page 342, post offices on page 345 and OTE (telephone) offices on page 344.

Most shops and offices are closed on public holidays and local festival days, with the exception of some shops within tourist resorts.

The dates of major local festivals are included in the Visitors' Checklists in each main town entry in this guide.

ADMISSION CHARGES

MOST STATE-RUN museums and archaeological sites charge an entrance fee of between 1.5 and 6 euros. Reductions are available, however, ranging from around 25 per cent for EU citizens aged 60 years and over (use your passport as proof of age) to 50 per cent for non-EU students armed with an international student identity card (ISIC) *(see p337)*.

Though most museums and sites are closed on public holidays, the ones that do remain open are free of charge.

EVENTS

THE ENGLISH-LANGUAGE paper *Athens News* has a What's On column, gazetting events all over the city and also those of special interest to children. The tourist office in Amerikis Street has a free monthly English-language magazine, *Now in Athens*, which has details of cultural events and entertainment in Athens, as does the weekly Time Out and Greek-language *Athinorama*.

A list of Greek festivals and cultural events is given on pages 42–6, but it is worth asking your nearest tourist office about what's happening locally. Other forms of entertainment include the outdoor cinema in summer, which is very popular with the Greeks; most films are in English with Greek subtitles. There are also

A typical sign about dress codes at a monastery

bars, discos and nightclubs in the resorts, as well as tavernas and *kafeneía* (coffee shops), found in every village and often the centre of social life.

RELIGION

GREECE IS ALMOST entirely Greek Orthodox. The symbols and rituals of the religion are deeply rooted in Greek culture and are visible everywhere. Saints' days are celebrated throughout Greece *(see p46)*, both locally and nationally.

The largest religious minorities are the Muslims of Rhodes and Kos, and the Catholics of Sýros and Tínos, though they constitute less than 1 per cent of the country's total population. Most other non-Orthodox places of worship are situated in Athens.

ETIQUETTE

LIKE ANYWHERE ELSE, common courtesy and respect is appreciated in Greece, so try speaking a few words of the language, even if your vocabulary only extends as far as the basics *(see pp396–400)*.

Though formal attire is rarely needed, modest clothing (trousers for men and skirts for women) is *de rigueur* for visits to churches and monasteries.

Topless sunbathing is generally tolerated, but nude bathing is officially restricted to a few designated beaches.

In restaurants, the service charge is always included in the bill, but tips are still appreciated – the custom is to

leave between 10 and 15 per cent. Public toilet attendants should also be tipped. Taxi drivers do not expect a tip, but they are not averse to them either; likewise hotel porters and chambermaids.

PHOTOGRAPHY

PHOTOGRAPHIC FILM is readily available in Greece, though it is often quite expensive in tourist areas and close to the major sights.

Taking photographs inside churches and monasteries is officially forbidden; within museums photography is usually permitted, but flashes and tripods are often not. In most cases where a stills camera is allowed, a video camera will also be fine, but you may have to pay an extra fee. At sites, museums or religious buildings it is best to gain permission before using a camera, as rules do vary.

A Greek priest

ELECTRICAL APPLIANCES

Two-pin adaptor, for use with all British appliances when in Greece

GREECE, LIKE OTHER European countries, runs on 220 volts/50 Hz AC. Plugs have two round pins, or three

round pins for appliances that need to be earthed. The adaptors required for British electrical appliances are difficult to find in Greece so bring one with you. Similarly, transformers are needed for North American equipment.

CONVERSION CHART

GREECE USES the metric system, with two small exceptions: sea distances are expressed in nautical miles and land is measured in *strémmata*, the equivalent of about 0.1 ha (0.25 acre).

Imperial to Metric
1 inch = 2.54 centimetres
1 foot = 30 centimetres
1 mile = 1.6 kilometres
1 ounce = 28 grams
1 pound = 454 grams
1 pint = 0.6 litres
1 gallon = 4.6 litres

Metric to Imperial
1 millimetre = 0.04 inches
1 centimetre = 0.4 inches
1 metre = 3 feet 3 inches
1 kilometre = 0.64 miles
1 gram = 0.04 ounces
1 kilogram = 2.2 pounds
1 litre = 1.8 pints

Personal Health and Security

GREECE IS ONE of the safest European countries to visit, with a time-honoured tradition of honesty that still survives despite the onslaught of mass tourism. But, like travelling anywhere else, it is still advisable to take out a comprehensive travel insurance policy. One place where danger is ever present, however, is on the road. Driving is a volatile matter in Greece, which now has the highest accident rate in Europe. Considerable caution is recommended, for drivers and pedestrians.

Fire service emblem

PERSONAL SECURITY

THE CRIME RATE in Greece is very low compared with other European countries. Nevertheless, a few precautions are worth taking, like keeping cars and hotel rooms locked, watching your handbag in public, and not keeping all your documents together in one place. If you do have anything stolen, contact the police or tourist police.

POLICE

GREECE'S POLICE are split into three forces: the regular police, the port police and the tourist police. The tourist police are the most useful for vacationers, combining normal police duties with tourist advice. Should you suffer a theft, lose your passport or have cause to complain about shops, restaurants, tour guides or taxi drivers, your case should first be made to them. As every tourist police office claims to have at least one English speaker, they can act as interpreters if the case needs to involve the local police. Their offices also offer maps, brochures, and advice on finding accommodation.

LEGAL ASSISTANCE FOR TOURISTS

EUROPEAN CONSUMERS' associations together with the European Commission have created a programme, known as **EKPIZO**, to inform tourists of their rights. Its aim is specifically to help vacationers who experience problems with hotels, campsites, travel

A policeman giving directions to vacationers

agencies and so forth. They will furnish tourists with the relevant information and, if necessary, arrange legal advice from lawyers in English, French or German. Contact the Crete office for their telephone numbers on the other islands.

MEDICAL TREATMENT AND INSURANCE

BRITISH and other EU citizens are entitled to free medical care in Greece on presentation of an E111 form (available from most UK post offices), and emergency treatment in public hospitals is free to all foreign nationals. Be aware, however, that public health facilities are limited on the islands and private clinics are expensive. Visitors are strongly advised to take out comprehensive travel insurance (available from travel agents, banks and insurance brokers) covering both private medical treatment and loss or theft of personal possessions. Be sure, too, to read the small print: not all policies, for instance,

will cover you for activities of a "dangerous" nature, such as motorcycling and trekking; not all policies will pay for doctors' or hospital fees direct, and only some will cover you for ambulances and emergency flights home. Paying for your flight with a credit card such as Visa or American Express will also provide limited travel insurance, including reimbursement of your air fare if the agent happens to go bankrupt.

HEALTH PRECAUTIONS

IT COSTS LITTLE or nothing to take a few sensible precautions when travelling abroad, and certain measures are essential if vacationing in the extreme heat of high summer. The most obvious thing to avoid is overexposure to the sun, particularly for the fair-skinned: wear a hat and good-quality sunglasses, as well as a high-factor suntan lotion. If you do burn, calamine lotion or aloe gel are soothing. Heat stroke is a real hazard for which medical attention should be sought immediately; heat exhaustion and dehydration (made worse by alcohol consumption) are also serious.

Be sure to drink plenty of water, even if you don't feel thirsty, and if in any doubt invest in a packet of electrolyte tablets (a mixture of potassium salts and glucose) available at any Greek pharmacy, to avoid dehydration and replace lost minerals.

Port policeman's uniform   **City policeman's uniform**

An ambulance with the emergency number emblazoned on its side

Fire engine

Police car

Always go prepared with an adequate supply of any medication you may need while away, as well as a copy of the prescription with the generic name of the drug – this is useful not only in case you run out, but also for the purposes of customs when you enter the country. Also be aware that codeine, a painkiller commonly found in headache tablets, is illegal in Greece.

Tap water in Greece is generally safe to drink, but in remote communities it is a good precaution to check with the locals. Bottled spring water is for sale throughout the islands, and often has the advantage of being chilled.

However tempting the sea may look, swimming after a meal is not recommended for at least two hours, since stomach cramps out at sea can

Pharmacy sign

be fatal. Underwater hazards to be aware of are weaver fish, jellyfish and sea urchins. The latter are not uncommon and are extremely unpleasant if trodden on. If you do tread on one, the spine will need to be extracted using olive oil and a sterilized needle. Jellyfish stings can be relieved by vinegar, bicarbonate of soda, or by various remedies sold at Greek pharmacies. Though a rare occurrence, the sand-dwelling weaver fish has a powerful sting, its poison causing extreme pain. The immediate treatment is to immerse the affected area in very hot water to dilute the venom's strength.

No inoculations are required for visitors to Greece, though tetanus and typhoid boosters may be recommended.

PHARMACIES

GREEK PHARMACISTS are highly qualified and can not only advise on minor ailments, but also dispense medication not usually available over the counter back home. Their premises, *farmakeía*, are identified by a red or green cross on a white background. Pharmacies are open from 8:30am to 2pm, but are usually closed in the afternoon and on Saturday mornings. However, in larger towns there is often a rota system to maintain a service throughout the day and also late at night. Details are posted in pharmacy windows, in both Greek and English.

EMERGENCY SERVICES

IN CASE OF EMERGENCIES the appropriate services to call are listed in the directory below. For accidents or other medical emergencies, a 24-hour ambulance service only operates within Athens. Outside Athens, in rural towns and on the islands, ambulances are rarely on 24-hour call. But, if necessary, patients can be transferred from island ESY (Greek National Health Service) hospitals or surgeries to a main ESY hospital in Athens by ambulance and ferry, or helicopter.

A complete list of ESY hospitals, private hospitals and clinics is available from the tourist police.

DIRECTORY

NATIONWIDE EMERGENCY NUMBERS

Police
(100.

Ambulance
(166.

Fire
(199.

Road assistance
(174.

Coastguard patrol
(108.

ATHENS EMERGENCY NUMBERS

Tourist police
(171.

Doctors
(1016.

Pharmacies
For information on 24-hour pharmacies:
(107 (central Athens).
(102 (suburbs).

Poison treatment centre
(01 779 3777.

EKPIZO BUREAU

Athens branch
Valtetsíou 4345, 10681 Athens.
(210 330 4444
FAX 210 330 0591.

Banking and Local Currency

Eurocheque logo

GREECE HAS NOW CONVERTED to the common European currency, the euro, which replaces the former drachma. Changing money from other currencies into euros is straightforward and can be done at banks or post offices. Even in small towns and resorts you can expect to find a car hire firm or travel agency that will change cash and travellers' cheques – albeit with a sizeable commission. Larger towns and tourist centres all have the usual banking facilities, including a growing number of cash machines (ATMs).

Visitors changing money at a foreign exchange bureau

BANKING HOURS

ALL BANKS ARE OPEN from 8am to 2pm Monday to Thursday, and from 8am to 1:30pm on Friday. In the larger cities and tourist resorts there is usually at least one bank that reopens its exchange desk for a few hours in the evening and on Saturday mornings during the summer season.

Cash machines, though seldom found outside the major towns and resorts, are in operation 24 hours a day. All banks are closed on public holidays (see p46) and may also be closed on any local festival days.

BANKS AND EXCHANGE FACILITIES

THERE ARE BANKS in all major towns and resorts, as well as exchange facilities at post offices (which tend to charge lower commissions and are found in the more remote areas of Greece), travel agents, hotels, tourist offices and car hire agencies. Always take your passport with you when cashing travellers' cheques, and check exchange rates and commission charges beforehand, as they vary greatly. In major towns and tourist areas you may find a foreign exchange machine

Foreign exchange machine

for changing money at any time of day or night. These operate in several languages, as do the ATMs.

CARDS, CHEQUES AND EUROCHEQUES

VISA, MASTERCARD (Access), American Express and Diners Club are the most widely accepted credit cards in Greece. They are the most convenient way to pay for air tickets, international ferry journeys, car hire, some hotels and larger purchases. Cheaper tavernas, shops and hotels as a rule do not accept credit cards.

You can get a cash advance on a foreign credit card at some banks, though the minimum amount is 44 euros, and you will need to take your passport with you as proof of identity. A credit card can be used for drawing local currency at cash machines. At a bank or ATM, a 1.5 per cent processing charge is usually levied for Visa, but none for other cards.

Cirrus and Plus debit card systems operate in Greece. Cash can be obtained using the Cirrus system at National Bank of Greece ATMs and the Plus system at Commercial Bank ATMs.

Travellers' cheques are the safest way to carry large sums of money. They are refundable if lost or stolen, though the process can be time-consuming. American Express and Travelex are the best-known brands of travellers' cheques in Greece. They usually incur two sets of commissions: one when you buy them (1–1.5 per cent) and another when you cash them. Rates for the latter vary considerably, so shop around

before changing your money. Travellers' cheques can be cashed at large post offices (see p345) – an important consideration if you are travelling to a rural area or remote island.

Eurocheques, available only to holders of a European bank account in the form of a chequebook, are honoured at banks and post offices throughout Greece, as well as many hotels, shops and travel agencies. There is no commission charged when cashing Eurocheques, though there is an annual fee of about £8 for holding a European account and a fee of about 2 per cent for each cheque used. All fees are debited directly from the account.

DIRECTORY

To report a lost or stolen credit card call the following numbers collect from Greece:

American Express
(00 44 1273 696933.

Diners Club
(00 44 1252 513500.

MasterCard
(00 800 11887 0303.

Visa
(00 800 11638 0304.

To report lost or stolen travellers' cheques call the following freephone numbers from Greece:

American Express
(00 800 44 127569.

Travelex
(00 800 44 131409 (toll free).

Visa
(00 800 44 128366.

THE EURO

INTRODUCTION OF the single European currency, the euro, is taking place in 12 of the 15 member states of the EU. Austria, Belgium, Finland, France, Germany, Greece, Ireland, Italy, Luxembourg, the Netherlands, Portugal and Spain chose to join the new currency; the UK, Denmark and Sweden stayed out, with an option to review their decision. The euro was introduced in most countries, but only for banking purposes, on 1 January, 1999. Greece adopted it on 1 January 2001. In all countries, a transition period saw euros and local currency used simultaneously.

In Greece, euro notes and coins came into circulation on 1 January 2002 and became the sole legal tender at the end of March 2002.

Bank Notes

Euro banknotes have seven denominations. The 5-euro note (grey in colour) is the smallest, followed by the 10-euro note (pink), 20-euro note (blue), 50-euro note (orange), 100-euro note (green), 200-euro note (yellow) and 500-euro note (purple). All notes show the stars of the European Union.

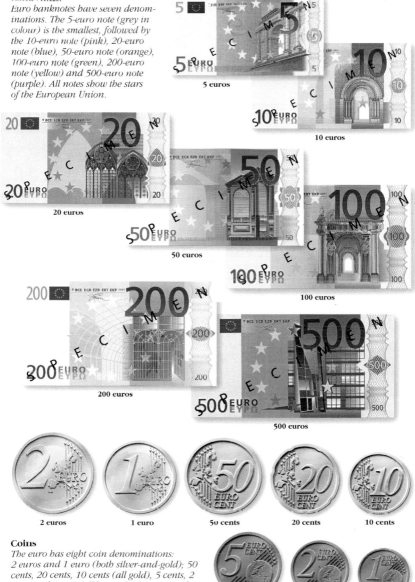

5 euros

10 euros

20 euros

50 euros

100 euros

200 euros

500 euros

2 euros | 1 euro | 50 cents | 20 cents | 10 cents

Coins

The euro has eight coin denominations: 2 euros and 1 euro (both silver-and-gold); 50 cents, 20 cents, 10 cents (all gold), 5 cents, 2 cents and 1 cent (all bronze). The reverse of each coin is the same in all Eurozone countries; the obverse is different in each country.

5 cents | 2 cents | 1 cent

Communications

Post office logo

THE GREEK NATIONAL telephone company is the OTE (Organismós Tilepikoinonión Elládos). Telecommunications have improved dramatically in recent years, and now there are direct lines to all major countries. These are often better than local lines, but the rates are among the highest in Europe. Greek post is reasonably reliable and efficient, especially from the larger towns and resorts; faxes are also easy to send and receive. The Greeks are avid newspaper readers, and in addition to a vast array of Greek publications, there are also a few good English-language papers and magazines.

TELEPHONES AND FAXES

PUBLIC TELEPHONES can be found in many locales – hotel foyers, telephone booths, street kiosks, or the local OTE office. Long-distance calls are best made in a telephone booth using a phonecard – available at any kiosk in a variety of different values. Alternatively, calls can be made at a metered phone in an OTE office, where you can also make reverse-charge calls. OTE offices are open daily from 7am to 10pm or midnight in the larger towns; or until around 3pm in smaller communities. Call charges are variable, but in general local calls are inexpensive, out-of-town domestic calls are surprisingly expensive, and long-distance calls are extortionate. You can ring the operator first for specific rates, as well as information about peak and cheap times, which vary depending on the country you are phoning.

Ship-to-shore and shore-to-ship calls can be made through INMARSAT; for information on this service call the marine operator from Greece on 158.

Faxes can be sent from OTE offices, a few city post offices, and some car hire and travel agencies, though expect to pay a heavy surcharge wherever you go. The easiest way to receive a fax is to become friendly with your nearest car hire or travel agency – both will usually oblige and keep faxes aside for you – otherwise the OTE office is the place to go.

RADIO AND TV

WITH THREE state-owned radio channels and a plethora of local stations, the airwaves are positively jammed in Greece, and reception is not always dependable. There are many Greek music stations to listen to, as well as classical music stations such as ER-3, one of the three state-run channels, which can be heard on 95.6 FM. Daily news summaries are broadcast in English, French and German, and with a shortwave radio you will be able to pick up the BBC World Service in most parts of Greece. Its frequency varies, but in the Greater Athens area it can be heard on 107.1 FM. Galaxy on 92.1 FM has CNN news summaries in English every two hours.

Greek TV is broadcast by two state-run, and several privately run, channels, plus a host of cable and satellite stations from across Europe. Most Greek stations cater to popular taste, with a mix of dubbed foreign soap operas, game shows, sport and films, Fortunately for visitors, foreign language films tend to be subtitled rather than dubbed.

Satellite stations CNN and Euronews televise international news in English round the clock. Guides that give deatails of the coming week's television programmes are published in all the English-language papers.

A public phone

USING A PHONECARD TELEPHONE IN GREECE

1 Lift the receiver and wait for a dialling tone.

2 Insert the phonecard.

3 The screen will display the number of units available, then tell you to key in the telephone number.

4 Key in the number and wait to be connected.

5 If the card runs out in mid-call, it will re-emerge; remove and insert another.

6 If you want to make another call, do not replace the receiver; simply press the follow-on call button and dial.

7 Replace the receiver after your call. When the card re-emerges, remove it.

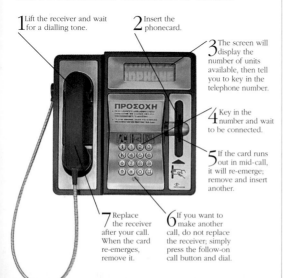

A pictorial telephone card

Red post box for express mail

Yellow post box for all other post

NEWSPAPERS AND MAGAZINES

THE TRUSTY corner *períptera* (kiosks), bookshops in larger towns and tourist shops in the resorts often sell day-old foreign newspapers and magazines, though the mark-up is substantial. Much cheaper, and also widely available, is the English-language paper published in Athens, *Athens News*, which is printed every day except Monday. The *Odyssey*, a bi-monthly, glossy magazine, is available in most of the resorts as well as the capital. These two publications are excellent sources of information on local entertainment, festivals and cultural goings-on, while also providing coverage of domestic and international news. The most popular Greek language newspapers are *Elefterotypía*, *Eléftheros Týpos* and *Kathemerini*.

POST

GREEK POST offices *(tachydromeía)* are generally open from 7:30am to 2pm Monday to Friday. Some main branches in the larger towns stay open as late as 8pm (main branches occasionally open for a few hours at the weekend as well).

All post offices are closed on public holidays (*see p46*). Those with an "Exchange" sign will change money in addition to the usual services.

Post boxes are usually bright yellow; those with two slots are marked *esorterikó*, meaning domestic, and *exoterikó*, meaning overseas. Bright red post boxes are reserved for express mail, for both domestic and overseas destinations. Express is a little more expensive, but cuts delivery time by a few days.

Stamp machine

Stamps *(gramma-tósima)* can be bought over the counter at post offices and also at *períptera*; the latter usually charge a 10 per cent commission.

Airmail letters from the Greek islands to most European countries take between three and six days, and anywhere from five days to a week or more to North America, Australia and New Zealand. Postcards always take a little longer, so if you are sending them, allow an additional couple of days to reach any destination.

The poste restante system – whereby mail can be sent to, and picked up from, a post office – is widely used in Greece. Mail should be clearly marked "Poste Restante", with the recipient's surname underlined so that it gets filed in the right place. A passport, or some other proof of identity, is needed when collecting the post, which is kept for a maximum of 30 days before being returned to the sender.

If you are sending a parcel from Greece to a non-EU country, do not seal it before going to the post office. The contents will need to be inspected by security before it is sent, and if the package is sealed they will unwrap it.

Athenians reading newspapers on a clothes line at a street kiosk

Shopping in Greece

Honey from Evvoia

SHOPPING IN THE GREEK ISLANDS can be an entertaining pastime, especially when you buy directly from the producer. This is often the case in the smaller villages, where crafts are a major source of income. Embroiderers and lace makers can be seen sitting outside their houses, and potters can be found in their workshops. Apart from these industries, and the food and drink produced locally, most other goods are imported to the islands and carry a heavy mark-up.

Olive-wood bowls and other souvenirs from Corfu Old Town

VAT AND TAX FREE SHOPPING

USUALLY INCLUDED in the price, FPA *(Fóros Prostitheménis Axías)* – the equivalent of VAT or sales tax – is about 18 per cent in Greece.

Visitors from outside the EU staying less than three months may claim this money back on purchases over 117 euros. A "Tax-Free Cheque" form must be completed in the store, a copy of which is then given to the customs authorities on departure. You may be asked to show your receipt or goods as proof of purchase.

OPENING HOURS

ALLOWING FOR PLENTY of exceptions, shops and boutiques are generally open on Monday, Wednesday and Saturday from 9am to 2:30pm, and on Tuesday, Thursday and Friday from 9am to 2pm and 5pm to 8pm. Supermarkets, found in all but the smallest communities, are often family-run and open long hours, typically Monday to Saturday from 8 or 9am to 8 or 9pm. Sunday shopping is possible in most tourist resorts. The corner *períptero*

(street kiosk), found in nearly every town, is open from around 7am to 11pm or midnight, selling everything from aspirins to ice cream.

Basket of herbs and spices from a market stall in Irákleio, Crete

MARKETS

MOST TOWNS in the Greek islands have their weekly street market *(laïki agorá)*, a colourful jumble of the freshest and best-value fruit and vegetables, herbs, fish, meat and poultry – often juxtaposed with a miscellany of shoes and underwear, fabrics, household items and sundry electronic equipment.

In larger towns, the street markets are in a different neighbourhood each day, usually opening early and packing up by about 1:30pm, in time for the afternoon siesta. Prices are generally cheaper than in the supermarkets, and a certain amount of bargaining is also acceptable, at least for non-perishable items.

AB (Alpha Vita) Supermarket logo

FOOD AND DRINK

CULINARY DELIGHTS to look out for in the shops and markets of the Greek islands include honey, pistachios, olives, herbs and spices. Good cheeses include the salty feta, and the sweet *anthótyro* from Crete; for something sugary, try the numerous pastries and biscuits (cookies) of the *zacharoplasteío*.

Greece is also well known for several of its wines and spirits. These include brandy, ouzo (an aniseed-flavoured spirit), retsina (a resinated wine) and, from Crete, the firewater known as raki.

SIZE CHART

Women's dresses, coats and skirts

Greek		44	46	48	50	52	54	(size)
GB/Australian		10	12	14	16	18	20	(size)
US		8	10	12	14	16	18	(size)

Men's suits, shirts and jumpers

Greek	44	46	48	50	52	54	56	(size)
GB/US	34	36	38	40	42	44	46	(inches)
Australian	87	92	97	102	107	112	117	(cm)

Women's shoes

Greek	36	37	38	39	40	41	(size)
GB	3	4	5	6	7	8	(size)
US/Australian	5	6	7	8	9	10	(size)

Men's shoes

Greek	40	41	42	43	44	45	(size)
GB/Australian	7	7 1/2	8	9	10	11	(size)
US	7 1/2	8	8 1/2	9 1/2	10 1/2	11 1/2	(size)

What to Buy in Greece

TRADITIONAL handicrafts, though not particularly cheap, do offer the most genuinely Greek souvenirs. These cover a range of items from finely wrought gold reproductions of ancient Minoan pendants to rustic pots, wooden spoons and handmade sandals. Leatherwork is particularly noted on the island of Crete, where the town of Chaniá *(see p248)* hosts a huge leather market. Among the islands renowned for their ceramics are Crete, Lésvos and Sífnos. Many villages throughout the Greek islands

Rug from Anógeia, Crete

produce brightly coloured embroidery *(kéntima)* and wall-hangings, which are often hung out for sale. You may also see thick *flokáti* rugs. They are handwoven from sheep or goat's wool, but are more often produced in the mountainous regions of mainland Greece than on the islands themselves. In the smaller island communities, crafts are often cottage industries, which earn the entire family a large chunk of its annual income during the summer. There is usually room for some bartering when buying from the villagers.

Gold jewellery *is sold mainly in larger towns. Modern designs are found in jewellers such as Lalaoúnis, and reproductions of ancient designs in museum gift shops.*

Icons *are generally sold in shops and monasteries. They range from very small portraits to substantial pictures. Some of the most beautiful, and expensive, use only age old traditional techniques and materials.*

Ornate utensils, *such as these wooden spoons, are found in traditional craft shops. As here, they are often hand-carved into the shapes of figures and produced from the rich-textured wood of the native olive tree.*

Komboloï, *or worry beads, are a traditional sight in Greece, the beads are counted as a way to relax. They are sold in souvenir shops and jewellers.*

Kitchenware *is found in most markets and in specialist shops. This copper coffee pot* (mpríki) *is used for making Greek coffee.*

Leather goods *are sold throughout Greece. The bags, backpacks and sandals make useful and good-value souvenirs.*

Ornamental ceramics *come in many shapes and finishes. Traditional earthenware, often simple, functional and unglazed, is frequently for sale on the outskirts of Athens and the larger towns of the islands.*

Special Interest Vacations and Outdoor Activities

Moped in Rhodes

IF YOU FEEL you want more of a focus to your vacation in the Greek islands, there are many organized tours and courses available that cater to special interests. You can visit ancient archaeological sites with a learned academic as your guide, you can improve your writing skills, paint the Greek landscape or develop your spirituality. All kinds of walking tours, as well as botanical and bird-watching expeditions, are available in the islands. Information on sailing and watersports and advice on choosing the perfect beach are covered on pages 350–51.

Visitors at the ancient theatre at Delos *(see pp214–15)*

ARCHAEOLOGICAL TOURS

FOR THOSE INTERESTED in Greece's glorious ancient past, a tour to some of the famous archaeological sites, accompanied by qualified archaeologists, can make for a fascinating and memorable vacation. In addition to visiting ruins, many tours take in Venetian fortresses, Byzantine churches, caves, archaeological museums and monasteries along the way. **Filoxenia** and **Pharos** organize tours with Minoan, Roman and medieval interests. The island of Crete is one of their main destinations, taking in sites at Réthymno *(see pp254–5)*, as well as the Minoan palace at Knosós *(see pp268–71)*.

CREATIVE VACATIONS

WITH ITS VIVID landscape and renowned quality of light, the Greek islands are an inspirational destination for artistic endeavour. Courses in creative writing, and drawing and painting, are available at all levels. The **Skyros Centre** *(see p112)*, on the island of the same name, offers two locations – one at the main town and another at the remote village of Atsítsa – for self-development and therapeutic vacations, including themes directed towards writing and painting. **Filoxenia** and **Pharos** also offer various creative vacations on Kýthira, Léros, Corfu and Crete.

Tourists visiting caves near Psychró, in Crete

Vamos, named after the village in Greece where it is based, offers traditional types of vacation, during which you stay in an authentic Greek house and learn to cook the regional specialities and produce local handicrafts.

NATURE VACATIONS

THE GREEK ISLANDS are rich in natural beauty, and you need not be a fanatical botanist or ornithologist to enjoy the stunning wild flowers and variety of birdlife. Spring is the best time to explore the countryside, when the colourful flowers are in bloom. It is also a good time to see the influx of migrating birds, which rest and feed in Greece on their journeys between Africa and Europe.

Peregrine Holidays is a specialist tour operator offering trips centred around bird-watching and botany. They have established tours to several islands. **Island Holidays** offers similarly themed tours on Crete. More information on the wildlife of Crete and other specialist tour operators is given on pages 242–3. These types of vacation also incorporate visits to nearby historical and archaeological sites into the tours.

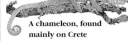

A chameleon, found mainly on Crete

WALKING

THE HILLS OF GREECE are a walker's paradise, particularly between March and June, when the countryside is verdant, the sun is not too hot and wild flowers abound. Many of the islands provide fine locations and scenery in which to walk. **Trekking Hellas** arranges walking holidays in the White Mountains of Crete, and on Andros and Tínos in the Cyclades. **Sherpa Expeditions** leads tours through the mountainous interior of Crete, and **Ramblers Holidays** offers walking in Crete, Ithaca, Chíos and Sámos. **Simply Crete**

Walkers climbing Mount Ídi in central Crete

arranges walking tours on Crete, as well as trips directed towards painting and wildlife

For the independent trekker, guides such as *Trekking in Greece* (Lonely Planet) and *The Mountains of Greece: A Walker's Guide* (Cicerone Press) are invaluable sources of information.

SPAS

GREECE IS WELL endowed with natural hot springs – a result of volcanic activity – and several islands have developed these as spas, offering such treatments as hydrotherapy, physiotherapy and hydromassage. The main centres are listed on the EOT's (Greek Tourist Office's) infor-

mation sheet *Spas In Greece*, and include Kos and Nísyros in the Dodecanese, Ikaría, Lésvos and Límnos in the Northeast Aegean group, Zákynthos in the Ionians and Kýthnos in the Cyclades.

CRUISES AND BOAT TRIPS

GREECE'S unique combination of natural beauty and fascinating history makes a cruising holiday both relaxing and stimulating. Greek cruises run between April and October, and there are a variety of options available, ranging from a full luxury cruise to short boat trips. Operators such as **Swan Hellenic**

Cruises in the UK, **Metro Tours** in the US, **Royal Olympic Cruises** in Athens and **Hellenic Holidays** *(see p359)* offer all-inclusive vacations on board large luxury liners, with guest speakers versed in a range of subjects from archaeology to marine biology. Such cruises tend to incorporate the Greek islands into extensive routes from Italy to the Middle East, or to the Black Sea.

At the other end of the spectrum, there are many less extensive boat trips from tourist centres to nearby islands and places of interest. Organized locally, these are best booked on the spot.

Daytrip boats in Mandráki Harbour, Rhodes

DIRECTORY

Filoxenia
Sourdock Hill, Barkisland,
Halifax, Yorkshire
HX4 0AG, UK.
☎ 01422 371796.
@ travel@filoxenia.co.uk

Hellenic Ornithological Society
Vasileos Irakleiou 24,
10682 Athens.
☎ 210 822 7937.

Island Holidays
Drummond Street, Comrie,
Perthshire PH6 2DS, UK.
☎ 01764 670107.
@ enquiries@
islandholidays.net

Metro Tours
484 Lowell St,

Peabody,
MA 01960, USA.
☎ (800) 221-2810.
w www.metrotours.com

Peregrine Holidays
(David Sayers Travel)
29a Main Street,
Oakham, Rutland LE15
9LR, UK.
☎ 01572 821330.
@ abrock3650@aol.com

Pharos
25–56 31st St, Astoria, NY
11102, USA.
☎ (718) 932-3960.
w www.pharostours.com

Ramblers Holidays
Box 43,
Welwyn Garden City,
Hertfordshire
AL8 6PQ, UK.

☎ 01707 331133.
@ info@ramblersholidays.
co.uk

Royal Olympic Cruises
Aktí Miaoúli 87,
18538 Piraeus.
☎ 210 429 1000.

Sherpa Expeditions
131a Heston Road,
Hounslow,
Middlesex TW5 0RF, UK.
☎ 020-8577 2717.
w www.
sherpaexpeditions.com

Simply Crete
King's House, Wood St,
Kingston-upon-Thames,
Surrey KT1 1SG, UK.
☎ 020-8541 2201.
w www.simplytravel.com

Swan Hellenic Cruises
Richmond House,
Perminus Terrace, South-
ampton SO14 3PN, UK.
☎ 0845 355 5111.
@ reservations@
swanhellenic.com

Trekking Hellas
Filellinon 7,
10557 Athens.
☎ 210 331 0323-26.
w www.trekking.gr

Waymark Holidays
44 Windsor Road, Slough,
Berkshire SL1 2EJ.
☎ 01753 516477.

Vamos
☎ 28250 23100.
w www.vamos.gr

Beaches and Watersports

W ITH HUNDREDS OF ISLANDS, crystal-clear seas and beaches of every kind, it is not surprising that so many water-lovers are attracted to Greece. Although people swim most of the year round, the main season for watersports is from late May to early November. All kinds of watersports can be enjoyed, especially in the larger and more developed resorts, and rental fees are still quite reasonable compared with other Mediterranean destinations. But if you prefer a more leisurely vacation, you can always choose from the many beautiful and tranquil beaches to be found on the islands.

Blue flag indicating a clean beach

Topless bathing is widespread, though nude bathing is still officially forbidden, except on a few designated beaches; it is never allowed within sight of a church.

The Greek seas are generally safe and delightful to swim in, though lifeguards are almost non-existent in Greece. Every year there are at least a few casualties, especially on windy days when the sea is rough and there are under-water currents. Sharks and stingrays are rare around beaches, but more common are sea urchins and jellyfish. Both can be painful, but are not particularly dangerous.

WATERSPORTS

W ITH SO MUCH coastline, facilities catering for watersports are numerous. Windsurfing has become very popular, and waters recommended for this include those around Corfu, Lefkáda and Zákynthos in the Ionian islands, Lésvos and Sámos in the Northeast Aegean, Kos in the Dodeca-nese, Náxos in the Cyclades and the coast around Crete. The **Hellenic Water-ski Federation** can offer the best advice. For a little more money you could take up water-skiing or jet-skiing; and at the larger resorts parasailing is also available. If you need instruction, you will find that many of the places that rent equipment also provide tuition.

Holiday company flags flying on "Golden Beach", Páros

BEACHES

B EACHES VARY GREATLY in the Greek islands, offering everything from shingle and volcanic rock to gravel and fine sand. The Cyclades and Ionian Islands are where the sandy beaches tend to be, and of these the best are usually on the south of the islands. Crete's beaches are also mostly sandy, but not exclusively. The Northeast Aegean and Sporades are a mixture of sandy and pebbly

beaches, and this is also true of the Dodecanese. Some islets, such as Chálki and Kastellórizo, have few or no beaches at all. But, in com-pensation, they often have exceptionally clear seas, which can be good for snorkelling.

Any beach with a Blue Flag (awarded annually by the Hellenic Society for the Protection of Nature, in con-junction with the European Union) is guaranteed to have its water tested every 15 days for cleanliness and purity, as well as meeting over a dozen other environmental criteria. These beaches tend to be among the best, and safest for children, though they can be very crowded. Also worth trying out are beaches recom-mended in the headings for each entry in this guide. Occasionally the main beach near the port of an island is run by the EOT (Greek Tourist Office). There will be a charge for its use, but it will be kept clean and often have the added benefit of showers.

Swimmers diving off the boards at a pool by the beach on Rhodes

Holiday-makers learning the skills of windsurfing in coastal waters

Hire centre for watersports equipment, Rhodes

SCUBA AND SNORKELLING

THE AMAZINGLY CLEAR waters of the Mediterranean and Aegean reveal a world of submarine life and archaeological remains. Snorkelling (see pp20–21) can be enjoyed almost anywhere along the coasts, though scuba diving is severely restricted. Designated areas for diving are around Crete, Rhodes, Kálymnos and Mýkonos, and also around most of the Ionian Islands. A complete list of places where it is permissible to dive with oxygen equipment can be obtained from the EOT, or by mail from the **Department of Underwater Archaeology** in Athens. Wherever you go snorkelling or diving, it is strictly forbidden to remove any antiquities you see, or even to photograph them.

SAILING HOLIDAYS

SAILING VACATIONS can be booked through yacht charter companies in Greece or abroad. The season runs from April to the end of October or early November, and itineraries are flexible. Charters fall into four main categories. Bareboat charter is without a skipper or crew and is available to those with previous sailing experience (contact the **Hellenic Professional and Bareboat Yacht Owners' Association**) Crewed charters range from the modest services of a skipper, assistant or cook to a yacht with a full crew. Sailing within a flotilla, typically in a group of around 6 to 12 yachts, provides the opportunity of independent sailing with the support of a lead boat, contactable by radio.

Learning the techniques of sailing

Thomas Cook and **Sunsail** both offer sailing holidays in a flotilla. They also offer the popular "combined vacation". This type of vacation mixes cruiser sailing with the added interest of coastal pursuits, such as shore-based dinghy sailing and windsurfing.

Sailing aboard a yacht in the Greek seas

TRAVEL INFORMATION

RELIABLY HOT, SUNNY WEATHER makes Greece an extremely popular destination for vacationers. During the warmer months (May to October), countless charter flights bring millions to the Greek islands, although it is also possible to reach Greece by car, rail or coach, and continue to the islands by ferry. While many of the larger islands are accessible by plane, the ferry network reaches even the remotest islands. This is matched by the bus service, which has frequent services on all major routes and local buses to the tiniest communities. Travelling around by car or motorcycle offers the most flexibility on larger islands, allowing the traveller to reach places that are inaccessible by public transport. But the roads in remoter parts can be rough and potentially dangerous *(see p360)*. If, however, you do not wish to rent a car, taxis provide another inexpensive option, and on many islands, taxi boats sail around coasts, offering pick-up and drop-off points along the way.

Olympic Airways passenger aeroplane

GETTING TO GREECE BY AIR

THE MAIN AIRLINES operating direct scheduled flights from London to Athens and Thessaloníki are **Olympic Airways** (the Greek national airline) and **British Airways**. Athens now has a new airport, Elefthérios Venizélos, which handles all international and domestic flights. The old airport (Hellinikon) is no longer used.

From Europe, there are around 20 international airports in Greece that can be reached directly. Only Crete, Rhodes and Corfu among the islands, and Athens and Thessaloníki on the mainland, handle both charter and scheduled flights. The other international airports can only be reached directly by charter flights.

Travellers with airport shopping

From outside Europe, all scheduled flights to Greece arrive in Athens, although only a few airlines offer direct flights – most will require changing planes, and often airlines, at a connecting European city. There are direct flights daily from New York operated by Olympic and **Delta**. From Australia, Olympic Airways operates flights out of Sydney, Brisbane and Melbourne. These generally necessitate a stop-off in Southeast Asia or Europe, but there are two direct flights a week leaving from Melbourne and Sydney. Flights from New Zealand are also via Melbourne or Sydney. Other carriers with services from Australasian cities to Athens include Qantas, **Singapore Airlines** and **KLM**.

Check-in desks at Athens' new Elefthérios Venizélos Airport

CHARTERS AND PACKAGE DEALS

CHARTER FLIGHTS to Greece are nearly all from within Europe, and mostly operate between May and October. Tickets are sold by travel agencies either as part of an all-inclusive package holiday or as a flight-only deal.

Although they tend to be the cheapest flights available, charters do carry certain restrictions: departure dates cannot be changed once booked and there are usually minimum and maximum limits to one's stay (typically between three days and a month). Another consideration if you plan to visit Turkey from Greece is that charter passengers can only go for a day trip; if you stay any longer you will forfeit the return portion of your air ticket.

Athens' new international airport

Booking agency in Athens

FLIGHT TIMES

FLYING TO ATHENS from London or Amsterdam takes about 3.5 hours; the journey time from Paris and Berlin is around 3 hours – the trip from Berlin being a little quicker. From Madrid it takes just over 4 hours and from Rome a little under 2 hours. There are direct flights to Athens from New York, which take 10 hours, although a non-direct flight can take more than 12. From Los Angeles the flight's duration is from 17 to 19 hours, depending on the European connection. From Sydney, via Bangkok, the flight takes around 19 hours.

AIR FARES

Departure gate symbol

FARES TO GREECE are generally at their highest from June to September, but how much you pay will depend more on the type of ticket you decide to purchase. Charters are usually the cheapest option during peak season, though discounted scheduled flights are also common and worth considering for longer visits or during the low season, when there are few charters available. Reasonable savings can also be made by booking an APEX (Advance Purchase Excursion) ticket well in advance but, like charters, these are subject to minimum and maximum limits to one's stay and other restrictions. Budget travellers can often pick up bargains through agents advertising in the national press, and cheap last-minute deals are also advertised on Teletext and Ceefax in the UK. Whoever you book through, be sure that the company is a fully bonded and licensed member of ABTA (the Association of British Travel Agents) or ASTA (the American Society of Travel Agents); this will ensure that you get home should the company go bankrupt during your stay, and should guarantee compensation. Note that domestic flights in Greece are subject to an airport tax (see p354).

ATHENS' NEW AIRPORT

GREECE'S LARGEST and most prestigious infrastructure development project for the new millennium opened to air traffic in 2001. Located at Spáta, 27 km (17 miles) northeast of the city centre, Athens' brand new airport now handles all the city's passenger and cargo flights. It has two runways, designed for simultaneous, round-the-clock operation, and a Main Terminal Building for all arrivals and departures. Arrivals are located on the ground floor (level 1) and departures on the first floor (level 2). The smaller Satellite Building is accessed along an underground corridor with moving walkways. The airport has been designed to allow for a 45-minute connection time between two scheduled flights.

The airport's modern business and service facilities include a shopping mall, restaurants and cafés in the Main Terminal Building and a four-star hotel within the airport complex. Car rental firms, banks, bureaux de change and travel agencies are located in the arrivals area.

TRANSPORT FROM ATHENS AIRPORT

A NEW SIX-LANE highway links the airport to the Athens City Ring Road. From the airport, the E95 bus runs to and

Ultramodern interior of Athens' new airport

from Plateía Syntágmatos in the city centre every 15 minutes with a journey time of about one hour. Bus E96 runs to and from Piraeus every 20 minutes, taking about 100 minutes. Tickets for both journeys cost around 3 euros. These tickets are in effect one-day travel cards and can also be used to travel around the city (see p291). A taxi-ride into town costs 12–15 euros.

There are plans to extend Athens' metro and main rail networks to the airport in time for the 2004 Olympic Games.

One of the smaller planes in Olympic's fleet, for short-haul flights

Athens' new airport, designed in the blue and white national colours

FLIGHT CONNECTIONS IN GREECE

A s WELL AS HAVING the largest number of international flights in Greece, Athens also has the most connecting air services to the islands. Both international and domestic flights now arrive at and depart from the main terminal at the city's Elefthérios Venizélos airport. Thessaloníki also handles scheduled flights, but only from within Europe. Greece's other international airports are served by charters only, again mostly from within Europe.

DOMESTIC FLIGHTS

G REECE'S DOMESTIC airline network is extensive. **Olympic Airways** and its affiliate, **Olympic Aviation**, operate most internal flights, though there are also a number of private companies, such as **Aegean Airways** and **Interjet**, providing services between Athens and some of the major island destinations. Fares for domestic flights are at least double the equivalent bus journey or deck-class ferry trip. Tickets and timetables for Olympic flights are available from any Olympic Airways office in Greece or abroad, as well as from most major travel agencies. Reservations are essential in peak season.

Olympic Airways operates direct flights from Athens to over two dozen islands, and from Thessaloníki, there are direct Olympic flights to nine of the islands. A number of inter-island services operate during the summer, and about a dozen of these fly through-out the year.

A small airport departure tax is charged on domestic flights of between 62 and 466 air miles. For "international" flights (that is, those over 466 air miles) the tax is doubled.

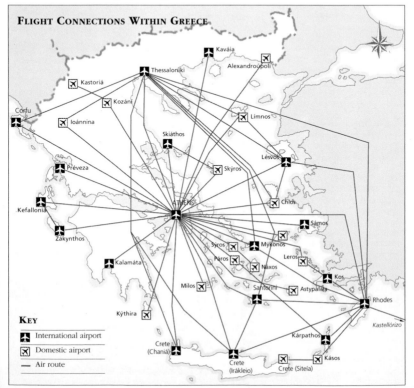

FLIGHT CONNECTIONS WITHIN GREECE

KEY

✈ International airport

⊠ Domestic airport

— Air route

ISLAND	DISTANCE	FLYING TIME	ISLAND	DISTANCE	FLYING TIME
Corfu	381 km (237 miles)	40 minutes	Crete (Chaniá)	318 km (198 miles)	45 minutes
Rhodes	426 km (265 miles)	45 minutes	Santoríni	228 km (142 miles)	40 minutes
Skýros	128 km (80 miles)	40 minutes	Kos	324 km (201 miles)	45 minutes
Skiáthos	135 km (84 miles)	30 minutes	Mýkonos	153 km (95 miles)	30 minutes
Límnos	252 km (157 miles)	45 minutes	Páros	157 km (98 miles)	35 minutes

DIRECTORY

ATHENS AIRPORT

Elefthérios Venizélos – Athens International Airport
5th km Spáta-Loutsa Ave., 10904 Spáta.
☎ 210 353 0000.
FAX 210 369 8883.
W www.aia.gr

OLYMPIC AIRWAYS

Arrivals and Departures
☎ 210 353 0000.
☎ 1440.

Athens Office
Syngroú 96, 11741 Athens.
☎ 210 926 7251.

Crete Office
Plateía Eleftherías, I rákleio.
☎ 28120 29191.

Rhodes Office
☎ 22410 24555.

Thessaloníki Office
Kountouriótou 3, Thessaloníki.
☎ 2310 368 311.
W www.olympic-airways.gr

OTHER AIRLINES

Aegean Airlines
Leof. Vouliagménis 572, 16451 Athens.
☎ 801 11 20000.
W www.aegeanair.com

Air Canada
Ziridi 10, 15124 Athens.
☎ 210 617 5321.
W www.aircanada.ca

Air France
Leof. Vouliagménis 18, 16674 Athens.
☎ 210 960 1100.
W www.airfrance.com

British Airways
Vouliagménis & Themistokleous 1, 16674 Athens.
☎ 210 890 6666.
(Phone for details of Qantas Airline services).
Thessaloníki:
☎ 2310 220 227.
W www.british airways.com

Delta Airlines
Othonos 4, 10557 Athens.
☎ 210 331 1668.
W www.delta.com

Easyjet
☎ 210 967 0000.
W www.easyjet.com

KLM
Vouliagménis 41, 16675 Athens.
☎ 210 926 7251.
W www.klm.com

Singapore Airlines
Xenofóntos 9, 10557 Athens
☎ 210 372 8000.
W www.singapore air.com

United Airlines
Syngroú 5, 11743 Athens.
☎ 210 924 2645.
W www.ual.com

PRIVATE AIRLINES (FOR DOMESTIC TRAVEL)

Greek Air Ltd
Efxenia Pontou 45, Ano Glyfada.
☎ 210 992 8108.

Interjet
Leof. Vouliagménis 6, 16674 Athens.
☎ 210 940 2151.

Olympic Aviation
Syngrou 96, 11741 Athens.
☎ 210 356 8600.
(reservations),
(or via Olympic Airways).

TRAVEL AGENCIES IN ATHENS

American Express Travel Services
Ermoú 2, 10225 Athens.
☎ 210 324 4975

Blue Star Ferries
Attica Premium, Attica Posidonos.
☎ 210 891 9935.

Ginis Vacances
3rd floor, Ermoú 23–25, 10563 Athens.
☎ 210 325 0401.

International Student and Youth Travel Service
1st floor,

Níkis 11, 10557 Athens.
☎ 210 322 1267.
@ isyts@travelling.gr

Oxygen Travel
Eslin 4, Athens.
☎ 210 641 0881.
@ angeki@eexi.gr

OLYMPIC AIRWAYS OFFICES ABROAD

Australia
37–49 Pitt Street, Suite 303, Level 3, Underwood House, Royal Exchange, Sydney, NSW 2001.
☎ (02) 9251 1047.

Canada
80 Bloor Street, Suite 502, Toronto, Ontario M5S F2V1.
☎ (416) 964 7137.

UK
11 Conduit Street, London W1R OLP.
☎ (020) 7399 1500.
☎ 0870 606 0460 *(reservations).*

USA
Satellite Airlines Terminal, 125 Park Avenue, New York, NY 10017.
☎ (718) 269 2200.

Travelling by Sea

Greece has always been a nation of seafarers and, with its hundreds of islands and thousands of miles of coastline, the sea has played an important part in the history of the country and continues to do so today. It is now a major source of revenue for Greece, with millions of vacationers choosing the idyllic Greek islands for their break. The network of ferries is a lifeline for the islanders, and for the tourist an enjoyable and relaxing way of island-hopping or reaching a single destination.

TRAVELLING TO GREECE BY SEA

There are regular year-round ferry crossings from the Italian ports of Ancona, Bari and Brindisi to the Greek ports of Igoumenítsa in Epirus and Pátra in the Peloponnese. During the summer, there are additional sailings from Venice and Trieste. Journey times and fares vary considerably, depending on the time of year, point of embarkation, ferry company and type of ticket. There are also reductions possible for students, travellers under 26 and railcard holders.

Other year-round ferry services include the route from Haifa in Israel, via Cyprus, to Rhodes and Piraeus (with a stop-off at Crete in summer). From Turkey's Aegean coast ferries operate year round between Kusadasi and Sámos, and Çeşme and Chíos, with additional summer sailings between Bodrum and Kos, Marmaris and Rhodes, and Ayvalık and Lésvos.

If you are transporting your car into Greece by ferry, you will require a vehicle registration document and, in summer,

Car ferry leaving from Mandráki harbour, on Nísyros

will need to reserve ahead. Addresses and numbers of agents for advance bookings are given on page 359.

GREEK FERRY SERVICE

The reputation of the Greek ferry service suffered as a result of the disaster in September 2000 when more than 80 people were drowned off the coast of Páros after their ferry sank. The government has now implemented stricter

checks on all ferries, which should result in higher safety standards in future.

The smaller ports have limited services, so check the timetable on arrival to see if you can get a ferry on the day and for the destination you want. The larger ports have many more services. Piraeus, the port of Athens, is Greece's busiest port and has many routes emanating from its harbour. The hub of activity is at Plateía Karaïskáki, where the majority of ticket agents reside, as well as the port police. A number of competing companies run the ferry services, each with its own agents handling bookings and enquiries. This makes the task of finding out when ferries sail, and from which dock, a more challenging one. The ferries are approximately grouped by destination, but when the port is busy ferries dock wherever space permits. So, finding your ferry usually involves studying the agency's information board or asking the port police *(limenarcheío)*.

In this guide, we show the direct ferry routes in high season on the individual island maps, pictorial maps for each island group, and the back endpaper for the country-wide network; high season is from June to August. In low season, expect all services to be significantly reduced and some routes to be suspended altogether. The routes on these maps should be taken as guidelines only – check local sources for the latest information.

The Greek Tourist Office's weekly schedules can serve as a useful guideline to departure times. Visit www.gtp. gr for information. Alternatively, ask at a local travel agency. Some of the English-language papers also print summer ferry schedules. Hydrofoils, catamarans, caïques and taxi boats supplement the ferry services *(see pp358–9)*.

FERRY TICKETS

Tickets for all ferry journeys can be purchased from the shipping line office, any authorized travel agency,

Motorcyclists waiting for a ferry at the port of Piraeus

Cruise ship sailing towards the harbour at Zákynthos

On major routes, ferries have essentially three classes, ranging from deck class to de luxe – the latter costing almost as much as flying.

First class usually entitles you to a two-bunk exterior cabin with bathroom facilities. A second-class ticket costs around 25 per cent less and gives you a three- or four-bunk cabin with washing facilities, such as a basin. Second-class cabins are usually within the interior of the vessel. A deck class ticket gives you access to most of the boat, including a lounge with reclining seats. But during the summer, on a warm, starry night, the deck is often the best place to be.

on the quayside, or on the ferry itself. All fares except first class are set by the Ministry of Transport, so a journey should cost the same amount regardless of which shipping line you choose. Advance booking is essential for a car in high season. For motorbikes and cars a supplement is also payable. Cars can cost as much as three or four times the passenger fare.

Children under two travel free, those aged from two to nine pay half fare, and once over the age of ten, children must pay the full adult fare.

FERRY COMPANY FUNNELS

The funnels of each company's fleet are bold and brightly coloured, and serve as beacons for travellers searching the harbour for their ferry. As each company is unlikely to have more than two or three boats in dock at a time – even in the busiest port, Piraeus – targeting the funnel is often the easiest way to find your ferry.

Minoan Lines

DANE Lines

ANEK Lines

GA Ferries

Ventouris Sea Lines

NEL Lines

PIRAEUS PORT MAP

This map shows the layout of the main harbour, with a guide to the quay you are likely to need for various destinations.

Piraeus Port Authority
📞 *210 422 6000.*

Coastal Service Timetables
📞 *1440.*

KEY TO DEPARTURE POINTS

◼	Argo-Saronic Islands
◼	Northeast Aegean Islands
◼	Dodecanese
◼	Cyclades
◼	Crete
◻	International ferries
◼	Hydrofoils and catamarans

For key to symbols see back flap

Hydrofoil, known as a "Flying Dolphin"

in the Aegean, mostly between the mainland port of Rafína and the islands of Andros, Tínos and Mýkonos. Costs are on a par with hydrofoils, and tickets should be bought from a travel agency a few days prior to sailing. But, if seats are available, they can be purchased on board.

Catamaran departure sign

HYDROFOILS AND CATAMARANS

SOME OF THE ISLANDS can be reached by Greece's 60 or so hydrofoils. The main operators are **Flying Dolphin** (run by Minoan Lines) and **Dodecanese Hydrofoils**, though all hydrofoils are known locally as "Flying Dolphins". They are twice as fast as a ferry but, as a consequence, are double the price.

The major drawback of hydrofoils is that most vessels only function in the summer months and are often cancelled if weather conditions are poor. In fact, on seas that are anything other than calm, hydrofoils are quite slow, and can prove a bad idea for those prone to seasickness.

Hydrofoils can accommodate around 140 passengers, but have no room for cars or

Catamaran

motorcycles. Advance booking is often essential, and it is as well to book as early as possible during high season. Tickets are bought from an agent or on the quayside, but rarely on board the vessel itself. Routes are around the mainland and Peloponnese coasts, and to island groups close to the mainland – the Argo-Saronic group, Evvoia and the Sporades, and to several islands within the Cyclades. There are also routes between Rhodes, in the Dodecanese, and Sámos, at the southern end of the Northeast Aegean.

Catamarans are a more recent innovation in Greece, offering an airline-type service in terms of seating, bar facilities and on-board television. They are also better designed for handicapped passengers. There are services around the Ionian Islands, and about half a dozen catamarans operating

TOURIST EXCURSIONS

MANY HOLIDAY RESORTS put on small excursion boats that take groups of tourists to out-of-the-way beaches and caves, or on day cruises and picnics. Routes and times are dictated by local conditions.

Passengers on a departing ferry

Up-to-date information and booking arrangements are available on arrival in the islands at any local travel agency or information centre.

An excursion caïque on the Dodecanese island of Sými

LOCAL INTER-ISLAND FERRIES

IN ADDITION to the large ferries that cover the main routes, there are smaller ferries making inter-island crossings in the summer. Local ferries, regardless of size, are subject to government price controls, but boats chartered by tourist agencies can charge what they like, and often prove expensive.

Taxi boat travelling around the coast of Spétses

These boats do, however, provide direct connections, which shortcut circuitous routes via mainland ports.

TAXI BOATS

TAXI BOATS (or caïques) are even more ad hoc, sailing along coastlines and making short trips between adjacent islands. They are usually only available during high season and, as the smallest vessels, are most prone to cancellation in adverse sea conditions. They tend to be more expensive than ferries, given the short distances involved, but often provide a route where few or no others are available.

Routes and itineraries are at the discretion of the boat owners, and the only place to determine if one is going your way is at the quayside.

DIRECTORY

UK & US AGENTS

Hellenic Holidays
1501 Broadway, Suite 1512,
New York, NY 10036.
(212) 944-8388.

HF Holidays
Imperial House, Edgeware Road,
London NW4 5AL.
020-8905 9558.
W www.hfholidays.co.uk

Viamare Travel Ltd
Graphic House, 2 Sumatra Rd,
London NW6 1PU.
020-7431 4560.
W www.viamare.com

HYDROFOIL AND CATAMARAN SERVICES

Flying Dolphin
Goúnari 2, Piraeus.
210 422 4775.

Dodecanese Hydrofoils
Australias 3,
85100 Rhodes.
22410 78052.

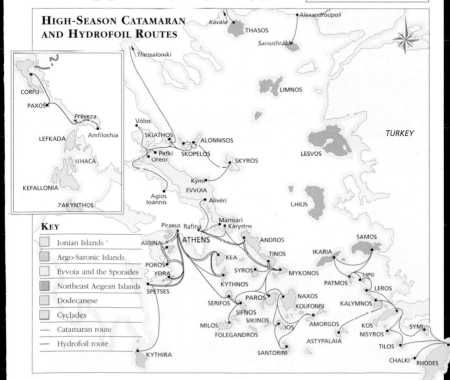

HIGH-SEASON CATAMARAN AND HYDROFOIL ROUTES

KEY

☐	Ionian Islands
☐	Argo-Saronic Islands
☐	Evvoia and the Sporades
☐	Northeast Aegean Islands
☐	Dodecanese
☐	Cyclades
—	Catamaran route
—	Hydrofoil route

Travelling by Road and Rail

T HERE HAS BEEN much upgrading of the roads on the islands but, particularly in remote areas, they can still be rough, and in some cases suitable only for four-wheel drive vehicles. Cars and motorcycles are easily rented though, and the extensive bus network is complemented by many taxis. Maps from local travel agents are less than reliable, however, and visitors are advised to bring their own: GeoCenter and Freytag & Berndt are both good.

You have priority

You have right of way

Do not use car horn

Wild animals crossing

Hairpin bend ahead

Roundabout (traffic circle)

TRAVELLING TO GREECE BY CAR

T HE MOST DIRECT overland route to Greece from the UK, via the former Yugoslavia, is currently not recommended to motorists. The alternative route is through France, Switzerland and Italy, and from there to Greece by ferry. Motoring organizations, such as the **AA**, **RAC** or **ELPA** (the Automobile and Touring Club of Greece), offer advice on routes and regulations. You need a full, valid national driving licence, and insurance cover (at least third party insurance is compulsory).

RULES OF THE ROAD

D RIVING IS ON the right in Greece and, with the exception of some rural back-roads, road signs conform to European norms. The speed limit on national highways is 120 km/h (75 mph) for cars; on country roads it is 90 km/h (55 mph) and in towns 50 km/h (30 mph). Seat belts are required by law and children under ten are not allowed in the front seat.

CAR HIRE

S CORES OF CAR RENTAL agencies in all main resorts offer a range of vehicles from small cars to minibuses. International companies such as **Avis** and **Budget** tend to be considerably more expensive than their local counterparts, though the latter are generally as reliable. Third party is the minimum insurance required by law, but personal accident insurance is strongly recommended. A full licence that has been held for at least one year is needed, and the minimum age requirement ranges from 21 to 25 years.

MOTORCYCLE, MOPED AND BICYCLE RENTAL

M OTORCYCLES AND MOPEDS are readily available to rent on the islands. The latter are ideal for short distances

Dual-language road sign

on flattish terrain, but for anything mountainous a motorcycle is a must. Make sure that the vehicle is in good condition before you set out and that the price includes adequate insurance cover; also check that your own travel insurance covers motorcycle accidents, as many do not.

The speed limit on national highways is 70 km/h (45 mph) for bikes up to 100 cc, and 90 km/h (55 mph) for larger bikes; helmets are compulsory.

Bicycles can also be rented in some resorts, though the steep mountainous terrain and hot sun can be deterrents to even the toughest enthusiast. Bicycles can, however, be transported free on most Greek ferries and buses.

PETROL (GAS) STATIONS

P ETROL STATIONS are plentiful in towns, though less so in rural areas – always set out with a full tank to be on the safe side. Fuel is sold by the litre, and there are usually three or four grades available: super (95 octane), unleaded, super unleaded and diesel, which is confusingly called *petrélaio*. Filling stations set

Sign for a petrol station

their own working hours, but generally they are open seven days a week from 7 or 8am to between 7 and 9pm.

Rack of bikes for hire, at the beach in Kos town

Passengers aboard a taxi truck on the island of Lipsí

TAXIS

TAXIS PROVIDE a very reasonably priced way of getting around on the islands. All taxis are metered, but for longer journeys a price can usually be negotiated per diem, or per trip. Drivers are generally amenable to dropping you off and picking you up a few hours later. Most rural villages have at least one taxi, and the best place to arrange for one is at the local *kafeneío* (café). Taxi trucks often take several passengers, each paying for their part of the journey.

TRAVELLING BY BUS AND COACH

INTERNATIONAL BUSES connect Greece with the rest of Europe, though fares are not as cheap as charter flights during the vacation season.

Greece's domestic bus system is operated by **KTEL** (Koinó Tameío Fispráxeon Leoforeíon), a syndicate of privately run companies that provides almost every community with services of some sort. In remote rural villages the bus might call once or twice a day, usually at the local taverna or *kafeneío*, while services between the larger centres are frequent and efficient. You can also usually rely on there being a bus service between the port and main town of any island, if the latter is situated inland.

On many of the larger islands travel agents offer a wide range of excursions on air-conditioned coaches, accompanied by qualified guides. These include trips to major archaeological and

historical sites, other towns and resorts, popular beaches, areas for established walks, such as the Samariá Gorge in Crete, and organized events, such as an evening out in a "typical Greek taverna".

Front view of a local bus on the island of Nísyros

TRAVELLING BY TRAIN

TRAVELLING TO GREECE by train from London takes over three days. The journey is via France, Switzerland and Italy, crossing by ferry to Corfu and the mainland port of Pátra.

Within Greece, the network is run by the **OSE** (Organismós Sidirodrómon Elládos). The system is restricted to the mainland, but there are useful routes out of Athens to Pátra, Vólos (for ferries to Skiáthos and Skópelos) and up the Attic coast to Evvoia.

The distinctive front end of an express train

General Index

Page numbers in **bold**
type refer to main entries.

A

AA Continental Road
Service 361
Access 342
Achílleion Palace
(Corfu) 69, **79**
Achilles **79**
Mólyvos 137
Skyros 112
Trojan War 52–3
Acropolis (Athens) 56,
279, **284–6**
restaurants 332
Acropolis (Líndos) 56,
192–3
Acropolis Museum
(Athens) 286
Actium, Battle of
(31 BC) 32
Adam, Sir Frederick
Mon Repos Villa
(Corfu) 75
Palaiokastrítsa 77
statue of 73
Adámas 233
Admission charges 338
Adoration of the Magi
(icon) 287
Adrína 109
Aegean Airlines 355
Aegean Islands *see*
Northeast Aegean
Islands
Aegina *see* Aígina
Aeneas 53
Aeschines 187
Aeschylus 28, 55
Afántou 191
Agáli 231
Agamemnon, King of
Mycenae 52
death 53
Mask of Agamemnon
282
Mycenae 25

Agathopés 219
Agesandros
Laocoön 182
Agía Anna (Náxos) 226
Agía Efpraxía (Ydra) 97
Agía Eiríni (Sýros) 219
Agía Eiríni Gorge
(Crete) 247
Agía Galíni (Crete) **259**
wildlife 242
Agía Marína (festival) 44
Agía Marína (Léros) 163
Agía Pákou (Sýros) 218
Agía Paraskeví (Spétses)
97
Agía Pelagía (Crete) **265**
hotels 306
Agía Pelagía (Kýthira)
99
Agía Rouméli (Samariá
Gorge) 251
restaurants 330
Agía Sofía Cave
(Kýthira) 99
Agía Theodóti (Ios) 230
Agía Triáda (Crete) **259**
wildlife 242
Agía Varvára (Kíni) 218
Agiásos 133, **136**
festivals 42
Agio Gála (Chíos) 148
Agioi Anárgyroi
(Spétses) 97
Agioi Apóstoloi
(Chaniá) 249
Agioi Apóstoloi
(festival) 44
Agioi Apóstoloi Pétros
kai Pávlos (festival) 44
Agioi Déka (Crete) 261
Agios Andréas
(Astypálaia) 170
Agios Antónios
(Nísyros) 171
Agios Antónis
(Tílos) 173
Agios Dimítrios
(festival) 45

Agios Dimítrios
(Kos) 168
Agios Efstrátios 131
Agios Fokás (Skýros)
113
Agios Fokás (Tínos)
209
Agios Geórgios
(Crete) 259
Agios Geórgios
(Folégandros) 231
Agios Geórgios (Lasíthi
Plateau) 273
Agios Geórgios
(Náxos) 226
Agios Geórgios (St
George's Day) 43
Agios Iákovos (Corfu
Town) 74
Agios Ioánnis
(Astypálaia) 170
Agios Ioánnis
(Ermoúpoli) 217
Agios Ioánnis (St John's
Day) 44
Agios Isídoros (Léros)
163
Agios Konstantínos kai
Agía Eléni (festival) 43
Agios Kírykos (Ikaría)
149
Agios Nektários
(Aígina) 93
Agios Nikítas (Lefkáda)
81
Agios Nikódimos
(festival) 44
Agios Nikólaos
(Aígina) 89
Agios Nikólaos
(Crete) **274**
hotels 306–7
restaurants 330–31
wildlife 243
Agios Nikólaos
(festival) 46
Agios Nikólaos
(Folégandros) 231

Agios Nikólaos
(Salamína) 92
Agios Nikólaos beach
(Sými) 175
Agios Panteleïmon
(Andros) 205
Agios Pávlos (Crete)
259
Agios Pétros (Andros)
206
Agios Pétros (Lefkáda)
81
Agios Spyrídon (Corfu
Old Town) **72**
festival 46
Street-by-Street map 70
Agios Vasíleios
(festival) 46
Agíou Panteleïmonos
Festival (Tílos) 44
Agíou Pnévmatos
(festival) 44
Agkístri 93
restaurants 323
Agnóntas 101, 109
Agora *see* Ancient Agora
(Athens)
Agorakritos 286
Agorastós, Antónios
108
Aígina 62, **92–3**
hotels 299
map 93
restaurants 323
Temple of Aphaia 92,
94–5
Aígina Museum 93
Aígina Town 90,
92–3
Aigisthos 53
Aínos, Mount *see* Mount
Aínos
Air Canada 355
Air France 355
Air travel **352–5**
flight connections in
Greece 354–5
Airport, Athens 352–5

Ajax 52
Akarnanians 81
Akrotírio Artemísio *see*
Cape Artemísio
Akrópoli *see* Acropolis
(Athens)
Akrotíri **237**
frescoes 237
Akrotíri Peninsula **247**
wildlife 242
Alcaeus 54
Alcman 54
Alcohol
duty-free allowances
336
Alexander the Great
23, 225
Acropolis (Líndos) 192
death 30
Hellenistic Greece
30–31
succeeds his father 29
Alexandria 30
Alexios I Comnenos,
Emperor 161, 229
Ali Pasha 37
Aliens' Bureau
(Athens) 337
Alimniá *see* Alimiá
Alimiá 195
Alínda 163
Alivéri 117
Alkamenes 286
Alkinoös, King 83
Alkmene 51
Alónnisos 24, **110**
hotels 300
restaurants 324
Alónnissos *see*
Alónnisos
Aloprónoia 231
Alpine refuges **296**, 297
Althaemenes of Crete
188
Alykés 87
Alykés saltpans 168
Alykí 126
Amári 257

Amári Valley, Tour of 257
Amazons 53
Amboise, Petrus d'
180, 185
Ambulances 341
American Embassy 339
American Express 342
American Express Travel
Services 355
American School of
Archaeology (Athens)
283
Ammon oracle 30
Amoopí 198
Ammoúdi 236
Amorgós **229**
hotels 304
restaurants 328
Amphitrite 50
Sanctuary of Poseidon
and Amphitrite (Tínos)
209
Anáfi 237
Anáktoro tis Knosoú *see*
Palace of Knosós
Análipsi 43
Anaphi *see* Anáfi
Anástasis (mosaic) 147
Anávatos 148
Ancient Agora (Athens)
57, 283
Ancient Chalkís 116
Ancient Delphi
Sanctuary of Delphi
28–9
Ancient Erétria 115, **117**
Ancient Ialyssós 177,
188
Ancient Kámeiros 176,
188
Ancient Palaiópoli 206
Ancient Phylakopi 233
Ancient Thásos **124–5**
map 125
Ancient Thíra 236–7
Andhros *see* Andros
Andíparos *see* Antíparos
Andípaxi *see* Antípaxos

Andípaxos *see* Antípaxos
Andrew, St 85
Andros **204–6**
  hotels 304
  map 205
  restaurants 328
Andros Town 204
Anemospiliá 272
Angelókastro 68
Angístri *see* Agkístri
Ano Merá 211
Ano Meriá 231
Ano Méros
  Tour of the Amári
  Valley 257
Ano Sagrí 227
Anógeia 13, **258–9**
Anóyia *see* Anógeia
Antikíthira *see*
  Antikýthira
Antikýthira 99
Antimácheia 169
Antíparos 18, 225
Antípaxoi *see* Antípaxos
Antípaxos 80
Antissa 132, **140**
Antony, Mark 32
Apartments, self-catering
  296
Apeíranthos 228
Apélla 199
Apéri 198
Aphaia 94
Aphrodite 50–51,
  98, 129
Aphrodite of Rhodes
  180
Apoíkia 204
Apókries 42
Apókrisi 220
Apollo
  Apóllon 228
  Delos 214
  Greek myths 51
  Oracle of 28
  Sífnos 221
Apóllon 228–9
Apollonía (Sífnos) 221

Apollonía (Mílos) 233
Aquariums
  Rhodes New Town
  186
Archaeological Museums
  Agios Nikólaos (Crete)
  274
  Ancient Erétria 117
  Andros Town 204
  Apeíranthos 228
  Archánes 272
  Argostóli 84
  Chalkída 116
  Chaniá 249
  Chóra 98
  Corfu Town 74–5
  Delos 214
  Ermoúpoli **216,** 217
  Firá 235
  Ierápetra 275
  Ioulís 219
  Irákleio 265, **266–7**
  Kástro 221
  Kos Town 167
  Mólyvos 137
  Mýkonos Town
  210, 211
  Mýrina 130
  Mytilíni Town 134
  National Archaeological
  Museum (Athens) 282
  Náxos Town 226
  Paroikiá 223
  Pláka 232, 233
  Póthia 164
  Réthymno 254
  Rhodes Old Town 179,
  180, 184
  Siteía 276
  Skýros Town 112
  Stavrós 82
  Thásos 124
  Tínos 209
  Vathý (Ithaca) 82
  Vathý (Sámos) 150
Archaeological tours 348
Archaía Agorá *see*
  Ancient Agora (Athens)

Archaía Chalkís *see*
  Ancient Chalkís
Archaía Erétria *see*
  Ancient Erétria
Archaía Ialyssós *see*
  Ancient Ialyssós
Archaía Kámeiros *see*
  Ancient Kámeiros
Archaía Palaiópoli *see*
  Ancient Palaiópoli
Archaía Fylakopí *see*
  Ancient Phylakopi
Archaía Thásos *see*
  Ancient Thásos
Archaía Thíra *see*
  Ancient Thíra
Archaic Period 26
Archánes 272
Archángelos 177, **190–91**
Archilochus 54, 223
  tomb of 224
Archimedes 31
Architecture
  Art Deco architecture
  of Lakkí 162
  kalývia (farmhouses)
  109
  mastic villages 144–5
  peristeriónes
  (dovecotes)
  of Tínos 209
  temples 56–7
  vernacular 18–19
Areos (Athens)
  hotels 308
Argéntis, Philip 143
Arginóntas 165
Argosaronikós *see* Argo-
  Saronic Islands
Argo-Saronic Islands
  89–99
  Aígina 92–5
  climate 47
  Exploring the Argo-
  Saronic Islands 90–91
  hotels 299
  Kýthira 98–9
  Póros 96

Argo-Saronic Islands
(cont.)
restaurants 323
Salamína 92
Spétses 97
Temple of Aphaia
(Aígina) 94–5
Ydra 96–7
Argostóli 84
Argus 83
Arhánes see Archánes
Ariadne 226
Arion 137
Aristophanes 54
Aristotle 28, 55, 141
Chalkída 116
death 30
school of philosophy 34
Arkádi Monastery see
Moní Arkadíou
Arkása 198
Armáthia 199
Armenistís 149
Armeós 218
Armólia 144
Arnás 206
Arsénios, St 225
Art
artists in Corfu 77
Cycladic 201, 207
Geometric pottery 26
painting holidays 348
vase painting 58–9
Art Deco architecture of
Lakkí 162
Artemídoros of Perge
236
Artemis 51, 169
Delos 214
Temple of Artemis
Tavrópolos
(Armenistís) 149
Artemísio, Cape see
Cape Artemísio
Artemisium, Battle of
(480 BC) 114, 119
Artemónas 221
Ascension Day 43

Asfendíou Villages 168
Asklepieíon 168
Asklepios 168, 187
Asklipieío 190
Asómatos 168
Asos 85
Assumption of the
Virgin (festival) 45
Assumption of the
Virgin (Theófilos) 121
Astipálaia see Astypálaia
Astipálca see Astypálaia
Astypálaia 18, 169, 170
hotels 302
restaurants 326
Aténi 206
Athena 50
Acropolis (Athens)
284, 286
Greek myths 51
olive trees 135
Trojan War 53
Athena Lemnia
(Pheidias) 29
Athenian League 214
Athenodoros
Laocoön 182
Athens 279–91
Acropolis 284–6
buses 288–9, 291,
361
emergency numbers
341
getting around
Athens 288–91
hotels 308–11
map 280–81
restaurants 332–3
temples 56
train stations 361
travel agencies 355
Athens Airport 352–5
Athens Festival 44
Atlantis 234
Atreus 53
Atsítsa 113
Attalos, King of
Pergamon 283

Attáviros, Mount see
Mount Attávyros
Aubusson, Pierre d' 185
Antimácheia 169
Moní Filerímou 188
Monólithos castle 189
Australia
Australian Embassy
339
Greek Tourist Offices
337
Olympic Airways
office 355
Autumn in Greece 45
Avars 34
Avgónyma 148
Avis 361
Avlémonas 99
Avlóna 199
Axes, Minoan double
266
Axieros 129
Ayía Galíni see Agía
Galíni
Ayía Triádha see Agía
Triáda
Ayios Nikólaos (Crete)
see Agios Nikólaos
Ayios Nikólaos (Paxós)
see Agios Nikólaos

B

Baby-sitting facilities
hotels 337
"Back Islands" 229
Balkan Wars 39
Báltiza (Spetses) 97
Bank notes 343
Banks 342
Barbarossa
Alónissos 110
Palaiochóra (Aígina) 93
Palaiochora (Kýthira)
99
Réthymno 254
Barozzi family 228–9
Bars 313

Basil the Bulgar Slayer,
Emperor 35
Beaches 350
The Bears (Adámas) 233
Belénis, Paríssis 163
Benákis, Antónos 287
Benákis, Emmanouíl
287
Benáki Museum
(Athens) 287
Benítses 69, 78
Betrayal in the Garden
(mosaic) 147
Bicycles
hiring 360
Bigot, Captain 170
Birds *see* Wildlife
Blue Caves
(Zákynthos) 87
Blue Star Ferries 355
Boats
cruises and boat trips
349
ferries 356–7
hydrofoils and
catamarans **358**, 359
local inter-island
ferries 359
sailing holidays 351
taxi boats 359
tourist excursions 358
Bond, James 79
Bouboulína, Laskarína
89
Bouboulína Museum
(Spétses Town) 97
Spétses 97
statue of 97
Bourtzi 104
Boyd-Hawes, Harriet
276
Brancusi, Constantin
The Kiss 207
Braque, Georges 204
Bread 317
Breakfast 314
Briseis 52
British Airways 355

British War Cemetery
(Léros) 163
Bronze Age 24
Cycladic art 201, **207**
Greek myths 50
Brooke, Rupert 112
grave 113
Budget (car hire) 361
Building materials 19
Bulgars 34
Buses 361
Athens **288–9**, 291
Byron, Lord
Cave of Antíparos 225
death 38
Byzantine Greece 34–5
Byzantine Museum
(Chíos Town) 143
Byzantine Museum
(Corfu Town) 73
Byzantine Museum
(Mytilíni) 134
Byzantine Museum
(Rhodes Old Town) 180
Byzantine Museum
(Zákynthos) 86

C
Caesar, Julius 32, 187
Cafés 313
Calderas
Nísyros 172
Santoríni 235
Calypso 162
Camping 296–7
Can Be Done Tours 337
Canada
Canadian Embassy 339
Greek Tourist Offices
337
Olympic Airways
office 355
Canal d'Amour (Sidári)
68, 77
Candlemas 46
Cape Artemísio 114, **119**
Cape Pouriá 112

Capuchin monks 216
Caravaggio 287
Carita, Raphael 79
Carnival Sunday 42
Carretto, Fabricius del
185
Cars
driving in Athens 290
driving to Greece 360
hiring **360**, 361
motoring organizations
361
petrol stations 360
road assistance 341
road signs 290, 360
rules of the road 360
safety 340
see also Tours by car
Caryatids 57
Cash machines 342
Cassius 187
Castel Rosso 101
Castle Museum
(Kastellórizo) 195
Castles
Antimácheia 169
Castle of the Knights
(Chorió, Kálymnos) 164
Castle of Knights
(Kos) 166
Castle of Lykomedes
(Skýros) 112
Chorió (Chálki) 194–5
Crusader castle
(Archángelos) 190
Faraklós (Rhodes) 190
Gardíki Castle (Corfu)
69, 78
Kástro (Chíos) 142–3
Kástro (Mólyvos) 137
Kástro (Mytilíni) 134
Kástro (Paroikiá) 223
Kritinía Castle
(Rhodes) 176, **189**
Monólithos (Rhodes)
189
Ovriókastro (Antissa)
140

Castles (cont.)
  Palaió Pylí (Kos) 169
  Palaiókastro (Andros) 206
  Skópelos 108
Castor and Pollux 129
Catacombs, Christian (Trypití) 233
Catamarans **358**, 359
Cathedrals
  Agía Triáda (Chaniá) 249
  Agios Christós (Póthia) 164
  Agios Iákovos (Corfu Town) 74
  Agios Konstantínos kai Eléni (Kastellórizo) 195
  Agios Minás (Irákleio) 264
  Aï-Giórgis (Ermoúpoli) 217
  Firá 235
  Mitrópoli (Corfu Old Town) 70, **74**
  Mitrópoli Zoodóchou Pigís (Náxos Town) 226
Cavafy, Constantine 40
Caves
  Agía Sofía Cave (Kýthira) 99
  Blue Caves (Zákynthos) 87
  Cave of Antíparos 225
  Cave of Seven Virgins (Kálymnos) 164
  Chrysospiliá (Folégandros) 231
  Cretan caves and the myth of Zeus 258
  Daskalió Cave (Kálymnos) 165
  Diktian Cave (Crete) 258, **273**
  Drogkaráti Cave (Kefalloniá) 85
  Ellinokamára Cave (Kásos) 199

Caves (cont.)
  Holy Cave of the Apocalypse (Pátmos) 159
  Idaian Cave (Crete) 258
  Kamáres Cave (Crete) 258
  Kolonóstilo (Kálymnos) 165
  Melissáni Cave-Lake (Kefalloniá) 85
  Mílatos Cave (Crete) 273
  Parastá Cave (Kastellórizo) 195
  Sellái Cave (Kásos) 199
  Sidári 77
  Trápeza Cave (Crete) 273
Cefalù 28
Cem, Prince 36–7
Cemeteries
  British War Cemetery (Léros) 163
  Commonwealth War Cemetery (Akrotíri Peninsula) 247
  German War Cemetery (Chaniá) 249
  Minoan (Archánes) 272
  Minoan (Réthymno) 255
Cephalloniá see Kefalloniá
Ceramics
  Geometric pottery 26
  vases and vase painting 58–9
  What to Buy in Greece 347
Cézanne, Paul 287
Chabeau 216
Chagall, Marc
  Daphnis and Chloe 134
Chain hotels **294**, 297
Chaironeia, Battle of (338 BC) 23, 29
Chalepás, Giannoúlis 164

Chalepás, Giannoúlis (cont.)
  Giannoúlis Chalepás Museum (Pýrgos) 209
  Sleeping Girl 40
Chálki (Dodecanese) **194–5**
  festivals 45
  hotels 302
  restaurants 326
Chalkí (Tragaía Valley, Naxos) 227
Chalkída 114, **116**
  festivals 43
Chalkís see Ancient Chalkís
Chalkós 98
Chandris Hotels 297
Chaniá **248–9**
  festivals 44
  hotels 307
  restaurants 331
Charáki 190–91
Chares of Líndos 186
Charging Bull (fresco) 270
Charkadió Grotto 173
Chármylos 169
Charter flights 352
Chatzi-Giánnis Méxis Museum (Spétses Town) 97
Chatzidákis, Mános 40
Chatzimichaïl, Theófilos see Theófilos Chatzimichaïl
Cheeses 320
Chersónisos 272
  hotels 307
"Chigi" vase 26–7
Children 337
  in restaurants 315
Chíos 63, **142–9**
  hotels 300
  map 142
  massacre at Chíos (1822) 38, **147**
  mastic villages 144–5

Chíos (cont.)
Néa Moní 146–7
restaurants 325
Chíos Town 142–3
Chivadolímni 233
Chlemoútsi Castle 35
Choklákia mosaics 194
Chóra (Amorgós) 229
Chóra (Astypálaia)
18, **170**
Chóra (Kýthira) 98
Chóra (Kýthnos) 220
Chóra (Pátmos) 158–9
Chóra (Samothráki)
128–9
Chóra Sfakíon see Sfakiá
Chorió (Chálki) 194–5
Chorió (Kálymnos) 164
Chorafákia (Crete)
restaurants 331
Chremonidean War 30
*Christ Washing the
Disciples' Feet* 146
Christian Catacombs
(Trypití) 233
Christmas 46
Christódoulos, Blessed
159
Agios Geórgios (Léros)
163
Monastery of St John
(Pátmos) 160
Palaió Pylí 169
Christoúgenna 46
Chrysí 275
Chrysí Aktí 225
Chrysólakkos 273
Chrysospiliá 231
Churches
dress code 339
photography in 339
see also Cathedrals *and
individual towns and
villages*
Churchill, Winston 40
Cigarettes
duty-free allowances
336

Cigarettes (cont.)
smoking 315
Civil War 40
Classical Greece 28–9
Clean Monday 42
Cleopatra, Queen of
Egypt 32
statue of 215
Climate 47
when to visit Greece
336
Clothes
in churches and
monasteries 339
in restaurants 315
size chart 346
what to bring 336
Club Mediterranée 297
Clymene 50
Coach travel 361
Coastguard patrol 341
Cocco clan 228–9
Cocco Pýrgos 228
Cockerell, C R 95
Coins 343
Colossus of Rhodes 31,
186
Commonwealth War
Cemetery (Akrotíri
Peninsula) 247
Communications 344–5
Communists 40
Community of
Mykonians 210
Constantine I, Emperor
32, 33, **35**
Agios Konstantínos kai
Agía Eléni 43
Constantine I, King 39
Constantine II, King 41
Constantine IX
Monomáchos,
Emperor 146
Constantinople 32, 34,
36, 38
Constitution 38
Convents see Monasteries
and convents

Conversion chart 339
Coracelli
*Odysseus's home-
coming* 83
Corfu 62, **68–79**
Achílleion Palace 79
festivals 46
hotels 298
map 68–9
Northern Corfu 76–7
restaurants 322
Southern Corfu 78–9
writers and artists 77
Corfu Reading Society
(Corfu Old Town)
Street-by-Street map
71
Corfu Town 66, 69,
70–75
map 75
Street-by-Street map
70–71
Corinth
League of Corinth 29
Roman Corinth 32–3
Corinth Canal 39
Corinthian temples 57
Cozzadini family 220
Crafts
What to Buy in Greece
347
Credit cards 343
in restaurants 314
Cretan Open-Air Museum
(Chersónisos) 272
Cretan School of
Painting 36, 73
Cretan wild goat 250
Crete 62, **241–77**
Battle of Crete (1941)
247
beaches 350
climate 47
Cretan caves and the
myth of Zeus 258
festivals 44
Flora and Fauna of
Crete 242–3

Crete (cont.)
food and drink 321
hotels 306–8
map 244–5
prehistoric Greece 24
restaurants 330–32
Samariá Gorge 250–51
vernacular architecture 18
Cricket Ground (Corfu Old Town)
Street-by-Street map 71
Crime 340
Crispi, Marco 230
Crispi family 228, 232
Cruises 349
Crusaders 34–5
Currency 343
Paper Money Museum (Corfu Old Town) 70
Currency exchange 342
Customs and excise 336
Cybele 31
Cyclades 201–39
Amorgós 229
Andros 204–6
beaches 350
climate 47
Cycladic art 207
Delos 214–15
festivals 44
Folégandros 231
hotels 304–6
Ios 230
Kéa 219
Kýthnos 220
map 202–3
Mílos 232–3
Mýkonos 210–13
Náxos 226–9
Páros 222–5
restaurants 328–30
Santoríni 234–9
Sérifos 220–21
Sífnos 221
Síkinos 230–31
Sýros 216–19
Tínos 208–9

Cycladic art 201, 207
Cycladic civilization 24
Cyclops 83
Cyprus 40

D
Daliánis, Chatzimichális 255
Damaskinós, Michaíl 261, 264
Damnóni 256
Danae 220
Dance
Skýros goat dance 113
Daphnis and Chloe (Chagall) 134
Darius I, King of Persia 27
Darius III, King of Persia 30
Dark Ages 26
Daskalió Cave 165
Daskalogiánnis, Ioánnis 255
Debit cards 342
Decorative Arts Museum (Rhodes Old Town) 180
Delacroix, Eugène
Scènes de Massacres de Scio 38, 143
Delavógias 206
Délfi, Mount see Mount Délfi
Delfini 218
Delian League 28
Delos 63, 214–15
map 214–15
Delphi see Ancient Delphi
Delphic Oracle 285
Delta Airlines 355
Demeter 50, 129
Demetrius 186
Demosthenes 55, 96
Department of Underwater Archaeology 351
Dhonoússa see Donoússa

Diafáni 199
Dialling codes 345
Díkti see Mount Díkti
Diktian Cave 258, 273
Dílos see Delos
Diners Club 342
Diogenes the Cynic 30, 55
Dionysía Festival (Náxos town) 45
Dionýsios (hermit) 151
Dionýsios, St 87
tomb of 86
Dionysos 50
House of the Masks (Delos) 215
statue of 167
Dionysos and Ariadne (mosaic) 249
Dírfys, Mount 102
Disabled travellers 337
in hotels 297
in restaurants 315
Discounts
students 337
Divani Hotels 297
Diving
safety 21
scuba diving 351
snorkelling 20, 351
Doctors 341
Dodecanese 40, 155–99
Astypálaia 170
beaches 350
Chálki 194–5
climate 47
hotels 302–4
Kálymnos 164–5
Kárpathos 198–9
Kastellórizo 195
Kos 166–9
Léros 162–3
Lipsí 162
map 156–7
Nísyros 170–72
Pátmos 158–61
restaurants 326–8
Rhodes 176–93

Dodecanese (cont.)
Sými 174–5
Tílos 173
Dodecanese, Treaty of
(1945) 175
Dodecanese Hydrofoils
359
Dodekánisa *see*
Dodecanese
Domátia
accommodation 294–5
Domestic air flights
354–5
Donoússa 229
Doric temples 57
Dragon houses 117
Drama 55
Dress code, in
restaurants 315
Drinks 321
Drogkaráti Cave 85
Drugs
customs requirements
336
prescription drugs 341
Dryopes tribe 220
Dryopída 220
Dryós 225
Dürer, Albrecht 287
Durrell, Gerald 77
Durrell, Lawrence 69, 77
Achílleion Palace
(Corfu) 79
Kalámi 76
Myrtiótissa 78
Rhodes New Town 186
Duty-free allowances 336
Dýstos, Lake 115

E
Easter 42–3
Niptír Ceremony 161
Ecology and Folk
Museum (Folégandros)
231
Efpalíneio Orygma 151
Egina *see* Aígina

Eisódia tis Theotókou 45
Ekatontapyliani
(Paroikiá) 222–3
EKPIZO 341
Elafonísi (Kýthira) *see*
Elafónisos (Kýthira)
Elafonísi (Palaióchora)
247
Elafonísi (Kýthira) 99
Electrical appliances 339
Eleftheriádis, Stratís
(Tériade) 134
Eleftheríou, Mános 15
Eléftherna 256
Elektra 53
Elgin, Lord 37
Elgin Marbles 41, 99
Eliá 211
Elijah, Prophet 44
Elizabeth, Empress of
Austria
Achílleion Palace
(Corfu) 69, **79**
Eloúnda *see* Eloúnta
Eloúnta **274**
hotels 307
wildlife 243
ELPA (Ellinikí Léschi
Periigíseon kai Afto-
kinítou) 361
Emmanuel Comnenus,
Emperor 205
Embassies 339
Emergency services 341
Emponas 176, **189**
Emporeiós (Nísyros) 171
Emporeiós (Kálymnos)
165
Enosis 38
Enosis Monument
(Corfu Town) 72
Entertainment
listings magazines 338
EOS (Ellinikós Oriva-
tikós Sýndesmos) 297
Ephialtes 28
Epic poetry 54
Epicurus 55

Epiphany 46
Episkopí (Kýthnos) 220
Episkopí (Ydra) 97
Eptá Pigés 177, **191**
Eptánisa *see* Ionian
Islands
Ereikoússa 77
Eresós 141
Erétria *see* Ancient
Erétria
Erikoúsa *see*
Ereikoússa
Erinna 173
Eris 50
Erystos 173
Ermoúpoli 216–17
Erymanthus *see* Mount
Erymanthus
Esplanade (Corfu Town)
72
Estiatória 312
Ethnikí Pinakothíki *see*
National Gallery of Art
(Athens)
Ethnikó Archaiologikó
Mouseío *see* National
Archaeological Museum
(Athens)
Etiquette 339
Euboea *see* Evvoia
Euboia *see* Evvoia
Euclid 55
Eumaeus 83
Eupalinos 151
Euripides 28, 55
Euro, the 41, 342–3
Eurocheques 342
Eurolines 361
European Union (EU) 15
Eurykleia 83
Eurystheus, King of
Mycenae 51
Evangelismós 43
Evangelístria 168
Evans, Sir Arthur 39
Ierápetra 275
Palace of Knosós 270–1
Evvia *see* Evvoia

Evvoia **114–19**
  festivals 43, 44
  hotels 300
  map 114–15
  restaurants 324
  see also Sporades and
  Evvoia
Exaltation of the True
  Cross 45
Exárcheia (Athens)
  hotels 308
  restaurants 332
Exekias 50
Exómpourgo 209
Express (taxis) 290
Eyina *see* Aigina

F

Faistós *see* Phaestos
Falásarna 246
Faliráki 177, 191
Faltáïts, Manos 112
Faltáits Museum
  (Skýros Town) 112
Faraklós 177, 190
Farángi Samariás *see*
  Samariá Gorge
Fasianós, Alékos 204
Fast food 314
Faxes 344
Fellós 206
Fengári, Mount *see*
  Mount Fengári
Ferries 356–7
  local inter-island
  ferries 359
  map *see* Back
  Endpaper
Festós *see* Phaestos
Filikí Etaireía 37, 38,
  39
Filóti 227
Filoxenia 349
Firá 203, **234–5**
Fire services 341
Fischer von Erlach,
  Johann Bernard 186

Fish
  Eating Fish on the
  Islands 318–19
Fiskárdo 67, 85
Flight connections in
  Greece 354–5
Flora and Fauna of
  Crete 242–3
Flowers
  Wild flowers on Crete
  243
Flying Dolphin 359
Fódele 265
Foínikas 218
Fokás, Nikifóros 205
Folégandhros *see*
  Folégandros
Folégandros 44, **231**
  hotels 304
Folégandros Town 231
Folk Art Museum
  (Skópelos) 108
Folk Museum (Agios
  Geórgios) 273
Folk Museum (Agios
  Nikólaos) 274
Folk Museum (Chalkída)
  116
Folk Museum (Kárystos)
  117
Folk Museum (Kými) 118
Folk Museum (Lefkáda
  Town) 81
Folk Museum
  (Léfkes, Paros) 224
Folk Museum (Mýkonos
  Town) **210**, 211
Folk Museum (Óthos)
  199
Folk Museum (Síkinos
  Town) **230**, 231
Folk Museum (Siteía) 276
Food and drink
  bread 317
  breakfast 314
  cheeses 320
  Classic Greek menu
  316–17

Food and drink (cont.)
  drinks 321
  Eating Fish on the
  Islands 318–19
  fast food or snacks 314
  olives 135
  ouzo 136
  picnics 315
  shops 346
  What to Eat on the
  Islands 320–21
  see also Restaurants
Foster, John 95
Foúrni (island) *see*
  Foúrnoi
Foúrni (Rhodes) 189
Foúrnoi (island) 149
  restaurants 325
Fowles, John 97
Frangokástello 255
Franks 34
Franz Josef, Emperor
  79
Frescoes
  Akrotíri 237
Freud, Sigmund 53
Fteliá 211
Funnels
  ferry companies 357
Furtwängler, Adolf 94
Fyrí Ammos 98

G

Gabriel, Archangel
  43, 45
Gáïos 67, **80**
Galaktopoleío 313
Galerius, Emperor 33
Galissás 218
Gardens *see* Parks and
  gardens
Gardíki Castle (Corfu)
  69, **78**
Garitsa Bay 75
Gatelluzi, Francesco
  134, 137
Gatelluzi clan 125

Gátsos, Níkos 15
Gávdos 247
Gávrio 206
Génis, Stylianós 175
Génnisis tis Theotókou
  (birth of the Virgin
  Mary) 45
Genoúpas, Rock of 159
Geological Museum
  (Apeíranthos) 228
Geology
  Mílos 233
  Nísyros 172
  Santoríni 235
Geometric pottery 26
George, St 43
Georgioúpoli 255
Gerakári
  Tour of the Amári
  Valley 257
Gérakas 110
German War Cemetery
  (Chaniá) 249
Germanós, Archbishop 39
Ghisi family 209
Ghisi, Geremia 229
Gialí 195
Gialós 230
Giamalákis, Dr 267
Giannoúlis Chalepás
  Museum (Pýrgos) 209
Ginis Vacances 355
Gioúchtas, Mount see
  Mount Gioúchtas
Glinádo 227
Glóssa 109
Glystéri 109
Goat dance, Skýros 113
Goats, Cretan wild 250
Gods, goddesses and
  heroes 50–51
Gorguet, A F 83
Gortringen, Hiller von
  236
Górtys 260–61
  Law Code of Górtys
  260
Goths 33

Goulandrís, Nikólaos and
  Dolly 287
Goulandrís family 204
Gourniá 276
Grámmata Bay 218
Gramvoúsa Peninsula
  246
Grand Masters
  Knights of St John
  183
Great Gods 128–9
"Great Idea" 38, 39
Great Lávra (Mount
  Athos) 34–5
Great Powers 38
El Greco 264
  birthplace 265
  icon of Christ 82
  The Landscape of the
  Gods-Trodden Mount
  Sinai 264
El Greco Park (Irákleio)
  264
Grecotel 297
Greek Air Ltd 355
Greek Camping Associ-
  ation 297
Greek language 14–15
Greek Orthodox Church
  14, 339
  Easter 42–3
  Niptír ceremony
  161
Greek Revolution see
  War of Independence
Greek Travel Pages
  297
Greek Yacht Brokers' and
  Consultants' Associ-
  ation 351
Gregory of Sými
  173, 192
Gríkos 159
Grótta 226
Gulf Air 355
Gyalí 171
Giália 204
Gýzis, Nikólaos 287

H
Hades 50
Hadrian, Emperor 32
Halbherr, Frederico 262
Hálki see Chálki
Hallerstein, Baron Haller
  von 95
Haniá see Chaniá
Hassan, Hadji 166
Health 340–41
Hector 52, 79
Hekate 129
Helen, St 35
  Agios Konstantínos kai
  Agía Eléni 43
  Ekatontapylianí
  (Paroikiá, Paros) 222
Helen of Troy 25, 260
  Acropolis (Líndos) 192
  Trojan War 50, 52, 79
Helios 50, 51
  Colossus of Rhodes 186
Hellas 290
Hellenic Holidays 359
Hellenic Ornithological
  Society 349
Hellenic Professional and
  Bareboat Yacht Owners'
  Association 351
Hellenic Water-ski
  Federation 351
Hellenic Yachting
  Federation 351
Hellenistic Greece 30–31
Hephaistos 130
Hera 50, 51, 152
Heraion 152
Herakleia see Irákleio
Herakleion see Irákleio
Herakles 168, 223
  Acropolis (Líndos)
  192
  Greek myths 50
  The Labours of
  Herakles 51
Hercules see Herakles
Heredia, Fernández de
  166

Hermes 50–51
 Ermoúpoli 216
 Trojan War 52
Hermes of Andros
 204
Herodotus 28, 54
Heroes 50–51
Hersónisos *see*
 Chersónisos
Herter, Ernst 79
Hesiod 54
Híos *see* Chíos
Hippocrates **168**
 Asklepieíon 168
 birthplace 169
 Ippokráteia (Kos) 44
 Kos 166
 statue of 167
Hipponax 54
Hiring
 cars **360**, 361
 motorbikes, mopeds
 and bicycles 360
Historic and Folk
 Museum (Alinda) 163
Historical and Folk Art
 Museum (Réthymno)
 254
Historical and Folk
 Museum (Argostóli) 84
Historical and Folk
 Museum (Mandráki)
 171
Historical Museum
 (Irákleio) 264
Historical Museum and
 Archives (Chaniá) 249
History 23–41
History and Folk
 Museum (Pláka) **232**,
 233
Hitchhiking 337
Holiday Care Service
 297, 337
Holidays, public 46
Holy Apostles Day 44
Homer 15, 260
 Iliad 27, 52, 54

Homer (cont.)
 Odyssey 27, 53, 54, 75,
 82
 tomb 230
Homeric kingdoms 26
Honeyguide Wildlife
 Holidays 243
Hoplite warriors 26–7
Hóra Sfakíon *see*
 Sfakiá
Horse of Troy 53
Hospitality of Abraham
 (fresco) 160
Hospitals 341
Hostels **296**, 297
Hotels **294–311**
 Argo-Saronic Islands
 299
 Athens 308–11
 baby-sitting services 337
 booking 295
 chain hotels **294**, 297
 Crete 306–8
 Cyclades 304–6
 disabled travellers 297
 Dodecanese 302–4
 domátia 294–5
 grading 295
 Ionian Islands 298–9
 monastery accom-
 modation 296
 Northeast Aegean
 Islands 300–301
 opening seasons 295
 prices 295
 restored settlements
 and buildings 294
 Sporades and Evvoia
 300
 tipping 339
House of Masks
 (Delos) 33
HSSPMS (Hellenic Society
 for the Study and
 Protection of Monk
 Seals) 110, 111
Hydra *see* Ydra
Hydrofoils 358, 359

I
Ialyssós *see* Ancient
 Ialyssós
Icon of St John 160
Icons
 School of Crete 36
 What to Buy in Greece
 347
Idi, Mount *see* Mount Idi
Idaian Cave 258
Idhra *see* Ydra
Idra *see* Ydra
Ierápetra 275
 hotels 307
 wildlife 243
Ifaisteía 131
Ignatius 222
Ikaría 149
Ikaris, Nikoláos
 Pythagóras statue 151
Ikaros 149
Iktinos 286
Iliad 27, 52, 54
Ilisia (Athens)
 hotels 309
Immortal Poetry
 (Tómpros) 112
Immunization 341
Independence Day 43
Inoculations 341
Inoussai *see* Oinoússes
Inoússes *see* Oinoússes
Insurance
 medical 340
 travel 340
Interjet 355
International Student
 and Youth Travel
 Service 337, 355
Ionian Academy 68
Ionian Islands 37,
 65–87
 beaches 350
 climate 47
 Corfu 68–79
 hotels 298–9
 Ithaca 82–3
 Kefalloniá 84–5

Ionian Islands (cont.)
  Lefkáda 81
  map 66–7
  Paxós 80
  restaurants 322–3
  Zákynthos 86–7
Ionic temples 57
Ios 230
  hotels 304
  restaurants 329
Ios Town 230
Ioulís (Ioulída) 219
Iphigeneia 52, 53
Ippokráteia (Kos) 44
Ipsus, Battle of
  (301 BC) 30
Irákleio 17, **264–7**
  hotels 307
  map 265
  restaurants 331
Irákleio Archeological
  Museum 265, **266–7**
Irákleia see Irákleio
Irakleion see Irákleio
Irakliá 229
Ireland
  Greek Tourist Offices
  337
  Irish Embassy 339
Irene, Empress 34,
  234
Iron Gates (Samariá
  Gorge) 251
Isidore of Miletus 222
Isídoros, St 143
Island Holidays 349
Issus 30
Istiaía 114, 119
Itanos 277
Ithaca **82–3**
  hotels 298
  legend of Odysseus's
  return to Ithaca 83
  map 82
  restaurants 322
Itháki see Ithaca
IYHF (Greece) 297
IYHF (UK) 297

J
Jason, St 75
Jellyfish stings 341
Jet-skiing 350
Jewellery
  What to Buy in
  Greece 347
John, St 44
John of Austria, Don 36
John the Divine, St
  Monastery of St John
  (Pátmos) 160–61
  Moní Ypsiloú 141
  Pátmos 63, 158, 159
John Palaiológos,
  Emperor 134
John the Russian, St 119
Jung, C G 53
Junta 16, 41
Justinian, Emperor
  134, 222
Justiniani Museum
  (Chíos Town) 143

K
Kabeirio 131
Kadmilos 129
Kafeneía 313
Kaiser's Throne (Corfu)
  78
Kalamáki 106–7
Kalámi 69, **76**
Kalamítsa 113
Kalamítsi 81
Kalávria 96
Kalávryta 39
Kaldáras, Apóstolos 15
Kálimnos see Kálymnos
Kallikrates 286
Kalloní 132, **140**
Kalogriá 113
Kaloí Liménes 260
Kalokairinós, Mínos 271
Kálymnos **164–5**
  hotels 302
  restaurants 326
  sponge-fishing 165

Kalypso see Calypso
Kalythiés 191
Kalývia (farmhouses)
  109
Kamáres 221
Kamáres Cave 258
Kamári (Ancient Thíra)
  237
Kamári (Kos) 169
Kámeiros see Ancient
  Kámeiros
Kamíni 97
Kámpos (Ikaría) 121,
  149
Kámpos (Pátmos) 159
Kámpos plain (Chíos)
  143
Kanála 220
Kanáris, Captain 143
Kánia 195
Kanóni 75
Kapileió 313
Kapodístrias, Ioánnis
  Aígina 92
  assassination 38
  becomes first President
  of Greece 38
  statue of 72–3
Kapsáli 98
Kara Ali, Admiral 143
Karakostís, Michaïl
  175
Karakostís, Nikítas 175
Karamanlís,
  Konstantínos 17, 41
Karavás 99
Karavostási 231
Kardáki
  Tour of the Amári
  Valley 257
Kardámaina 169
Karfí 273
Karlóvasi 153
Kárpathos 16, **198–9**
  festivals 42, 45
  hotels 302
  map 198
  restaurants 326

Kárpathos Town 198
Kárystos 115, **117**
Kásos 199
  hotels 302
  restaurants 327
Kassiópi 69, **76**
Kássos *see* Kásos
Kastélli (Crete) *see*
  Kastélli Kissámou
Kastélli (Kálymnos)
  165
Kastélli (Pátmos) 158
Kastélli Kissámou **246**
  hotels 307
Kastellórizo **195**
  hotels 302
  restaurants 327
Kastráki 226
Kástro (Kefalloniá) 84
Kástro (Sífnos) 221
Kástro (Thásos) 127
Kástro architecture 18
Katápola 229
Katasáris 173
Katharí Deftéra 42
Káto Chóra 99
Káto Katákoilos 206
Katsadiás (Lipsí) 162
Kazantzákis, Níkos 272
  Náxos Town 226
  Zorba the Greek 40, 93
  Kazantzákis Museum
  (Myrtiá) 272
Kéa **219**
  festivals 44
  hotels 304
Kechriás 105
Kefalloniá 14, **84–5**
  hotels 298
  map 84
  restaurants 322
Kefaloniá *see* Kefalloniá
Kéfalos 169
Kéntros 229
Kentrótas, Geórgios 233
Kéos *see* Kéa
Kerketéfs, Mount *see*
  Mount Kerketéfs

Kérkyra *see* Corfu
Kéros-Sýros culture 24,
  207
Khálki *see* Chálki
Khaniá *see* Chaniá
Khersónisos *see*
  Chersónisos
Khíos *see* Chíos
Kiliç Ali, Admiral 150
Kímolos 233
Kíni 218
The Kiss (Brancusi) 207
Kitchenware
  What to Buy in
  Greece 347
Kíthira *see* Kýthira
Kleoboulos 192
Klídonas 44
KLM 355
Klontzás, Geórgios 174
Klytemnestra 53
Knights of Rhodes
  (Knights of St John)
  36–7, **184–5**
  Acropolis (Líndos) 192
  Ancient Ialyssós 188
  Antimácheia 169
  Chorió 195
  Dodecanese 155
  Faráklos 177
  Grand Masters 183
  Kastellórizo 195
  Kos 166
  Léros 162
  Mandráki 171
  Palace of the Grand
  Masters (Rhodes)
  182–3
  Rhodes 63, 176
  Rhodes Old Town
  178, 179
  Street of the Knights
  (Rhodes) 184–5
  Tílos 173
Knights of St John *see*
  Knights of Rhodes
Knosós *see* Palace of
  Knosós

Knossos *see* Palace of
  Knosós
Koímisis tis Theotókou
  (Mount Kerketéfs) 153
Koímisis tis Theotókou
  (Assumption of the
  Virgin) 45
Kokkári 152–3
Kokkinókastro 110
Kókkinos, Irene and
  Michális 164
Kolonáki (Athens)
  hotels 309
  restaurants 332–3
Kolonóstilo 165
Kolympári 246
Kolympíthres 201, 209
Komiakí 228
Kommós 260
Kontiás 123, 131
Koraïs, Adamántios
  143
Korisíon Lagoon 68, **78**
Korissía 219
Kornáros, Ioánnis
  Lord, Thou Art Great
  277
Kos **166–9**
  festivals 44
  hotels 302–3
  map 166–7
  restaurants 327
Kos Town 166–7
Koskinoú 16, 177, **191**
Kosmos 290
Koufoníssi 229
Koukáki (Athens)
  hotels 309
Koukounariés 104
Kounoupidianá (Crete)
  restaurants 331
Kournás, Lake 255
Kouros 26
Kournochóri 227
Kourtaliótiko gorge
  wildlife 242
Koútsouras (Crete)
  restaurants 331

Kri-kri (Cretan wild goat) 250
Kríti *see* Crete
Kritinía (Rhodes) 189
Kritinía Castle (Rhodes) 176, **189**
Kritsá 275
Kronos 152, 258
Krýa Váthra 129
Kydonia 248
Kykládes *see* Cyclades
Kými 115, **118**
Kyrá Panagiá 113, 199
Kyrrestes, Andronikos 209, 283
Kýthera *see* Kýthira
Kýthira 98–9
 hotels 299
 map 98
 restaurants 323
Kýthnos **220–21**
 hotels 304–5
 restaurants 329

L

Labour Day 43
Ladikó Bay 191
Lady of Phylakopi 232
Laertes 83
Laganás 87
Lagáda (Amorgós) 229
Lagáda (Mílos) 233
Lagoúdi 168
Lákka 80
Lakkí **162–3**
 Art Deco architecture 162
Lámpi 159
The Landscape of the Gods-Trodden Mount Sinai (El Greco) 264
Language 14–15
Laocoön 182
Lárdos 193
Lárdos Bay 193
Lasíthi Plateau 14, 245, **273**
 wildlife 243

Lássi 84
Latináki 231
Lató 275
Lausanne, Treaty of (1923) 39
Law Code of Górtys 260
League of Corinth 29
Lear, Edward 77
Leather goods
 What to Buy in Greece 347
Lefkáda 67, **81**
 hotels 298
 map 81
 restaurants 322
Lefkas *see* Lefkáda
Léfkes 224
Lefkós 199
Legal assistance for tourists 340
Léger, Fernand 134
Leighton, Lord 53
Leipsoí *see* Lipsí
Lemnos *see* Límnos
Lent 42
Leo III, Pope 34
Leo IX, Pope 35
Lepanto, Battle of (1571) 36
Lépoura 117
Lernaean hydra 51
Léros 162–3
 hotels 303
 map 163
 restaurants 327
Lesbos *see* Lésvos
Lesseps, Mathieu de 72
Lesvian *pýrgoi* (fortified towers) 18
Lésvos **132–41**
 Eastern Lésvos 136–7
 festivals 42
 hotels 301
 map 132–3
 olive growing 135
 restaurants 325
 Western Lésvos 140–41

Leto 214
Leuktra, Battle of (371 BC) 29
Ligonéri 97
Liménas 124
Limín Chersonísou *see* Chersónisos
Límni 114, **119**
Limnonári 109
Límnos **130–31**
 hotels 301
 map 130
 restaurants 325
Linariá 113
Líndos 177, **192–3**
 festivals 44
Lipsí **162**
 restaurants 327
Lipsí Town 162
Lipsós *see* Lipsí
Lissós 247
Listings magazines 338
The Liston (Corfu Old Town) **72**
 Street-by-Street map 71
Literature 54–5
Livádi (Aígina) 93
Livádi (Astypálaia) 170
Livádi (Donoússa) 229
Livádi (Folégandros) 231
Livádi (Sérifos) 221
Livádia (Tílos) 173
Livádi Geranoú (Pátmos) 159
Loggerhead turtles 87
Logothétis, Lykoúrgos 151
Lois, Caesar 162
Lord, Thou Art Great (Kornáros) 277
Louis, Spyrídon 39
Louis XIII, King of France 217
Louis XVIII, King of France 233
Loutrá (Kýthnos) 220
Loutrá (Nísyros) 171
Loutrá Aidipsoú 114, **119**

Loutrá Giáltron 119
Loutráki 109
Loutró (Crete) **255**
 hotels 307
Luke (hermit) 127
Luke, St 133, 136
Lycian tomb
 (Kastellórizo) 195
Lykavittós Hill (Athens)
 279
 restaurants 333
Lykourgos 27, 285
Lysias 55
Lýtras, Nikifóros 287
Lýtras, Nikólaos 287

M
Magaziá 112
Magazines **345**
 entertainments listings
 338
Mageirió 312
Maitland, Sir Thomas 73
Maitland Rotunda (Corfu
 Town) 73
Makrygiánni (Athens)
 hotels 309
Mália **273**
 wildlife 243
Maltezána 170
Mamidakis Hotels of
 Greece 297
Mandráki (Nísyros) 170–71
Mandráki (Skíathos) 105
Mandráki Harbour
 (Rhodes) 186
Mandrákia (Mílos) 202
Manganári 230
Mános, Grigórios 73
Mantamádos 133, **136–7**
Manuel II Palaiológos,
 Emperor 125, 127
Maps
 Aígina 93
 Ancient Thásos 125
 Andros 205
 Argo-Saronic Islands
 90–91

Maps (cont.)
 Athens 280–81
 Athens: Getting around
 288
 Athens transport links
 291
 Byzantine Greece 34
 catamaran and
 hydrofoil routes 359
 Chíos 142
 Classical Greece 28
 Corfu 68–9
 Corfu Old Town 70–71
 Corfu Town 75
 Crete 244–5
 Cyclades 202–3
 Dark Ages and Archaic
 Period 26
 Delos 214–15
 Dodecanese 156–7
 Emerging Greek State
 38
 Europe and North
 Africa 11
 Evvoia 114–15
 ferries *see* Back
 Endpaper
 flight connections
 within Greece 354
 Flora and Fauna of
 Crete 242–3
 Greece 10–11
 Greece in 1493 36
 Greek islands 62–3
 Hellenistic Greece
 30–31
 Ionian Islands 66–7
 Irákleio 265
 Ithaca 82
 Kárpathos 198
 Kefalloniá 84
 Kos 166–7
 Kýthira 98
 Lefkáda 81
 Léros 163
 Lésvos 132–3
 Límnos 130
 mastic villages 144

Maps (cont.)
 Mílos 232
 Mýkonos 211
 Náxos 227
 Nísyros 171
 Northeast Aegean
 Islands 122–3
 Páros 223
 Pátmos 158
 Piraeus port 357
 prehistoric Greece 24
 Rhodes 176–7
 Rhodes New Town 187
 Rhodes Old Town 178–9
 Roman Greece 32 3
 Samariá Gorge 250 51
 Sámos 150
 Santoríni 234
 Skiáthos 104
 Skópelos 108
 Skýros 113
 Sporades and Evvoia
 102–3
 Sými 174
 Sýros 216
 Thásos 124
 Tínos 208
 Tour of the Amári
 Valley 257
 Zákynthos 86
Maráthi 211
Marathon, Battle of
 (490 BC) 27
Marathoúnta 175
Margarítes 256
Marinátos, Professor
 Spyrídon 237
Marine life **20–21**
 marine wildlife in the
 Sporades 111
Maritime Museum
 (Andros Town) 204
Maritime Museum
 (Sými Town) 174
Maritime Museum of the
 Aegean (Mýkonos
 Town) **210**, 211
Markets 346

Mármara 224
Márpissa 224
Martinákia 220
Mask of Agamemnon 282
Mastercard 342
Mastic 145
Mastic villages 144–5
Mastichári 169
Mastichochória *see*
  Mastic Villages
Mátala **260**
  hotels 308
Mathráki 77
Matrona, St 143
Mausoleum of
  Halicarnassus 30
Mavrogénous, Mantó 210
May Day 43
Medical insurance 340
Medical treatment 340
Medieval Rhodes and
  Ancient Rhodes
  Exhibitions (Rhodes
  Old Town) 180
Megáli Evdomáda 43
Megálo Chorió 173
Megálo Kazavíti 127
Megálos Gialós 193
Meganísi 81
  hotels 298
Meganíssi *see* Meganísi
Mégaro Ghisi Museum
  (Firá) 235
Megiste *see* Kastellórizo
Megísti *see* Kastellórizo
Mehmet II, Sultan 36
Mélanes Valley 227
Melissáni Cave-Lake 85
Melói 158
Meltémi wind 44
Menelaos, King of
  Sparta 50
  Mátala 260
  Trojan War 50, 79
Menetés 198
Ménites 205
Mérichas 220
Merkoúri, Melína 41

Méronas, Tour of the
  Amari Valley 257
Mesará, Gulf of 242
Mesariá 205
Mesaktí 123
Mestá 144–5
Metamórfosi 45
Metamórfosis tou Sotíros
  (Skópelos) 109
Metaxás, Anastásios 45,
  287
Metóchi 165
Metro (Athens) 289, 291
Metro Tours 349
Méxis, Chatzi-Giánnis 97
Meyísti *see* Kastellórizo
Mezedopoleío 313
Miaoúlis, Admiral
  Andréas 89, 216
Michael, Archangel 45,
  136, 175
Michaíl Angelos
  Komninós II 77, 78
Míkonos *see* Mýkonos
Mikrí Vígla 226
Mikró Chorió 173
Mílatos Cave 273
Miller, Henry 77
Mílos **232–3**
  geology 233
  hotels 305
  map 232
  restaurants 329
Minoa (Amorgós) 229
Minoan cemetery
  (Réthymno) 255
Minoan civilization
  24–5
  Archánes 272
  double axes 266
  Gourniá 276
  Irákleio Archeological
  Museum 266
  Palace of Knosós
  268–71
  Palace of Mália 273
  Phaestos 262–3
  Zákros 277

Minos, King 271
Minotaur 271
Miró, Joan 134
Mithridates 32, 214
Mitrópoli (Corfu Old
  Town) **74**
  Street-by-Street map 70
Móchlos 276
Modern Greece 38–9
Modigliani, Amedeo 207
Mohammed the
  Conqueror 137
Mólos 112, 225
Mólyvos (Míthymna)
  121–122, 132, **137**
Mon Repos Villa (Corfu)
  75
Monasteries and convents
  accommodation in 296
  dress code 339
  opening hours 338
  photography in 339
  Agía Varvára (Kíni) 218
  Agios Ioánnis
  (Ermoúpoli) 217
  Great Lávra (Mount
  Athos) 34–5
  Koímisis tis Theotókou
  (Mount Kerketéfs) 153
  Metamórfosis tou
  Sotíros (Skópelos) 109
  Monastery of St John
  (Pátmos) 158, **160–61**
  Moní Agías Marínas
  (Kéa) 219
  Moní Agías Theodótis
  (Ios) 230
  Moní Agías Triádas
  (Akrotíri Peninsula) 247
  Moní Agíou Antoníou
  (Páros) 224
  Moní Agíou Ioánni
  (Kos) 169
  Moní Agíos Ioánnis sto
  Gkremó (Kýthira) 98
  Moní Agíou
  Panteleïmonos
  (Tílos) 173

Monasteries and
convents (cont.)
Moní Agíou Andréa
(Kefalloniá) 84–5
Moní Agíou
Charalámpou
(Skiáthos) 105
Moní Agíou Georgíou
(Skýros) 112
Moní Agíou Ioánnou
(Crete) 256
Moní Agíou Ioánnou
Prodrómou (Chálki) 195
Moní Agíou Theodórou
(Kýthira) 99
Moní Arkadíou (Crete)
256
Moní Asomáton
(Crete) 257
Moní Christoú tou
Dásous (Páros) 225
Moní Chrysoskalítissas
(Palaióchora) 246, **247**
Moní Episkopís
(Síkinos) 230–31
Moní Evangelistrías
(Mount Kerketéfs) 153
Moní Evangelismoú
(Skiáthos) 105
Moní Evangelistrías
(Skópelos) 109
Moní Faneroménis
(Apóllon) 228
Moní Faneroménis
(Gourniá) 276
Moní Faneroménis
(Lefkáda Town) 81
Moní Faneroménis
(Salamína) 92
Moní Filerímou
(Rhodes) 177, **188**
Moní Galatáki (Límni)
119
Moní Gouvernétou
(Akrotíri Peninsula) 247
Moní Katholikoú
(Akrotíri Peninsula)
247

Monasteries and
convents (cont.)
Moní Kechrovouníou
(Tínos) 209
Moní Leimónos
(Kallóni) 140
Moní Longovárdas
(Páros) 224
Moní Megális Panagías
(Sámos) 151
Moní Moúndon
(Chíos) 149
Moní Palaiokástrou
(Mýkonos) 211
Moní Panachrántou
(Andros) 205
Moní Panagía
(Ydra) 97
Moní Panagías Chozo-
viótissas (Amorgós) 229
Moní Panagías Goniás
(Crete) 246
Moní Panagias
Kounístras (Skiáthos)
105
Moní Panagiás Spilianís
(Mandráki) 171
Moní Panagías Spilianís
(Pythagóreio) 151
Moní Perivolís
(Lésvos) 140
Moní Préveli (Crete)
242, **256**
Moní Skiádi (Rhodes)
176, **189**
Moní Sotíra (Kými) 118
Moní Taxiárchi Michaïl
Panormíti (Sými) 175
Moní Taxiarchón
(Mantamádos) 136
Moní Taxiarchón
(Sérifos) 221
Monasteries and
convents (cont.)
Moní Taxiarchón
(Skópelos) 109
Moní Thárri (Rhodes)
176, **190**

Moní Theotókou
(Palaiokastrítsa) 77
Moní Timíou
Prodrómou (Skópelos)
109
Moní tis Panagías
tis Anafonítrias
(Zákynthos) 87
Moní Toploú (Crete)
277
Moní Archangélou
Michaïl (Thásos) 126–7
Moní Tsampíkas
(Rhodes) 191
Moní Vrontisíou
(Crete) 261
Moní Ypsiloú (Lésvos)
132, **141**
Moní Zoödóchou Pigís
(Kalavría) 96
Néa Moní (Chíos) 122,
146–7
Panagía i Tourlianí
(Mýkonos) 211
Profítis Ilías (Ydra) 97
Zoödóchos Pigís
(Andros) 206
Monastiráki (Athens)
282
hotels 309
restaurants 333
Money **343**
banks 342
credit cards **342**
currency exchange 342
debit cards 342
travellers' cheques 342
Moní (Aígina) 93
Moní see Monasteries
and convents
Monk seals 111
Monodéntri 162
Monólithos 176, **189**
Monte Smith (Rhodes
New Town) 187
Moore, Henry
*Three Standing
Figures* 207

Mopeds
  hiring 360
Moraïtidis, Aléxandros
  105
Mosaics
  Choklákia mosaics
    194
  Néa Moní 146–7
Moschophoros (Calf-
  bearer) 286
Motorbikes
  hiring 360
Motoring organizations
  361
Moúdros 131
Mount Aínos 85
Mount Attávyros
  189
Mount Délfi 109
Mount Díkti
  wildlife 243
Mount Erymanthus
  51
Mount Fengári 129
Mount Gioúchtas 272
Mount Idi 50, **258**
Mount Kerketéfs 153
Mount Kýnthos 214
Mount Ochi 115
Mount Oros 93
Mount Paloúki 109
Mount Pantokrátor 69,
  76
Mouseío Kykladikís kai
  Archaías Ellinikís
  Téchnis see Museum of
  Cycladic Art (Athens)
Mouseío Mpénaki see
  Benáki Museum
  (Athens)
Mousodákis, Aglaïnós
  159
Moutsoúna 228
Mozart, W A 217
Mpatsí 206
Mpenítses see Benítses
Mpoumpoulína see
  Bouboulína

Municipal Art Gallery
  (Mýkonos) **210**, 211
Municipal Museum
  (Skýros Town) 112
Murad Reis 186
Museums and galleries
  admission charges
    338
  opening hours 338
  photography in
    339
  Acropolis Museum
    (Athens) 286
  Aígina Museum 93
  Archaeological Museum
    (Agios Nikólaos) 274
  Archaeological Museum
    (Ancient Erétria) 117
  Archaeological Museum
    (Andros Town) 204
  Archaeological Museum
    (Apeíranthos) 228
  Archaeological Museum
    (Archánes) 272
  Archaeological Museum
    (Argostóli) 84
  Archaeological Museum
    (Chalkída) 116
  Archaeological Museum
    (Chaniá) 249
  Archaeological Museum
    (Chóra) 98
  Archaeological Museum
    (Corfu Town) 74–5
  Archaeological Museum
    (Delos) 214
  Archaeological Museum
    (Ermoúpoli) **216**, 217
  Archaeological Museum
    (Firá) 235
  Archaeological Museum
    (Ierápetra) 275
  Archaeological Museum
    (Ioulís) 219
  Archaeological Museum
    (Kástro) 221
  Archaeological Museum
    (Kos Town) 167

Museums and galleries
  (cont.)
  Archaeological Museum
    (Tínos) 209
  Archaeological Museum
    (Mólyvos) 137
  Archaeological Museum
    (Mýkonos Town) **210**,
    211
  Archaeological Museum
    (Mýrina) 130
  Archaeological Museum
    (Mytilíni) 134
  Archaeological Museum
    (Náxos Town) 226
  Archaeological Museum
    (Paroikiá) 223
  Archaeological Museum
    (Pláka) **232**, 233
  Archaeological Museum
    (Póthia) 164
  Archaeological Museum
    (Réthymno) 254
  Archaeological Museum
    (Rhodes Town) 179,
    180, 184
  Archaeological Museum
    (Siteía) 276
  Archaeological Museum
    (Skýros Town) 112
  Archaeological Museum
    (Stavrós) 82
  Archaeological Museum
    (Thásos) 124
  Archaeological Museum
    (Vathý, Ithaca) 82
  Archaeological Museum
    (Vathý, Sámos) 150
  Benáki Museum
    (Athens) 287
  Bouboulína Museum
    (Spétses Town) 97
  Byzantine Museum
    (Chíos Town) 143
  Byzantine Museum
    (Corfu Town) 73
  Byzantine Museum
    (Mytilíni) 134

Museums and galleries
(cont.)
Byzantine Museum
(Rhodes Old Town) 180
Byzantine Museum
(Zákynthos) 86
Castle Museum
(Kastellórizo) 195
Chatzi Giánnis Méxis
Museum (Spétses
Town) 97
Cretan Open-Air
Museum (Chersónisos)
272
Decorative Arts
Museum (Rhodes Old
Town) 180
Ecology and Folk
Museum (Folégandros)
231
Faltáits Museum
(Skýros Town) 112
Folk Art Museum
(Skópelos) 108
Folk Museum (Agios
Geórgios) 273
Folk Museum (Agios
Nikólaos) 274
Folk Museum
(Chalkída) 116
Folk Museum
(Kárystos) 117
Folk Museum (Kými)
118
Folk Museum (Lefkáda
Town) 81
Folk Museum
(Léfkes) 224
Folk Museum (Mýkonos
Town) 210, 211
Folk Museum (Othos)
199
Folk Museum (Síkinos
Town) 230, 231
Folk Museum (Siteía)
276
Geological Museum
(Apeíranthos) 228

Museums and galleries
(cont.)
Giannoúlis Chalepás
Museum (Pýrgos)
209
Historic and Folk
Museum (Alínda) 163
Historical and Folk Art
Museum (Réthymno)
254
Historical and Folk
Museum (Argostóli)
84
Historical and Folk
Museum (Mandráki) 171
Historical Museum
(Iráklcio) 264
Historical Museum
and Archives (Chaniá)
249
History and Folk
Museum (Pláka) 232,
233
Irákleio Archeological
Museum 265, 266–7
Justiniani Museum
(Chíos Town) 143
Kazantzákis Museum
(Myrtiá) 272
Maritime Museum of
the Aegean (Mýkonos
Town) 210, 211
Maritime Museum
(Andros Town) 204
Maritime Museum
(Sými Town) 174
Medieval Rhodes and
Ancient Rhodes
Exhibitions (Rhodes
Old Town) 180
Mégaro Ghisi Museum
(Firá) 235
Municipal Art Gallery
(Mýkonos) 210, 211
Museum of Asiatic Art
(Corfu Town) 73
Museum of Cretan
Ethnology (Vóroi) 259

Museums and galleries
(cont.)
Museum of Cycladic
Art (Athens) 287
Museum of Modern
Art (Andros Town) 204
Museum of Natural
History (Irákleio) 265
Museum of Popular
Arts and Folklore
(Sífnos) 221
Museum of Religious
Art (Irákleio) 264
Museum of Rural Life
(Chersónisos) 272
National Archaeological
Museum (Athens) 282
National Gallery of Art
(Athens) 287
Naval Museum
(Chaniá) 248
Nikofóreion
Ecclesiastical Museum
(Lipsí Town) 162
Palaeontological
Museum (Megálo
Chorió) 173
Pántheon (Líndos) 192,
193
Papadiamántis
Museum (Skiáthos
Town) 105
Paper Money Museum
(Corfu Old Town) 70, 73
Philip Argéntis Museum
(Chíos Town) 143
Phonograph Museum
(Lefkáda Town) 81
Solomós Museum
(Zákynthos) 86
Sými Museum (Sými
Town) 174
Tériade Museum
(Mytilíni) 134
Vágis Museum
(Potamiá) 126
Vamvakáris Museum
(Ermoúpoli) 217

Music
  Markos Vamvakáris
  217
Muslims 339
Mussolini, Benito 45
  Lakkí 155, **162–3**
  Palace of the Grand
  Masters (Rhodes)
  182
Mustapha Pasha 181
Mycenae
  Trojan War 52
Mycenaean civilization
  24–5
Mýkonos 17,
  210–13
  hotels 305
  map 211
  restaurants 329
Mýkonos Town 210
Mýloi 227
Mylopótamos 99
Mylopótas 230
Mýrina 130
Myrsíni 228
Myrivílis, Strátis 133
  birthplace 137
Mýronas *see* Méronas
Myrtiá 272
Myrtiés 165
Myrtiótissa 68, 78
Mýrtou Bay 85
Mystrás 35
Myths 50–51
Mytilíni (town) 17, 133,
  134
Mytilíni (island) *see*
  Lésvos

N

Náfpaktos, Peace of
  (217 BC) 31
Name days 46
Naós tis Afaías *see*
  Temple of Aphaia
Náousa 224
Napoleon I, Emperor
  143, 224

Napoleon I, Emperor
(cont.)
  Napoleon's House
  (Ierápetra) 275
  Rhodes 185, 187
National Archaeological
  Museum (Athens) 282
National Gallery of Art
  (Athens) 287
National Naval Academy
  (Póros) 96
NATO 40
Nature vacations 348
Naturetrek 243
Naval Museum (Chaniá)
  248
Navaríno, Battle of
  (1827)· 38
Náxos **226–9**
  hotels 305
  map 227
  restaurants 329
Náxos, Dukes of 222
Náxos Town **226**
  festivals 44, 45
Nazis 175
Néa Kaméni 235, 237
Néa Moní 122, **146–7**
Nea Stýra 115
Nektários, Archbishop 93
Nemean lion 51
Neolithic 24
Néos Kósmos (Athens)
  hotels 309
Nerá 165
Nero, Emperor 32, 76
New Fortress (Corfu
  Town) 74
New Zealand Embassy 339
Newspapers 345
Nída Plateau 258
Nikariá *see* Ikaría
Nikariás 149
Nike 31
Nikiá 171, 172
Nikofóreion
  Ecclesiastical Museum
  (Lipsí Town) 162

Nílos (hermit) 151
Nimporió 194
Nio *see* Ios
Niptír Ceremony 161
Nisiá Anatolikoú
  Aigaíou *see*
  Northeast Aegean
  Islands
Níssiros *see* Nísyros
Nísyros **170–71**
  geology 172
  hotels 303
  map 171
  restaurants 327
Noel-Baker family 114,
  119
Nointel, Marquis de 225
Normans 35
Northeast Aegean
  Islands **121–53**
  beaches 350
  Chíos 142–9
  climate 47
  hotels 300–301
  Lésvos 132–41
  Límnos 130–31
  map 122–3
  restaurants 325–6
  Sámos 150–53
  Samothráki 128–9
  Thásos 124–7
Noúlia 175
Nude bathing 339, 350
Nydrí 81

O

Ochi, Mount *see* Mount
  Ochi
Ochi Day 45
Ochthoniá 115, **118**
Odysseus 65
  Ithaca 82
  legend of Odysseus's
  return to Ithaca 83
  Lipsí 162
  Pontikonísi 75
  Odysseus's homecoming
  (Coracelli) 83

Odysseus's Palace
  (Ithaca) 82
Odyssey 27, 53, 54, 75,
  83
Oía 236
Oinoússes 149
Old Fortress (Corfu
  Town) 74
Olives
  olive growing in
    Greece 135
  types of olive 135
Oloús 274
Olympic Airways 355
Olympic Aviation 355
Olympic Games 39
Olýmpoi 145
Olympos 16, 199
  festivals 45
  traditions of 199
Omalós Plateau
  wildlife 242
Omónoia (Athens)
  hotels 310
  restaurants 333
Omorfi Ekklisía (Aígina)
  93
Onassis, Aristotle 40, 41
Opening hours 338
  banks 342
  shops 346
Opening seasons
  hotels 295
Oracle of Apollo 28
Oratory 55
Order of the Knights of
  St John see Knights of
  Rhodes
Orestes 53
Ormos Abrám 228
Ormos Achíli 113
Ormos Aigiális 229
Oropédio Lasithíou see
  Lasíthi Plateau
Oros, Mount see Mount
  Oros
Orsini, Grand Master 190
Ortelius, Abraham 23

Orthodox Church see
  Greek Orthodox Church
OSE 361
Othonoí 77
Othos 198–9
Otto, King 117
  Athens 279
  portrait of 38
  Royal Palace
    (Athens) 38
Ottoman Greece 35,
  36–7
Outdoor activities
  348–9
Ouzerí 313
Ouzo 136
Oxygen Travel 355

P

Package holidays 352
Pagoménos, Ioánnis 247
Painting see Art
Painting holidays 348
Palace of the Grand
  Masters (Rhodes) 182–3
Palace of Knosós 245,
  268–71
  excavations 39
  history 25, 271
  Timeline 271
  Visitors' Checklist 269
Palace of Mália 273
Palace of St Michael and
  St George (Corfu Old
  Town) 73
  Street-by-Street map 71
Palaeolithic civilization
  24
Palaeontological
  Museum (Megálo
  Chorió) 173
Palaiá Alónnisos 110
Palaiá Kaméni 235, 237
Palaíkastro 277
Palaió Pylí 169
Palaiochóra (Aígina) 90,
  93

Palaióchora (Crete)
  246–7
  hotels 308
Palaióchora (Kýthira) 99
Palaiokastrítsa 68, 77
Palaiókastro (Andros)
  206
Palaiologína, María 134
Palaiópoli (Andros) see
  Ancient Palaiópoli
Palaiópoli (Samothráki)
  128–9
Palamedes 137
Paleóhora see
  Palaióchora (Crete)
Paleókhora see
  Palaióchora (Crete)
Pallás 193
Pallavicini 254
Páloi 171
Paloúki, Mount see
  Mount Paloúki
Pan 85, 125
Pan-hellenic Socialist
  Movement (PASOK)
  14, 41
Panagiá 126
Panagía i Tourlianí 211
Pánormos Bay 211
Panteleïmon, Agios
  205
Pántheon (Líndos) 192,
  193
Pantokrátor, Mount see
  Mount Pantokrátor
Papadiamántis,
  Aléxandros 105
Papadiamántis,
  Aléxandros (cont.)
Papadiamántis Museum
  (Skiáthos Town) 105
  statue of 104
Papadópoulos, Colonel
  41
Papáfragkas 233
Papandréou, Andréas
  17, 41
Papandréou, Geórgios 4(

Papanikoláou, Dr
  Geórgios 118
Paper Money Museum
  (Corfu Old Town) **73**
  Street-by-Street map
  70
Paradise 211
Paradise (fresco) 275
Parágka 211
Paralía Väï *see* Väï
  Beach
Parastá Cave 195
Paris 50
  Trojan War 52, 53, 79
Parks and gardens
  Achílleion Palace
  (Corfu) 79
  Esplanade (Corfu
  Town) 72
  El Greco Park
  (Irákleio) 264
  Kárpathos park
  (Kárpathos) 198
  Public Gardens
  (Chaniá) 249
  Rodíni Park (Rhodes
  Town) 187
Paroikiá 222–3
Páros 13, **222–5**
  beaches 350   -
  hotels 305
  map 223
  restaurants 329
Parthenon (Athens) **286**
  frieze 28
  history 28
  Venetians damage 37
Pasiphaë 271
PASOK 14, 41
Passports 336
Patitíri 110
Pátmos 63, 155, **158–61**
  festivals 42, 44
  hotels 303
  map 158
  restaurants 327
Patroklos 52
Paul, St 44, 261

Paul, St (cont.)
  Corinth 32
  St Paul's Bay (Líndos)
  193
  sermon on Areopagos
  hill 285
Pausanias
  Guide to Greece 33, 54
Paxí *see* Paxós
Paximádia islands
  259
Paxoí *see* Paxós
Paxós 80
  restaurants 323
Peake, Sir Charles 73
Pédi bay 175
Péfkos 113, 193
Peisistratos 27
Pelagía, Sister 208, 209
Pélekas 78
Pélla 30, 40
Peloponnesian War 28
Penelope 83
Pentecost (Pentikostí) 44
Penthesilea 53
Péra Kástro 164
Pérdika 93
Peregrine Holidays
  349
Perfumes
  duty-free allowances
  336
Perikles 28
  Acropolis (Athens)
  284–5
  Athens 279
  Parthenon (Athens) 286
Períssa 237
Peristeriónas (dovecotes)
  209
Persephone 50
Perseus 220
Personal security 340
Petaloúdes (Páros)
  225
Petaloúdes (Rhodes)
  177, **188**
Peter, St 44

Pétra 132, **140**
  Women's Rural
  Tourism Cooperative
  297
Petrified forest (Lésvos)
  141
Petrol stations 360
Pétros the Pelican 210
Phaestos 262–3
Phaestos Disc 262
Pharmacies 341
Pharos 349
Pheidias
  Athena Lemnia 29
  Parthenon (Athens) 56,
  286
Pherekydes 218
Philakopí 232–3
Philip II, King of
  Macedon 28
  Battle of Chaironeia
  (338 BC) 23
  Demosthenes attacks
  55
  League of Corinth 29
  Pélla 40
  tomb of 29
Philip V, King of
  Macedon 31
Philip Argéntis Museum
  (Chíos Town) 143
Philoctetes 131
Philosophers 55
Pholegandros *see*
  Folégandros
Phonecards 344
Phonograph Museum
  (Lefkáda Town) 81
Photography 339
Phylakopi *see* Ancient
  Phylakopi
Picasso, Pablo 134, 204,
  207
  *Woman in a White
  Dress* 287
Picnics 315
Piraeus
  port map 357

Piraeus (cont.)
  telephone numbers
    357, 359
Píso Livadi 225
Pláka (Athens) **283**
  hotels 310–11
  restaurants 333
Pláka (Eloúnta) 274
Pláka (Mílos) 232–3
Pláka (Náxos) 226
Plakiás 15, **256**
  hotels 308
Plakotós 230
Plataiaí, Battle of
  (479 BC) 27
Plátanos (Kálymnos)
  165
Plátanos (Léros) 163
Plateía Dimarcheíou
  (Corfu Town) 74
Plato 28, 55
  Academy 29, 34
Pláton, Nikólaos 277
Platýs Gialós (Lipsí)
  162
Platýs Gialós
  (Mýkonos) 211
Platýs Gialós (Sífnos)
  221
Plomári 133, **136**
Poetry 54
Poison treatment centre
  (Athens) 341
Police **340**, 341
Pólis Bay 82
Polítis, Charles 287
Polióchni 151
Polydoros
  Laocoön 182
Polykrates
  Delos 214
  Heraion 152
  Pythagóreio 151
  Sámos 150
Polyrínia 246
Polyvotis 170
Póntamos 194
Pontikonísi 75

Póros **96**
  restaurants 323
Poros, King of India 31
Póros Town 89, 96
Portianoú 131
Pórto Longós 80
Poseidon 50
  Acropolis (Athens) 284
  Nísyros 170
  and Odysseus 83
  Paxos 80
  Pontikonísi 75
  Sanctuary of Poseidon
    and Amphitrite (Tínos)
    209
  statue of 119
Poseidonía 218–19
Postal services 344
Poste restante 345
Potamiá 126
Póthia 164
Pottery *see* Ceramics
Poulákis, Theódoros 175
Poúnta 225
Pouriá 112
Prehistoric Greece 24–5
Préveli, Abbot 256
Préveli (Crete) 241, **256**,
  259
Préveli Monastery *see*
  Moní Préveli
Priam, King of Troy 52,
  53
Pródromos 224
Profítis Ilías (festival) 44
Profítis Ilías (Ýdra) 97
Prokópi 114, **119**
Prometheus 50
Protomagiá 43
Psará 149
Psarotavérna 313
Psáthi 230
Psérimos 165
Psilí Ammos 159
Psiloreítis *see* Mount Idi
Psistariá 313
Psyrrí 282
Ptolemy II, Pharaoh 129

Public holidays 46
Pure Crete 243
Pylos 52
Pyrgí 144
  women's rural tourism
    cooperative 297
Pýrgos 209
Pyropolitís
  statue of 80
Pyrros, King of Epirus
  30
Pythagoras 151
Pythagóras statue
  (Ikaris) 151
Pythagóreio 17, **151**

Q
Qantas 352
Quirini family 170

R
RAC 361
Rachídi 229
RADAR 297, 337
Radio 344
Rail Europe (InterRail)
  361
Railways 361
Rainfall 47
Ramblers Holidays 349
Raphael 55
Religion 14, **339**
  deities and mysteries
    of Samothráki 129
  gods, goddesses and
    heroes 50–51
Rembrandt 209, 287
Réni Koskinoú 191
Residents' permits 336
Restaurants 312–33
  Argo-Saronic Islands
    323
  Athens 332–3
  cafés and bars 313
  children in 315
  Classic Greek menu

Restaurants (cont.)
316–17
clothes 315
Crete 330–32
Cyclades 328–30
Dodecanese 326–8
dress code 315
how to pay 314
Ionian Islands 322–3
Northeast Aegean
Islands 325–6
reservations 314
service and tipping 315
smoking 315
Sporades and Evvoia
324
tavernas 312–13
tipping 339
types of 312
vegetarian food 315
wheelchair access 315
wine 314
Restored settlements
and buildings
accommodation in 294
Réthimno see Réthymno
Réthymno 241, 244,
254–5
hotels 308
restaurants 332
Réthymno Festival 44
Réthymnon see Réthymno
Rhea 258
Rhodes 63, 156, **176–93**
Colossus of Rhodes
31, 186
Eastern Rhodes 190–91
festivals 44
hotels 303
Knights of St John 184–5
Líndos 192–3
map 176–7
Palace of the Grand
Masters 182–3
restaurants 327–8
Rhodes New Town
186–7
siege of (1522) 185

Rhodes (cont.)
Street-by-Street map:
Rhodes Old Town
178–9
Street of the Knights
184–5
Venetian and Ottoman
Greece 36–7
vernacular architecture
19
Western Rhodes 188–9
Rhodes New Town 177,
186–7
map 187
Rhodes Old Town
178–81
Palace of the Grand
Masters (Rhodes)
182–3
Street-by-Street map
178–9
Street of the Knights
184–5
Rhoikos 152
Rína 165
Road assistance 341
Road signs 290, 360
Road travel 360–61
Ródhos see Rhodes
Rodíni Park (Rhodes
Town) 187
Ródos see Rhodes
Roman Greece 32–3
Kos Town 166–7
Roxane 31
Royal Olympic Cruises
349
Rubens, Peter Paul 209
Rudolph, Archduke 79
Rules of the road 360
Rural tourism **296**, 297

S
Safety 340
snorkelling 21
Sailing holidays 351
St Paul's Bay 193
Salamína 92

Salamína Town 92
Salamis see Salamína
Salamis, Battle of (480
BC) 89, **92**
*Salvation of Souls on the
Ladder to Heaven*
(mural) 149
Samariá Gorge 62,
250–51
wildlife 242
Samariá Village 251
Samariás see Samariá
Gorge
Sámi 65, **85**
Sámos **150–53**
hotels 301
map 150
restaurants 325–6
Samothrace see
Samothráki
Samothráki **128–9**
hotels 301
restaurants 326
Sanctuary of the Great
Gods (Samothráki) 56,
128–9
Sanctuary of Poseidon
and Amphitrite (Tínos)
209
Santoríni 15, 25, **234–9**
geology 235
hotels 305–6
map 234
restaurants 330
Sanudo, Marco 231
Sappho 27, 54, **141**
Lésvos 132
Sarakíniko 233
Sardeli 162
Sariá 199
Saronic Islands see Argo-
Saronic Islands
*Scènes de Massacres de
Scio* (Delacroix) **38**,
143
Schinoússa 229
Schliemann, Heinrich
38

Scuba diving 351
Sea urchin stings 341
Seals, monk 111
Seasons 42–5
Seféris, George 41
Self-catering apartments
 and villas 296
Sérifos 220–21
 hotels 306
 restaurants 330
Scriphos see Sérifos
Seven Wonders of the
 Ancient World 30, 186
Sèvres, Treaty of (1920)
 39
Sfakiá 244, 255
 restaurants 332
Sherpa Expeditions 349
Shopping 346–7
 food and drink 346
 markets 346
 opening hours 338, 346
 VAT and tax free
  shopping 346
 What to Buy in Greece
  347
Siána 176, 189
Sidári 68, 77
Sideróportes (Samariá
 Gorge) 251
Siestas 338
Sífnos 221
 archontiká (town
  houses) 18
 hotels 306
 restaurants 330
Sígri 132, 141
Síkinos 230–31
 hotels 306
Síkinos Town 230
Silenus 285
Siligknákis, Abbot 277
Sími see Sými
Simítis, Kóstas 41
Simonídeia Festival
 (Kea) 44
Simonides 44
Simply Crete 349

Singapore Airlines 355
Siphnos see Sifnos
Síros see Sýros
Sísi 273
Siteía 245, 276
 hotels 308
 restaurants 332
 wildlife 243
Sitía see Siteía
Size chart 346
Skála 158
Skála Eresoú 132, 141
Skála Kameírou 176,
 189
Skála Potamiás 126
Skalochóri 140
Skhinoússa see
 Schinoússa
Skiáthos 104–5
 hotels 300
 map 104
 restaurants 324
Skiáthos Town 102,
 104–5
Skinoússa see
 Schinoússa
Skíros see Skýros
Skópelos 62, 108–9
 hotels 300
 map 108
 restaurants 324
Skópelos Town 108
Skordílis 220
Skoulás, Manólis 259
Skoulás, Vasíleios 259
Skrivánou, Léna
 Léna's House (Mýkonos
  Town) 210, 211
Skýros 112–13
 festivals 42
 goat dance 113
 hotels 300
 map 113
 restaurants 324
Skýros Town 103, 112
Slavs 34
Sleeping Girl (Chalepás)
 40

Smith, Sir Sidney 187
Smoking 315
Smyrna 39
Snacks 314
Snorkelling 20, 351
 safety 21
Sóchos, Antónios 209
Society for the
 Advancement of Travel
 for the Handicapped
 (SATH) 337
Socrates 28, 55
 trial and execution 29
Solomós, Dionýsios 77
 Solomós Museum
  (Zákynthos) 86
Solon 26
Sophocles 28, 54, 55
Sossipater, St 75
Sotíras 127
Soúda 256
 restaurants 332
Soúgia 247
Soúyia see Soúgia
Sparta 28
Spas 349
Specialist holidays 348–9
Speed limits 360
Spétsai see Spétses
Spétses 97
 hotels 299
 restaurants 323
Spétses, Battle of (1822)
 45
Spétses Town 97
Spíli
 hotels 308
Spinalónga 274
Sponge-fishing 165
Sporades and Evvoia
 101–19
 Alónnisos 110
 beaches 350
 climate 47
 Evvoia 114–19
 Exploring the
  Sporades and Evvoia
  102–3

Sporades and Evvoia
(cont.)
hotels 300
marine wildlife 111
restaurants 324
Skiáthos 104–5
Skópelos 108–9
Skýros 112–13
Sporades Marine Park
111
Sporádhes see Sporades
and Evvoia
Sports 350–51
Spring in Greece 42–3
Spyrídon, St 46
tomb of 70, **72**
STA Travel 337
Stamatópoulos,
Efstrátios see Myrivílis,
Strátis
Stathátos, Otto and
Athiná 287
Stathátou, Eléni 282
Stathmós Laríssis
(Athens)
hotels 311
Stavrós (Ithaca) 66, **82**
Stavrós (Tínos) 209
Stéfanos crater 172
Stégna 190
Stení 102, 115, **118**
Steniés 204
Stings, marine creatures
341
Street of the Knights
(Rhodes) 184–5
Stréfi Hill (Athens)
hotels 311
Students 337
Stymfalían birds 51
Stýra 117
Styx, River 79
Suleiman the
Magnificent, Sultan 93
Ancient Ialyssós 188
conquest of Rhodes
155, 179
Mosque of Suleiman

Suleiman the Magnificent,
Sultan (cont.)
the Magnificent (Rhodes
Old Town) 181
Sulla 32
Summer in Greece 44–5
Sunbathing 340
topless 339
Sunsail 351
Sunshine 47
Super Paradise 211
Susa 31
Swan Hellenic Cruises 349
Swimming 350
children's safety 337
safety 341
Sykamiá 218
Sykaminiá 133, **137**
Sými 155, 157, **174–5**
hotels 303–4
map 174
restaurants 328
Sými Museum (Sými
Town) 174
Sými Town 174–5
Sýnaxis tis Theotókou 46
Syntágma (Athens)
hotels 311
restaurants 333
Syra see Sýros
Sýros **216–19**
hotels 306
map 216
restaurants 330

T

Taliadoúros,
Mastrodiákis 175
Tavernas 313
Taxes, VAT 346
Taxiarchón Michaíl
kai Gavriíl 45
Taxi boats 359
Taxis 361
Athens **290,** 291
tipping 339
Telemachos 83

Télendos 165
restaurants 328
Telephones **344,** 345
Television 344
Télos see Tílos
Temperatures 47
Temples
Acropolis (Athens) 56
Acropolis (Rhodes) 56
architecture 56–7
Sanctuary of the Great
Gods (Samothráki) 56
Temple of Aphaia
(Aígina) 56, 62, 92,
94–5
Temple of Apollo
(Aígina Town) 93
Temple of Apollo
(Delos) 56
Temple of Artemis
(Corfu) 75
Temple of Athena
(Górtys) 261
Temple of Athena Nike
(Athens) 284
Temple of Athena
Polias and Zeus Poliefs
(Ancient Ialyssós) 188
Temple of Athena
Poliouchos (Ancient
Thásos) 125
Temple of Dionysos
(Ancient Thásos) 125
Temple of Hera
(Olympia) 27
Temple of Hera
(Sámos) 56
Temple of Lindian
Athena (Líndos) 56
Temple of Poseidon
(Kalavría) 96
Temple of Pythian
Apollo (Górtys)
261
Ténos see Tínos
Tenrag Yacht Charters
351
Tériade 134

Tériade Museum
  (Mytilíni) 134
Thalassa Charter and
  Yacht Brokers 351
Thásos **124–7**
  Ancient Thásos 124–5
  hotels 301
  map 124
  restaurants 326
Thásos Town 124–5
Thássos *see* Thásos
Theatre 55
Theft 340
Themistokles 92
Theodora, St 70, **74**
Theodoros 152
Theodosius I, Emperor
  33
Theofánia (Epiphany)
  46
Theófilos Chatzimichaïl
  133
  Alexander the Great 23
  *Assumption of the
  Virgin* 121
  Theófilos Museum
  (Mytilíni) 134
Theoktísti, St 223
Theológos 127
Theophrastos 141
Thérma (Ikaría) 149
Thermá (Samothráki)
  129
Thérma Lefkádas 149
Thérmes Kalithéas 191
Thermiá *see* Kýthnos
Thermopylae, Battle of
  (480 BC) 27
Theseus
  Greek myths 50
  and the Minotaur 271
  Náxos 226
  Skýros 112
Thessaloníki 34
Thetis 79
Thíra *see* Ancient Thíra;
  Santoríni
Thirasía 237

Thiseío (Athens)
  restaurants 333
Tholária 229
Thomas Cook 342, 351
Three Standing Figures
  (Moore) 207
Thrónos
  Tour of the Amári
  Valley 257
Thucydides 54
Tigkáki 168
Tílos **173**
  festivals 44
  hotels 304
  restaurants 328
Time zones 338
Tínos **208–9**
  hotels 306
  map 208
  peristeiónas (dove-
  cotes) 209
  restaurants 330
Tínos Town 44, **208**
Tipping 339
  in restaurants 315
Tiryns 25
Titus, St 261
Tobacco
  duty-free allowances
  336
Tómpros, Michális 204
  Immortal Poetry 112
  Unknown Sailor 204
Topless bathing 339, 350
Toploú Monastery *see*
  Moní Toploú
Tourist Guide of Greece
  297
Tourist information 338
Tourist offices 337
Tourist police
  340, 341
Tours by car
  Amári Valley 257
Tragaía Valley 227
Trains 361
Transfiguration of Christ
  45

Trápeza Cave 273
Travel **352–61**
  air 352–5
  Argo-Saronic Islands
  91
  buses 361
  coaches 361
  Crete 244
  Cyclades 202
  Dodecanese 157
  getting around Athens
  288–91
  Ionian Islands 67
  Northeast Aegean
  Islands 123
  road 360–61
  sea 356–9
  Sporades and Evvoia
  103
  taxis **290**, 291, 361
  trains 361
Travel agencies
  Athens 355
Travellers' cheques 342
  in restaurants 314
Treis Ekklisiés 224
Treís Mpoúkes 113
Trekking Hellas 349
Triandáros 201
Tripolitsá 38
Tripscope 297, 337
Trojan Horse 53
Trojan War 50, **52–3**
Trolleybuses
  Athens **289**, 291
Troy 25
Tsampíka 191
Tsaroúchis, Giánnis
  40
Tsiliví 87
Turtles, loggerhead
  87
Twentieth-century
  Greece **40–41**
Týlissos 265
Tzanáki 170
Tzermiádo 273
Tziá *see* Kéa

U

Ulysses Tours Inc. 351
United Kingdom
  Greek Tourist Offices
  337
  Olympic Airways
  office 355
  United Kingdom
  Embassy 339
United States of America
  Embassy 339
  Greek Tourist Offices
  337
  Olympic Airways
  office 355
Unknown Sailor
  (Tómbros) 204

V

Vagiá 159
Vágis, Polýgnotos 126
  Vágis Museum
  (Potamiá) 126
Váï Beach 277
Valtíza *see* Baltíza
Válvis, Dimítrios 226
Vamos 349
Vamvakáris, Márkos 217
  Vamvakáris Museum
  (Ermoúpoli) 217
Van Dyck, Sir Anthony
  287
Vapória 217
Vári 219
Varsamiá 206
Vases and vase painting
  58–9
Vasilikí 81
VAT 346
Vathás, Thomás 159
Vathý (Astypálaia) 170
Vathý (Ithaca) 82
Vathý (Sámos) 150
Vathý (Sífnos) 221
Vátos 68, **78**
Vatoússa 140
Vávyloi 145

Vegetarian food
  in restaurants 315
Venetian Greece 34, **36–7**
Venizélos, Elefthérios
  17, **39**, 249, 259
  Athens airport 252–3
  Crete 241
  statue of 265
  tomb of 247
Venus de Milo 232, 233
Verdi, Giuseppe 217
Vernacular architecture
  18–19
Véssa 144
Viamare Travel Ltd 359
Victor Emmanuel III,
  King of Italy 182
Vígla 231
Vignoli, Admiral Vignolo
  de 183, 184
Vilaragut, Diomede de
  184
Villaret, Foulkes de 183
Villas, self-catering 296
Villeneuve, Grand
  Master del 183
Villiers de l'Isle Adam,
  Grand Master 185
Villon, Jacques 134
Virgil
  Aeneid 52
Virgin Mary
  festivals 43, 45, 46
Visa (credit cards) 343
Visas 336
Vitális, Geórgios 209, 217
Vizári
  Tour of the Amári
  Valley 257
Vlachérna 65, 75
Volcanoes
  Nísyros 172
  Santoríni 235
Volissós 148
Vóreies Sporádes *see*
  Sporades and Evvoia
Voúdia 233
Voúlgaris, Ioánnis 209

Vourkári 219
Vourliótes 153
Vréllas 97
Vrontádo 217
Vroukoúnda 199
Vryókastro 220

W

Walking 348–9
  in Athens 290
War of Independence
  23, **38–9**, 89
  massacre at Chíos
  (1822) 147
Water, drinking 341
Water-skiing 350
Watersports 350–51
Weather 47
  when to visit Greece
  336
Weaver fish stings 341
Wheelchair access *see*
  Disabled travellers
"White Terror" 40
Whitsun 44
Wildlife
  Alykés Saltpans 168
  Aquarium (Rhodes
  New Town) 186
  flora and fauna of
  Crete 242–3
  Korisíon Lagoon 78
  kri-kri (Cretan wild
  goat) 250
  loggerhead turtles
  87
  marine life 20–21
  marine wildlife in the
  Sporades 111
  nature vacations 348
  Sporades Marine Park
  111
Wildlife Travel 243
Wilhelm II, Kaiser
  Achílleion Palace
  (Corfu) 79
  Kaiser's Throne
  (Corfu) 78

Windmills 19
Windsurfing 350
Wine **321**
  duty-free allowances
  336
  in restaurants 314
Winter in Greece 46
Women travellers 337
Women's Rural Tourism
  Cooperatives **296**, 297
World War I 38, 39
World War II 40
  Alimiá 195
  Ancient Ialyssós 188
  Ano Méros 257
  Anógeia 258
  battle of Crete (1941)
  247
  Moní Préveli (Crete)
  256
  Moní Toploú (Crete)
  277
  Treaty of the
  Dodecanese 175
Writers **54–5**
  in Corfu 77
Writing holidays 348

X
Xálki *see* Chálki
Xaniá *see* Chaniá
Xerxes, King of Persia
  92, 119
Xíos *see* Chíos
Xirókampos 163
Xylokeratídi 229
Xylóskalo (Samariá
  Gorge) 250
Xyloúris, Níkos 259

Y
Ydra **96–7**
  hotels 299
  restaurants 323
Ydra Town 96–7
Youth hostels **296**,
  297
Ypapantí 46
Ypsosis tou Timíou
  Stavroú 45

Z
Zacharoplasteío 313
Zákinthos *see*
  Zákynthos
Zákros **277**
  restaurants 332
  wildlife 243
Zákynthos **86–7**
  hotels 299
  map 86
  restaurants 323
Zákynthos Town 86
Zante *see* Zákynthos
Zante Hotels 297
Zarós 261
  hotels 308
Zarós Gorge 261
Zeus
  Cretan caves and the
  myth of Zeus 258
  Diktian Cave 273
  Greek myths 50
  Heraion 152
  Trojan War 52
Ziá 168
Ziller, Ernst 216
Zoödóchos Pigí
  206

Acknowledgments

DORLING KINDERSLEY would like to thank the following people whose contributions and assistance have made the preparation of this book possible.

MAIN CONTRIBUTORS

MARC DUBIN is an American expatriate who divides his time between London and Sámos. Since 1978 he has travelled in every province of Greece. He has written or contributed to numerous guides to Greece, covering such diverse topics as trekking and contemporary Greek music.

STEPHANIE FERGUSON, a freelance journalist and travel writer, has hopped around almost 50 Greek islands. She became bewitched by Greece after a holiday 20 years ago and since then has contributed to eight guide books and written travel features on Greece for several national publications.

MIKE GERRARD is a travel writer and broadcaster who has written several guides to various parts of Greece, which he has been visiting annually since 1964.

ANDY HARRIS is a travel and food journalist based in Athens. He is the author of *A Taste of the Aegean*.

TANYA TSIKAS is a Canadian writer and travel guide editor. Married to a Greek, she has spent time in Crete and currently lives in Oxford.

DEPUTY EDITORIAL DIRECTOR
Douglas Amrine

DEPUTY ART DIRECTOR Gillian Allan

MANAGING EDITOR Georgina Matthews

MANAGING ART EDITOR Annette Jacobs

ADDITIONAL ILLUSTRATIONS

Richard Bonson, Louise Boulton, Gary Cross, Kevin Goold, Roger Hutchins, Claire Littlejohn.

DESIGN AND EDITORIAL ASSISTANCE

Hilary Bird, Elspeth Collier, Catherine Day, Jim Evoy, Emily Green, Emily Hatchwell, Leanne Hogbin, Kim Inglis, Lorien Kite, Esther Labi, Felicity Laughton, Andreas Michael, Ella Milroy, Lisa Minsky, Robert Mitchell, Adam Moore, Jennifer Mussett, Eva Petrou, Tamsin Pender, Jake Reimann, Ellen Root, Simon Ryder, Rita Selvaggio, Claire Stewart, Claire Tennant-Scull, Amanda Tomeh, Andy Wilkinson.

DORLING KINDERSLEY would also like to thank the following for their assistance: The Greek Wine Bureau, Odysea.

ADDITIONAL RESEARCH

Anna Antoniou, Garifalia Boussiopoulou, Anastasia Caramanis, Michelle Crawford, Magda Dimouti, Shirley Durant, Panos Gotsi, Zoi Groummouti, Peter Millett, Tasos Schizas, Garifalia Tsiola, Veronica Wood.

ARTWORK REFERENCE

Ideal Photo S.A., The Image Bank, Melissa Publishing House, Tony Stone Worldwide.

ADDITIONAL PHOTOGRAPHY

Jane Burton, Frank Greenaway, Derek Hall, Dave King, Neil Lucas, National History Museum, Stephen Oliver, Roger Philips, Kim Sayer, Clive Steeter, Harry Taylor, Kim Taylor, Mathew Ward, Jerry Young.

PHOTOGRAPHY PERMISSIONS

DORLING KINDERSLEY would like to thank the following for their assistance and kind permission to photograph at their establishments:

Nelly Dimoglou Folk Dance Theatre, Rhodes; Museum of Greek Folk Art, Athens; Karpathos Museum; Markos Vamvakaris Museum, Syros; Kymi Folk Museum, Evvoia; Stavros Kois's House, Syros. Also all other cathedrals, churches, museums, hotels, restaurants, shops, galleries, and sights too numerous to thank individually.

PICTURE CREDITS

t = top; tl = top left; tlc = top left centre; tc = top centre; trc = top right centre; tr = top right; cla = centre left above; ca = centre above; cra = centre right above; cl = centre left; c = centre; cr = centre right; clb = centre right below; cb = centre below; crb = centre right below; bl = bottom left; b = bottom; bc = bottom centre; bcl = bottom centre left; br = bottom right; d = detail.

Works of art have been reproduced with the permission of the following copyright holders: © ADAGP, Paris and DACS, London 1997 *The Kiss* Constantin

Brancusi 207br. The work of art *Three Standing Figures*, Henry Moore (1947) 207bl is reproduced by permission of the Henry Moore Foundation.

The publisher would like to thank the following individuals, companies and picture libraries for permission to reproduce their photographs:

AISA ARCHIVO ICONGRAFICO, Barcelona: Museo Archeologique, Bari 55tr; Museo Archeologique, Florence 52tl; AKG, London· 186b, 284t; Antiquario Palatino 51bl; British Museum 285b; Erich Lessing Akademie der Bildenden Künste, Vienna 52c; Musée du Louvre 51tl; Naples Archaeological Museum 141b; National Archeological Museum, Athens 24–5(d), 25t; Staatliche Kunstsammlungen, Albertinum, Dresden 29crb, Liebighaus, Frankfurt/Main 31c; Staatliche Antikensammlungen und Glyptotek, München 50b; Mykonos Museum 53t; ANCIENT ART AND ARCHITECTURE: 27ca, 28t, 32t, 32ca, 33cl, 35t, 54cb, 54b(d), 95b; ANTIKENMUSEUM BASEL UND SAMMLUNG LUDWIG: 58–9; APERION: John Hios 43c; ARGYROPOULOS PHOTO PRESS: 43t, 45cr, 46t, 46cb, Athens International Airport: 352cr/b, 353cr, 354.

BENAKI MUSEUM: 23b, 34ca, 37t, 37c, 39ca, 287b; PAUL BERNARD: 31t; BIBLIOTHÈQUE NATIONAL, Paris: Caoursin folio 175 4c(d), 36–7(d), Caoursin folio 33 185bl, Caoursin folio 79 185br; BODLEIAN LIBRARY, Oxford: MS Canon Misc 378 170v 32cb; BRIDGEMAN ART LIBRARY, London: Birmingham City Museums and Art Galleries *Pheidias Completing the Parthenon Frieze*, Sir Lawrence Alma-Tadema 56t; Bibliothèque Nationale, Paris *The Author Guillaume Caoursin, Vice Chancellor of the Order of St John of Jerusalem Dedicating his Book to Pierre d'Aubusson, Grand Master of the Order of St John of Jerusalem who is Seated Surrounded by High Dignitaries of the Order* (1483), illustrated by the Master of Cardinal of Bourbon Lat 6067 f 3v 22(d); British Museum, London *Cup, Tondo, with Scene of Huntsmen Returning Home* 27cb, *Greek Vase Showing Diver About to Enter the Sea in Search of Sponges* (c.500 BC) 165br; Fitzwilliam Museum, University of Cambridge *Figurine of Demosthenes*, Enoch Wood of Burslem (c.1790) (lead glazed earthenware) 55tl,

Attic Red-figured Pelike: Pigs, Swineherd and Odysseus, Pig Painter (470–60BC) 83bl; Freud Museum, London *Figure of Artemis from Myrina*, Greek, Hellenistic Period (2nd century BC) 214tl; Giraudon/Louvre Paris *Alexander the Great, Portrait Head* (3rd century BC) Greek (marble) 30tr; House of Masks, Delos *Mosaic of Dionysus riding a Leopard* (c.AD 180) 33t; Kunsthistorisches Museum, Vienna *Elizabeth of Bavaria, Wife of Emperor Franz Joseph I of Austria*, Franz Xavier Winterhalter 79c(d); Lauros-Giraudon/Louvre, Paris *Rhodes Winged Victory of Samothrace* (early 2nd century BC) 128c; Louvre, Paris *Double Bust of Aristophanes and Sophocles* (15th century) 54t; National Archaeological Museum, Athens *Bronze Satue of Poseidon* (c.460–450 BC) photo Bernard Cox 50c; Private Collection *Two-tiered Icon of the Virgin and Child and Two Saints*, Cretan School (15th century) 36cl; Victoria and Albert Museum, London *Corfu*, Edward Lear 77b; © THE BRITISH MUSEUM: 24clb, 25cb, 26tl, 28cb, 29clb, 51tr(d), 51br, 53c(d), 58tl, 59tl, 59tr, 135cra.

CAMERA PRESS, London: ANAG 41tl, 41bl; Christopher Simon Sykes 73t; Wim Swaan 215t; TANYA COLBOURNE: 350t; BRUCE COLEMAN LTD.: Philip van de Berg 243cl; Luiz Claudio Marigo 87t; Natalio Feneck 111ca; Gordon Langsbury 243bl; Andrew J Purcell 20ca; Kim Taylor 111bl; World Wildlife Fund for Nature 111t; Konrad Wothe 243br.

C M DIXON PHOTO RESOURCES: 25ca; Glyptotek, Munich 30tr; MARC DUBIN: 18t, 19bla, 19bra, 44tl, 170t, 195t, 195b, 219b, 229c, 231b, 248b.

ECOLE FRANÇAISE D'ATHÈNES: 214tr; ECOLE NATIONALE SUPERIEURE DES BEAUX ARTS, Paris: *Delphes Restauration du Sanctuaire Envoi*, Tournaire (1894) 28–9; EKDOTIKI ATHINON: 3, 24crb, 160b, 183b(d), 184bl(d); ELIA: 105b; JANICE ENGLISH: 188t, 189t, 189b, 190c, 190b; ET ARCHIVE: National Archaeology Museum, Naples 30ca; EUROPEAN COMMISSION: 343; MARY EVANS PICTURE LIBRARY: 83cr, 83bc, 83br, 129b, 152b.

FERENS ART GALLERY: Hull City Museums and Art Galleries and Archives *Electra at the Tomb of Agamennon* (1869), Lord

Frederick Leighton 53b.

GIRAUDON, Paris: Chateau Ecouen *Retour d'Ulysse* Ecole Siennoise 83cl; Louvre Paris 58c, *Scène de Massacres de Scio,* Eugene Delacroix 38ca(d), 143b(d); Musée Nationale Gustave Moreau *Hesiode et Les Muses,* Gustave Moreau 54ca; Musée d'Art Catalan, Barcelona 285cb; NICHOLAS P GOULANDRIS FOUNDATION MUSEUM OF CYCLADIC AND ANCIENT GREEK ART: 207tl, 207tc, 207tr, 207cl, 207cr,280b,287t; RONALD GRANT ARCHIVE: *Zorba the Greek,* 20th Century Fox 272b.

ROBERT HARDING PICTURE LIBRARY: David Beatty 42br; Tony Gervis 42ca, 42bl; Adam Woolfitt 44c; HELIO PHOTO: 94ca; HELLENIC POST SERVICE: 41cla; HELLENIC WAR MUSEUM, Athens: 247t; HISTORICAL MUSEUM OF CRETE, Irákleio: *Landscape of the Gods-Trodden Mount Sinai,* El Greco 264tr; MICHAEL HOLFORD: British Museum 30cb, 50t; HULTON GETTY COLLECTION: 39cb(d); Central Press Photo 40clb(d).

IDEAL PHOTO SA: T Dassios 297c; A Pappas 231t; C Vergas 43clb, 43br, 44tr, 79b, 113b, 157t; IMAGES COLOUR LIBRARY: 90t, 266bl; IMPACT PHOTOS: Jeremy Nicholl 348b; Caroline Penn 43bl.

CAROL KANE: 194br; GULIA KLIMI: 45t; KOSTOS KONTOS: 24cr, 40cra, 40cla, 43crb, 46ca, 159b, 160c, 184br, 289b, 341t, 351c.

FRANK LANE PICTURES: Eric and David Hoskings 242bl; ILIAS LALAOUNIS: 347cla.

MAGNUM PHOTOS LTD.: Constantine Manos 42t; MANSELL COLLECTION: 50–1.

NATIONAL GALLERY OF VICTORIA, Melbourne: *Greek by the Inscriptions Painter Challidian* Felton Bequest (1956) 52b; NATIONAL HISTORICAL MUSEUM: 36t, 38t, 38–9(d), 39t, 40b; NATURAL IMAGE: Bob Gibbons 243tl; Peter Wilson 250tl; NATURE PHOTOGRAPHERS: Brinsley Burbridge 243tr; Robin Bush 243cr; Michael J Hammett 20tr; Paul Sterry 111br, 243tc; ANTONIS NICOLOPOULOS: 350c, 351b.

OLYMPIC AIRWAYS: 352t; ORONOZ ARCHIVO FOTOGRAFICO: Biblioteca National Madrid *Invasions Bulgares Historia Matriksiscronica FIIIV* 34cb(d); Charlottenberg, Berlin 52tr; El Escorial, Madrid *Battle of Lepanto,* Cambiaso Luca

36cr(d); Museo Julia 51c(d); Musée du Louvre 58b; Museo Vaticano 55b, 59bl; OXFORD SCIENTIFIC FILMS: Paul Kay 21tr.

ROMYLOS PARISIS: City of Athens Museum 38cb; PICTOR INTERNATIONAL: 44b; PICTURES: 42crb, 350br; PLANET EARTH PICTURES: Wendy Dennis 242c; Jim Greenfield 21cb; Ken Lucas 111cb; Marty Snyderman 21tl; PRIVATE COLLECTION: 277c; POPPERFOTO: 40crb, 41cra, 41br.

REX FEATURES: Sipa Press/C Brown 41tr.

SCALA, Florence: Gallerie degli Uffizi 26cb; Museo Archeologico, Firenze 27t; Museo Mandralisca Cefalu 28ca; Museo Nationale Tarquinia 59br; Museo de Villa Giulia 26–7, 58tr; SPECTRUM COLOUR LIBRARY: 250tl; MARIA STEFOSSI: 16bl.

TAP (SERVICE ARCHAEOLOGICAL RECEIPTS FUND) HELLENIC REPUBLIC MINISTRY OF CULTURE: 1st Epharat of Antiquities 41cb, 56br, 284cb, 284b, 285t, 285ca; Acropolis Museum 286tl, 286tr; Andros Archaeological Museum 204cl; Agios Nikolaos Archaeological Museum 274c; 2nd Epharat of Antiquities 62bl, 94t, 94cb, 94b, 95t, 95c; Chalkida Archaeological Museum 116c; Chania Archaeological Museum 249c; Corfu Archaeological Museum 65t, 75c; Eretreia Archaeological Museum 5t, 115b, 117c; 5th Epharat of Byzantine Antiquities 35c; 14th Epharat of Byzantine Antiquities 133t, 136t, 140b; 4th Epharat of Byzantine Antiquities 14c, 161tr, 161c, 161b, 195c; 18th Epharat of Antiquities 124t, 125t, 125b; 19th Epharat of Antiquities 128b, 129ca, 129cb; Ikia Varelizidenas 121c; Irakleio Archaeological Museum 262bl, 266t, 266ca, 266cb, 267t, 267c, 268br; 20th Epharat of Antiquities 131b; 21st Epharat of Antiquities 63t, 152t, 152c, 214b, 215ca, 215bl, 215br, 223c, 226cl, 236cb, 237c, 348ca; 22nd Epharat of Antiquities 167b, 168t, 168c, 176t, 182tl, 182tr, 182c, 182b, 183t, 183c, 192t, 192cr; 23rd Epharat of Antiquities 245t, 259c, 260c, 260b, 261 all, 262t, 262c, 262br, 263 all, 268t, 268c, 268bl, 269tl, 269tr, 269b, 270t, 270c, 270b, 271b, 217t; 24th Epharat of Antiquities 273c; Kos Archaeological Museum 168b; Milos Archaeological Museum 232t; Mykonos Archaeological Museum 210tr; National Archeological Museum, Athens 24t, 26tr, 237b, 282c; Naxos Archaeological Museum 226t; Nea Moni Archaeological Museum 63ca; Numismatic Museum of

Athens 271c; Rhodes Archaeological Museum 180cb; Vathy Archaeological Museum, Samos 150cr; 2nd Epharat of Byzantine Antiquities 209c, 217t, 220t, 223b, 247c; 7th Epharat of Byzantine Antiquities 105t; 6th Epharat of Byzantine Antiquities 85c; Thessaloniki Archaeological Museum 29t; Thira Archaeological Museum 234tl; 3rd Epharat of Byzantine Antiquities 140b, 148tl, 149c, 151b; 13th Epharat of Byzantine Antiquities 146–7 all, 257cra, 273b, 275t; Tinos Archaeological Museum 208t; 3rd Epharat of Antiquities 283b; TERIADE MUSEUM: *Dafnis and Chloe,* Marc Chagall ©ADAGP, Paris and DACS, London 1997; TRAVEL INK: Nigel Bowen-Morris 238–9; TRAVEL LIBRARY: Faltaits Museum 112tr; YANNIS

TSAROUCHIS FOUNDATION: Private Collection *Barber Shop in Marousi,* Yannis Tsarouchis (1947) 40u.
WERNER FORMAN ARCHIVE: Thessaloniki Archaeological Musem 34t; LORRAINE WILSON: 62br; PETER WILSON: 16c, 57bl, 63b, 284ca; BRIAN WOODYATT:14b.

JACKET
Front - DK PICTURE LIBRARY: Linda Whitwam cb, bla; ROBERT HARDING PICTURE LIBRARY: Paul Henning bc; MASTERFILE, UK: Garry Black main image. Back - DK PICTURE LIBRARY: Max Alexander b, Rupert Horrox t. Spine: MASTERFILE, UK: Garry Black.

All other images © Dorling Kindersley. For further information see: www.dkimages.com

Phrase Book

THERE IS NO universally accepted system for representing the modern Greek language in the Roman alphabet. The system of transliteration adopted in this guide is the one used by the Greek Government. Though not yet fully applied throughout Greece, most of the street and place names have been transliterated according to this system. For Classical names this guide uses the k, os, on and f spelling, in keeping with the modern system of transliteration. In a few cases, such as Socrates, the more familiar Latin form has been used. Classical names do not have accents. Where a well-known English form of a name exists, such as Athens or Corfu, this has been used. Variations in transliteration are given in the index.

GUIDELINES FOR PRONUNCIATION

The accent over Greek and transliterated words indicates the stressed syllable. In this guide the accent is not written over capital letters nor over monosyllables, except for question words and the conjunction ή (meaning "or"). In the right-hand "Pronunciation" column below, the syllable to stress is given in bold type.

On the following pages, the English is given in the left-hand column with the Greek and its transliteration in the middle column. The right-hand column provides a literal system of pronounciation and indicates the stressed syllable in bold.

THE GREEK ALPHABET

Α α	A a	**arm**
Β β	V v	**vote**
Γ γ	G g	**y**ear (when followed by e and i sounds) **n**o (when followed by ξ or γ)
Δ δ	D d	**th**at
Ε ε	E e	**egg**
Ζ ζ	Z z	**zoo**
Η η	I i	bel**ie**ve
Θ θ	Th th	**th**ink
Ι ι	I i	bel**ie**ve
Κ κ	K k	**k**id
Λ λ	L l	**l**and
Μ μ	M m	**m**an
Ν ν	N n	**n**o
Ξ ξ	X x	ta**x**i
Ο ο	O o	**fox**
Π π	P p	**p**ort
Ρ ρ	R r	**r**oom
Σ σ	S s	**s**orry (zero when followed by μ)
ς	s	(used at end of word)
Τ τ	T t	**t**ea
Υ υ	Y y	bel**ie**ve
Φ φ	F f	**f**ish
Χ χ	Ch ch	lo**ch** in most cases, but **h**e when followed by a, e or i sounds
Ψ ψ	Ps ps	ma**ps**
Ω ω	O o	**fox**

COMBINATIONS OF LETTERS

In Greek there are two-letter vowels that are pronounced as one sound:

Αι αι	Ai ai	**egg**
Ει ει	Ei ei	bel**ie**ve
Οι οι	Oi oi	bel**ie**ve
Ου ου	Ou ou	l**u**te

There are also some two-letter consonants that are pronounced as one sound:

Μπ μπ	Mp mp	**b**ut, sometimes nu**mb**er in the middle of a word
Ντ ντ	Nt nt	**d**esk, sometimes u**nd**er in the middle of a word
Γκ γκ	Gk gk	**g**o, sometimes bi**ng**o in the middle of a word
Γξ γξ	nx	a**nx**iety
Τζ τζ	Tz tz	ha**nds**
Τσ τσ	Ts ts	i**t's**
Γγ γγ	Gg gg	bi**ng**o

IN AN EMERGENCY

Help!	Βοήθεια! Voitheia	vo-**e**-theea
Stop!	Σταματήστε! Stamatiste	sta-ma-**tee**-steh
Call a doctor!	Φωνάξτε ένα γιατρό Fonáxte éna giatró	fo-**nak**-steh **e**-na ya-**tro**
Call an ambulance/ the police/the fire brigade!	Καλέστε το ασθενοφόρο/την αστυνομία/την πυροσβεστική Kaléste to asthenofóro/tin astynomía/tin pyrosvestiki	ka-**le**-steh to as-the-no-**fo**-ro/teen as-ti-no-**mia**/teen pee-ro-zve-stee-**kee**
Where is the nearest telephone/hospital/ pharmacy?	Πού είναι το πλησιέστερο τήλέφωνο/νοσοκο-μείο/φαρμακείο; Poú einai to plisiés-tero tiléfono/ nosoko-meio/farmakeio?	**poo ce**-ne to plee-see-**e**-ste-ro tee-le-pho-no/no-so-ko-**mee**-o/far-ma-**kee**-o?

COMMUNICATION ESSENTIALS

Yes	Ναι Nai	neh
No	Όχι Ochi	**o**-chee
Please	Παρακαλώ Parakaló	pa-ra-ka-**lo**
Thank you	Ευχαριστώ Efcharistó	ef-cha-ree-**sto**
You are welcome	Παρακαλώ Parakaló	pa-ra-ka-**lo**
OK/alright	Εντάξει Entáxei	en-**dak**-zee
Excuse me	Με συγχωρείτε Me synchoreíte	me seen-cho-**ree**-teh
Hello	Γειά σας Geiá sas	**yeea** sas
Goodbye	Αντίο Antío	an-**dee**-o
Good morning	Καλημέρα Kaliméra	ka-lee-**me**-ra
Good night	Καληνύχτα Kalinýchta	ka-lee-**neech**-ta
Morning	Πρωί Proí	pro-**ee**
Afternoon	Απόγευμα Apógevma	a-**po**-yev-ma
Evening	Βράδυ Vrádi	**vrath**-i
This morning	Σήμερα το πρωί Símera to proi	**see**-me-ra to pro-**ee**
Yesterday	Χθές Chthés	chthes
Today	Σήμερα Símera	**see**-me-ra
Tomorrow	Αύριο Avrio	**av**-ree-o
Here	Εδώ Edó	ed-**o**
There	Εκεί Ekeí	e-**kee**
What?	Τι; Ti?	t**ee**?
Why?	Γιατί; Giatí?	ya-t**ee**?
Where?	Πού; Poú?	p**oo**?
How?	Πώς; Pós?	p**os**?
Wait!	Περίμενε! Perímene!	pe-**ree**-me-neh

USEFUL PHRASES

How are you?	Τί κάνεις;	tee **ka**-nees
	Tí káneis?	
Very well, thank you	Πολύ καλά,	po-lee ka-**la**, ef-cha-
	ευχαριστώ	ree-**sto**
	Polý kalá, efcharistó	
How do you do?	Πώς είστε;	pos **res**-te?
	Pós eíste?	
Pleased to meet you	Χαίρω πολύ	**che**-ro po-**lee**
	Chaíro polý	
What is your name?	Πώς λέγεστε;	pos le-**ye**-ste?
	Pós légeste?	
Where is/are ?	Πού είναι;	poo ee-ne?
	Poú eínai?	
How far is it to...?	Πόσο απέχει... ;	po-so a-pe-**chee**?
	Póso apéchei...?	
How do I get to?	Πώς μπορώ να	pos bo-**ro**-na **pa**-o?
	πάω.... ;	
	Pos mporó na páo...?	
Do you speak	Μιλάτε Αγγλικά;	mee-**la**-te an-glee-**ka**?
English?	Miláte Anglika?	
I understand	Καταλαβαίνω	ka-ta-la-**ve**-no
	Katalavaino	
I don't understand	Δεν καταλαβαίνω	then ka-ta-la-**ve**-no
	Den katalavaíno	
Could you speak	Μιλάτε λίγο πιο	mee-**la**-te lee-go pyo
slowly?	αργά παρακαλώ;	ar-**ga** pa-ra-ka-**lo**?
	Miláte lígo pio argá	
	parakaló?	
I'm sorry	Με συγχωρείτε	me seen-cho-ree-teh
	Me synchoreíte	
Does anyone have a	Έχει κανένας	**e**-chee ka-**ne**-nas
key?	κλειδί;	klee-**dee**?
	Echei kanénas	
	kleidí?	

USEFUL WORDS

big	Μεγάλο	me-**ga**-lo
	Megálo	
small	Μικρό	mi-**kro**
	Mikró	
hot	Ζεστό	zes-**to**
	Zestó	
cold	Κρύο	**kree**-o
	Krýo	
good	Καλό	ka-**lo**
	Kaló	
bad	Κακό	ka-**ko**
	Kakó	
enough	Αρκετά	ar-ke-**ta**
	Arketá	
well	Καλά	ka-**la**
	Kalá	
open	Ανοιχτά	a-neech-**ta**
	Anoichtá	
closed	Κλειστά	klee-**sta**
	Kleistá	
left	Αριστερά	a-ree-ste-**ra**
	Aristerá	
right	Δεξιά	dek-see-**a**
	Dexiá	
straight on	Ευθεία	ef-**thee**-a
	Efthcía	
between	Ανάμεσα / Μεταξύ	a-**na**-me-sa/me-tak-
	Anámesa / Metaxý	see
on the corner of.....	Στη γωνία του...	stee go-nee-a too
	Sti gonía tou...	
near	Κοντά	kon-**da**
	Kontá	
far	Μακριά	ma-kree-a
	Makriá	
up	Επάνω	e-**pa**-no
	Epáno	
down	Κάτω	**ka**-to
	Káto	
early	Νωρίς	no-**rees**
	Norís	
late	Αργά	ar-**ga**
	Argá	
entrance	Η είσοδος	ee **ce**-so-thos
	I eísodos	
exit	Η έξοδος	ee **e**-kso-dos
	I éxodos	
toilet	Οι τουαλέτες /WC	ee-too-a-**le**-tes
	Oi toualétes / WC	
occupied/engaged	Κατειλημμένη	ka-tee-lee-**me**-nee
	Kateiliméni	

unoccupied/vacant	Ελεύθερη	e-**lef**-the-ree
	Eléftheri	
free/no charge	Δωρεάν	tho-re-**an**
	Doreán	
in/out	Μέσα /Έξω	me-sa/**ek**-so
	Mésa/ Exo	

MAKING A TELEPHONE CALL

Where is the nearest	Πού βρίσκεται ο	poo vrees-ke-teh o
public telephone ?	πλησιέστερος	plee-see-**e**-ste-ros
	τηλεφωνικός	tee-le-fo-ni-**kos** tha-
	θάλαμος;	la-mos?
	Poú vrísketai o	
	plisiésteros	
	tilefonikós thalamos?	
I would like to place	Θα ήθελα να κάνω	tha ee-the-la na **ka**-
a long-distance call	ένα υπεραστικό	no **e**-na ee-pe-ra-sti-
	τηλεφώνημα	**ko** tee-le **fo**-nee-ma
	Tha íthela na káno éna	
	yperastikó tilefónima	
I would like to	Θα ήθελα να	tha **ce**-the-la na chre-
reverse the charges	χρεώσω το	**o**-so to tee-le-**fo** nee-
	τηλεφώνημα στον	ma ston pa-ra-lep-tee
	παραλήπτη	
	Tha íthela na	
	chreóso to tilefónima	
	ston paralípti	
I will try again later	Θα ξανατηλεφωνήσω	tha ksa-na-tee-le-fo-
	αργότερα	**ni**-so ar-**go**-te ra
	Tha xanatilefoníso	
	argótera	
Can I leave a	Μπορείτε να του	bo-**ree**-te na too a-
message?	αφήσετε ένα	**fee**-se-teh **e**-na mee-
	μήνυμα;	nee-ma?
	Mporeite na tou	
	afisete éna minyma?	
Could you speak up	Μιλάτε δυνατότερα	mee-**la**-teh dee-na-**to**-
a little please?	παρακαλώ;	te-ra, pa-ra-ka-**lo**
	Miláte dynatótera,	
	parakaló	
Local call	Τοπικό τηλεφώνημα	to-pi-**ko** tee-le-**fo**-
	Topikó tilefónima	nee-ma
Hold on	Περιμένετε	pe-ri-**me**-ne-teh
	Periménete	
OTE telephone office	Ο ΟΤΕ / Το	o O-**TE** / To tee-le-fo-
	τηλεφωνείο	nee-o
	O OTE / To	
	tilefoneío	
Phone box/kiosk	Ο τηλεφωνικός	o tee-le-fo-ni-**kos** tha-
	θάλαμος	la-mos
	O tilefonikós	
	thálamos	
Phone card	Η τηλεκάρτα	ee tee-le-**kar**-ta
	I tilekárta	

SHOPPING

How much does this	Πόσο κάνει;	po-so **ka**-nee?
cost?	Póso kánei?	
I would like...	Θα ήθελα...	tha **ce**-the-la...
	Tha íthela...	
Do you have.....?	Έχετε...;	**e**-che-teh
	Echete...?	
I am just looking	Απλώς κοιτάω	a-plos kee-**ta**-o
	Aplós koitáo	
Do you take credit	Δέχεστε πιστωτικές	the-ches-teh pee-sto-
cards/travellers'	κάρτες/travellers'	tee-kes **kar**-tes/
cheques?	cheques;	travellers' cheques?
	Décheste pistotikés	
	kartes/travellers	
	cheques?	
What time do you	Ποτέ ανοίγετε/	po-teh a-nee-ye-teh/
open/close?	κλείνετε;	klee-ne-teh?
	Póte anoigete/	
	kleinete?	
Can you ship this	Μπορείτε να το	bo-**ree**-teh na to
overseas?	στείλετε στο	stee-le-teh sto e-xo-
	εξωτερικό;	te-ree ko?
	Mporeite na to	
	steilete sto	
	exoterikó?	
This one	Αυτό εδώ	af-**to** e-**do**
	Aftó edó	
That one	Εκείνο	e-**kee**-no
	Ekeíno	

expensive	Ακριβό Akrinó	a-kree-vo
cheap	Φθηνό Fthinó	fthee-no
size	Το μέγεθος Το mégethos	to me-ge-thos
white	Λευκό Lefkó	lef-ko
black	Μαύρο Mávro	mav-ro
red	Κόκκινο Kókkino	ko-kee-no
yellow	Κίτρινο Kítrino	kee-tree-no
green	Πράσινο Prásino	pra-see-no
blue	Μπλε Mple	bleh

TYPES OF SHOP

antique shop	Μαγαζί με αντίκες Magazí me antíkes	ma-ga-zee me an-dee-kes
bakery	Ο φούρνος Ο foúrnos	o foor-nos
bank	Η τράπεζα Ι trápeza	ee tra-pe-za
bazaar	Το παζάρι Το pazári	to pa-za-ree
bookshop	Το βιβλιοπωλείο Το vivliopoleío	to vee-vlee-o-po-lee-o
butcher	Το κρεοπωλείο Το kreopoleío	to kre-o-po-lee-o
cake shop	Το ζαχαροπλαστείο Το zacharoplasteío	to za-cha-ro-pla-stee-o
cheese shop	Μαγαζί με αλλαντικά Magazí me allantiká	ma-ga-zee me a-lan-dee-ka
department store	Πολυκάταστημα Polykatástima	Po-lee-ka-ta-stee-ma
fishmarket	Το ιχθυοπωλείο/ ψαράδικο Το ichthyopoleío/ psarádiko	to eech-thee-o-po-lee-o /psa-rá-dee-ko
greengrocer	Το μανάβικο Το manáviko	to ma-na-vee-ko
hairdresser	Το κομμωτήριο Το kommotírio	to ko-mo-tee-ree-o
kiosk	Το περίπτερο Το períptero	to pe-reep-te-ro
leather shop	Μαγαζί με δερμάτινα είδη Magazí me dermátina eídi	ma-ga-zee me ther-ma-tee-na ee-thee
street market	Η λαϊκή αγορά Ι laïkí agorá	ee la-ee-kee a-go-ra
newsagent	Ο εφημεριδοπώλης Ο efimeridopólis	O e-fee-me-ree-tho-po-lees
pharmacy	Το φαρμακείο Το farmakeío	to far-ma-kee-o
post office	Το ταχυδρομείο Το tachydromeío	to ta-chee-thro-mee-o
shoe shop	Κατάστημα υποδημάτων Katástima ypodimáton	ka-ta-stee-ma ee-po-dee-ma-ton
souvenir shop	Μαγαζί με "souvenir" Magazí me "souvenir"	ma-ga-zee meh "souvenir"
supermarket	Σουπερμάρκετ/ Υπεραγορά "Supermarket"/ Yperagorá	"Supermarket" / ee-per-a-go-ra
tobacconist	Είδη καπνιστού Eídi kapnistoú	Ee-thee kap-nees
travel agent	Το ταξειδιωτικό γραφείο Το taxeidiotikó grafeío	to tak-see-thy-o-tee-ko gra-fee-o

SIGHTSEEING

tourist information	Ο ΕΟΤ Ο ΕΟΤ	o E-OT
tourist police	Η τουριστική αστυνομία Ι touristikí astynomía	ee too-rees-tee-kee a-stee-no-mee-a
archaeological	αρχαιολογικός archaiologikós	ar-che-o-lo-yee-kos

art gallery	Η γκαλερί Ι gkalerí	ee ga-le-ree
beach	Η παραλία Ι paralía	ee pa-ra-lee-a
Byzantine	βυζαντινός vyzantinós	vee-zan-dee-nos
castle	Το κάστρο Το kástro	to ka-stro
cathedral	Η μητρόπολη Ι mitrópoli	ee mee-tro-po-lee
cave	Το σπήλαιο Το spílaio	to spee-le-o
church	Η εκκλησία Ι ekklisía	ee e-klee-see-a
folk art	λαϊκή τέχνη laïkí téchni	la-ee-kee tech-nee
fountain	Το συντριβάνι Το syntriváni	to seen-dree-va-nee
hill	Ο λόφος Ο lófos	o lo-fos
historical	ιστορικός istorikós	ee-sto-ree-kos
island	Το νησί Το nisí	to nee-see
lake	Η λίμνη Ι límni	ee leem-nee
library	Η βιβλιοθήκη Ι vivliothíki	ee veev-lee-o-thee-kee
mansion	Η έπαυλις Ι épavlis	ee e-pav-lees
monastery	Μονή moní	mo-ni
mountain	Το βουνό Το vounó	to voo-no
municipal	δημοτικός dimotikós	thee-mo-tee-kos
museum	Το μουσείο Το mouseío	to moo-see-o
national	εθνικός ethnikós	eth-nee-kos
park	Το πάρκο Το párko	to par-ko
garden	Ο κήπος Ο kípos	o kee-pos
gorge	Το φαράγγι Το farángi	to fa-ran-gee
grave of.....	Ο τάφος του... Ο táfos tou...	o ta-fos too
river	Το ποτάμι Το potámi	to po-ta-mee
road	Ο δρόμος Ο drómos	o thro-mos
saint	άγιος/αγίου/αγία/ αγίες ágios/ágioi/agía/agies	a-yee-os/a-yee-ee/a-yee-a/a-yee-es
spring	Η πηγή Ι pigí	ee pee-yee
square	Η πλατεία Ι plateía	ee pla-tee-a
stadium	Το στάδιο Το stádio	to sta-thee-o
statue	Το άγαλμα Το ágalma	to a-gal-ma
theatre	Το θέατρο Το théatro	to the-a-tro
town hall	Το δημαρχείο Το dimarcheío	To thee-mar-chee-o
closed on public holidays	κλειστό τις αργίες kleistó tis argíes	klee-sto tees aryee-es

TRANSPORT

When does the .... leave?	Πότε φεύγει το ....; Póte févgei to...?	po-teh fev-yee to...?
Where is the bus stop?	Πού είναι η στάση του λεωφορείου; Poú eínai i stási tou leoforeíou?	poo ee-neh ee sta-see too le-o-fo-ree-oo?
Is there a bus to..?	Υπάρχει λεωφορείο για....; Ypárchei leoforeío gia...?	ee-par-chee le-o-fo-ree-o yia...?
ticket office	Εκδοτήρια εισιτηρίων Ekdotiria eisitiríon	Ek-tho-tee-reea ee-see-tee-ree-on
return ticket	Εισιτήριο με επιστροφή Eisitírio me epistrofí	ee-see-tee-ree-o meh e-pee-stro-fee
single journey	Απλό εισιτήριο Apló eisitírio	a-plo ee-see-tee-reeo

bus station	Ο σταθμός λεωφορείων Ο stathmós leoforeíon	o stath-mos leo-fo-ree-on
bus ticket	Εισιτήριο λεωφορείου Eisitirio leoforeíou	ee-see-tee-ree-o leo fo-ree-oo
trolley bus	Το τρόλλεϋ To trólley	to tro-le-ee
port	Το λιμάνι To limáni	to lee ma-nee
train/metro	Το τρένο To tréno	to tre-no
railway station	σιδηροδρομικός σταθμός sidirodromikós stathmós	see-thee-ro-thro-mee-kos stath-mos
moped	Το μοτοποδήλατο / το μηχανάκι To motopodílato / To michanáki	to mo-to-po-thee-la-to/to mee-cha-na-kee
bicycle	Το ποδήλατο To podilato	to po-thee-la to
taxi	Το ταξί To taxí	to tak-see
airport	Το αεροδρόμιο To aerodrómio	to a-e-ro-thro-mee-o
ferry	Το φερυμπότ To "ferry-boat"	to fe-ree-bot
hydrofoil	Το δελφίνι / Το υδροπτέρυγο To delfíni / To ydroptérygo	to del-fee-nee / To ee-throp-te-ree-go
catamaran	Το καταμαράν To katamaráii	to catamaran
for hire	Ενοικιάζονται Enoikiázontai	e-nee-kya-zon-deh

Staying in a Hotel

Do you have a vacant room?	Έχετε δωμάτια; Echete domátia?	e-che-teh tho-ma-tee-a?
double room with double bed	Δίκλινο με διπλό κρεβάτι Diklino me dipló kreváti	thee klee-no meh thee-plo kre-va-tee
twin room	Δίκλινο με μονά κρεβάτια Diklino me moná krevátia	thee-klee-no meh mo-na kre-vat-ya
single room	Μονόκλινο Monóklino	mo-no-klee no
room with a bath	Δωμάτιο με μπάνιο Domátio me mpánio	tho-ma-tee-o meh ban-yo
shower	Το ντους To douz	To dooz
porter	Ο πορτιέρης O portiéris	o por-tye-rees
key	Το κλειδί To kleidí	to klee-dee
I have a reservation	Εχω κάνει κράτηση Echo kánei krátisi	e-cho ka-nee kra tee-see
room with a sea view/balcony	Δωμάτιο με θέα στη θάλασσα/μπαλκόνι Domátio me théa sti thálassa/mpalkóni	tho-ma tee o mch the-a stee tha-la-sa/bal- ko-nee
Does the price include breakfast?	Το πρωινό συμπεριλαμβάνεται στην τιμή; To proïnó symperilamvánetai stin timí?	to pro ee-no seem-be-ree-lam-va-ne-teh steen tee-mee?

Eating Out

Have you got a table?	Έχετε τραπέζι; Echete trapézi?	e che te tra-pe-zee?
I want to reserve a table	Θέλω να κρατήσω ένα τραπέζι Thélo na kratíso éna trapézi	the-lo na kra-tee-so e-na tra-pe-zee
The bill, please	Τον λογαριασμό, παρακαλώ Ton logariazmó parakaló	ton lo-gar-yas-mo pa-ra-ka-lo
I am a vegetarian	Είμαι χορτοφάγος Eímai chortofágos	ee-meh chor to fa-gos
What is fresh today?	Τί φρέσκο έχετε σήμερα; Ti frésko échete símera?	tee fres-ko e-che-teh see-me-ra?

waiter/waitress	Κύριε / Γκαρσόν / Κυρία (female) Kýrie/Garson"/Kyría	Kee-ree-eh/Gar son/Kee-ree-a
menu	Ο κατάλογος O katálogos	o ka-ta-lo-gos
cover charge	Το κουβέρ To "couvert"	to koo-ver
wine list	Ο κατάλογος με τα οινοπνευματώδη O katálogos me ta oinopnevmatódi	o ka-ta-lo-gos meh ta ee-no-pnev-ma
glass	Το ποτήρι To potíri	to po-tee-ree
bottle	Το μπουκάλι To mpoukáli	to bou-ka-lee
knife	Το μαχαίρι To machairi	to ma-che-ree
fork	Το πηρούνι To piroúni	to pee-roo-nee
spoon	Το κουτάλι To koutáli	to koo-ta-lee
breakfast	Το πρωινό To proïnó	to pro-ee-no
lunch	Το μεσημεριανό To mesimerianó	to me-see-mer-ya-no
dinner	Το δείπνο To deipno	to theep-no
main course	Το κυρίως γεύμα To kyríos gévma	to kee-ree-os yev-ma
starter/first course	Τα ορεκτικά Ta orektiká	ta o-rek-tee ka
dessert	Το γλυκό To glykó	to ylee-ko
dish of the day	Το πιάτο της ημέρας To piáto tis iméras	to pya-to tees ee me-ras
bar	Το μπαρ To "bar"	To bar
taverna	Η ταβέρνα I tavérna	ee ta-ver-na
café	Το καφενείο To kafeneío	to ka-fe-nee-o
fish taverna	Η ψαροταβέρνα I psarotavérna	ee psa-ro-ta-ver-na
grill house	Η ψησταριά I psistariá	ee psee-sta-rya
wine shop	Το οινοπώλειο To oinopoleio	to ee-no-po-lee-o
dairy shop	Το γαλακτοπωλείο To galaktopoleío	to ga-la-kto-po-lee-o
restaurant	Το εστιατόριο To estiatório	to e-stee-a-to-ree-o
ouzeri	Το ουζερί To ouzerí	to oo-ze-ree
meze shop	Το μεζεδοπωλείο To mezedopoleio	To me-ze-do-po-lee-o
take away kebabs	Το σουβλατζίδικο To souvlatzidiko	To soo-vlat-zee-dee-ko
rare	Ελάχιστα ψημένο Eláchista psiméno	e-lach-ees-ta psee-me-no
medium	Μέτρια ψημένο Métria psiméno	met-ree-a psee-me-no
well done	Καλοψημένο Kalopsiméno	ka-lo-psee-me-no

Basic Food and Drink

coffee	Ο καφές O Kafés	o ka-fes
with milk	με γάλα me gála	me ga-la
black coffee	σκέτος skétos	ske-tos
without sugar	χωρίς ζάχαρη choris záchari	cho-rees za-cha-ree
medium sweet	μέτριος métrios	me-tree-os
very sweet	γλυκύς glykýs	glee-kees
tea	τσάι tsái	tsa-ee
hot chocolate	ζεστή σοκολάτα zestí sokoláta	ze-stee so-ko-la-ta
wine	κρασί krasí	kra-see
red	κόκκινο kókkino	ko-kee-no
white	λευκό lefkó	lef-ko
rosé	ροζέ rozé	ro-ze

raki	Το ρακί / Το rakí	to ra-kee
ouzo	Το ούζο / Το oúzo	to oo-zo
retsina	Η ρετσίνα / I retsína	ee ret-see-na
water	Το νερό / Το neró	to ne-ro
octopus	Το χταπόδι / Το chtapódi	to chta-po-dee
fish	Το ψάρι / Το psári	to psa-ree
cheese	Το τυρί / Το tyrí	to tee-ree
halloumi	Το χαλούμι / Το chaloúmi	to cha-loo-mee
feta	Η φέτα / I féta	ee fe-ta
bread	Το ψωμί / Το psomí	to pso-mee
bean soup	Η φασολάδα / I fasoláda	ee fa-so-la-da
houmous	Το χούμους / Το houmous	to choo-moos
halva	Ο χαλβάς / Ο chalvás	o chal-vas
meat kebabs	Ο γύρος / Ο gýros	o yee-ros
Turkish delight	Το λουκούμι / Το loukoúmi	to loo-koo-mee
baklava	Ο μπακλαβάς / Ο mpaklavás	o bak-la-vas
klephtiko	Το κλέφτικο / Το kléftiko	to klef-tee-ko

NUMBERS

1	ένα / éna	e-na
2	δύο / dýo	thee-o
3	τρία / tría	tree-a
4	τέσσερα / téssera	te-se-ra
5	πέντε / pénte	pen-deh
6	έξι / éxi	ek-si
7	επτά / eptá	ep-ta
8	οχτώ / ochtó	och-to
9	εννέα / ennéa	e-ne-a
10	δέκα / déka	the-ka
11	έντεκα / énteka	en-de-ka
12	δώδεκα / dódeka	tho-the-ka
13	δεκατρία / dekatría	de-ka-tree-a
14	δεκατέσσερα / dekatéssera	the-ka-tes-se-ra
15	δεκαπέντε / dekapénte	the-ka-pen-de
16	δεκαέξι / dekaéxi	the-ka-ek-si
17	δεκαεπτά / dekaeptá	the-ka-ep-ta
18	δεκαοχτώ / dekaochtó	the-ka-och-to
19	δεκαεννέα / dekaennéa	the-ka-e-ne-a
20	είκοσι / eíkosi	ee-ko-see
21	εικοσιένα / eikosiéna	ee-ko-see-e-na
30	τριάντα / triánta	tree-an-da
40	σαράντα / saránta	sa-ran-da
50	πενήντα / peninta	pe-neen-da
60	εξήντα / exínta	ek-seen-da
70	εβδομήντα / evdominta	ev-tho-meen-da
80	ογδόντα / ogdónta	og-thon-da
90	ενενήντα / eneninta	e-ne-neen-da
100	εκατό / ekató	e-ka-to
200	διακόσια / diakósia	thya-kos-ya
1,000	χίλια / chília	cheel-ya
2,000	δύο χιλιάδες / dýo chiliádes	thee-o cheel-ya-thes
1,000,000	ένα εκατομμύριο / éna ekatommýrio	e-na e-ka-to-mee-ree-o

TIME, DAYS AND DATES

one minute	ένα λεπτό / éna leptó	e-na lep-to
one hour	μία ώρα / mía óra	mee-a o-ra
half an hour	μισή ώρα / misí óra	mee-see o-ra
quarter of an hour	ένα τέταρτο / éna tétarto	e-na te-tar-to
half past one	μία και μισή / mía kai misí	mee-a keh mee-see
quarter past one	μία και τέταρτο / mía kai tétarto	mee-a keh te-tar-to
ten past one	μία και δέκα / mía kai déka	mee-a keh the-ka
quarter to two	δύο παρά τέταρτο / dýo pará tétarto	thee-o pa-ra te-tar-to
ten to two	δύο παρά δέκα / dýo pará déka	thee-o pa-ra the-ka
a day	μία μέρα / mía méra	mee-a me-ra
a week	μία εβδομάδα / mía evdomáda	mee-a ev-tho-ma-tha
a month	ένας μήνας / énas mínas	e-nas mee-nas
a year	ένας χρόνος / énas chrónos	e-nas chro-nos
Monday	Δευτέρα / Deftéra	thef-te-ra
Tuesday	Τρίτη / Tríti	tree-tee
Wednesday	Τετάρτη / Tetárti	te-tar-tee
Thursday	Πέμπτη / Pémpti	pemp-tee
Friday	Παρασκευή / Paraskeví	pa-ras-ke-vee
Saturday	Σάββατο / Sávvato	sa-va-to
Sunday	Κυριακή / Kyriakí	keer-ee-a-kee
January	Ιανουάριος / Ianouários	ee-a-noo-a-ree-os
February	Φεβρουάριος / Fevrouários	fev-roo-a-ree-os
March	Μάρτιος / Mártios	mar-tee-os
April	Απρίλιος / Aprílios	a-pree-lee-os
May	Μάιος / Máios	ma-ee-os
June	Ιούνιος / Ioúnios	ee-oo-nee-os
July	Ιούλιος / Ioúlios	ee-oo-lee-os
August	Αύγουστος / Avgoustos	av-goo-stos
September	Σεπτέμβριος / Septémvrios	sep-tem-vree-os
October	Οκτώβριος / Októvrios	ok-to-vree-os
November	Νοέμβριος / Noémvrios	no-em-vree-os
December	Δεκέμβριος / Dekémvrios	the-kem-vree-os

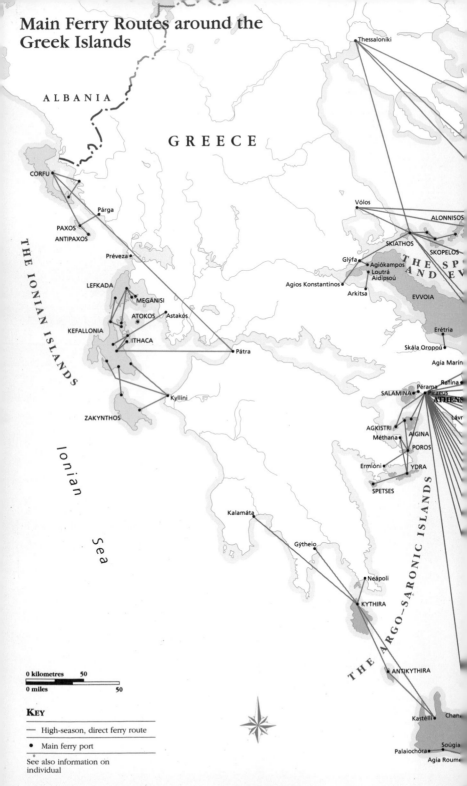

Main Ferry Routes around the Greek Islands

ALBANIA

GREECE

Thessaloníki

CORFU

Párga

PAXOS

ANTIPAXOS

Préveza

LEFKADA

MEGANISI

ATOKOS   Astakós

ITHACA

KEFALLONIA

Pátra

Kyllíni

ZAKYNTHOS

THE IONIAN ISLANDS

Ionian Sea

Vólos

ALONNISOS

SKIATHOS

SKOPELOS

Glýfa

Agiókampos

Loutrá Aidipsoú

Agios Konstantinos

Arkítsa

EVVOIA

THE SP AND EV

Erétria

Skála Oropoú

Agía Marín

Rafína

SALAMINA   Pérama   Piraeus

AGKISTRI   ATHENS

Méthana   AIGINA   Lávr

POROS

Ermióni   YDRA

SPETSES

Kalamáta

Gýtheio

Neápoli

KYTHIRA

THE ARGO-SARONIC ISLANDS

ANTIKYTHIRA

Kastélli   Chan

Soúgia

Palaiochóra   Agía Roume

GAVDO

0 kilometres   50

0 miles   50